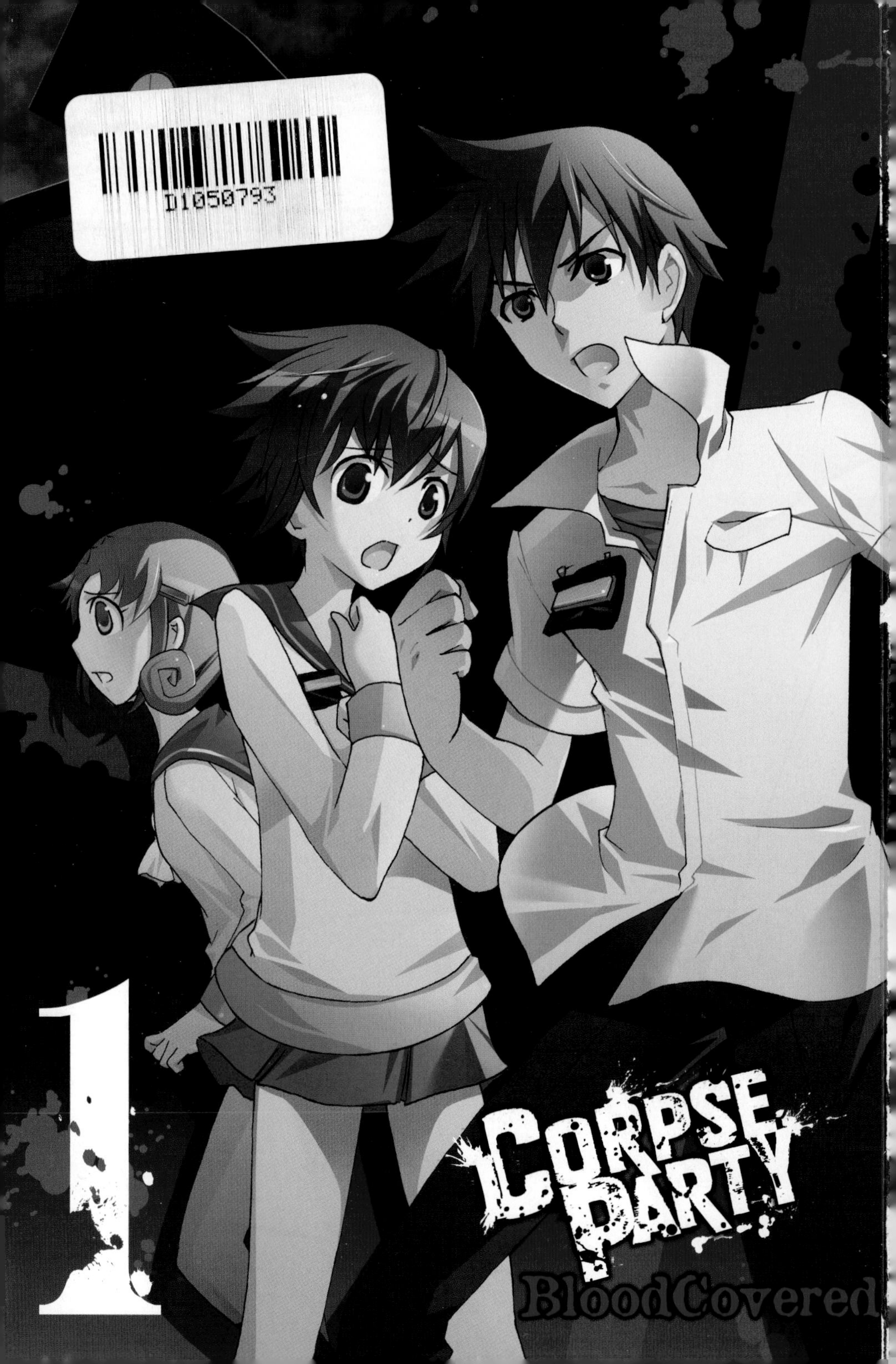
1
CORPSE PARTY
Blood Covered

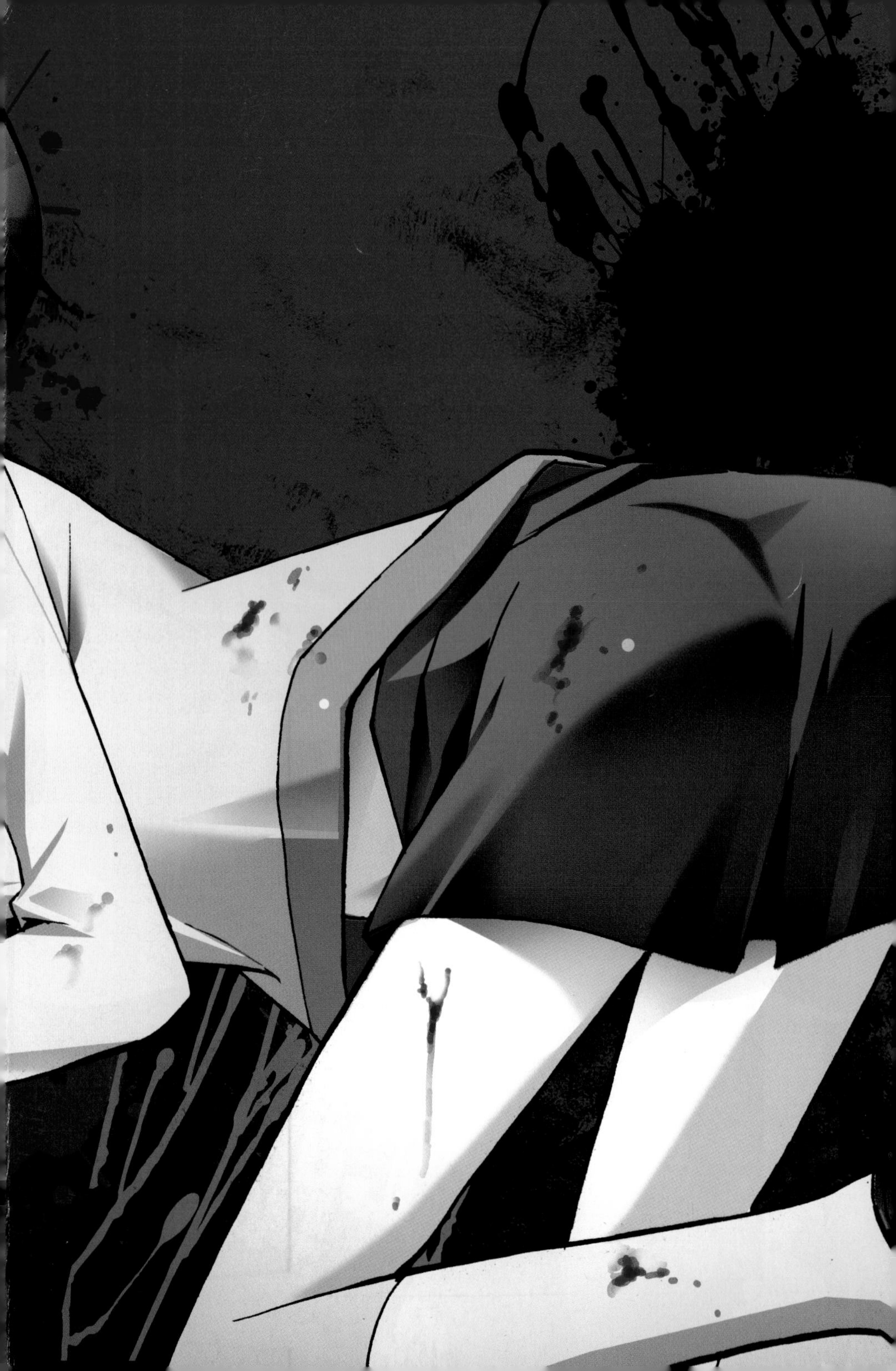

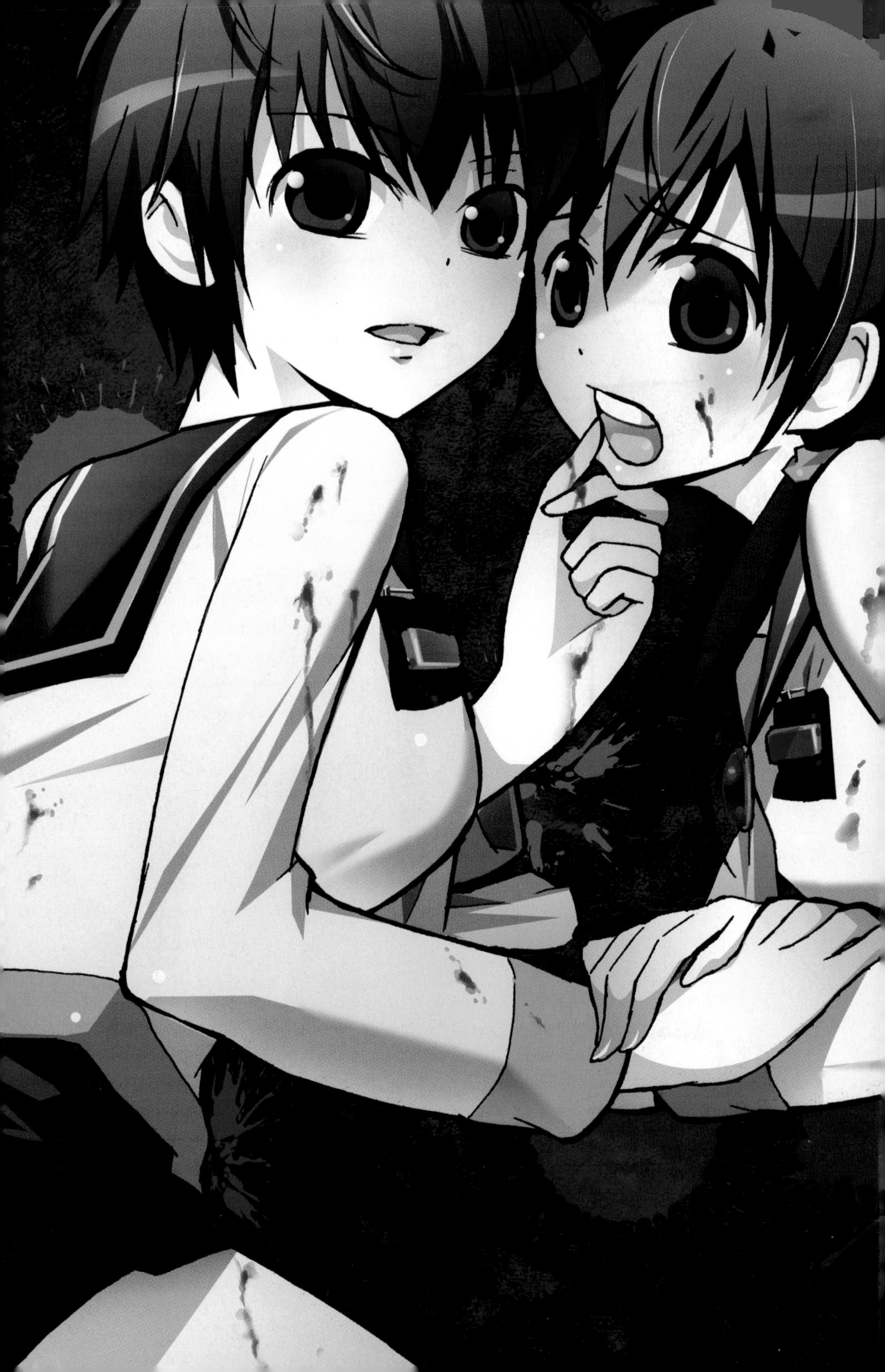

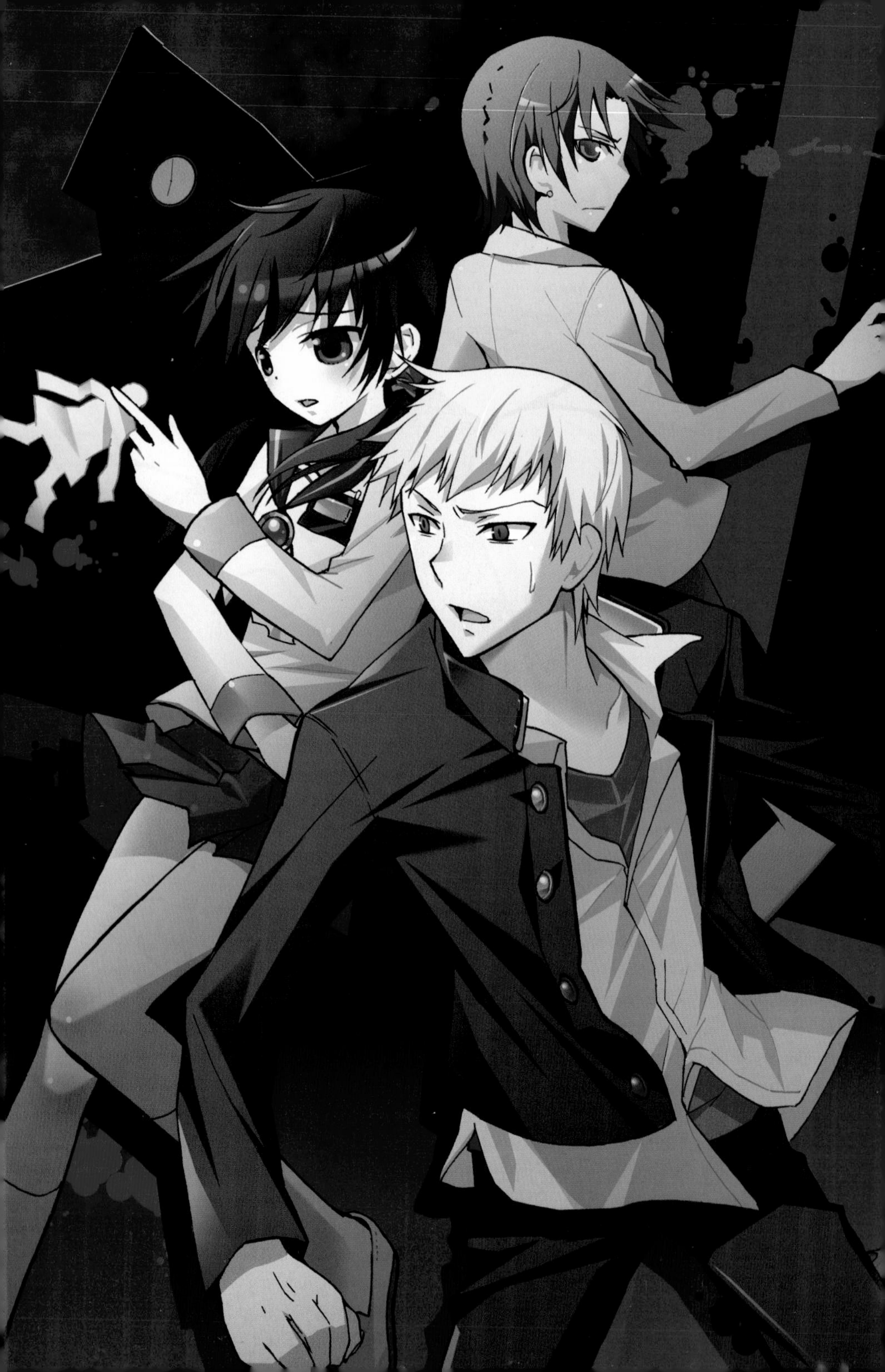

BloodCovered Contents

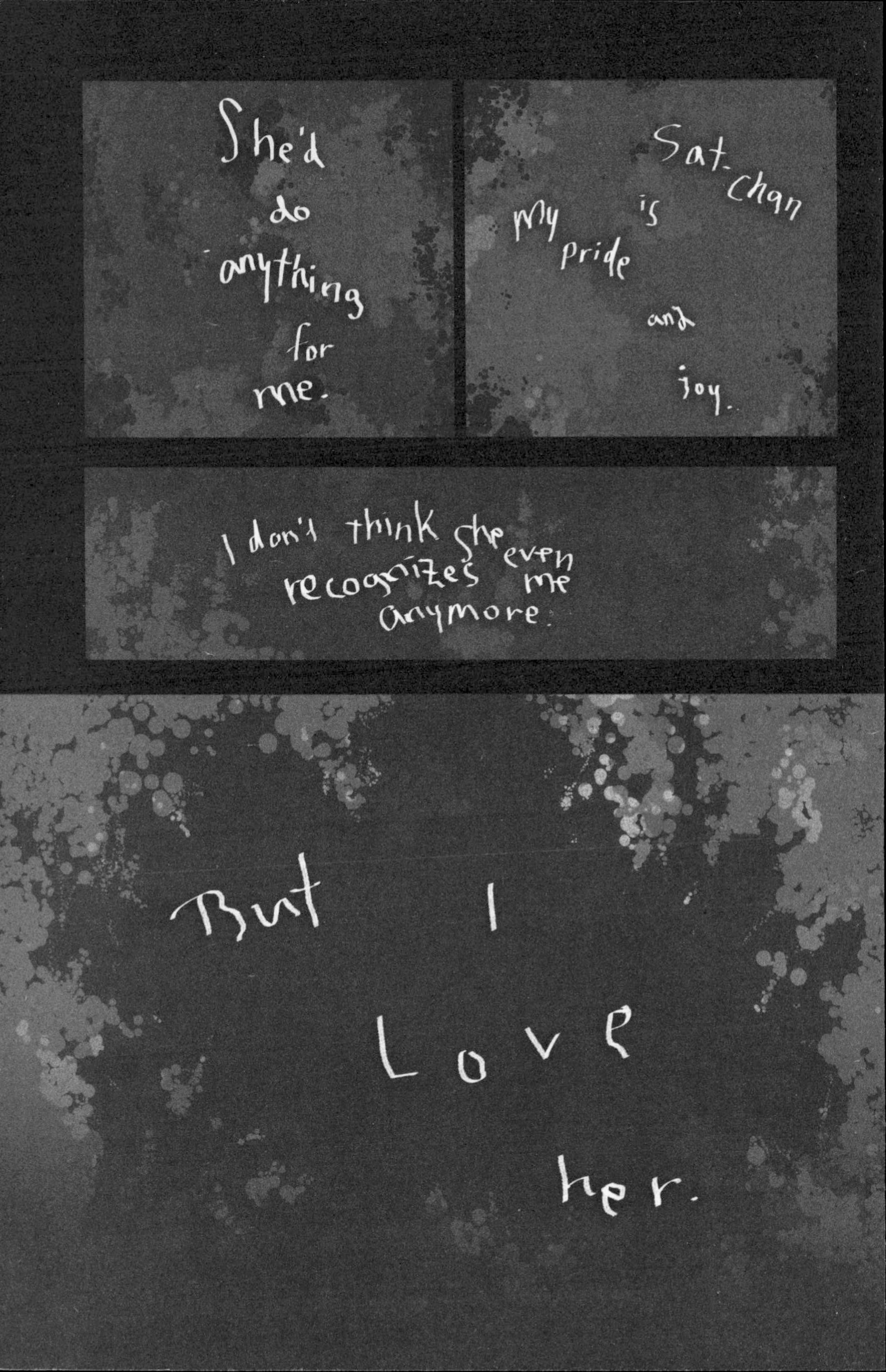
Sat-chan is my pride and joy.
She'd do anything for me.
I don't think she even recognizes me anymore.
But I Love her.

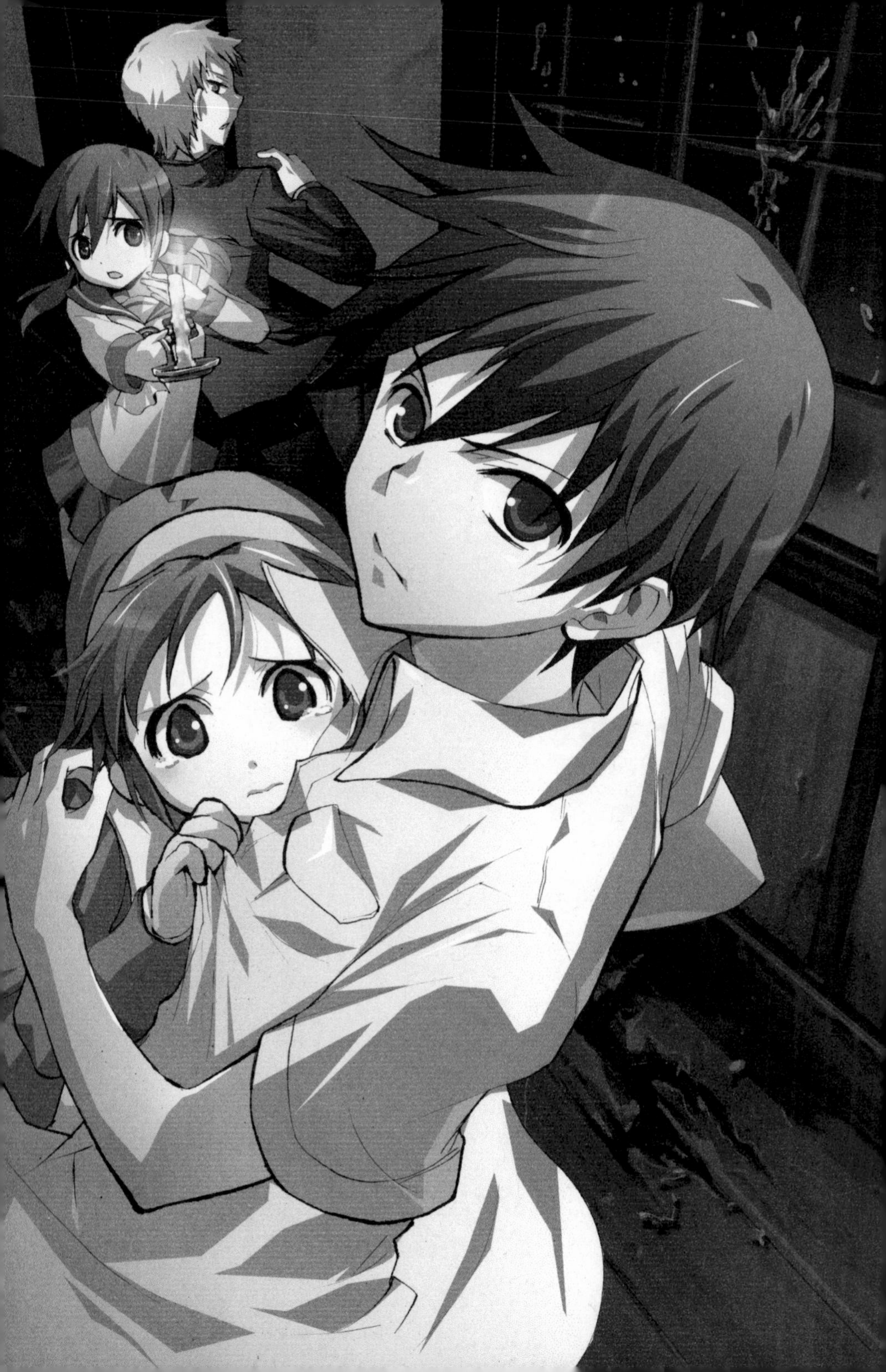

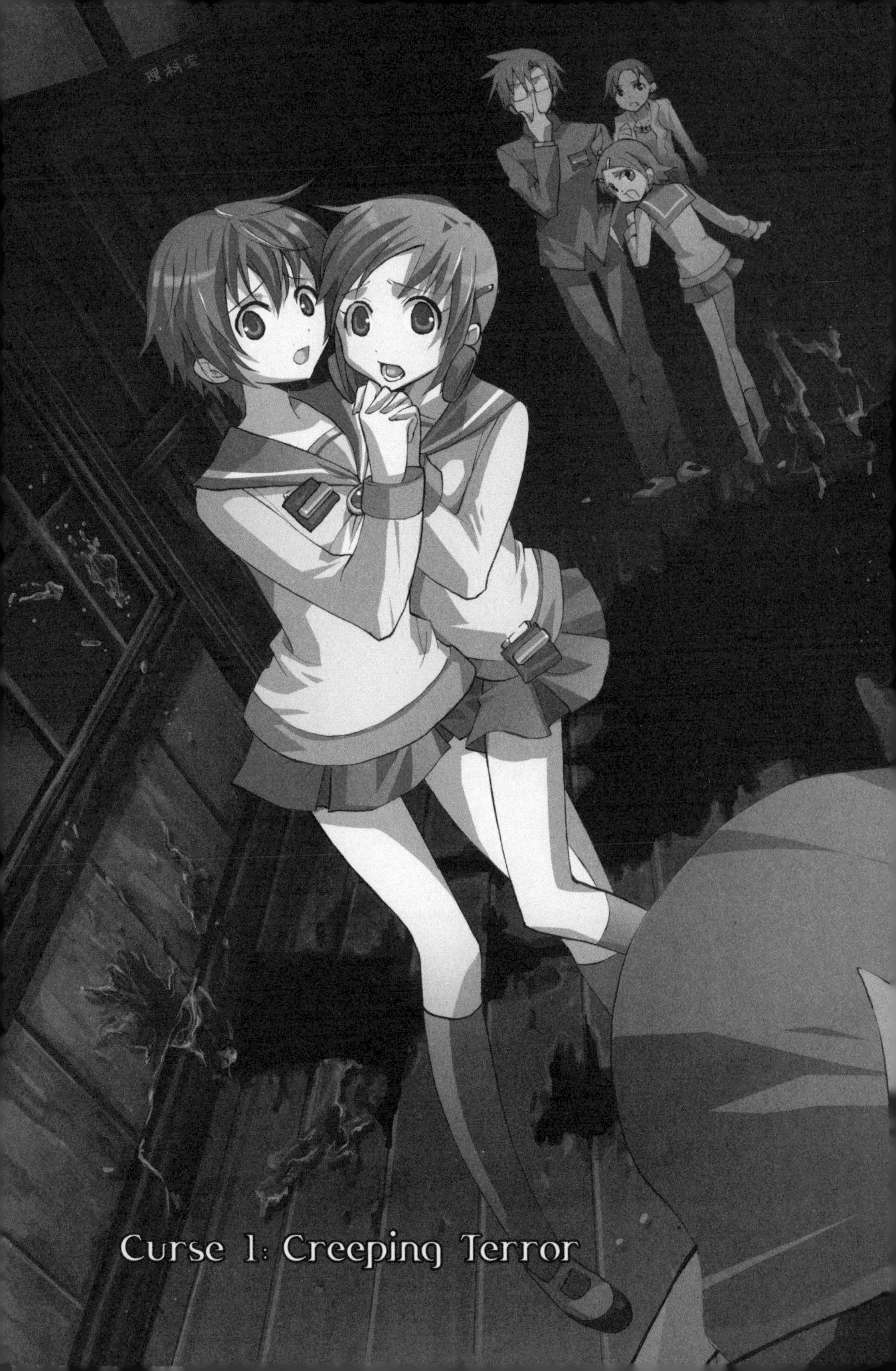
理科室

Curse 1: Creeping Terror

CORPSE PARTY
Blood Covered

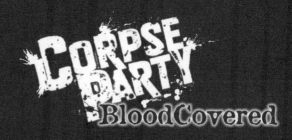

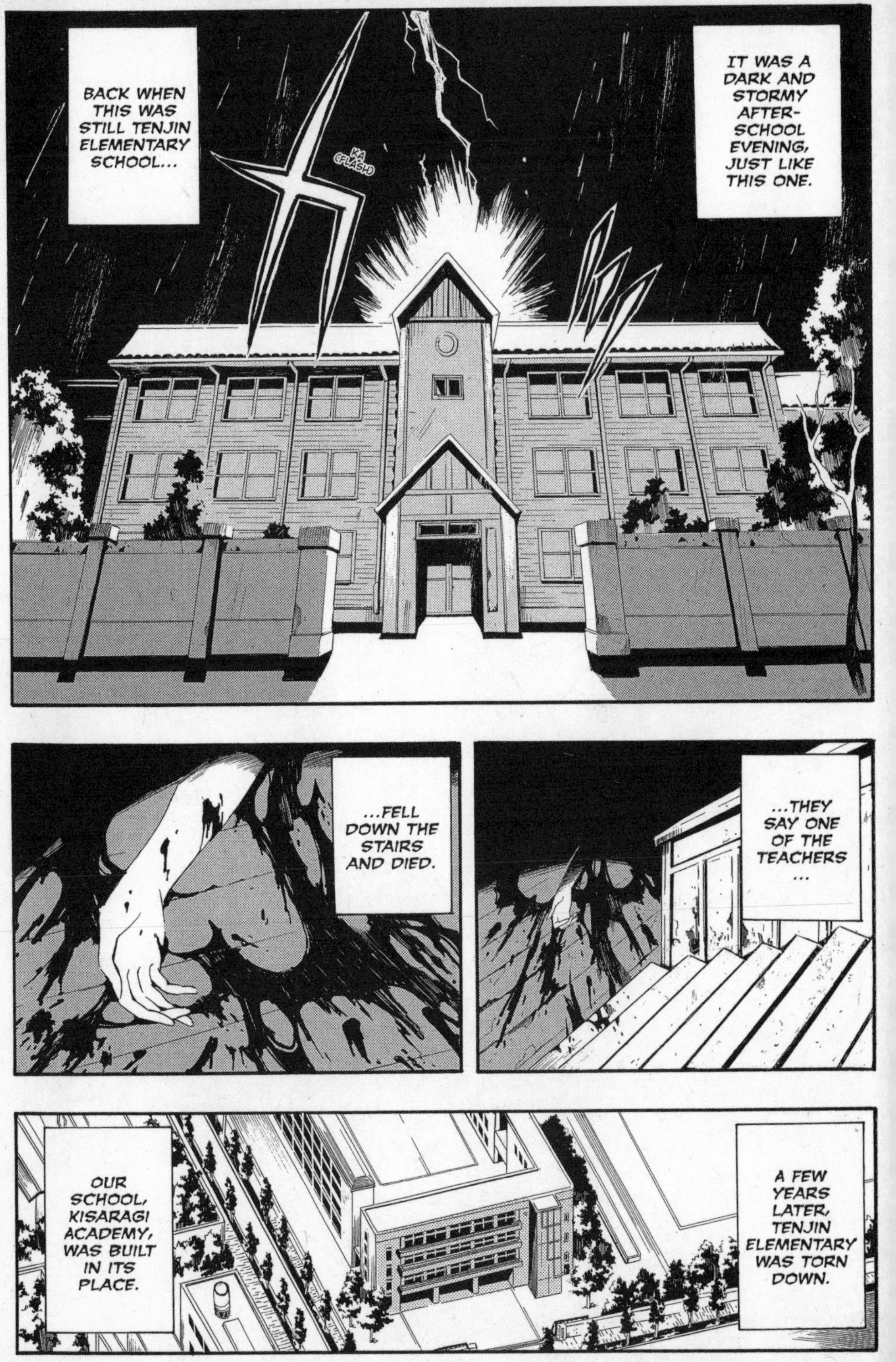
IT WAS A DARK AND STORMY AFTER-SCHOOL EVENING, JUST LIKE THIS ONE.
KA (FLASH)
BACK WHEN THIS WAS STILL TENJIN ELEMENTARY SCHOOL...
...THEY SAY ONE OF THE TEACHERS ...
...FELL DOWN THE STAIRS AND DIED.
A FEW YEARS LATER, TENJIN ELEMENTARY WAS TORN DOWN.
OUR SCHOOL, KISARAGI ACADEMY, WAS BUILT IN ITS PLACE.

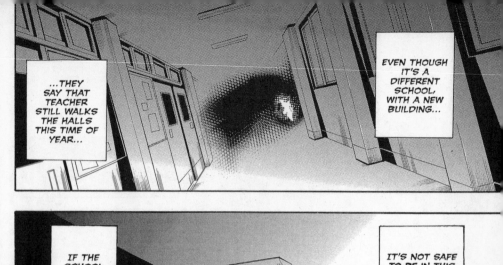

EVEN THOUGH IT'S A DIFFERENT SCHOOL, WITH A NEW BUILDING...
...THEY SAY THAT TEACHER STILL WALKS THE HALLS THIS TIME OF YEAR...
IT'S NOT SAFE TO BE IN THIS SCHOOL AFTER THE CLOCK STRIKES SEVEN.
IF THE SCHOOL GOES DARK IN A BLACKOUT...
...THAT TEACHER WILL APPEAR...

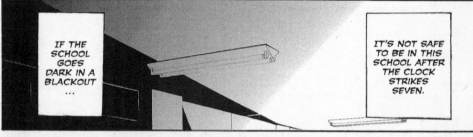

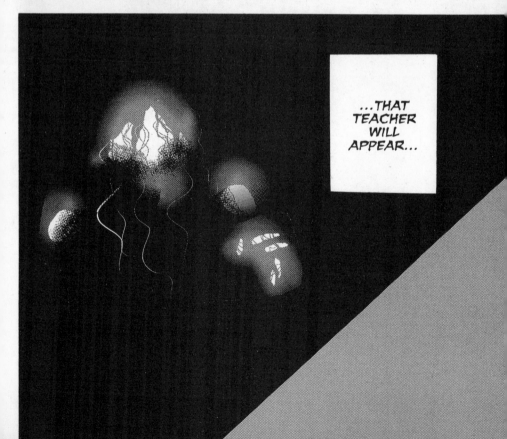

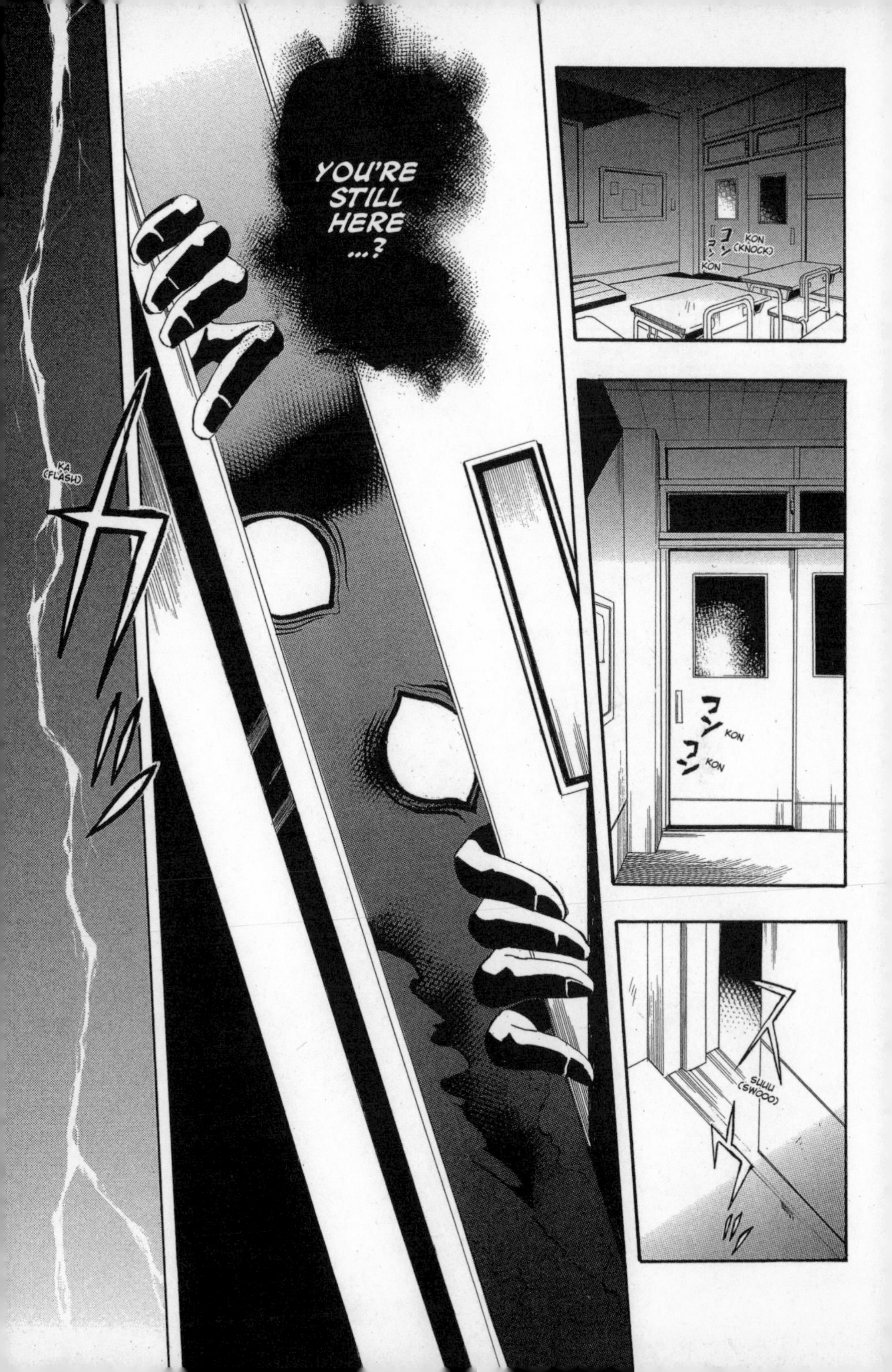
コンコン
KON (KNOCK)
KON
コン
KON
コン
KON
SUUU (SWOOO)
YOU'RE STILL HERE ...?
KA (FLASH)

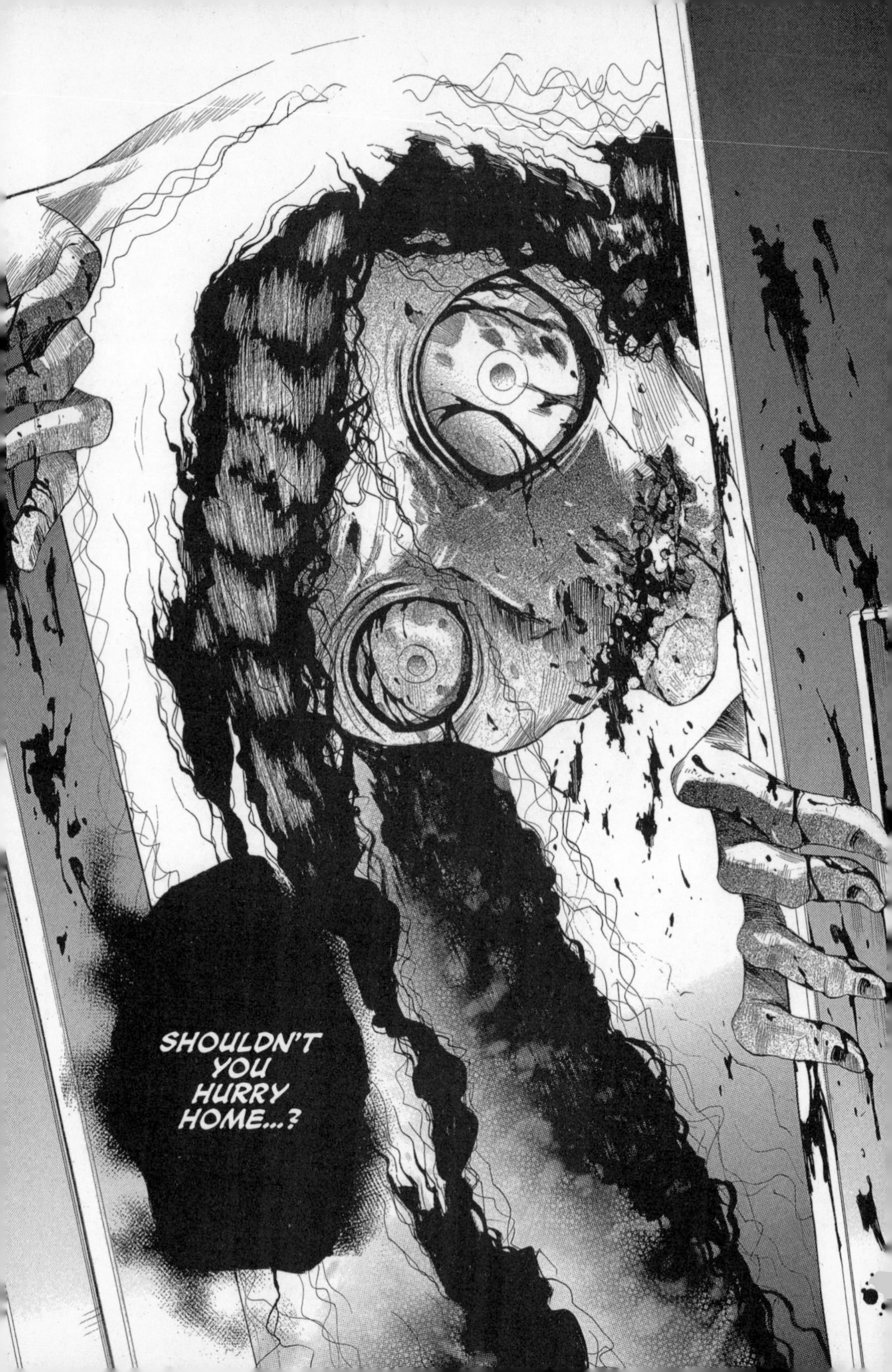
SHOULDN'T YOU HURRY HOME...?

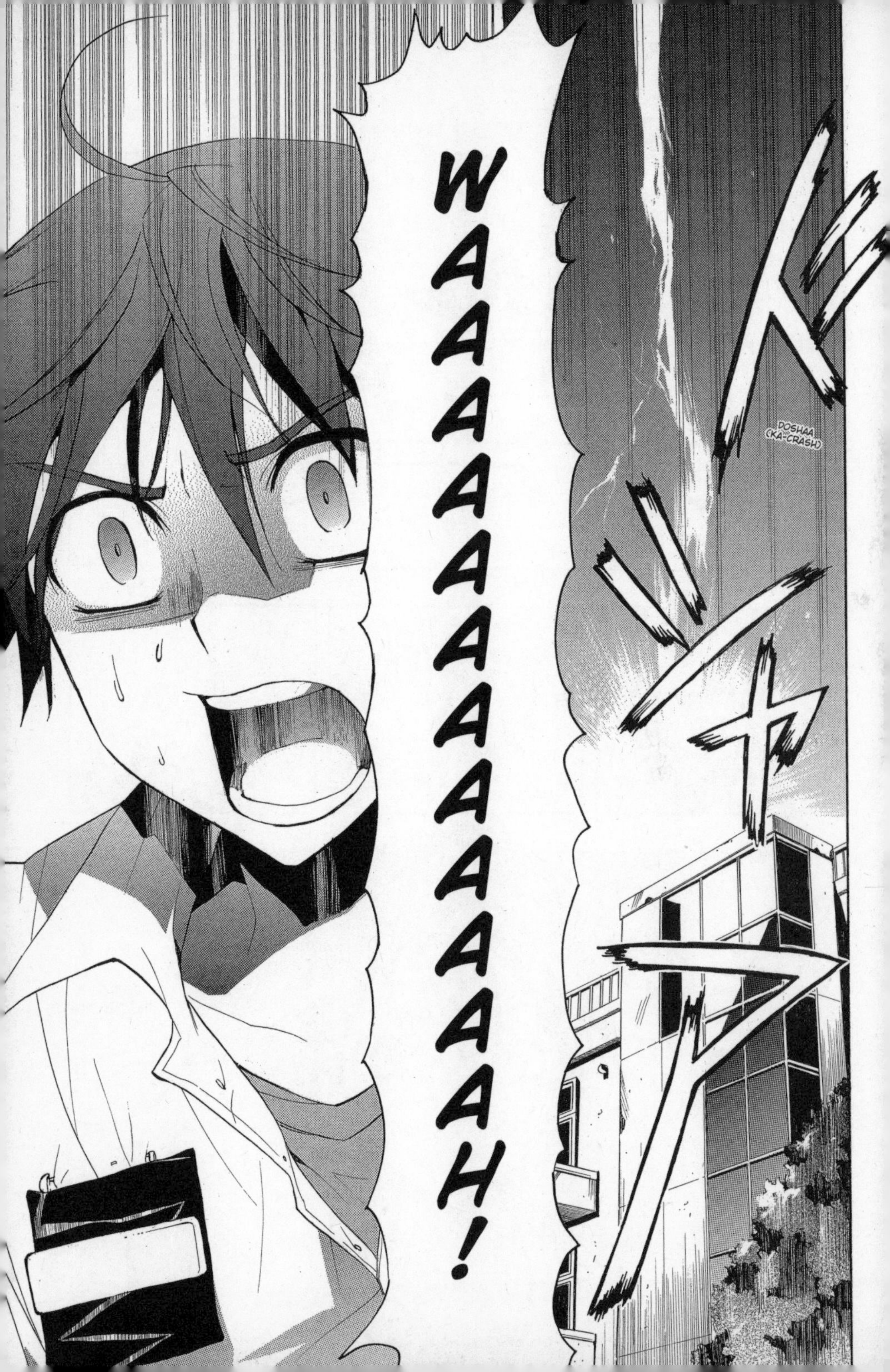
DOSHAA (KA-CRASH)
WAAAAAAAAAAAAAAH!

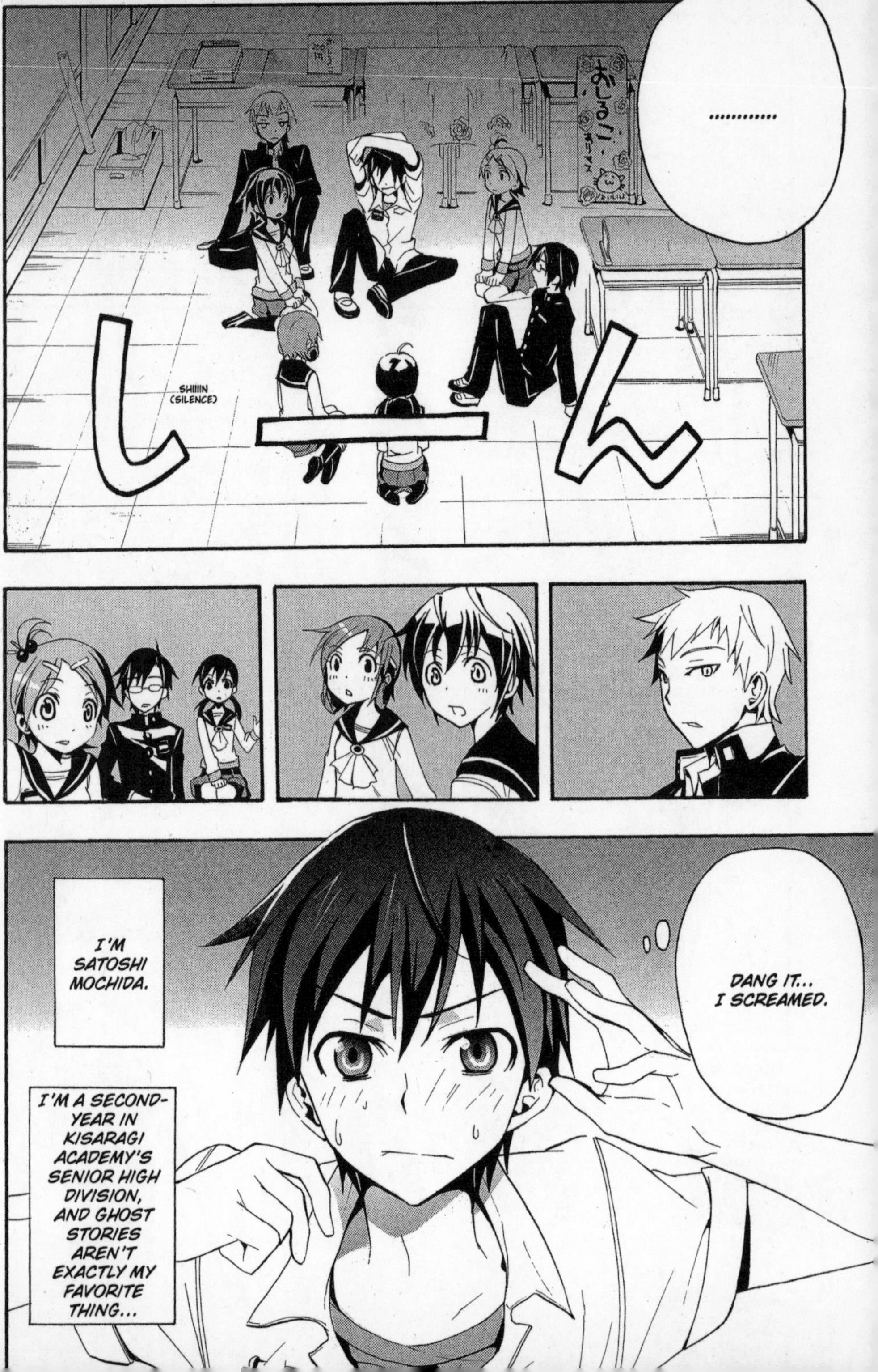
SIGN: RED BEAN SOUP 200 YEN / WE HAVE RED BEAN SOUP! IT'S YUMMY!
....
しーん
SHIIIIN (SILENCE)
DANG IT... I SCREAMED.
I'M SATOSHI MOCHIDA.
I'M A SECOND-YEAR IN KISARAGI ACADEMY'S SENIOR HIGH DIVISION, AND GHOST STORIES AREN'T EXACTLY MY FAVORITE THING...

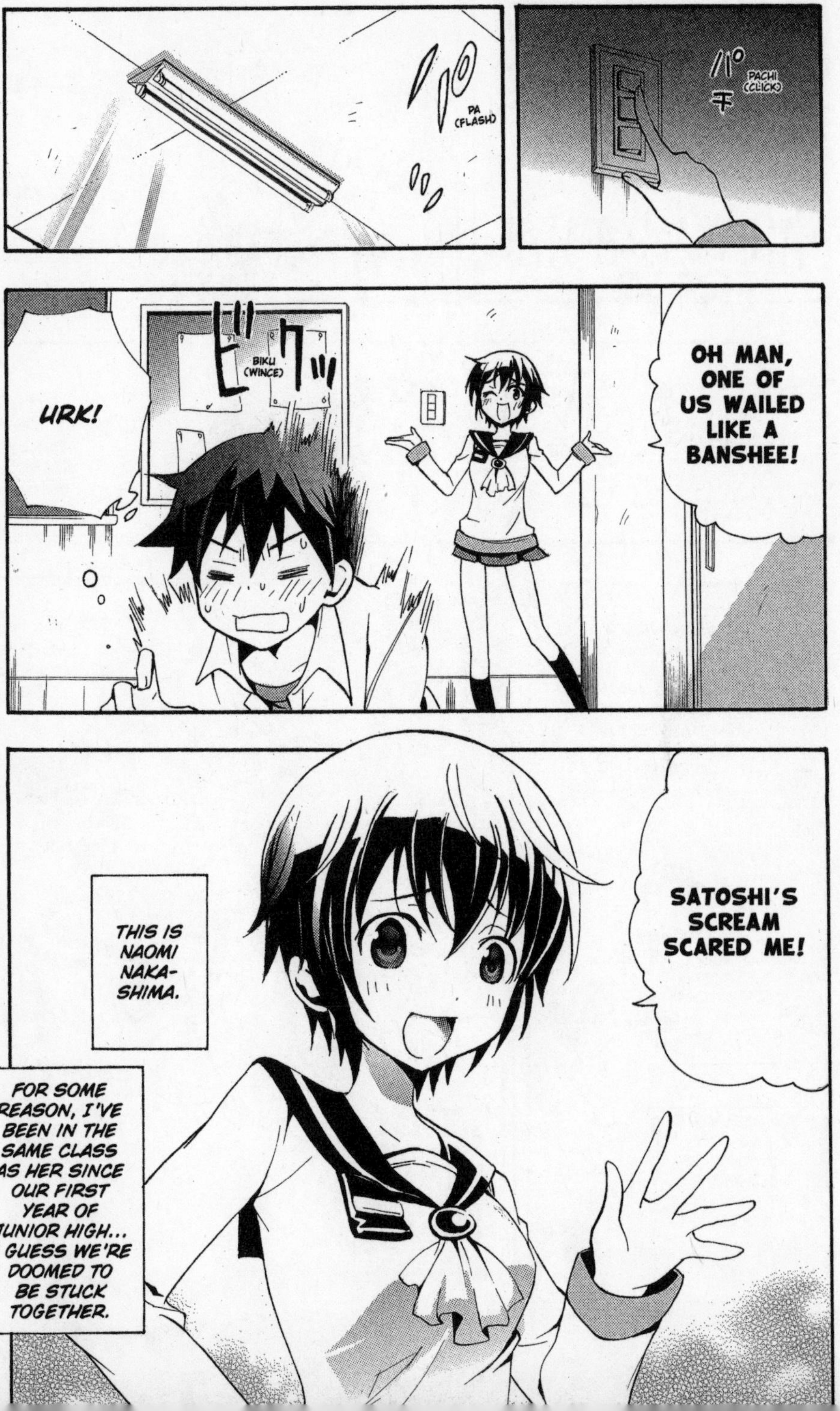
パチ
PACHI (CLICK)
パ
PA (FLASH)
OH MAN, ONE OF US WAILED LIKE A BANSHEE!
ビクッ
BIKU (WINCE)
URK!
SATOSHI'S SCREAM SCARED ME!
THIS IS NAOMI NAKA-SHIMA.
FOR SOME REASON, I'VE BEEN IN THE SAME CLASS AS HER SINCE OUR FIRST YEAR OF JUNIOR HIGH... I GUESS WE'RE DOOMED TO BE STUCK TOGETHER.

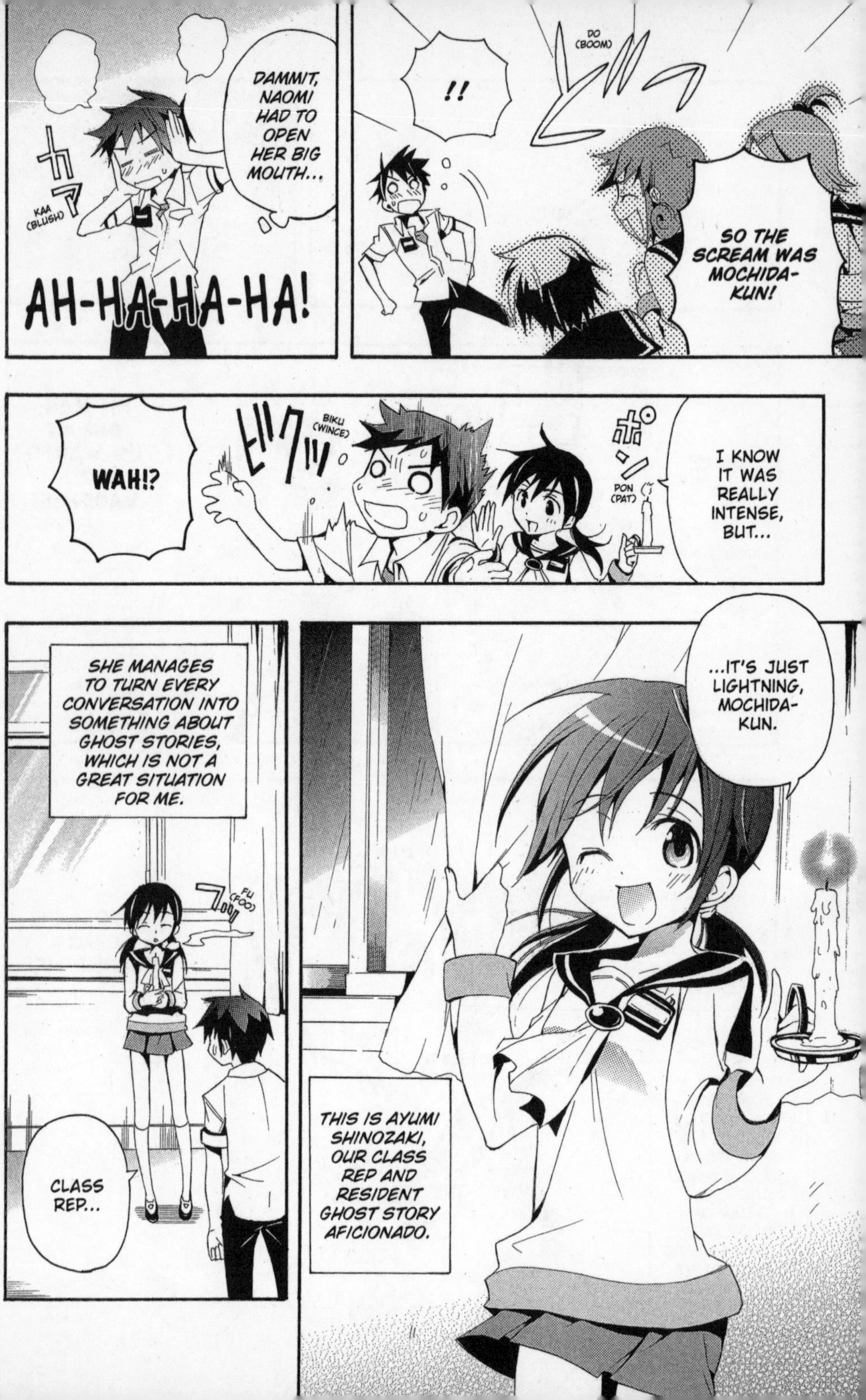
DO (BOOM)
!!
SO THE SCREAM WAS MOCHIDA-KUN!
DAMMIT, NAOMI HAD TO OPEN HER BIG MOUTH...
KAA (BLUSH)
AH-HA-HA-HA!
I KNOW IT WAS REALLY INTENSE, BUT...
PON (PAT)
BIKU (WINCE)
WAH!?
...IT'S JUST LIGHTNING, MOCHIDA-KUN.
THIS IS AYUMI SHINOZAKI, OUR CLASS REP AND RESIDENT GHOST STORY AFICIONADO.
SHE MANAGES TO TURN EVERY CONVERSATION INTO SOMETHING ABOUT GHOST STORIES, WHICH IS NOT A GREAT SITUATION FOR ME.
FU (FOO)
CLASS REP...

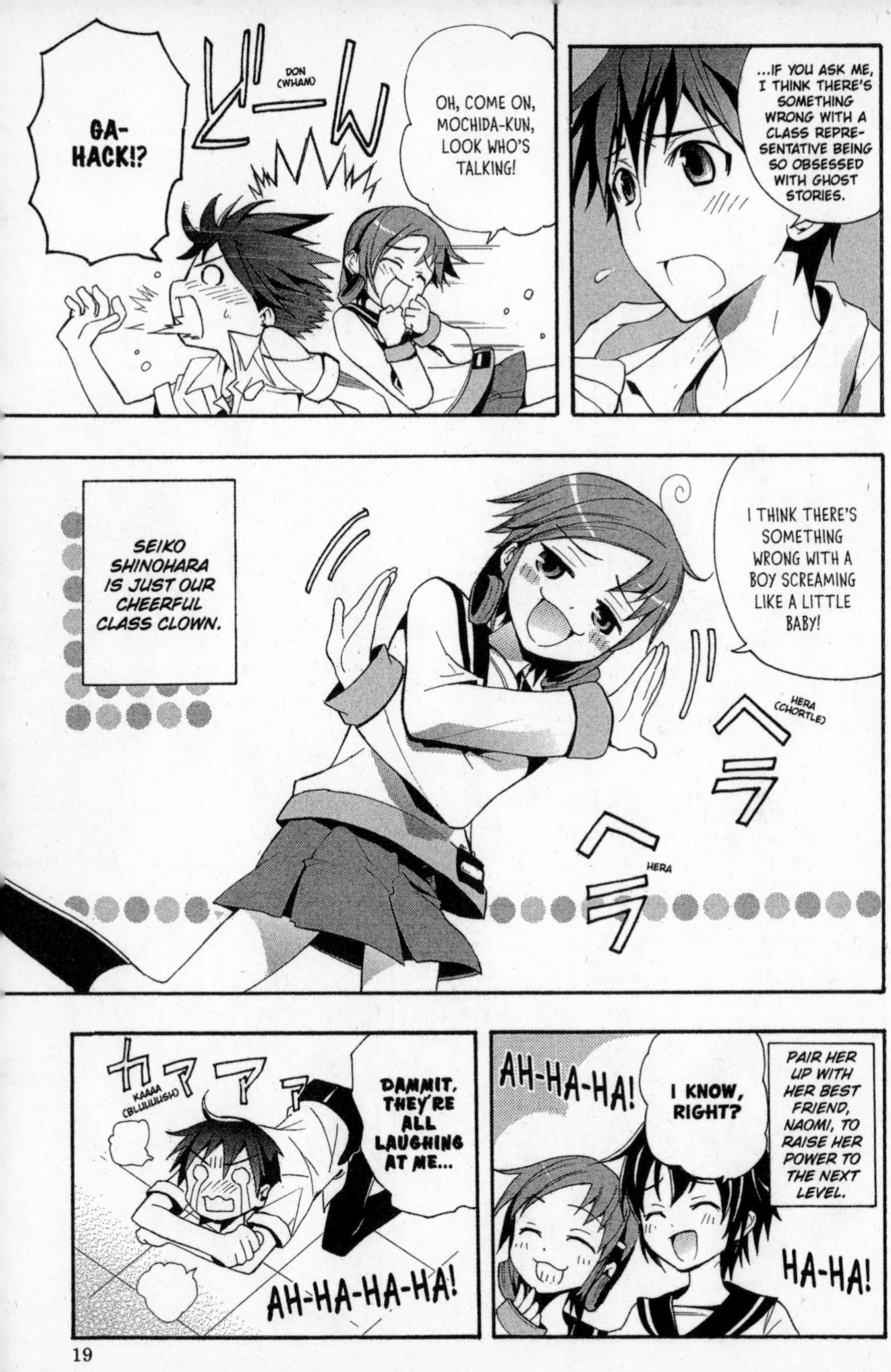
...IF YOU ASK ME, I THINK THERE'S SOMETHING WRONG WITH A CLASS REPRE-SENTATIVE BEING SO OBSESSED WITH GHOST STORIES.
OH, COME ON, MOCHIDA-KUN, LOOK WHO'S TALKING!
DON (WHAM)
GA-HACK!?
I THINK THERE'S SOMETHING WRONG WITH A BOY SCREAMING LIKE A LITTLE BABY!
HERA (CHORTLE)
HERA
SEIKO SHINOHARA IS JUST OUR CHEERFUL CLASS CLOWN.
PAIR HER UP WITH HER BEST FRIEND, NAOMI, TO RAISE HER POWER TO THE NEXT LEVEL.
I KNOW, RIGHT?
AH-HA-HA!
HA-HA!
DAMMIT, THEY'RE ALL LAUGHING AT ME...
KAAAA (BLUUUUSH)
AH-HA-HA-HA!

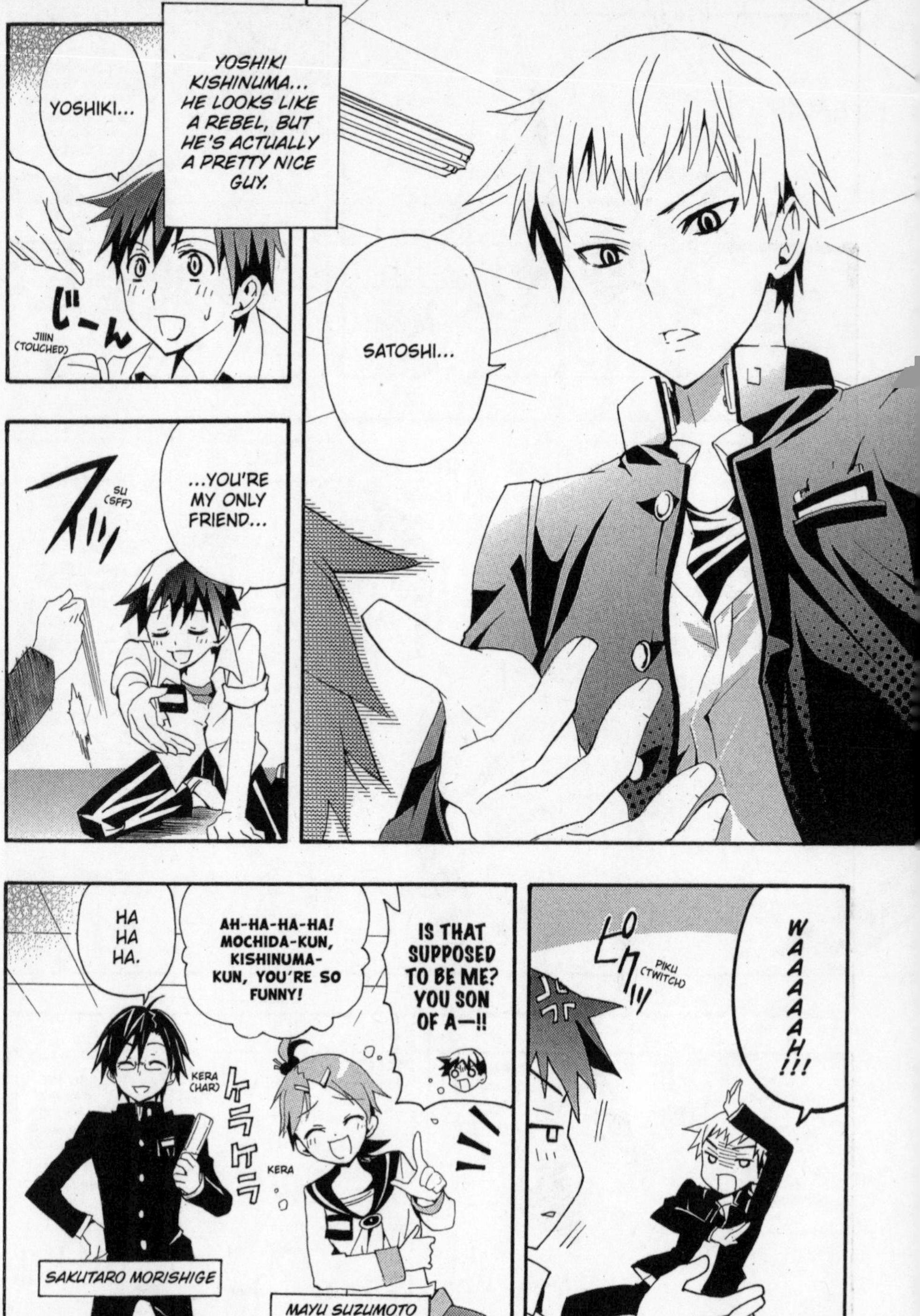
SATOSHI...
YOSHIKI KISHINUMA... HE LOOKS LIKE A REBEL, BUT HE'S ACTUALLY A PRETTY NICE GUY.
YOSHIKI...
JIIN (TOUCHED)
...YOU'RE MY ONLY FRIEND...
SU (SFF)
PIKU (TWITCH)
WAAAAAAH!!!
IS THAT SUPPOSED TO BE ME? YOU SON OF A—!!
AH-HA-HA-HA! MOCHIDA-KUN, KISHINUMA-KUN, YOU'RE SO FUNNY!
HA HA HA.
KERA (HAR)
KERA
SAKUTARO MORISHIGE
MAYU SUZUMOTO

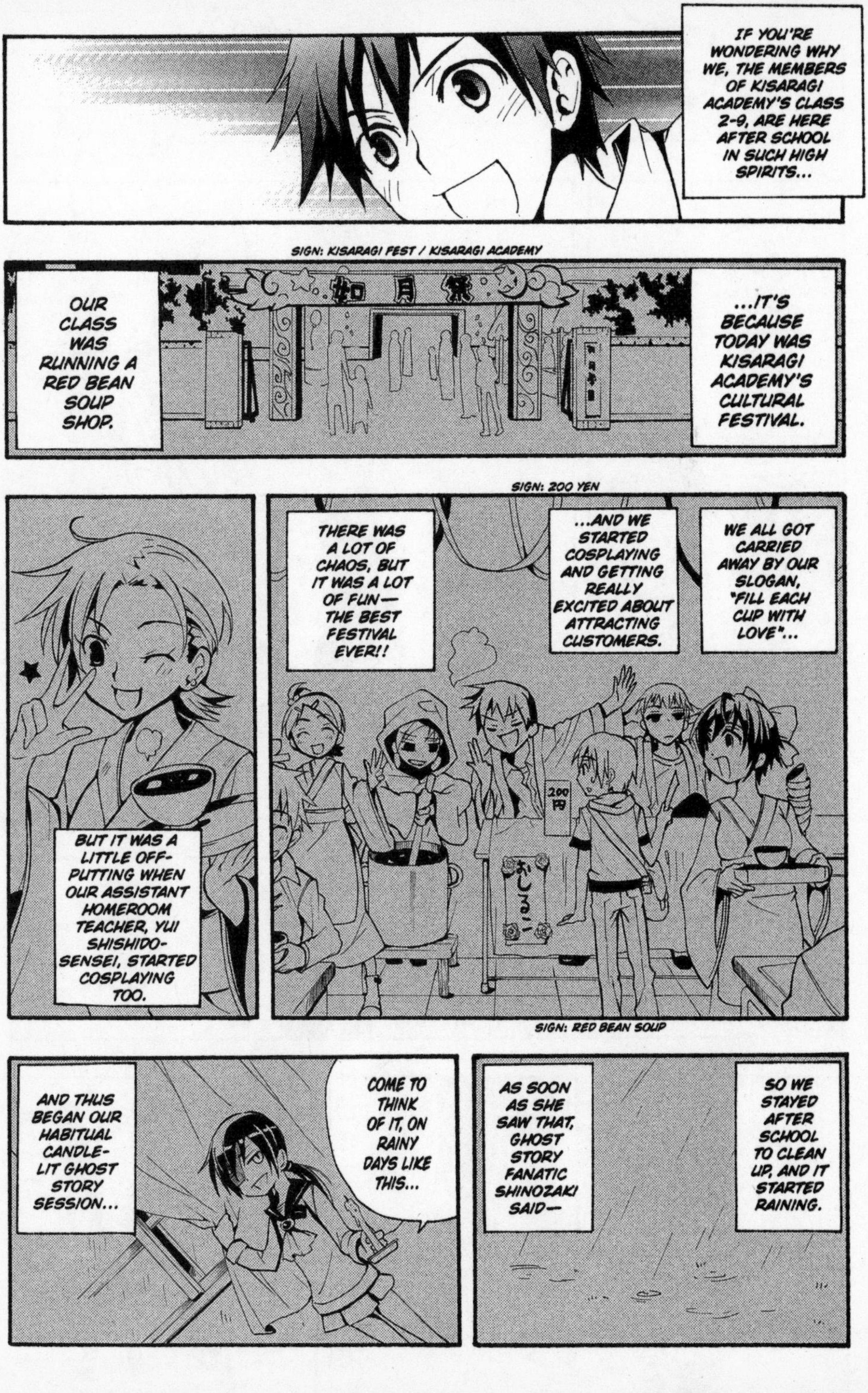
IF YOU'RE WONDERING WHY WE, THE MEMBERS OF KISARAGI ACADEMY'S CLASS 2-9, ARE HERE AFTER SCHOOL IN SUCH HIGH SPIRITS...
SIGN: KISARAGI FEST / KISARAGI ACADEMY
...IT'S BECAUSE TODAY WAS KISARAGI ACADEMY'S CULTURAL FESTIVAL.
OUR CLASS WAS RUNNING A RED BEAN SOUP SHOP.
SIGN: 200 YEN
WE ALL GOT CARRIED AWAY BY OUR SLOGAN, "FILL EACH CUP WITH LOVE"...
...AND WE STARTED COSPLAYING AND GETTING REALLY EXCITED ABOUT ATTRACTING CUSTOMERS.
THERE WAS A LOT OF CHAOS, BUT IT WAS A LOT OF FUN—THE BEST FESTIVAL EVER!!
SIGN: RED BEAN SOUP
BUT IT WAS A LITTLE OFF-PUTTING WHEN OUR ASSISTANT HOMEROOM TEACHER, YUI SHISHIDO-SENSEI, STARTED COSPLAYING TOO.
SO WE STAYED AFTER SCHOOL TO CLEAN UP, AND IT STARTED RAINING.
AS SOON AS SHE SAW THAT, GHOST STORY FANATIC SHINOZAKI SAID—
COME TO THINK OF IT, ON RAINY DAYS LIKE THIS...
AND THUS BEGAN OUR HABITUAL CANDLE-LIT GHOST STORY SESSION...

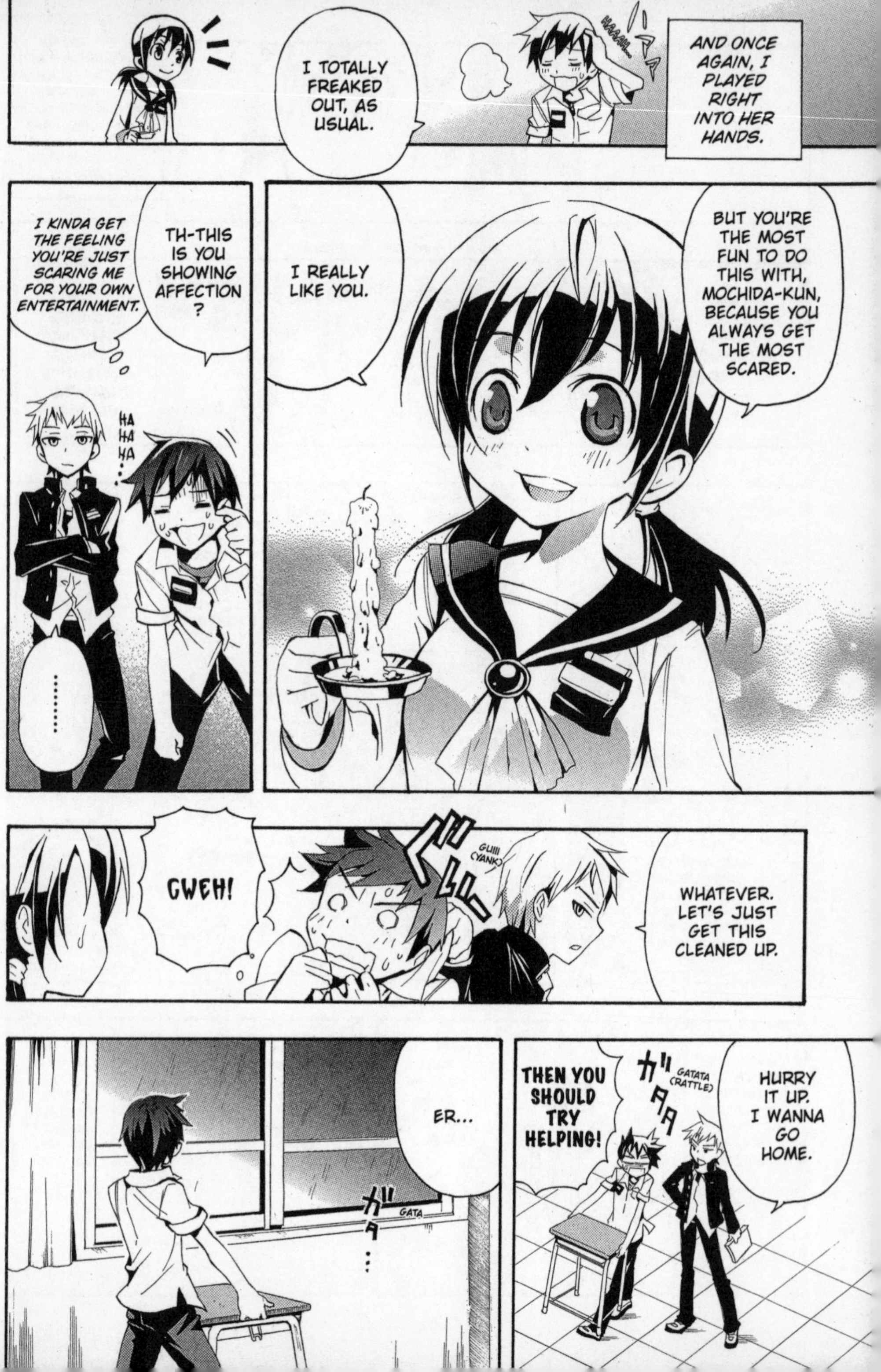
AND ONCE AGAIN, I PLAYED RIGHT INTO HER HANDS.
HAAAH...
I TOTALLY FREAKED OUT, AS USUAL.
BUT YOU'RE THE MOST FUN TO DO THIS WITH, MOCHIDA-KUN, BECAUSE YOU ALWAYS GET THE MOST SCARED.
I REALLY LIKE YOU.
TH-THIS IS YOU SHOWING AFFECTION?
I KINDA GET THE FEELING YOU'RE JUST SCARING ME FOR YOUR OWN ENTERTAINMENT.
HA HA HA
......
WHATEVER. LET'S JUST GET THIS CLEANED UP.
GUIII (YANK)
GWEH!
HURRY IT UP. I WANNA GO HOME.
GATATA (RATTLE)
THEN YOU SHOULD TRY HELPING!
ER...
GATA

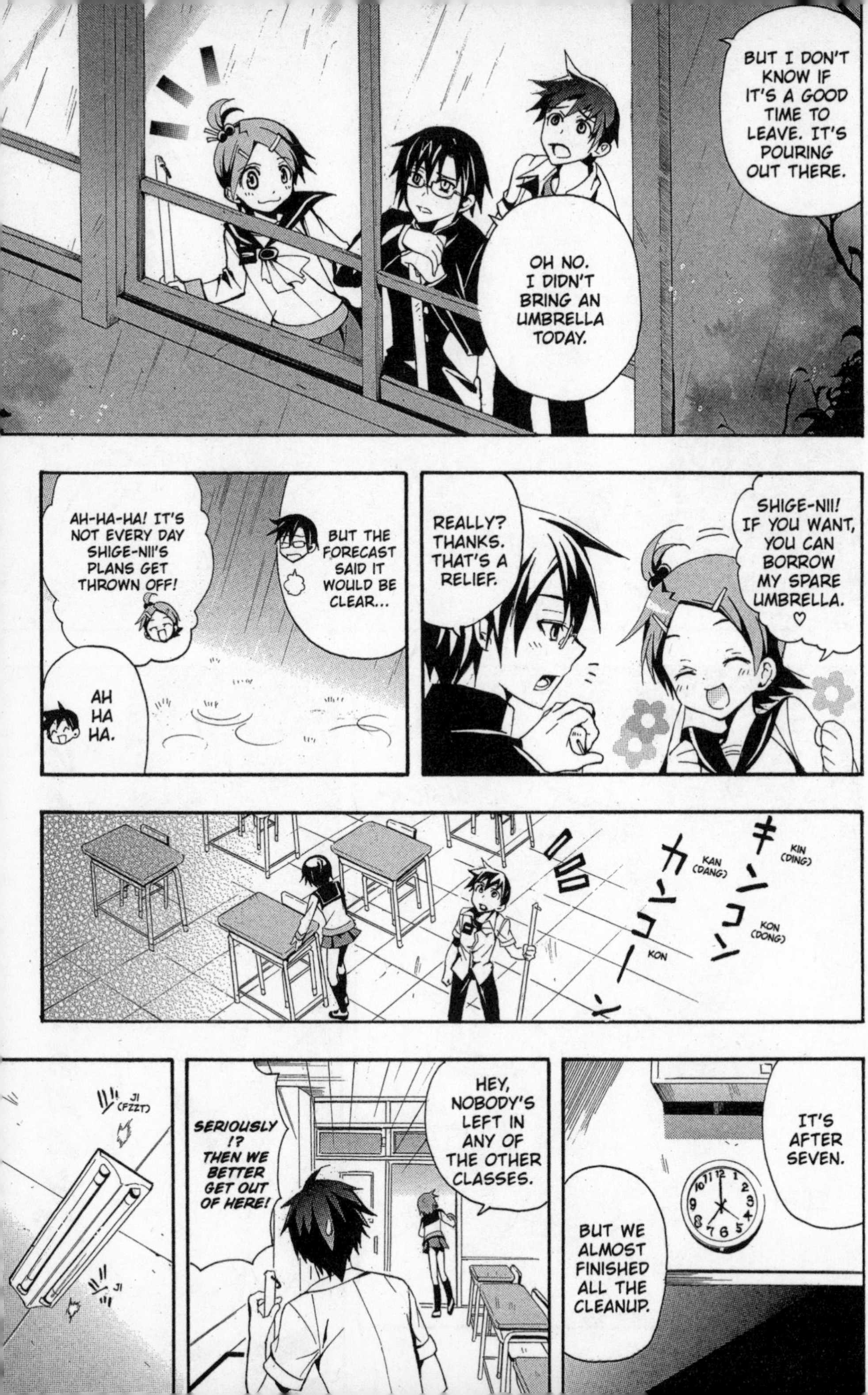
BUT I DON'T KNOW IF IT'S A GOOD TIME TO LEAVE. IT'S POURING OUT THERE.
OH NO. I DIDN'T BRING AN UMBRELLA TODAY.
SHIGE-NII! IF YOU WANT, YOU CAN BORROW MY SPARE UMBRELLA. ♡
REALLY? THANKS. THAT'S A RELIEF.
BUT THE FORECAST SAID IT WOULD BE CLEAR...
AH-HA-HA! IT'S NOT EVERY DAY SHIGE-NII'S PLANS GET THROWN OFF!
AH HA HA.
KIN (DING)
KON (DONG)
KAN (DANG)
KON
IT'S AFTER SEVEN.
BUT WE ALMOST FINISHED ALL THE CLEANUP.
HEY, NOBODY'S LEFT IN ANY OF THE OTHER CLASSES.
SERIOUSLY!? THEN WE BETTER GET OUT OF HERE!
JI (FZZT)
JI

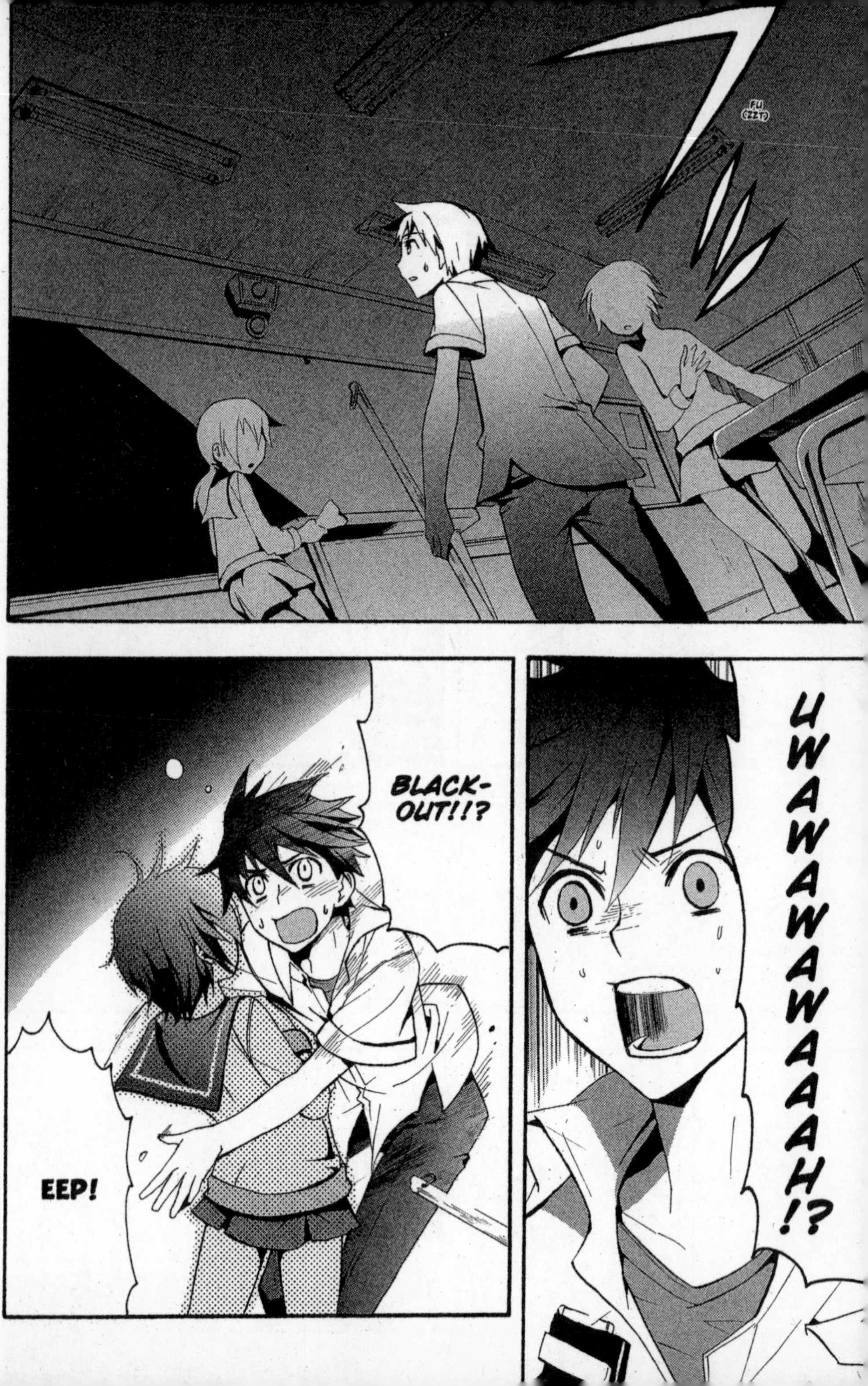
FU (ZZT)
UWAWAWAWAWAAAAH!?
BLACK-OUT!!?
EEP!

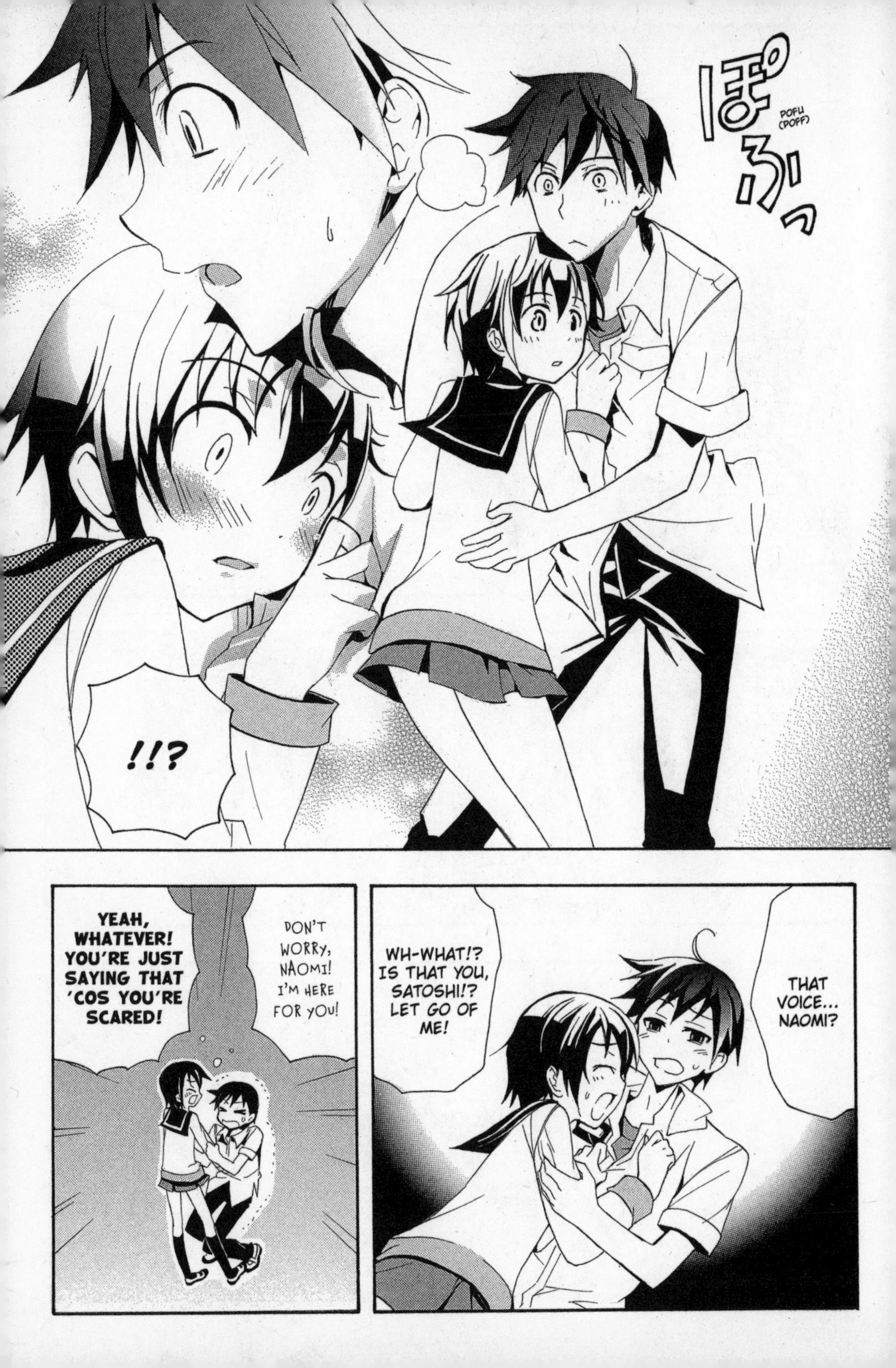
ぽふっ
POFU (POFF)
!!?
THAT VOICE... NAOMI?
WH-WHAT!? IS THAT YOU, SATOSHI!? LET GO OF ME!
DON'T WORRY, NAOMI! I'M HERE FOR YOU!
YEAH, WHATEVER! YOU'RE JUST SAYING THAT 'COS YOU'RE SCARED!

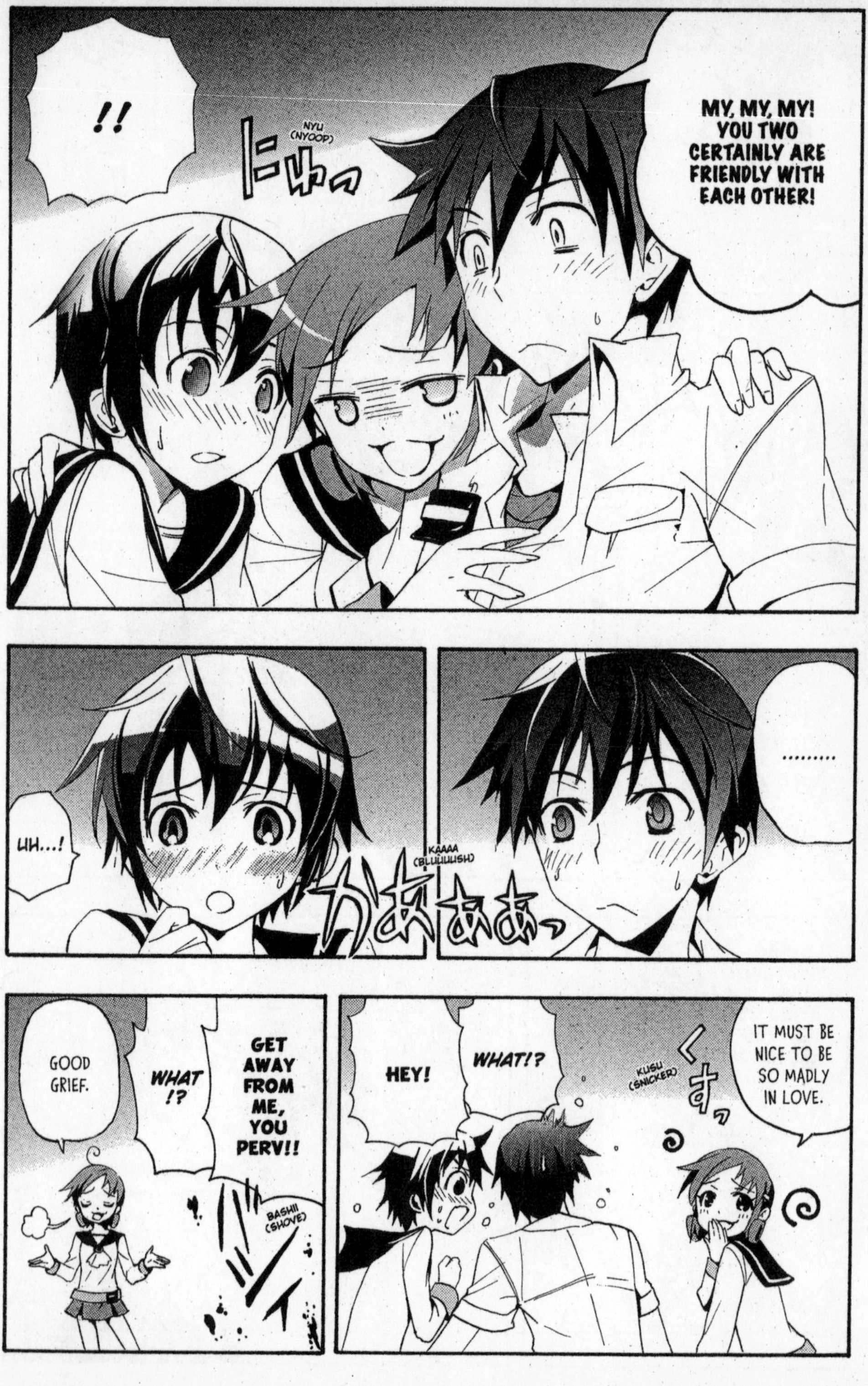
MY, MY, MY! YOU TWO CERTAINLY ARE FRIENDLY WITH EACH OTHER!
にゅっ
NYU (NYOOP)
!!
....
かあああっ
KAAAA (BLUUUUSH)
UH...!
IT MUST BE NICE TO BE SO MADLY IN LOVE.
くすっ
KUSU (SNICKER)
WHAT!?
HEY!
GET AWAY FROM ME, YOU PERV!!
BASHII (SHOVE)
WHAT !?
GOOD GRIEF.

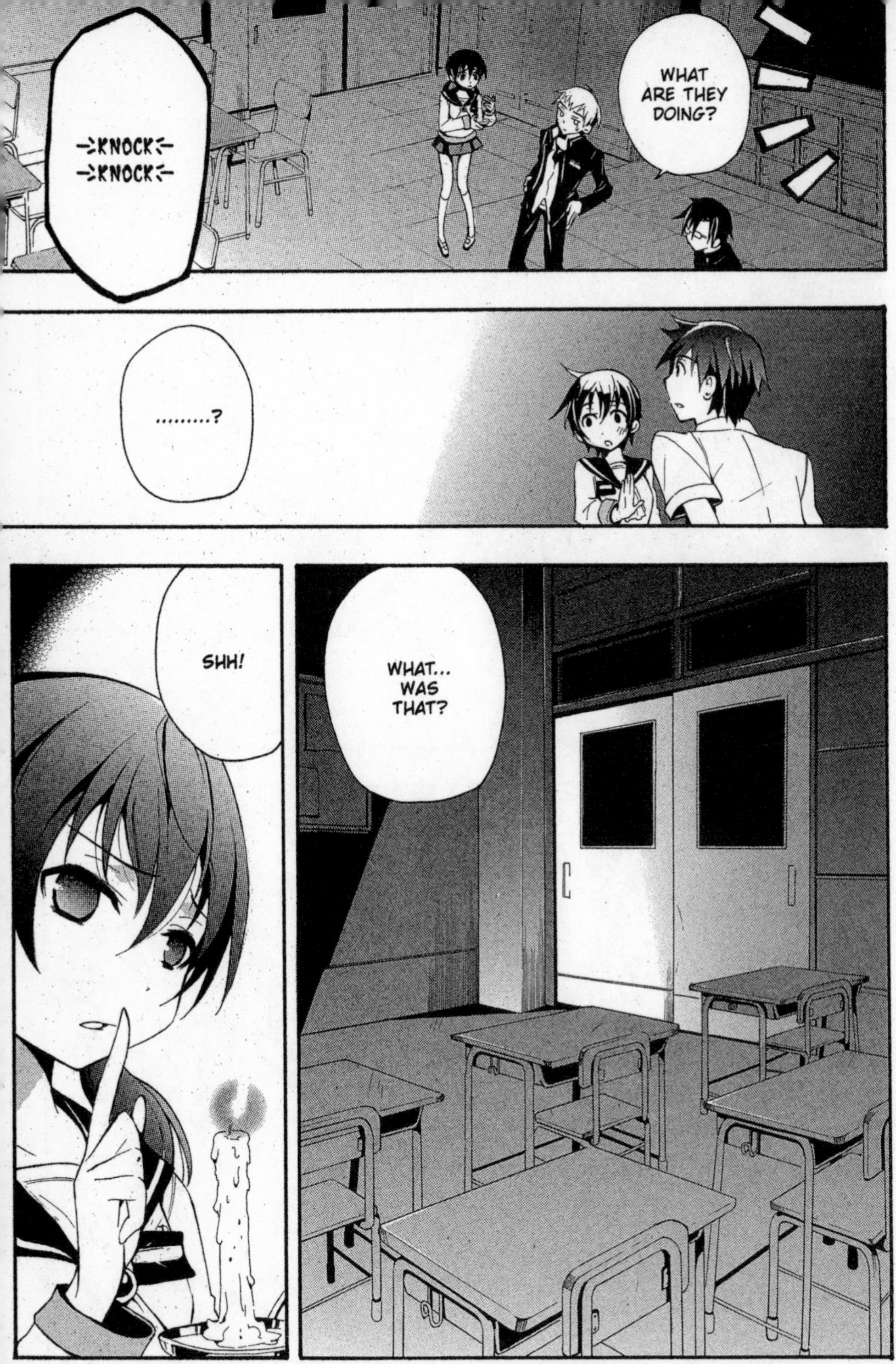
WHAT ARE THEY DOING?
-KNOCK-
-KNOCK-
.........?
WHAT... WAS THAT?
SHH!

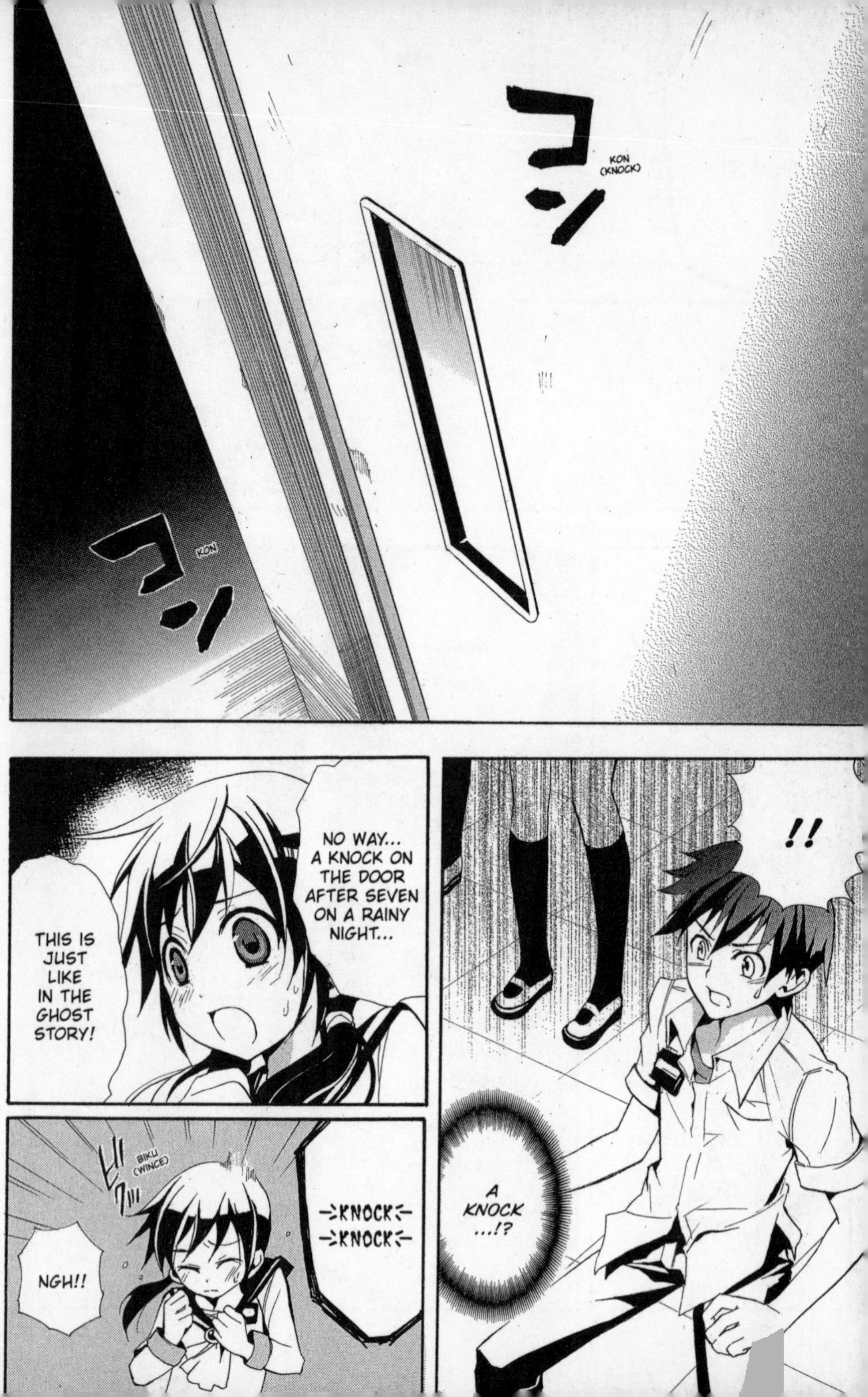
KON (KNOCK)
KON
!!
A KNOCK ...!?
NO WAY... A KNOCK ON THE DOOR AFTER SEVEN ON A RAINY NIGHT...
THIS IS JUST LIKE IN THE GHOST STORY!
KNOCK KNOCK
BIKU (WINCE)
NGH!!

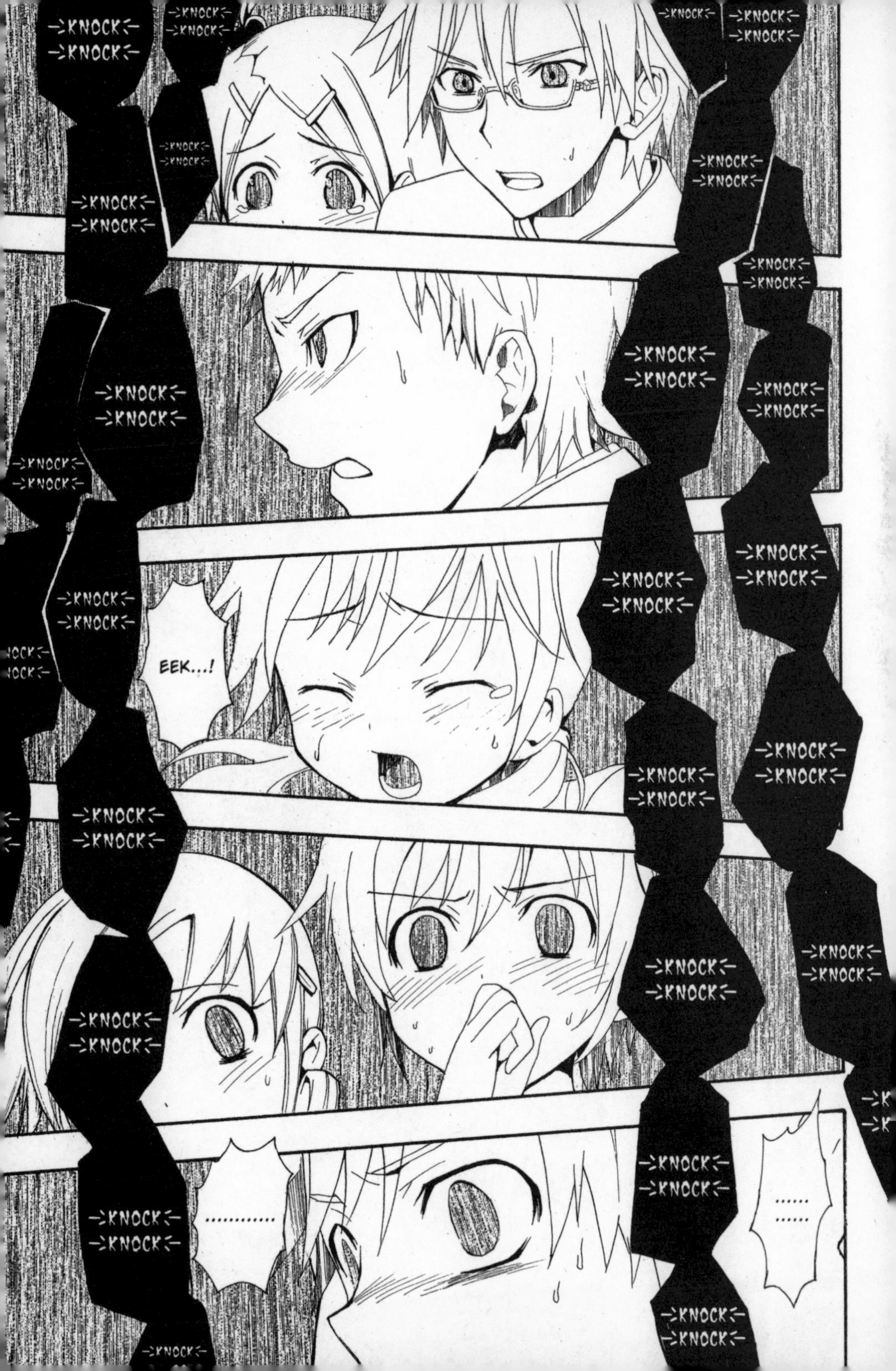
KNOCK KNOCK
KNOCK KNOCK
KNOCK KNOCK
KNOCK KNOCK
KNOCK KNOCK
KNOCK KNOCK
KNOCK KNOCK
KNOCK KNOCK
KNOCK KNOCK
KNOCK KNOCK
KNOCK KNOCK
KNOCK KNOCK
KNOCK KNOCK
KNOCK KNOCK
KNOCK KNOCK
EEK...!
KNOCK KNOCK
KNOCK KNOCK
KNOCK KNOCK
KNOCK KNOCK
KNOCK KNOCK
KNOCK KNOCK
KNOCK KNOCK
....
KNOCK KNOCK
....
KNOCK KNOCK
KNOCK

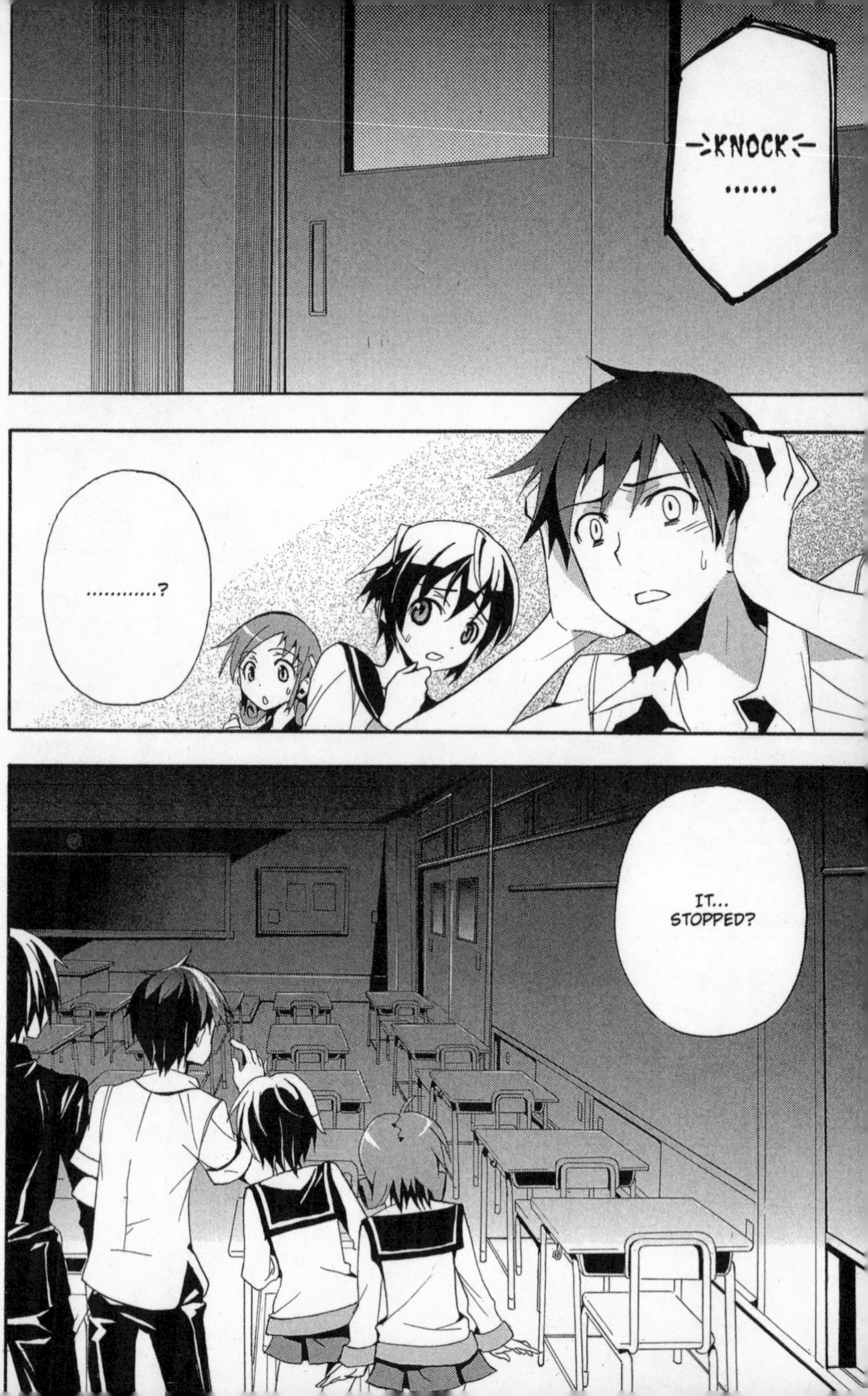
KNOCK
......
............?
IT... STOPPED?

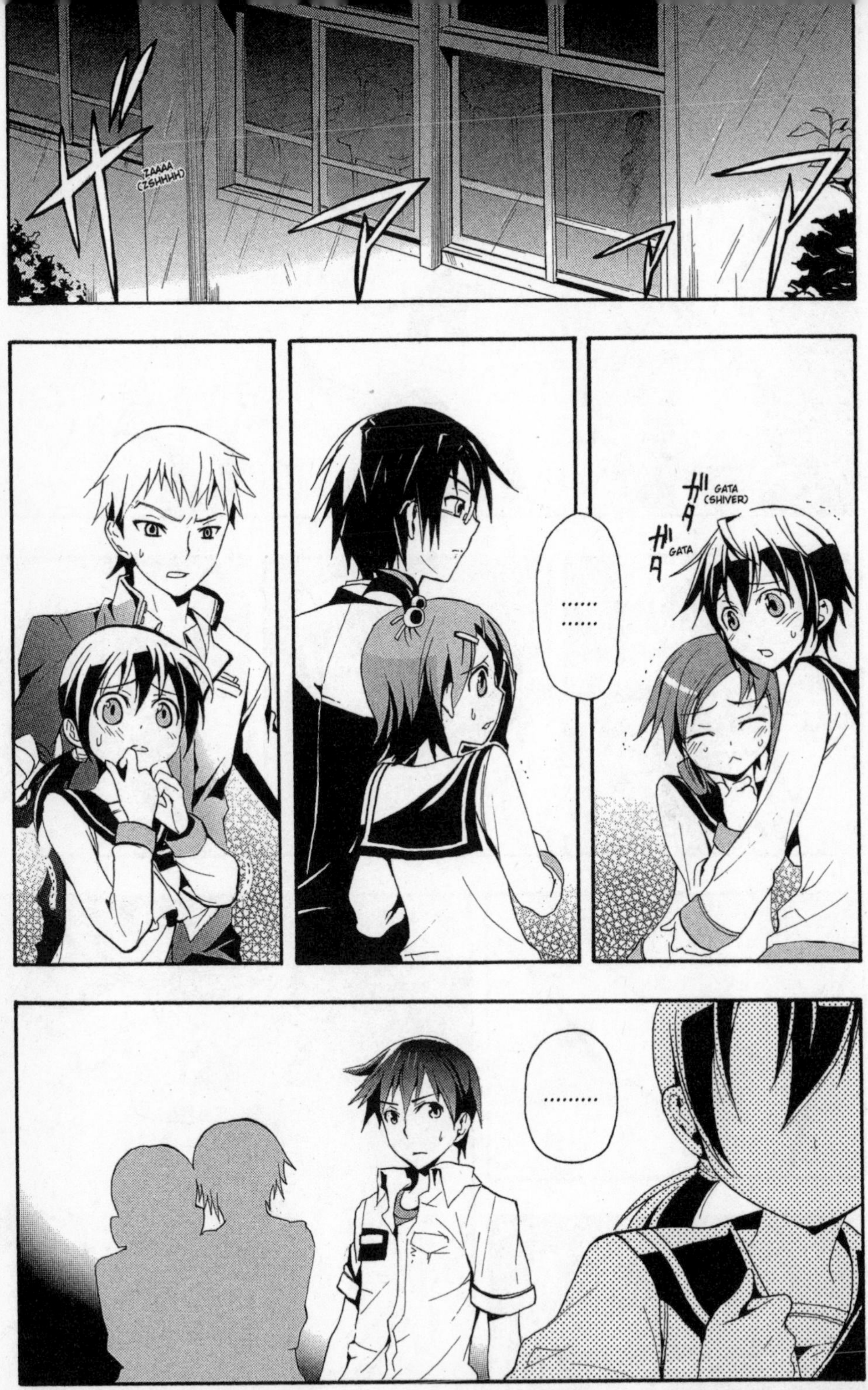
ZAAAA (ZSHHHH)
GATA (SHIVER)
GATA
......
......
....

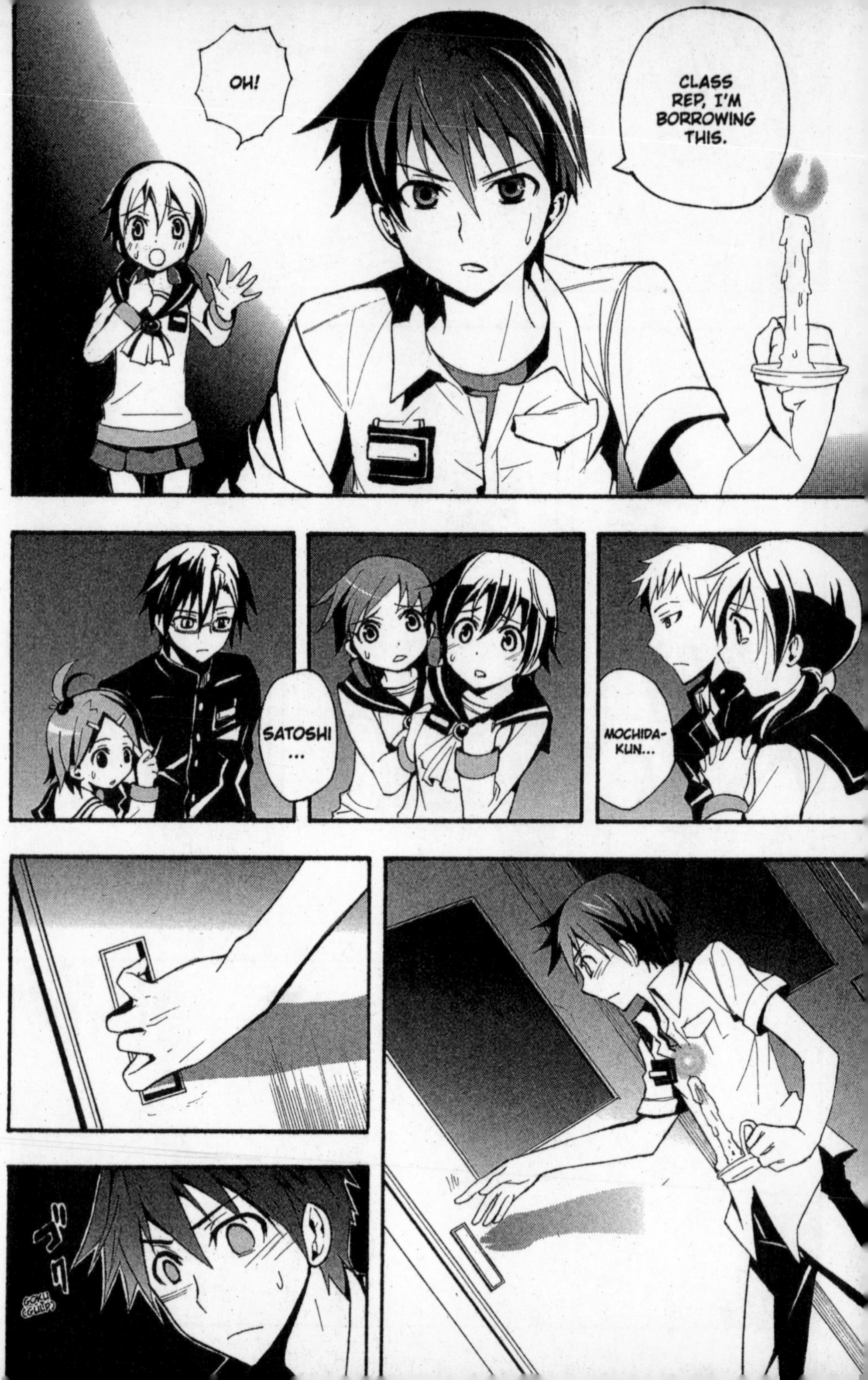
CLASS REP, I'M BORROWING THIS.
OH!
MOCHIDA-KUN...
SATOSHI ...
GOKU (GULP)

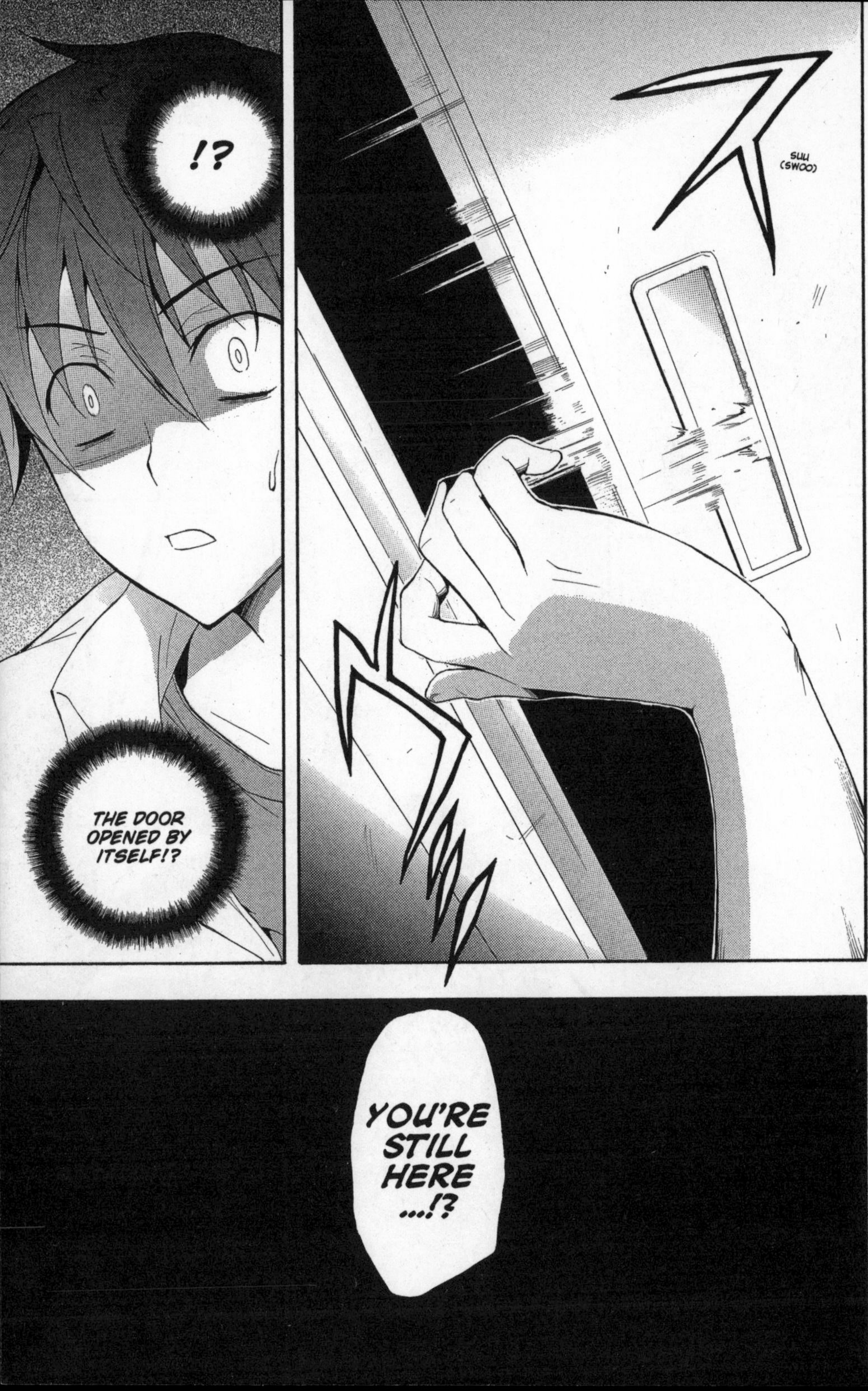
SUU
(SWOO)
!?
THE DOOR OPENED BY ITSELF!?
YOU'RE STILL HERE ...!?

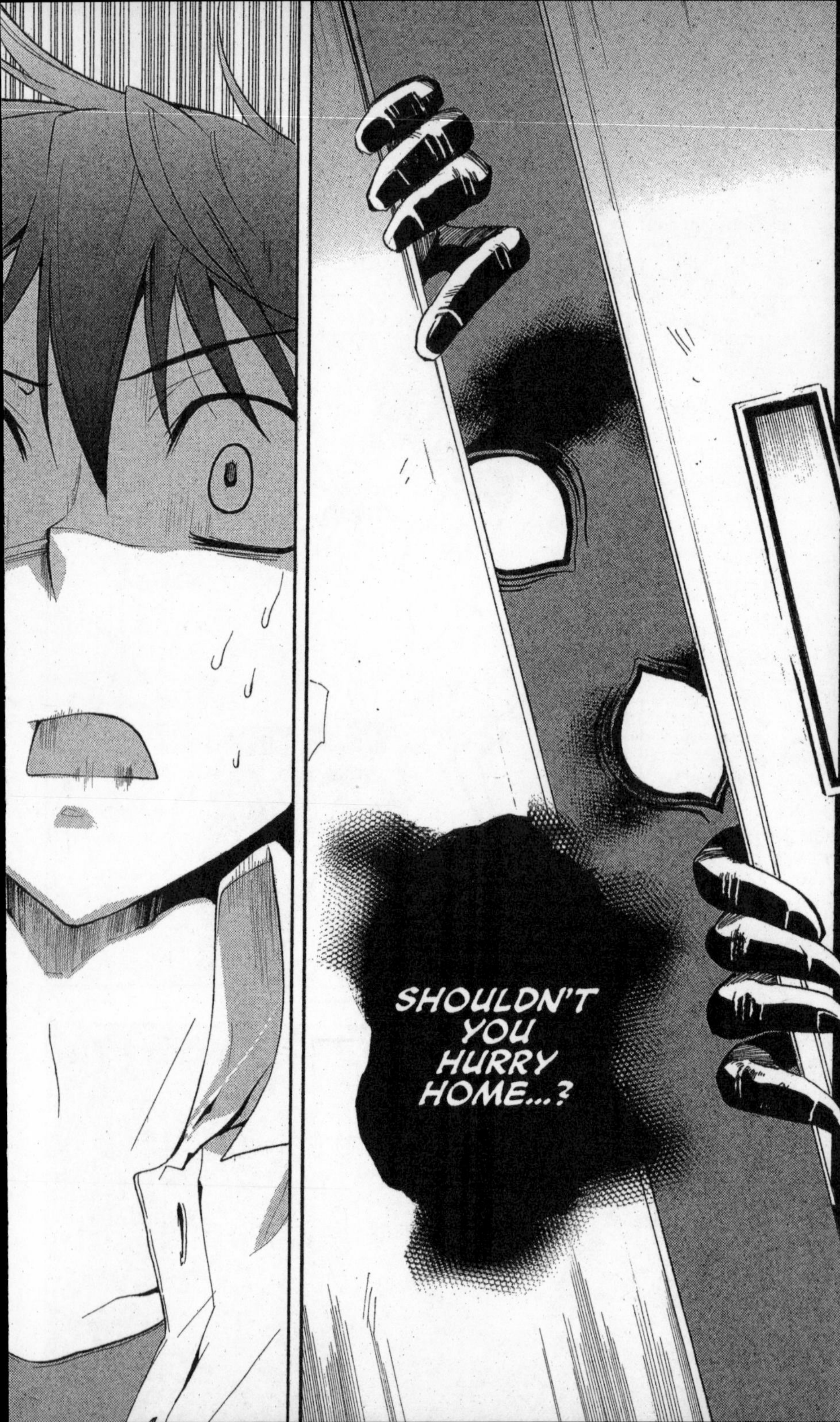
SHOULDN'T YOU HURRY HOME...?

WAAAAAH!

AAAAAAAAH!

HEE-HEE-HEE...

PA (FLASH)

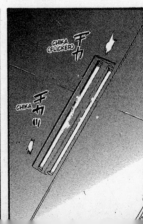

CHIKA (FLICKER)

CHIKA

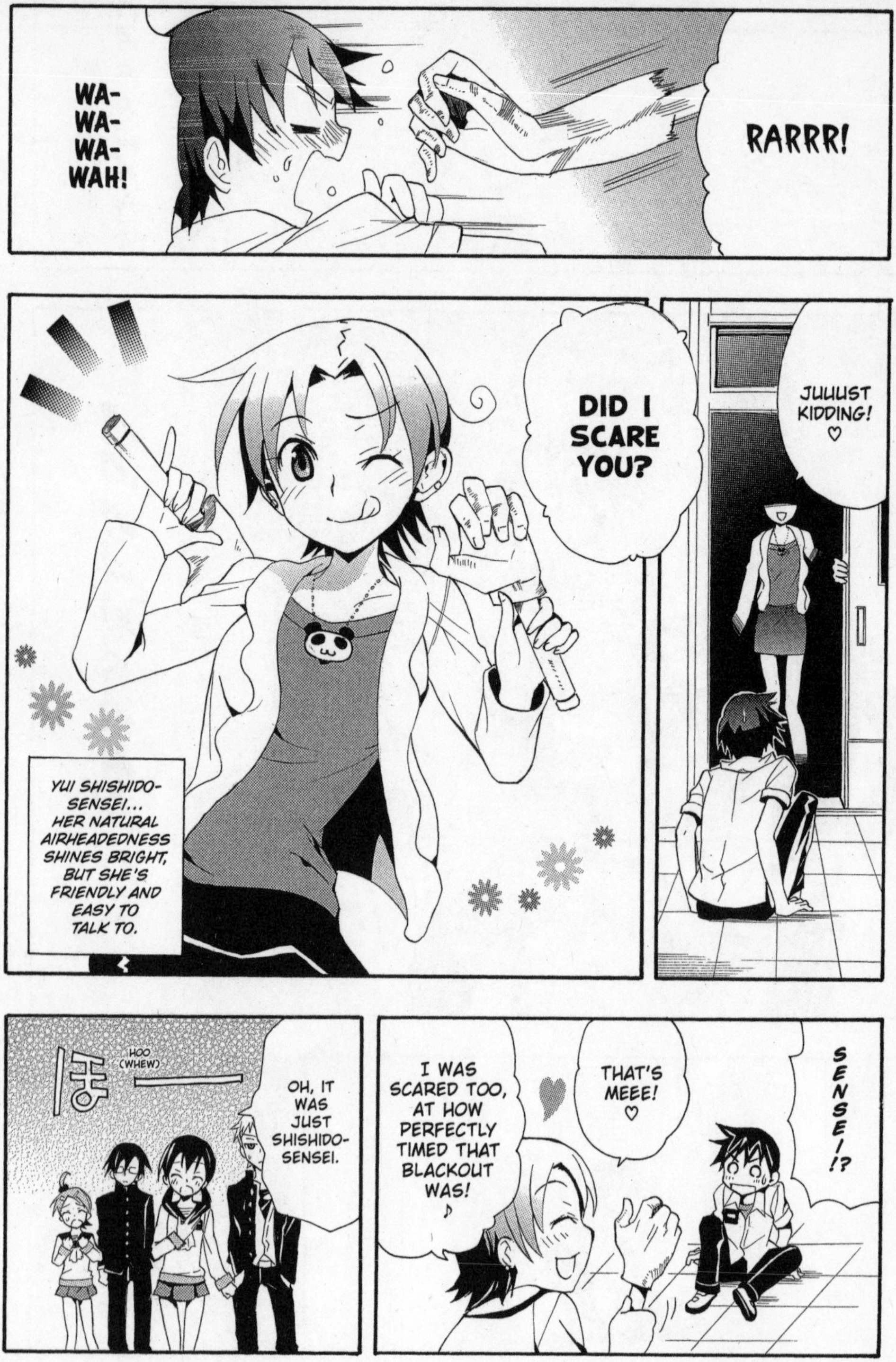
RARRR!
WA-WA-WA-WAH!
JUUUST KIDDING! ♡
DID I SCARE YOU?
YUI SHISHIDO-SENSEI... HER NATURAL AIRHEADEDNESS SHINES BRIGHT, BUT SHE'S FRIENDLY AND EASY TO TALK TO.
SENSEI!?
THAT'S MEEE! ♡
I WAS SCARED TOO, AT HOW PERFECTLY TIMED THAT BLACKOUT WAS! ♪
OH, IT WAS JUST SHISHIDO-SENSEI.
ほー
HOO (WHEW)

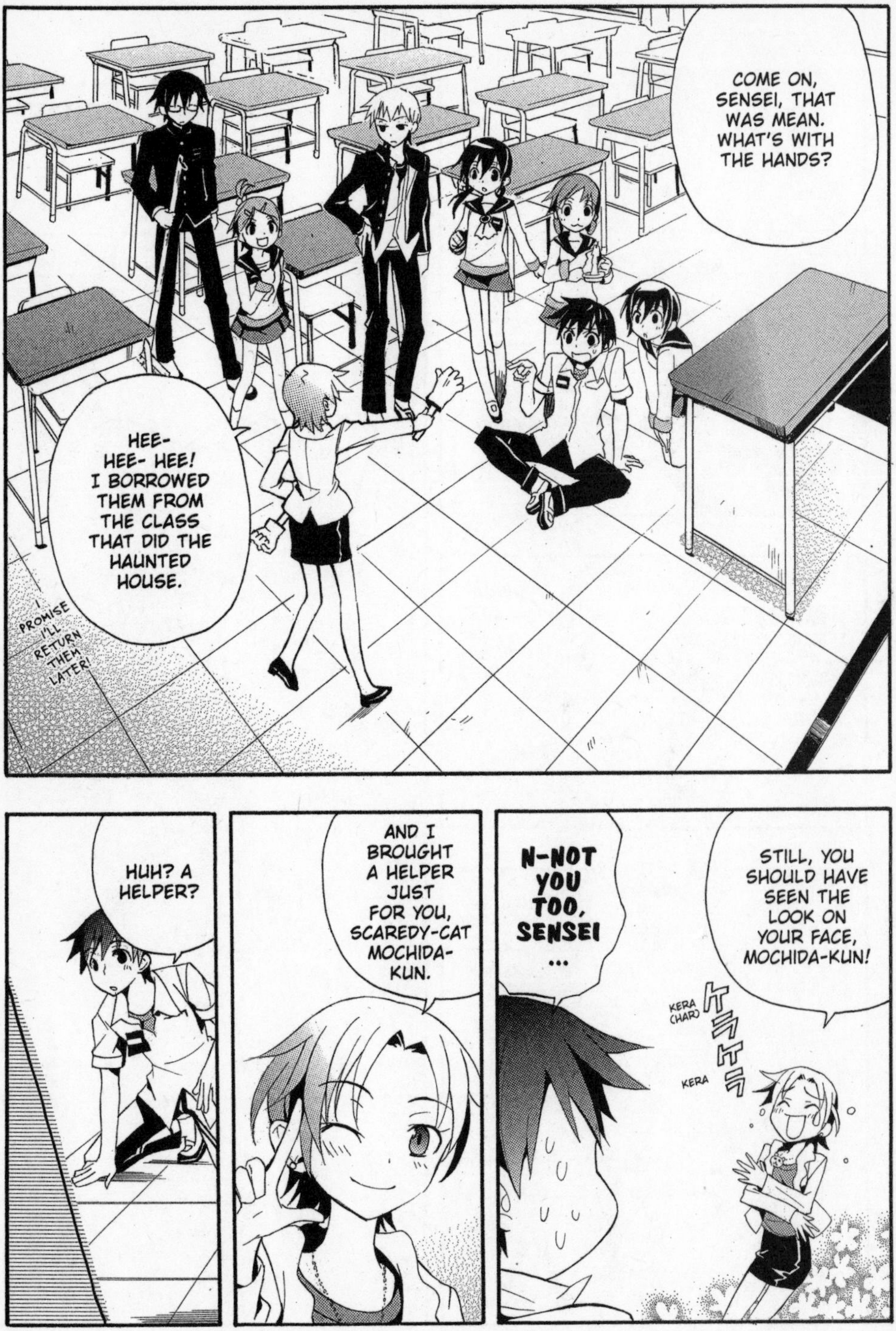
COME ON, SENSEI, THAT WAS MEAN. WHAT'S WITH THE HANDS?
HEE-HEE- HEE! I BORROWED THEM FROM THE CLASS THAT DID THE HAUNTED HOUSE.
I PROMISE I'LL RETURN THEM LATER!
STILL, YOU SHOULD HAVE SEEN THE LOOK ON YOUR FACE, MOCHIDA-KUN!
KERA (CHAR)
KERA
N-NOT YOU TOO, SENSEI ...
AND I BROUGHT A HELPER JUST FOR YOU, SCAREDY-CAT MOCHIDA-KUN.
HUH? A HELPER?

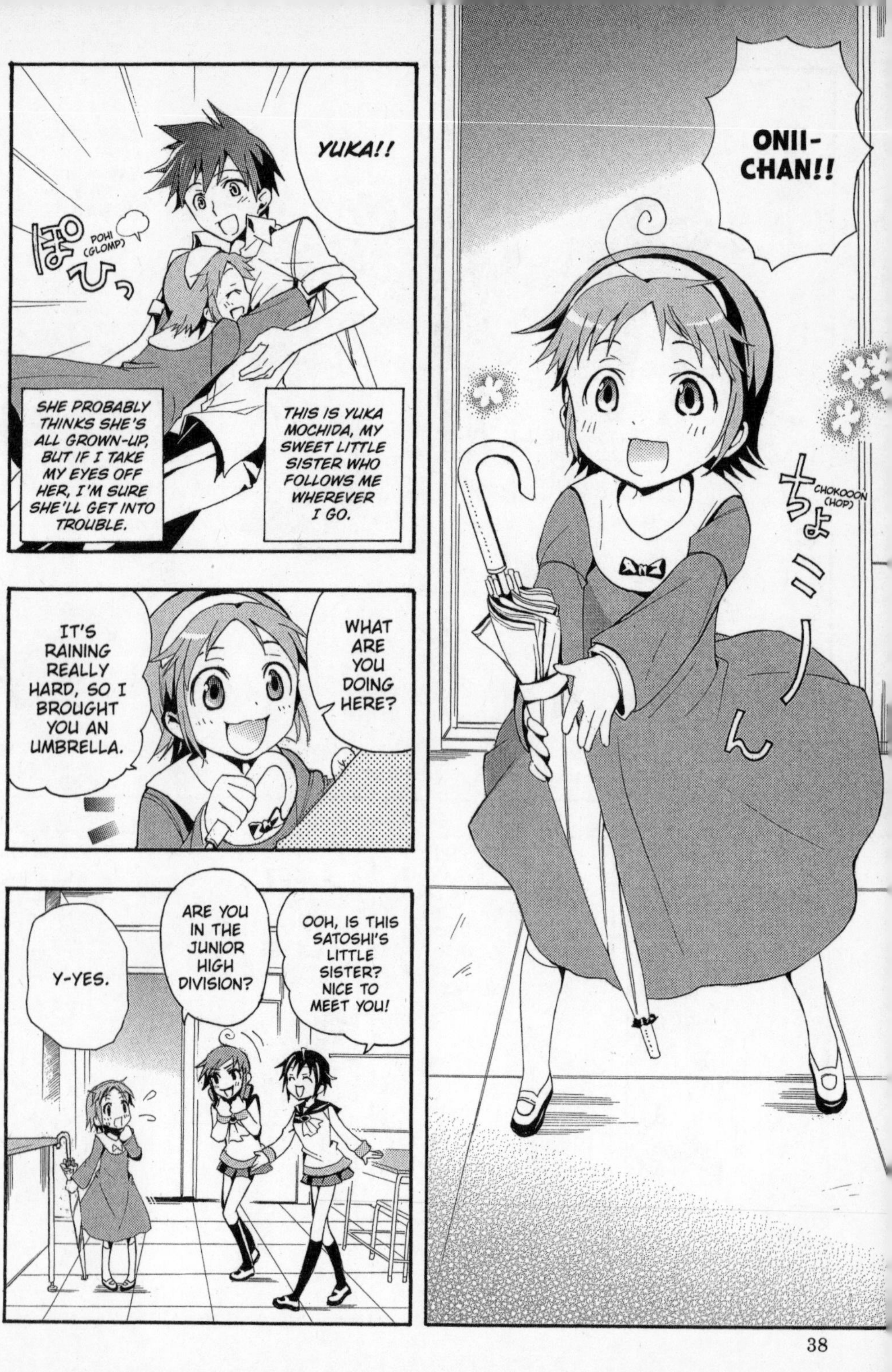

ONII-CHAN!!
ちょこーん
CHOKOOON (HOP)
YUKA!!
ぽひっ
POHI (GLOMP)
THIS IS YUKA MOCHIDA, MY SWEET LITTLE SISTER WHO FOLLOWS ME WHEREVER I GO.
SHE PROBABLY THINKS SHE'S ALL GROWN-UP, BUT IF I TAKE MY EYES OFF HER, I'M SURE SHE'LL GET INTO TROUBLE.
WHAT ARE YOU DOING HERE?
IT'S RAINING REALLY HARD, SO I BROUGHT YOU AN UMBRELLA.
OOH, IS THIS SATOSHI'S LITTLE SISTER? NICE TO MEET YOU!
ARE YOU IN THE JUNIOR HIGH DIVISION?
Y-YES.

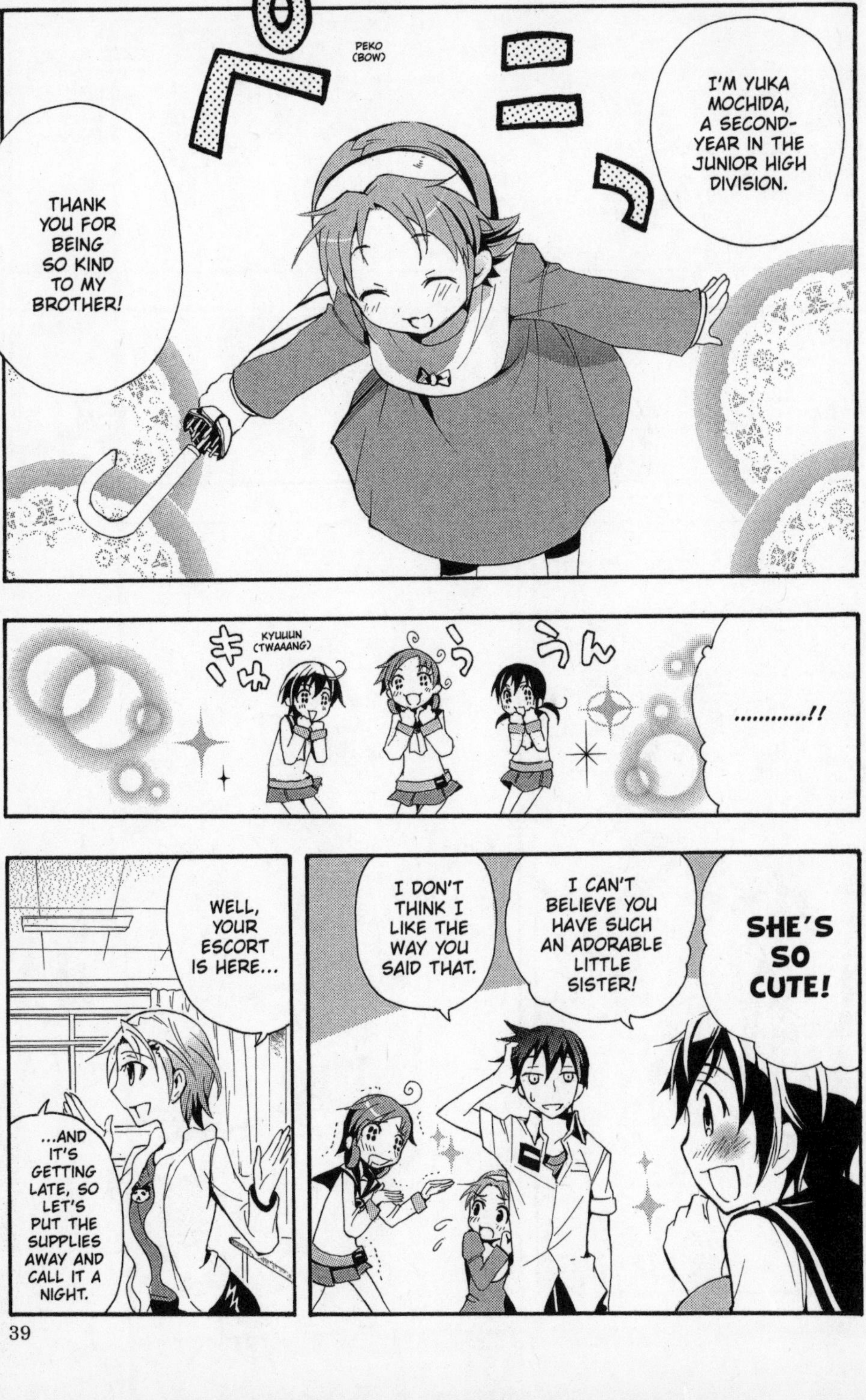

I'M YUKA MOCHIDA, A SECOND-YEAR IN THE JUNIOR HIGH DIVISION.
PEKO (BOW)
THANK YOU FOR BEING SO KIND TO MY BROTHER!
............!!
KYUUUN (TWAAANG)
SHE'S SO CUTE!
I CAN'T BELIEVE YOU HAVE SUCH AN ADORABLE LITTLE SISTER!
I DON'T THINK I LIKE THE WAY YOU SAID THAT.
WELL, YOUR ESCORT IS HERE...
...AND IT'S GETTING LATE, SO LET'S PUT THE SUPPLIES AWAY AND CALL IT A NIGHT.

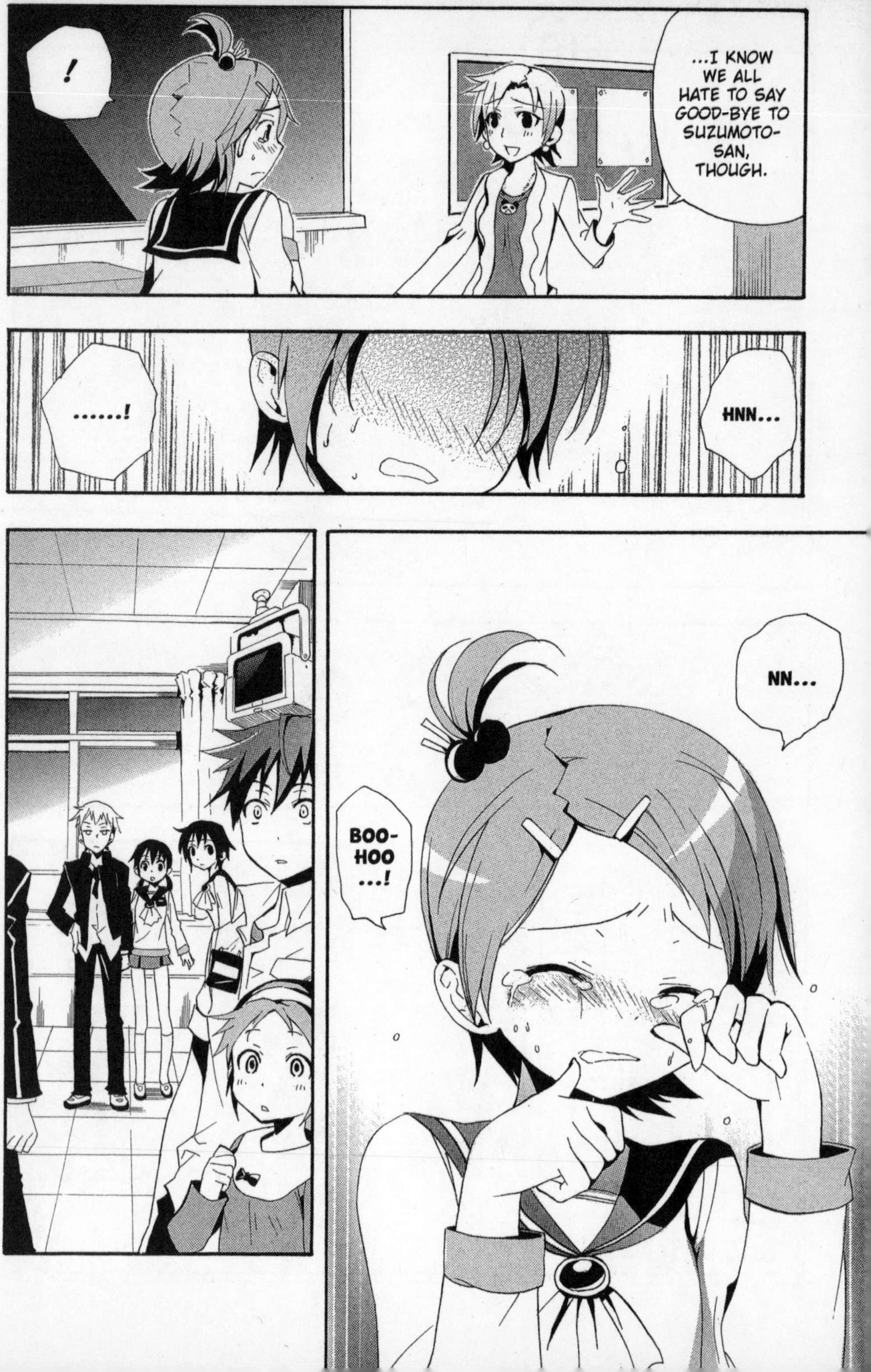
...I KNOW WE ALL HATE TO SAY GOOD-BYE TO SUZUMOTO-SAN, THOUGH.
!
HNN...
......!
NN...
BOO-HOO...!

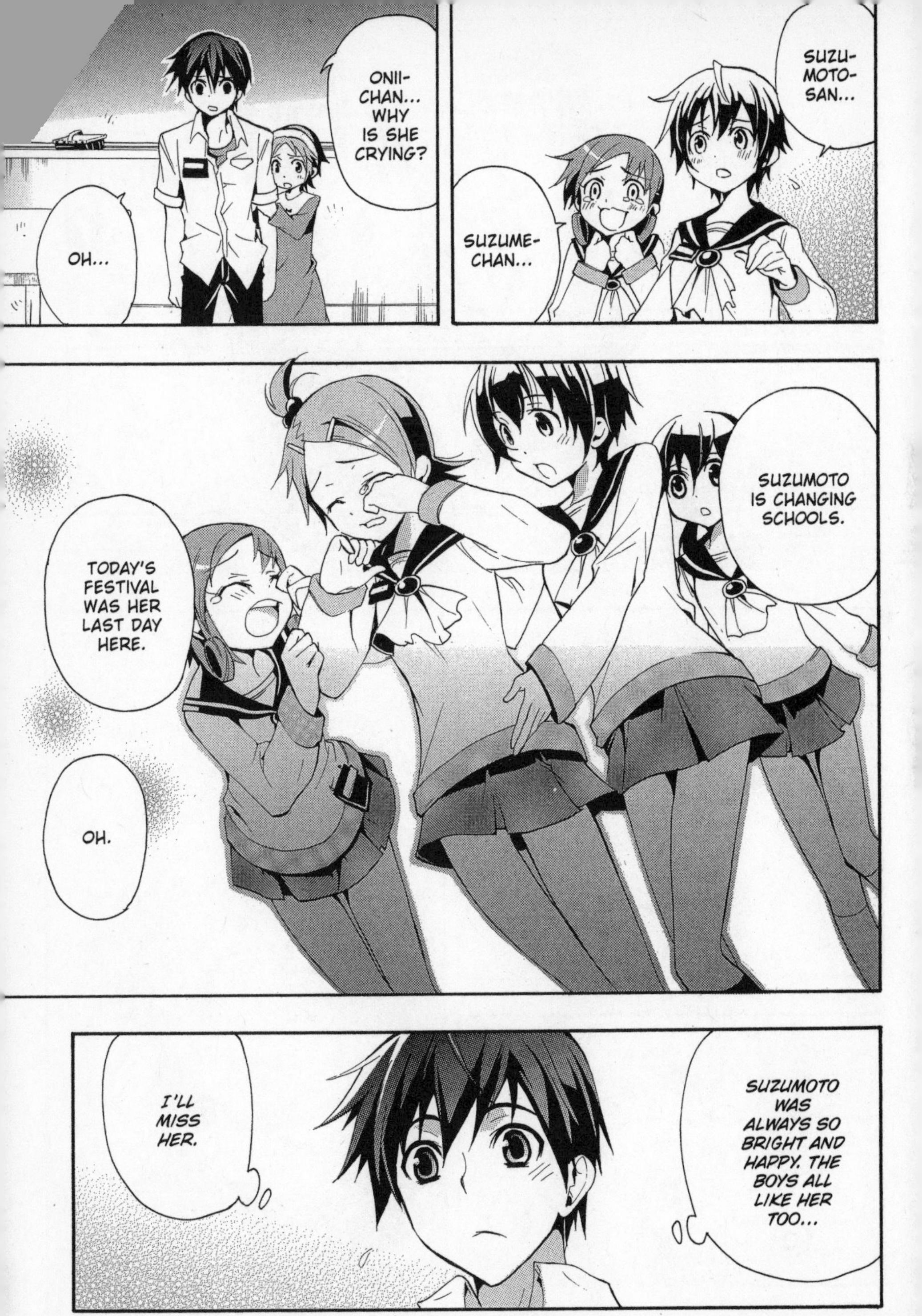
SUZU-MOTO-SAN...
SUZUME-CHAN...
ONII-CHAN... WHY IS SHE CRYING?
OH...
SUZUMOTO IS CHANGING SCHOOLS.
TODAY'S FESTIVAL WAS HER LAST DAY HERE.
OH.
SUZUMOTO WAS ALWAYS SO BRIGHT AND HAPPY. THE BOYS ALL LIKE HER TOO...
I'LL MISS HER.

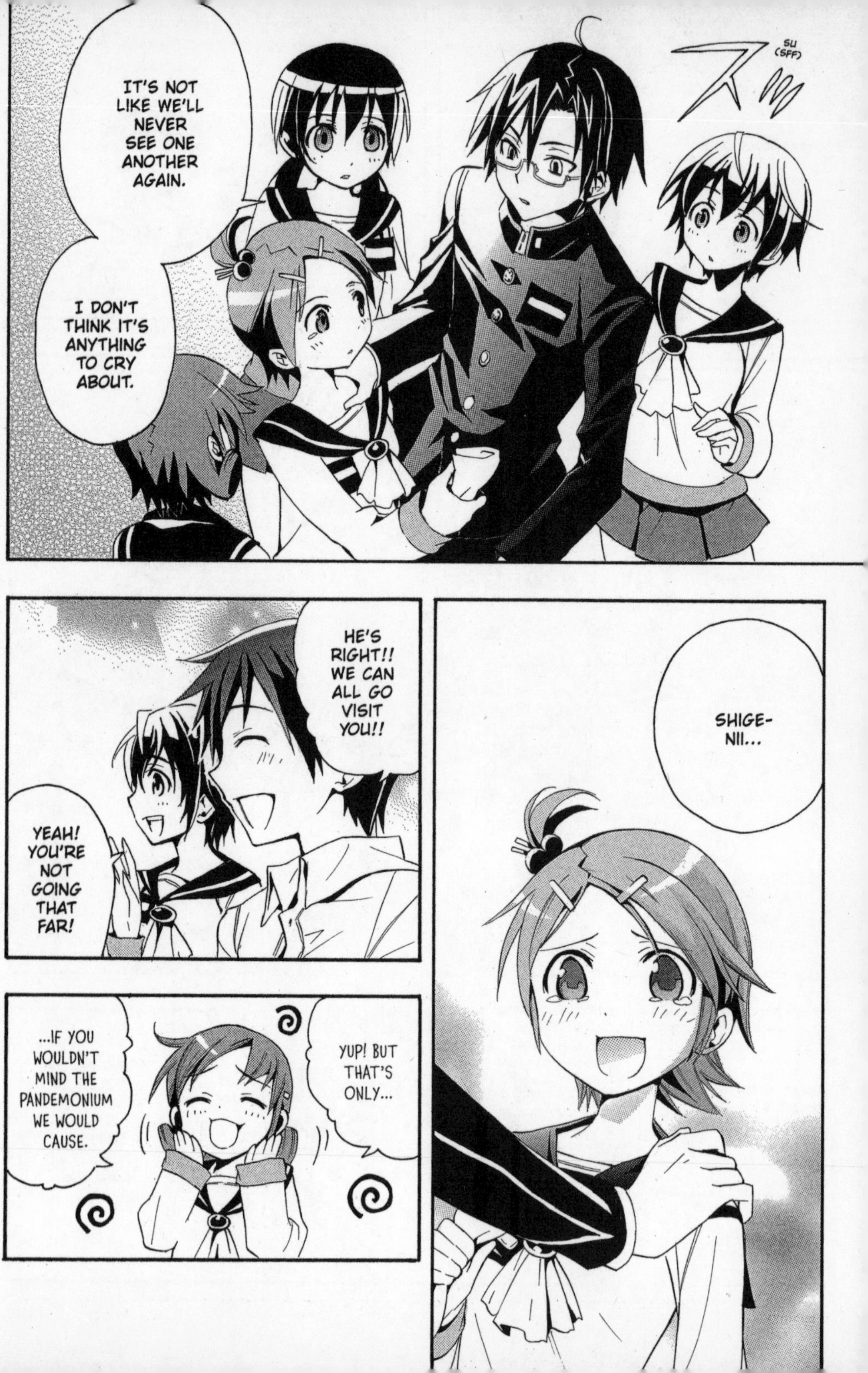
SU (SFF)
IT'S NOT LIKE WE'LL NEVER SEE ONE ANOTHER AGAIN.
I DON'T THINK IT'S ANYTHING TO CRY ABOUT.
SHIGE-NII...
HE'S RIGHT!! WE CAN ALL GO VISIT YOU!!
YEAH! YOU'RE NOT GOING THAT FAR!
YUP! BUT THAT'S ONLY...
...IF YOU WOULDN'T MIND THE PANDEMONIUM WE WOULD CAUSE.

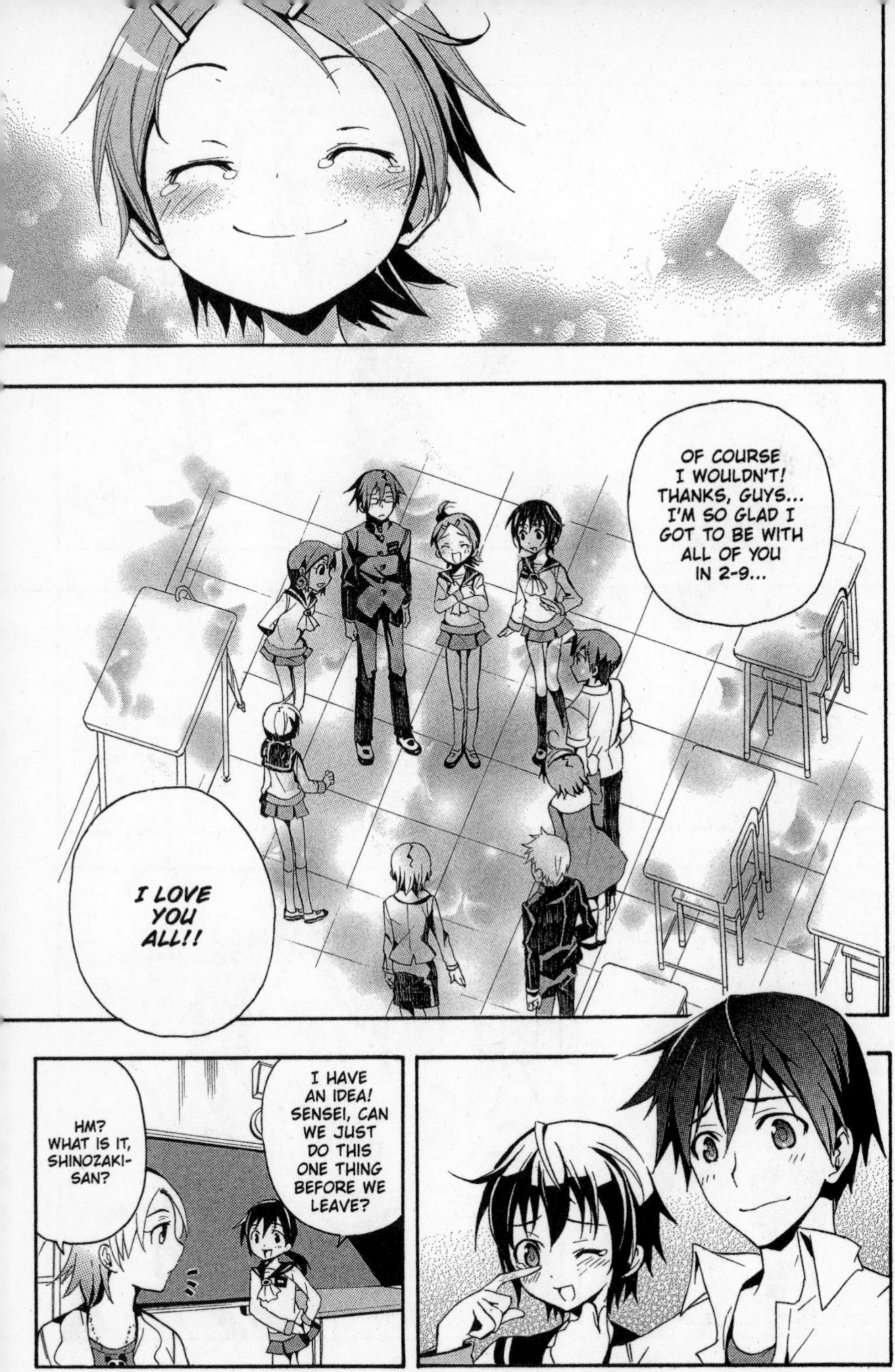
OF COURSE I WOULDN'T! THANKS, GUYS... I'M SO GLAD I GOT TO BE WITH ALL OF YOU IN 2-9...
I LOVE YOU ALL!!
I HAVE AN IDEA! SENSEI, CAN WE JUST DO THIS ONE THING BEFORE WE LEAVE?
HM? WHAT IS IT, SHINOZAKI-SAN?

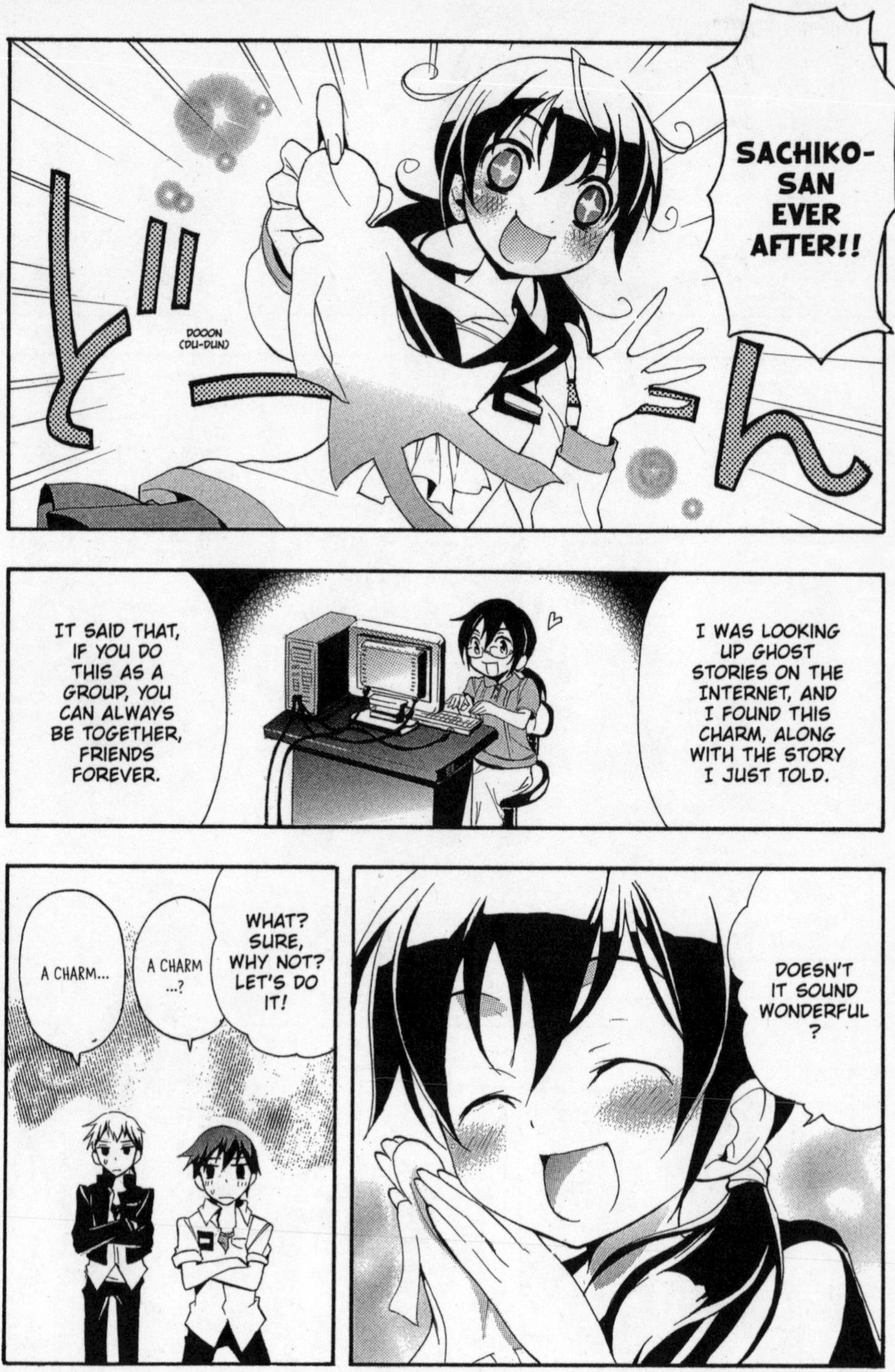
SACHIKO-SAN EVER AFTER!!
DOOON (DU-DUN)
I WAS LOOKING UP GHOST STORIES ON THE INTERNET, AND I FOUND THIS CHARM, ALONG WITH THE STORY I JUST TOLD.
IT SAID THAT, IF YOU DO THIS AS A GROUP, YOU CAN ALWAYS BE TOGETHER, FRIENDS FOREVER.
DOESN'T IT SOUND WONDERFUL?
WHAT? SURE, WHY NOT? LET'S DO IT!
A CHARM ...?
A CHARM...

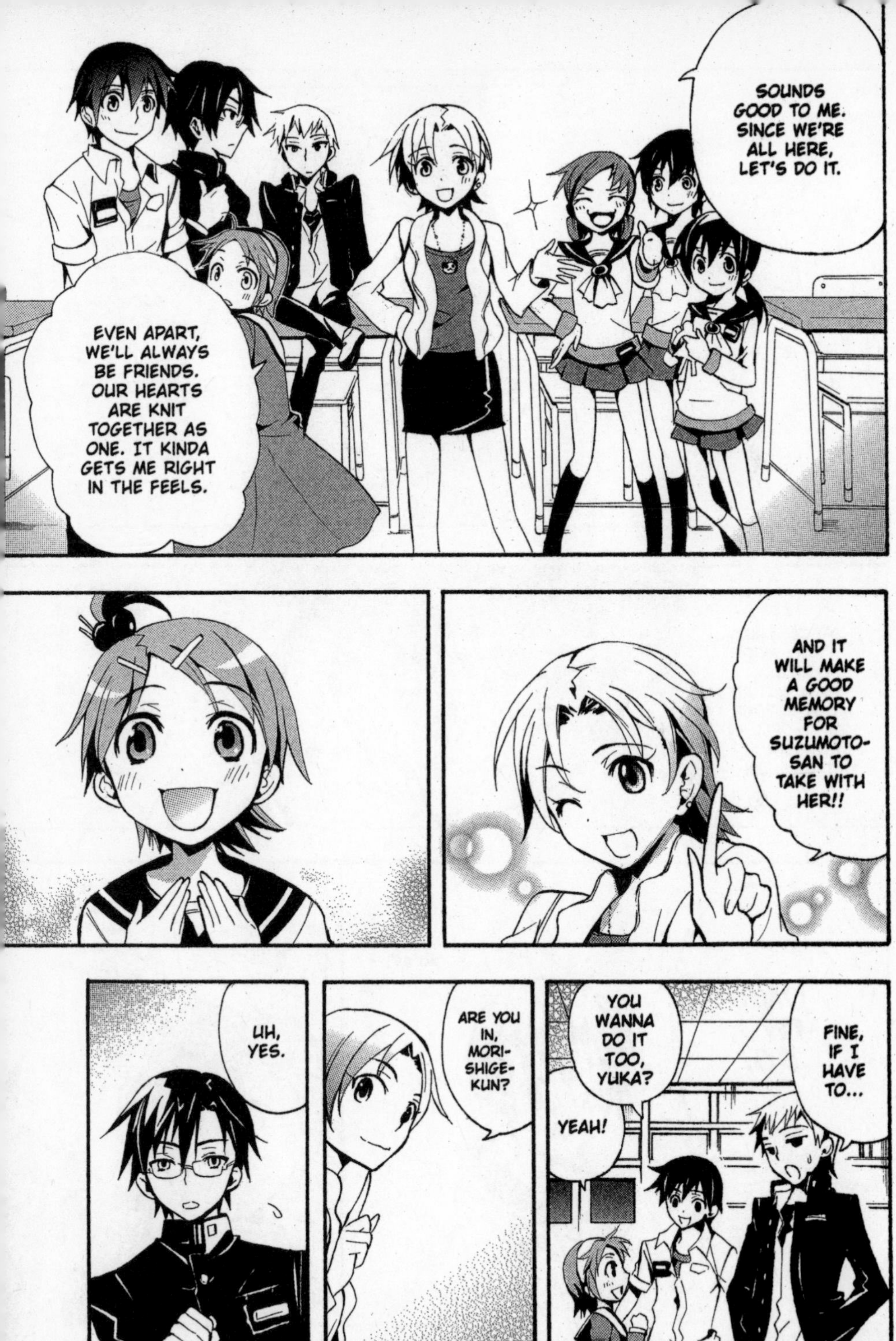
SOUNDS GOOD TO ME. SINCE WE'RE ALL HERE, LET'S DO IT.
EVEN APART, WE'LL ALWAYS BE FRIENDS. OUR HEARTS ARE KNIT TOGETHER AS ONE. IT KINDA GETS ME RIGHT IN THE FEELS.
AND IT WILL MAKE A GOOD MEMORY FOR SUZUMOTO-SAN TO TAKE WITH HER!!
FINE, IF I HAVE TO...
YOU WANNA DO IT TOO, YUKA?
YEAH!
ARE YOU IN, MORI-SHIGE-KUN?
UH, YES.

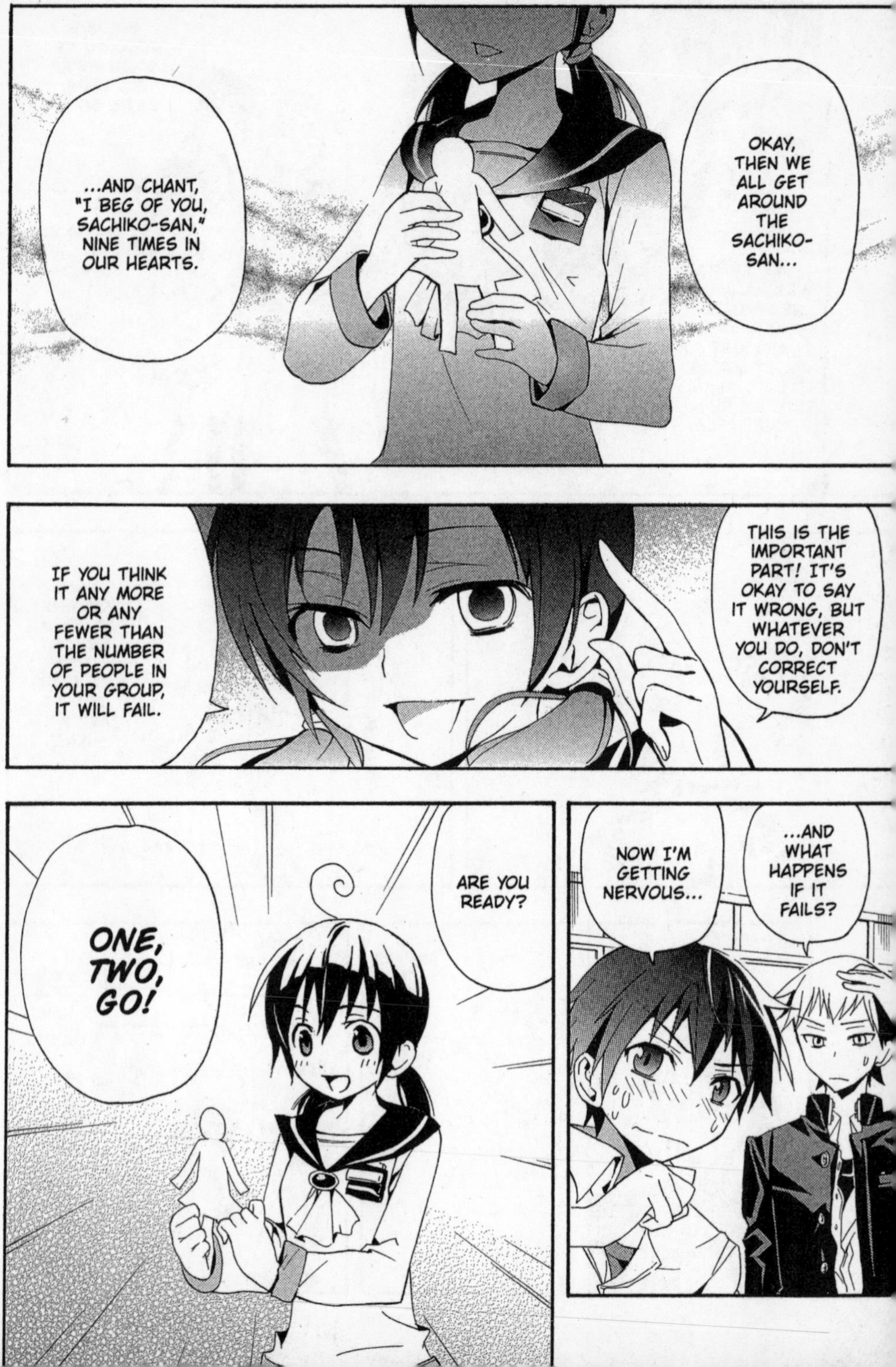
OKAY, THEN WE ALL GET AROUND THE SACHIKO-SAN...
...AND CHANT, "I BEG OF YOU, SACHIKO-SAN," NINE TIMES IN OUR HEARTS.
THIS IS THE IMPORTANT PART! IT'S OKAY TO SAY IT WRONG, BUT WHATEVER YOU DO, DON'T CORRECT YOURSELF.
IF YOU THINK IT ANY MORE OR ANY FEWER THAN THE NUMBER OF PEOPLE IN YOUR GROUP, IT WILL FAIL.
...AND WHAT HAPPENS IF IT FAILS?
NOW I'M GETTING NERVOUS...
ARE YOU READY?
ONE, TWO, GO!

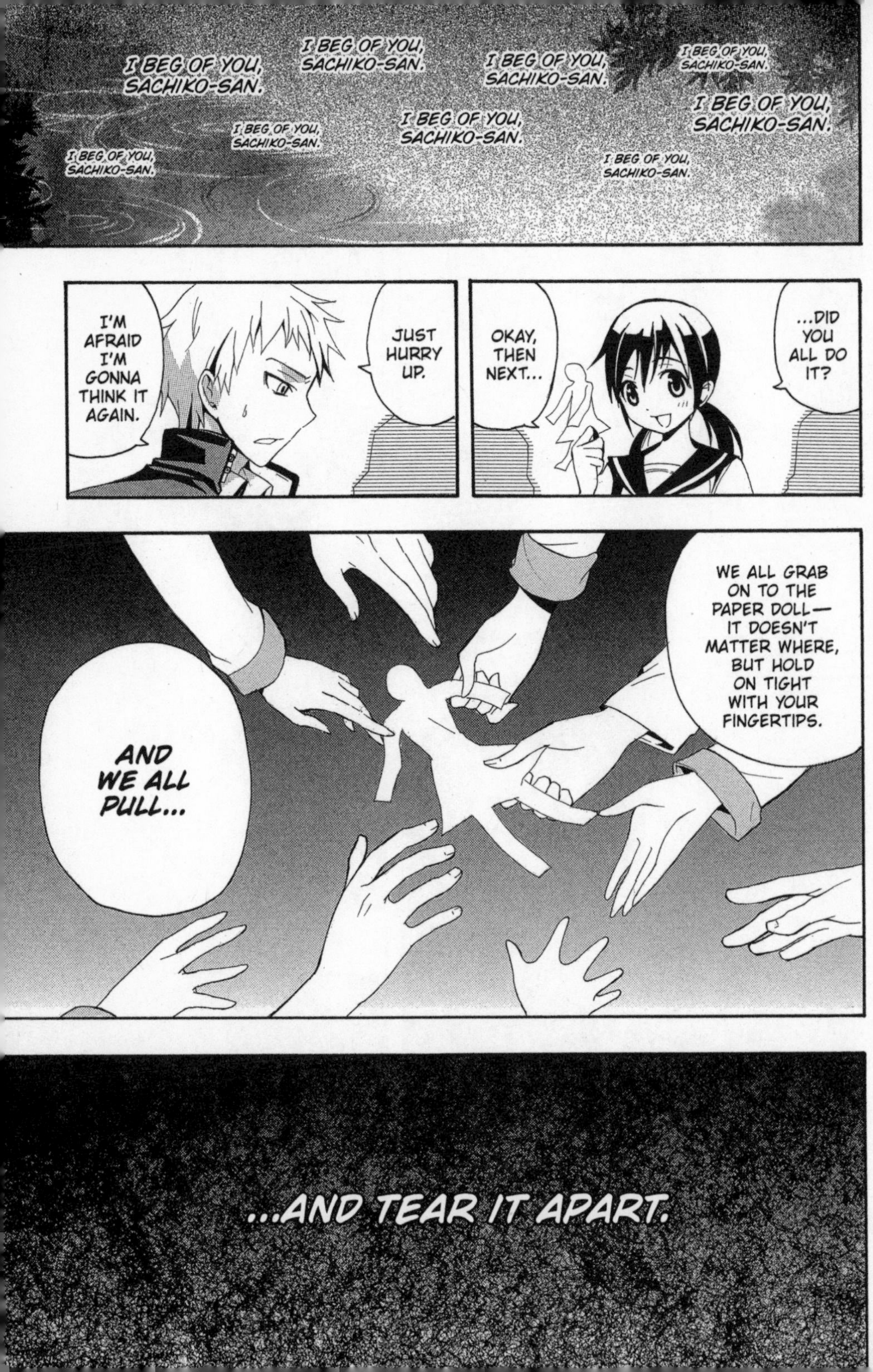
I BEG OF YOU, SACHIKO-SAN.
I BEG OF YOU, SACHIKO-SAN.
I BEG OF YOU, SACHIKO-SAN.
I BEG OF YOU, SACHIKO-SAN.
I BEG OF YOU, SACHIKO-SAN.
I BEG OF YOU, SACHIKO-SAN.
I BEG OF YOU, SACHIKO-SAN.
I BEG OF YOU, SACHIKO-SAN.
...DID YOU ALL DO IT?
OKAY, THEN NEXT...
JUST HURRY UP.
I'M AFRAID I'M GONNA THINK IT AGAIN.
WE ALL GRAB ON TO THE PAPER DOLL— IT DOESN'T MATTER WHERE, BUT HOLD ON TIGHT WITH YOUR FINGERTIPS.
AND WE ALL PULL...
...AND TEAR IT APART.

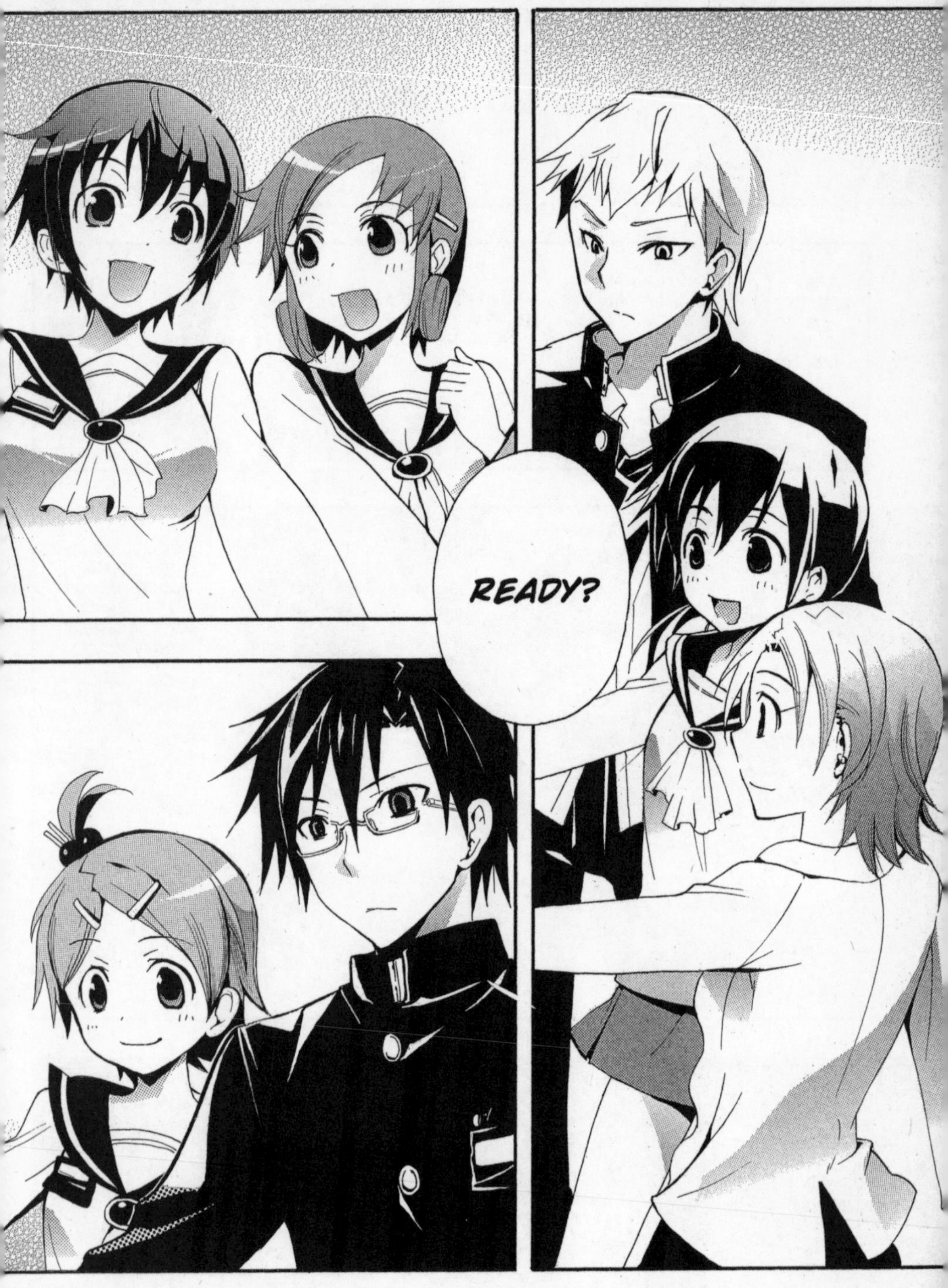
READY?

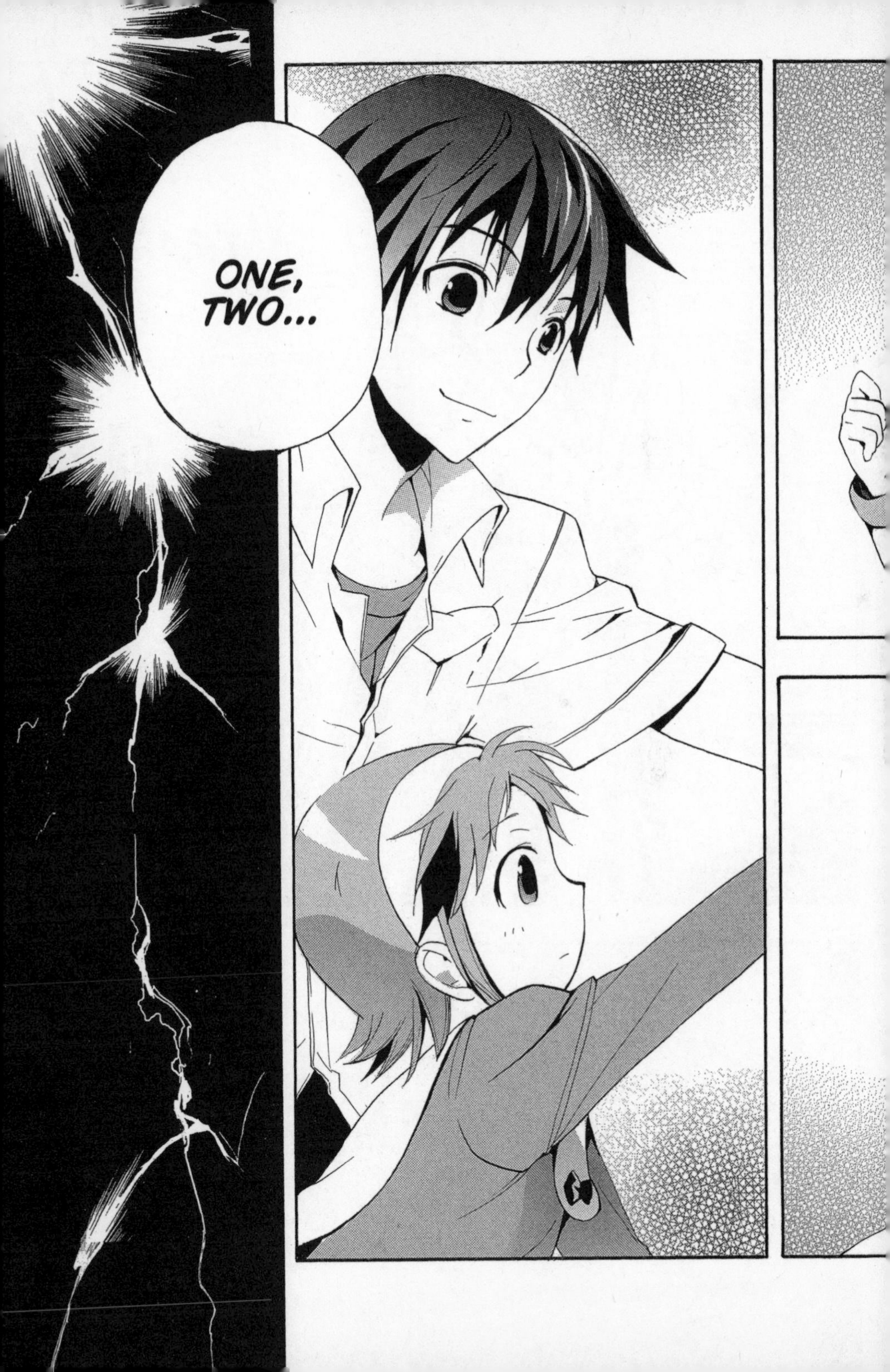
ONE, TWO...

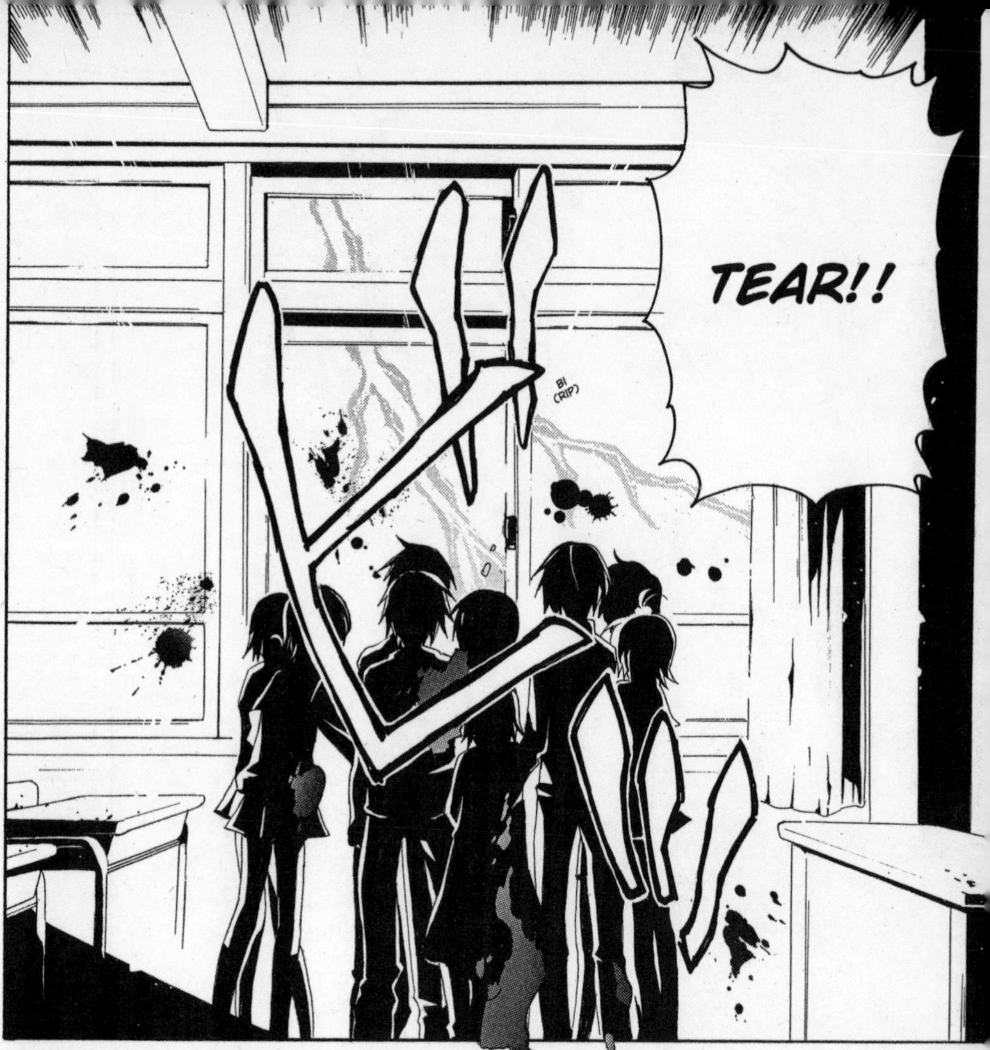
TEAR!!
BI
(RIP)
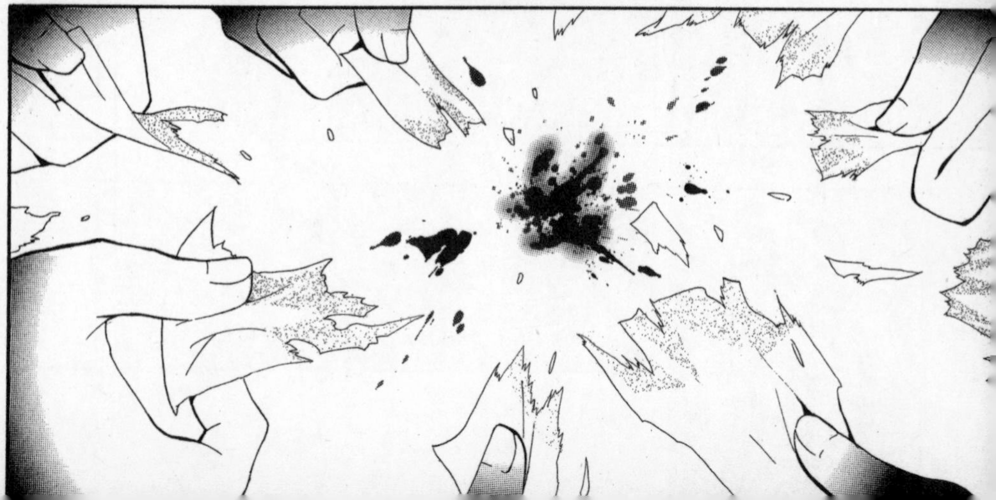

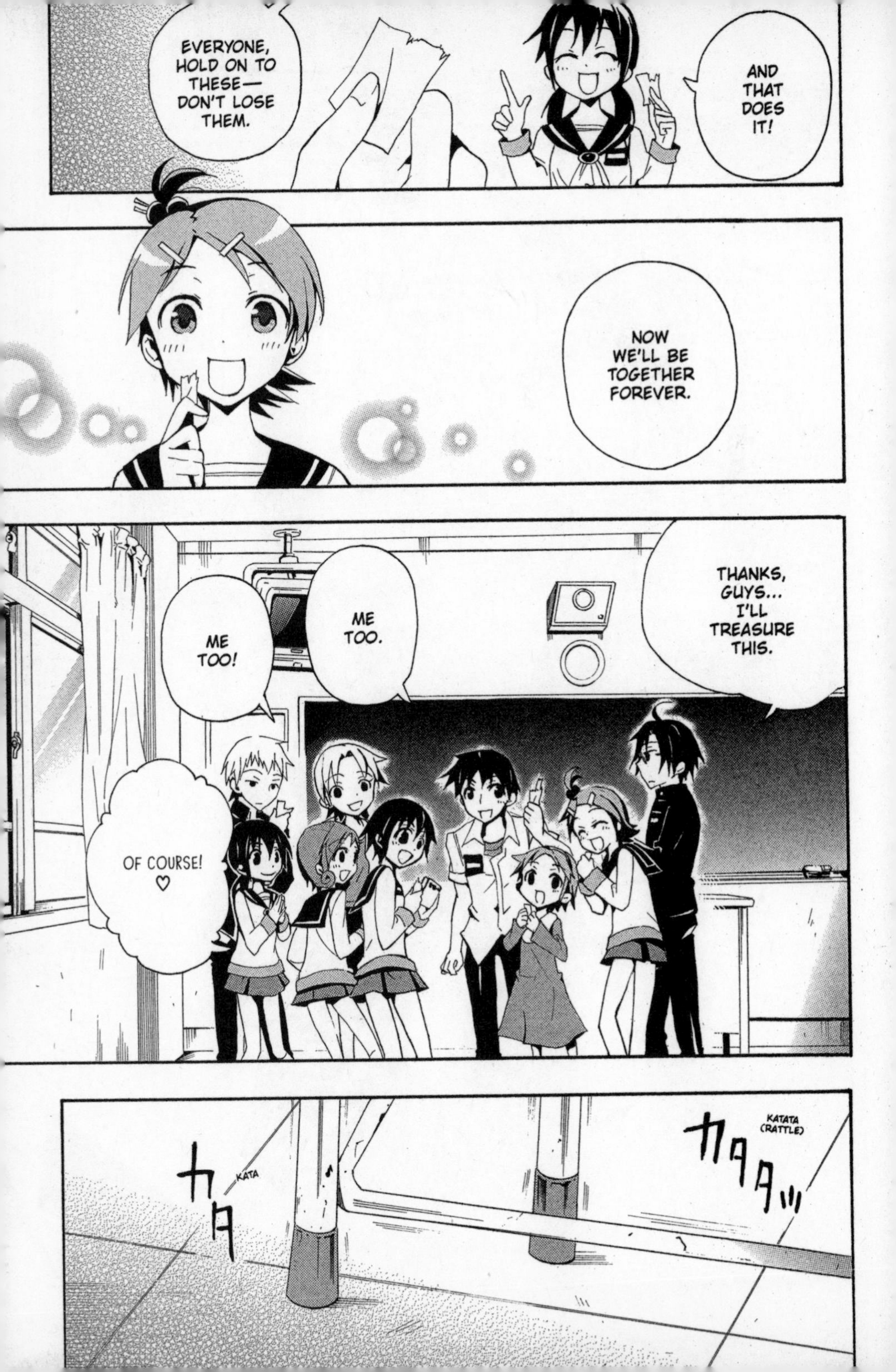
AND THAT DOES IT!
EVERYONE, HOLD ON TO THESE— DON'T LOSE THEM.
NOW WE'LL BE TOGETHER FOREVER.
THANKS, GUYS... I'LL TREASURE THIS.
ME TOO.
ME TOO!
OF COURSE! ♡
カタタッ
KATATA (RATTLE)
カタ
KATA

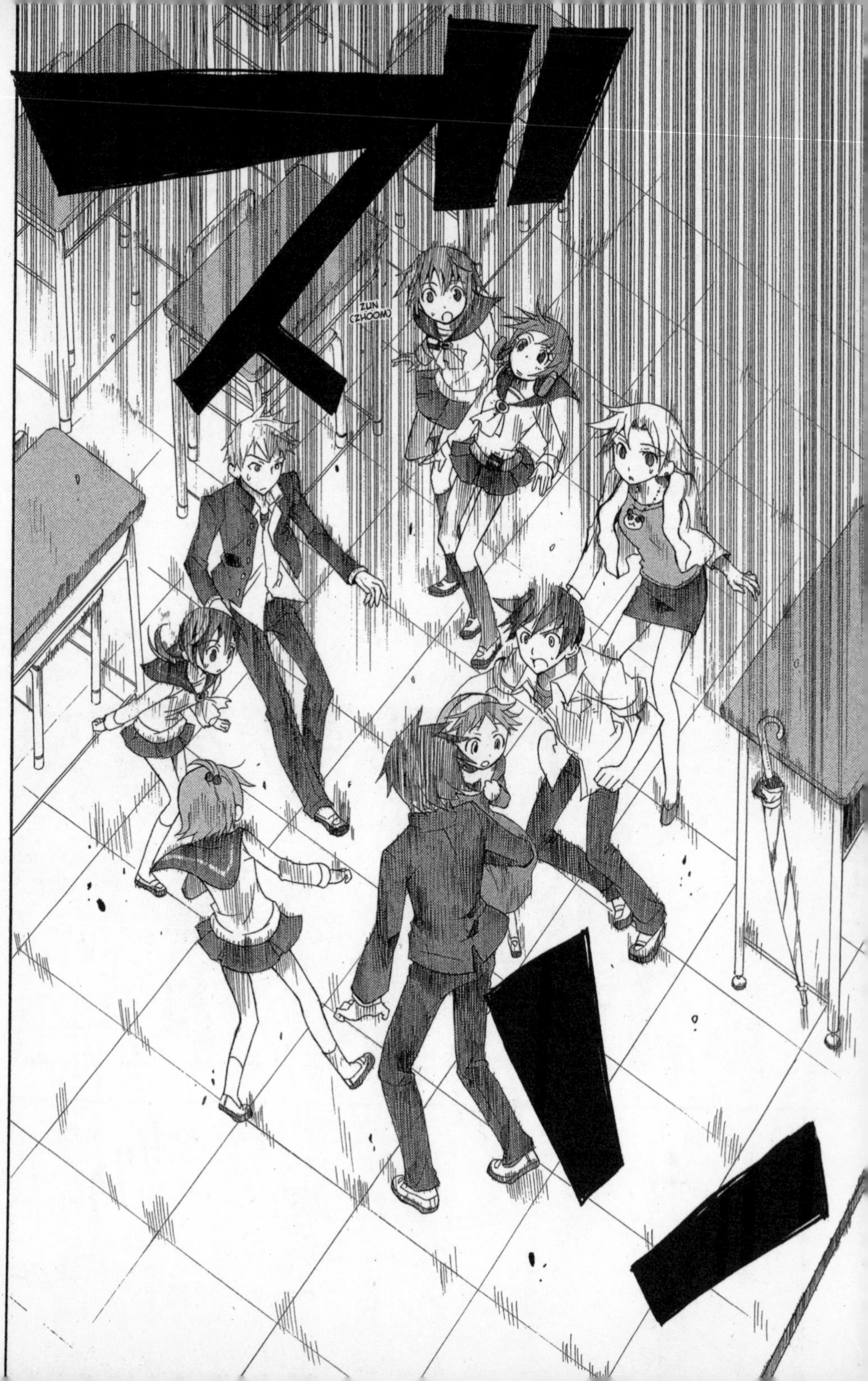
ZUN
(ZHOOM)

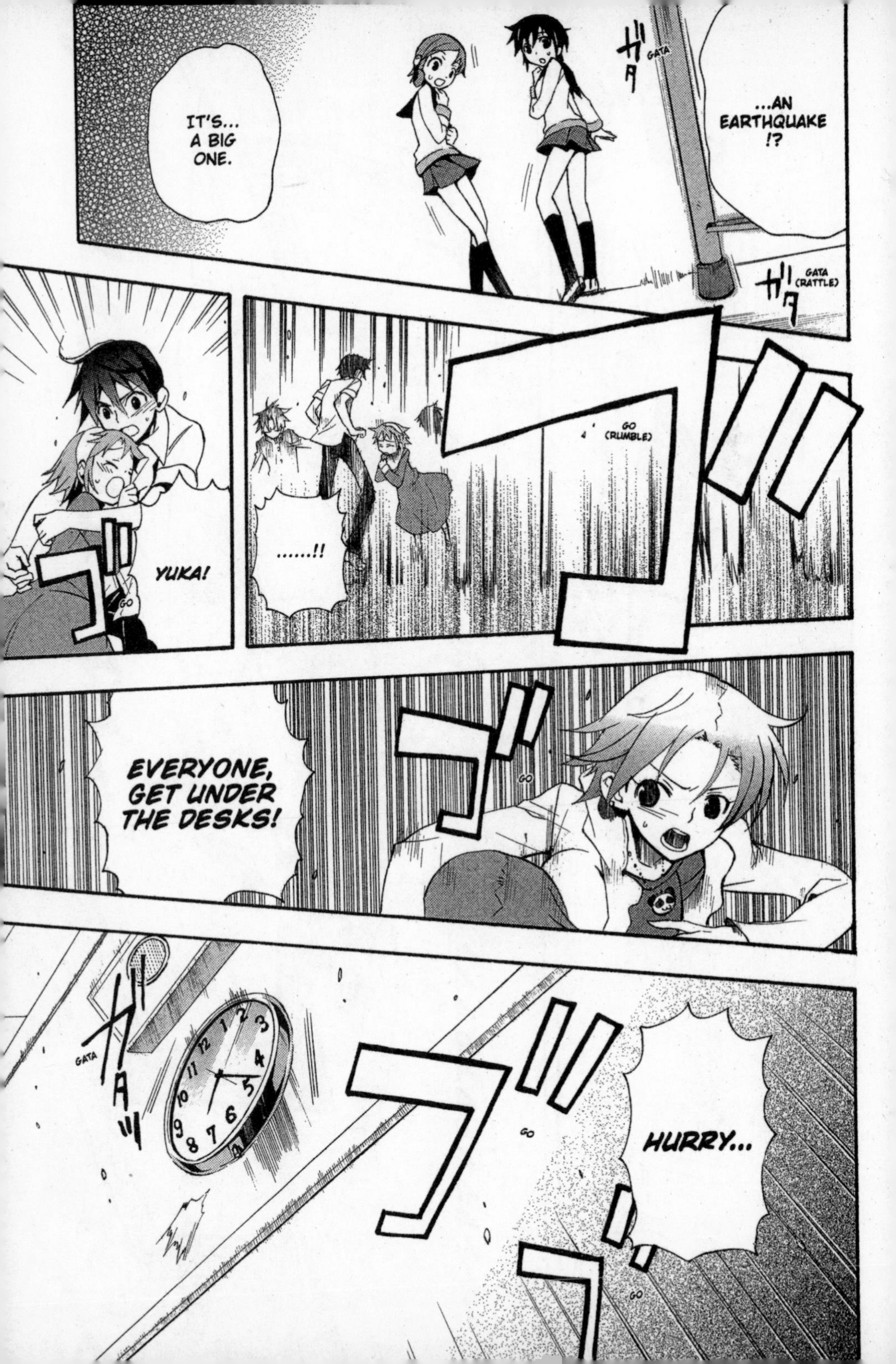

GATA
...AN EARTHQUAKE !?
IT'S... A BIG ONE.
GATA (RATTLE)
GO (RUMBLE)
......!!
YUKA!
GO
GO
EVERYONE, GET UNDER THE DESKS!
HURRY...
GO
GO
GATA

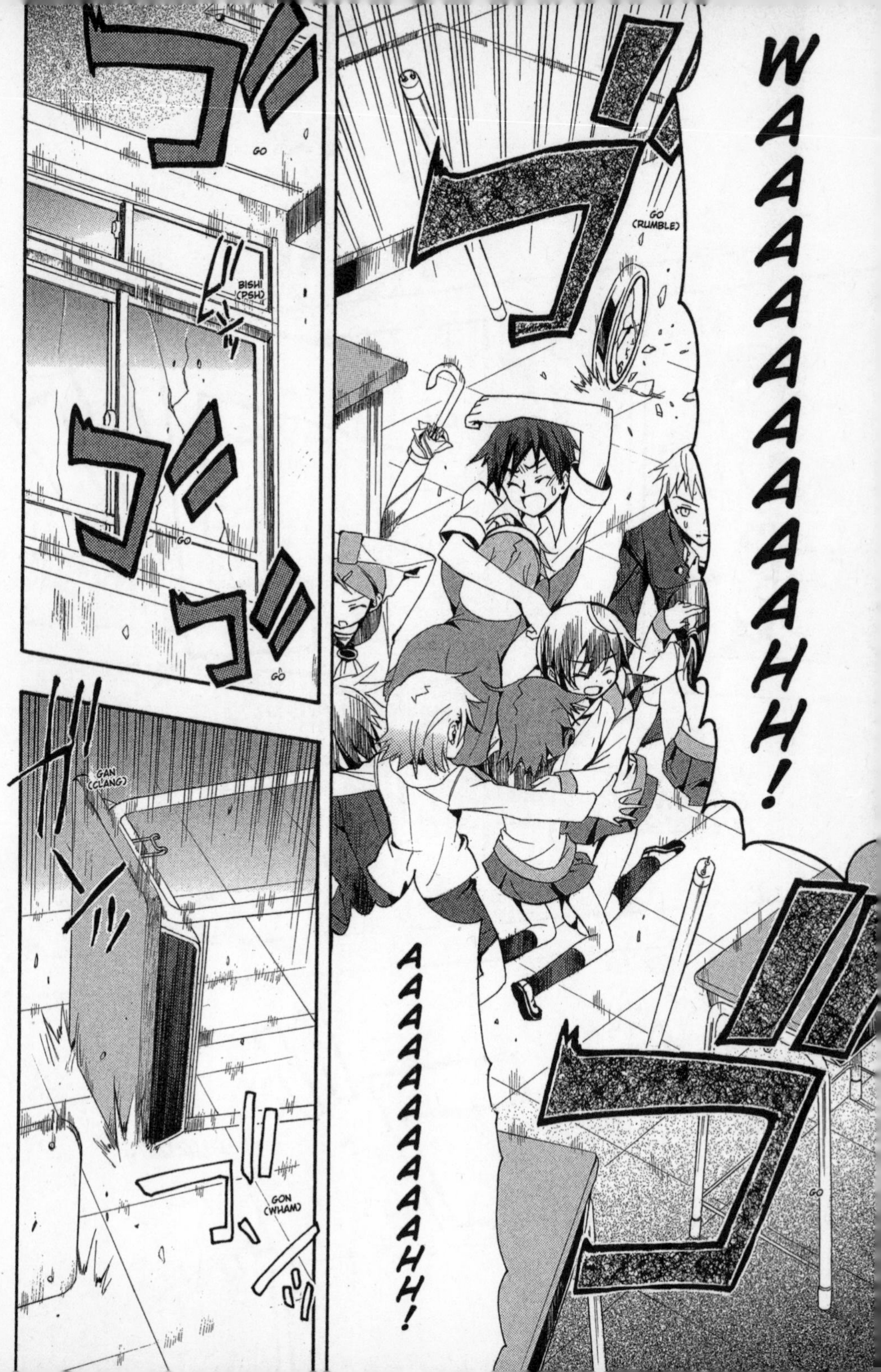
WAAAAAAAAAAHH!
GO (RUMBLE)
AAAAAAAAAAHH!
GO
GO
BISHI (PSH)
GO
GO
GAN (CLANG)
GON (WHAM)

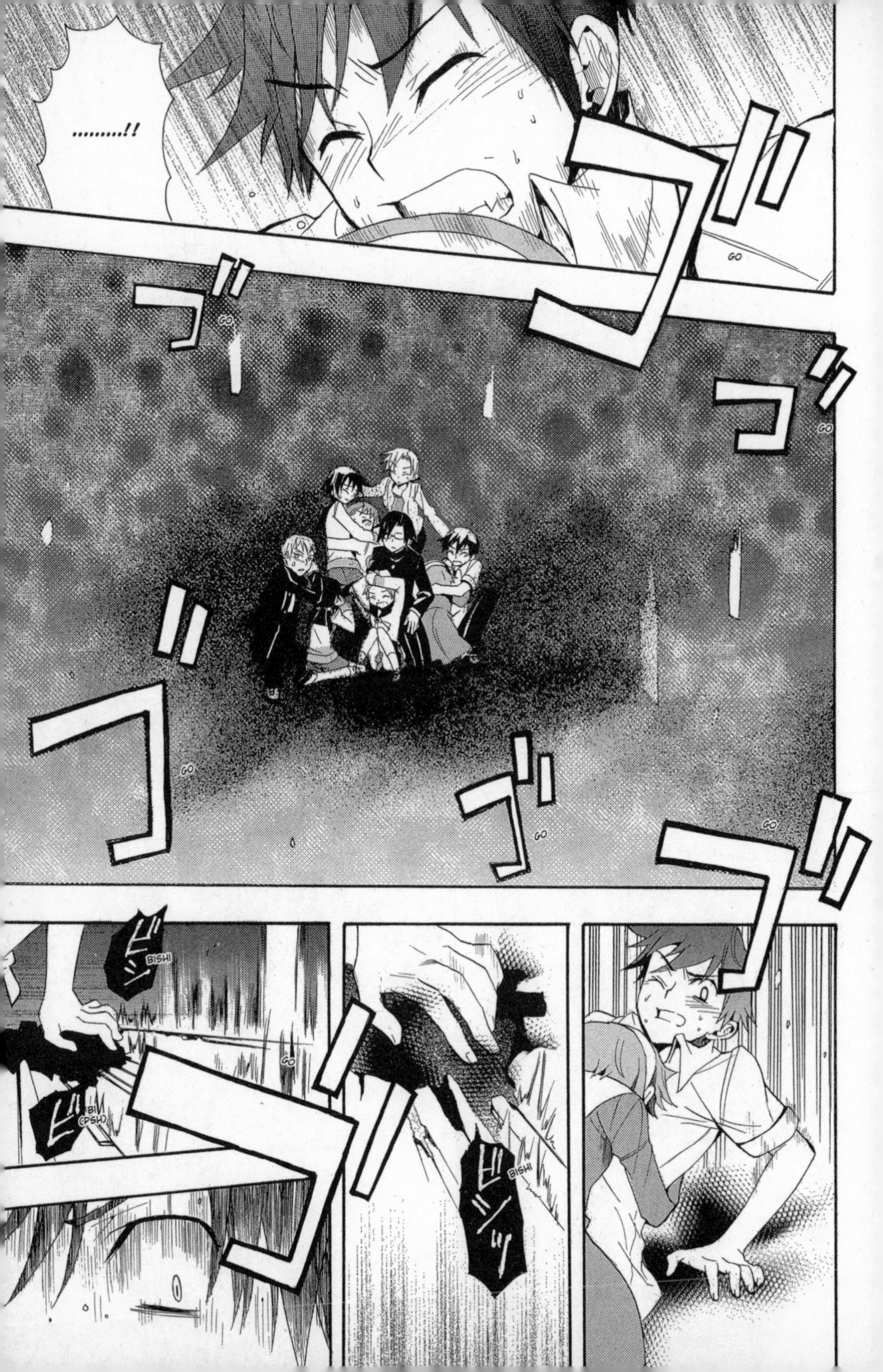
.........!!
GO
GO
GO
GO
GO
GO
BISHI
BISHI
BISHI (PSH)
GO

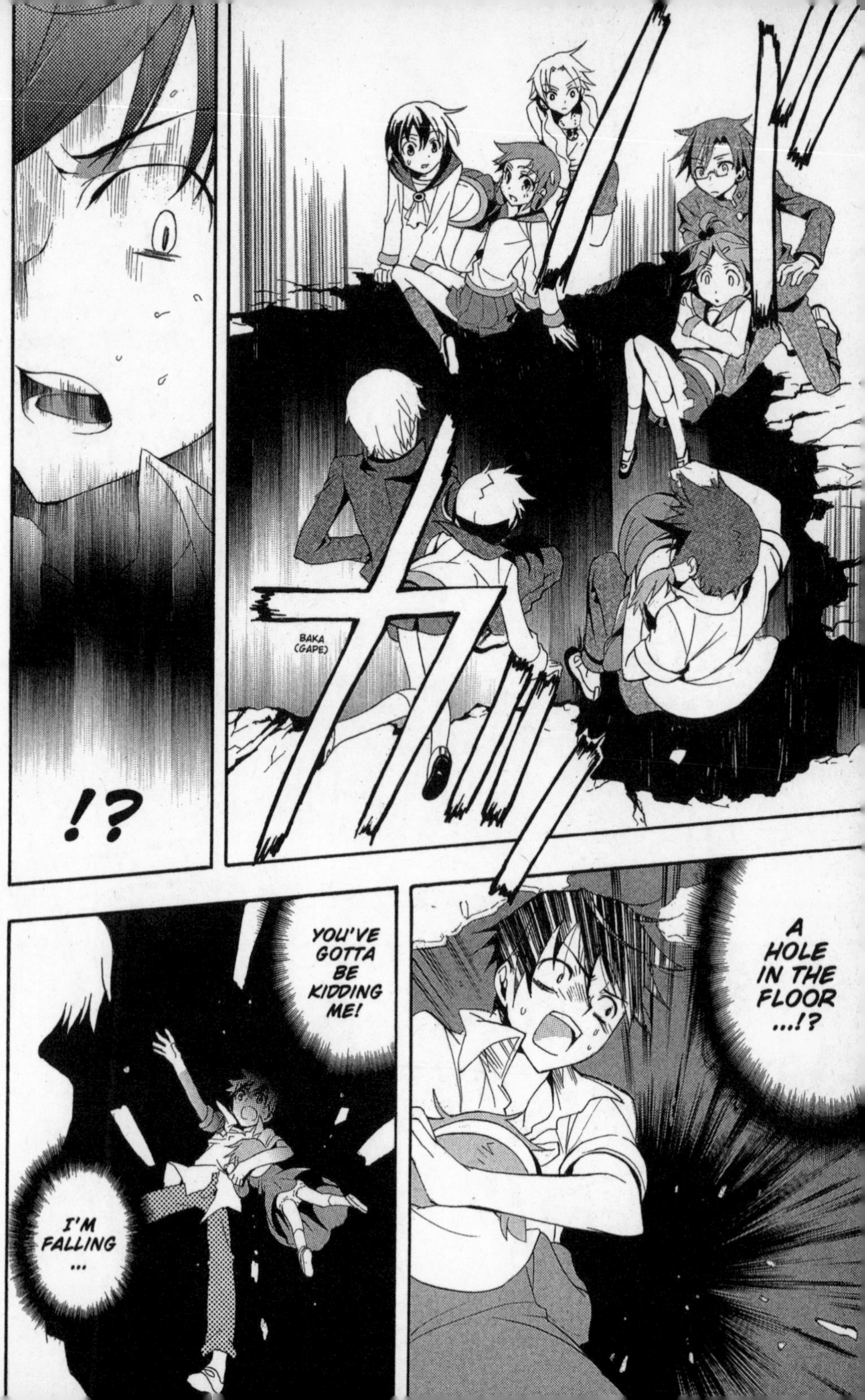
BAKA (GAPE)
!?
A HOLE IN THE FLOOR ...!?
YOU'VE GOTTA BE KIDDING ME!
I'M FALLING ...

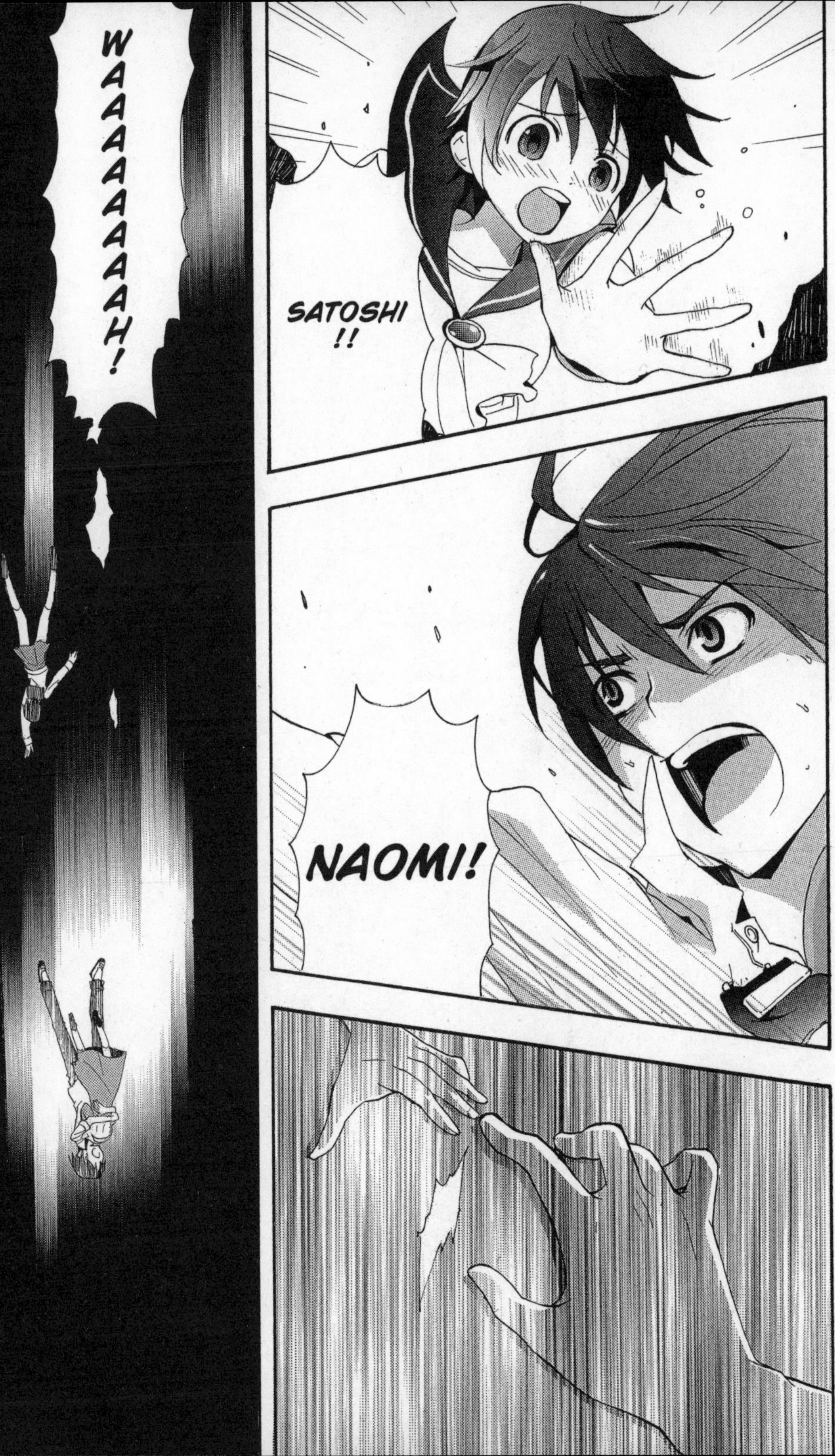
SATOSHI!!
NAOMI!
WAAAAAAAAH!

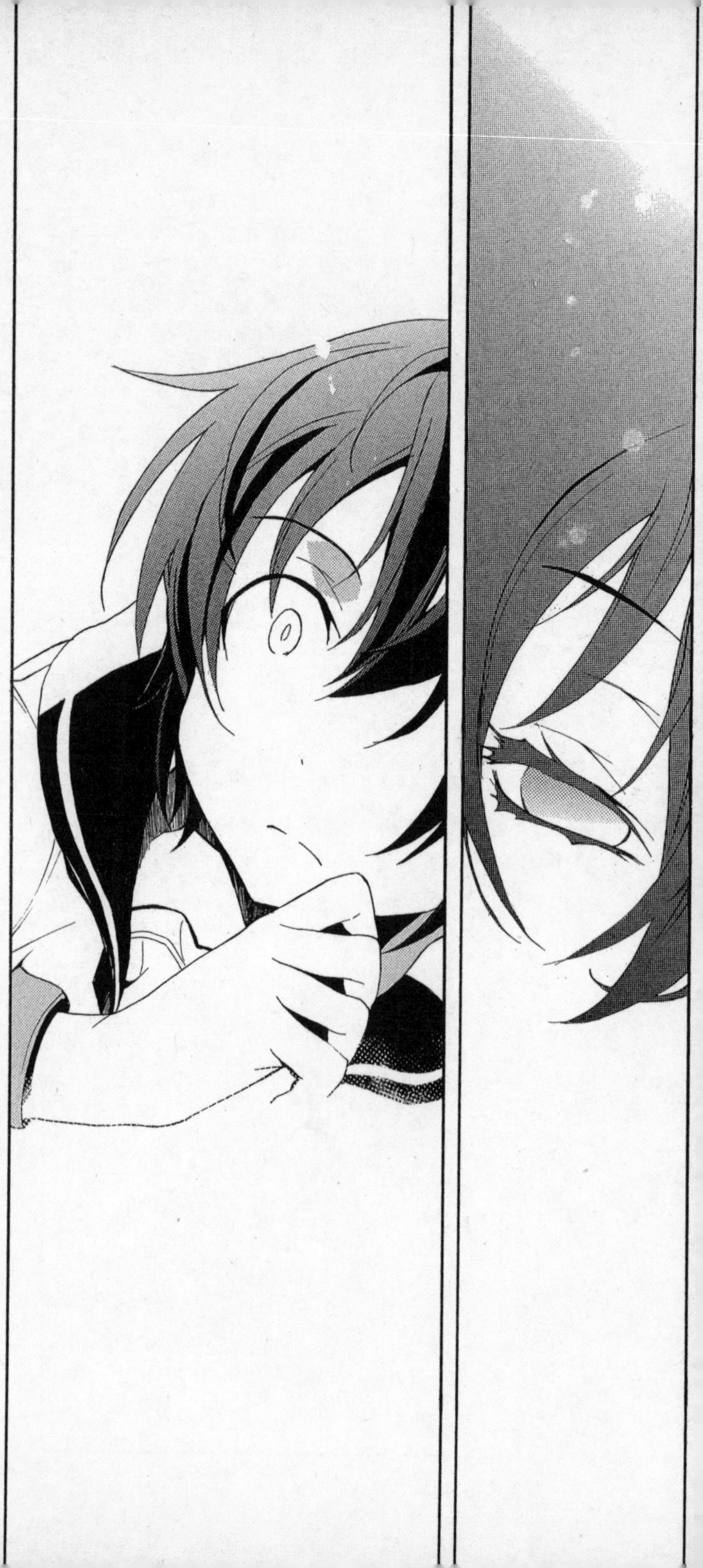

OW! NNGH... I TWISTED MY ANKLE...

BUT I THINK I'M OKAY EVERYWHERE ELSE...

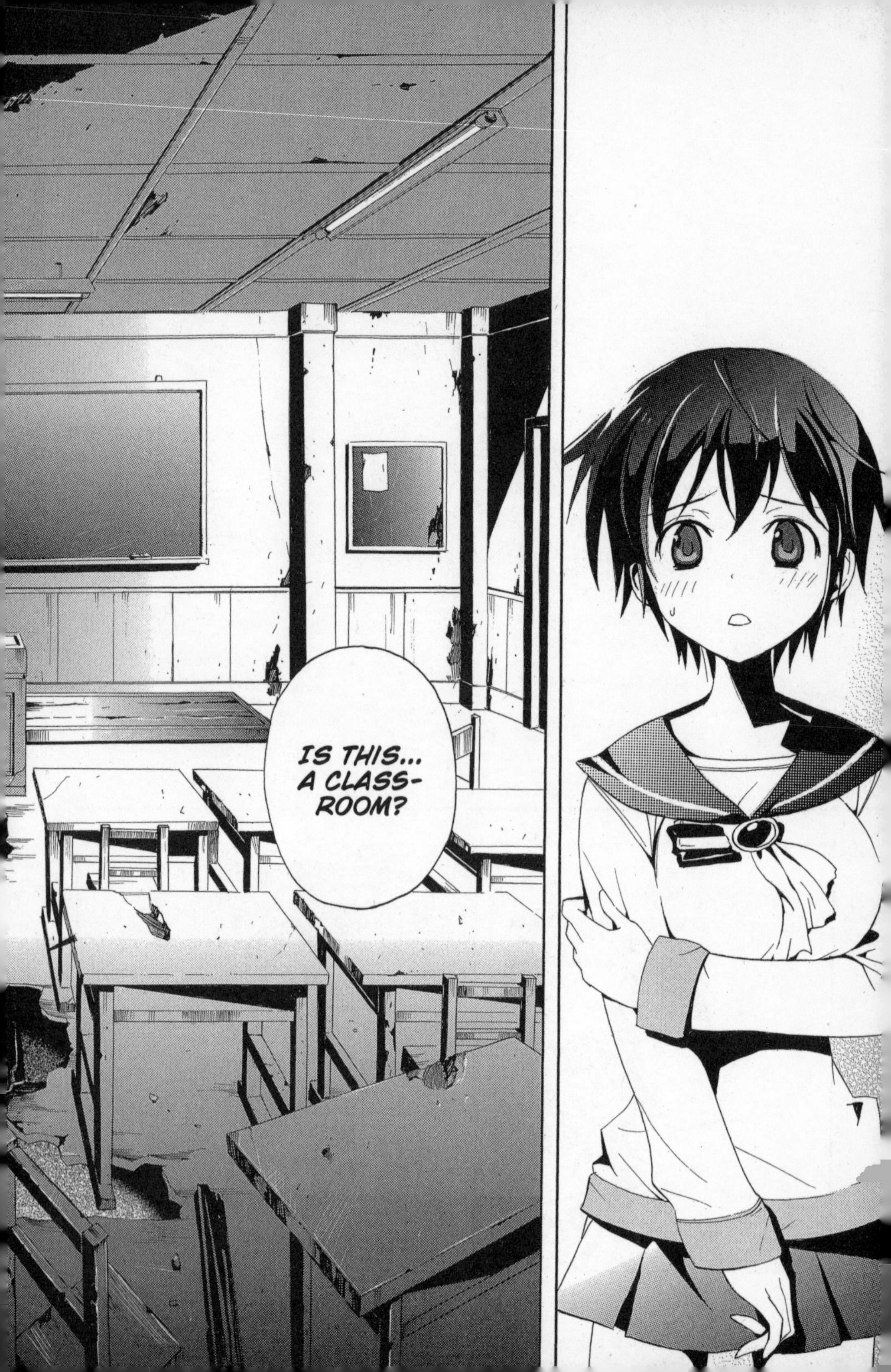
IS THIS... A CLASS-ROOM?

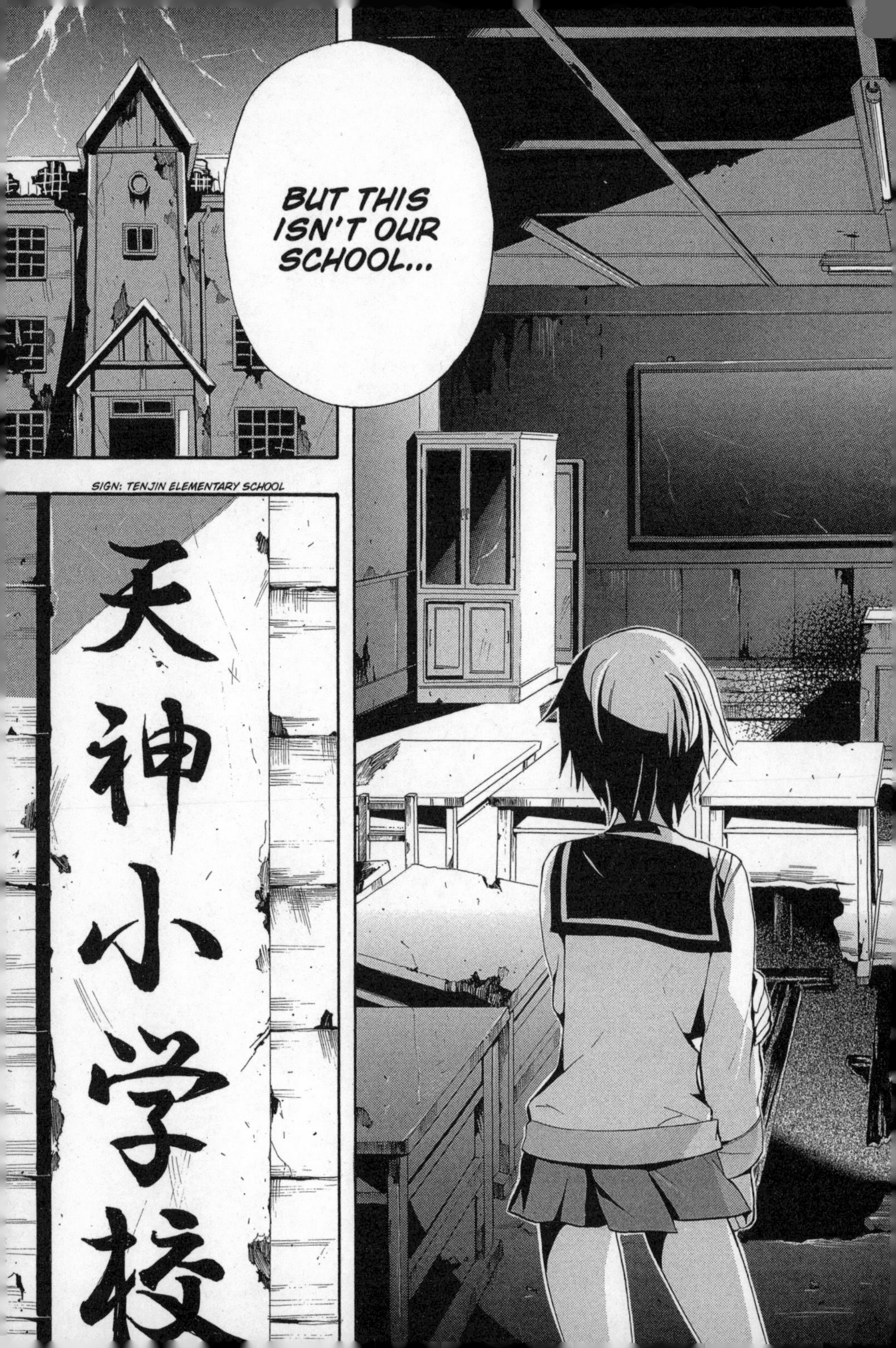
BUT THIS ISN'T OUR SCHOOL...
SIGN: TENJIN ELEMENTARY SCHOOL
天神小学校

CORPSE PARTY
Blood Covered

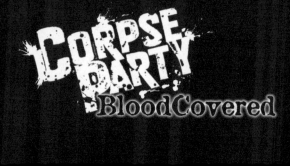

Curse 2: Tenjin Elementary School

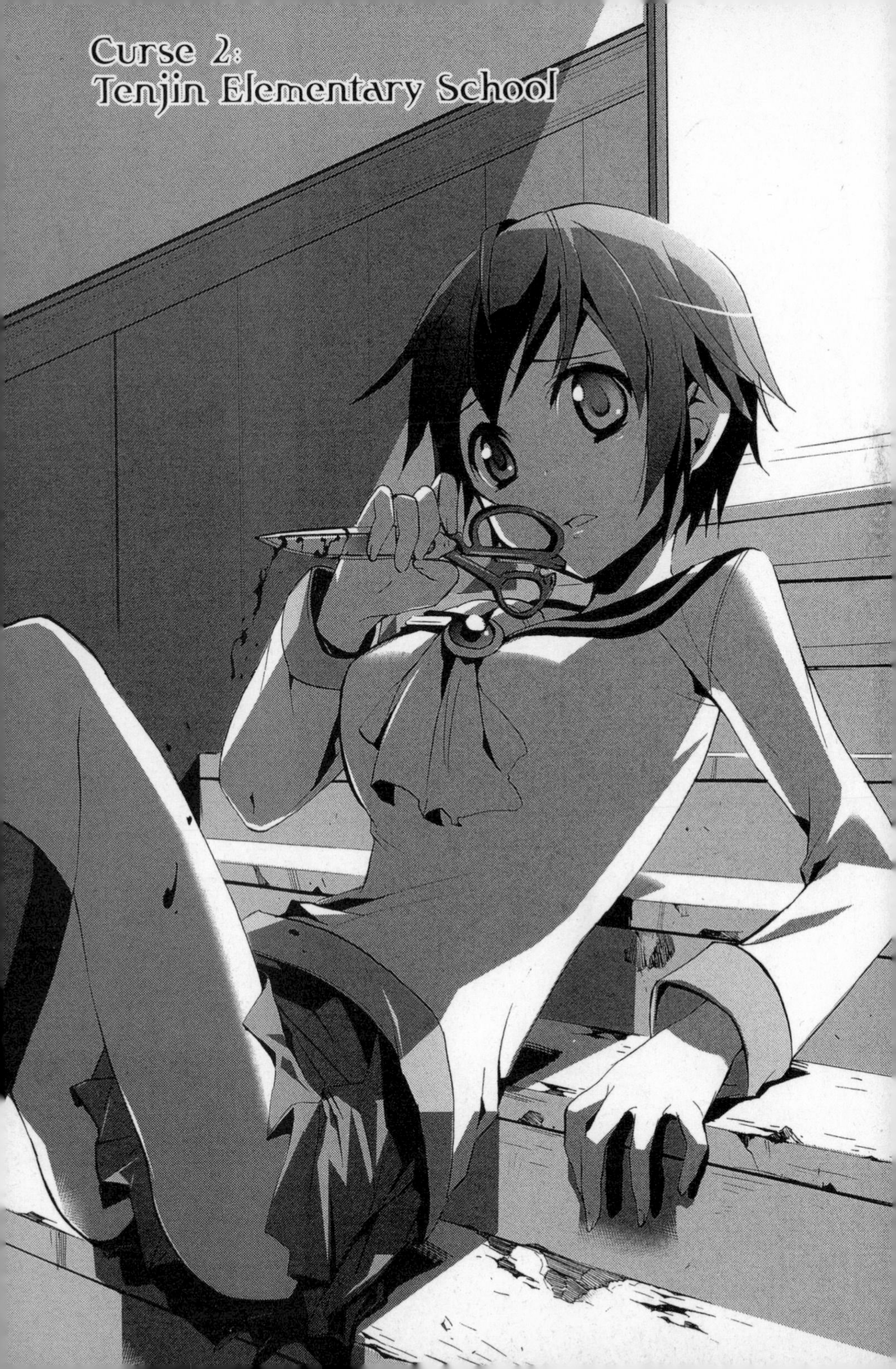

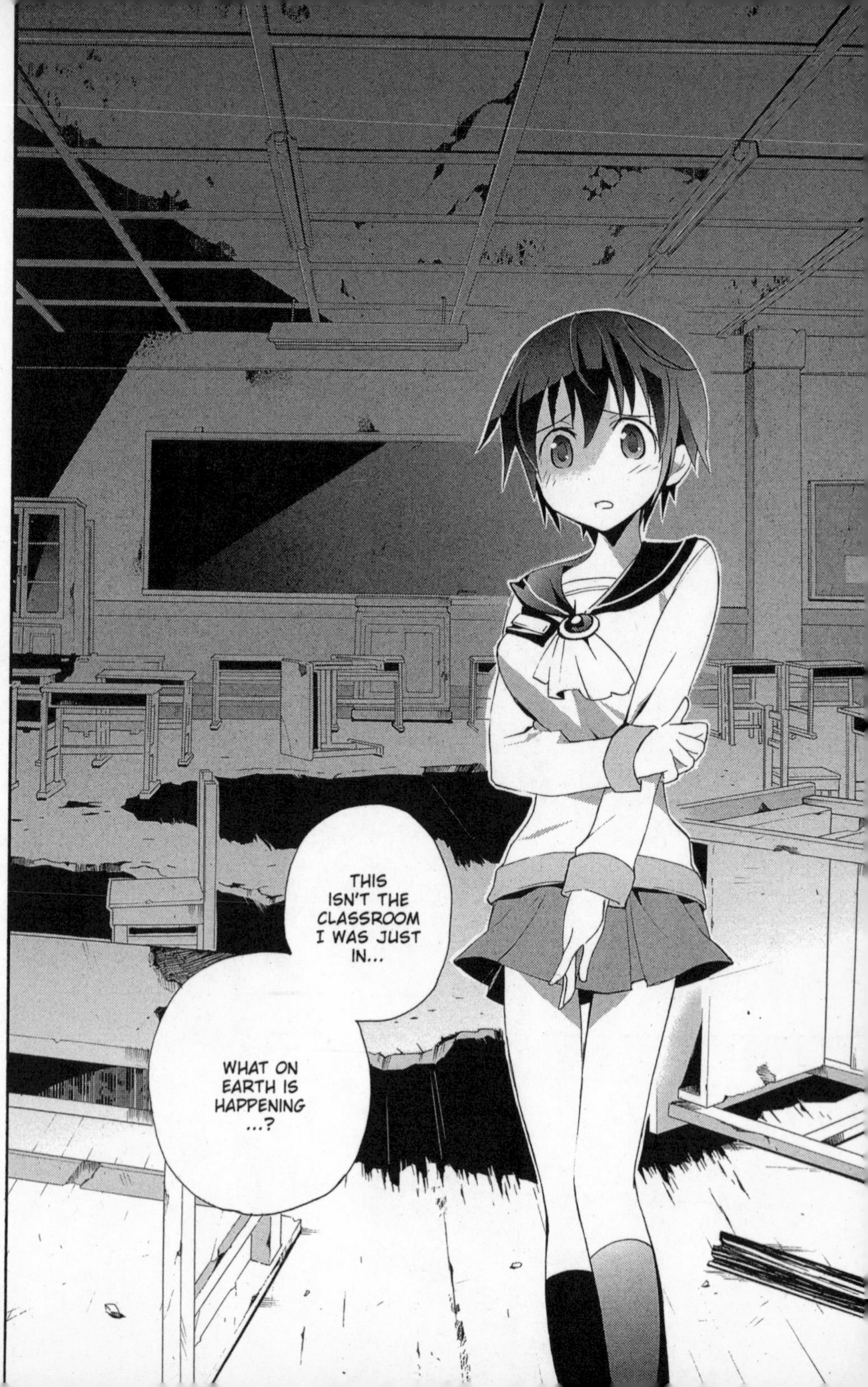
THIS ISN'T THE CLASSROOM I WAS JUST IN...
WHAT ON EARTH IS HAPPENING ...?

ZUKI
(STING)

GUSHA
(SCRUNCH)

OUCH!

NNGH...
MY
ANKLE
HURTS...

PA
(FLASH)

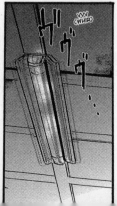

VVV
(WHIR)

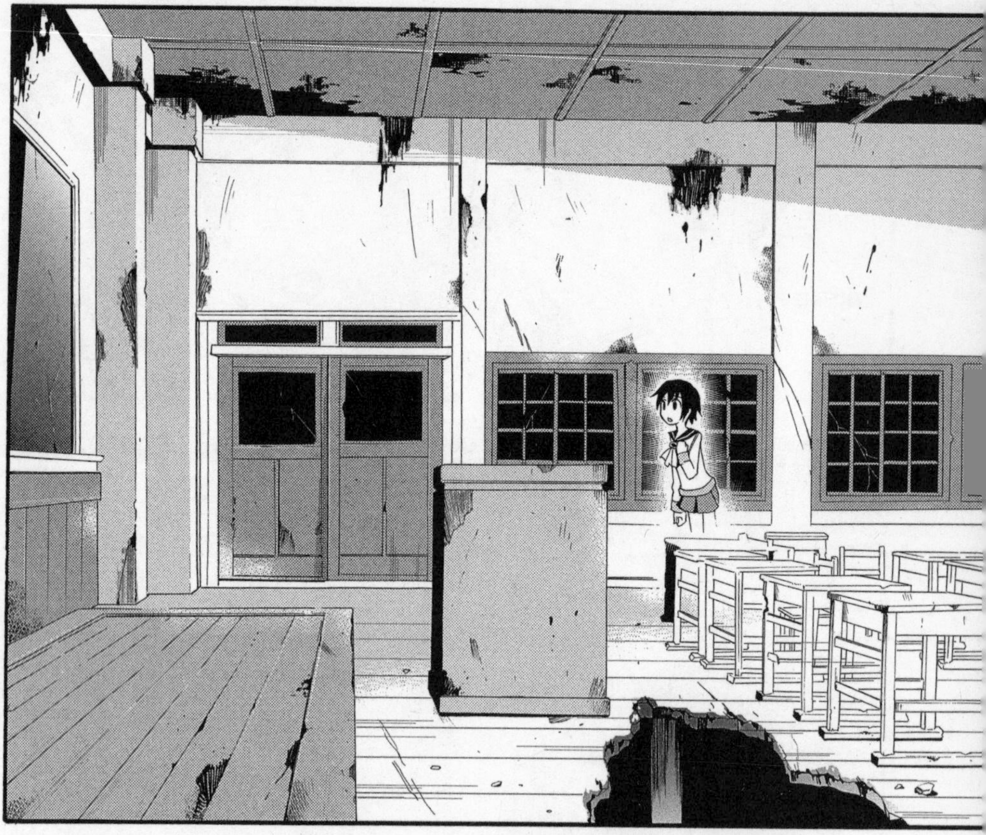
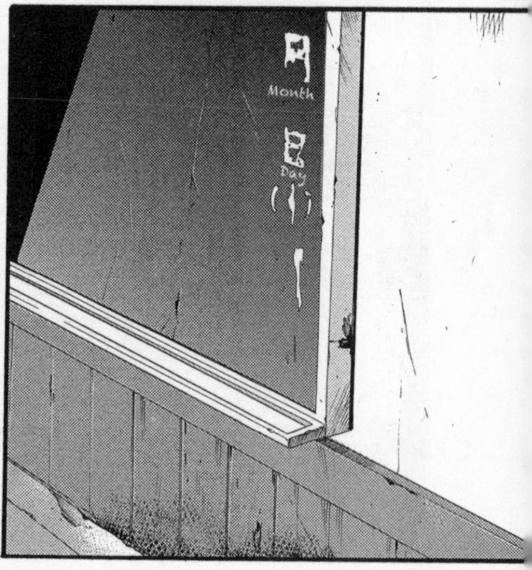
Month
Day
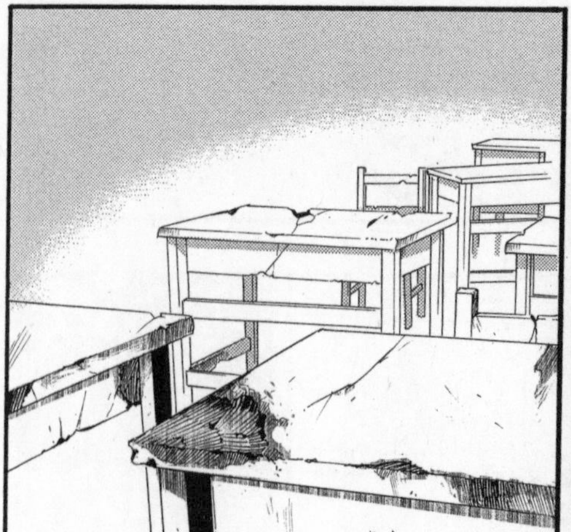

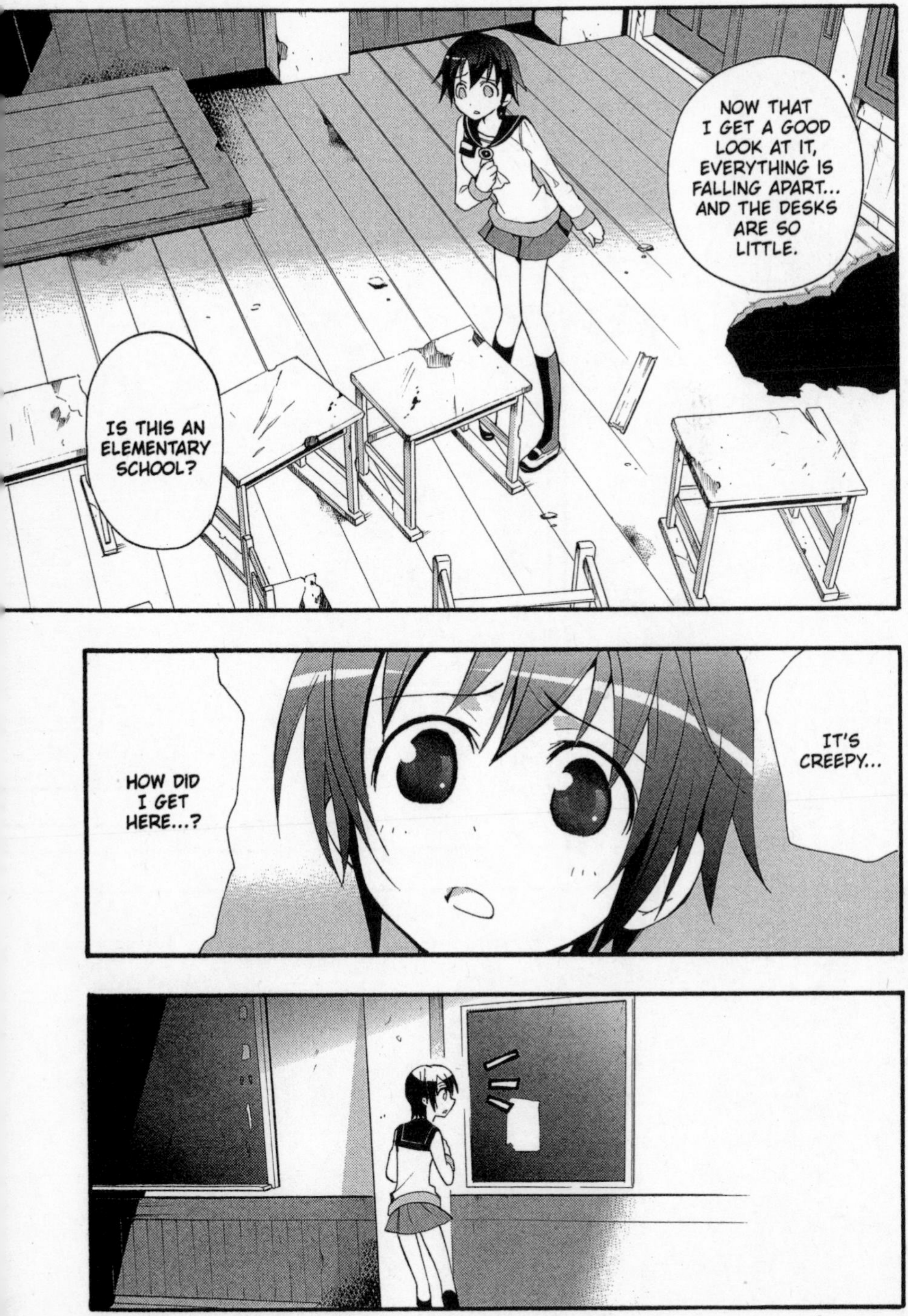
NOW THAT I GET A GOOD LOOK AT IT, EVERYTHING IS FALLING APART... AND THE DESKS ARE SO LITTLE.
IS THIS AN ELEMENTARY SCHOOL?
IT'S CREEPY...
HOW DID I GET HERE...?

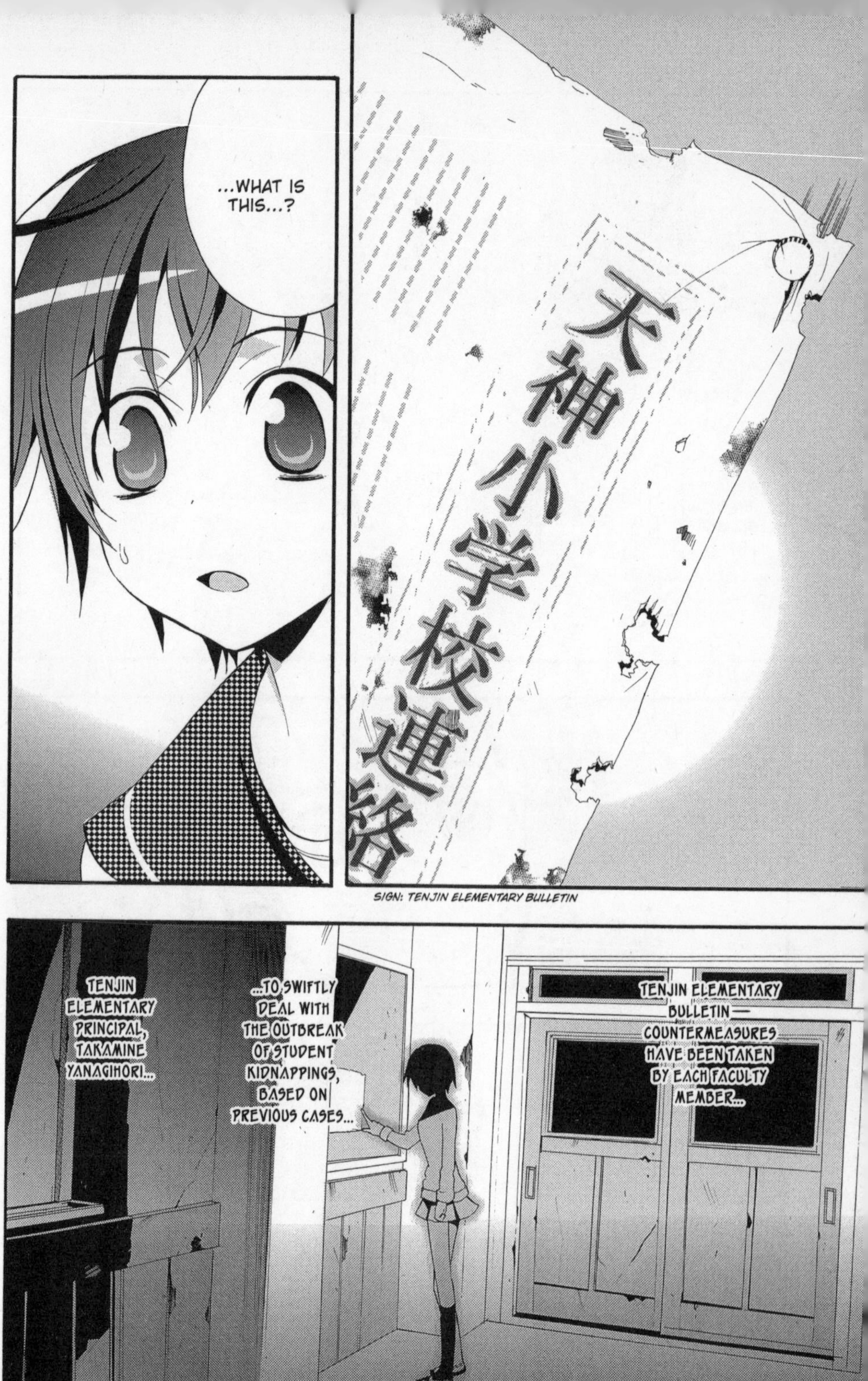
天神小学校連絡
SIGN: TENJIN ELEMENTARY BULLETIN
...WHAT IS THIS...?
TENJIN ELEMENTARY BULLETIN— COUNTERMEASURES HAVE BEEN TAKEN BY EACH FACULTY MEMBER...
...TO SWIFTLY DEAL WITH THE OUTBREAK OF STUDENT KIDNAPPINGS, BASED ON PREVIOUS CASES...
TENJIN ELEMENTARY PRINCIPAL, TAKAMINE YANAGIHORI...

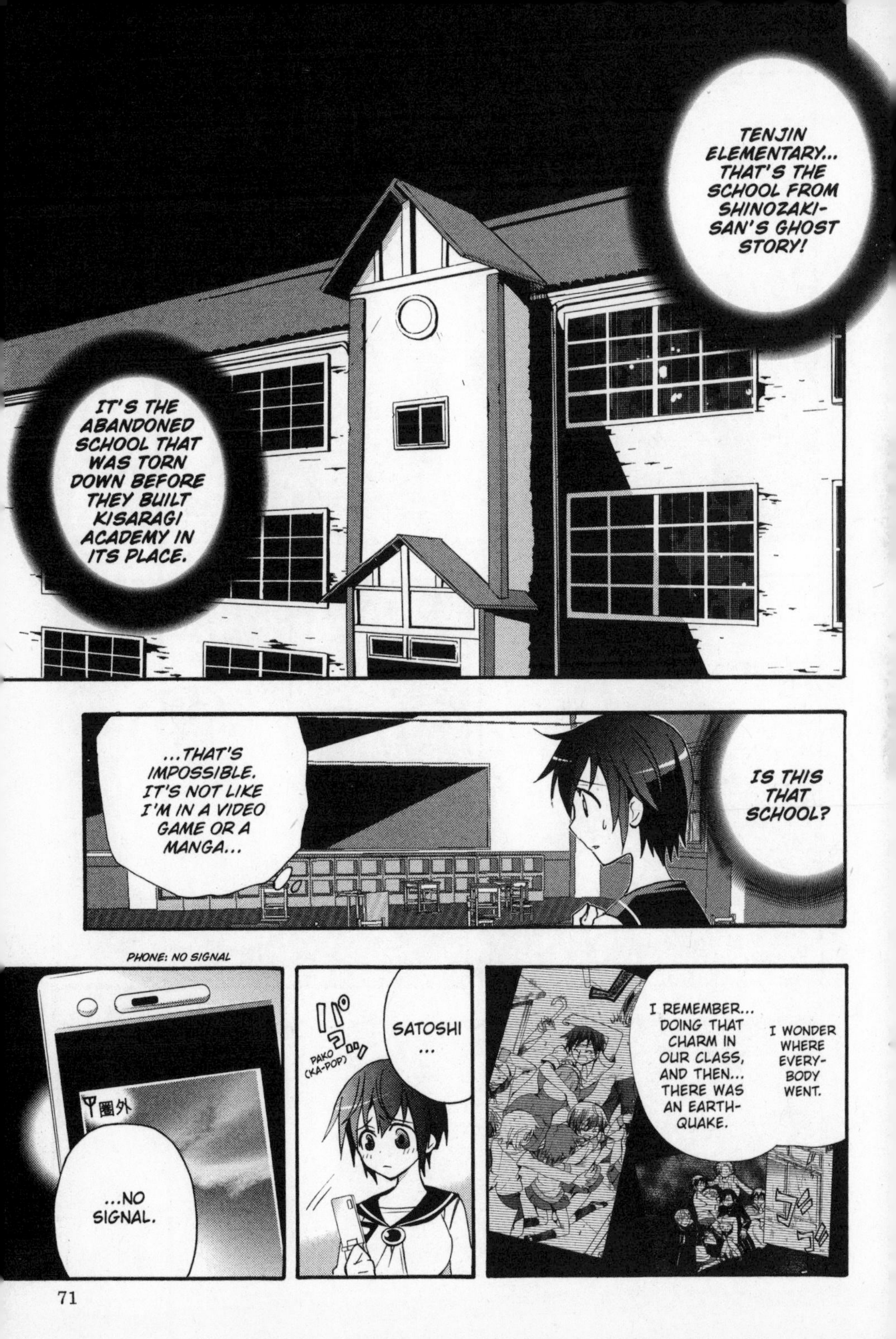
TENJIN ELEMENTARY... THAT'S THE SCHOOL FROM SHINOZAKI-SAN'S GHOST STORY!
IT'S THE ABANDONED SCHOOL THAT WAS TORN DOWN BEFORE THEY BUILT KISARAGI ACADEMY IN ITS PLACE.
IS THIS THAT SCHOOL?
...THAT'S IMPOSSIBLE. IT'S NOT LIKE I'M IN A VIDEO GAME OR A MANGA...
I WONDER WHERE EVERY-BODY WENT.
I REMEMBER... DOING THAT CHARM IN OUR CLASS, AND THEN... THERE WAS AN EARTH-QUAKE.
SATOSHI ...
パコッ
PAKO (KA-POP)
PHONE: NO SIGNAL
圏外
...NO SIGNAL.

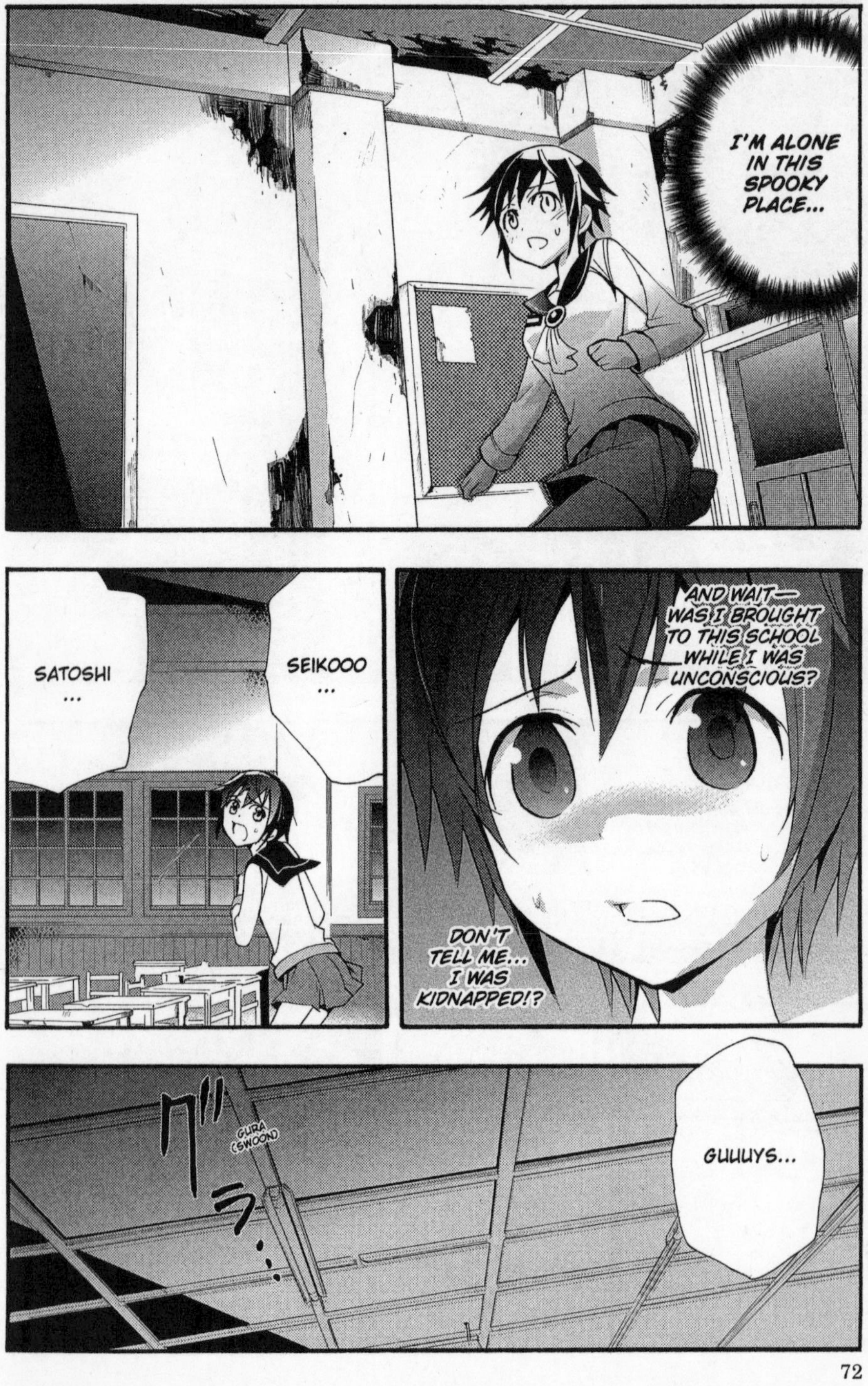
I'M ALONE IN THIS SPOOKY PLACE...
AND WAIT— WAS I BROUGHT TO THIS SCHOOL WHILE I WAS UNCONSCIOUS?
DON'T TELL ME... I WAS KIDNAPPED!?
SEIKOOO ...
SATOSHI ...
GUUUYS...
グラ...
GURA (SWOON)

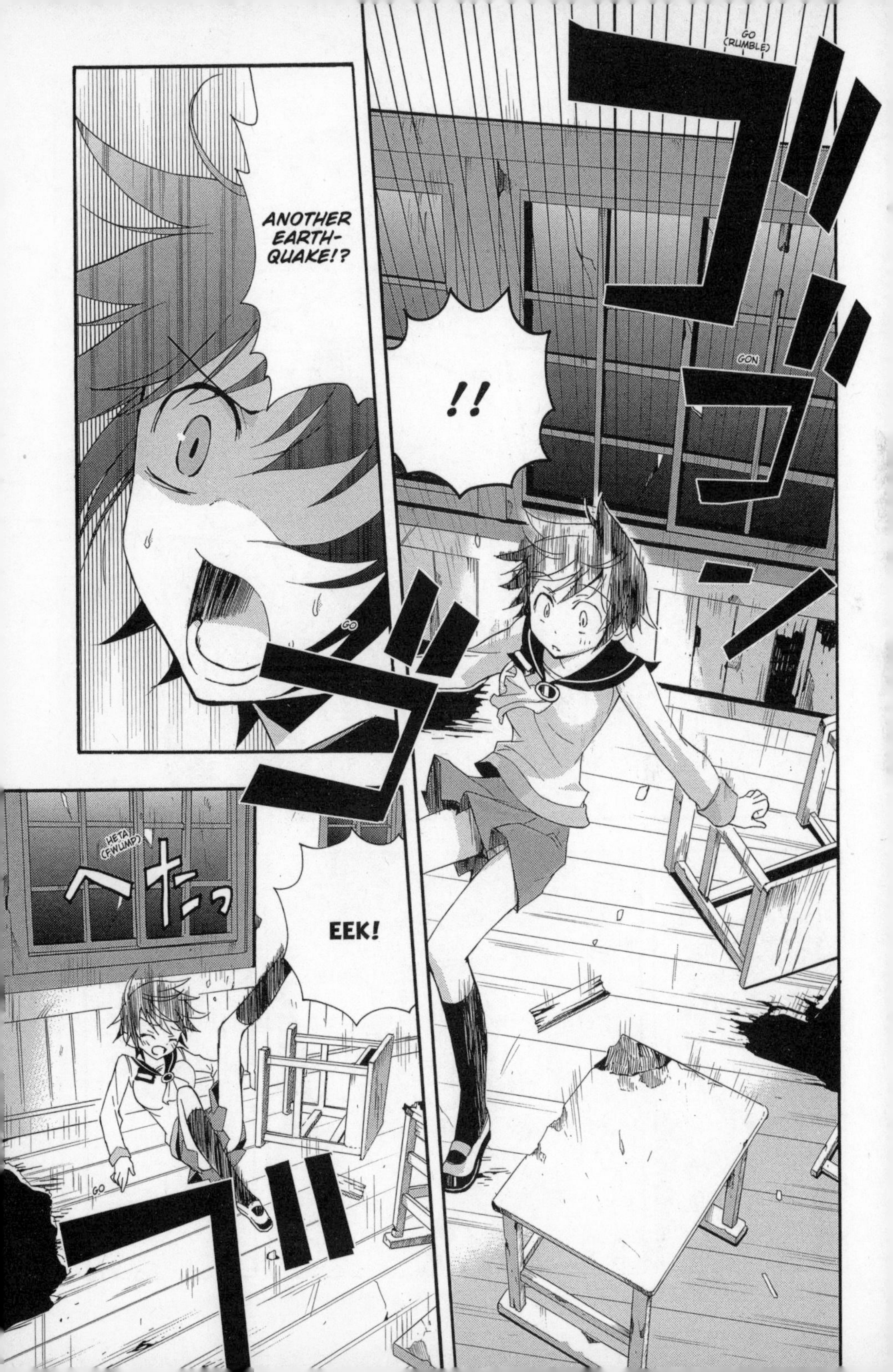
GO (RUMBLE)
GON
!!
GO
ANOTHER EARTH-QUAKE!?
HETA (FWUMP)
EEK!
GO

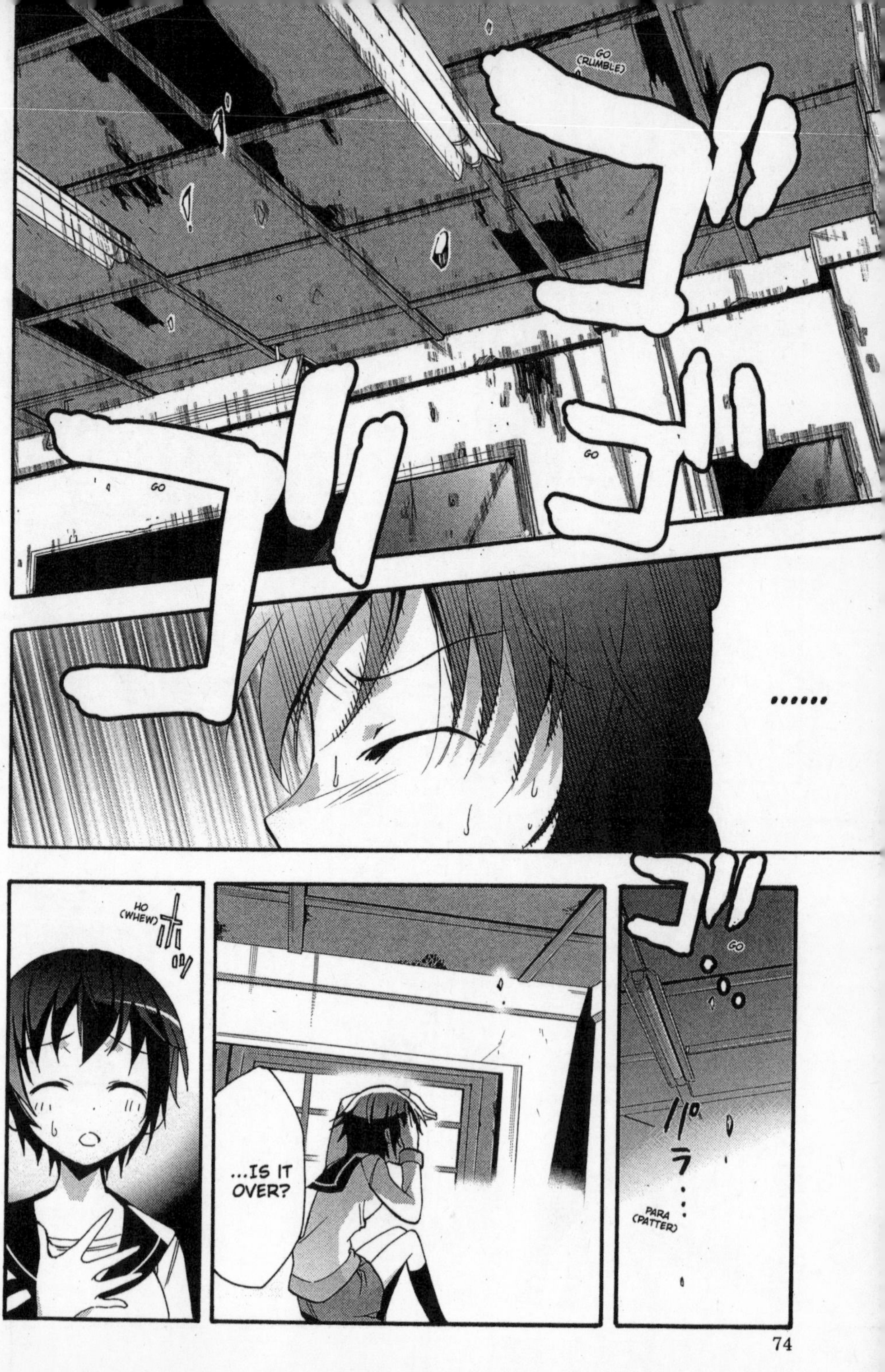
GO (RUMBLE)
GO
GO
......
GO
PARA (PATTER)
...IS IT OVER?
HO (WHEW)

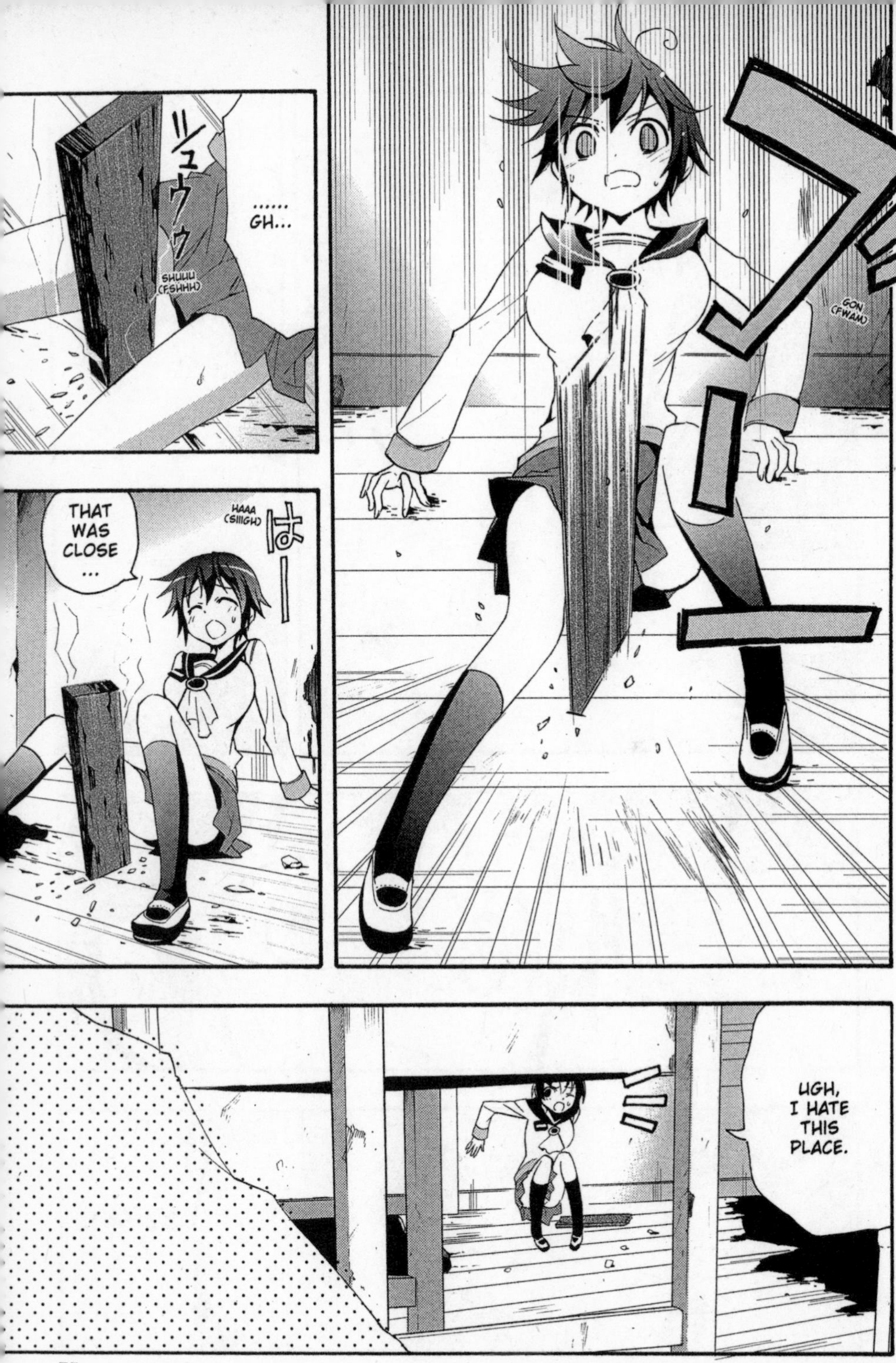
GON (FWAM)
シュウウ
SHUUU (FSHHH)
......GH...
THAT WAS CLOSE...
はー
HAAA (SIIIGH)
UGH, I HATE THIS PLACE.

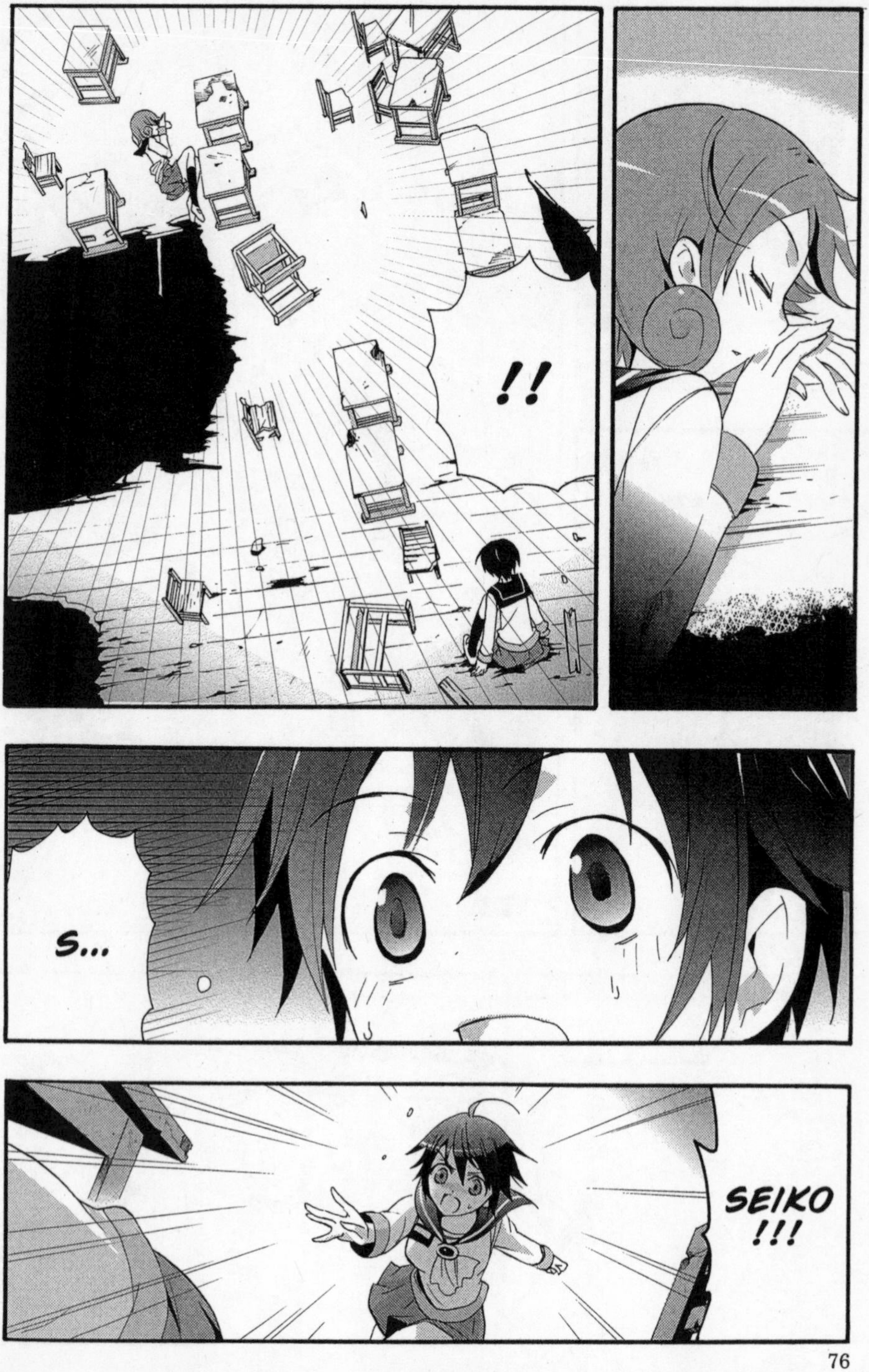
!!
S...
SEIKO !!!

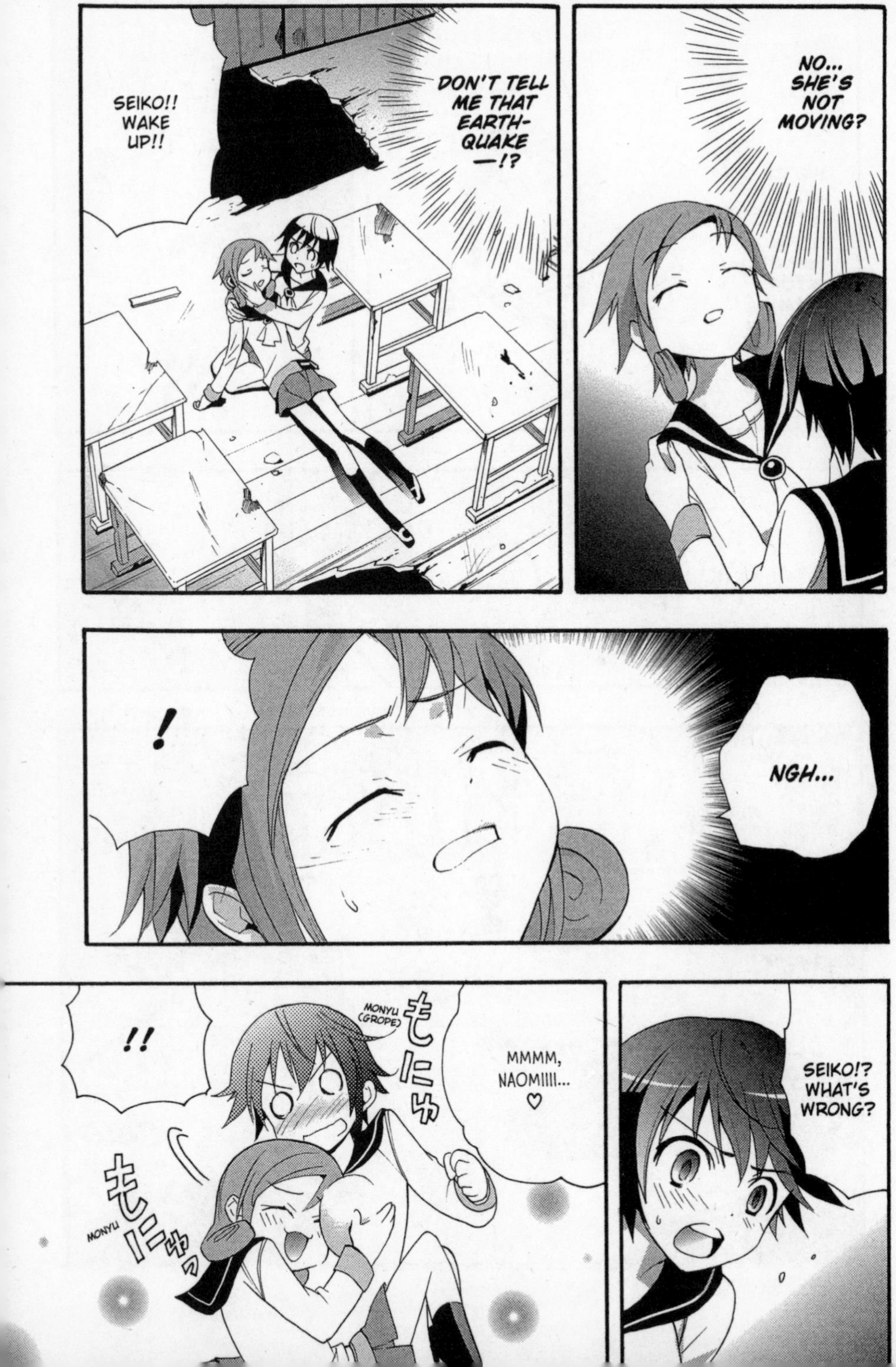
NO... SHE'S NOT MOVING?
DON'T TELL ME THAT EARTH-QUAKE —!?
SEIKO!! WAKE UP!!
NGH...
!
SEIKO!? WHAT'S WRONG?
MMMM, NAOMIIII... ♡
もにゅ
MONYU (GROPE)
!!
もにゅっ
MONYU

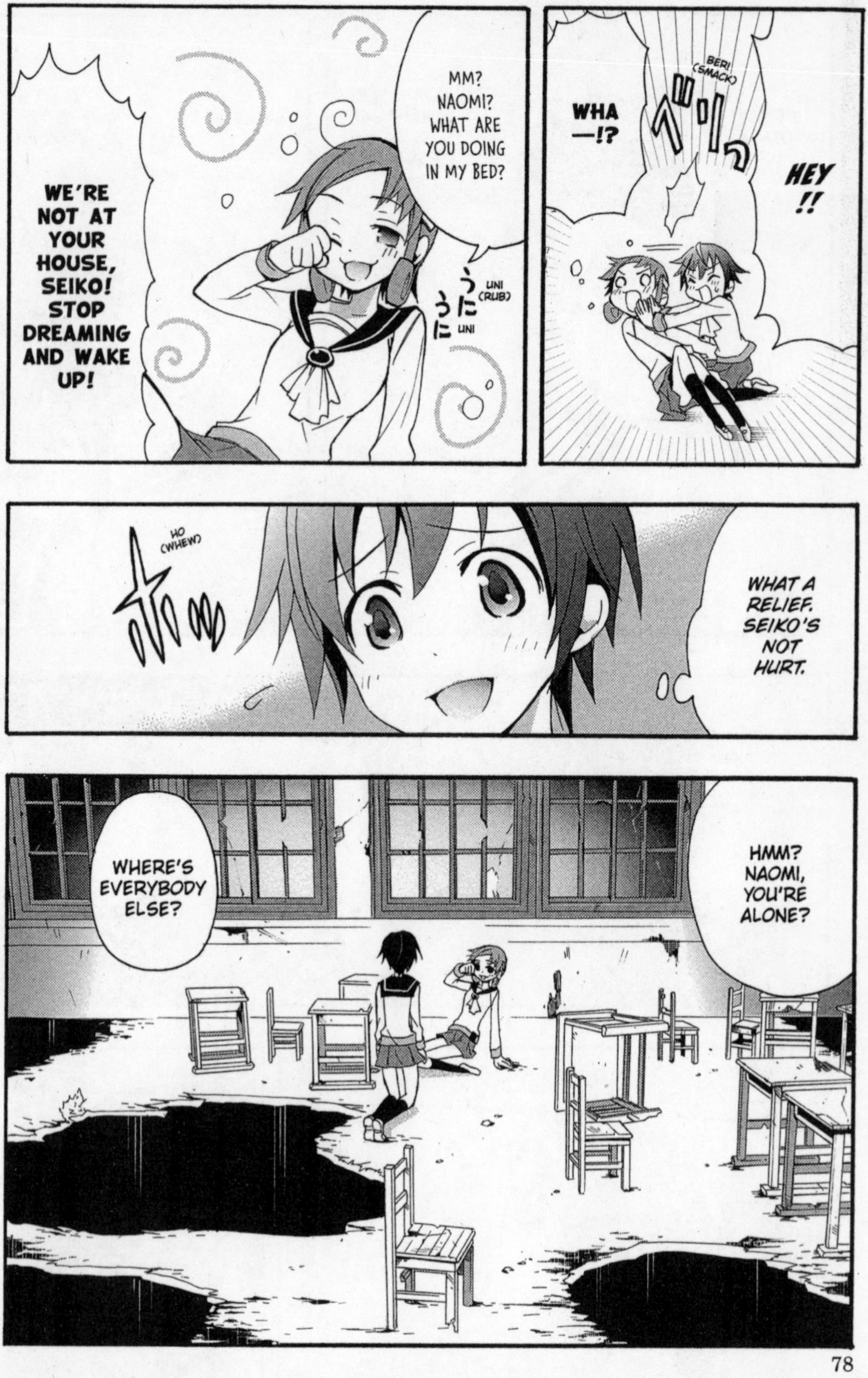

BERI (SMACK)
HEY!!
WHA—!?
MM? NAOMI? WHAT ARE YOU DOING IN MY BED?
UNI (RUB) UNI
WE'RE NOT AT YOUR HOUSE, SEIKO! STOP DREAMING AND WAKE UP!
WHAT A RELIEF. SEIKO'S NOT HURT.
HO (WHEW)
HMM? NAOMI, YOU'RE ALONE?
WHERE'S EVERYBODY ELSE?

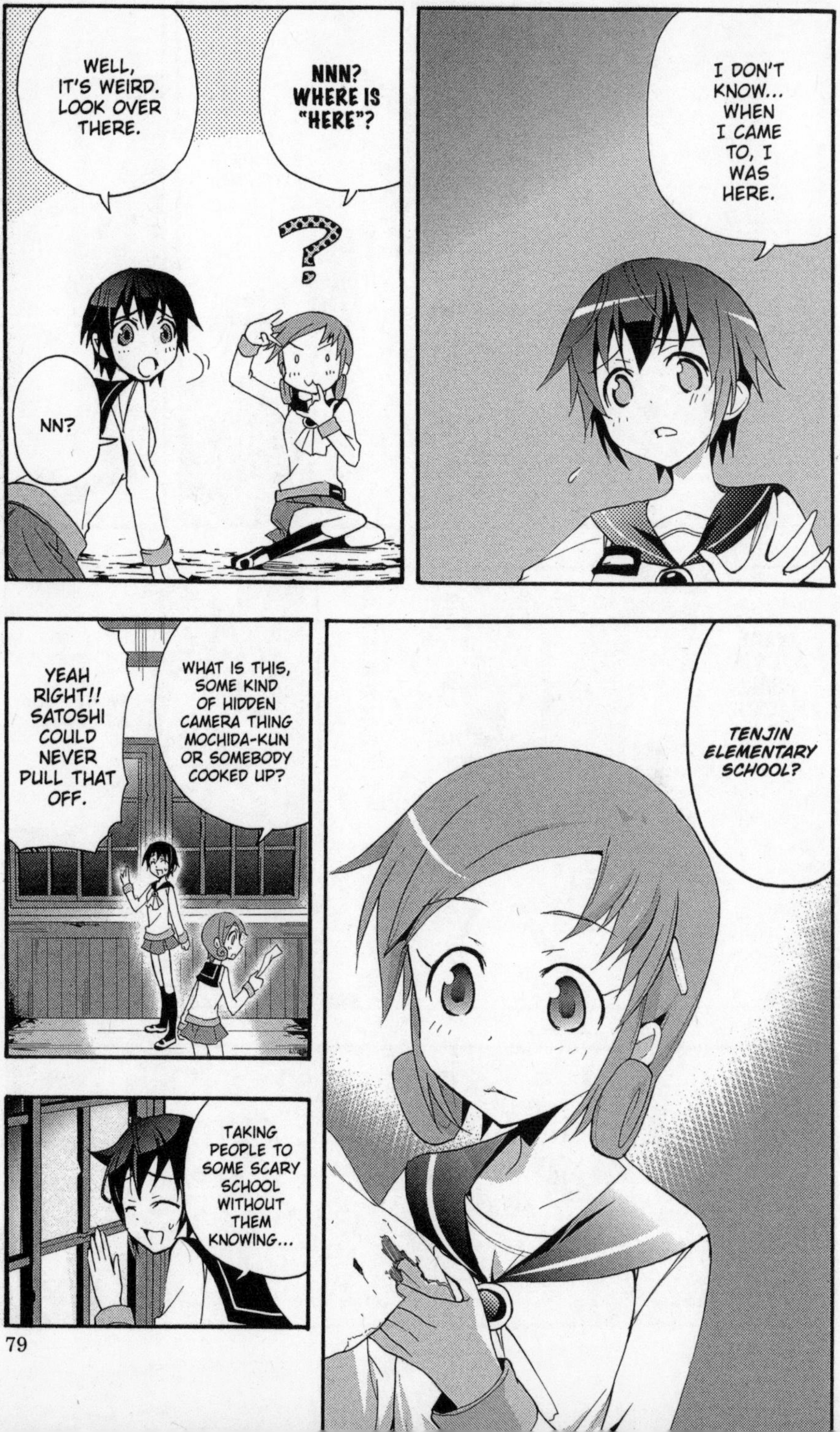
I DON'T KNOW... WHEN I CAME TO, I WAS HERE.
NNN? WHERE IS "HERE"?
WELL, IT'S WEIRD. LOOK OVER THERE.
NN?
TENJIN ELEMENTARY SCHOOL?
WHAT IS THIS, SOME KIND OF HIDDEN CAMERA THING MOCHIDA-KUN OR SOMEBODY COOKED UP?
YEAH RIGHT!! SATOSHI COULD NEVER PULL THAT OFF.
TAKING PEOPLE TO SOME SCARY SCHOOL WITHOUT THEM KNOWING...

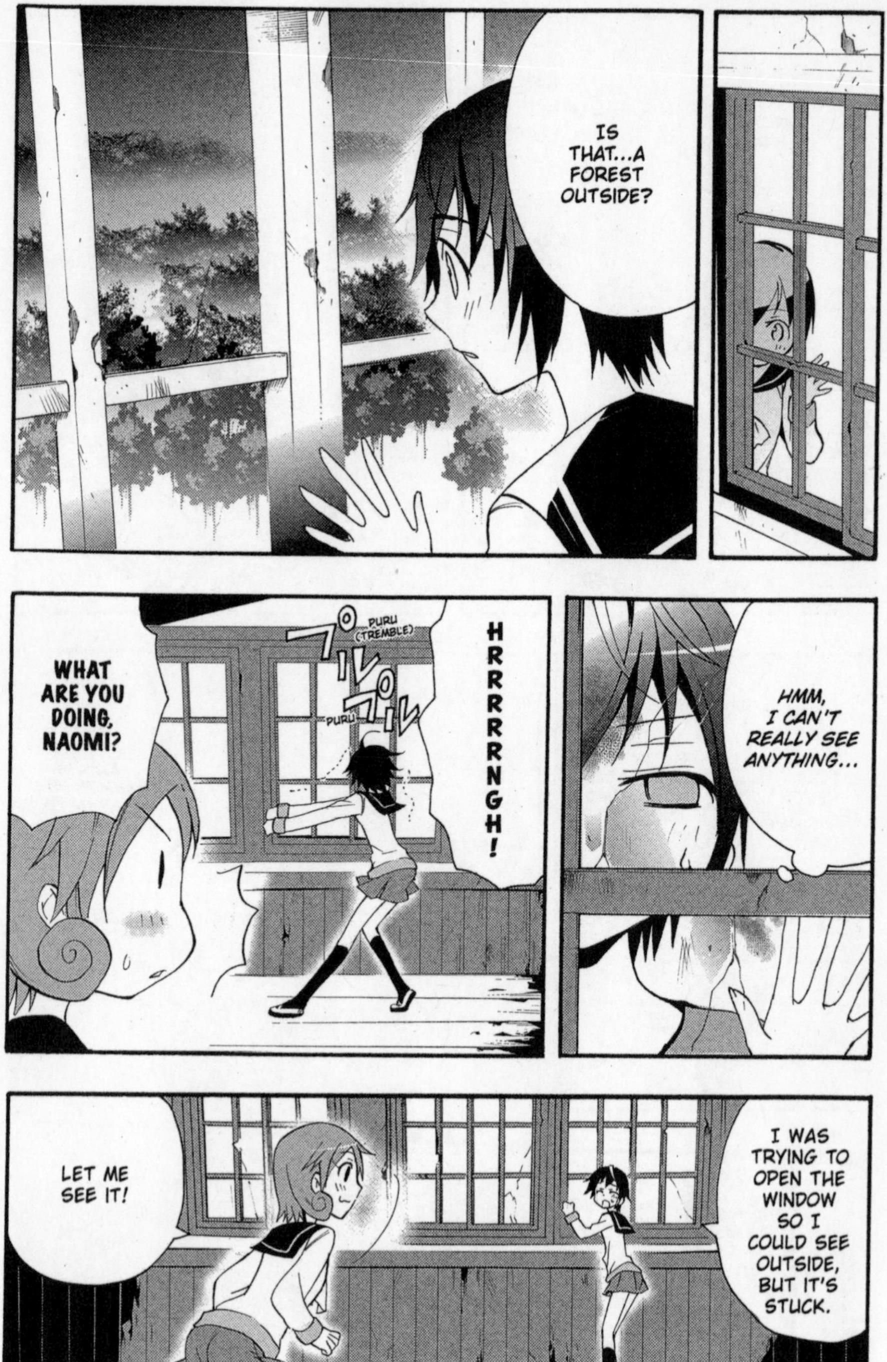
IS THAT...A FOREST OUTSIDE?
HMM, I CAN'T REALLY SEE ANYTHING...
HRRRRRNGH!
PURU (TREMBLE)
PURU
WHAT ARE YOU DOING, NAOMI?
I WAS TRYING TO OPEN THE WINDOW SO I COULD SEE OUTSIDE, BUT IT'S STUCK.
LET ME SEE IT!

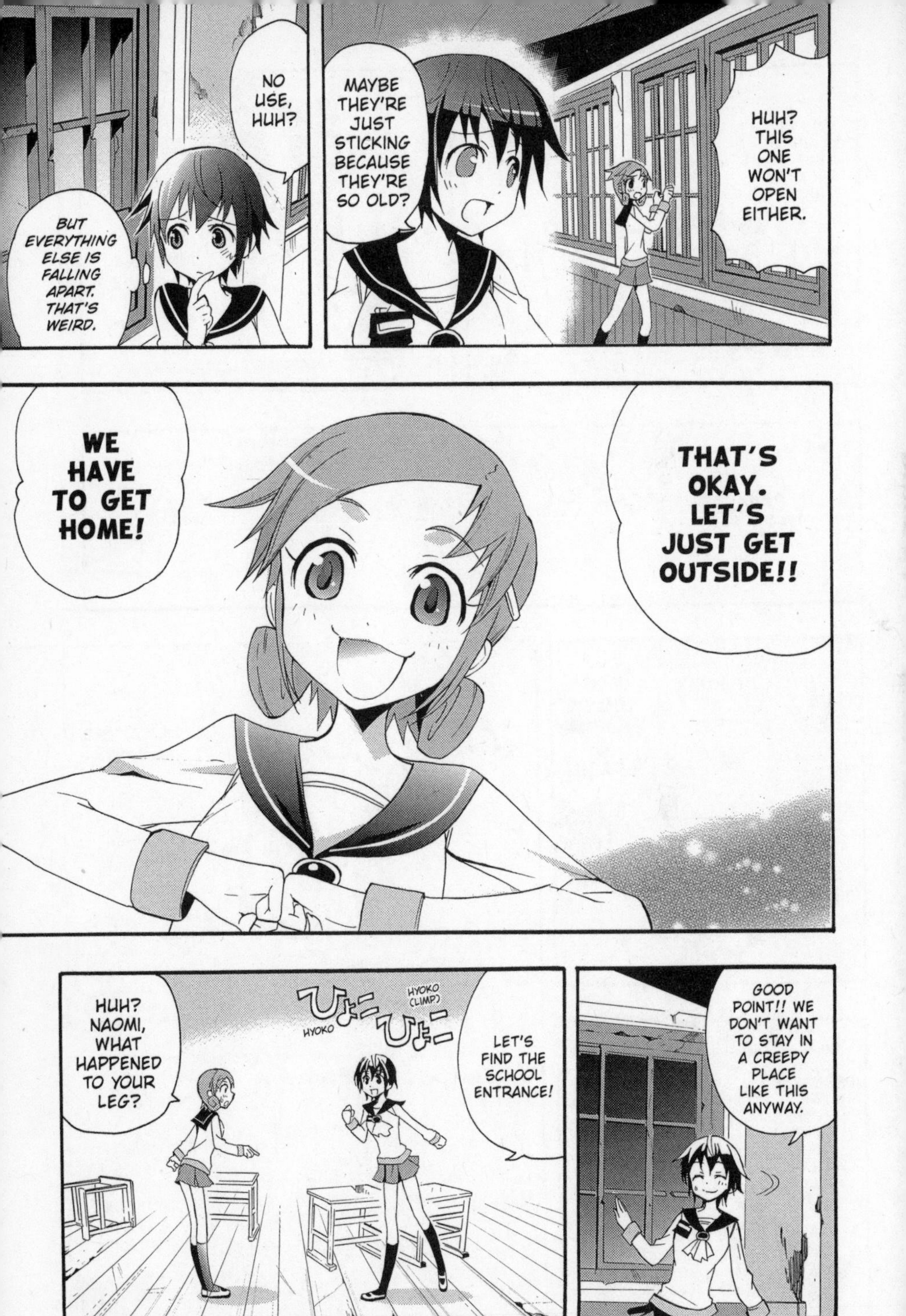
HUH? THIS ONE WON'T OPEN EITHER.
MAYBE THEY'RE JUST STICKING BECAUSE THEY'RE SO OLD?
NO USE, HUH?
BUT EVERYTHING ELSE IS FALLING APART. THAT'S WEIRD.
THAT'S OKAY. LET'S JUST GET OUTSIDE!!
WE HAVE TO GET HOME!
GOOD POINT!! WE DON'T WANT TO STAY IN A CREEPY PLACE LIKE THIS ANYWAY.
LET'S FIND THE SCHOOL ENTRANCE!
HYOKO (LIMP)
HYOKO
HUH? NAOMI, WHAT HAPPENED TO YOUR LEG?

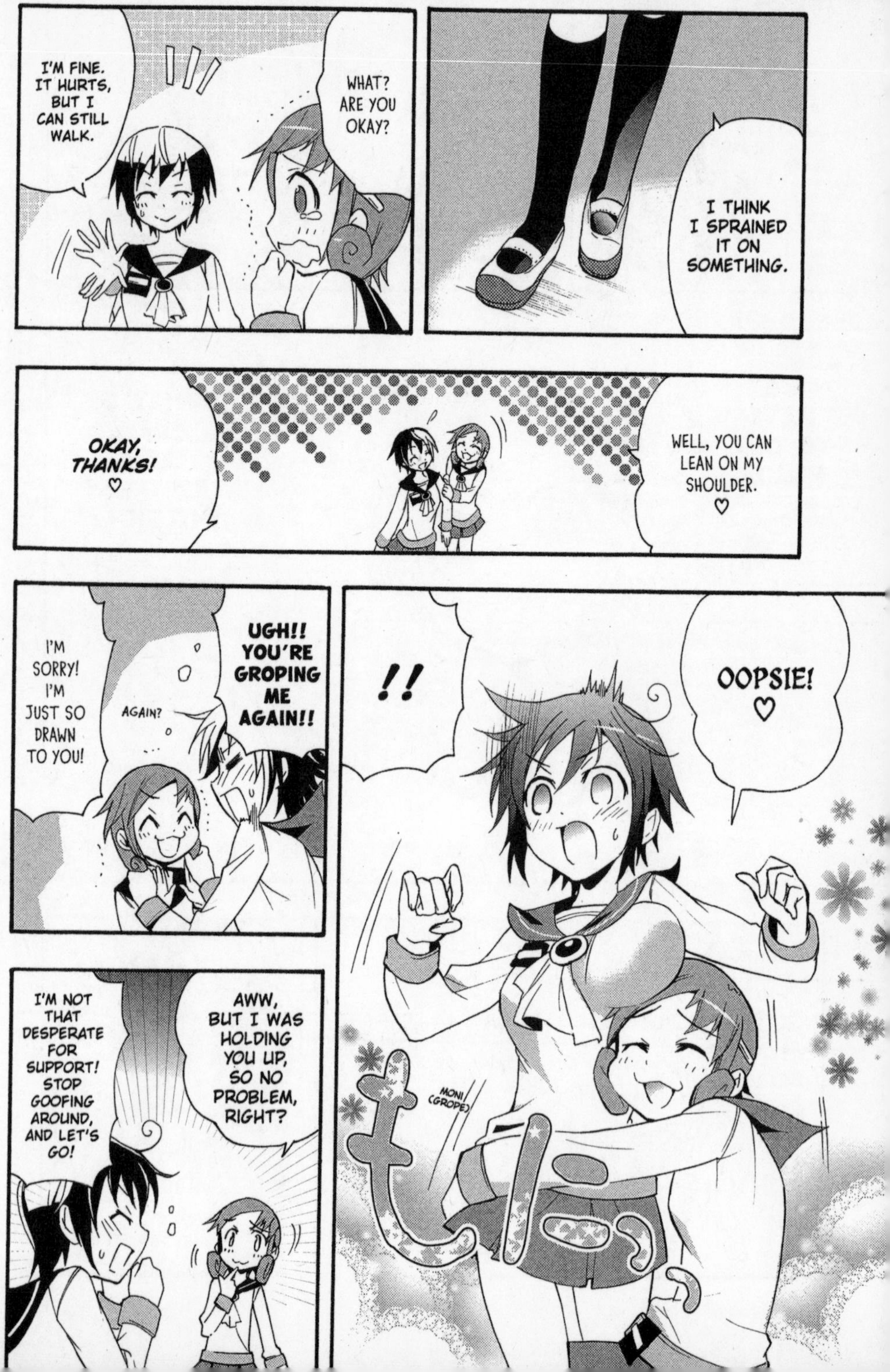
I THINK I SPRAINED IT ON SOMETHING.
WHAT? ARE YOU OKAY?
I'M FINE. IT HURTS, BUT I CAN STILL WALK.
WELL, YOU CAN LEAN ON MY SHOULDER. ♡
OKAY, THANKS! ♡
OOPSIE! ♡
!!
MONI (GROPE)
UGH!! YOU'RE GROPING ME AGAIN!!
AGAIN?
I'M SORRY! I'M JUST SO DRAWN TO YOU!
AWW, BUT I WAS HOLDING YOU UP, SO NO PROBLEM, RIGHT?
I'M NOT THAT DESPERATE FOR SUPPORT! STOP GOOFING AROUND, AND LET'S GO!

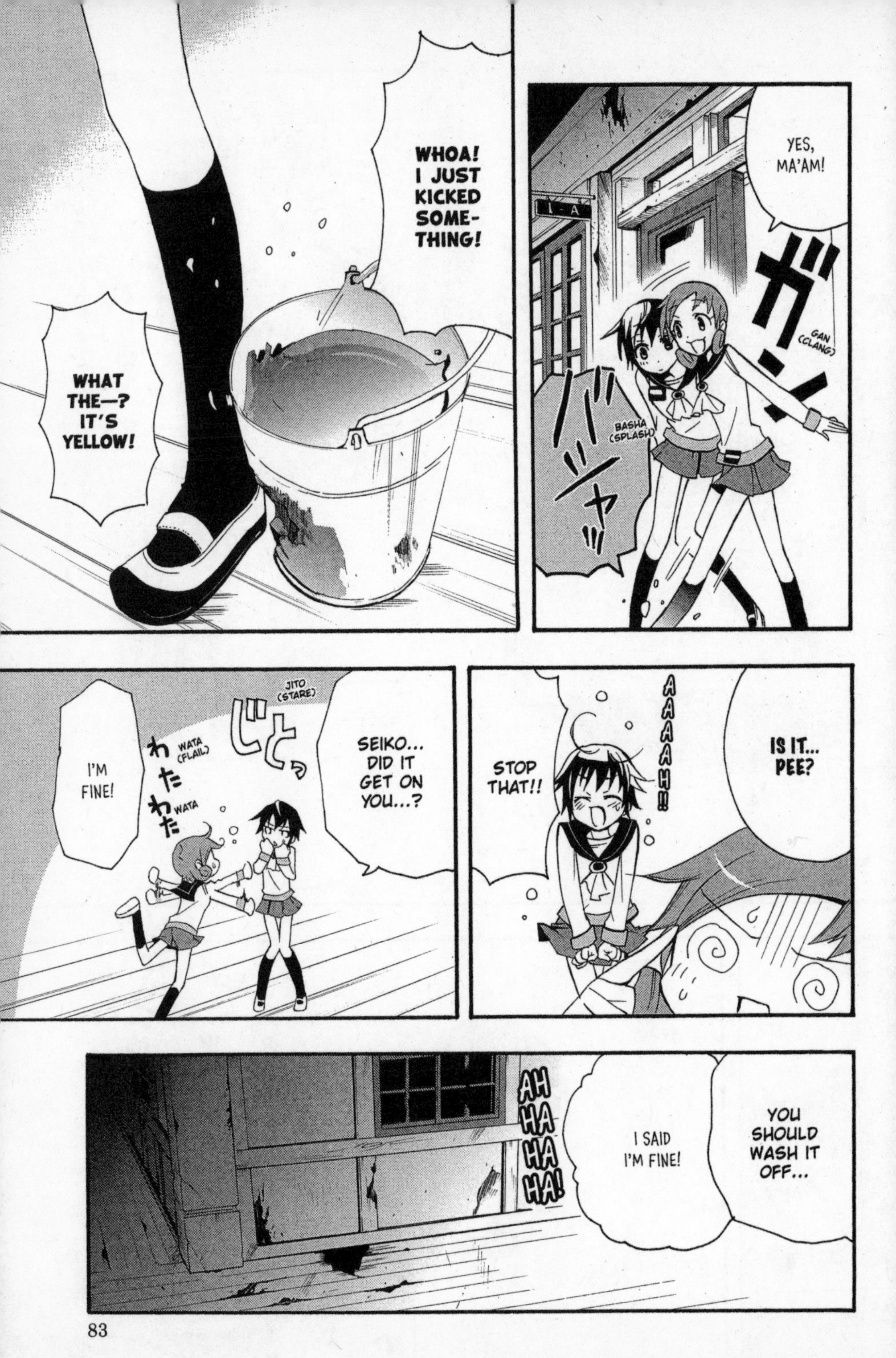

YES, MA'AM!
1-A
ガン
GAN (CLANG)
バシャ
BASHA (SPLASH)
WHOA! I JUST KICKED SOME-THING!
WHAT THE—? IT'S YELLOW!
IS IT... PEE?
AAAAAAH!!
STOP THAT!!
SEIKO... DID IT GET ON YOU...?
じとっ
JITO (STARE)
わたわた
WATA (FLAIL) WATA
I'M FINE!
YOU SHOULD WASH IT OFF...
I SAID I'M FINE!
AH HA HA HA HA!

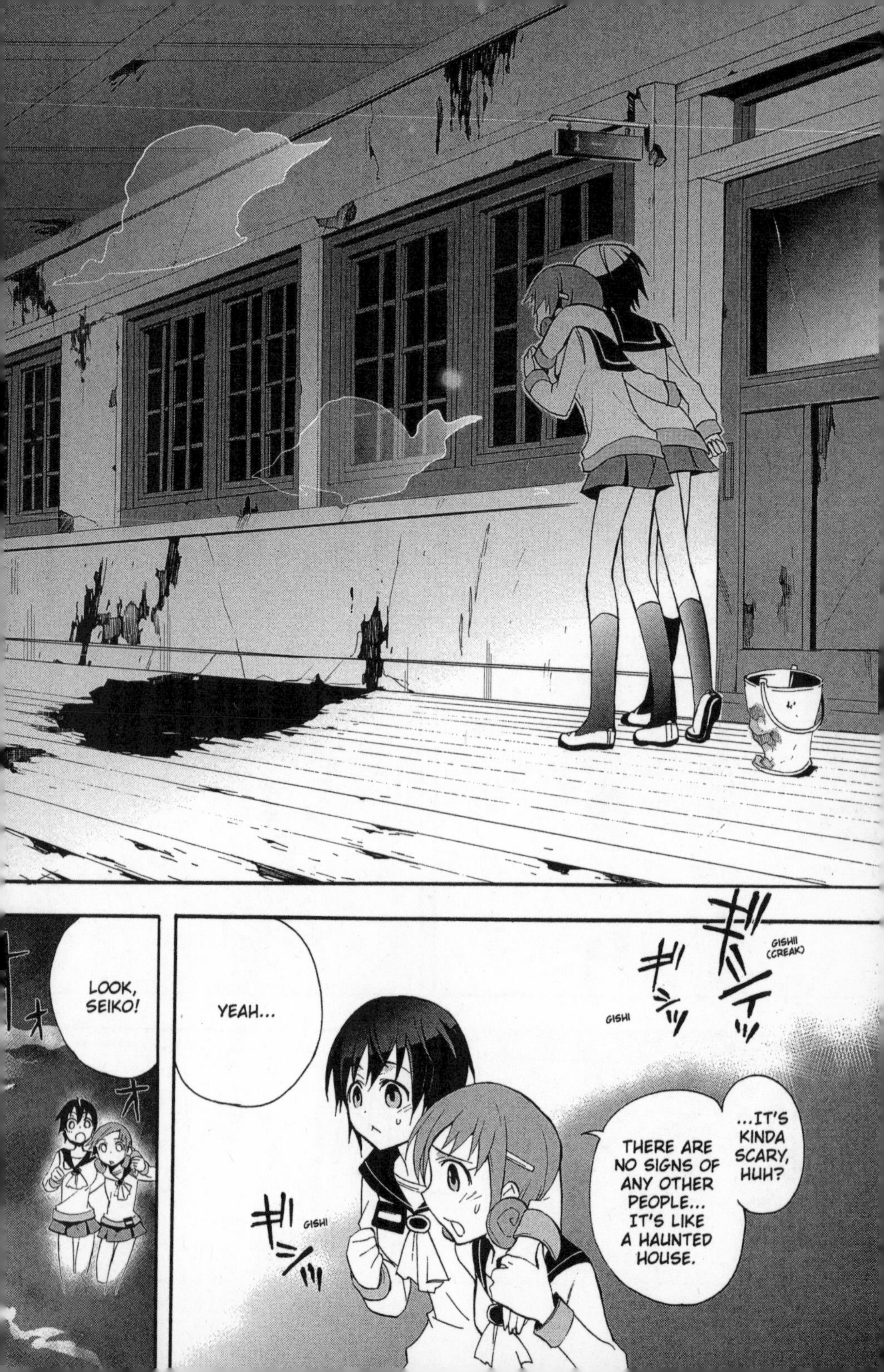
GISHII (CREAK)
GISHI
...IT'S KINDA SCARY, HUH?
THERE ARE NO SIGNS OF ANY OTHER PEOPLE... IT'S LIKE A HAUNTED HOUSE.
YEAH...
GISHI
LOOK, SEIKO!

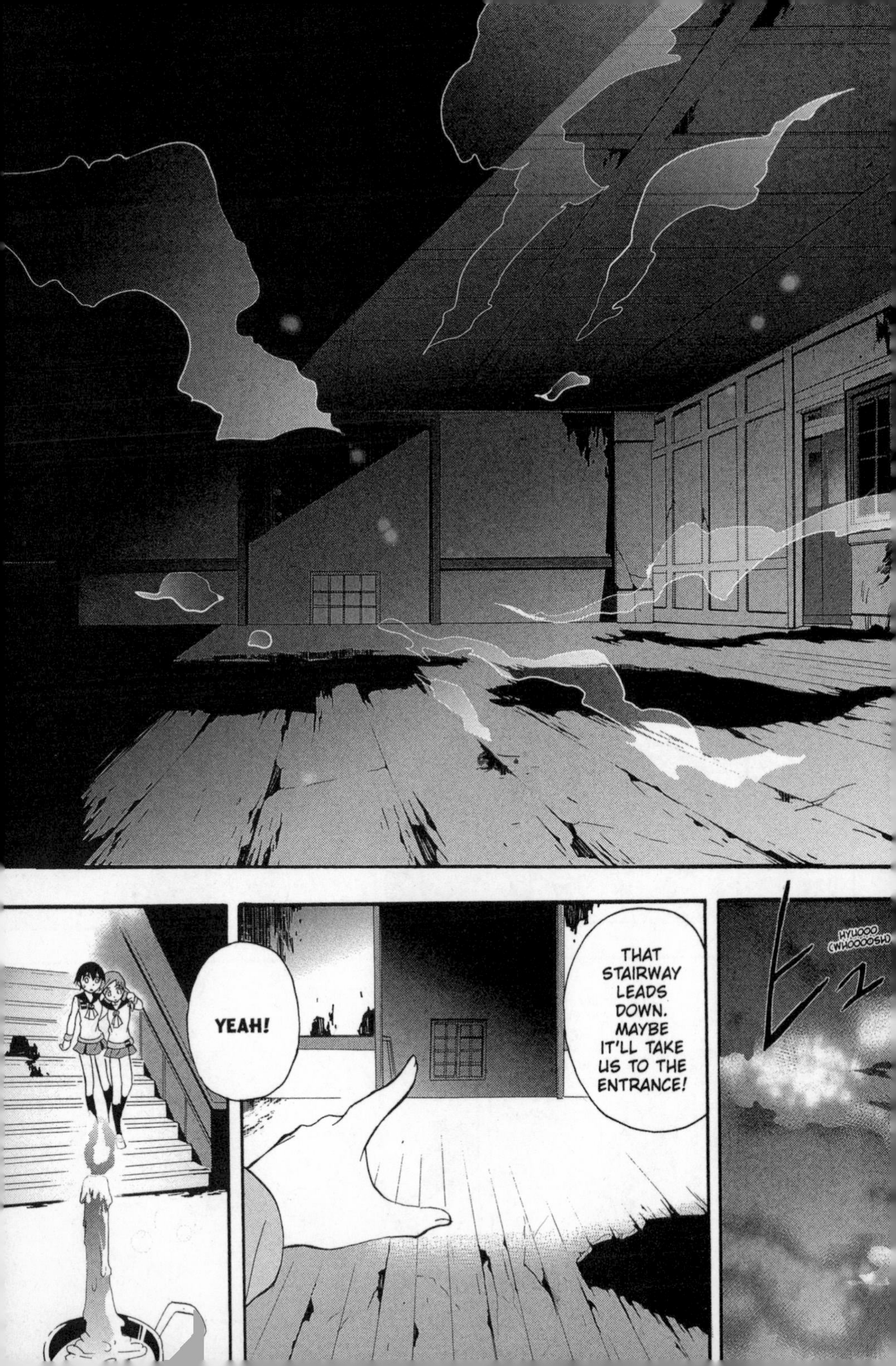
HYUOOO
(WHOOOOSH)
THAT STAIRWAY LEADS DOWN. MAYBE IT'LL TAKE US TO THE ENTRANCE!
YEAH!

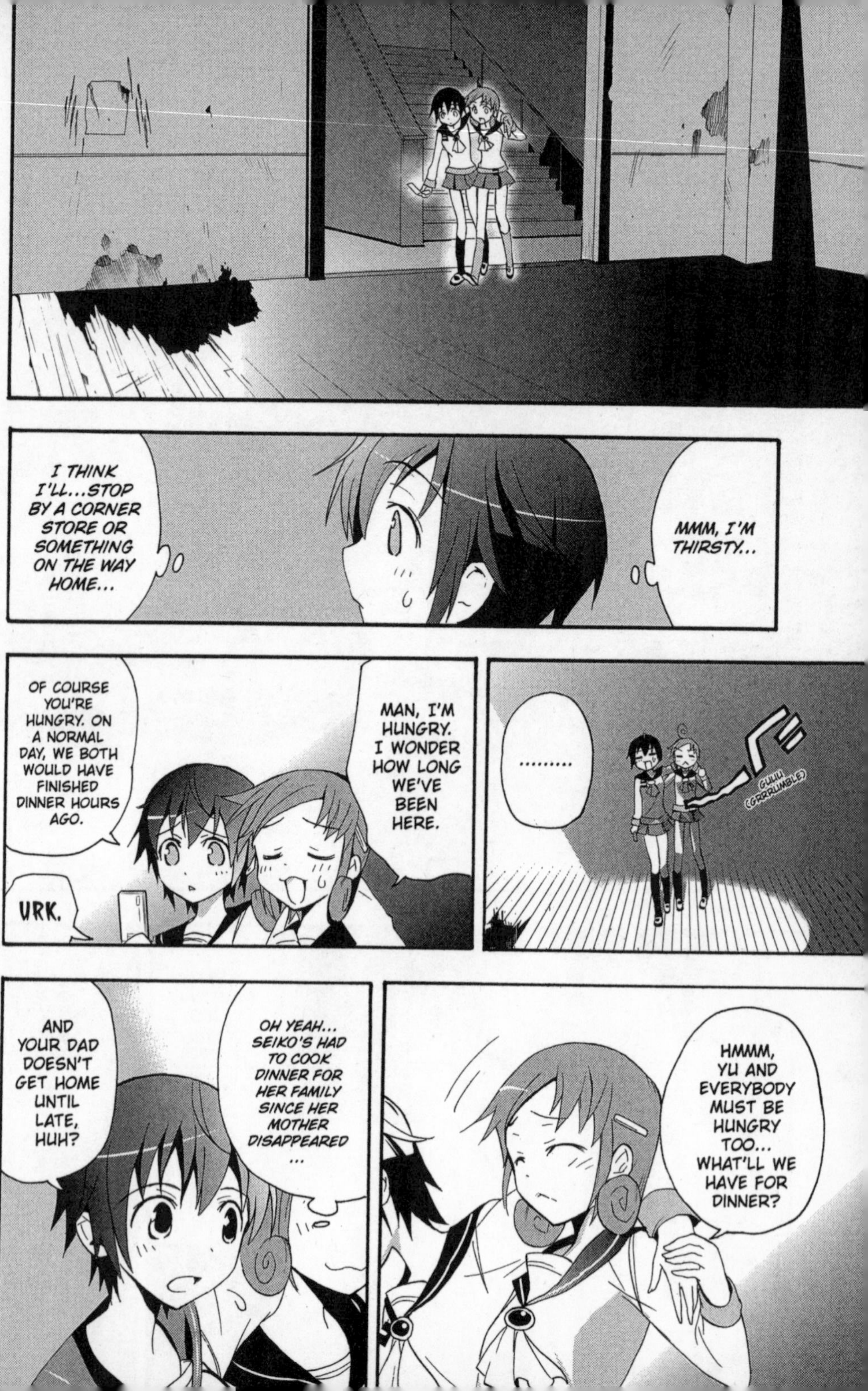
MMM, I'M THIRSTY...
I THINK I'LL...STOP BY A CORNER STORE OR SOMETHING ON THE WAY HOME...
....
GULUU (GRRRUMBLE)
MAN, I'M HUNGRY. I WONDER HOW LONG WE'VE BEEN HERE.
OF COURSE YOU'RE HUNGRY. ON A NORMAL DAY, WE BOTH WOULD HAVE FINISHED DINNER HOURS AGO.
URK.
HMMM, YU AND EVERYBODY MUST BE HUNGRY TOO... WHAT'LL WE HAVE FOR DINNER?
OH YEAH... SEIKO'S HAD TO COOK DINNER FOR HER FAMILY SINCE HER MOTHER DISAPPEARED...
AND YOUR DAD DOESN'T GET HOME UNTIL LATE, HUH?

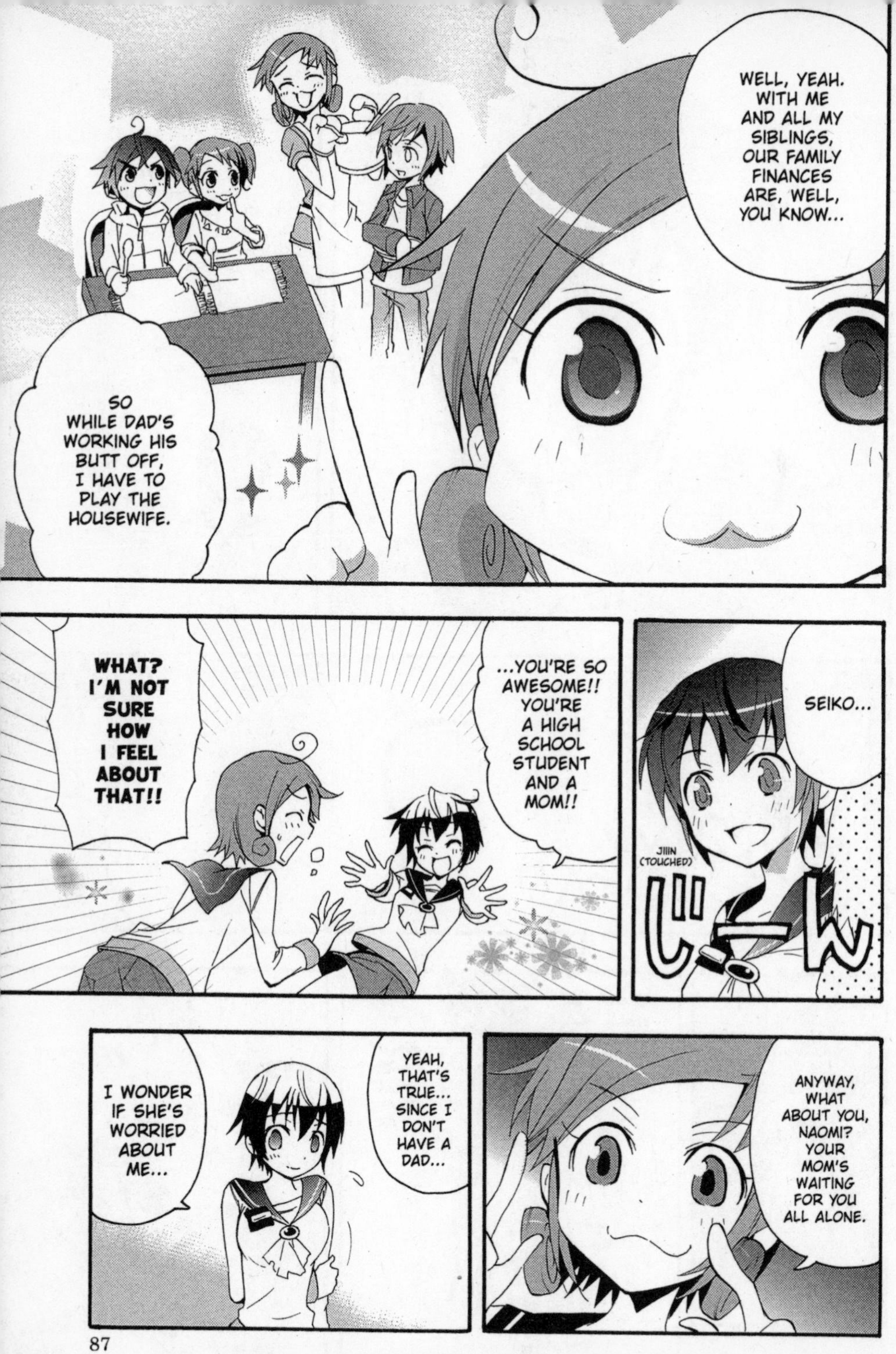
WELL, YEAH. WITH ME AND ALL MY SIBLINGS, OUR FAMILY FINANCES ARE, WELL, YOU KNOW...
SO WHILE DAD'S WORKING HIS BUTT OFF, I HAVE TO PLAY THE HOUSEWIFE.
SEIKO...
JIIN (TOUCHED)
じーん
...YOU'RE SO AWESOME!! YOU'RE A HIGH SCHOOL STUDENT AND A MOM!!
WHAT? I'M NOT SURE HOW I FEEL ABOUT THAT!!
ANYWAY, WHAT ABOUT YOU, NAOMI? YOUR MOM'S WAITING FOR YOU ALL ALONE.
YEAH, THAT'S TRUE... SINCE I DON'T HAVE A DAD...
I WONDER IF SHE'S WORRIED ABOUT ME...

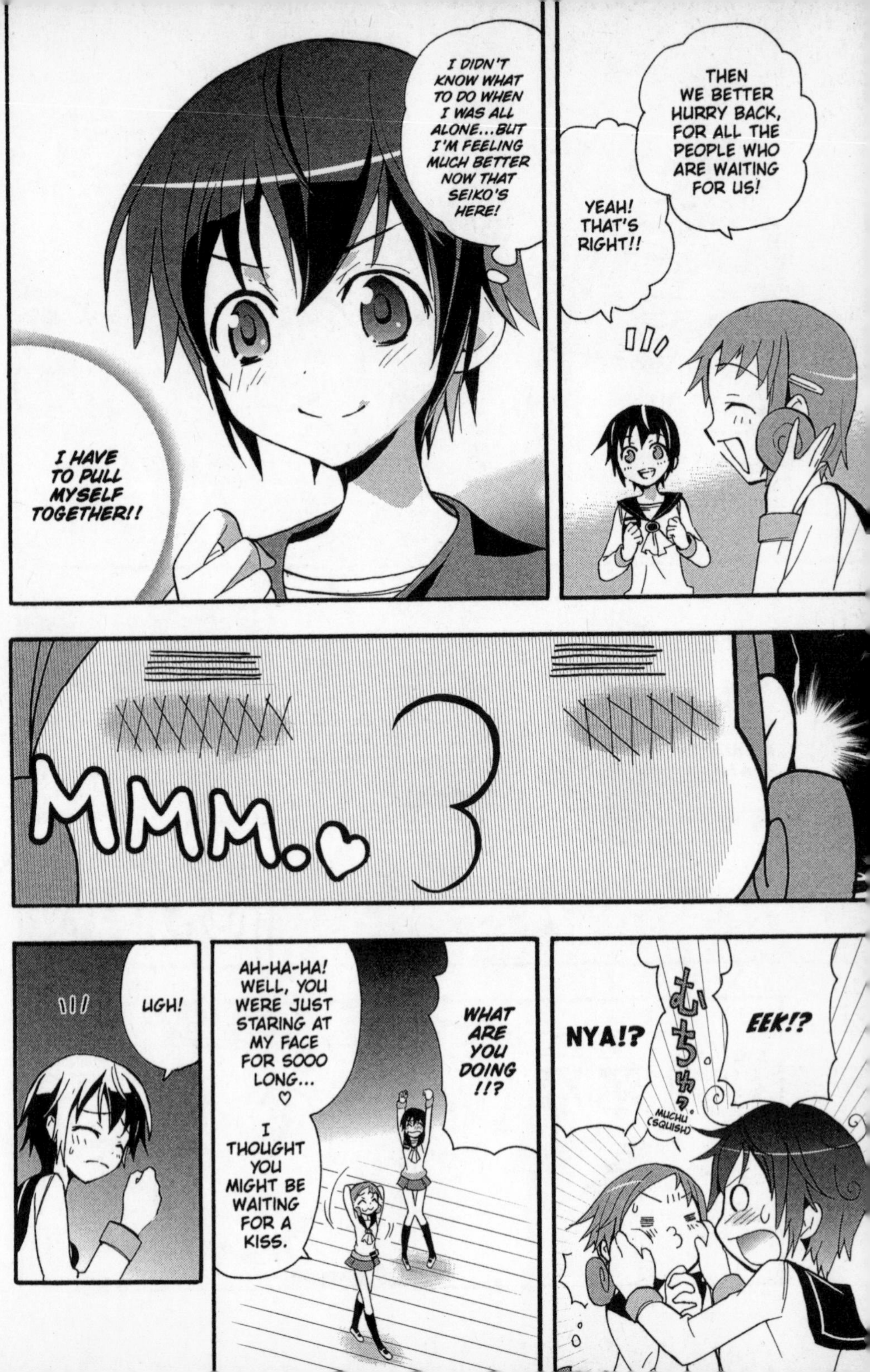
THEN WE BETTER HURRY BACK, FOR ALL THE PEOPLE WHO ARE WAITING FOR US!
YEAH! THAT'S RIGHT!!
I DIDN'T KNOW WHAT TO DO WHEN I WAS ALL ALONE...BUT I'M FEELING MUCH BETTER NOW THAT SEIKO'S HERE!
I HAVE TO PULL MYSELF TOGETHER!!
MMM.♥
EEK!?
むちゅ
NYA!?
MUCHU (SQUISH)
WHAT ARE YOU DOING!!?
AH-HA-HA! WELL, YOU WERE JUST STARING AT MY FACE FOR SOOO LONG...♡
I THOUGHT YOU MIGHT BE WAITING FOR A KISS.
UGH!

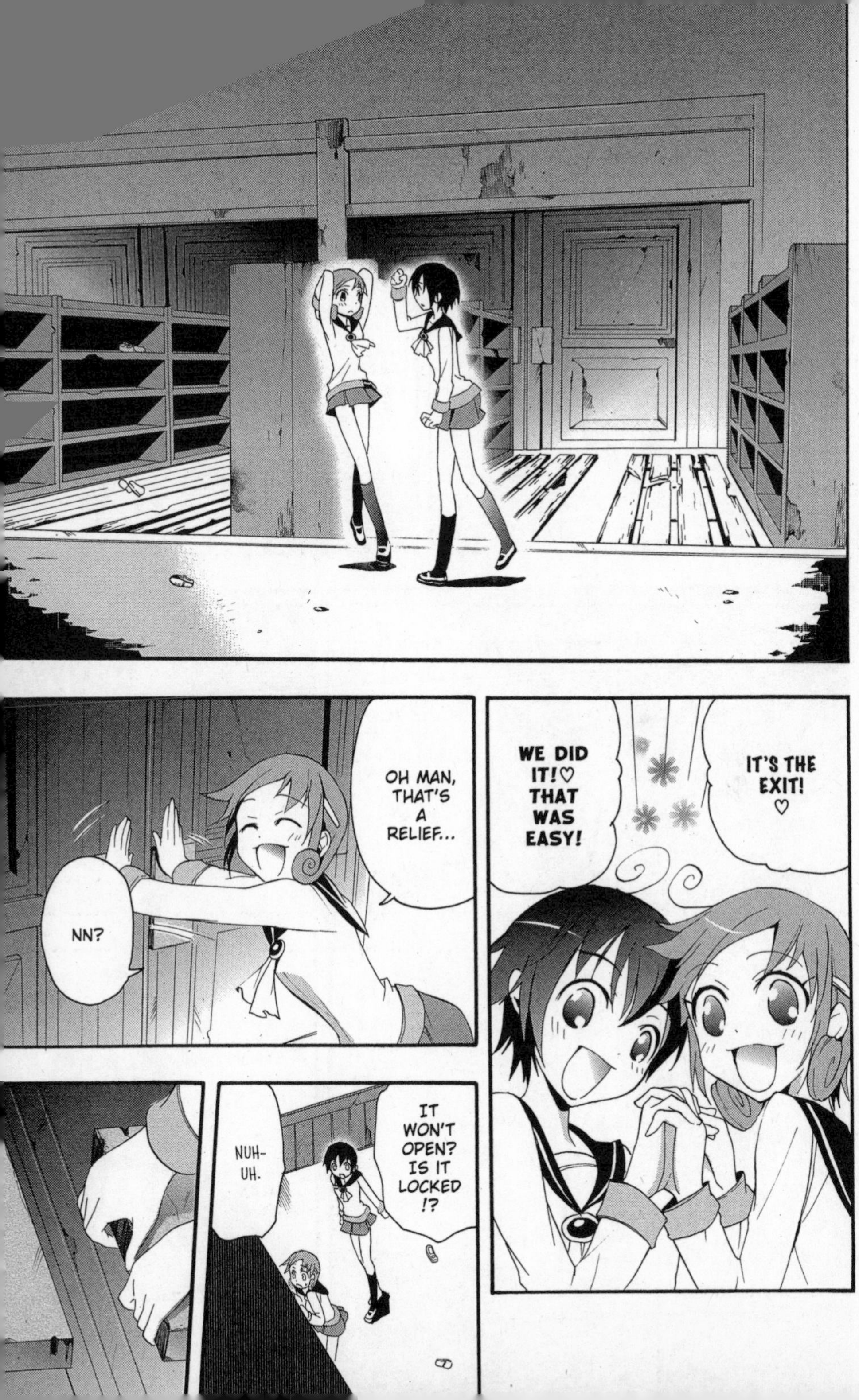
IT'S THE EXIT! ♡
WE DID IT! ♡ THAT WAS EASY!
OH MAN, THAT'S A RELIEF...
NN?
IT WON'T OPEN? IS IT LOCKED !?
NUH-UH.

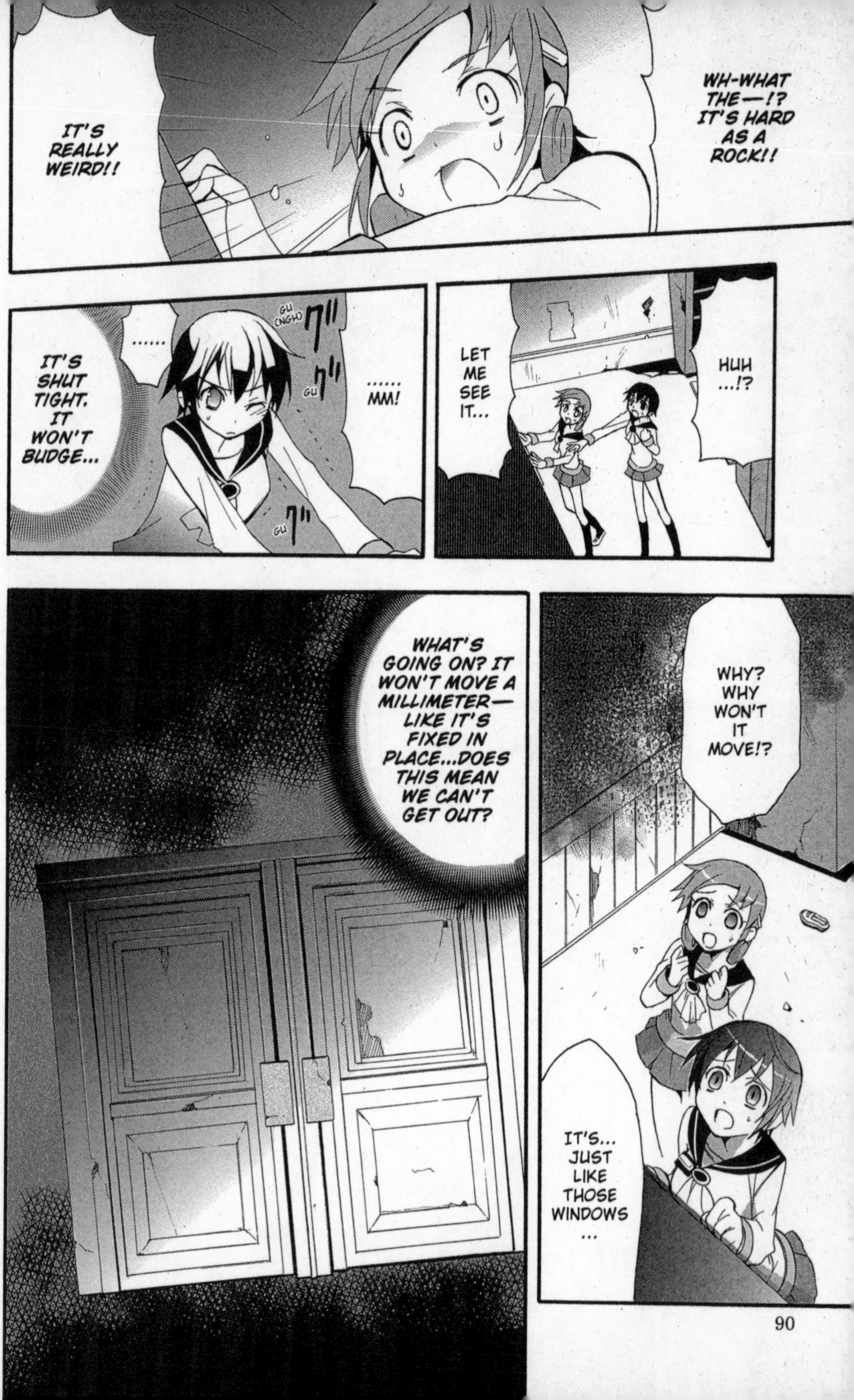
WH-WHAT THE—!? IT'S HARD AS A ROCK!!
IT'S REALLY WEIRD!!
HUH ...!?
LET ME SEE IT...
......MM!
GU (NGH)
GU
GU
......
IT'S SHUT TIGHT. IT WON'T BUDGE...
WHY? WHY WON'T IT MOVE!?
IT'S... JUST LIKE THOSE WINDOWS ...
WHAT'S GOING ON? IT WON'T MOVE A MILLIMETER—LIKE IT'S FIXED IN PLACE...DOES THIS MEAN WE CAN'T GET OUT?

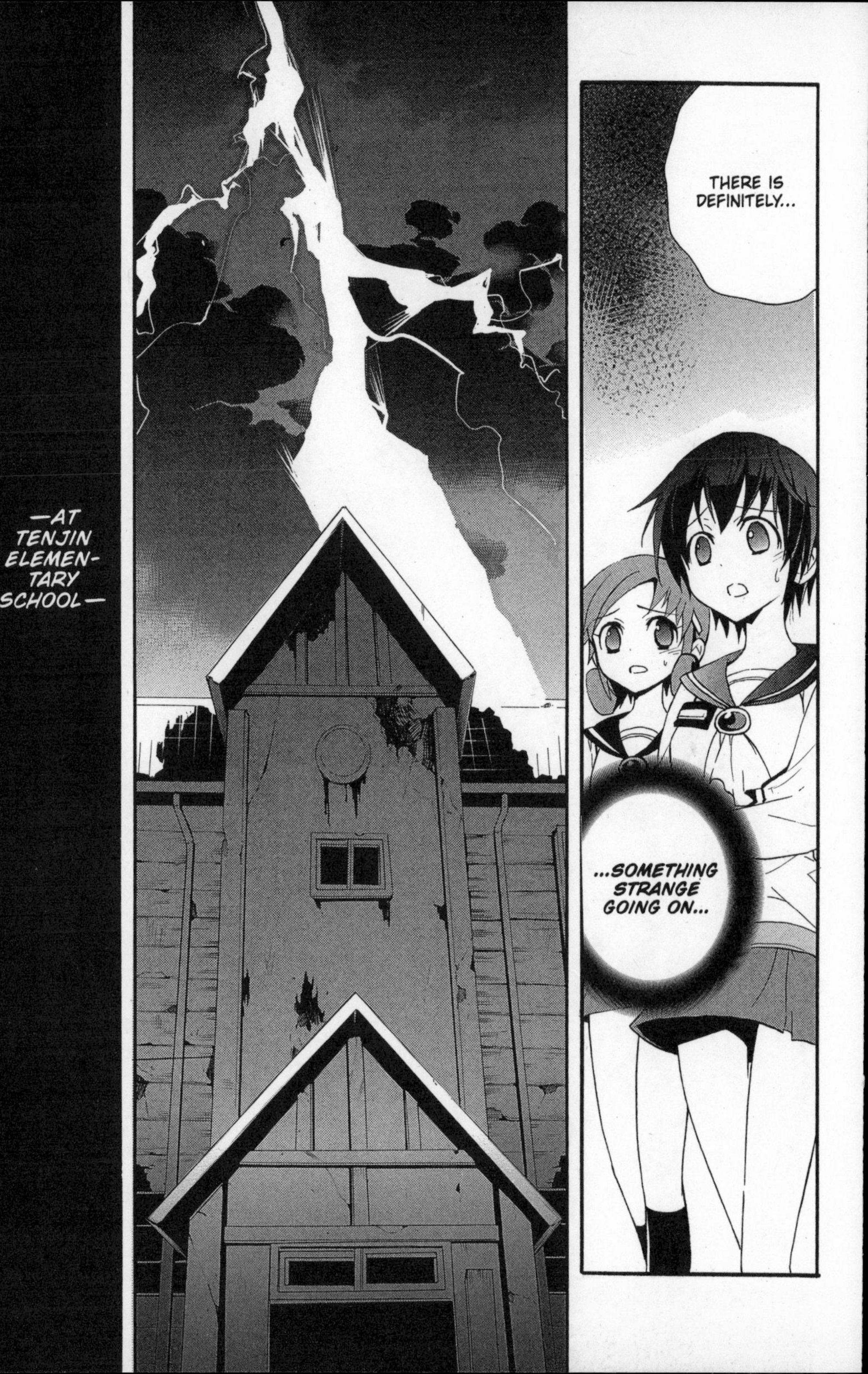
THERE IS DEFINITELY...
...SOMETHING STRANGE GOING ON...
—AT TENJIN ELEMENTARY SCHOOL—

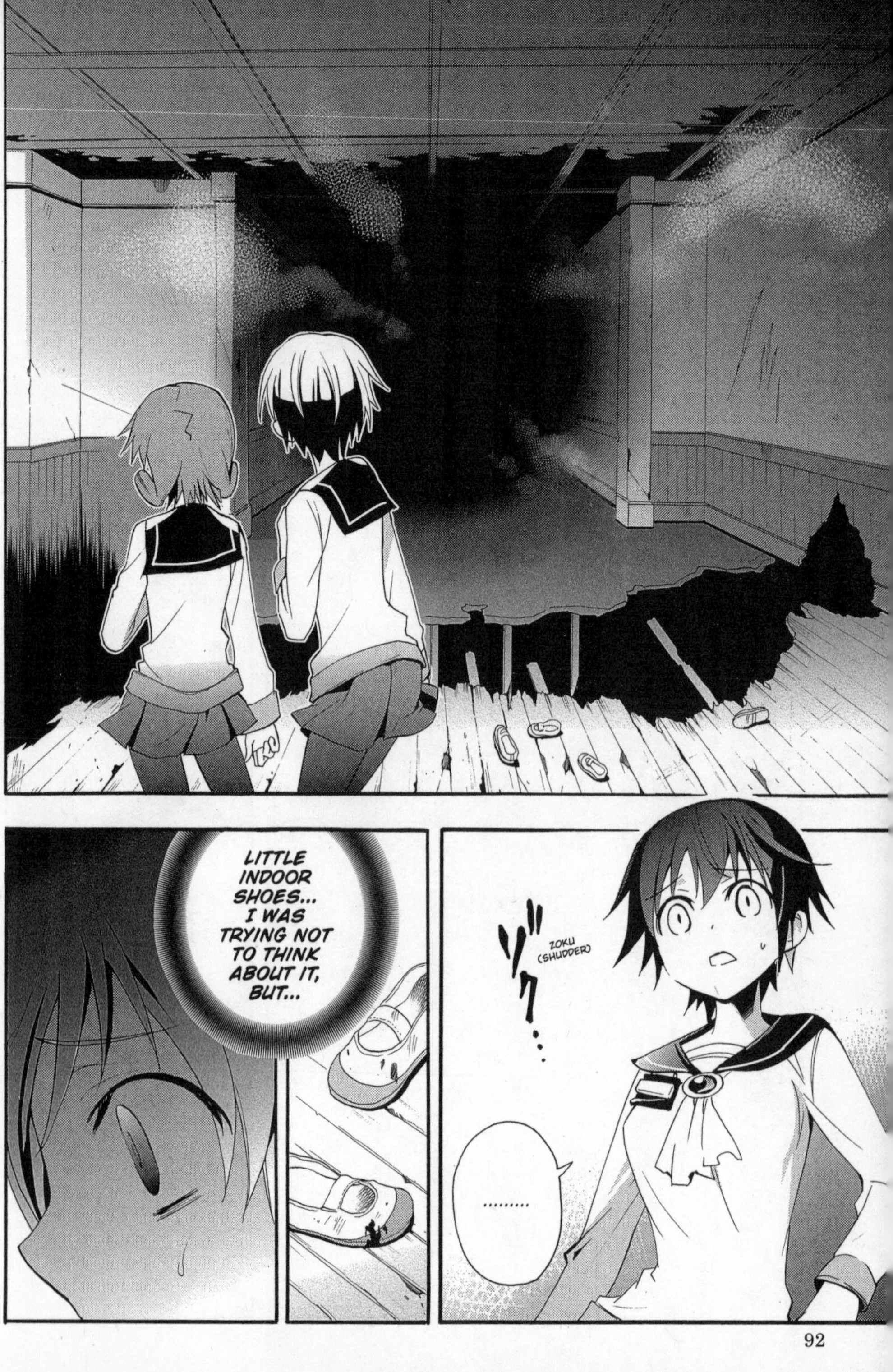
ZOKU (SHUDDER)
....
LITTLE INDOOR SHOES... I WAS TRYING NOT TO THINK ABOUT IT, BUT...

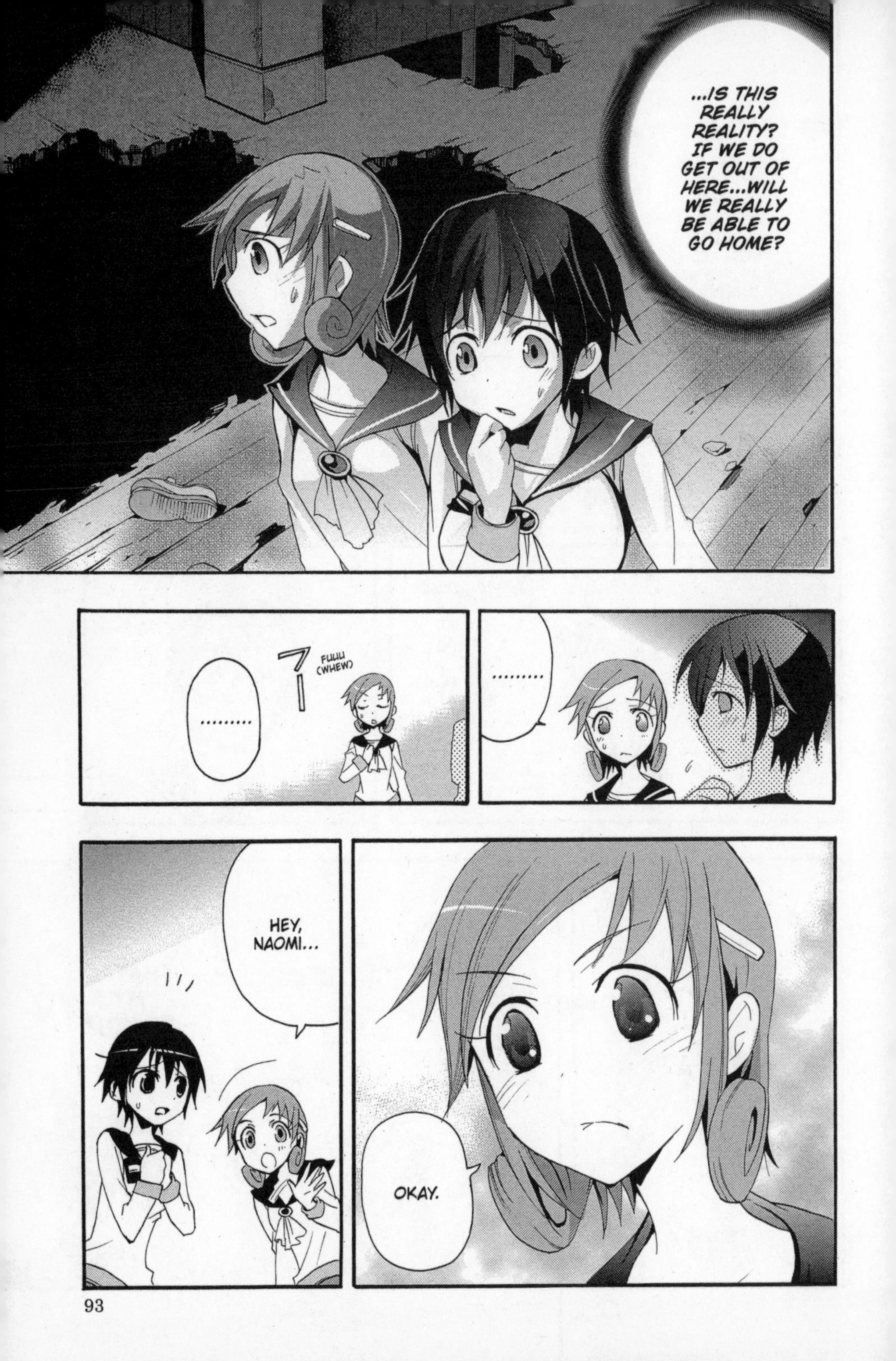
...IS THIS REALLY REALITY? IF WE DO GET OUT OF HERE...WILL WE REALLY BE ABLE TO GO HOME?
....
FUUU (WHEW)
....
OKAY.
HEY, NAOMI...

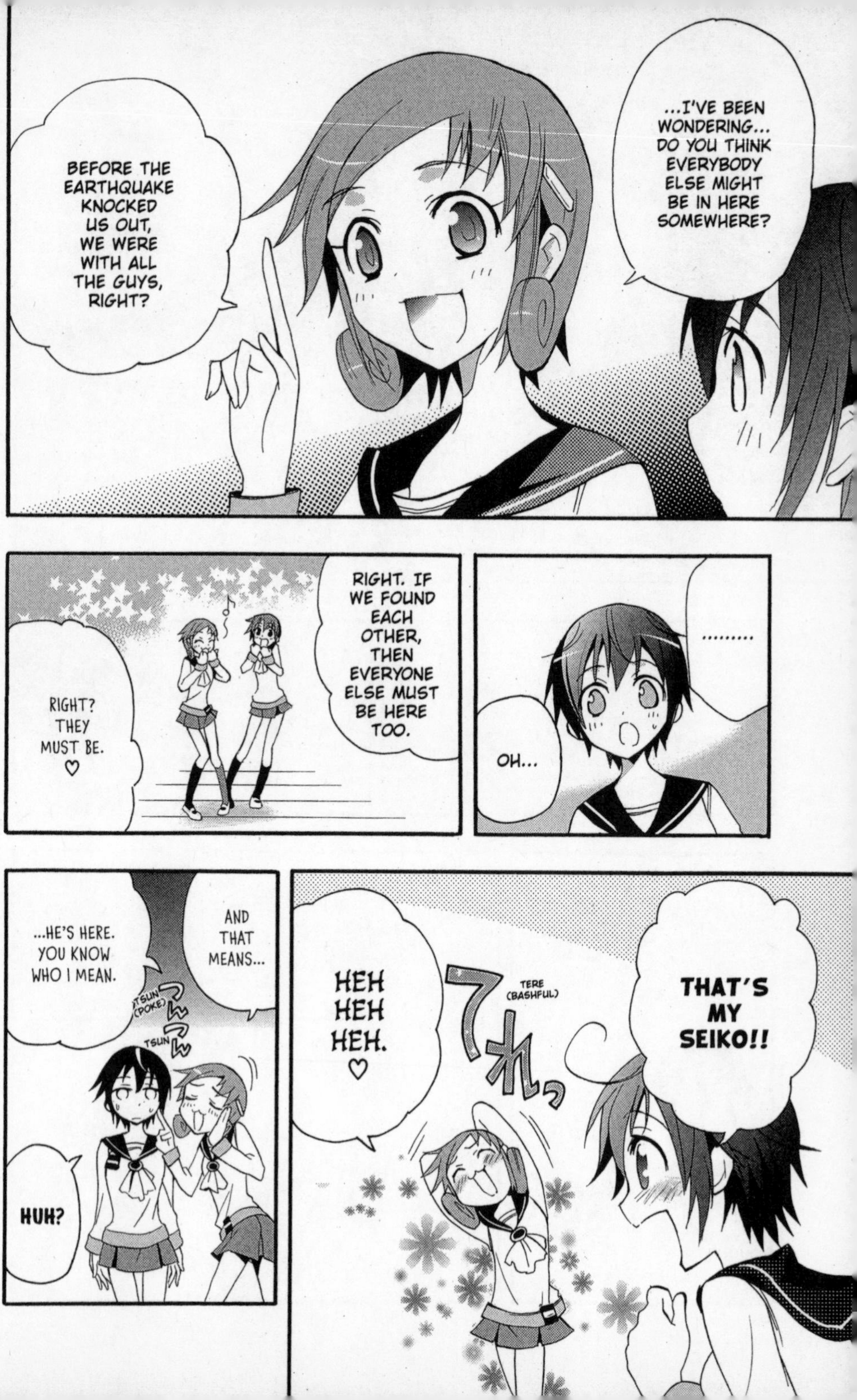
...I'VE BEEN WONDERING... DO YOU THINK EVERYBODY ELSE MIGHT BE IN HERE SOMEWHERE?
BEFORE THE EARTHQUAKE KNOCKED US OUT, WE WERE WITH ALL THE GUYS, RIGHT?
....
OH...
RIGHT. IF WE FOUND EACH OTHER, THEN EVERYONE ELSE MUST BE HERE TOO.
RIGHT? THEY MUST BE. ♡
THAT'S MY SEIKO!!
TERE (BASHFUL)
HEH HEH HEH. ♡
AND THAT MEANS...
...HE'S HERE. YOU KNOW WHO I MEAN.
TSUN (POKE)
TSUN
HUH?

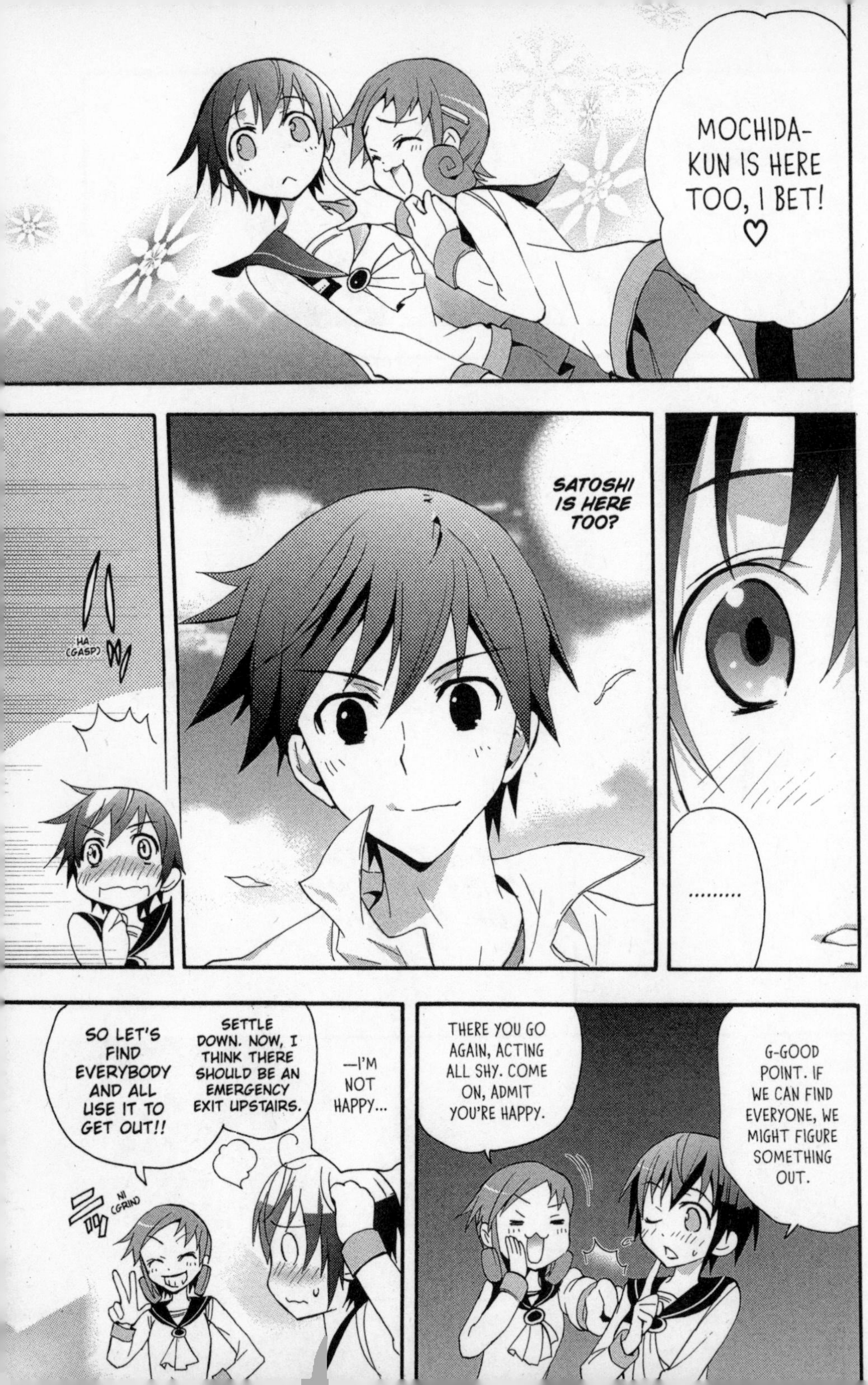
MOCHIDA-KUN IS HERE TOO, I BET! ♡
....
SATOSHI IS HERE TOO?
HA (GASP)
G-GOOD POINT. IF WE CAN FIND EVERYONE, WE MIGHT FIGURE SOMETHING OUT.
THERE YOU GO AGAIN, ACTING ALL SHY. COME ON, ADMIT YOU'RE HAPPY.
—I'M NOT HAPPY...
SETTLE DOWN. NOW, I THINK THERE SHOULD BE AN EMERGENCY EXIT UPSTAIRS.
SO LET'S FIND EVERYBODY AND ALL USE IT TO GET OUT!!
NI (GRIN)

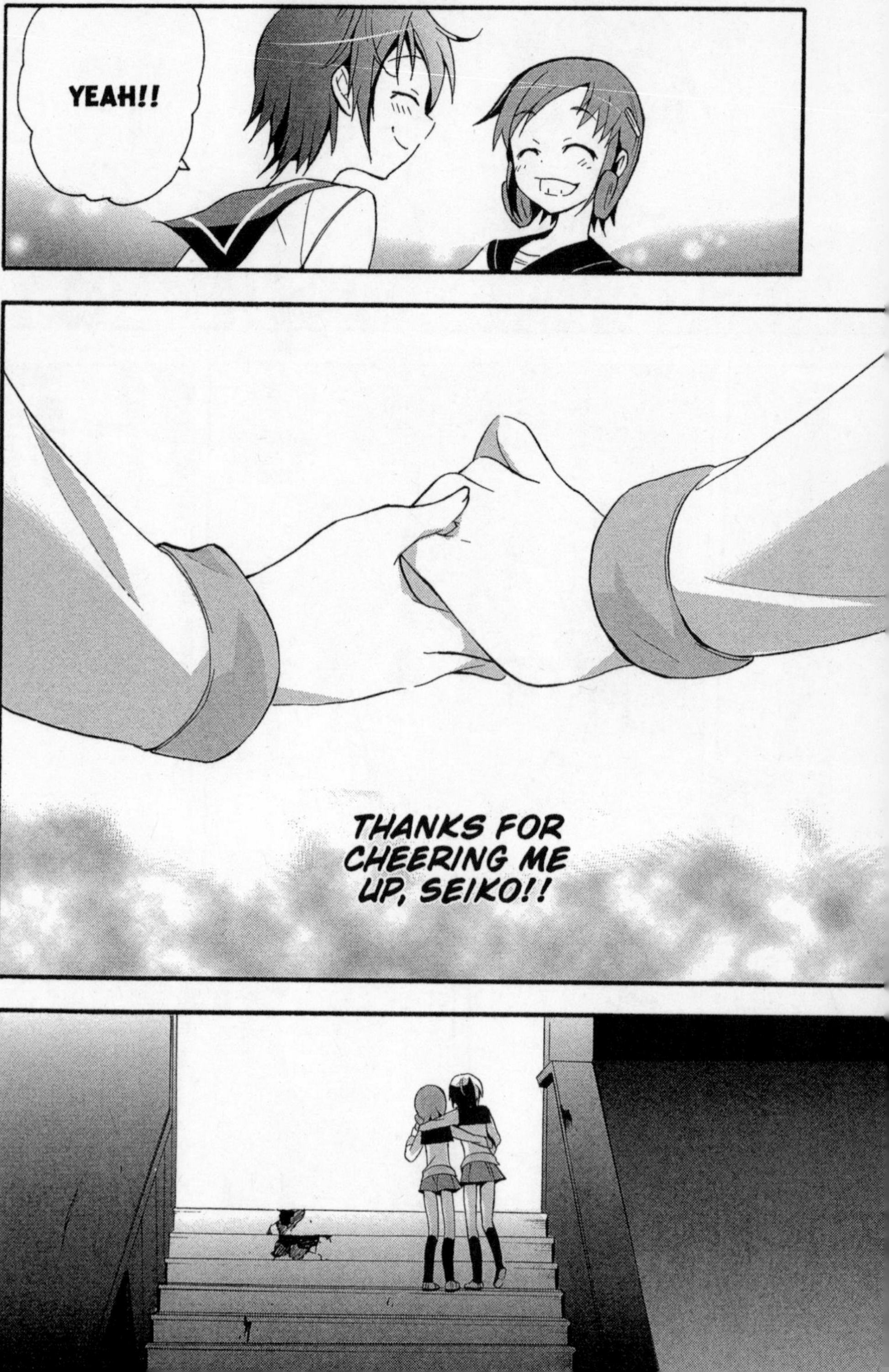
YEAH!!
THANKS FOR CHEERING ME UP, SEIKO!!

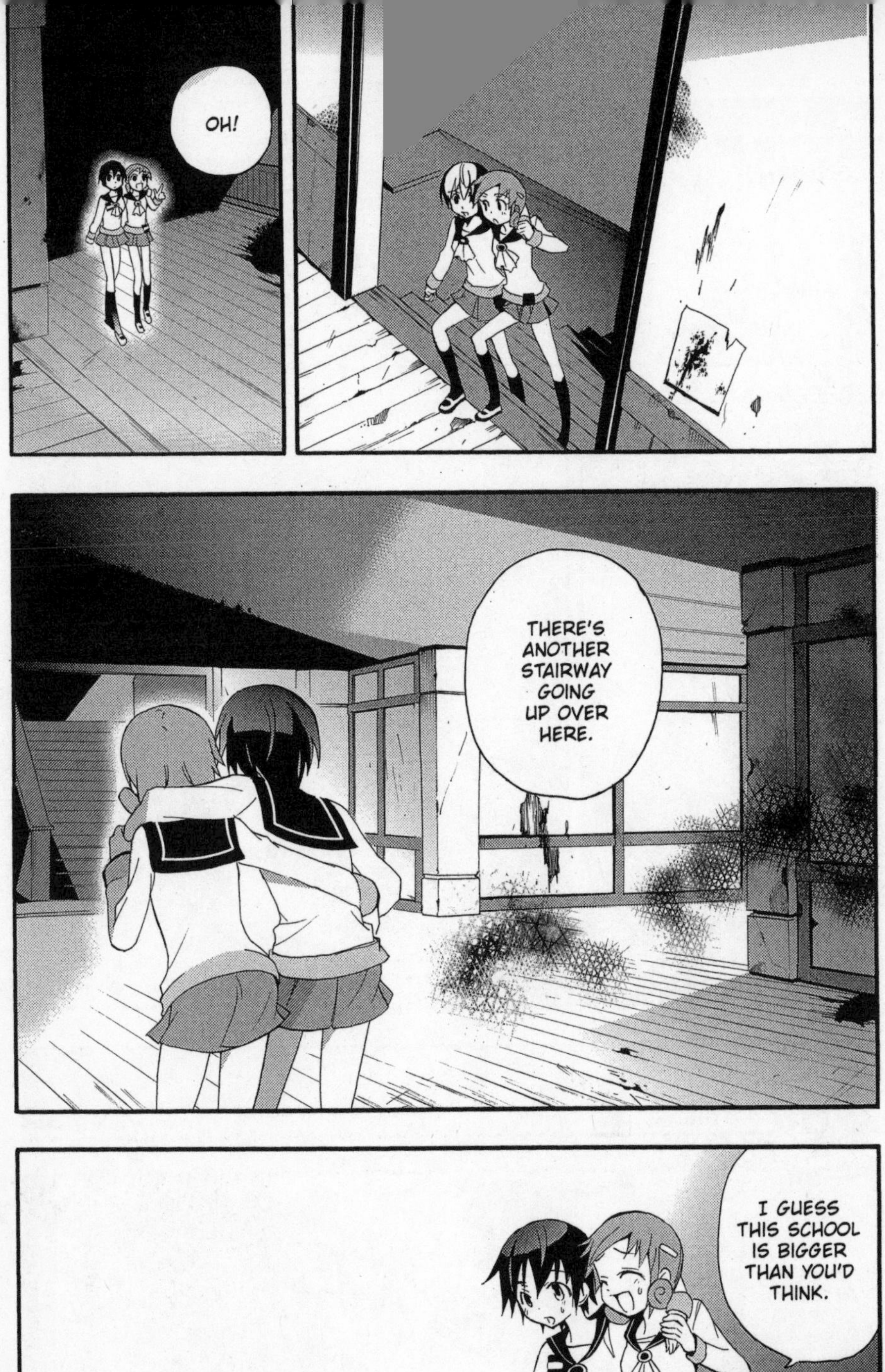
OH!
THERE'S ANOTHER STAIRWAY GOING UP OVER HERE.
I GUESS THIS SCHOOL IS BIGGER THAN YOU'D THINK.

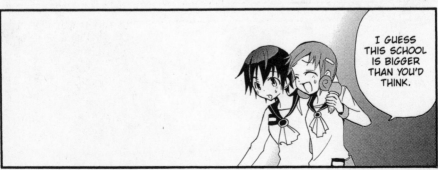

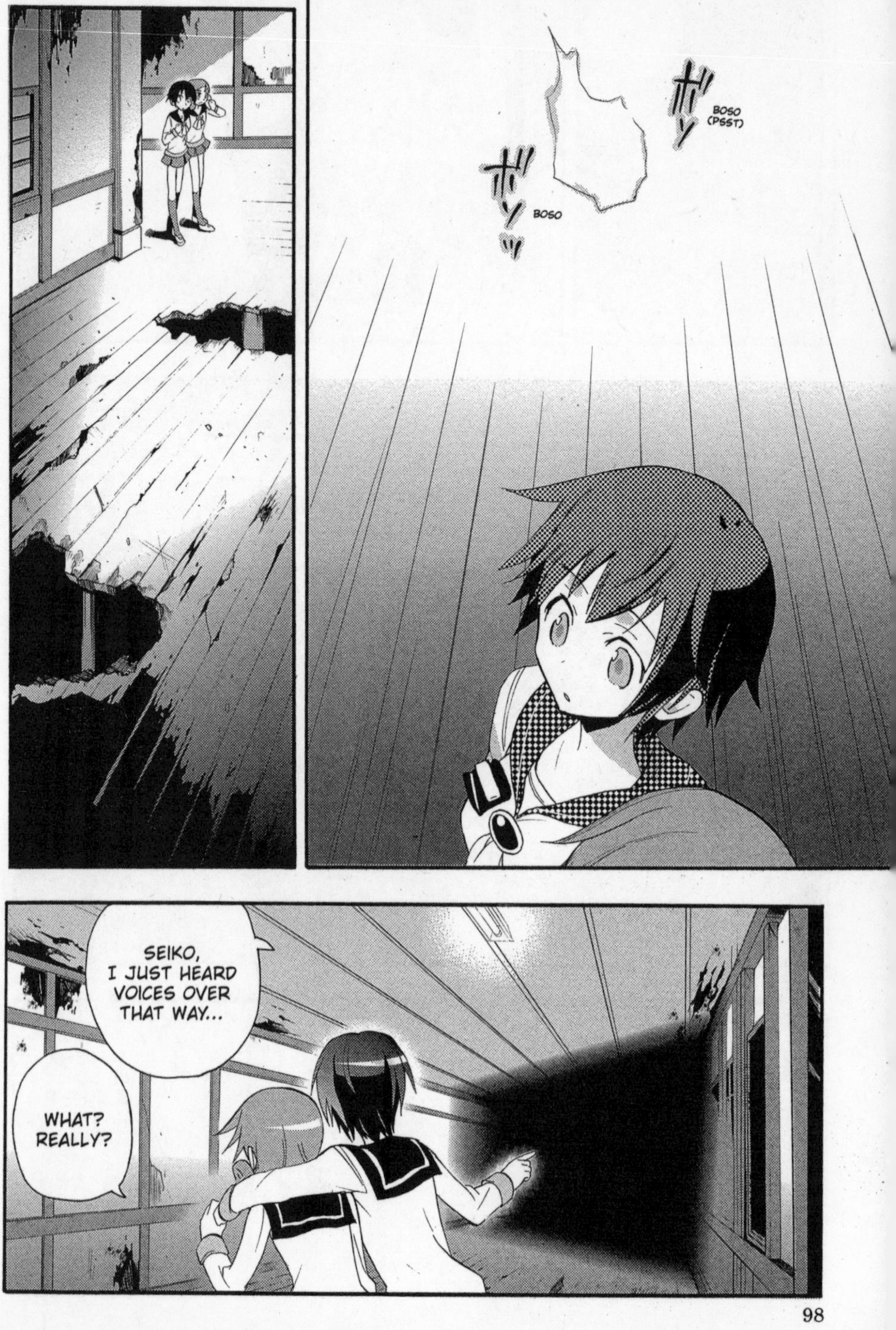
ボソ
BOSO (PSST)
ボソッ
BOSO
SEIKO, I JUST HEARD VOICES OVER THAT WAY...
WHAT? REALLY?

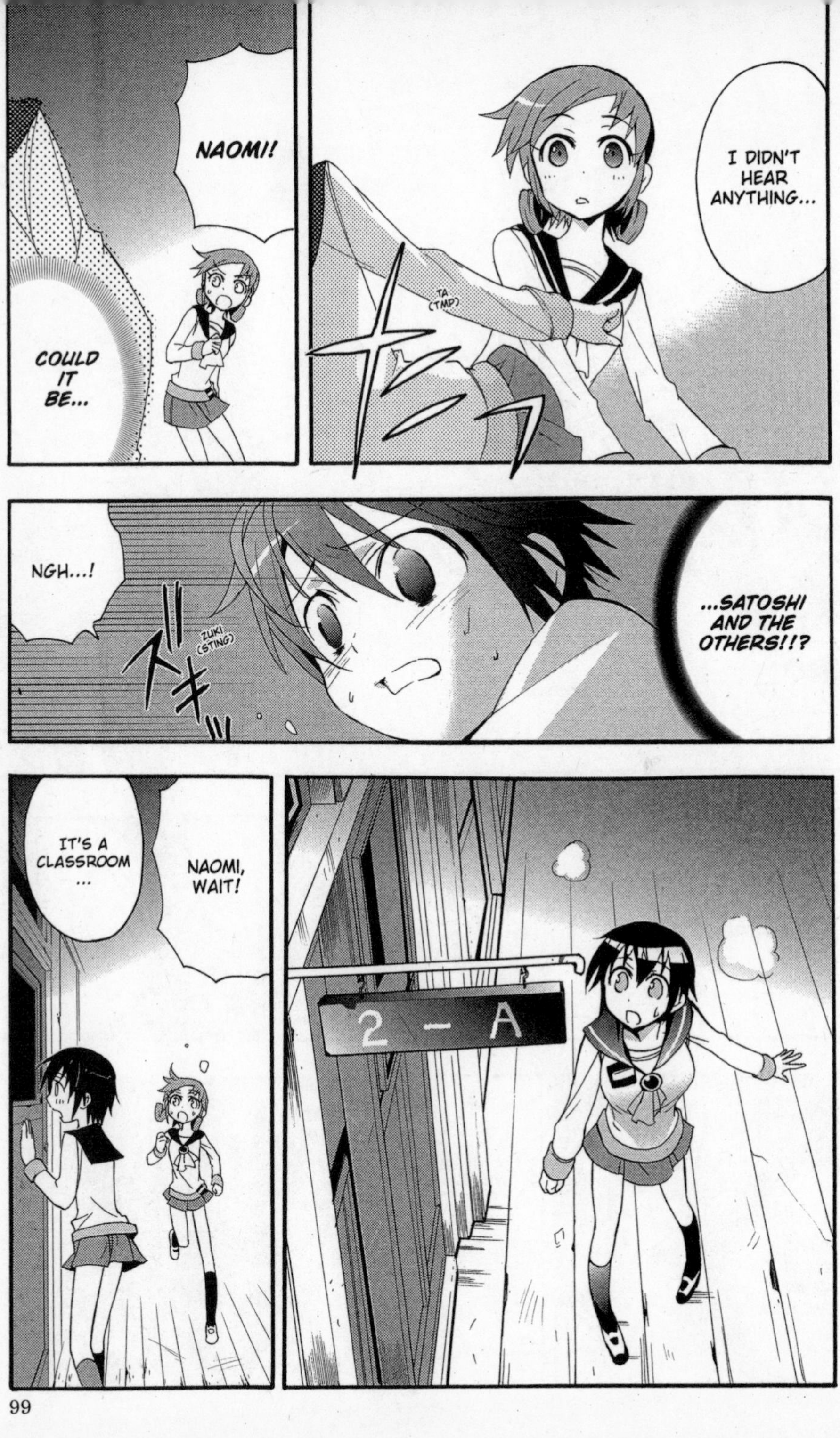
I DIDN'T HEAR ANYTHING...
TA (TMP)
NAOMI!
COULD IT BE...
...SATOSHI AND THE OTHERS!!?
ZUKI (STING)
NGH...!
2 - A
NAOMI, WAIT!
IT'S A CLASSROOM ...

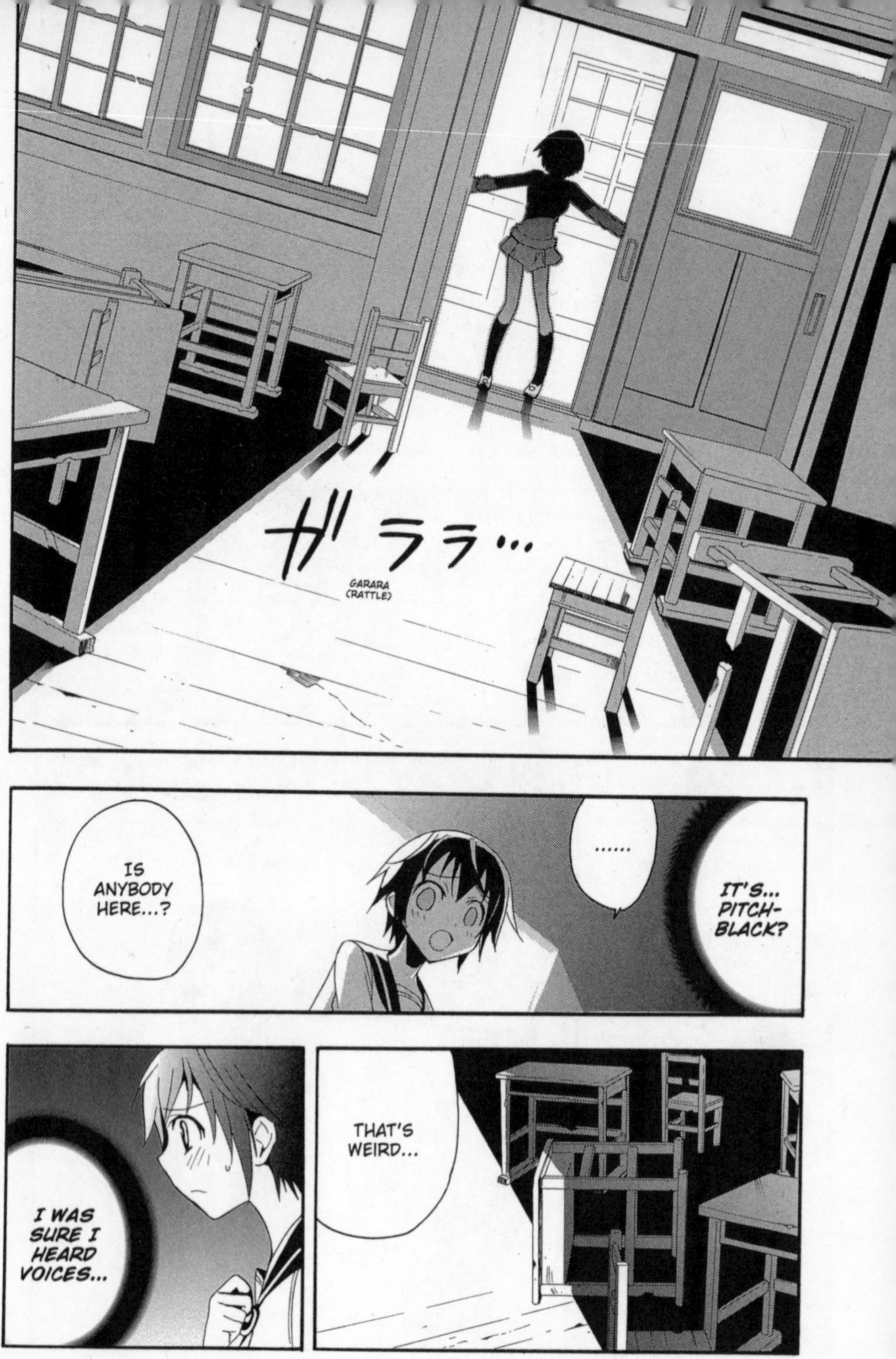
ガララ…
GARARA (RATTLE)
IT'S... PITCH-BLACK?
......
IS ANYBODY HERE...?
THAT'S WEIRD...
I WAS SURE I HEARD VOICES...

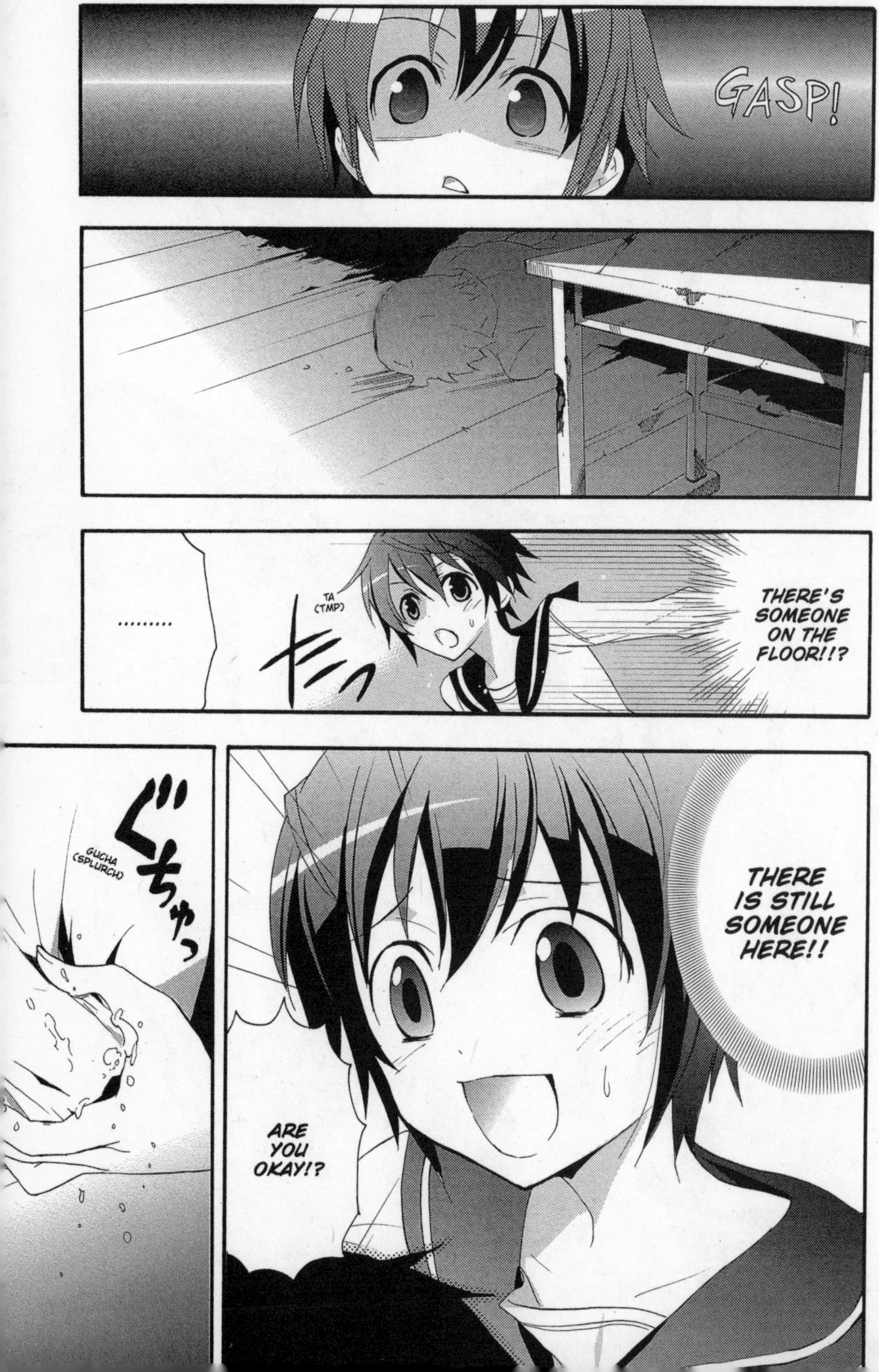

GASP!
THERE'S SOMEONE ON THE FLOOR!!?
たっ
TA (TMP)
....
THERE IS STILL SOMEONE HERE!!
ARE YOU OKAY!?
ぐちゃっ
GUCHA (SPLURCH)

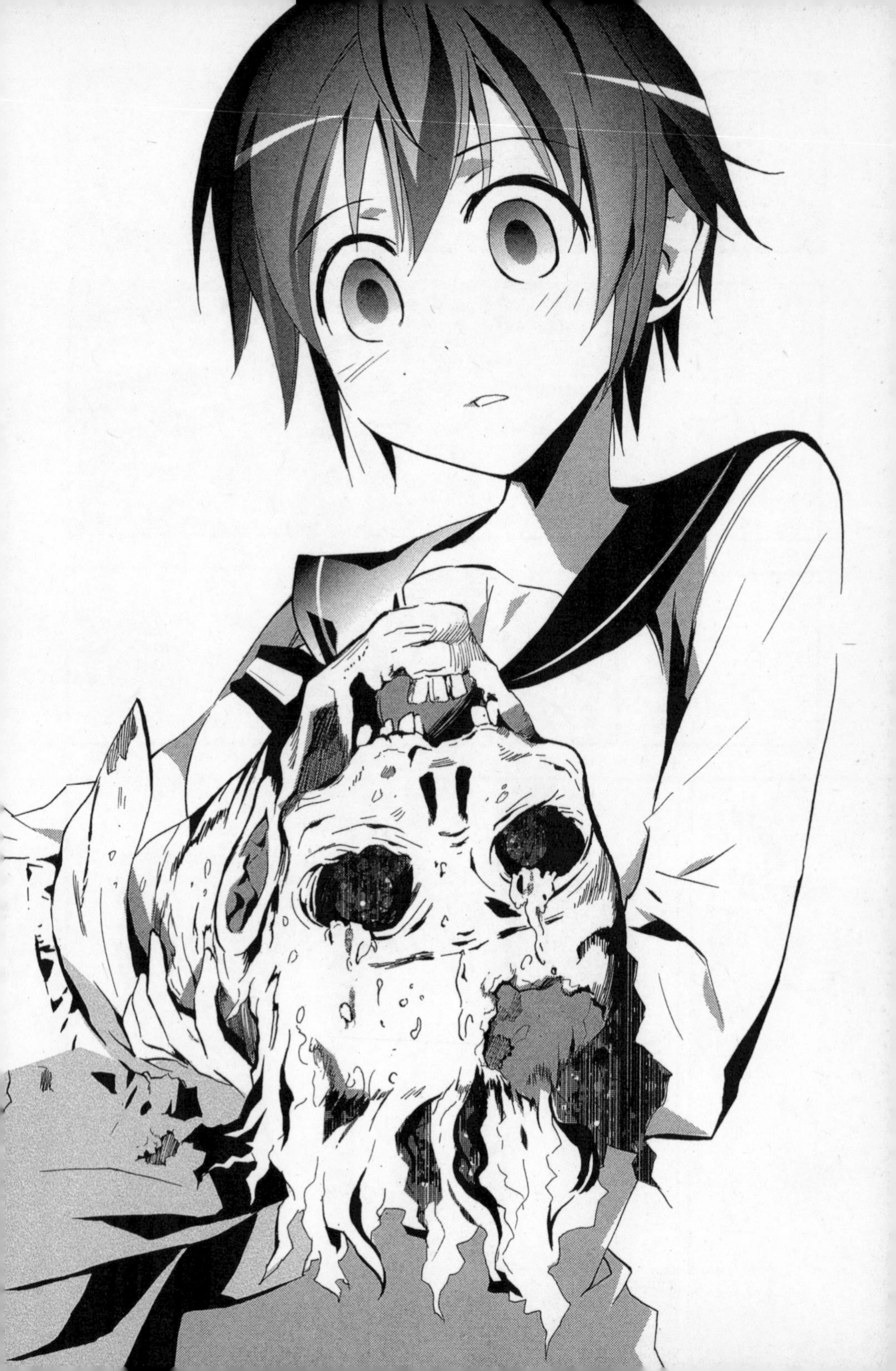

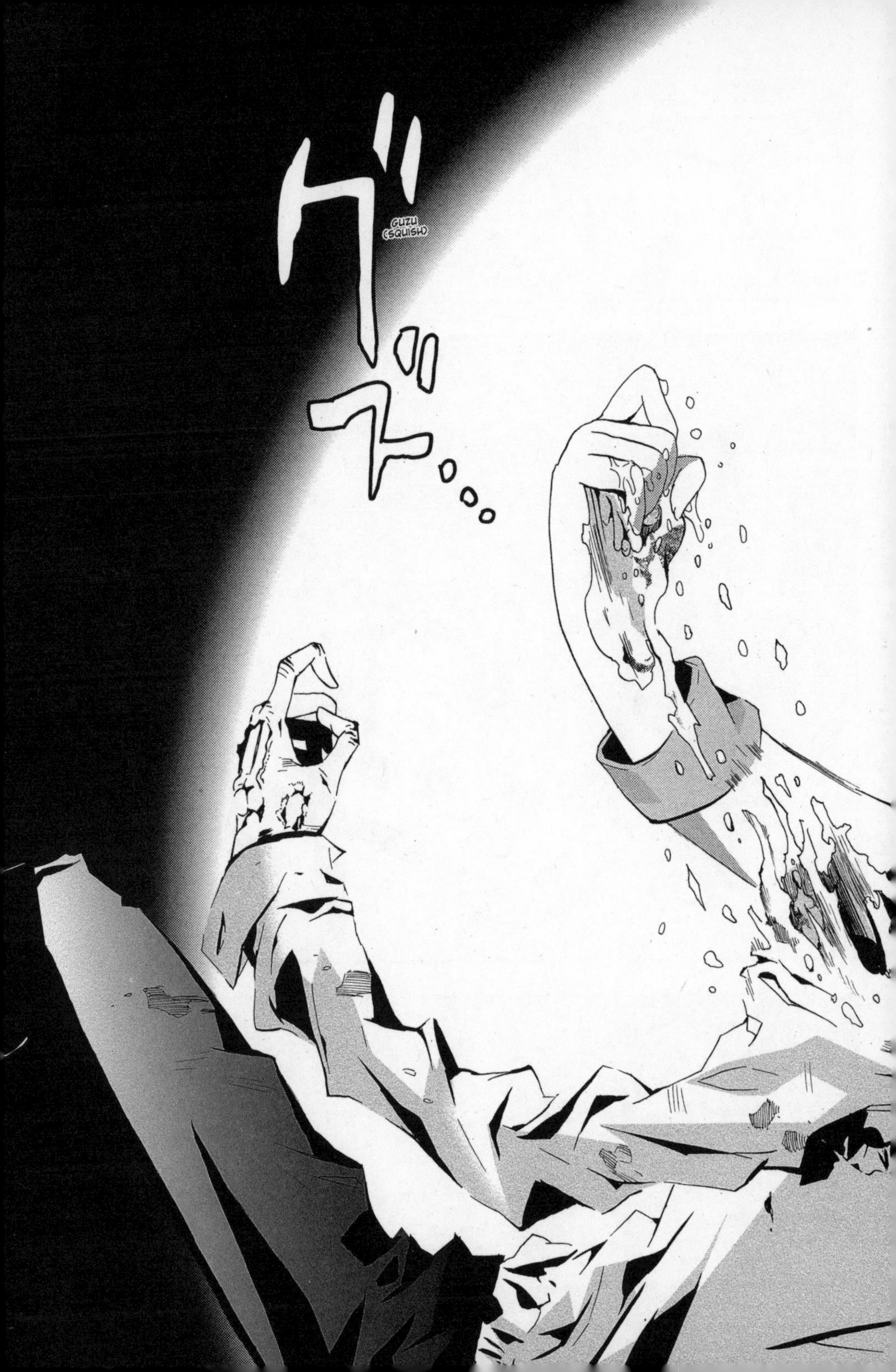

グズ…
GUZU (SQUISH)

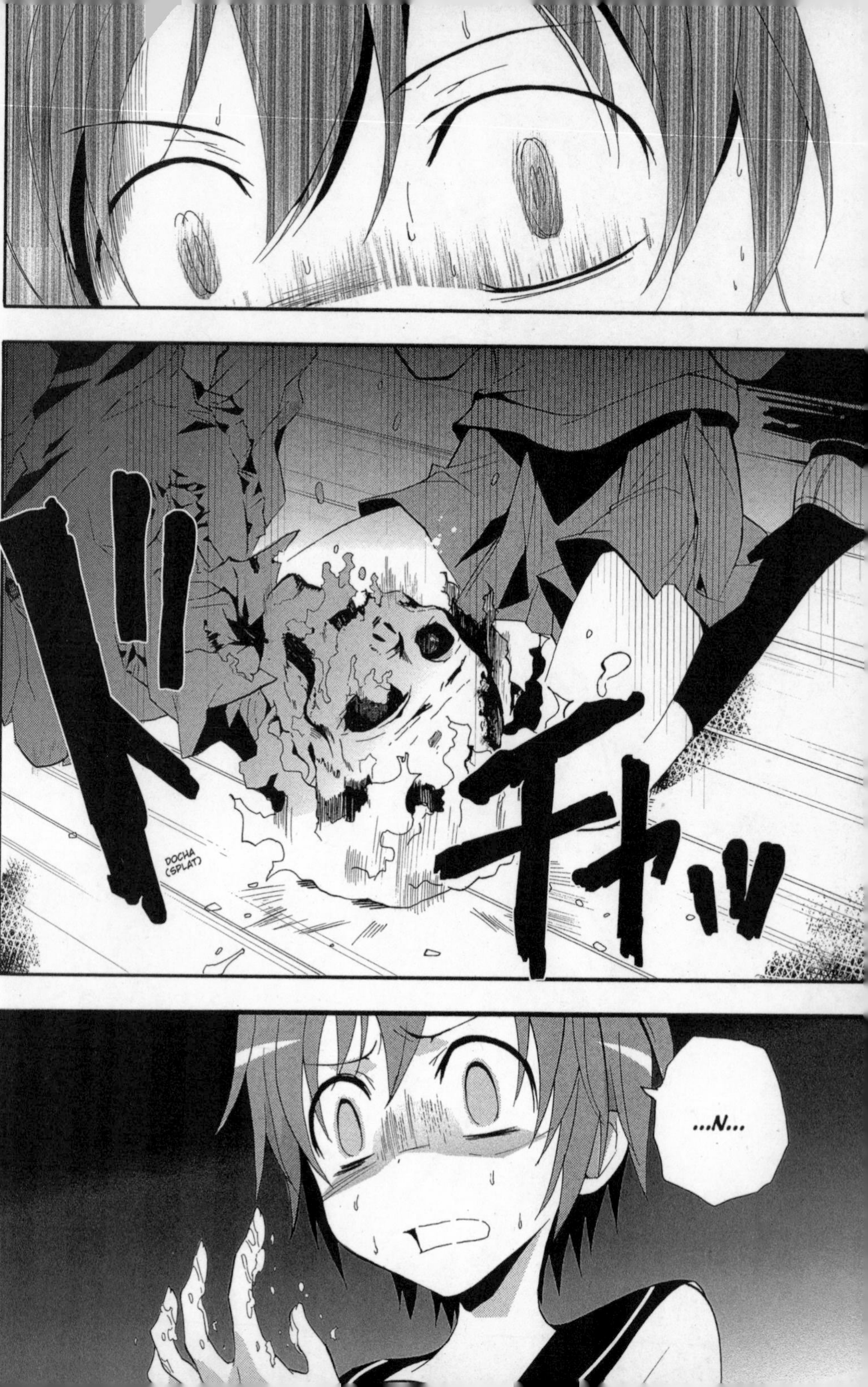
ドチャッ
DOCHA (SPLAT)
...N...

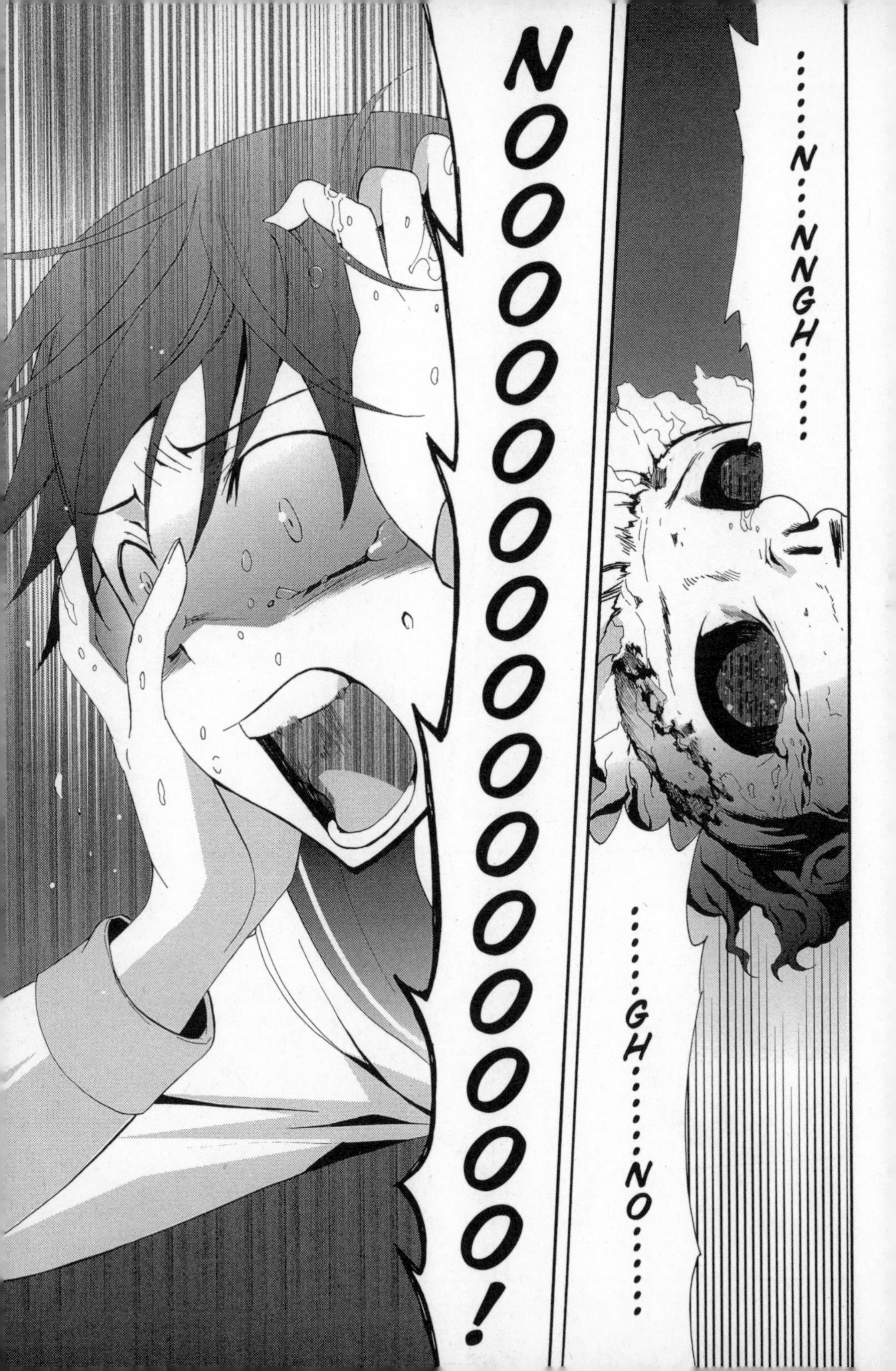
......N..NNGH......
......GH......NO......
NOOOOOOOOOOOOOOOOO!

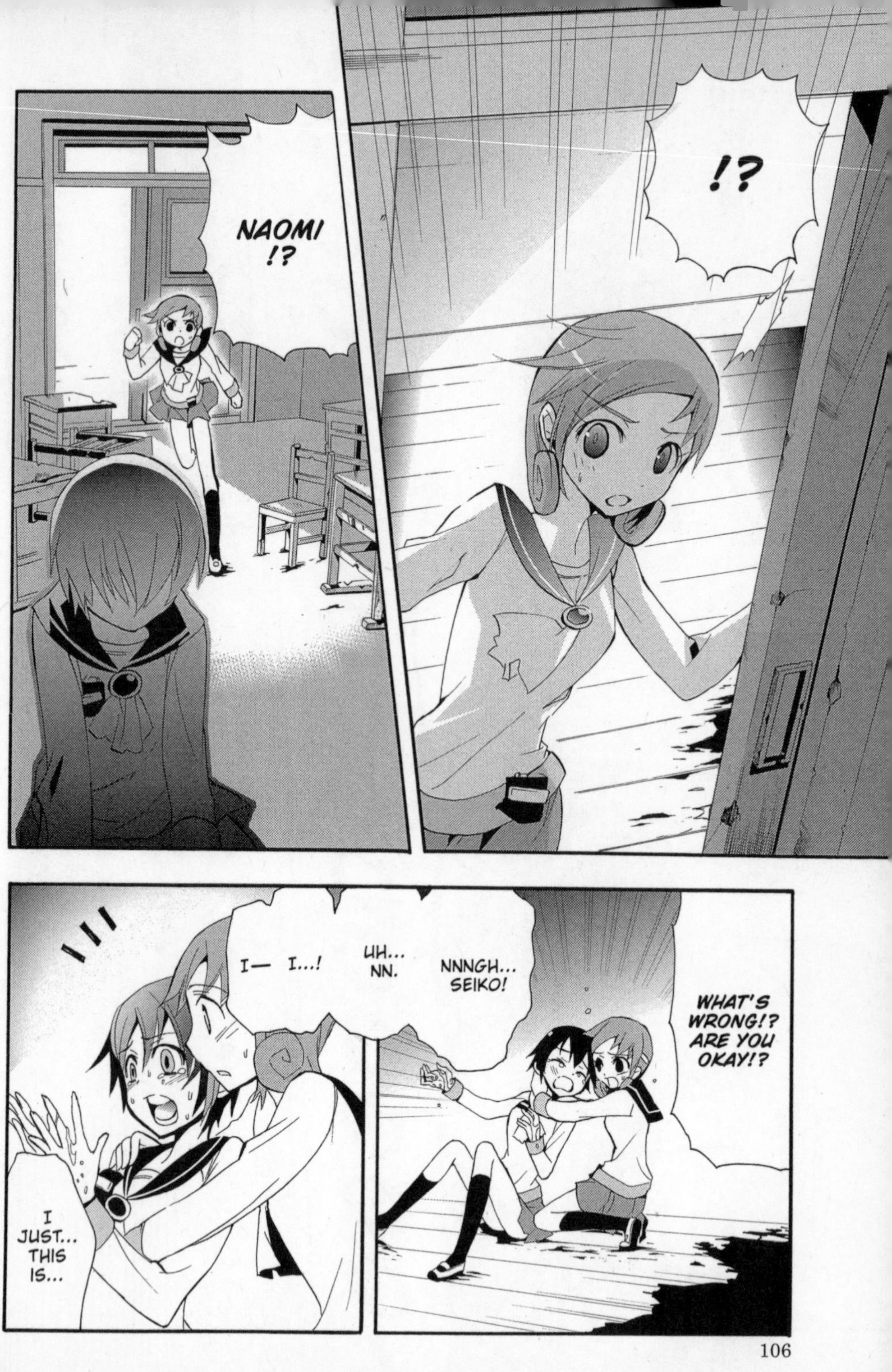
!?
NAOMI !?
WHAT'S WRONG!? ARE YOU OKAY!?
NNNGH... SEIKO!
UH... NN.
I— I...!
I JUST... THIS IS...

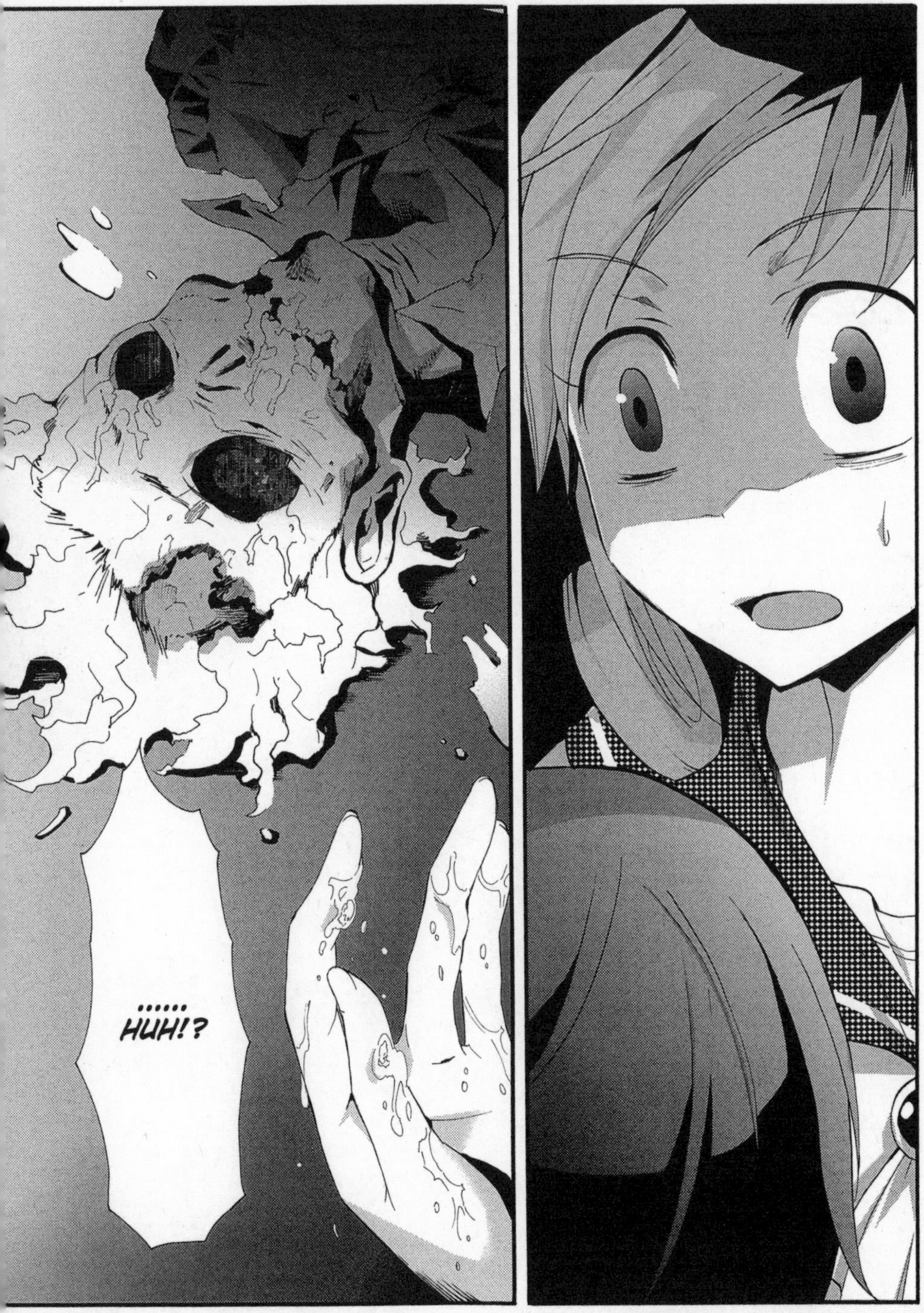
......
HUH!?

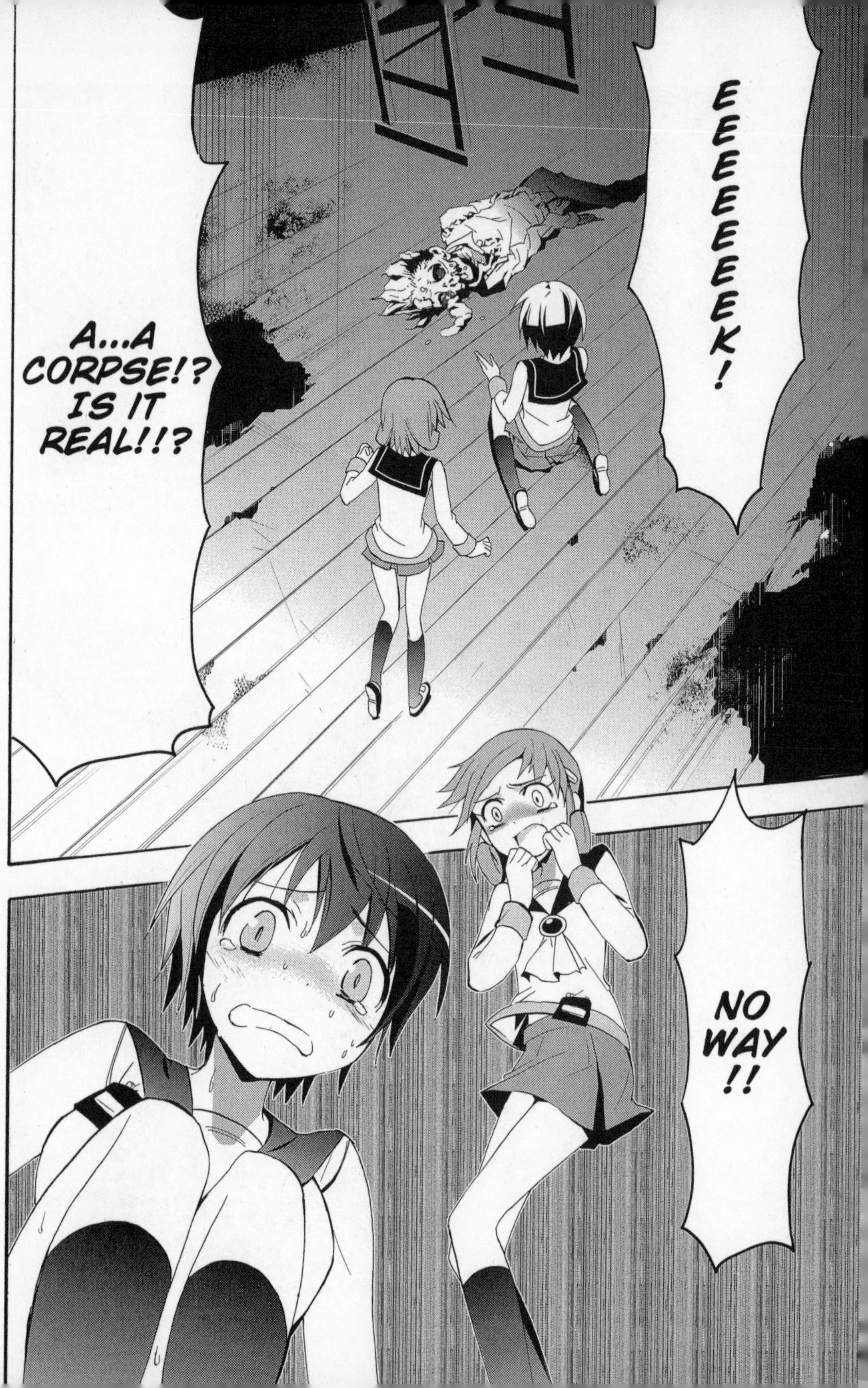
EEEEEEEK!
A...A CORPSE!? IS IT REAL!!?
NO WAY!!

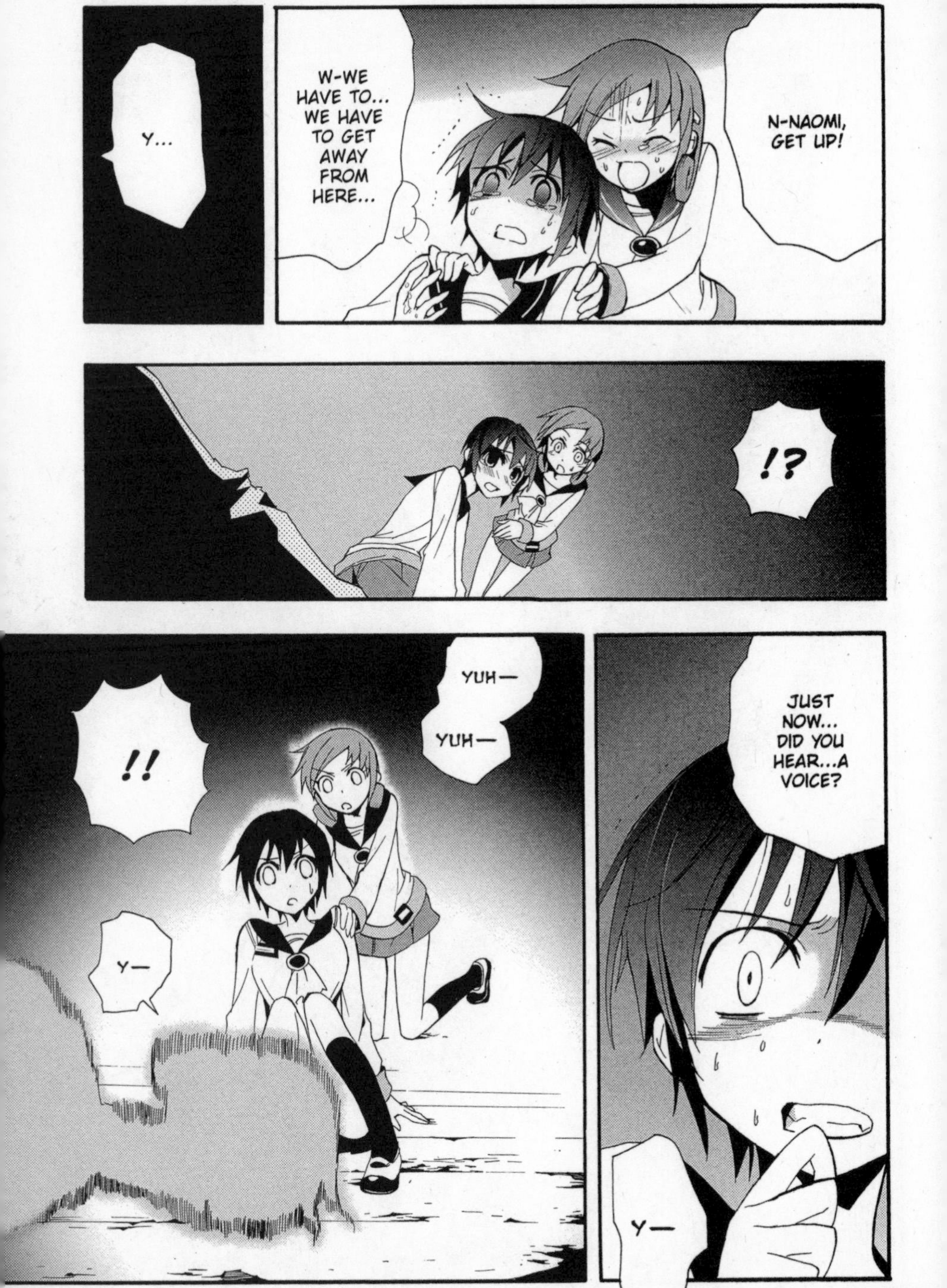
N-NAOMI, GET UP!
W-WE HAVE TO... WE HAVE TO GET AWAY FROM HERE...
Y...
!?
JUST NOW... DID YOU HEAR...A VOICE?
Y—
YUH—
YUH—
!!
Y—

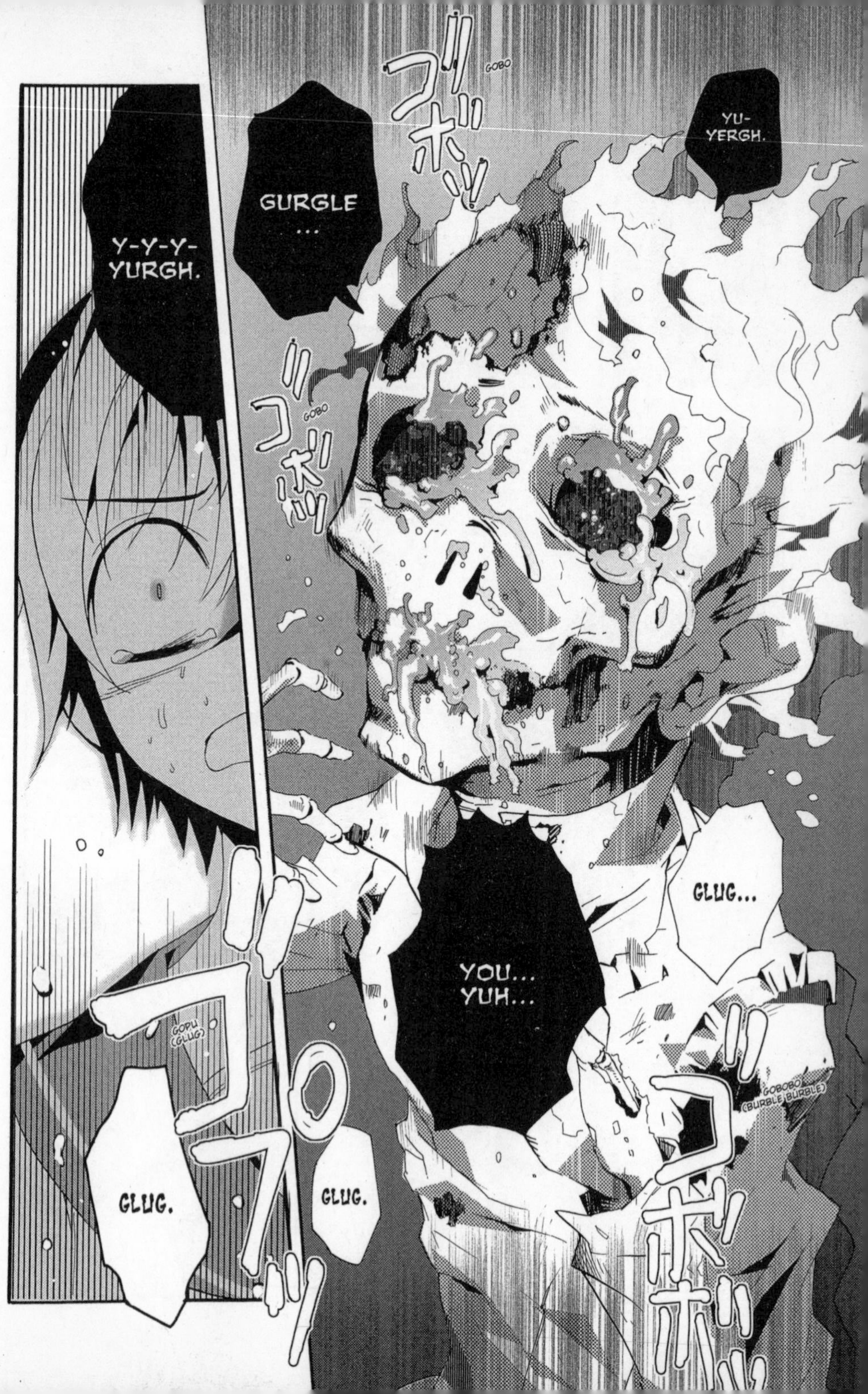
YU-
YERGH.
ゴボッ
GOBO
GURGLE
...
ゴボッ
GOBO
GLUG...
YOU...
YUH...
ゴボボッ
GOBOBO
(BURBLE BURBLE)
GLUG.
ゴプッ
GOPU
(GLUG)
Y-Y-Y-Y-
YURGH.
GLUG.

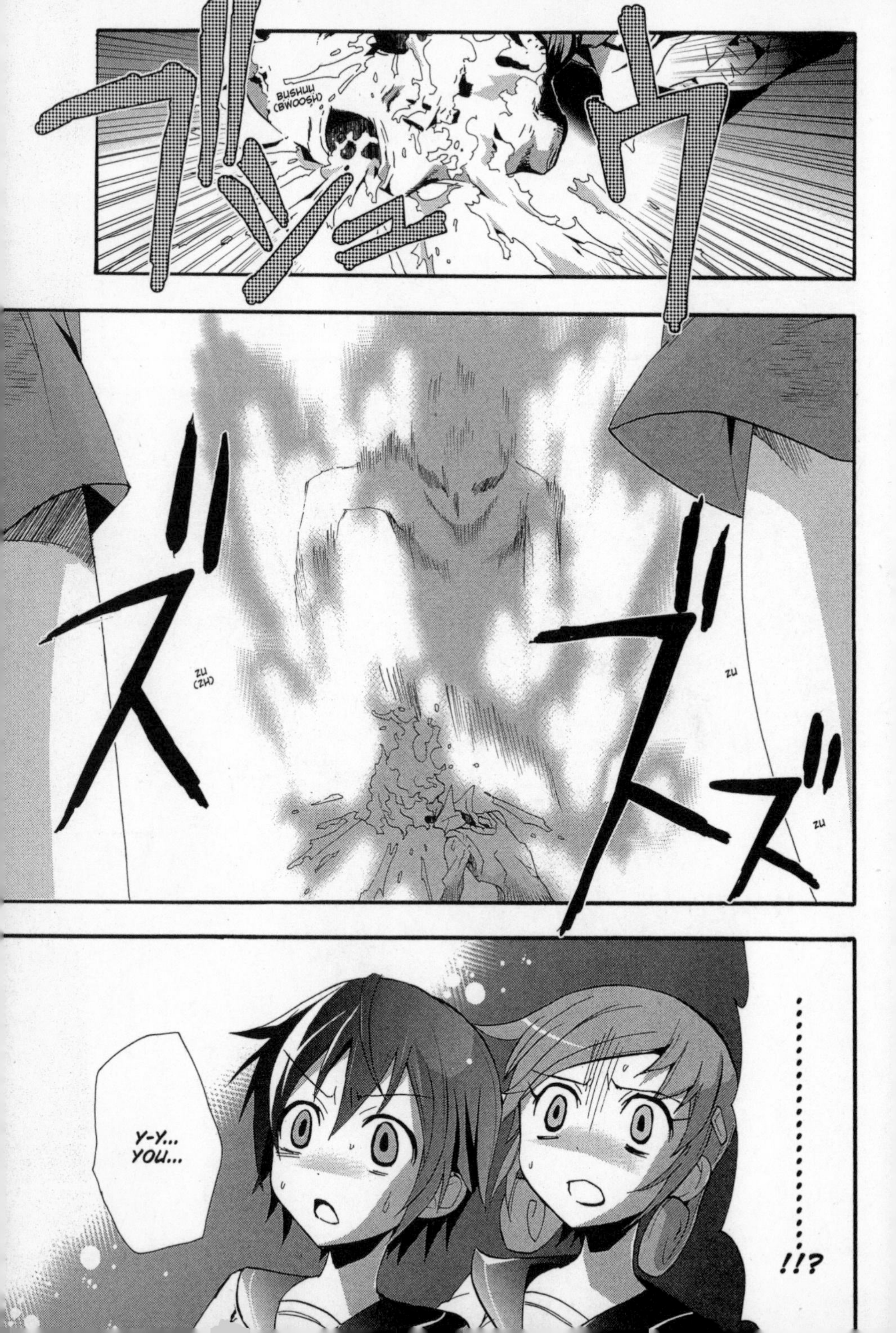
BUSHUU (BWOOSH)
ZU
ZU
ZU (ZH)
......!!?
Y-Y... YOU...

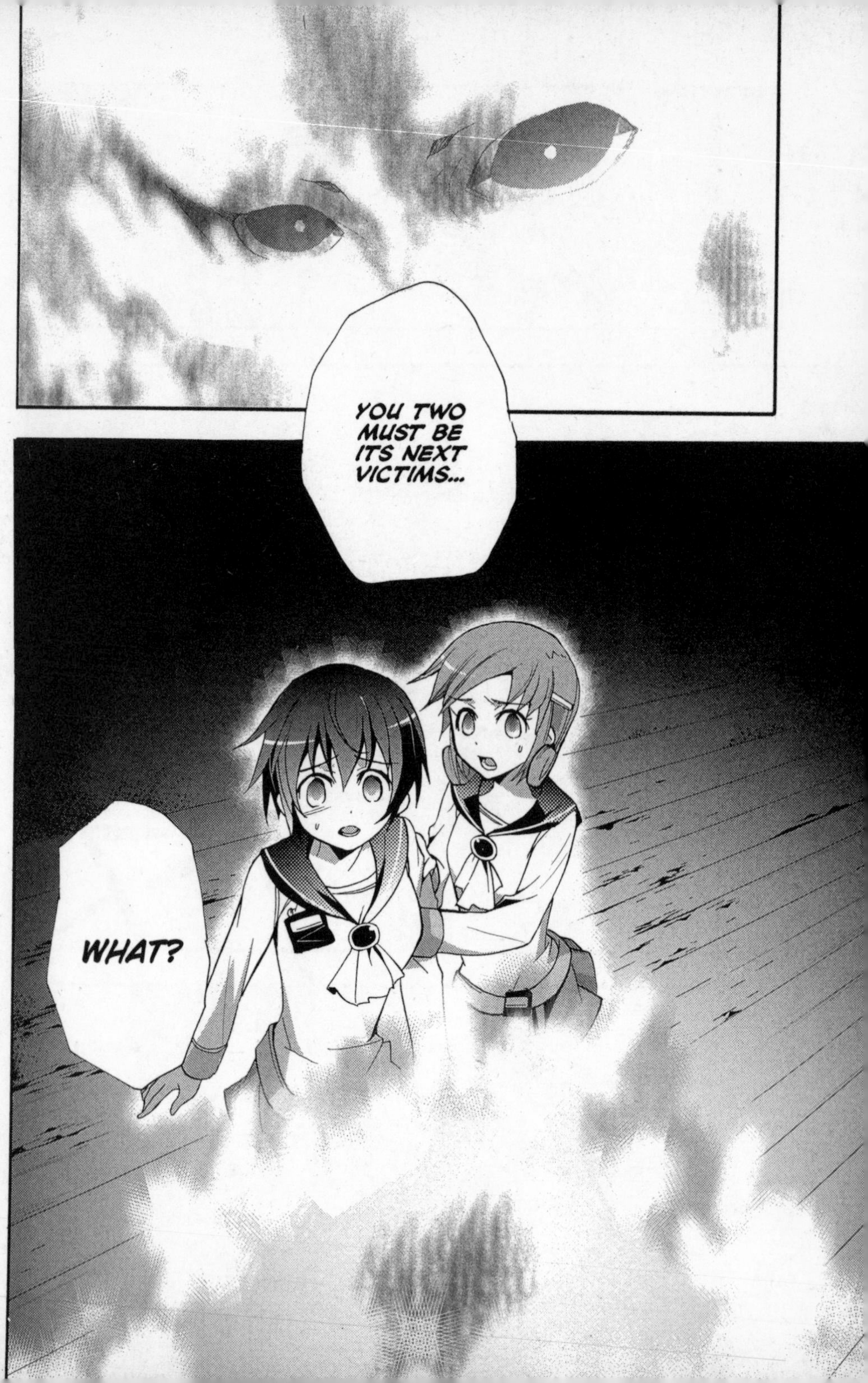
YOU TWO MUST BE ITS NEXT VICTIMS...
WHAT?

a list of corpses/01

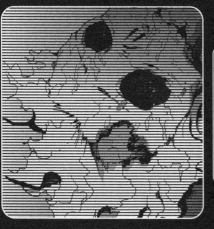

Male student, Class 3-4
Hikoito Public High School, Misato City

Died from blood loss after being
fatally wounded by one of the traps on
campus. Still calls for help to escape
the eternal torment that continues even
after his death.

CORPSE PARTY

Blood Covered

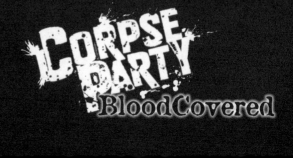

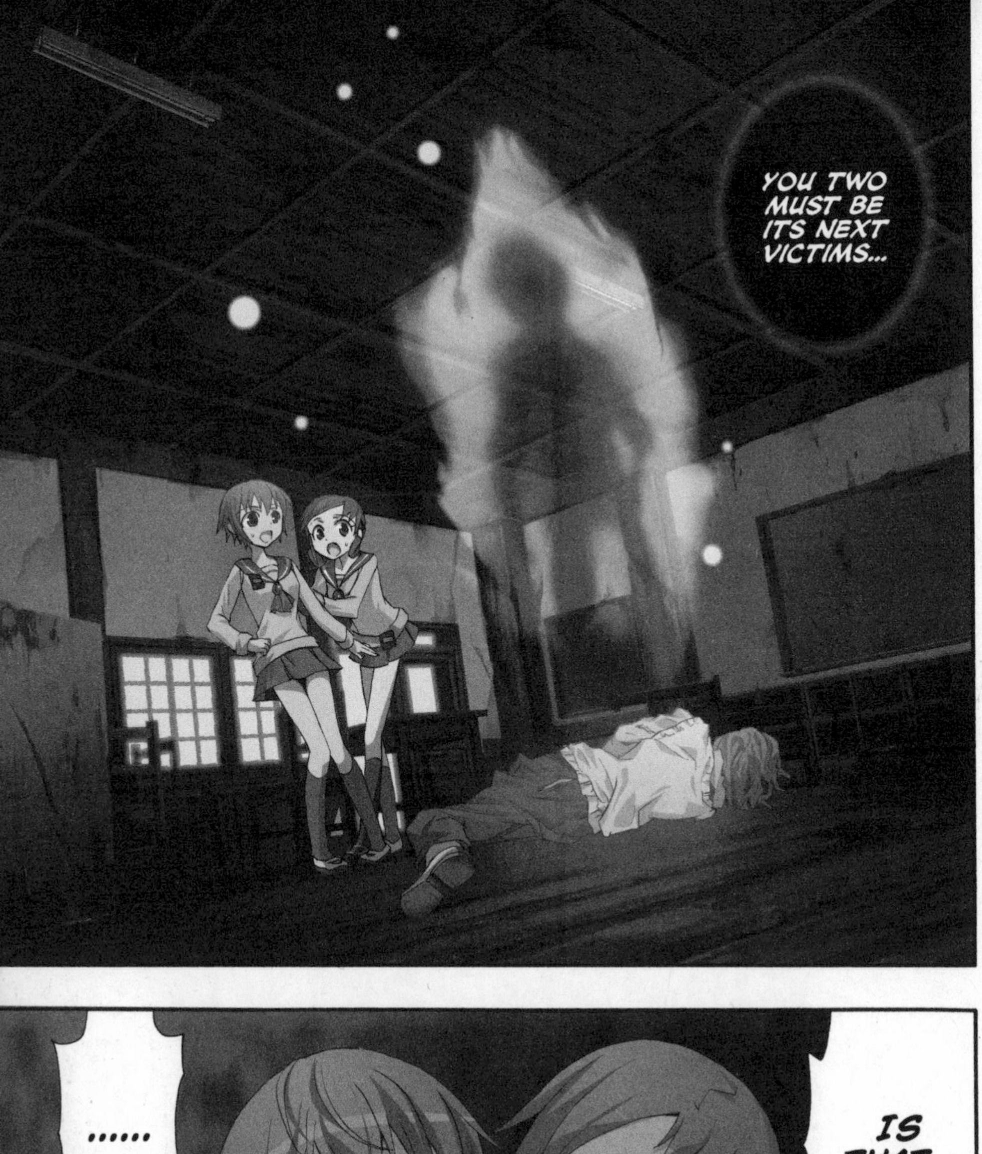
YOU TWO MUST BE ITS NEXT VICTIMS...

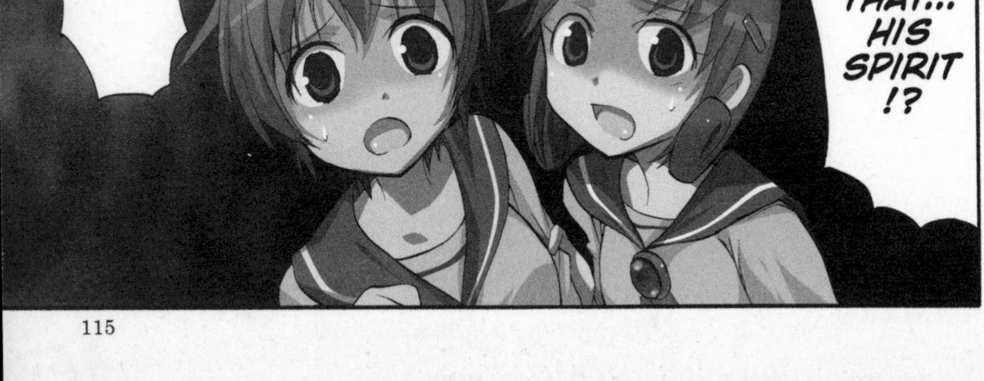
IS THAT... HIS SPIRIT !?
......

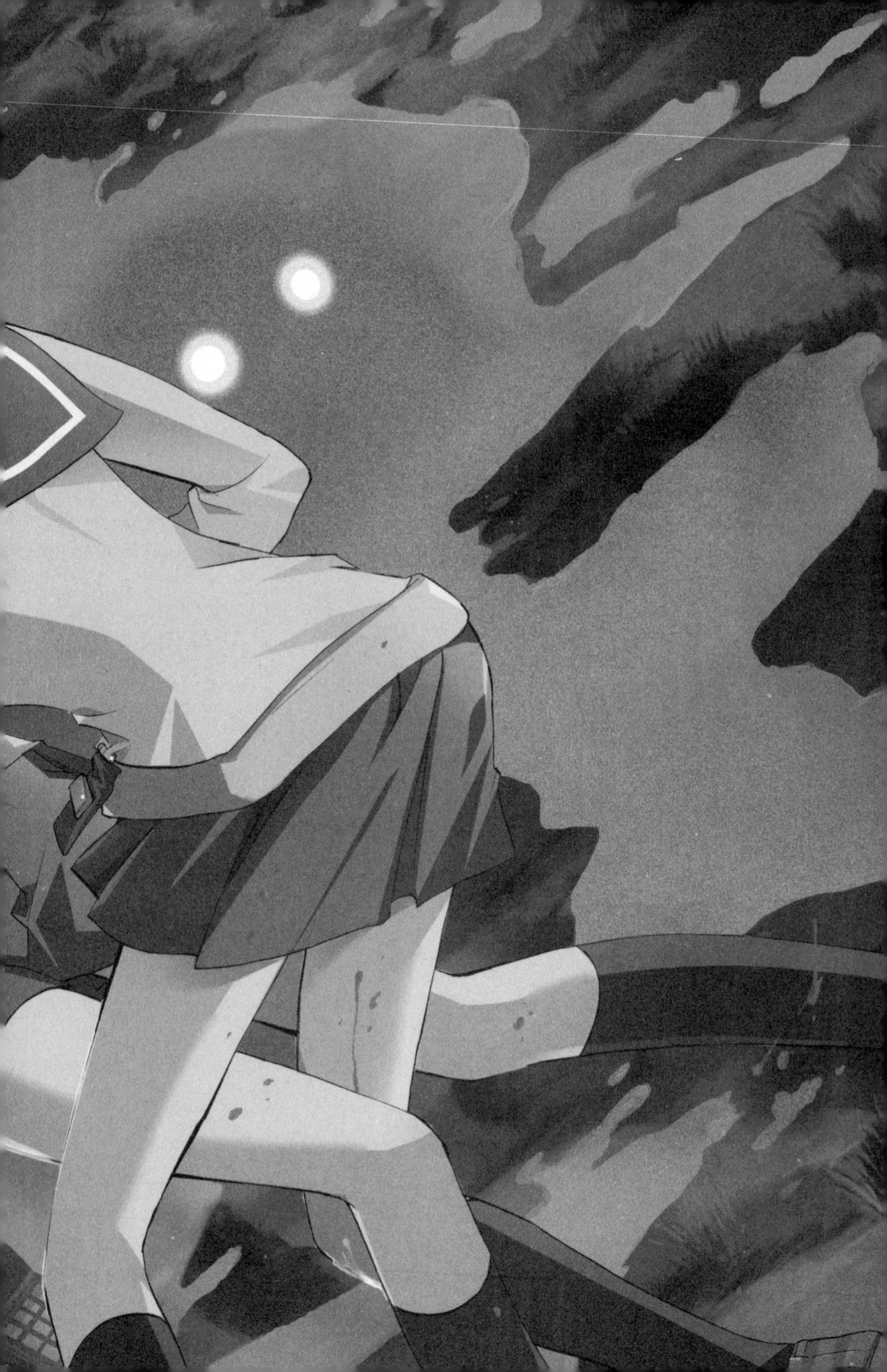

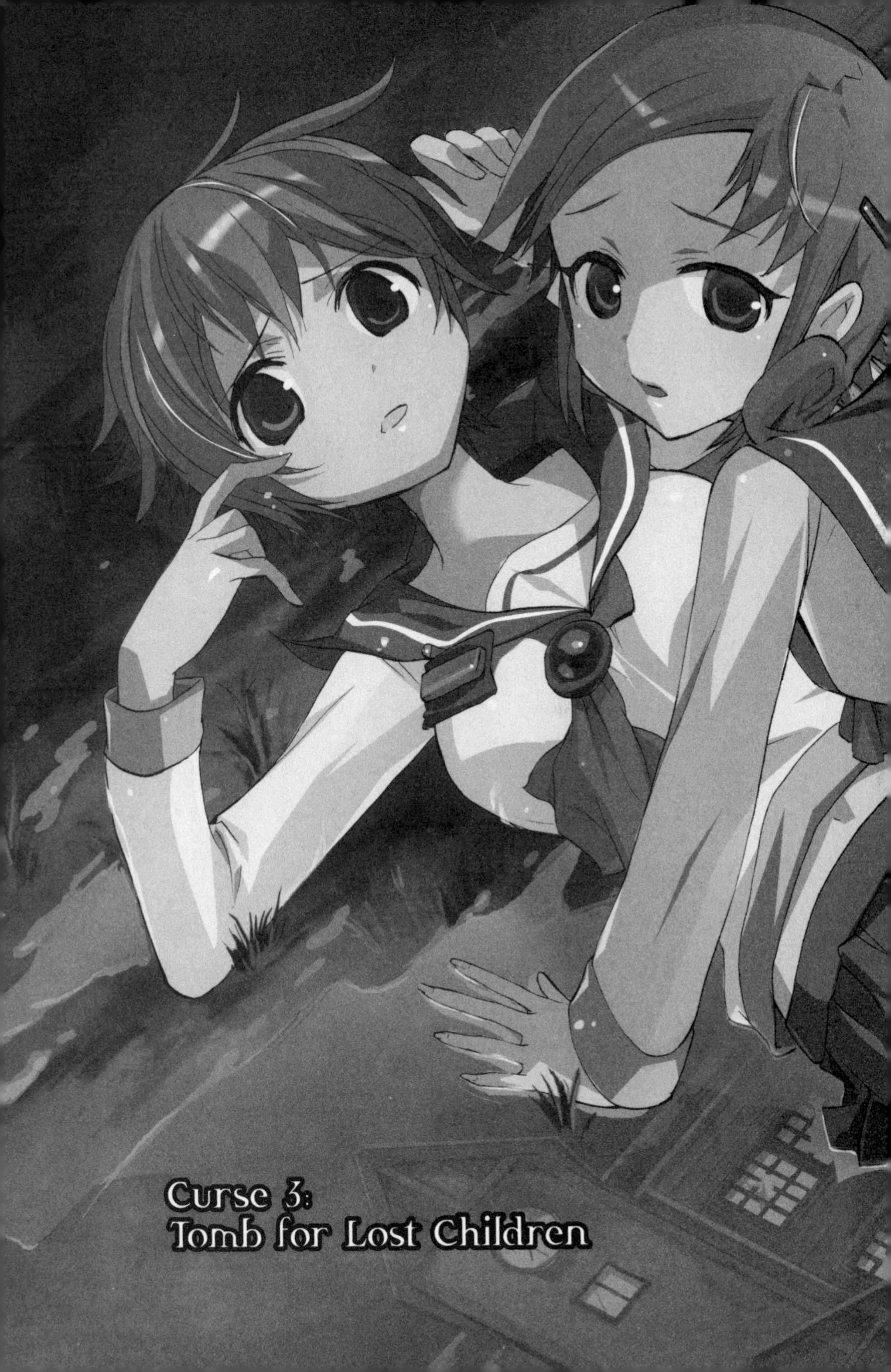

Curse 3:
Tomb for Lost Children

WHO... WHO ARE YOU...?

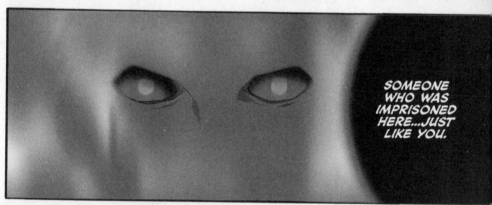

SOMEONE WHO WAS IMPRISONED HERE...JUST LIKE YOU.

THIS SCHOOL EXISTS OUTSIDE THE WORLD THAT YOU CAME FROM.

IMPRISONED ...!?

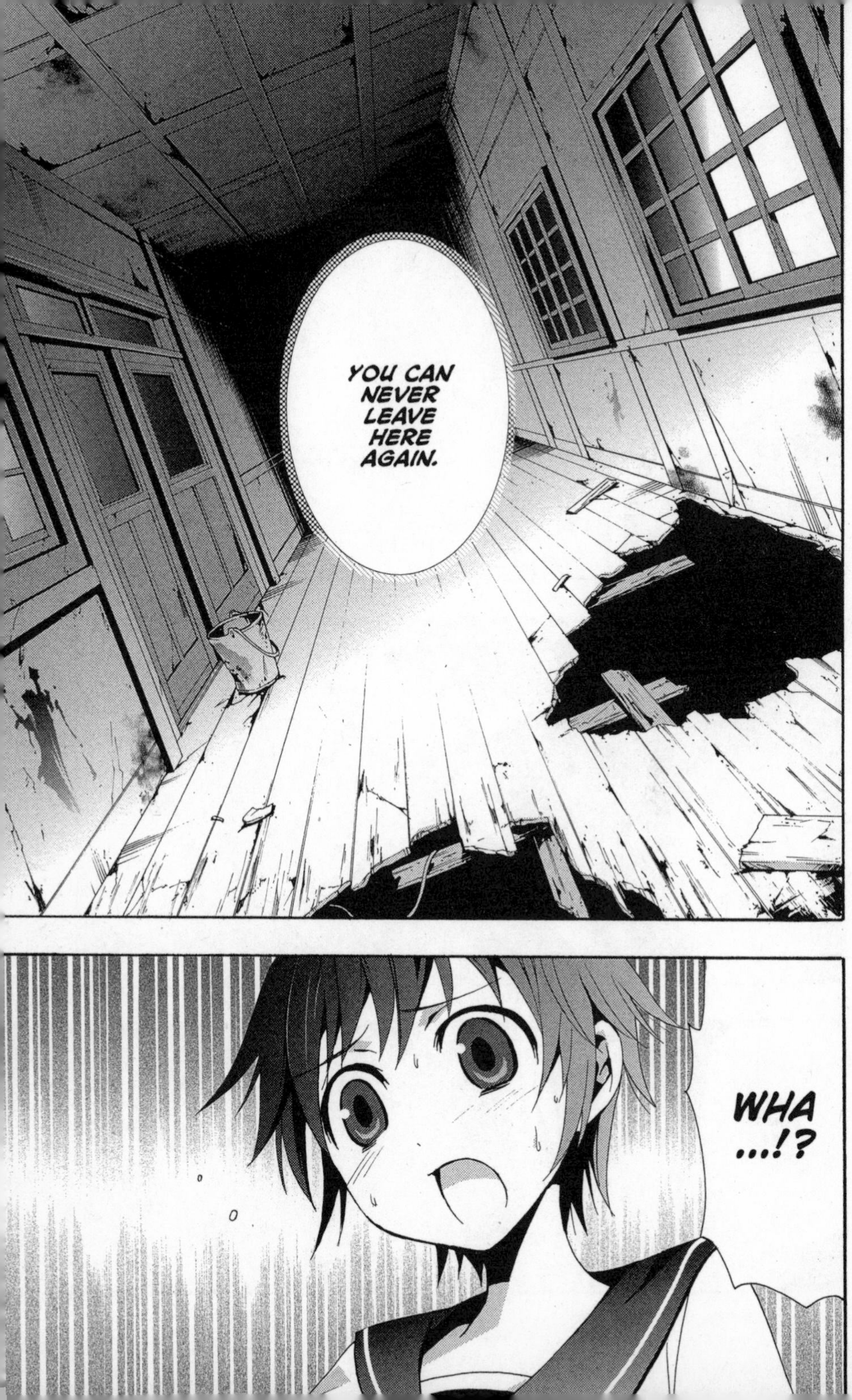
YOU CAN NEVER LEAVE HERE AGAIN.
WHA ...!?

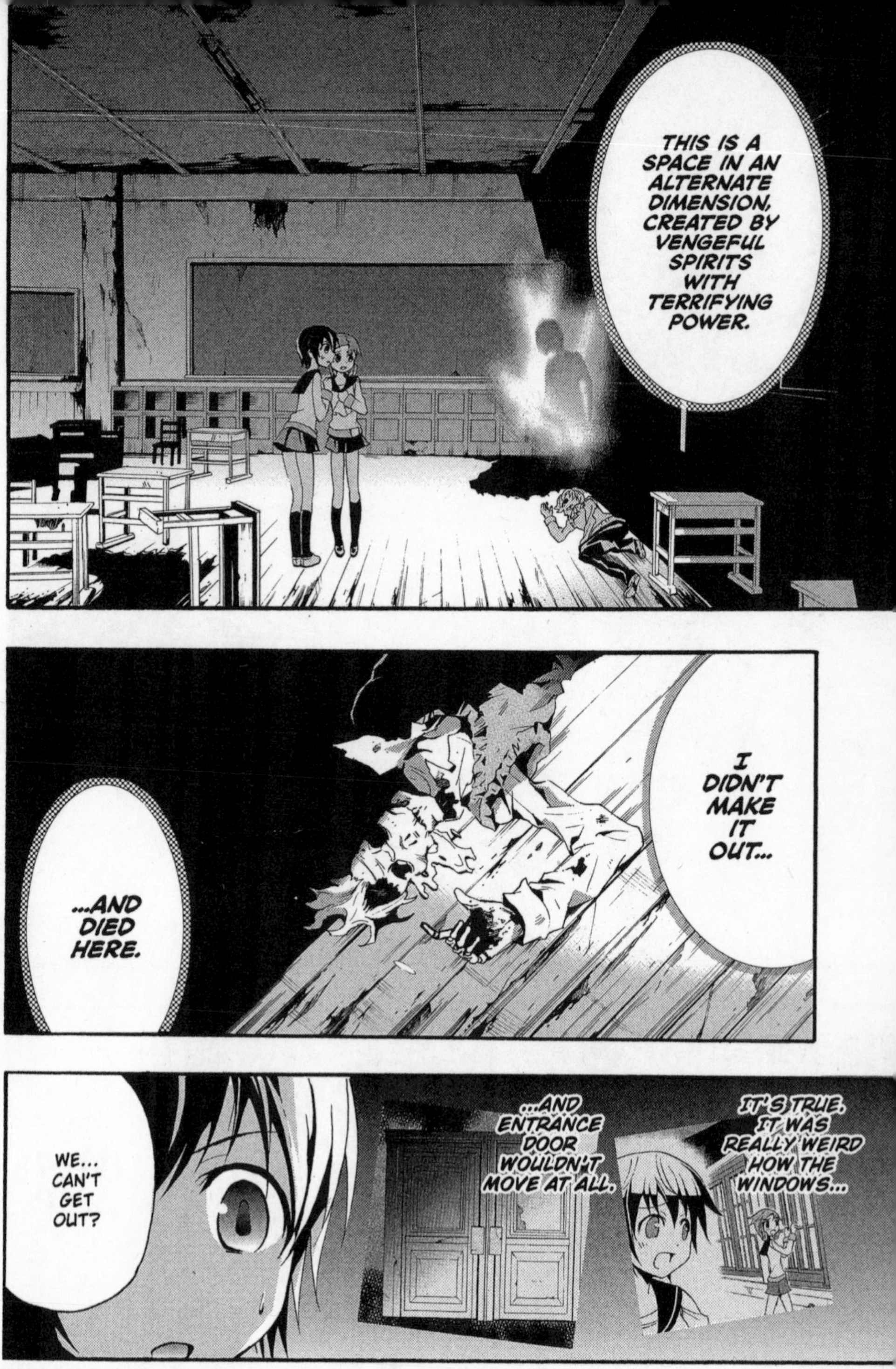
THIS IS A SPACE IN AN ALTERNATE DIMENSION, CREATED BY VENGEFUL SPIRITS WITH TERRIFYING POWER.
I DIDN'T MAKE IT OUT...
...AND DIED HERE.
IT'S TRUE. IT WAS REALLY WEIRD HOW THE WINDOWS...
...AND ENTRANCE DOOR WOULDN'T MOVE AT ALL.
WE... CAN'T GET OUT?

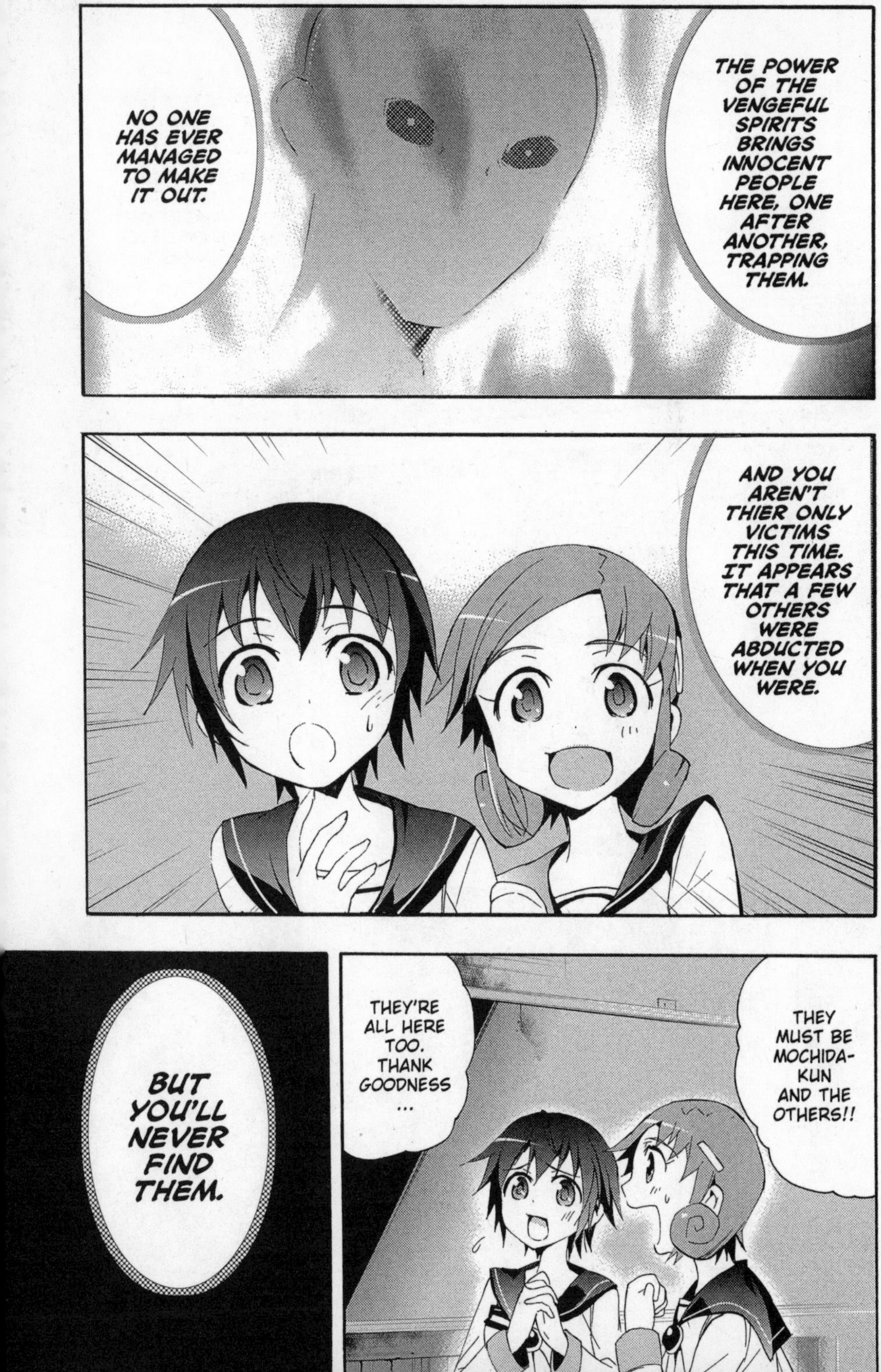
THE POWER OF THE VENGEFUL SPIRITS BRINGS INNOCENT PEOPLE HERE, ONE AFTER ANOTHER, TRAPPING THEM.
NO ONE HAS EVER MANAGED TO MAKE IT OUT.
AND YOU AREN'T THIER ONLY VICTIMS THIS TIME. IT APPEARS THAT A FEW OTHERS WERE ABDUCTED WHEN YOU WERE.
THEY MUST BE MOCHIDA-KUN AND THE OTHERS!!
THEY'RE ALL HERE TOO. THANK GOODNESS ...
BUT YOU'LL NEVER FIND THEM.

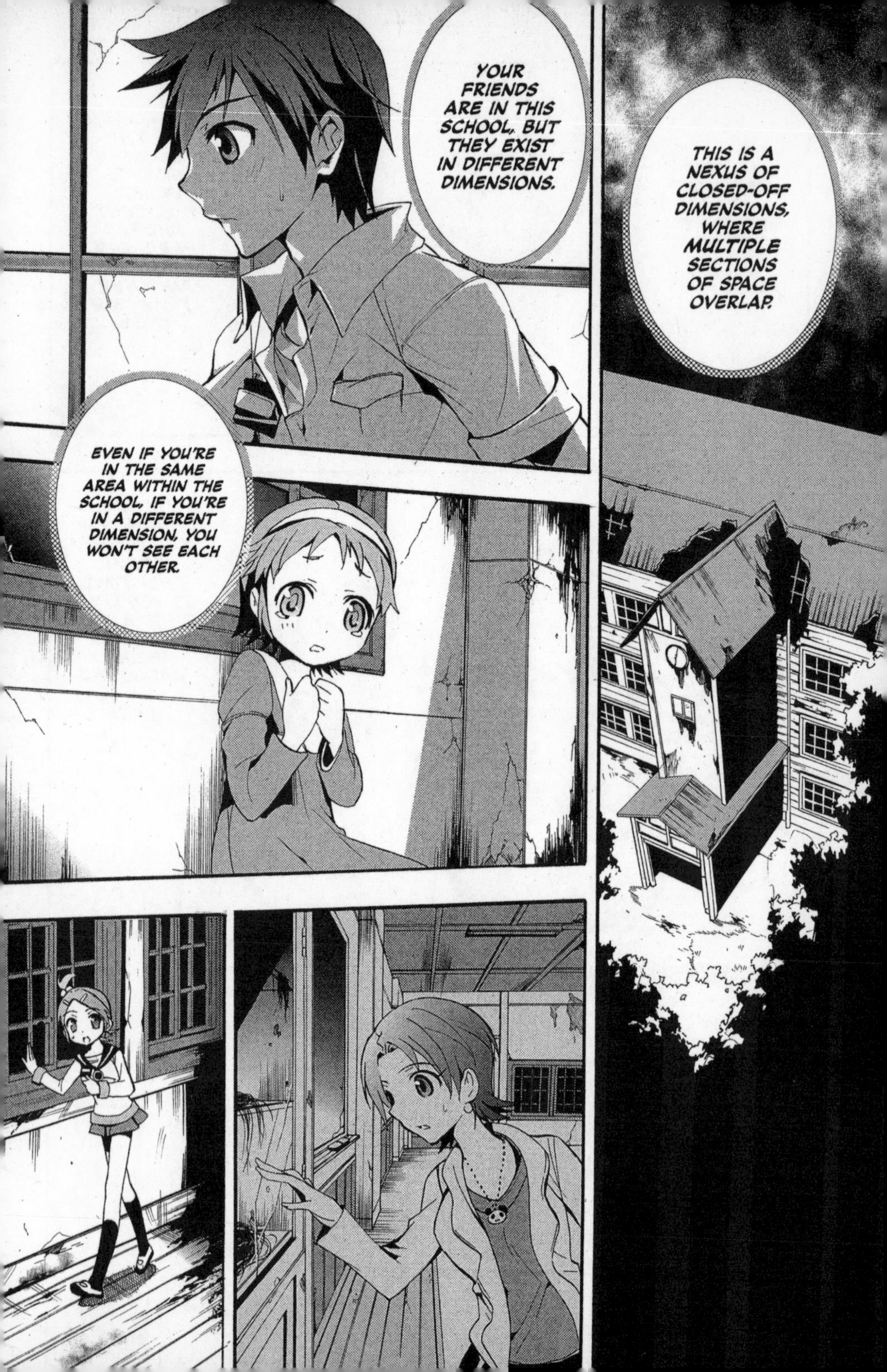
THIS IS A NEXUS OF CLOSED-OFF DIMENSIONS, WHERE MULTIPLE SECTIONS OF SPACE OVERLAP.
YOUR FRIENDS ARE IN THIS SCHOOL, BUT THEY EXIST IN DIFFERENT DIMENSIONS.
EVEN IF YOU'RE IN THE SAME AREA WITHIN THE SCHOOL, IF YOU'RE IN A DIFFERENT DIMENSION, YOU WON'T SEE EACH OTHER.

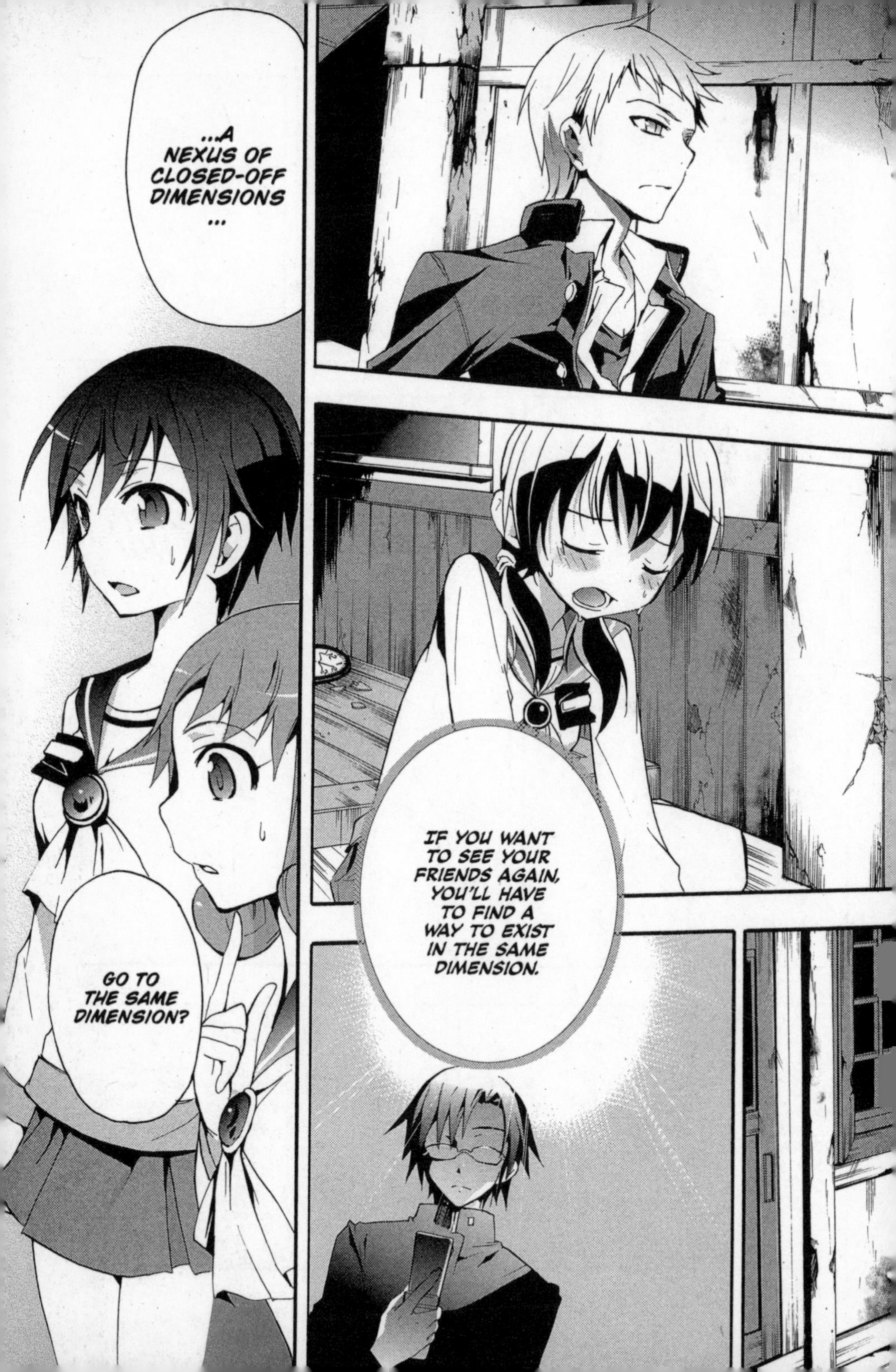
...A NEXUS OF CLOSED-OFF DIMENSIONS ...
IF YOU WANT TO SEE YOUR FRIENDS AGAIN, YOU'LL HAVE TO FIND A WAY TO EXIST IN THE SAME DIMENSION.
GO TO THE SAME DIMENSION?

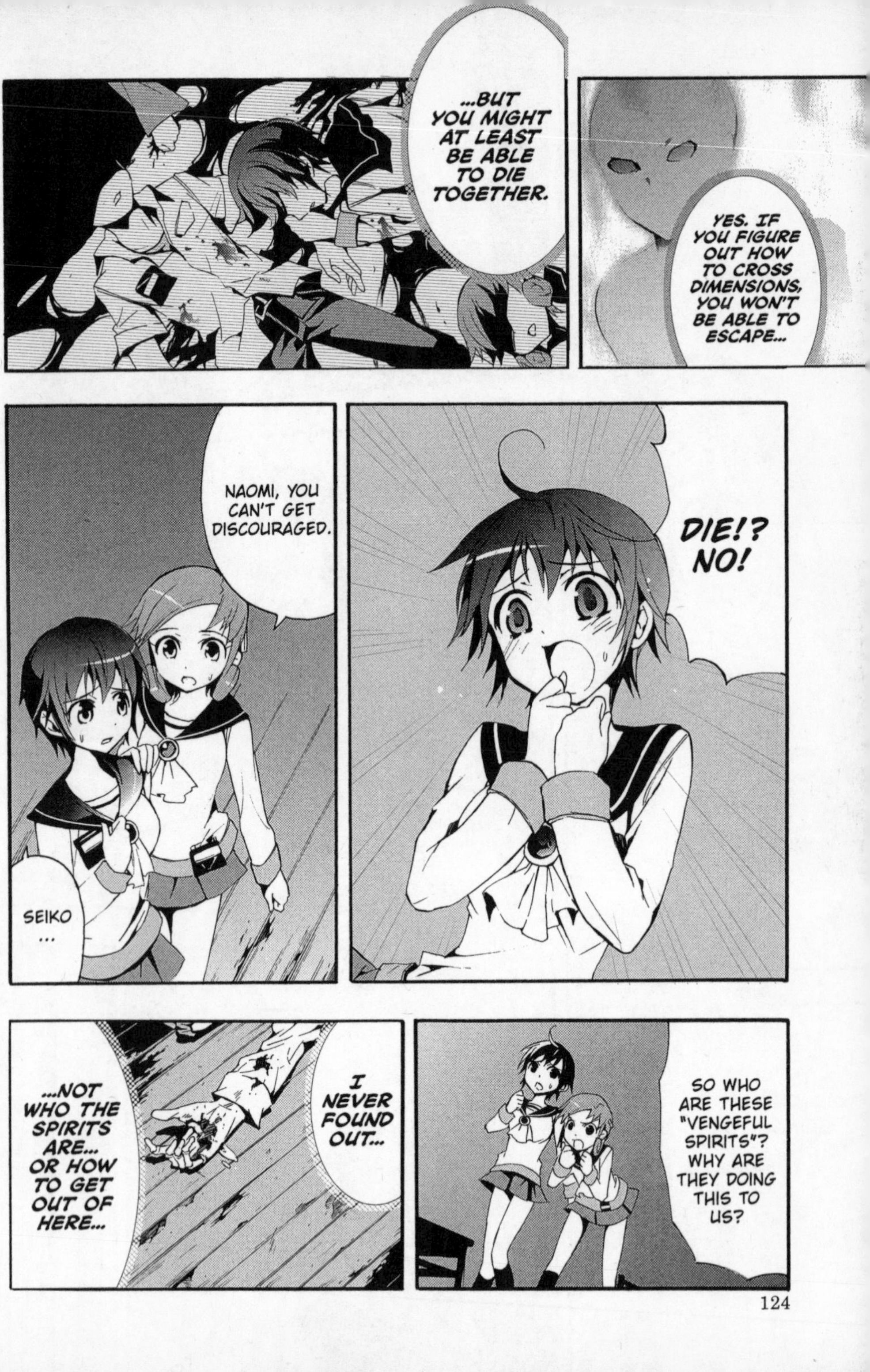
YES. IF YOU FIGURE OUT HOW TO CROSS DIMENSIONS, YOU WON'T BE ABLE TO ESCAPE...
...BUT YOU MIGHT AT LEAST BE ABLE TO DIE TOGETHER.
DIE!? NO!
NAOMI, YOU CAN'T GET DISCOURAGED.
SEIKO ...
SO WHO ARE THESE "VENGEFUL SPIRITS"? WHY ARE THEY DOING THIS TO US?
I NEVER FOUND OUT...
...NOT WHO THE SPIRITS ARE... OR HOW TO GET OUT OF HERE...

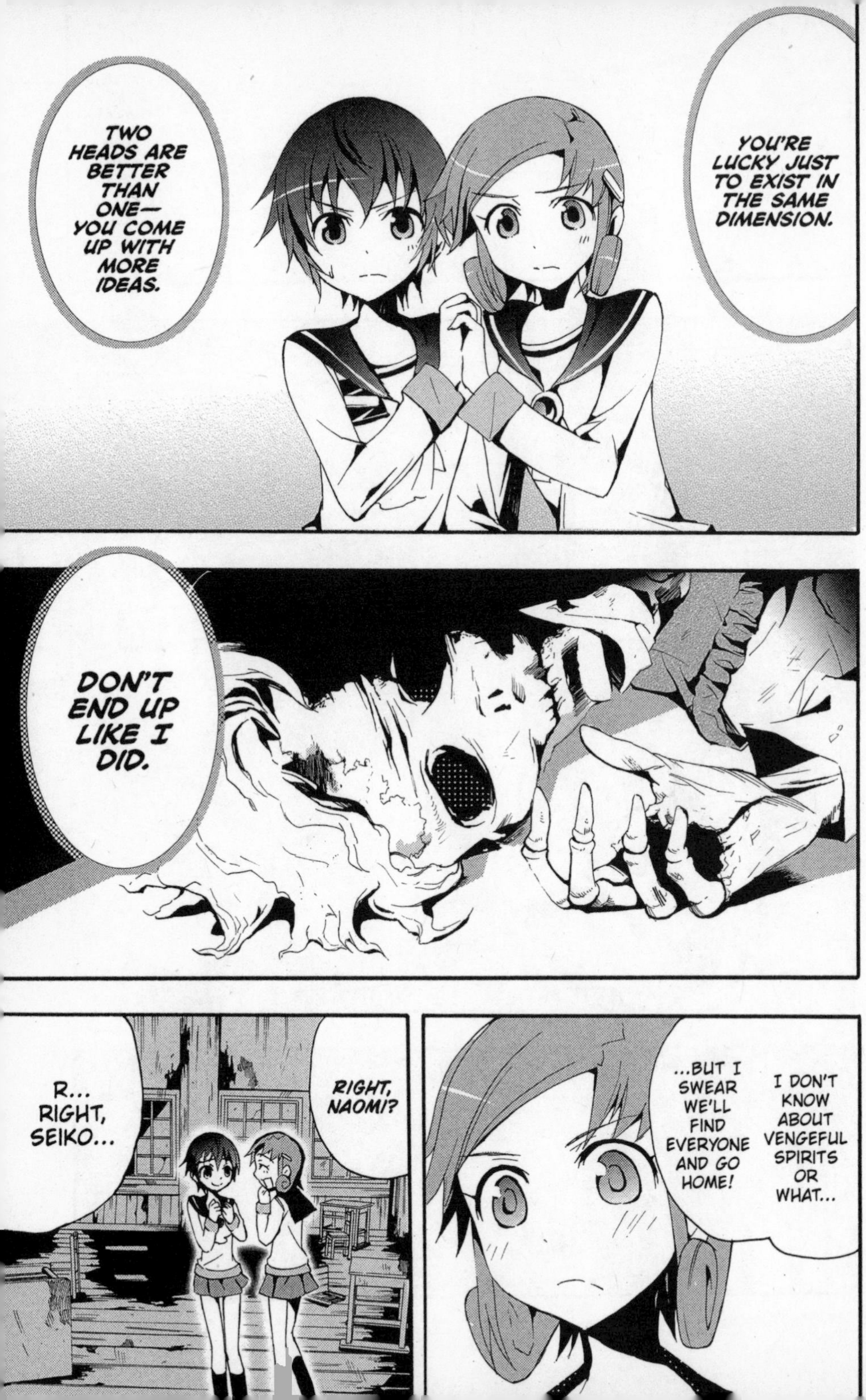
YOU'RE LUCKY JUST TO EXIST IN THE SAME DIMENSION.
TWO HEADS ARE BETTER THAN ONE—YOU COME UP WITH MORE IDEAS.
DON'T END UP LIKE I DID.
I DON'T KNOW ABOUT VENGEFUL SPIRITS OR WHAT...
...BUT I SWEAR WE'LL FIND EVERYONE AND GO HOME!
RIGHT, NAOMI?
R... RIGHT, SEIKO...

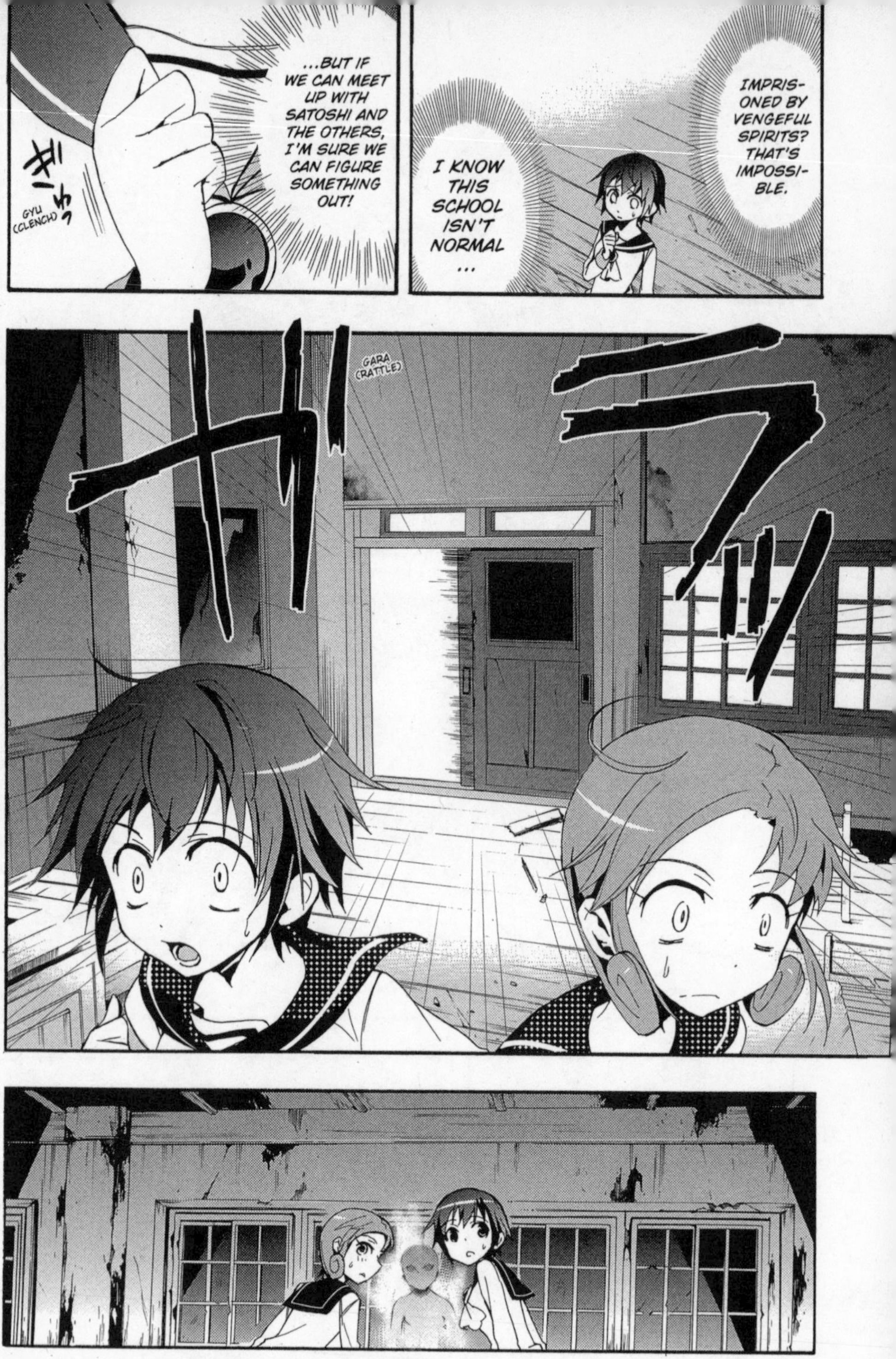
IMPRISONED BY VENGEFUL SPIRITS? THAT'S IMPOSSIBLE.
I KNOW THIS SCHOOL ISN'T NORMAL...
...BUT IF WE CAN MEET UP WITH SATOSHI AND THE OTHERS, I'M SURE WE CAN FIGURE SOMETHING OUT!
GYU (CLENCH)
GARA (RATTLE)

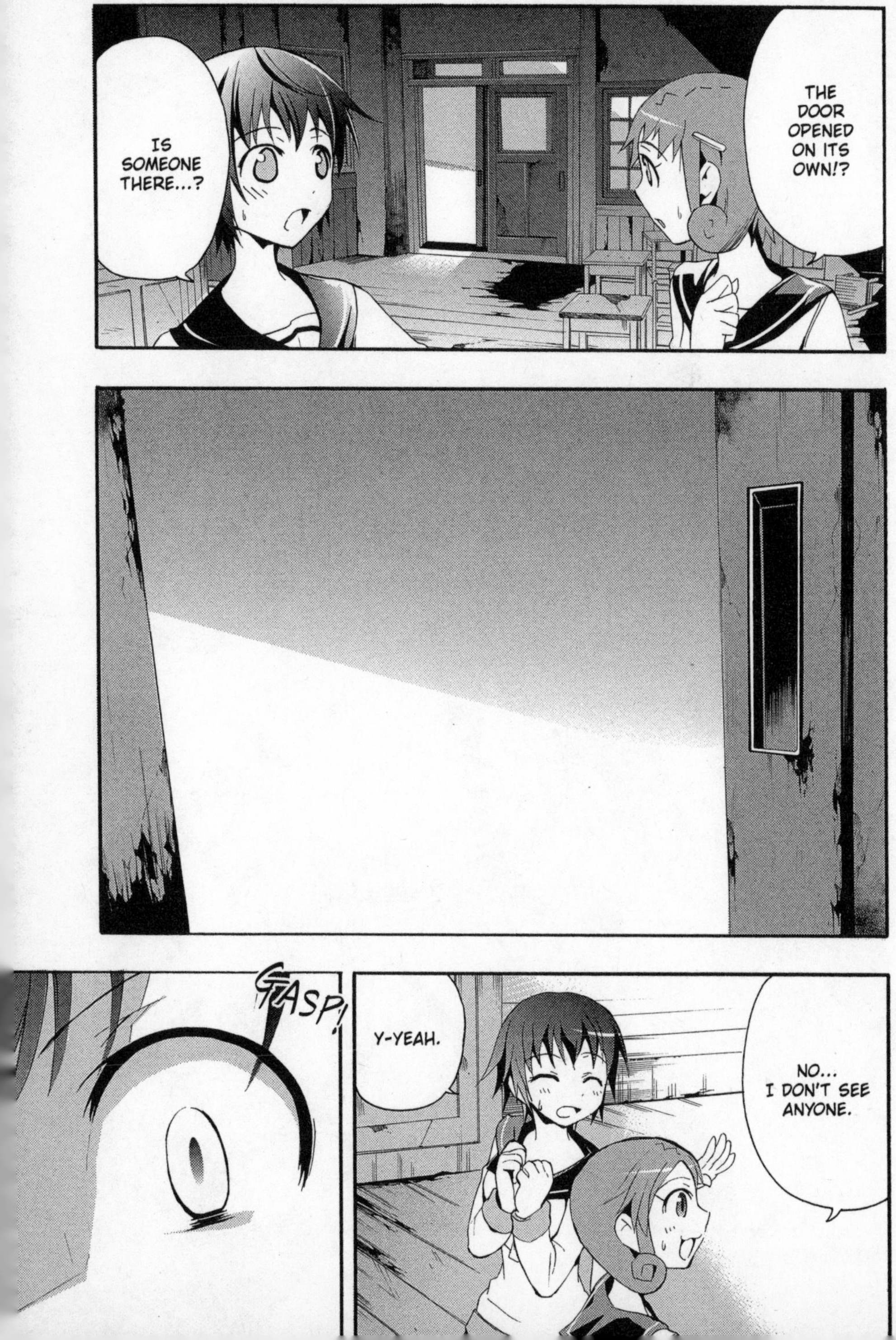
THE DOOR OPENED ON ITS OWN!?
IS SOMEONE THERE...?
NO... I DON'T SEE ANYONE.
Y-YEAH.
GASP!

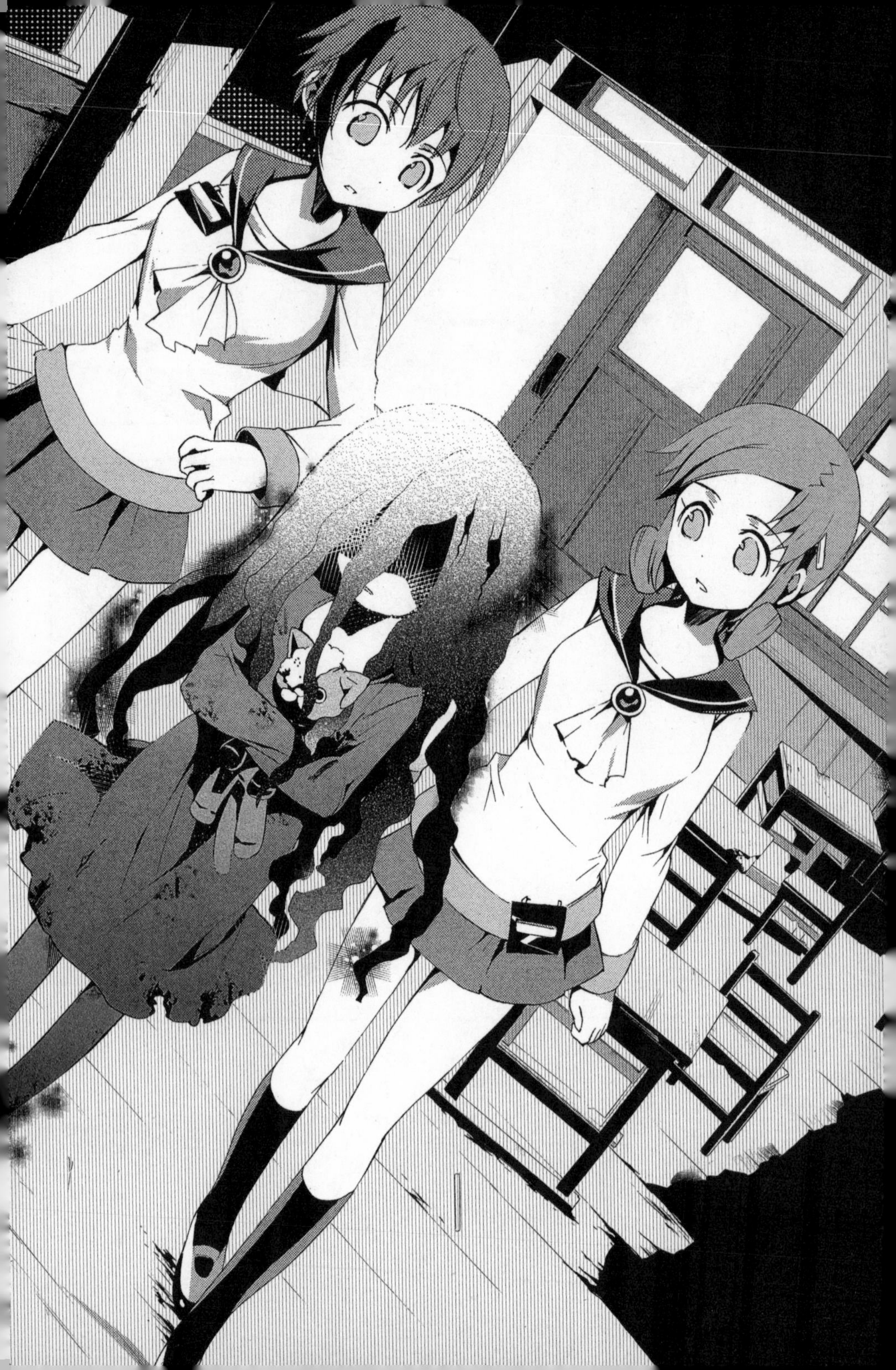

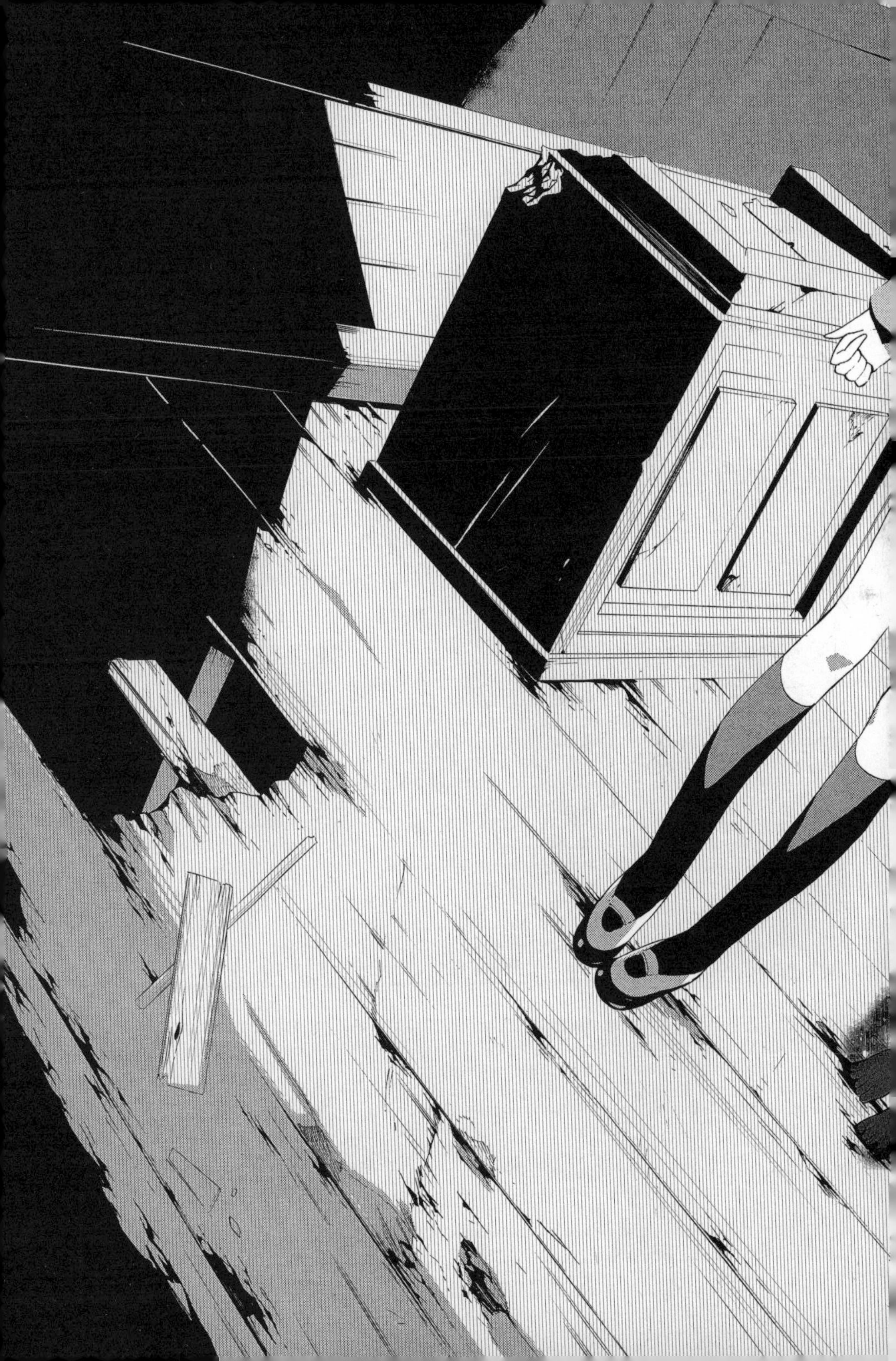

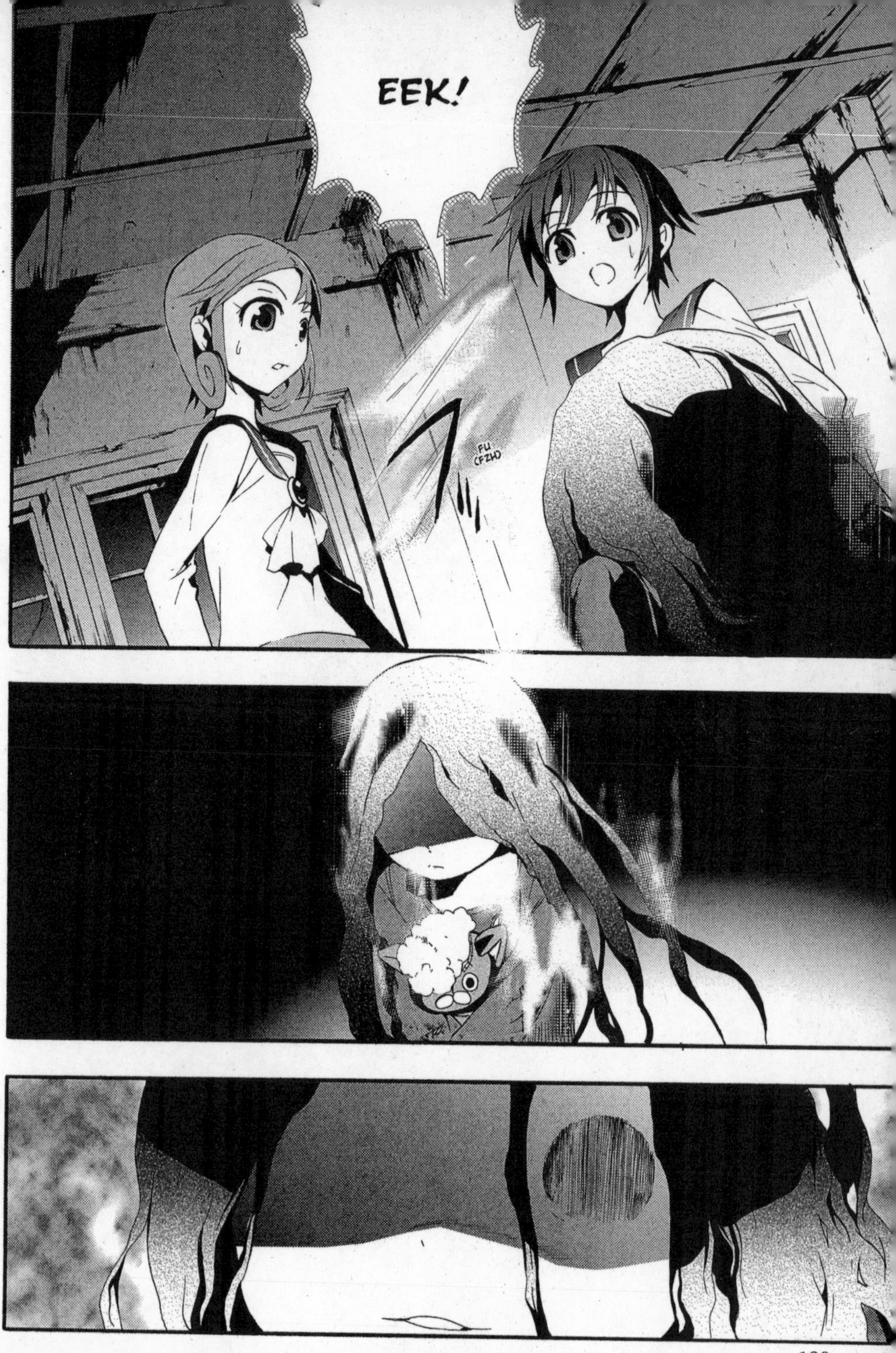
EEK!
FU (FZH)

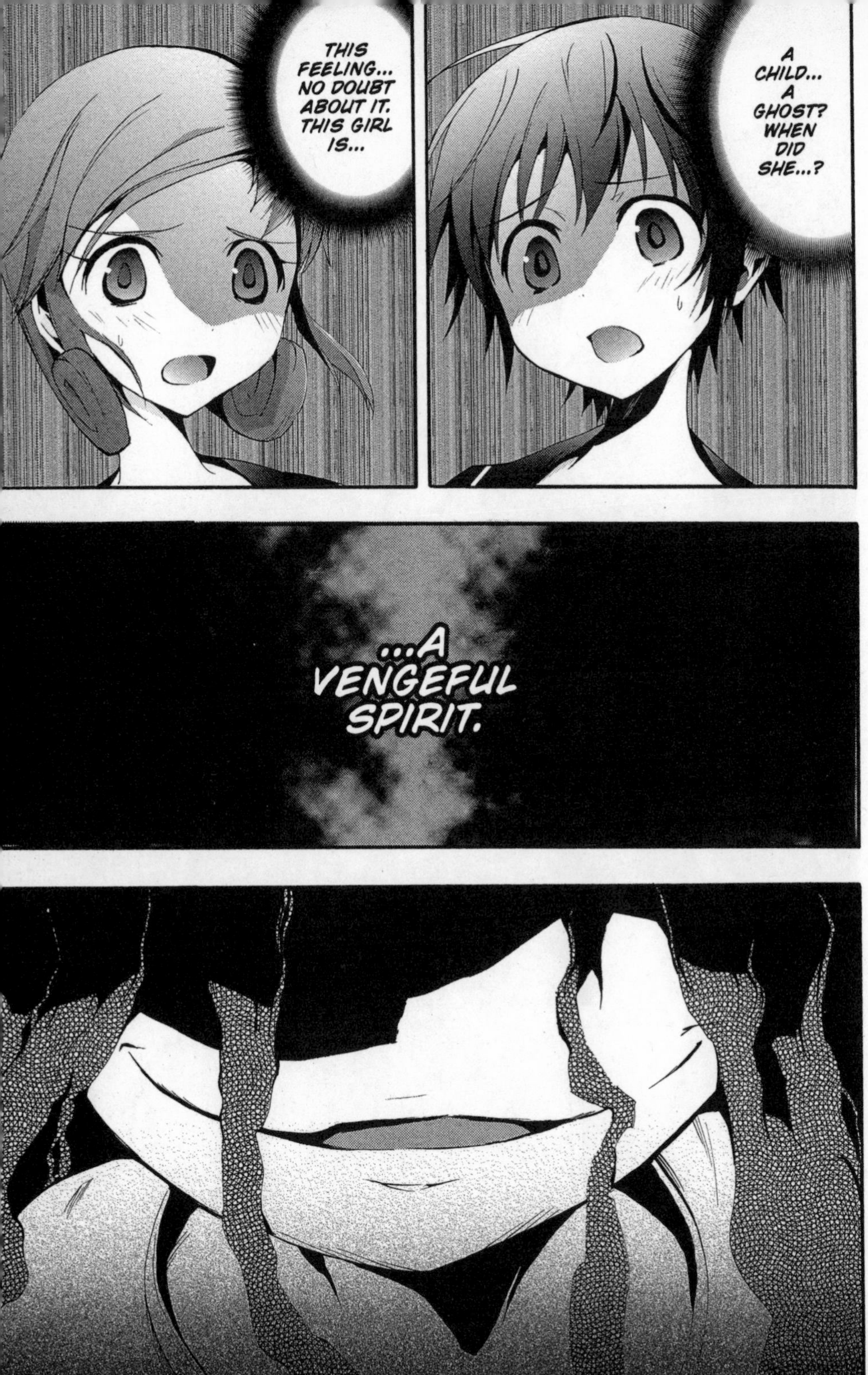
A CHILD... A GHOST? WHEN DID SHE...?
THIS FEELING... NO DOUBT ABOUT IT. THIS GIRL IS...
...A VENGEFUL SPIRIT.

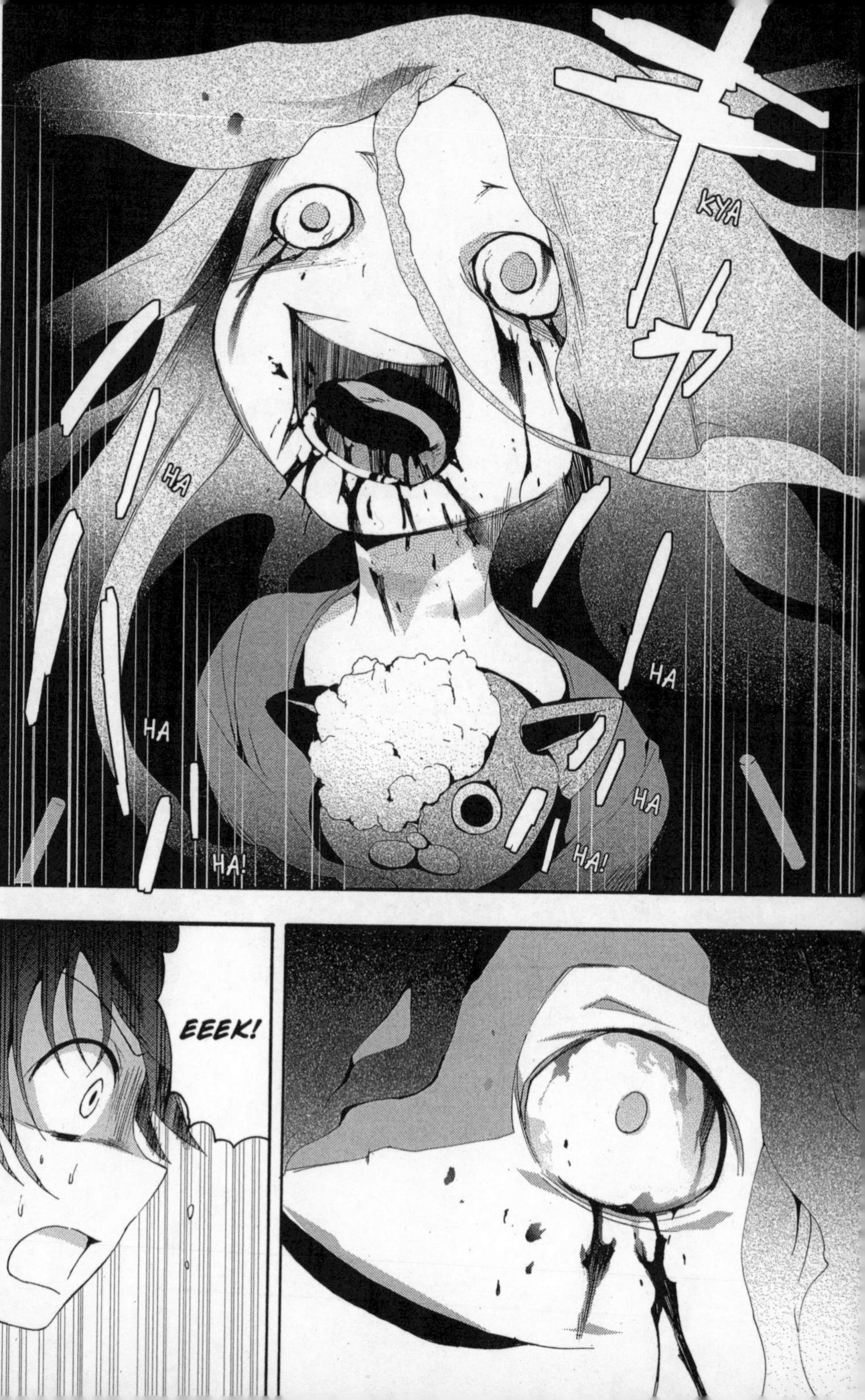
KYA
HA
HA
HA!
HA
HA
HA!
EEEK!

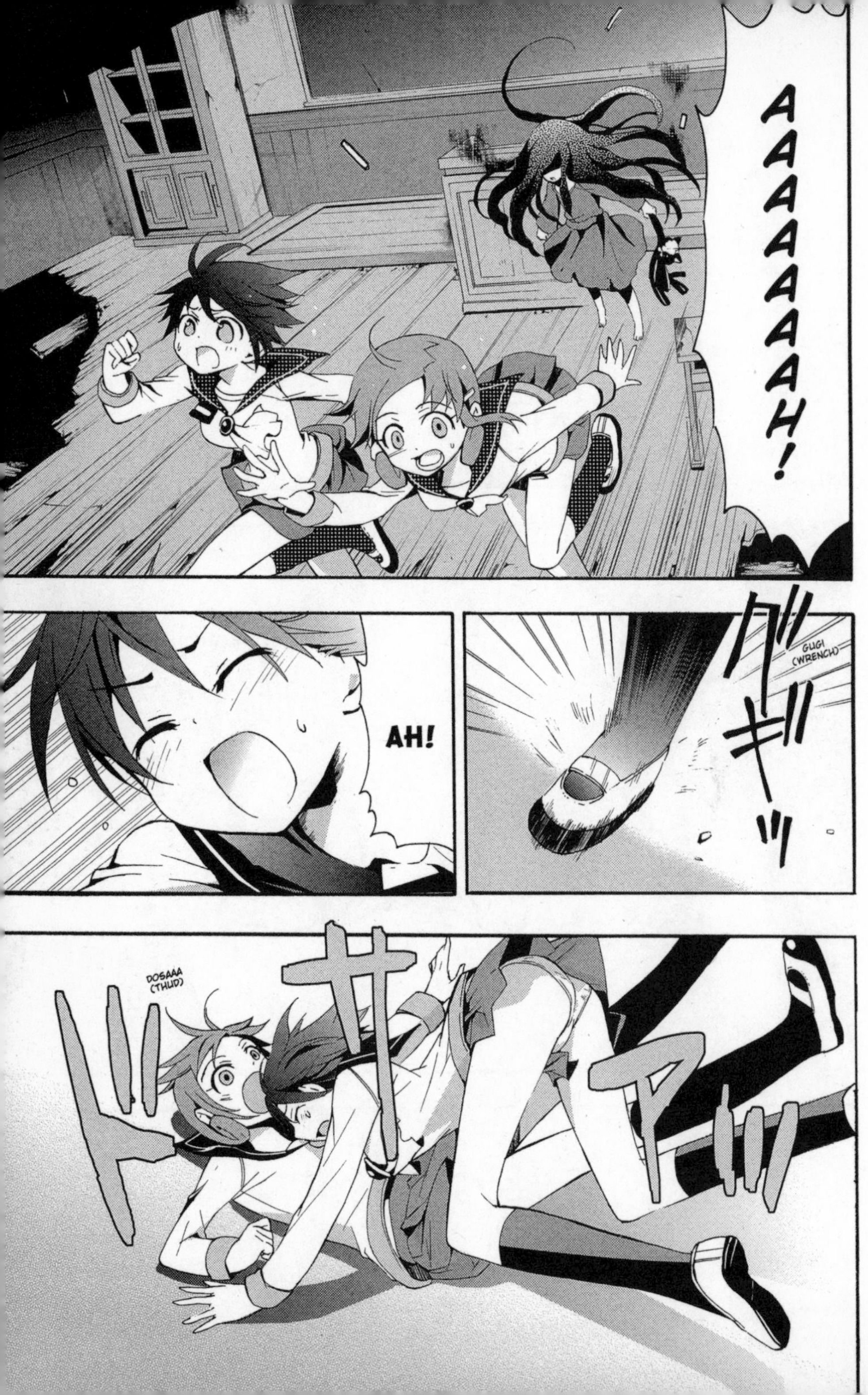
AAAAAAAAH!
GUGI (WRENCH)
AH!
DOSAAA (THUD)

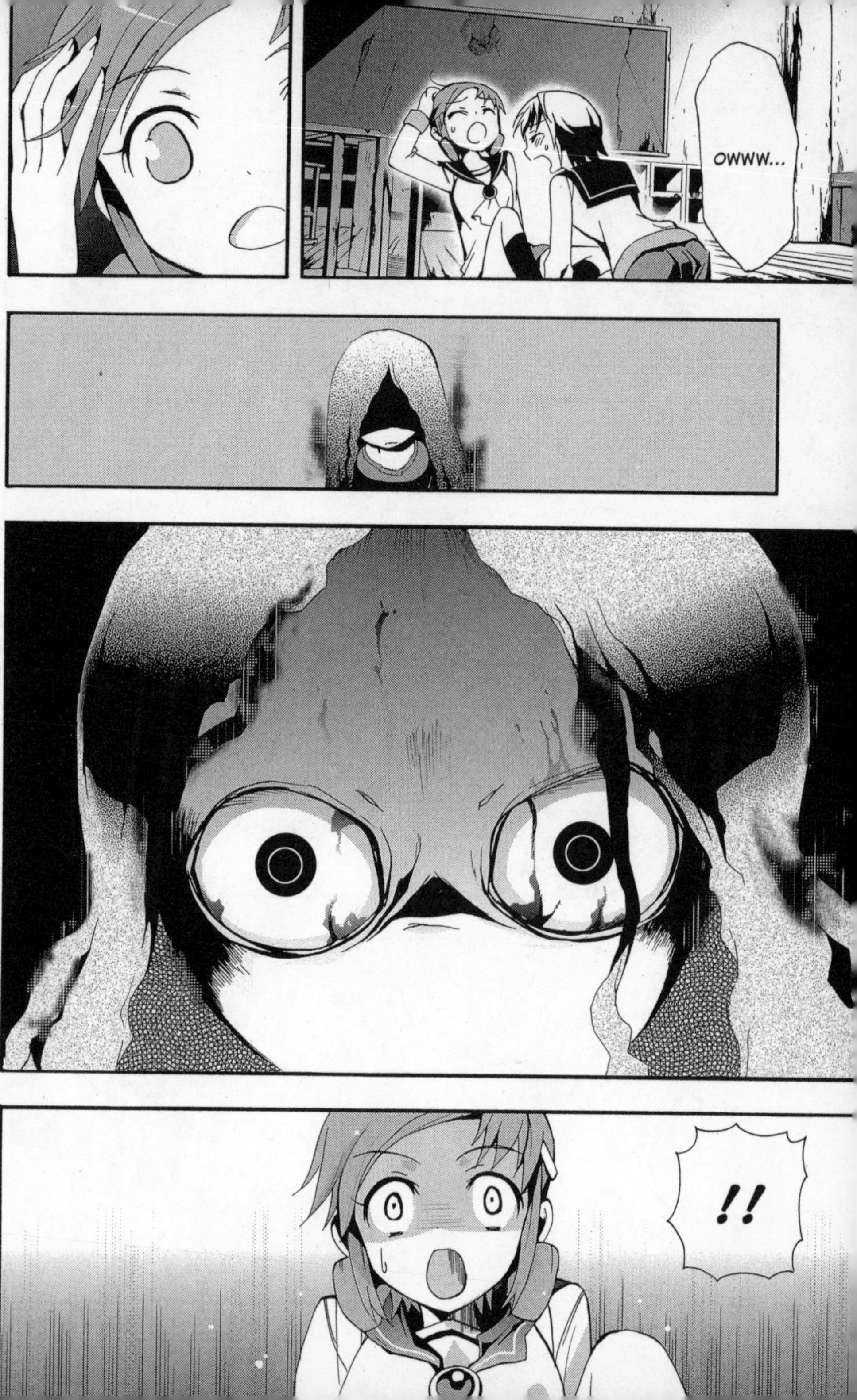
OWWW...
!!

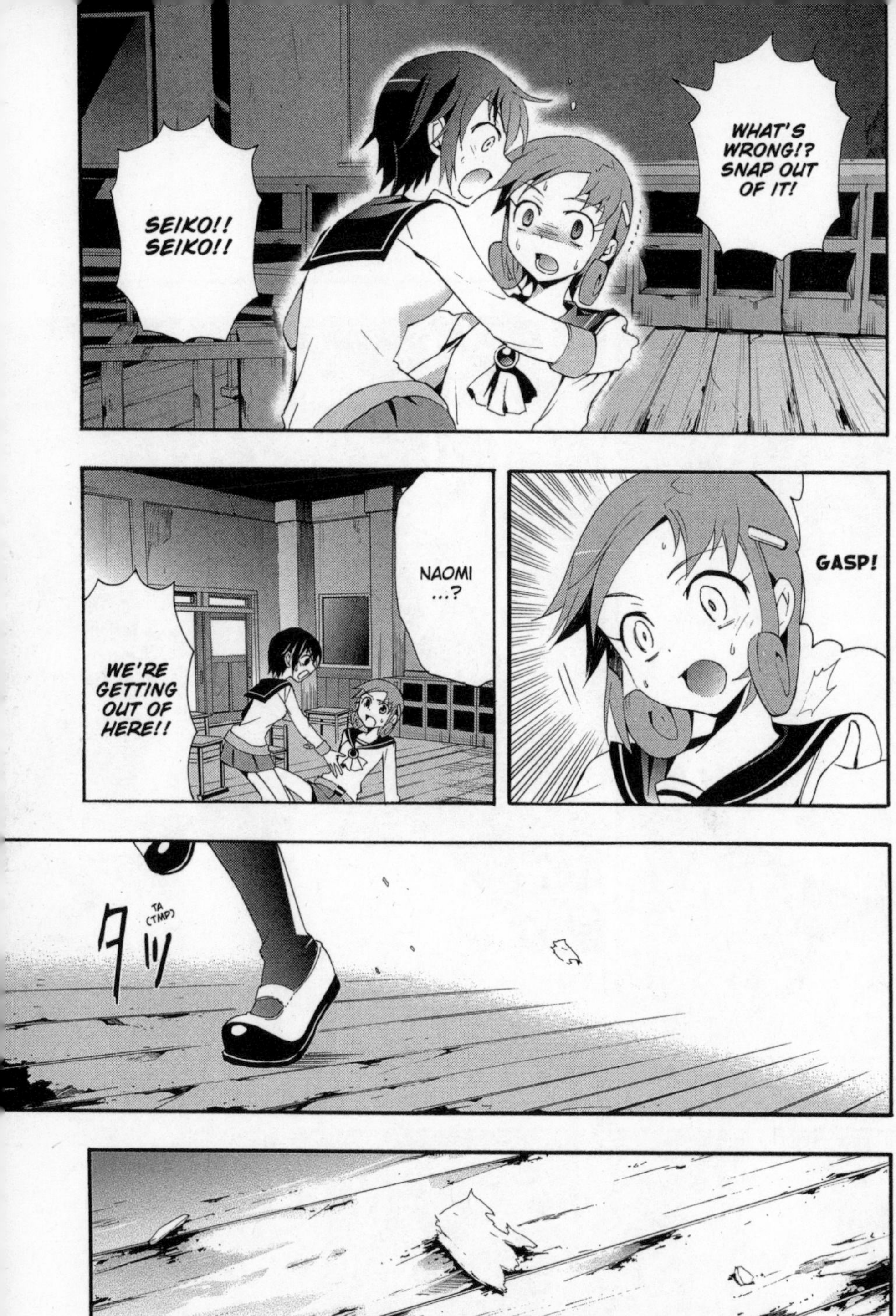
WHAT'S WRONG!? SNAP OUT OF IT!
SEIKO!! SEIKO!!
GASP!
NAOMI ...?
WE'RE GETTING OUT OF HERE!!
TA (TMP)

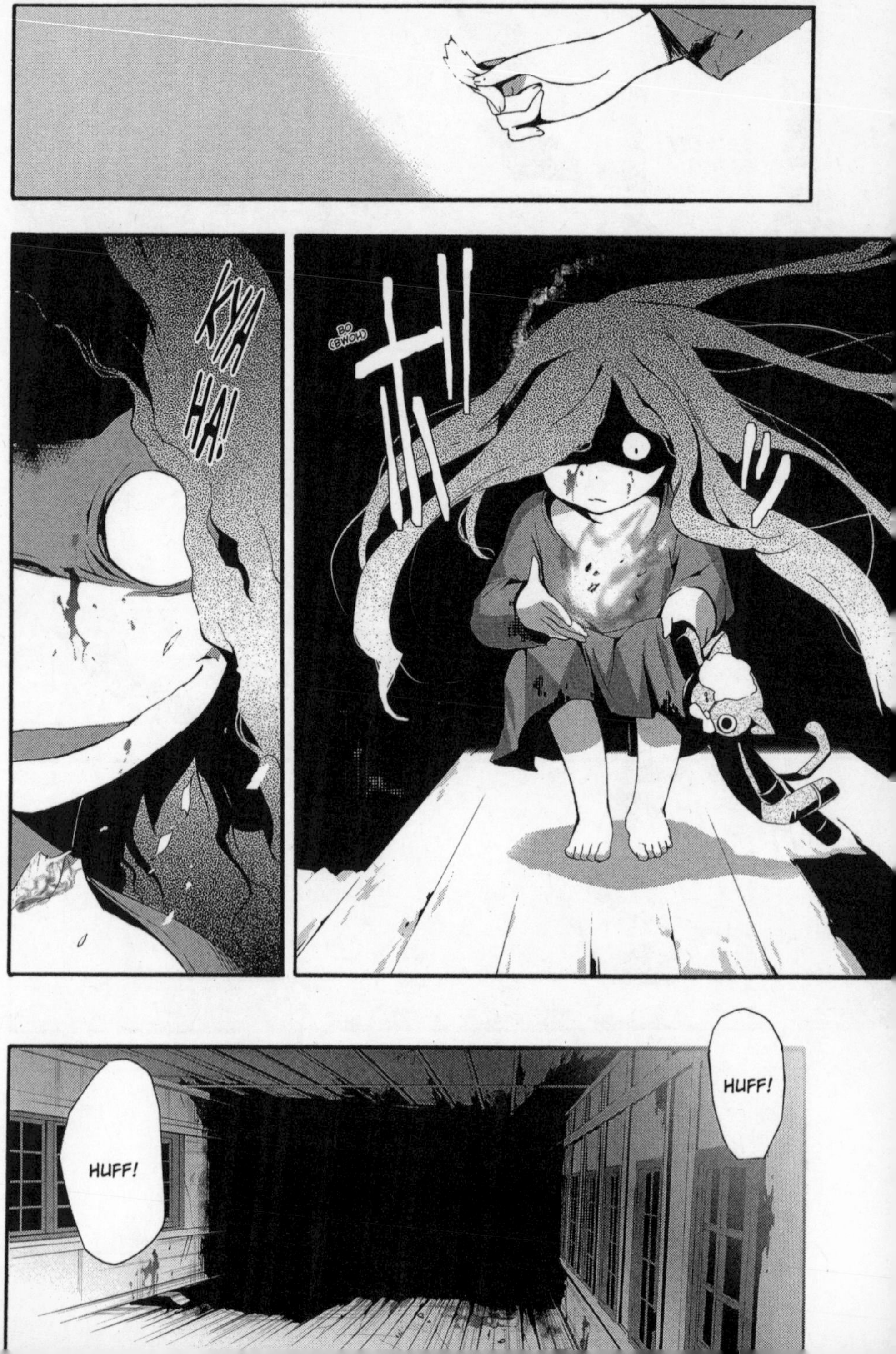
BO (BWOH)
KYAHA HA!
HUFF!
HUFF!

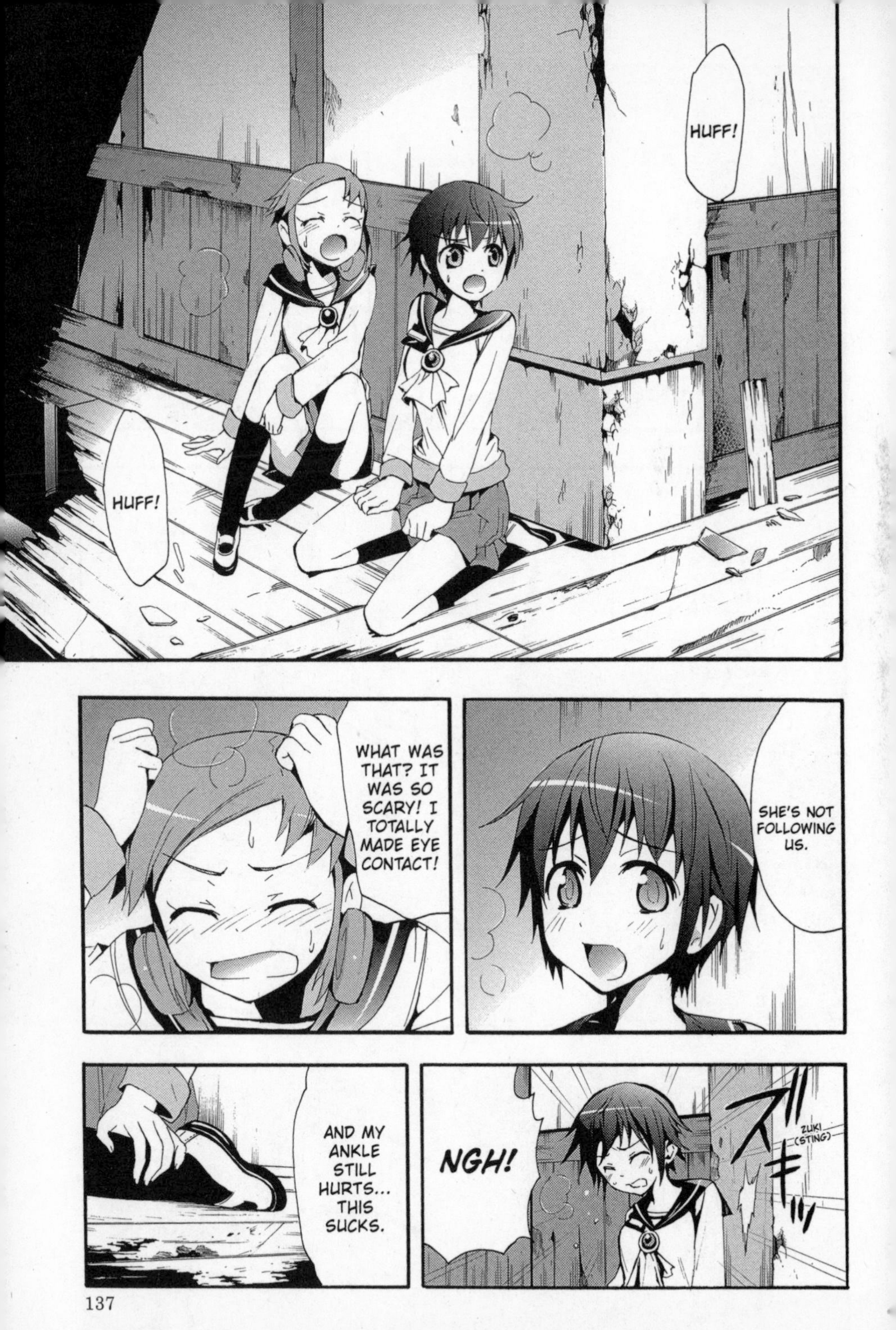
HUFF!
HUFF!
SHE'S NOT FOLLOWING US.
WHAT WAS THAT? IT WAS SO SCARY! I TOTALLY MADE EYE CONTACT!
ZUKI (STING)
NGH!
AND MY ANKLE STILL HURTS... THIS SUCKS.

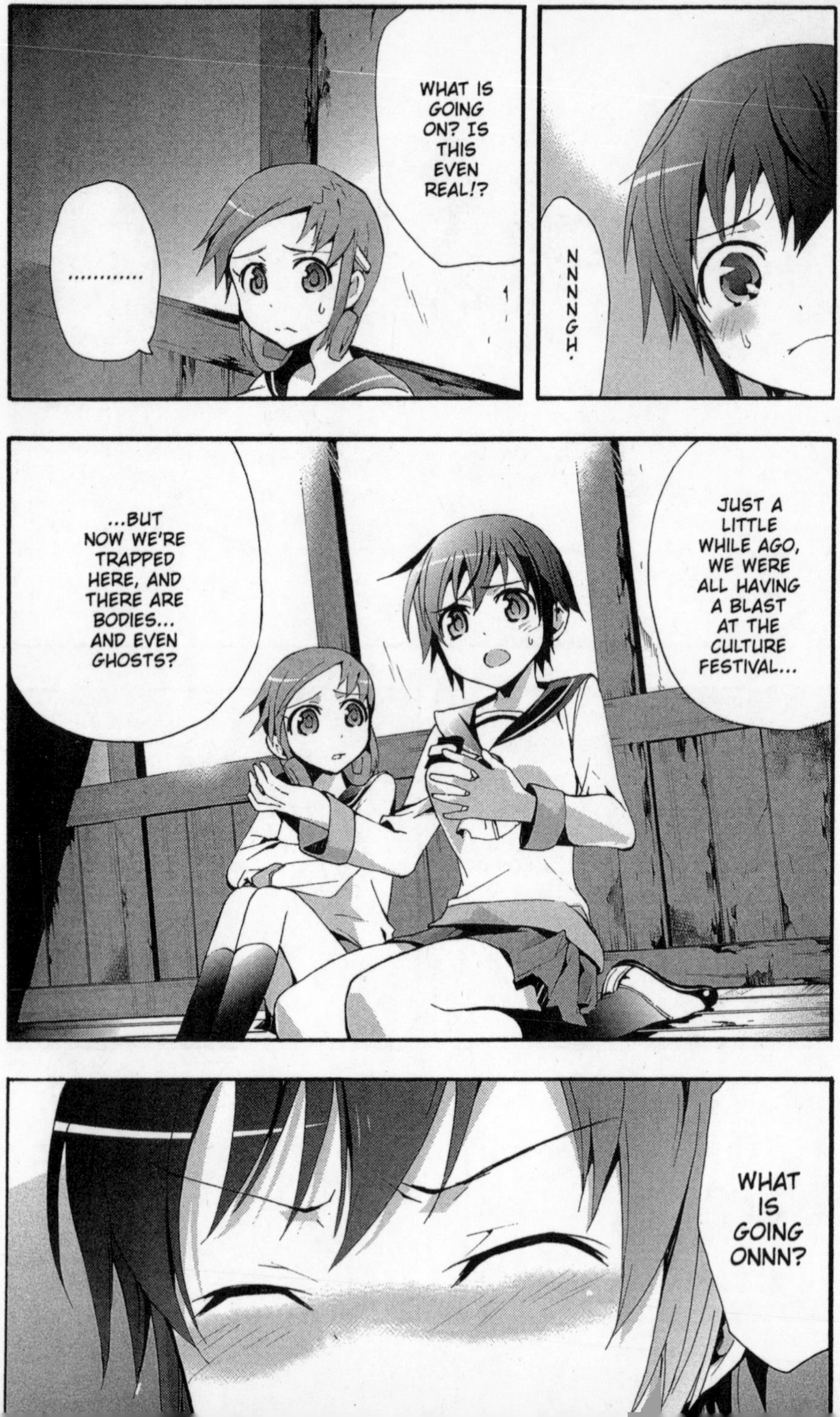
NNNNGH.
WHAT IS GOING ON? IS THIS EVEN REAL!?
....
JUST A LITTLE WHILE AGO, WE WERE ALL HAVING A BLAST AT THE CULTURE FESTIVAL...
...BUT NOW WE'RE TRAPPED HERE, AND THERE ARE BODIES... AND EVEN GHOSTS?
WHAT IS GOING ONNN?

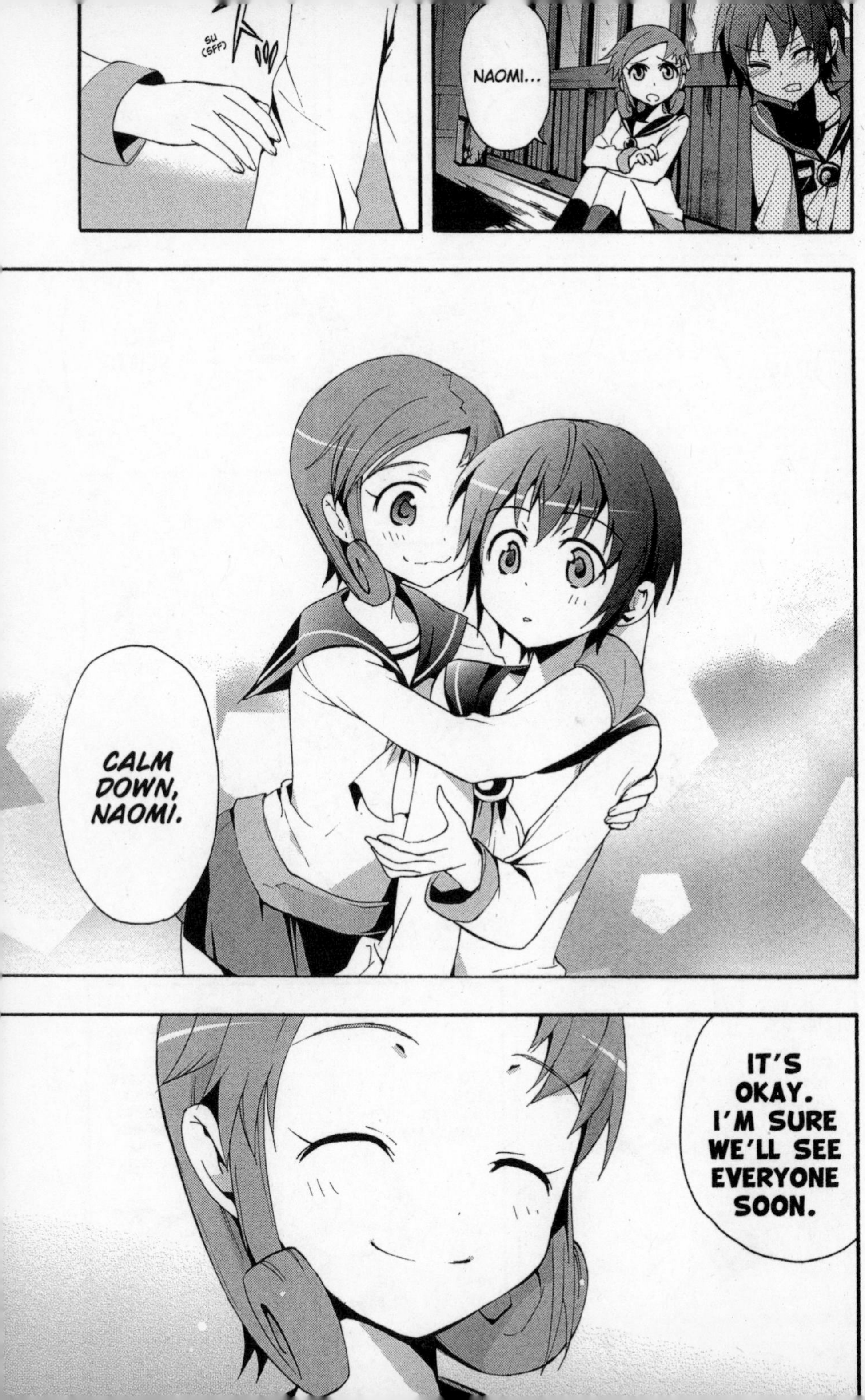
NAOMI...
SU (SFF)
CALM DOWN, NAOMI.
IT'S OKAY. I'M SURE WE'LL SEE EVERYONE SOON.

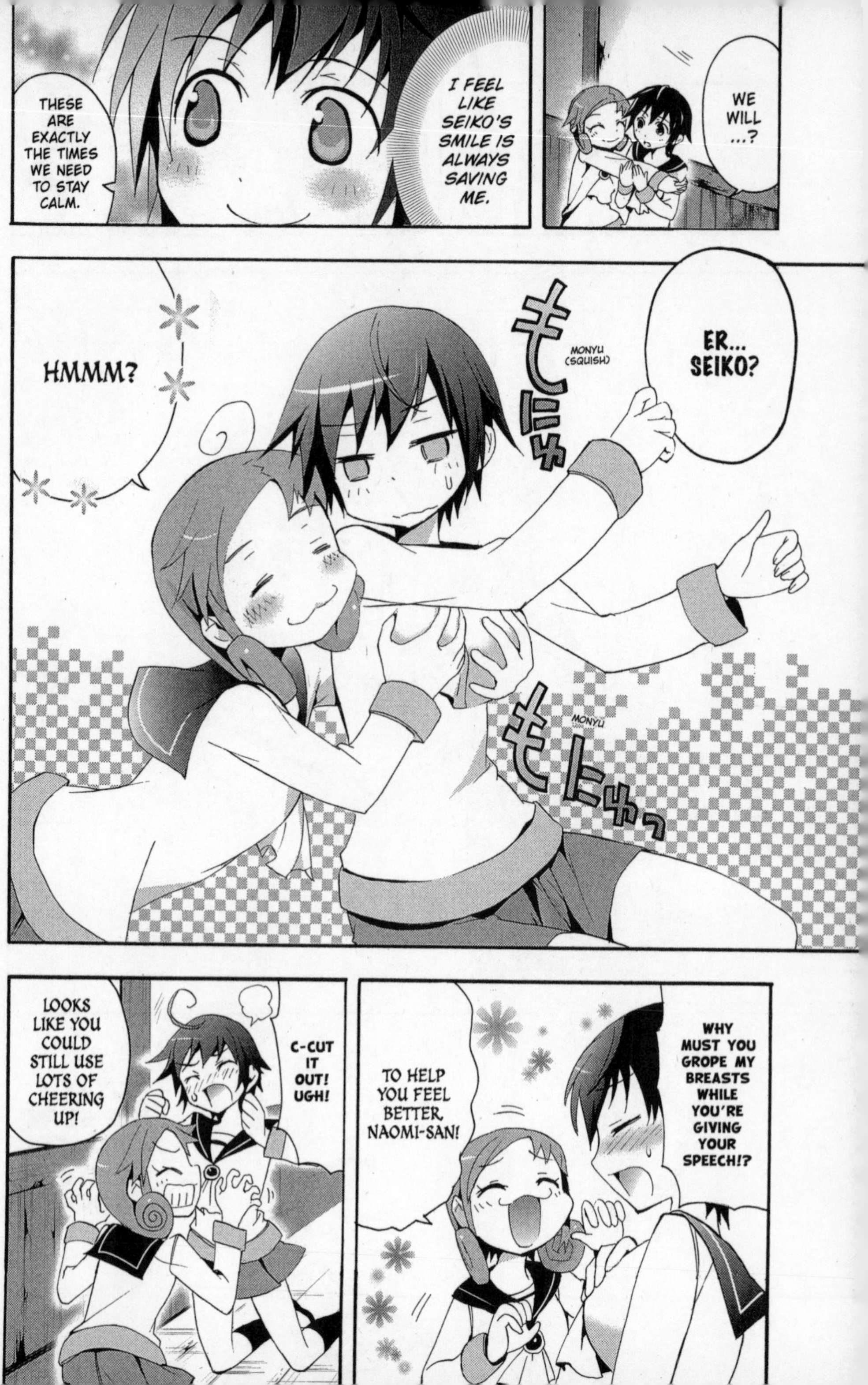

WE WILL ...?
I FEEL LIKE SEIKO'S SMILE IS ALWAYS SAVING ME.
THESE ARE EXACTLY THE TIMES WE NEED TO STAY CALM.
ER... SEIKO?
もにゅ
MONYU (SQUISH)
HMMM?
もにゅっ
MONYU
WHY MUST YOU GROPE MY BREASTS WHILE YOU'RE GIVING YOUR SPEECH!?
TO HELP YOU FEEL BETTER, NAOMI-SAN!
C-CUT IT OUT! UGH!
LOOKS LIKE YOU COULD STILL USE LOTS OF CHEERING UP!

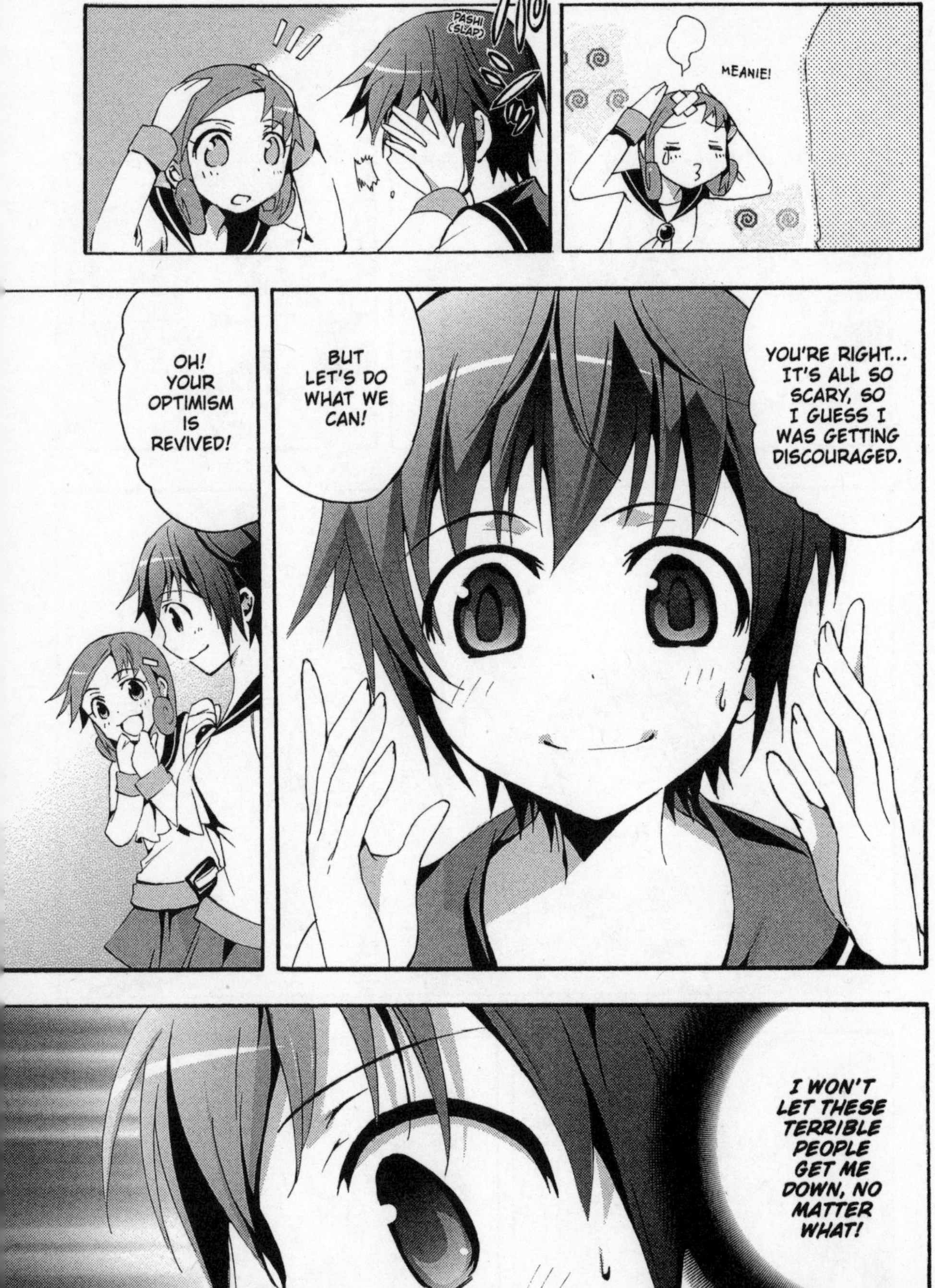
MEANIE!
PASHI (SLAP)
YOU'RE RIGHT... IT'S ALL SO SCARY, SO I GUESS I WAS GETTING DISCOURAGED.
BUT LET'S DO WHAT WE CAN!
OH! YOUR OPTIMISM IS REVIVED!
I WON'T LET THESE TERRIBLE PEOPLE GET ME DOWN, NO MATTER WHAT!

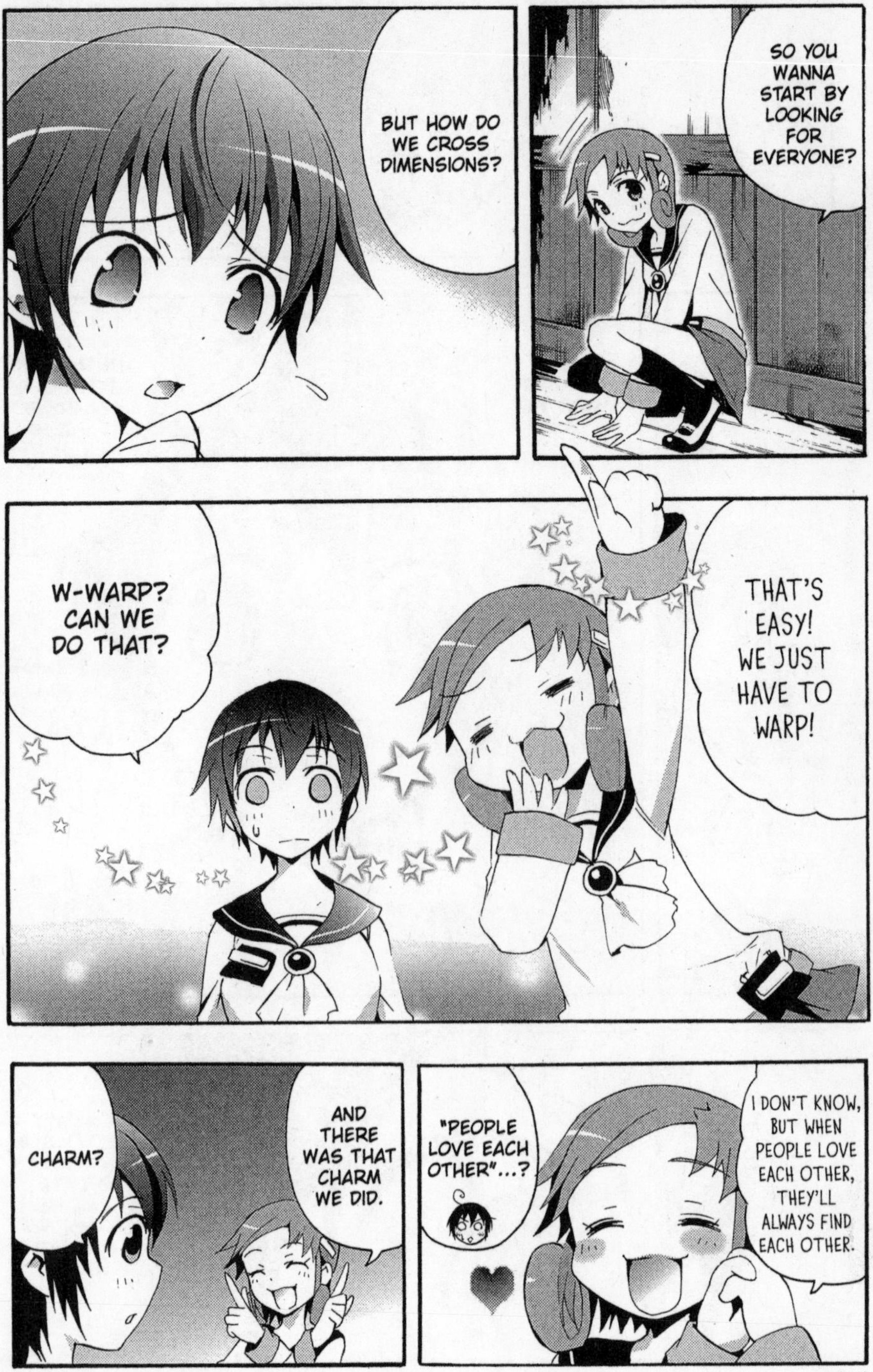
SO YOU WANNA START BY LOOKING FOR EVERYONE?
BUT HOW DO WE CROSS DIMENSIONS?
THAT'S EASY! WE JUST HAVE TO WARP!
W-WARP? CAN WE DO THAT?
I DON'T KNOW, BUT WHEN PEOPLE LOVE EACH OTHER, THEY'LL ALWAYS FIND EACH OTHER.
"PEOPLE LOVE EACH OTHER"...?
AND THERE WAS THAT CHARM WE DID.
CHARM?

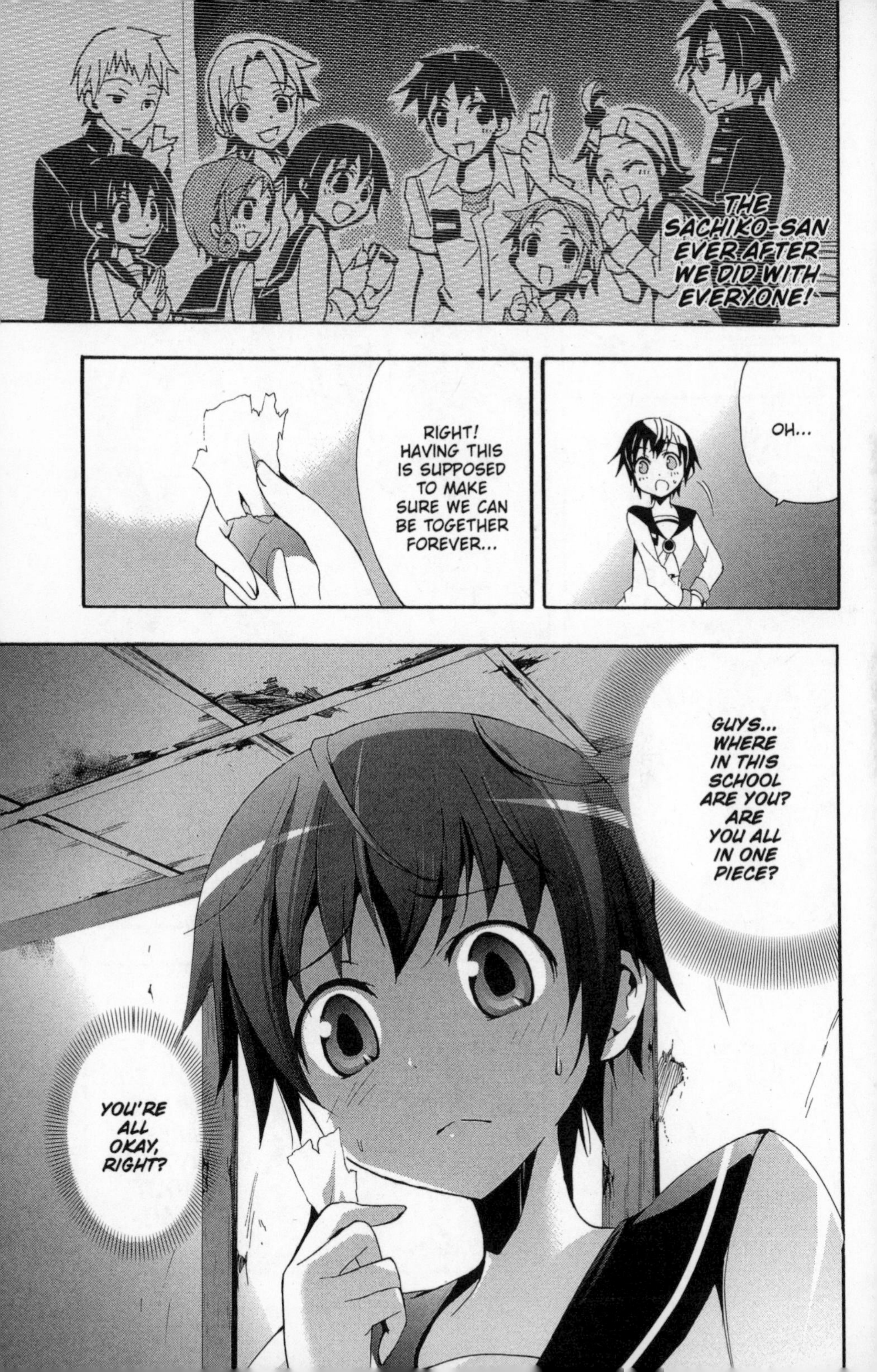
THE SACHIKO-SAN EVER AFTER WE DID WITH EVERYONE!
OH...
RIGHT! HAVING THIS IS SUPPOSED TO MAKE SURE WE CAN BE TOGETHER FOREVER...
GUYS... WHERE IN THIS SCHOOL ARE YOU? ARE YOU ALL IN ONE PIECE?
YOU'RE ALL OKAY, RIGHT?

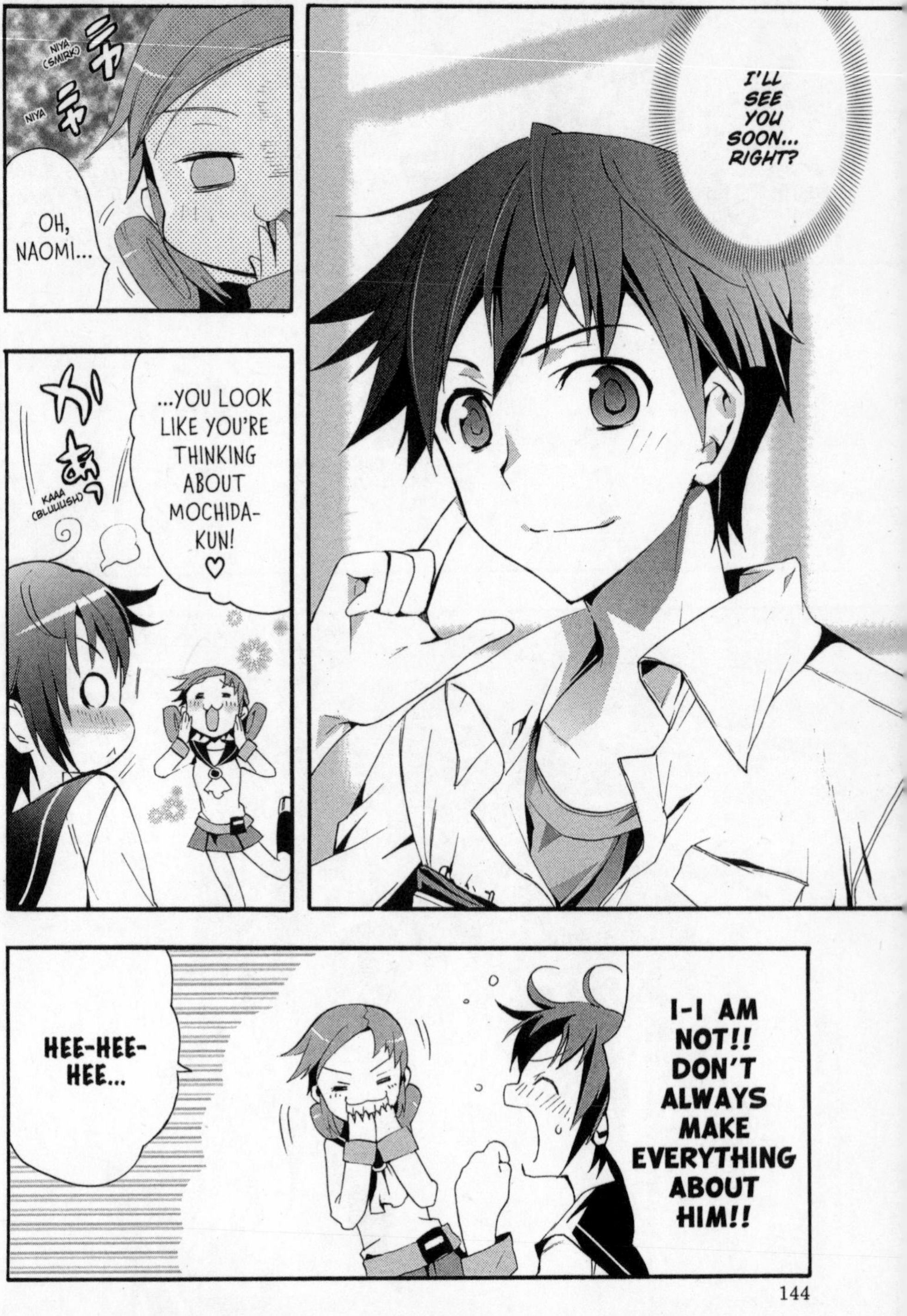
I'LL SEE YOU SOON... RIGHT?
ニヤ
NIYA (SMIRK)
ニヤ
NIYA
OH, NAOMI...
...YOU LOOK LIKE YOU'RE THINKING ABOUT MOCHIDA-KUN! ♡
かあっ
KAAA (BLUUUSH)
I-I AM NOT!! DON'T ALWAYS MAKE EVERYTHING ABOUT HIM!!
HEE-HEE-HEE...

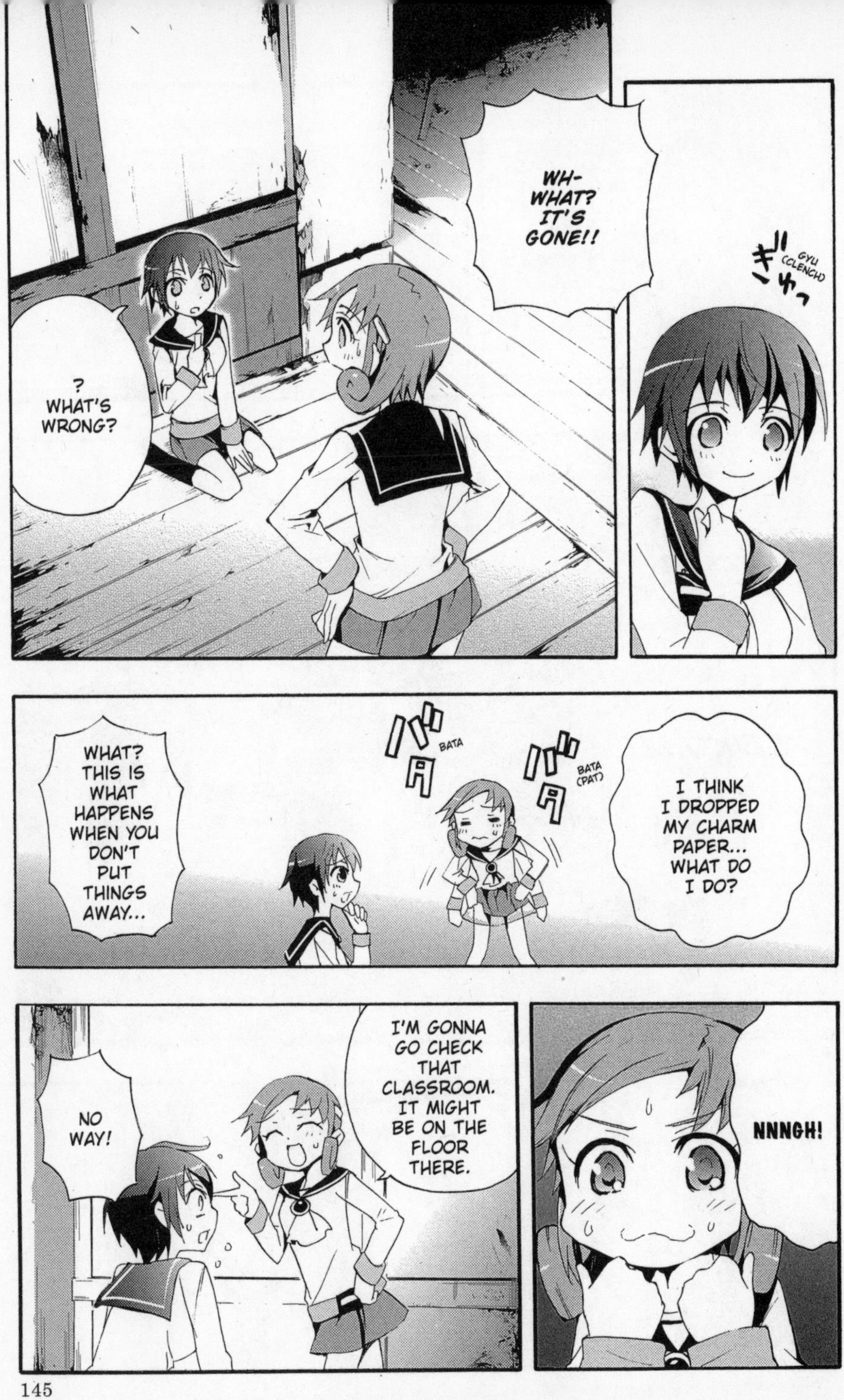
ぎゅっ
GYU (CLENCH)
WH-WHAT? IT'S GONE!!
? WHAT'S WRONG?
I THINK I DROPPED MY CHARM PAPER... WHAT DO I DO?
バタ
BATA (PAT)
バタ
BATA
WHAT? THIS IS WHAT HAPPENS WHEN YOU DON'T PUT THINGS AWAY...
NNNGH!
I'M GONNA GO CHECK THAT CLASSROOM. IT MIGHT BE ON THE FLOOR THERE.
NO WAY!

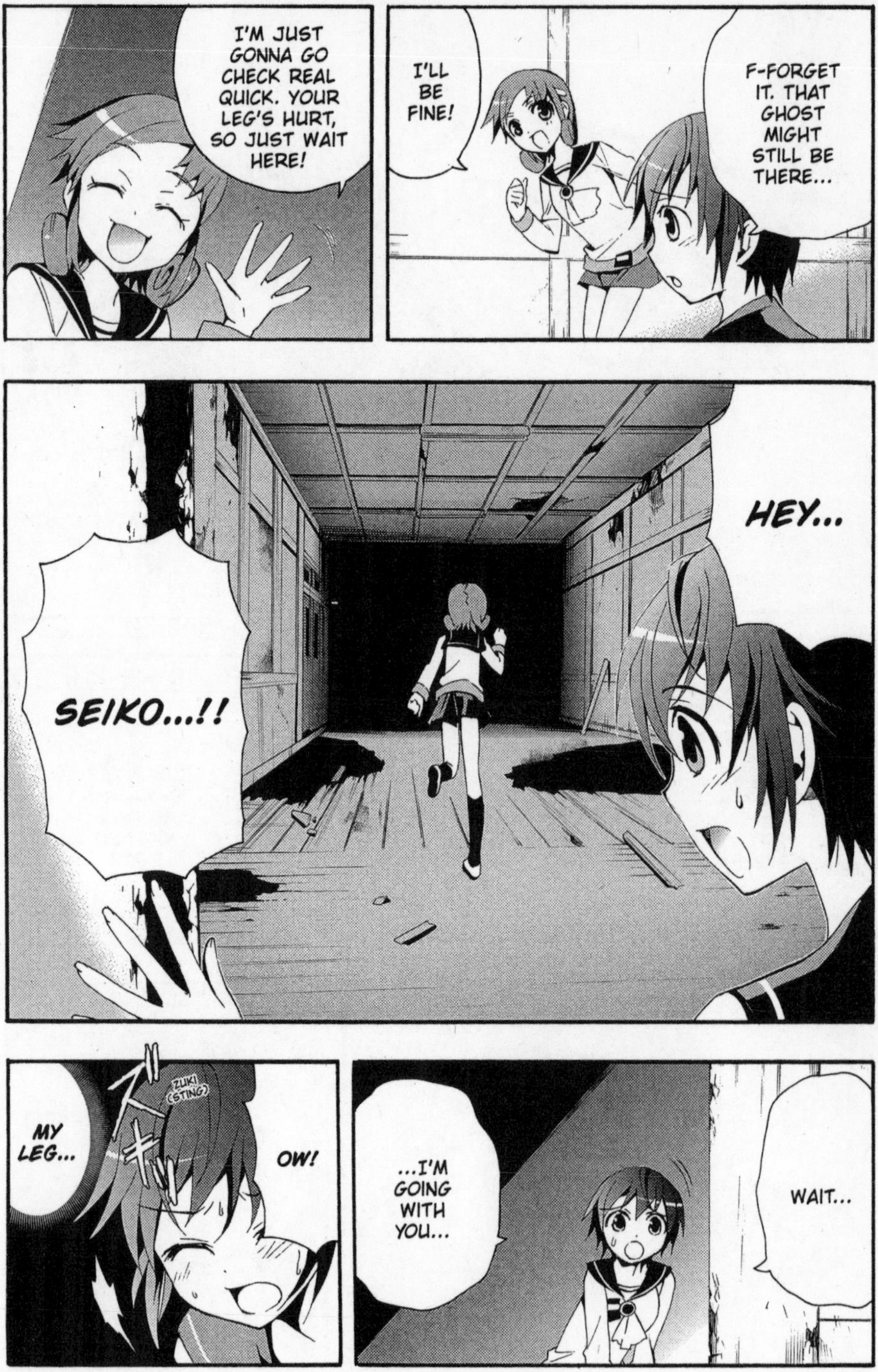
F-FORGET IT. THAT GHOST MIGHT STILL BE THERE...
I'LL BE FINE!
I'M JUST GONNA GO CHECK REAL QUICK. YOUR LEG'S HURT, SO JUST WAIT HERE!
HEY...
SEIKO...!!
WAIT...
...I'M GOING WITH YOU...
OW!
ZUKI (STING)
MY LEG...

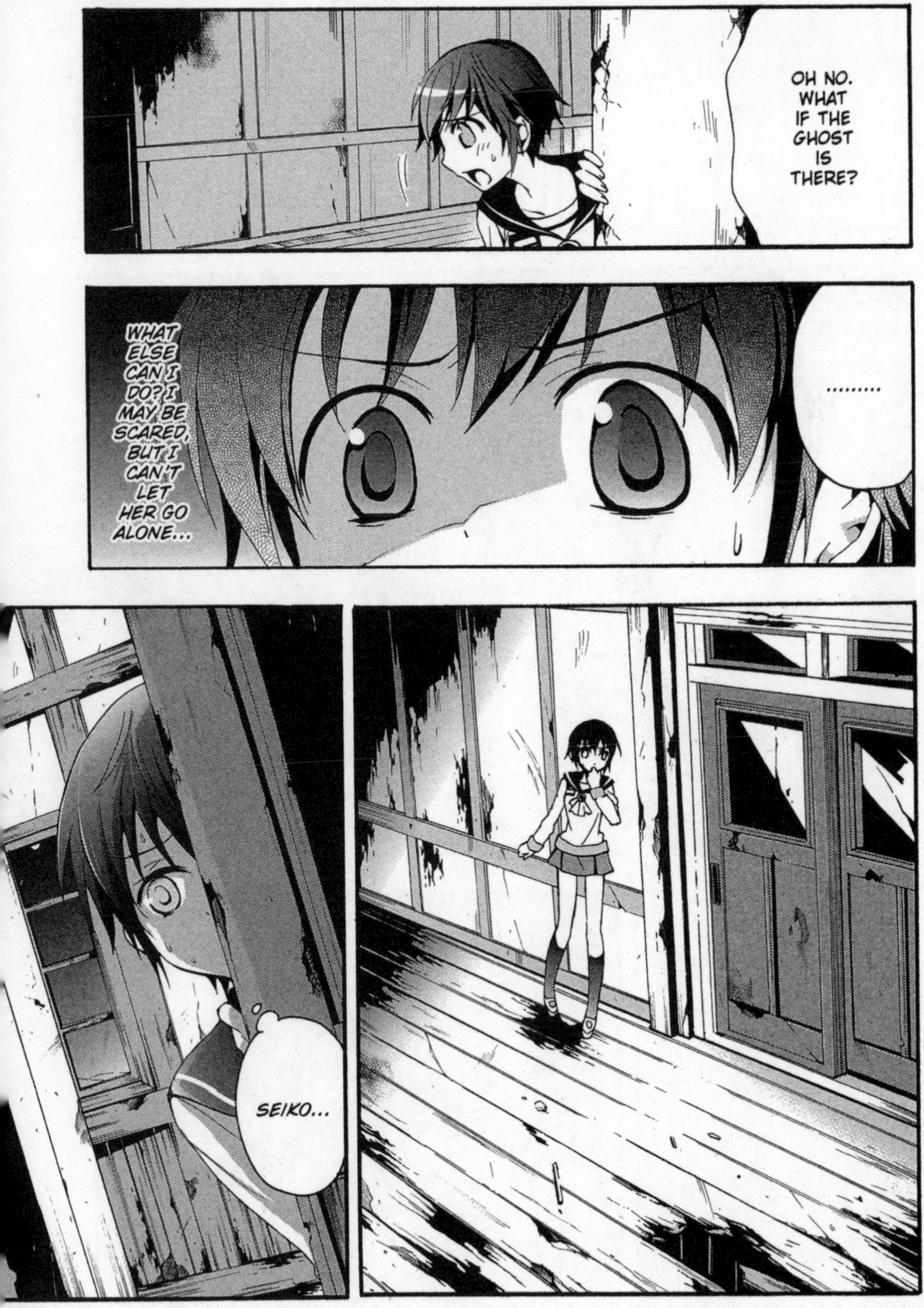
OH NO. WHAT IF THE GHOST IS THERE?
....
WHAT ELSE CAN I DO? I MAY BE SCARED, BUT I CAN'T LET HER GO ALONE...
SEIKO...

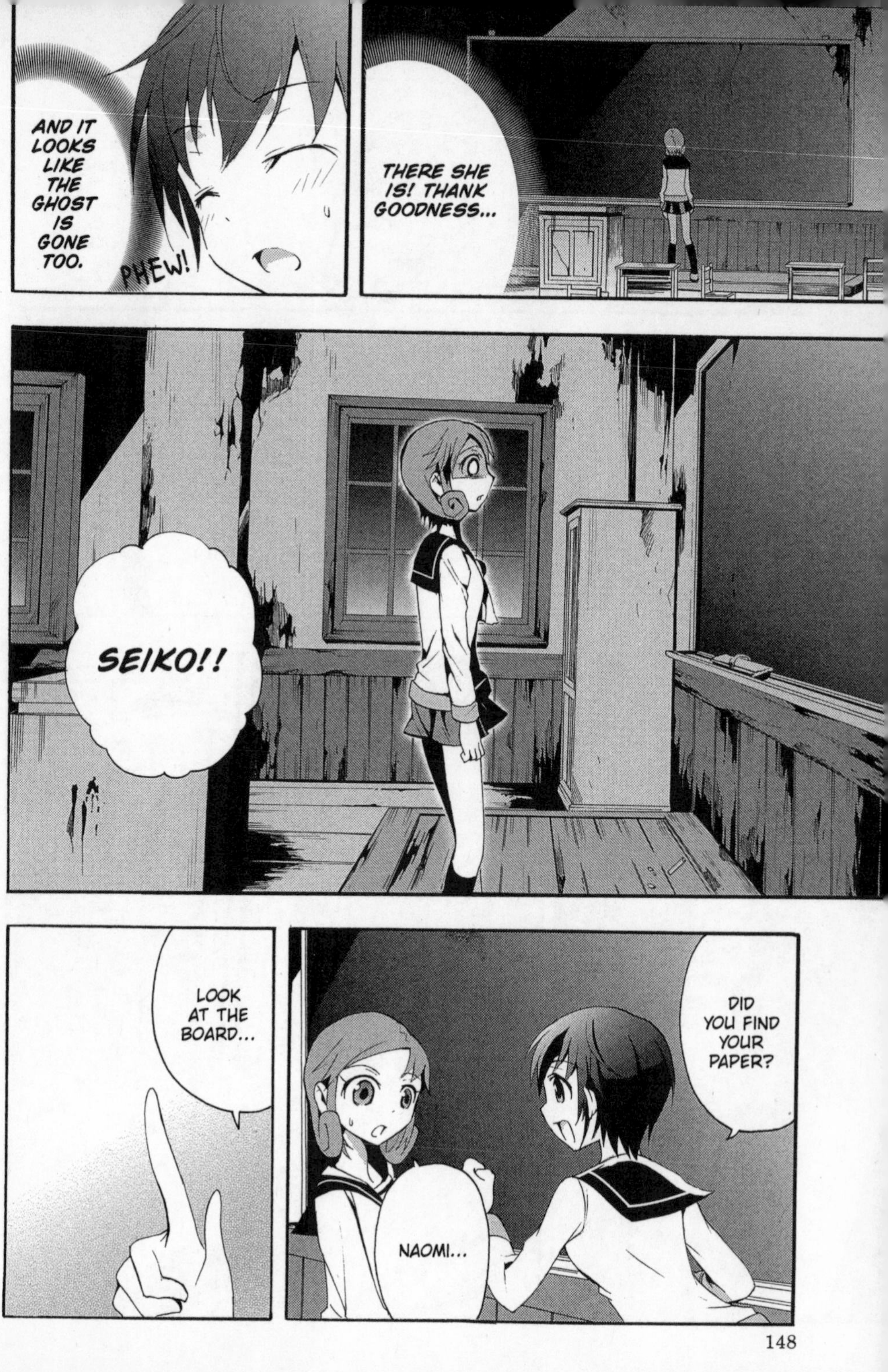
THERE SHE IS! THANK GOODNESS...
AND IT LOOKS LIKE THE GHOST IS GONE TOO.
PHEW!
SEIKO!!
DID YOU FIND YOUR PAPER?
NAOMI...
LOOK AT THE BOARD...

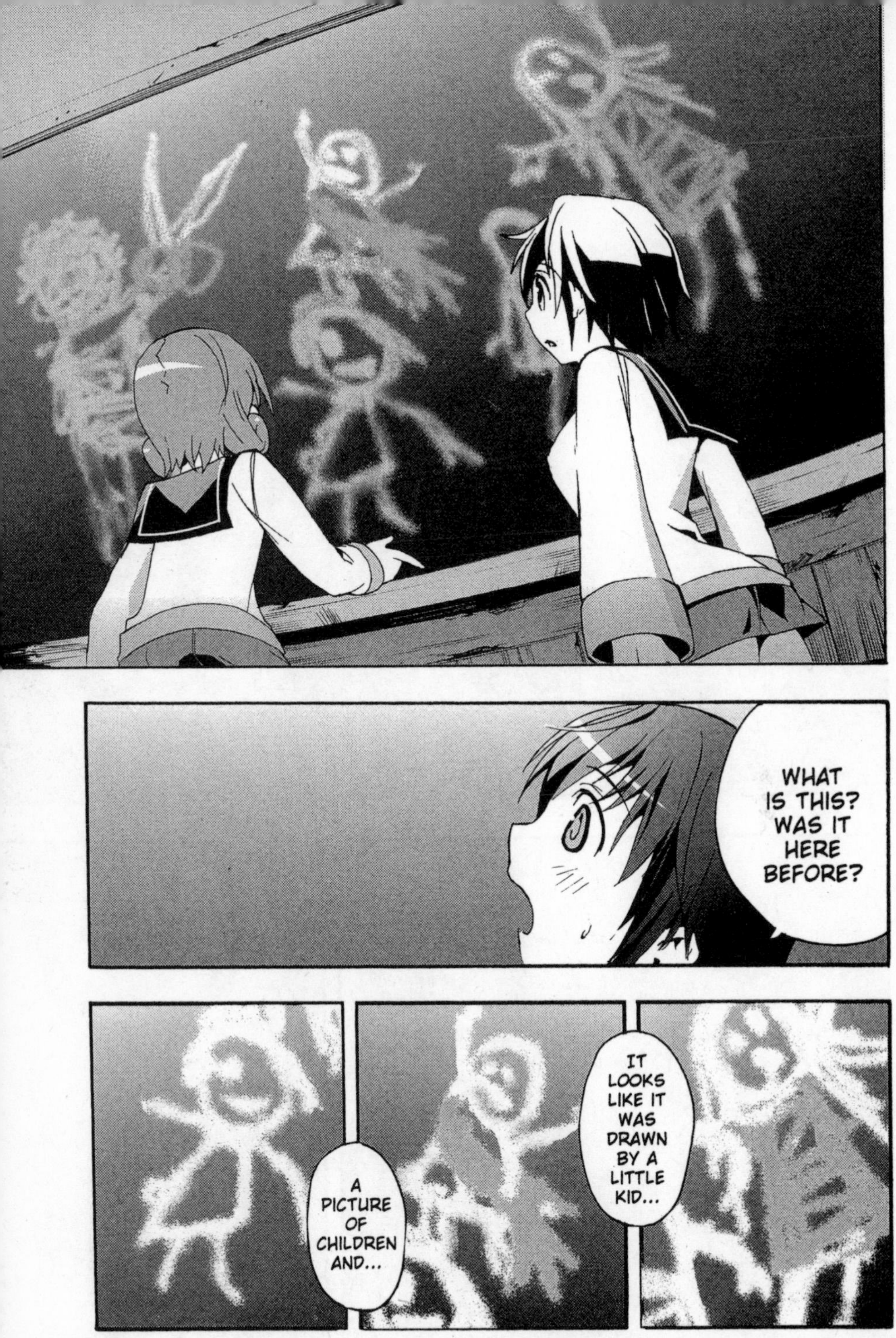
WHAT IS THIS? WAS IT HERE BEFORE?
IT LOOKS LIKE IT WAS DRAWN BY A LITTLE KID...
A PICTURE OF CHILDREN AND...

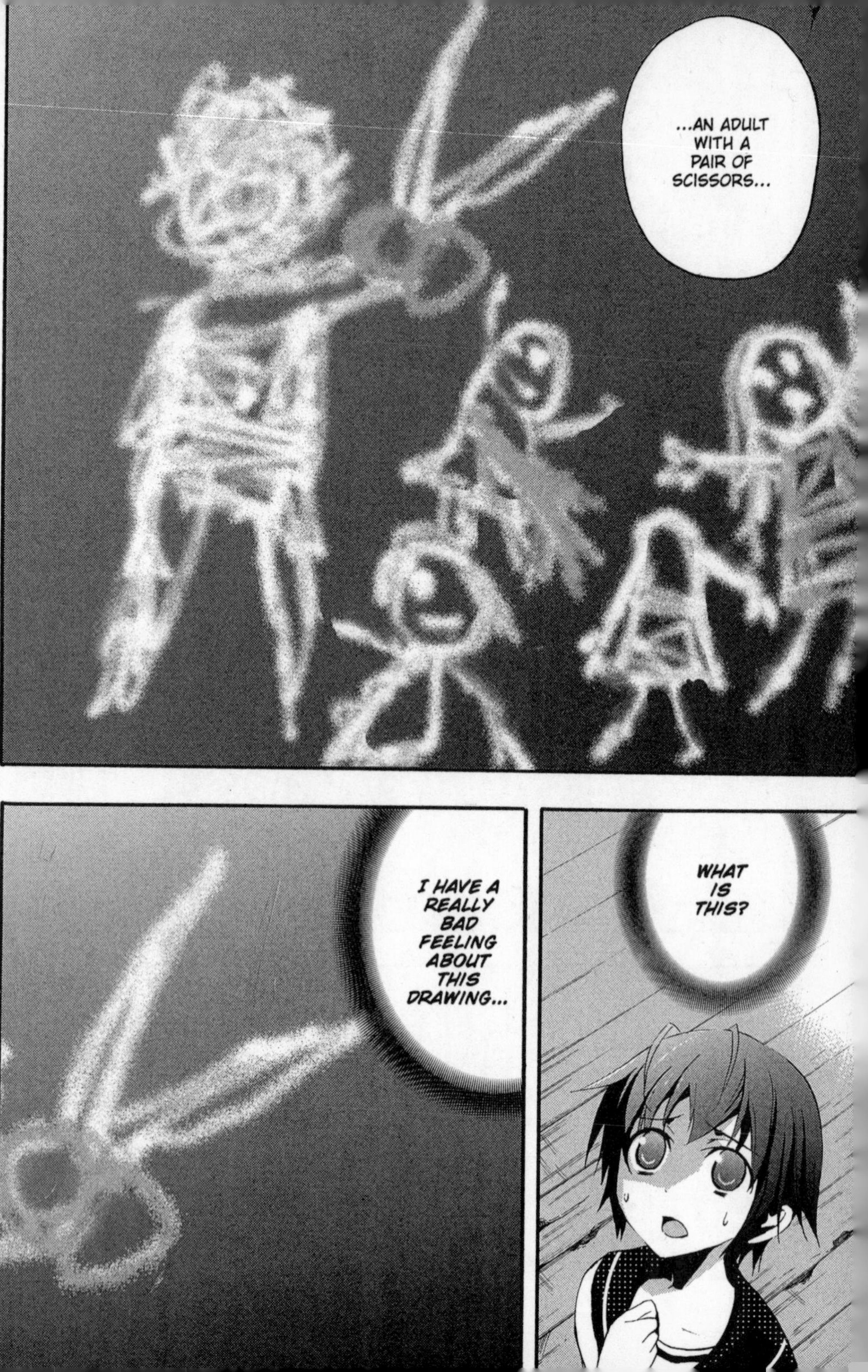
...AN ADULT WITH A PAIR OF SCISSORS...
WHAT IS THIS?
I HAVE A REALLY BAD FEELING ABOUT THIS DRAWING...

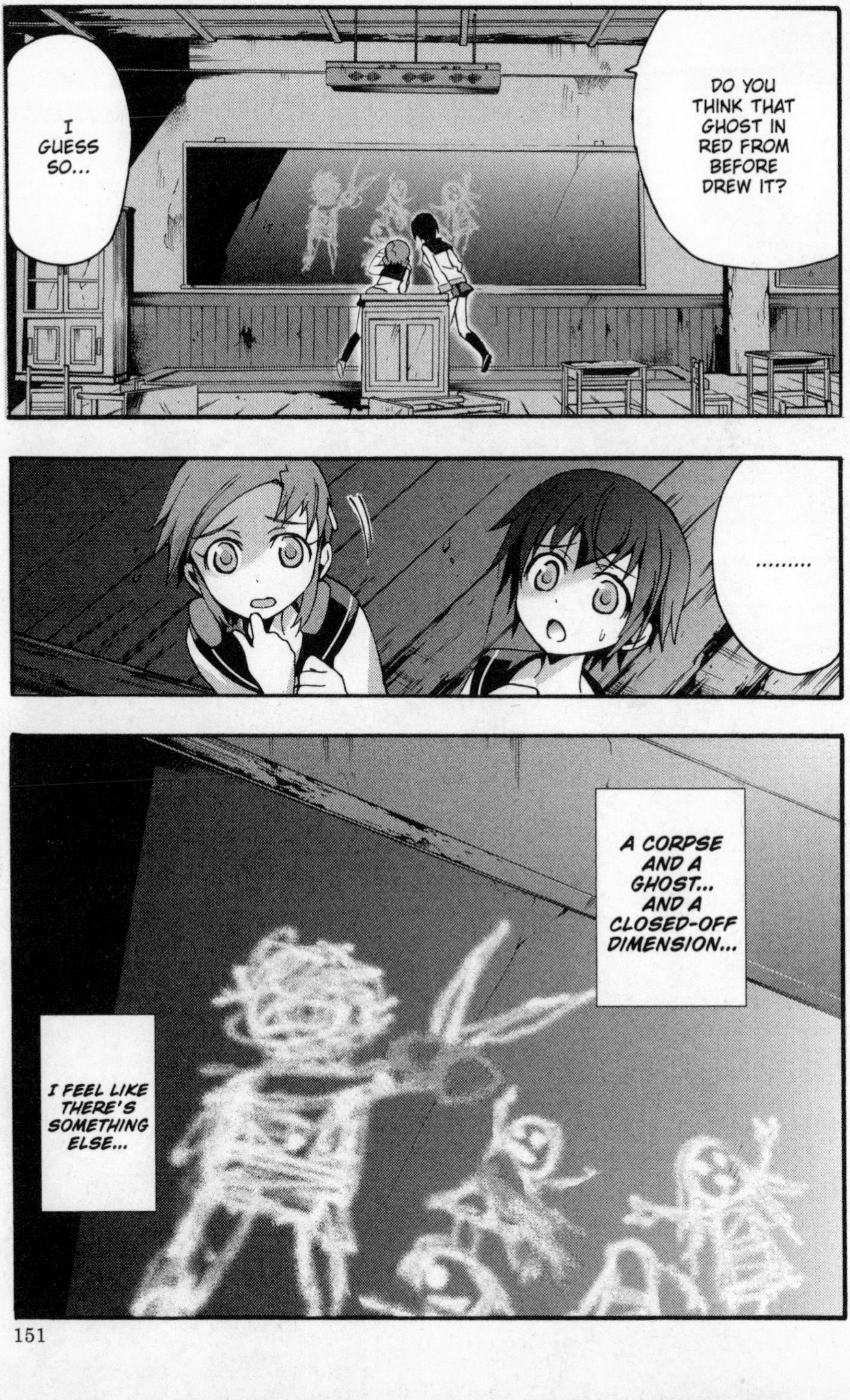
DO YOU THINK THAT GHOST IN RED FROM BEFORE DREW IT?
I GUESS SO...
....
A CORPSE AND A GHOST... AND A CLOSED-OFF DIMENSION...
I FEEL LIKE THERE'S SOMETHING ELSE...

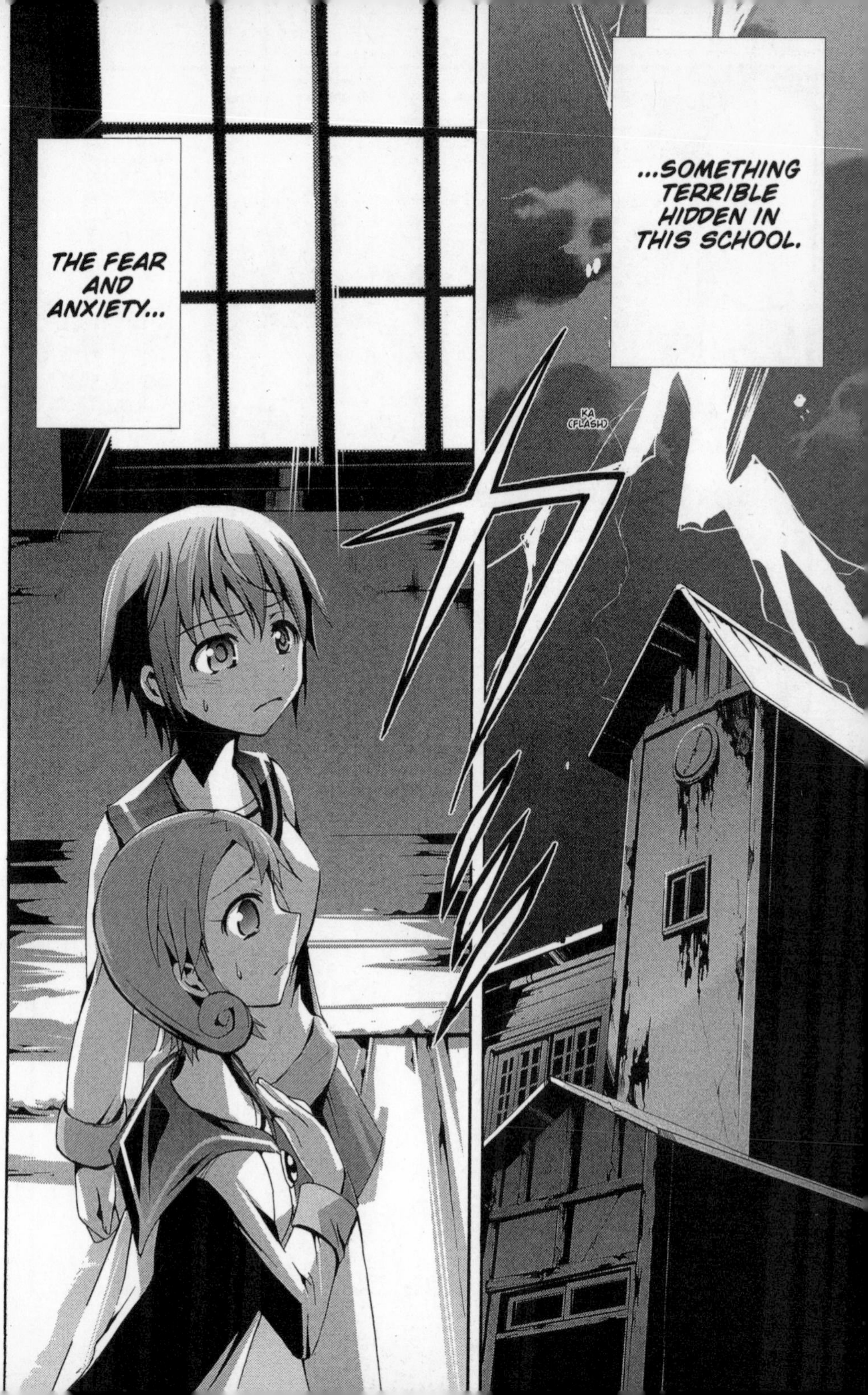
THE FEAR AND ANXIETY...
...SOMETHING TERRIBLE HIDDEN IN THIS SCHOOL.
KA (FLASH)

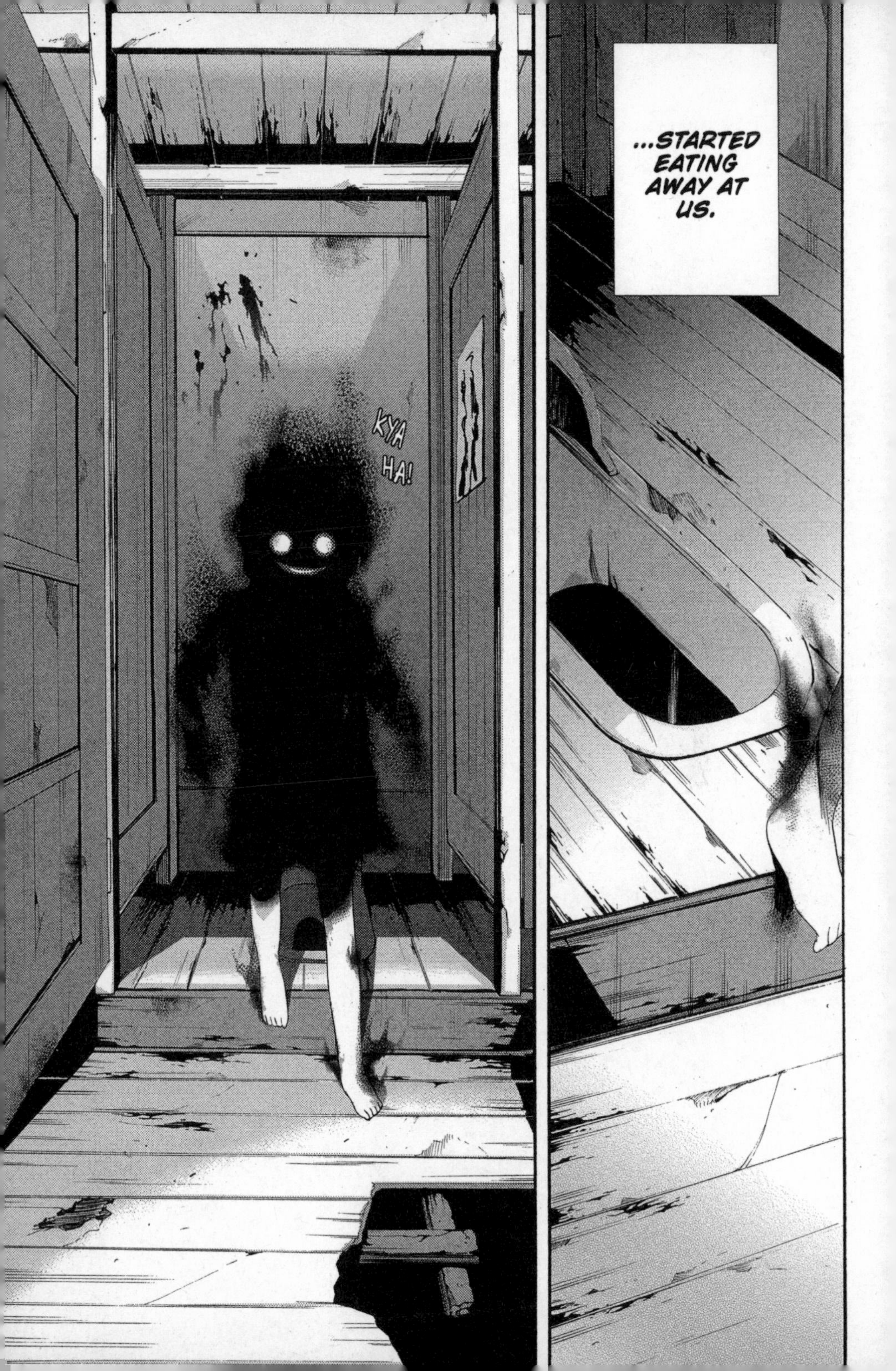
...STARTED EATING AWAY AT US.
KYA HA!

a list of ghosts/01

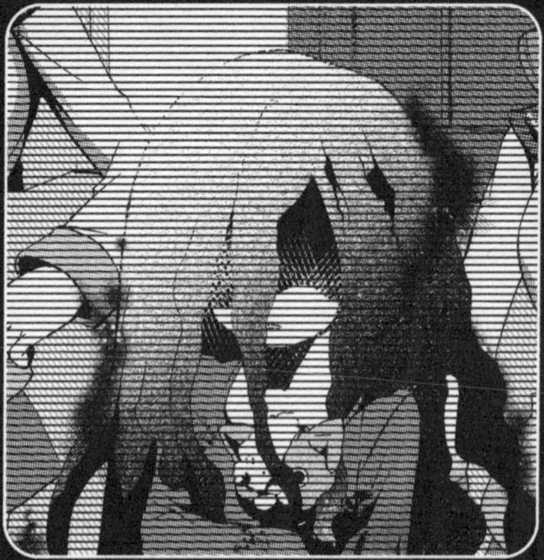

A child's ghost wearing red. Surprised Naomi and Seiko in Class 2-A's room. Based on the fact that she was laughing, it's possible that she was actually only playing. She left some seemingly important drawings on the blackboard and vanished.

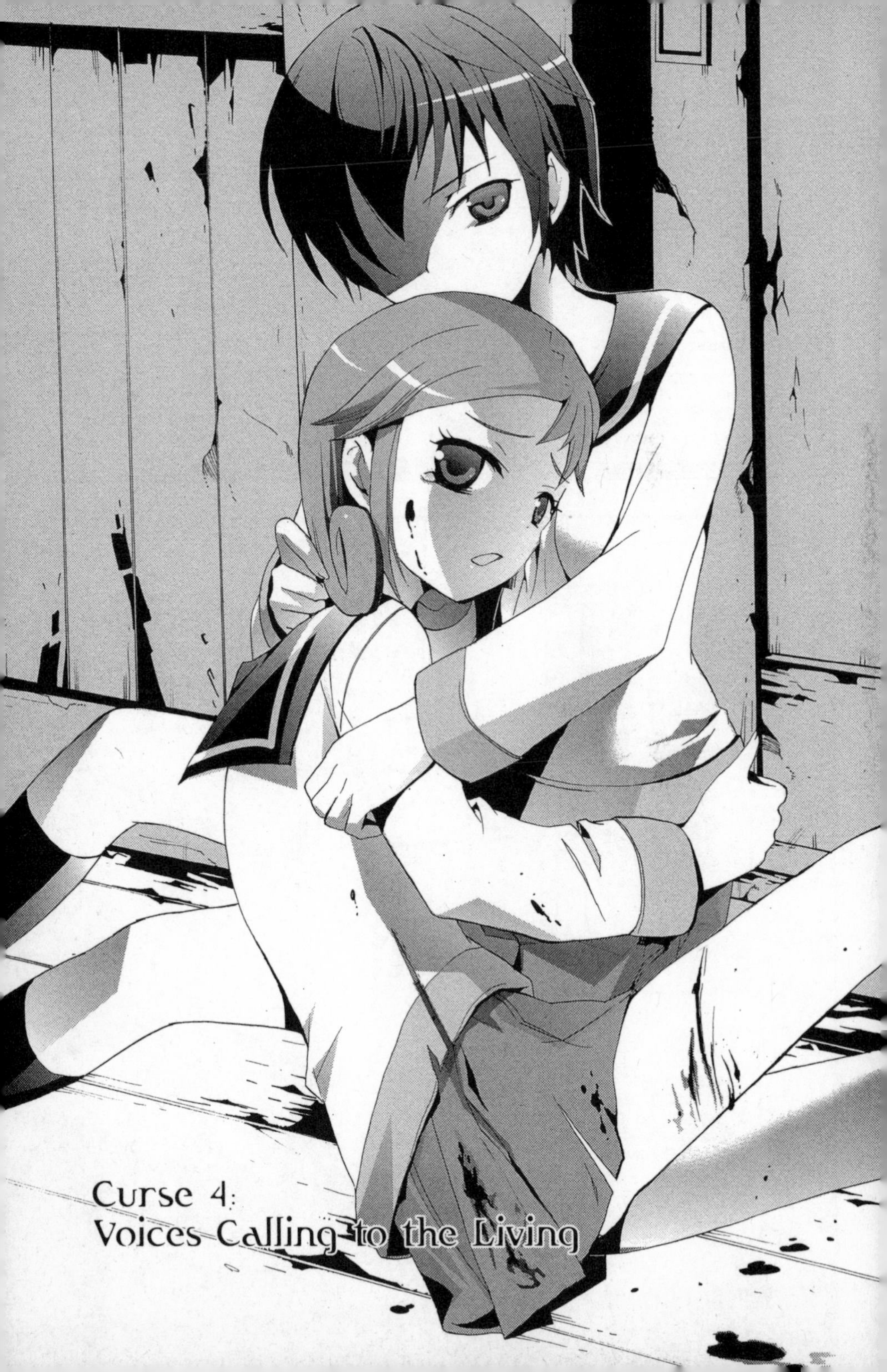
Curse 4:
Voices Calling to the Living

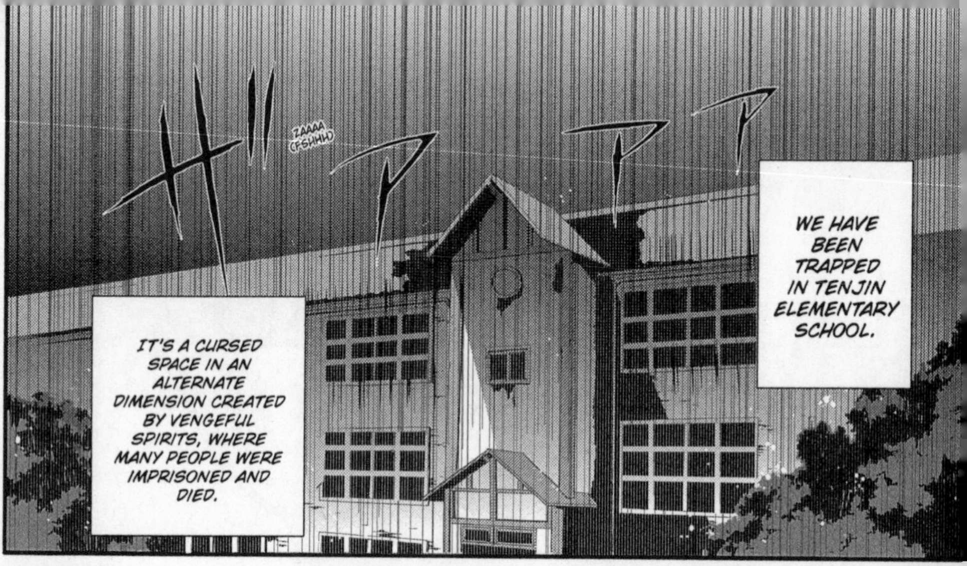
ZAAAA (FSHHH)
WE HAVE BEEN TRAPPED IN TENJIN ELEMENTARY SCHOOL.
IT'S A CURSED SPACE IN AN ALTERNATE DIMENSION CREATED BY VENGEFUL SPIRITS, WHERE MANY PEOPLE WERE IMPRISONED AND DIED.

PAPER : MON. TUE. WED. THU. FRI. SAT.

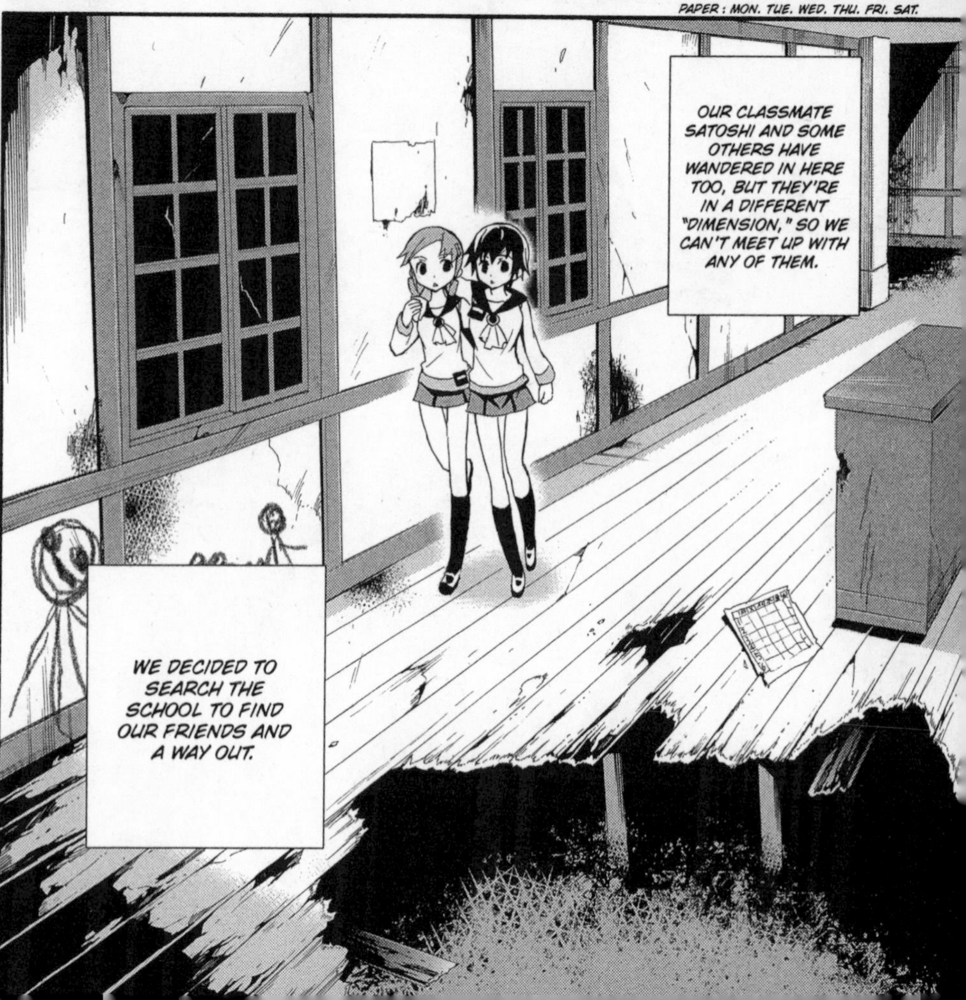
OUR CLASSMATE SATOSHI AND SOME OTHERS HAVE WANDERED IN HERE TOO, BUT THEY'RE IN A DIFFERENT "DIMENSION," SO WE CAN'T MEET UP WITH ANY OF THEM.
WE DECIDED TO SEARCH THE SCHOOL TO FIND OUR FRIENDS AND A WAY OUT.

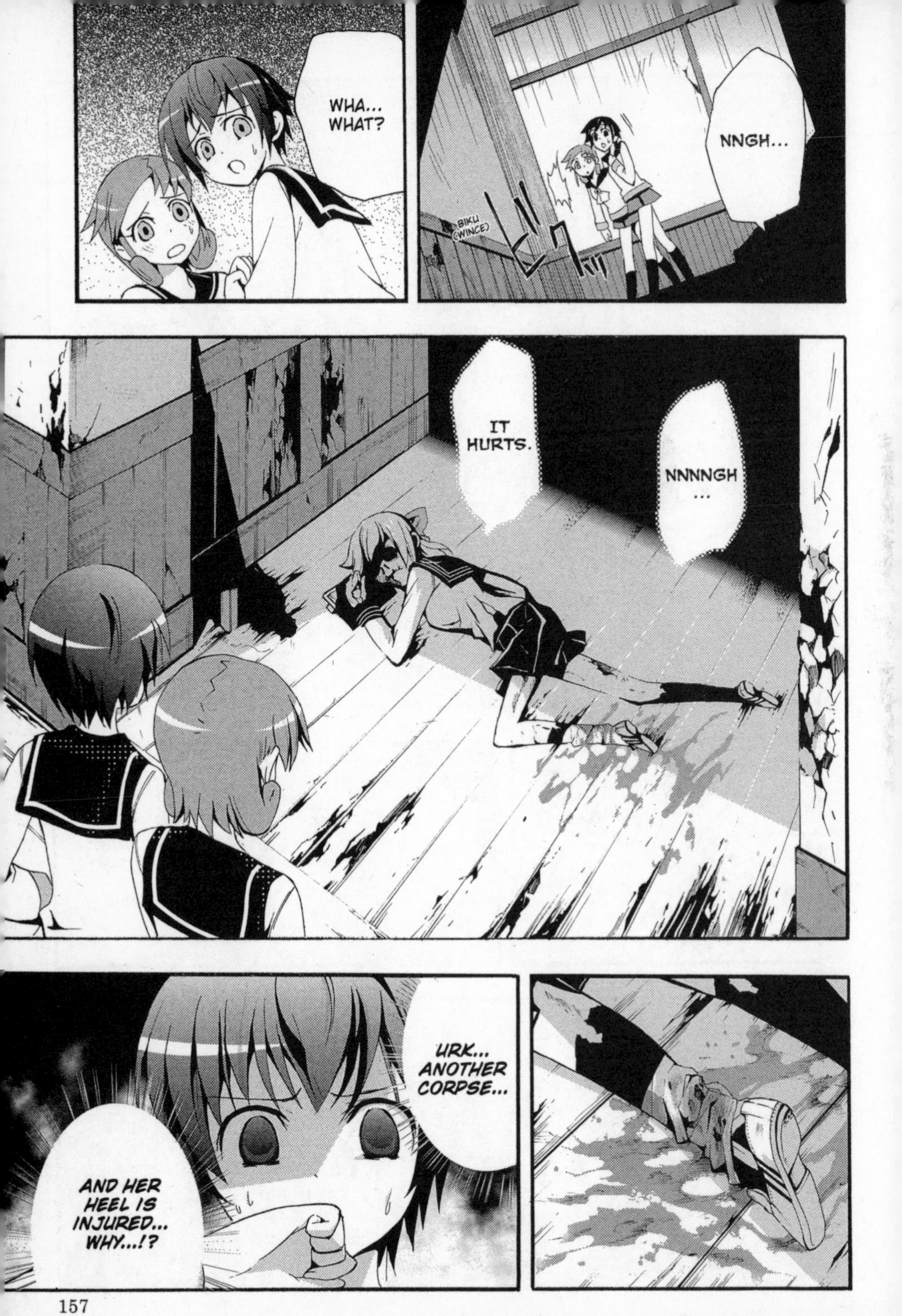
NNGH...
BIKU (WINCE)
WHA... WHAT?
NNNNGH ...
IT HURTS.
URK... ANOTHER CORPSE...
AND HER HEEL IS INJURED... WHY...!?

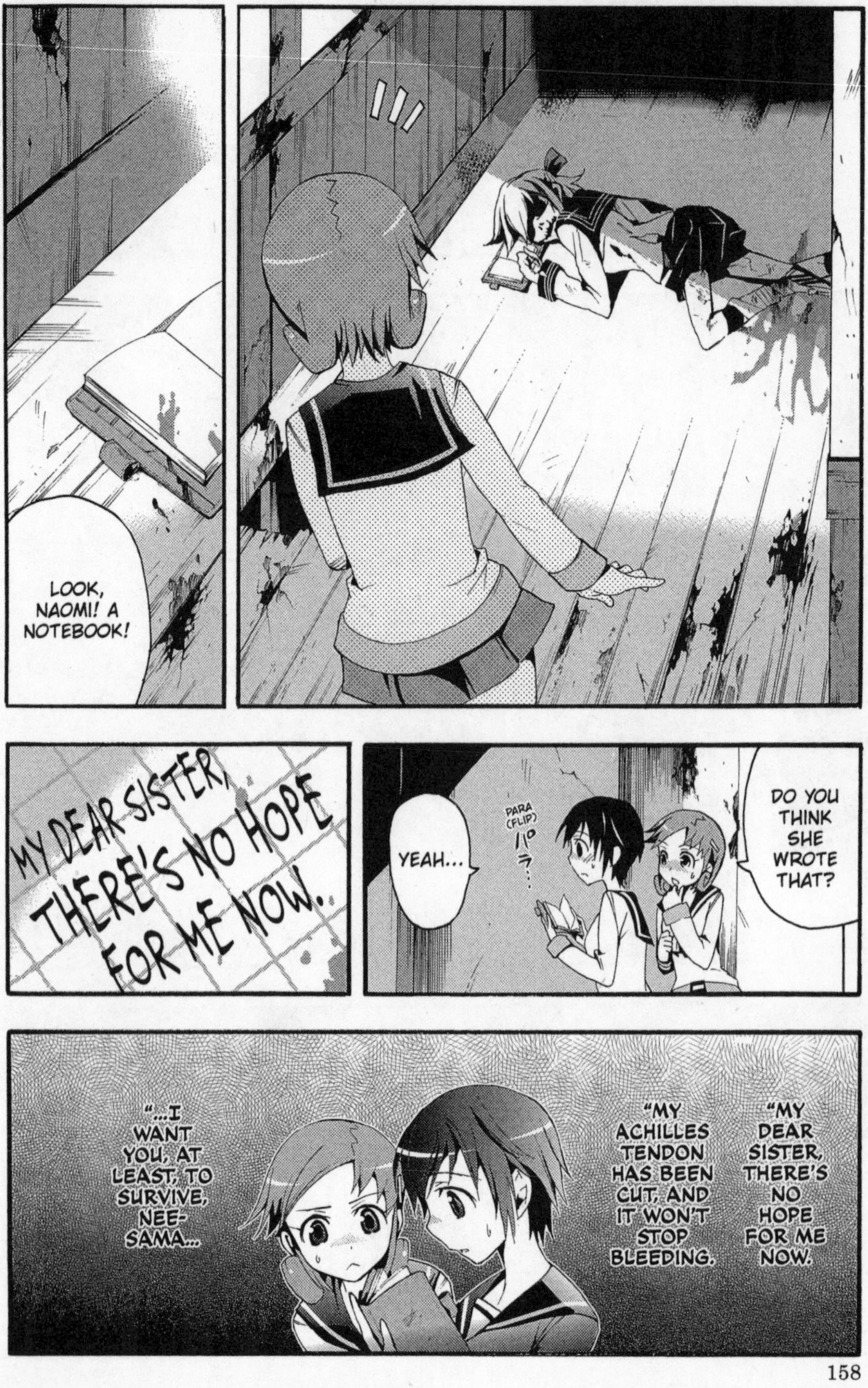
LOOK, NAOMI! A NOTEBOOK!
DO YOU THINK SHE WROTE THAT?
PARA (FLIP) パラ…
YEAH...
MY DEAR SISTER, THERE'S NO HOPE FOR ME NOW..
"MY DEAR SISTER, THERE'S NO HOPE FOR ME NOW.
"MY ACHILLES TENDON HAS BEEN CUT, AND IT WON'T STOP BLEEDING.
"...I WANT YOU, AT LEAST, TO SURVIVE, NEE-SAMA...

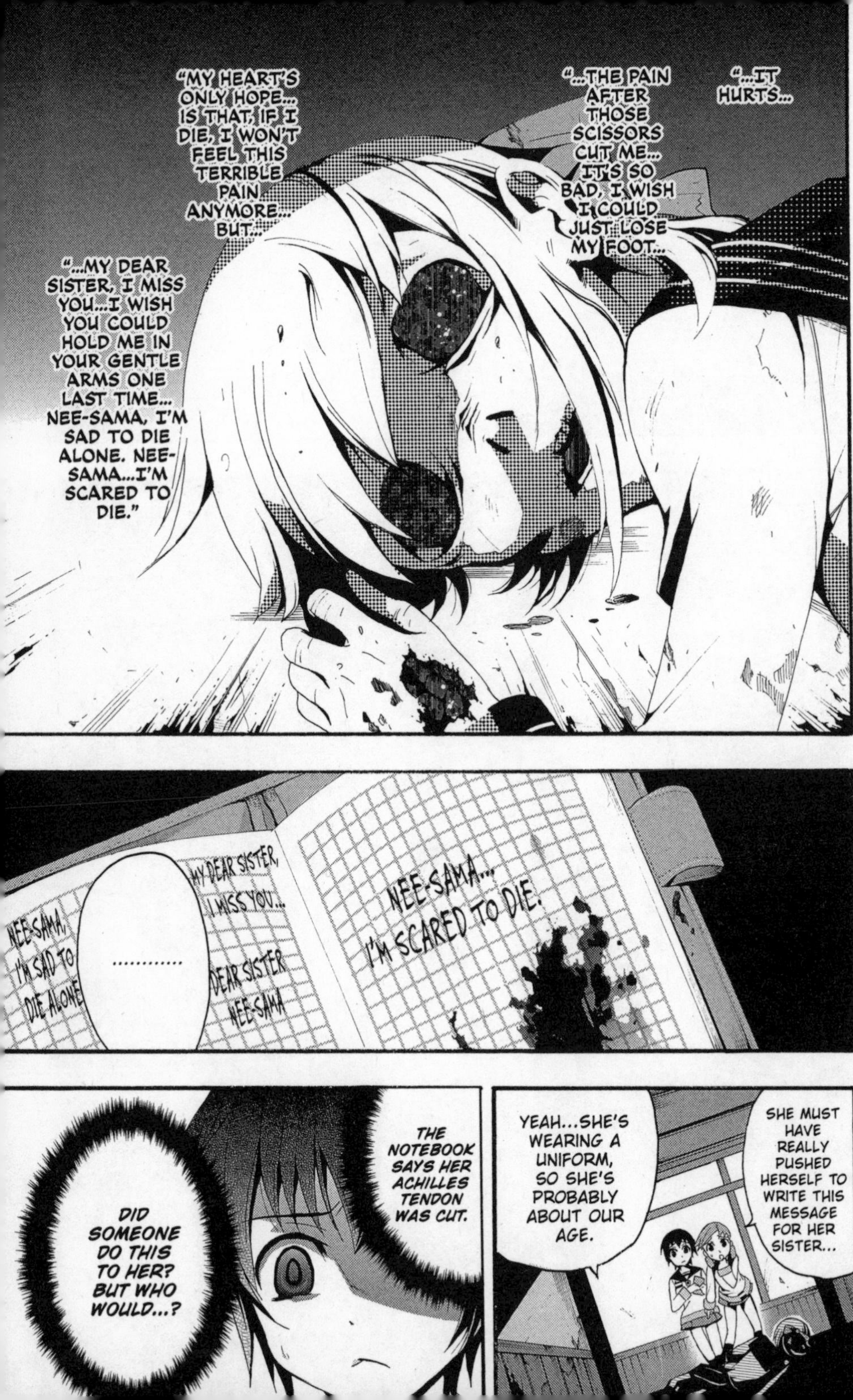
"...IT HURTS...
"...THE PAIN AFTER THOSE SCISSORS CUT ME... IT'S SO BAD, I WISH I COULD JUST LOSE MY FOOT...
"MY HEART'S ONLY HOPE... IS THAT, IF I DIE, I WON'T FEEL THIS TERRIBLE PAIN ANYMORE... BUT...
"...MY DEAR SISTER, I MISS YOU...I WISH YOU COULD HOLD ME IN YOUR GENTLE ARMS ONE LAST TIME... NEE-SAMA, I'M SAD TO DIE ALONE. NEE-SAMA...I'M SCARED TO DIE."
NEE-SAMA... I'M SCARED TO DIE.
MY DEAR SISTER, I MISS YOU...
DEAR SISTER NEE-SAMA
....
NEE-SAMA, I'M SAD TO DIE ALONE
SHE MUST HAVE REALLY PUSHED HERSELF TO WRITE THIS MESSAGE FOR HER SISTER...
YEAH...SHE'S WEARING A UNIFORM, SO SHE'S PROBABLY ABOUT OUR AGE.
THE NOTEBOOK SAYS HER ACHILLES TENDON WAS CUT.
DID SOMEONE DO THIS TO HER? BUT WHO WOULD...?

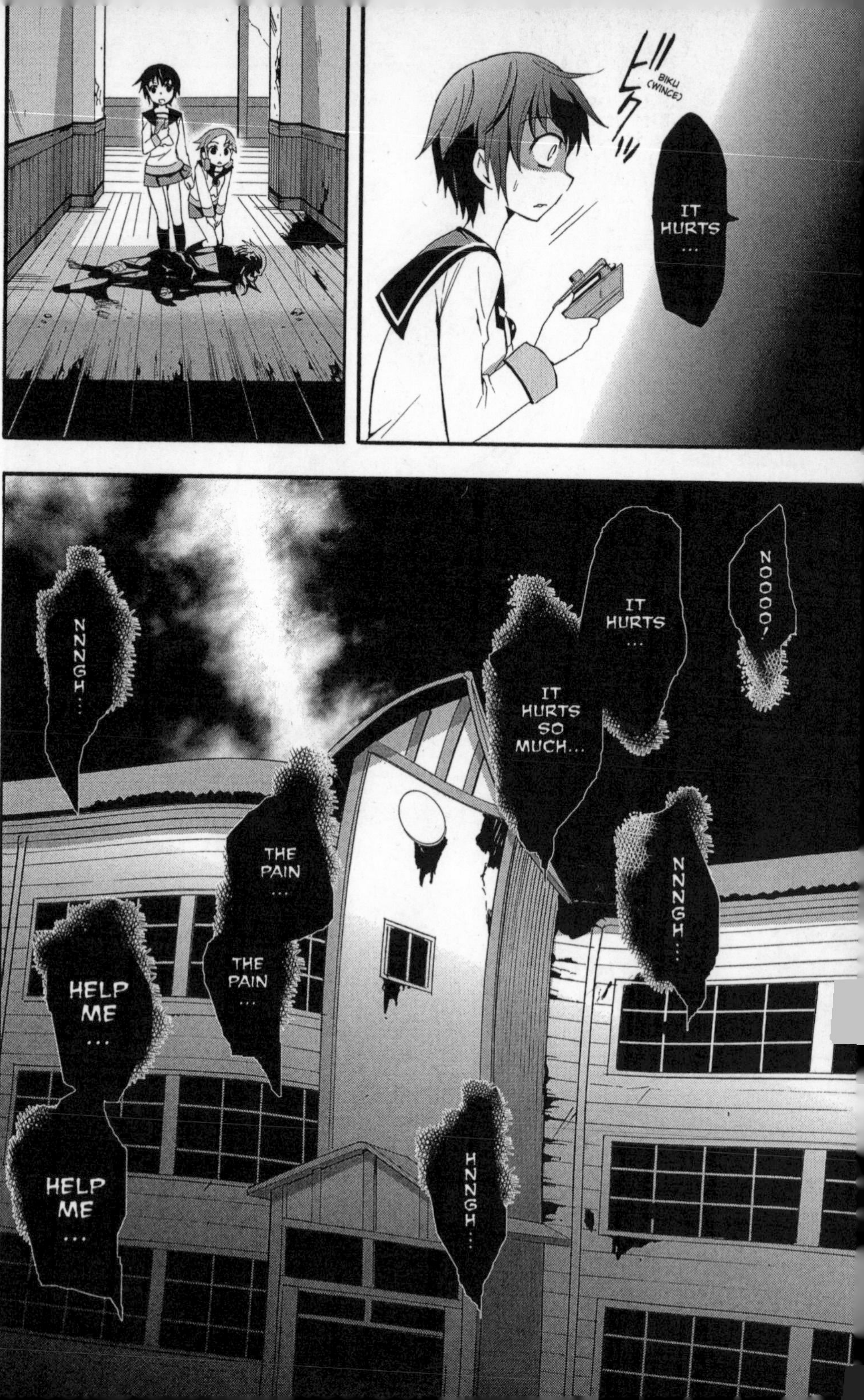
BIKU (WINCE)
IT HURTS...
NOOOO!
IT HURTS...
IT HURTS SO MUCH...
NNNGH...
NNNGH...
THE PAIN...
THE PAIN...
HNNGH...
HELP ME...
HELP ME...

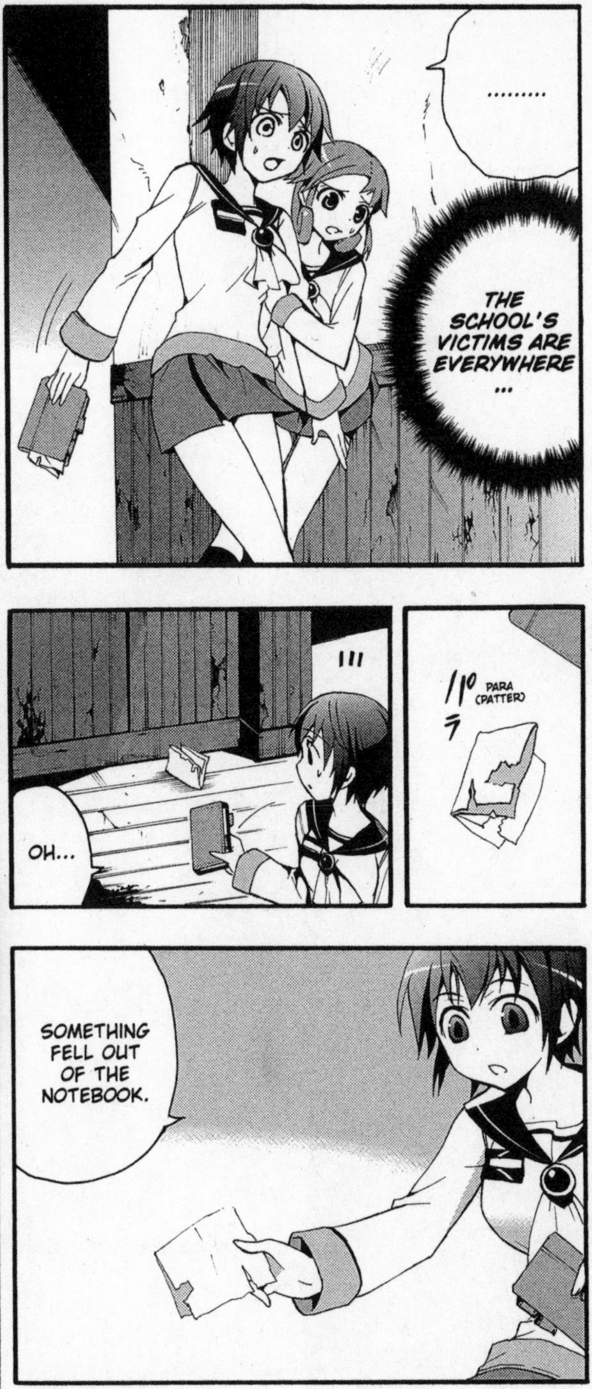
....
THE SCHOOL'S VICTIMS ARE EVERYWHERE ...
PARA (PATTER)
OH...
SOMETHING FELL OUT OF THE NOTEBOOK.

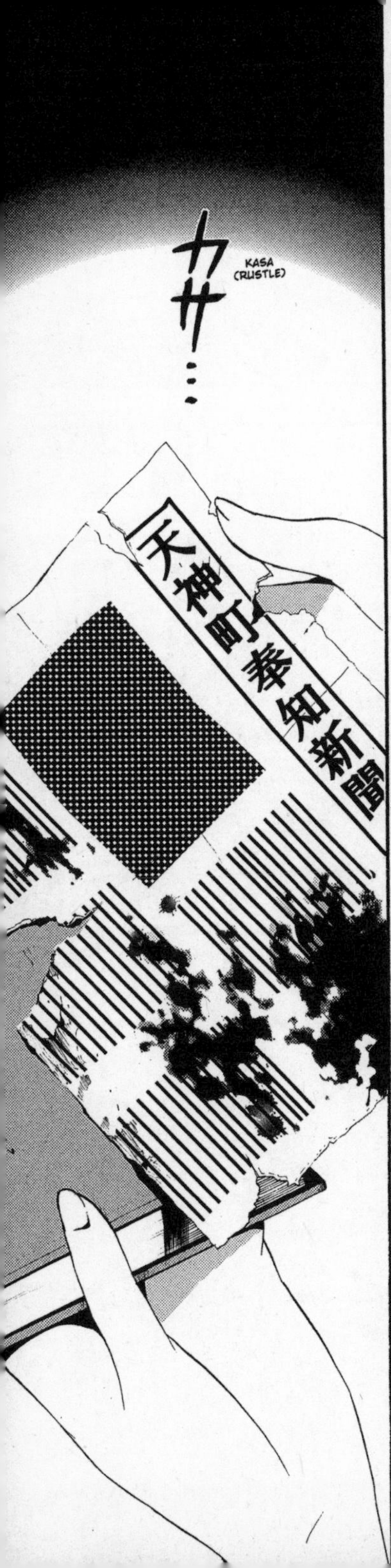
KASA (RUSTLE)
天神町奉知新聞

PAPER: TENJIN TIDINGS

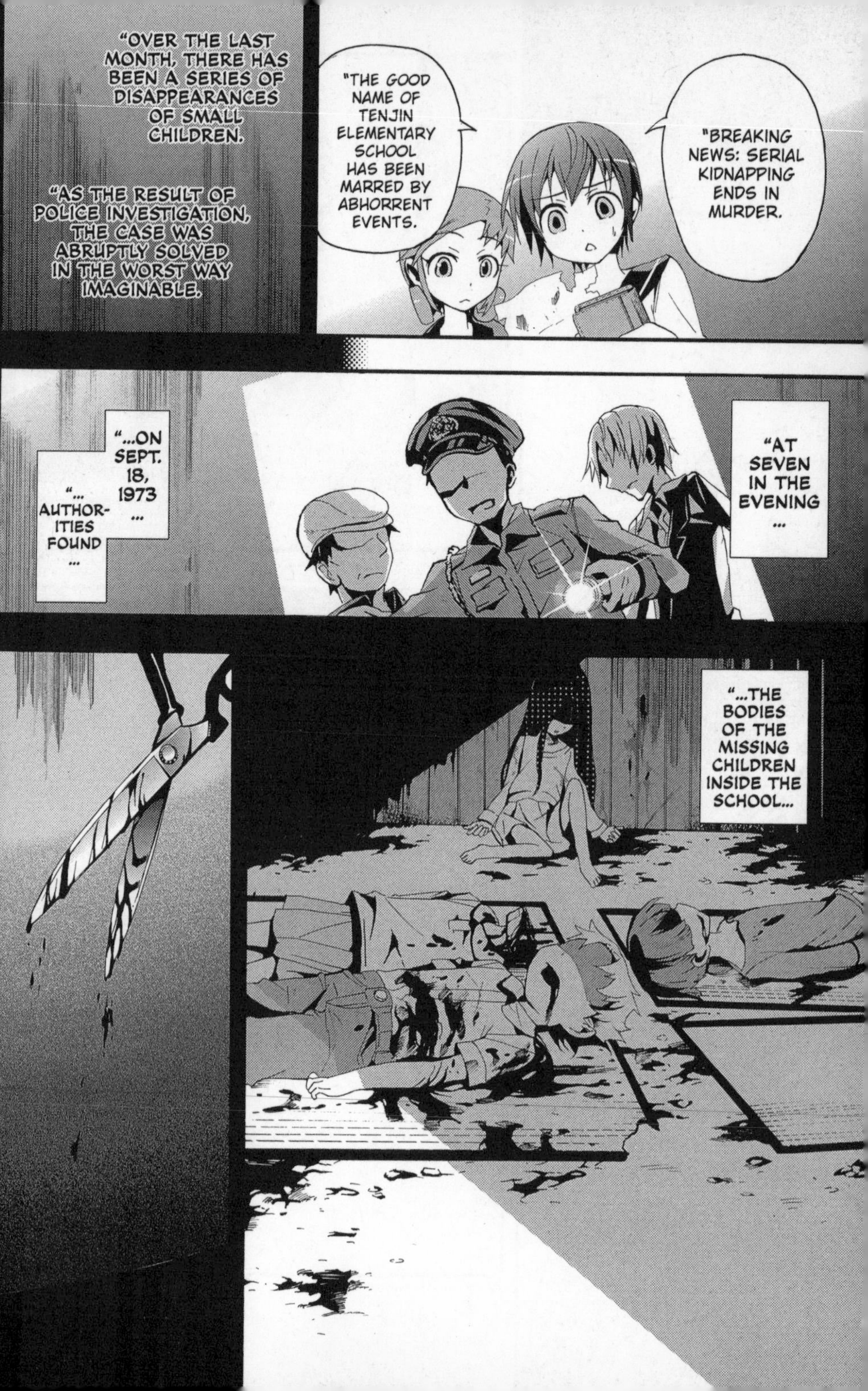
"BREAKING NEWS: SERIAL KIDNAPPING ENDS IN MURDER.
"THE GOOD NAME OF TENJIN ELEMENTARY SCHOOL HAS BEEN MARRED BY ABHORRENT EVENTS.
"OVER THE LAST MONTH, THERE HAS BEEN A SERIES OF DISAPPEARANCES OF SMALL CHILDREN.
"AS THE RESULT OF POLICE INVESTIGATION, THE CASE WAS ABRUPTLY SOLVED IN THE WORST WAY IMAGINABLE.
"AT SEVEN IN THE EVENING ...
"...ON SEPT. 18, 1973 ...
"... AUTHORITIES FOUND ...
"...THE BODIES OF THE MISSING CHILDREN INSIDE THE SCHOOL...

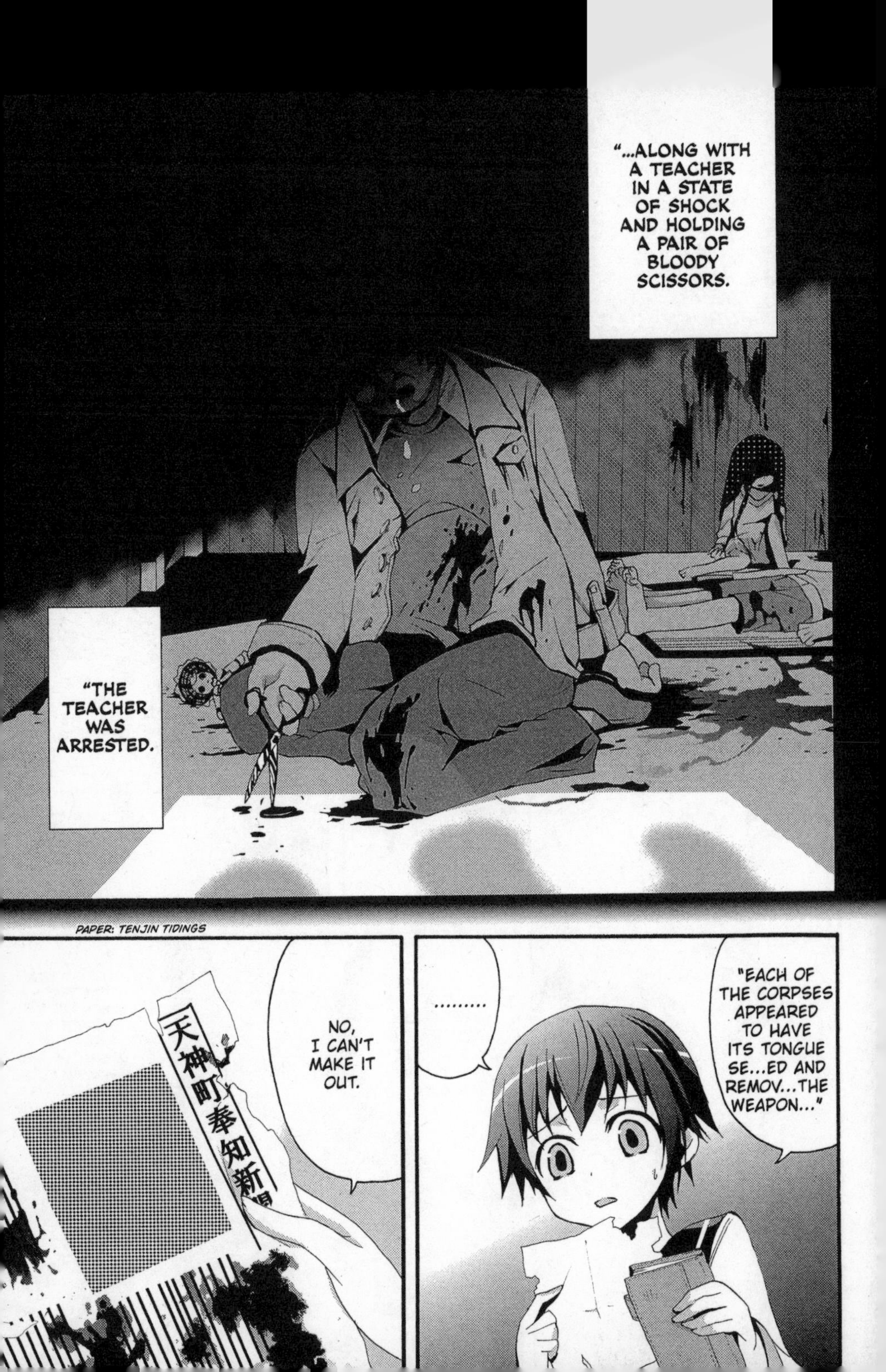
"...ALONG WITH A TEACHER IN A STATE OF SHOCK AND HOLDING A PAIR OF BLOODY SCISSORS.
"THE TEACHER WAS ARRESTED.
PAPER: TENJIN TIDINGS
"EACH OF THE CORPSES APPEARED TO HAVE ITS TONGUE SE...ED AND REMOV...THE WEAPON..."
....
NO, I CAN'T MAKE IT OUT.
天神町奉知新

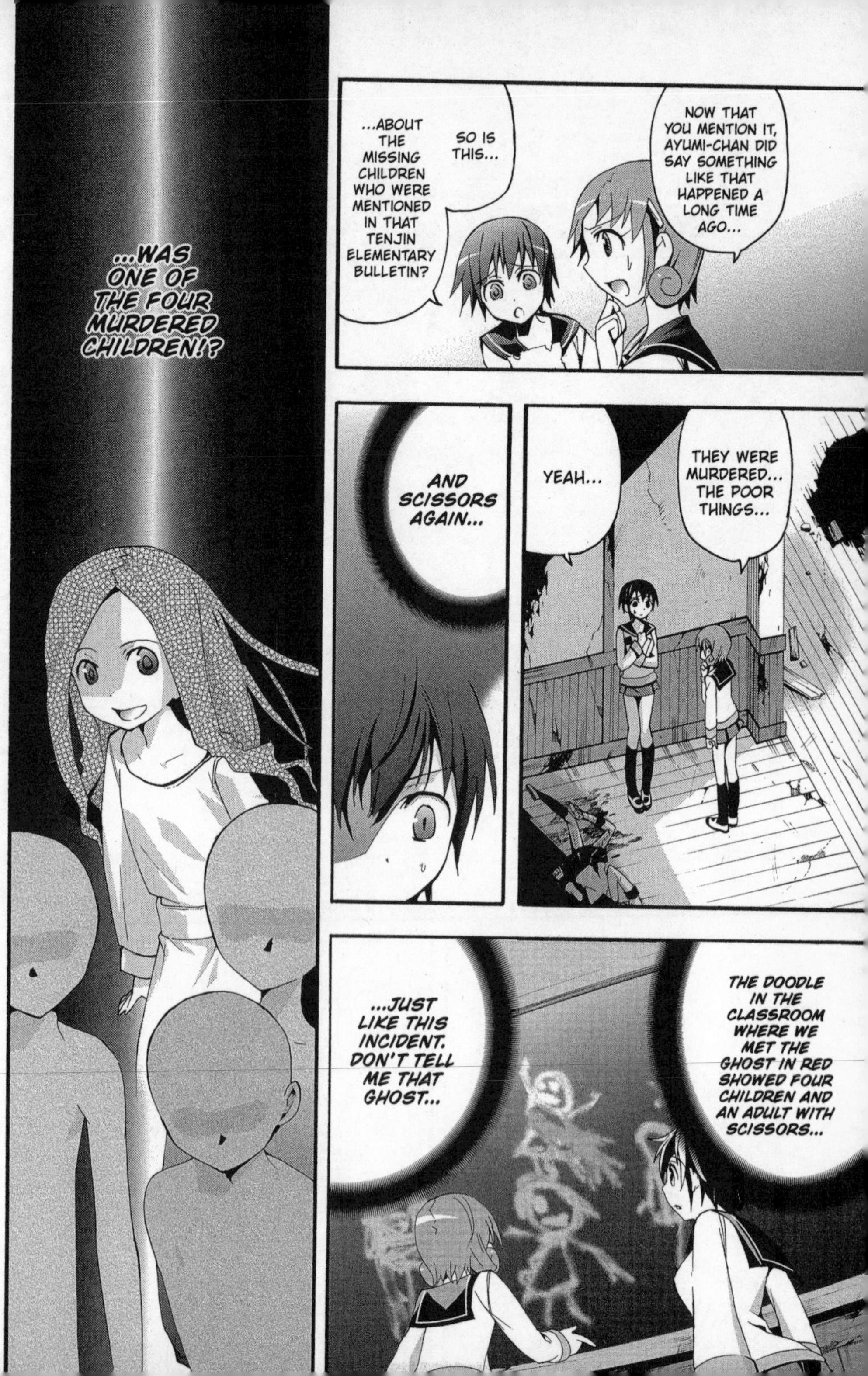
NOW THAT YOU MENTION IT, AYUMI-CHAN DID SAY SOMETHING LIKE THAT HAPPENED A LONG TIME AGO...
SO IS THIS... ...ABOUT THE MISSING CHILDREN WHO WERE MENTIONED IN THAT TENJIN ELEMENTARY BULLETIN?
THEY WERE MURDERED... THE POOR THINGS...
YEAH...
AND SCISSORS AGAIN...
THE DOODLE IN THE CLASSROOM WHERE WE MET THE GHOST IN RED SHOWED FOUR CHILDREN AND AN ADULT WITH SCISSORS...
...JUST LIKE THIS INCIDENT. DON'T TELL ME THAT GHOST...
...WAS ONE OF THE FOUR MURDERED CHILDREN!?

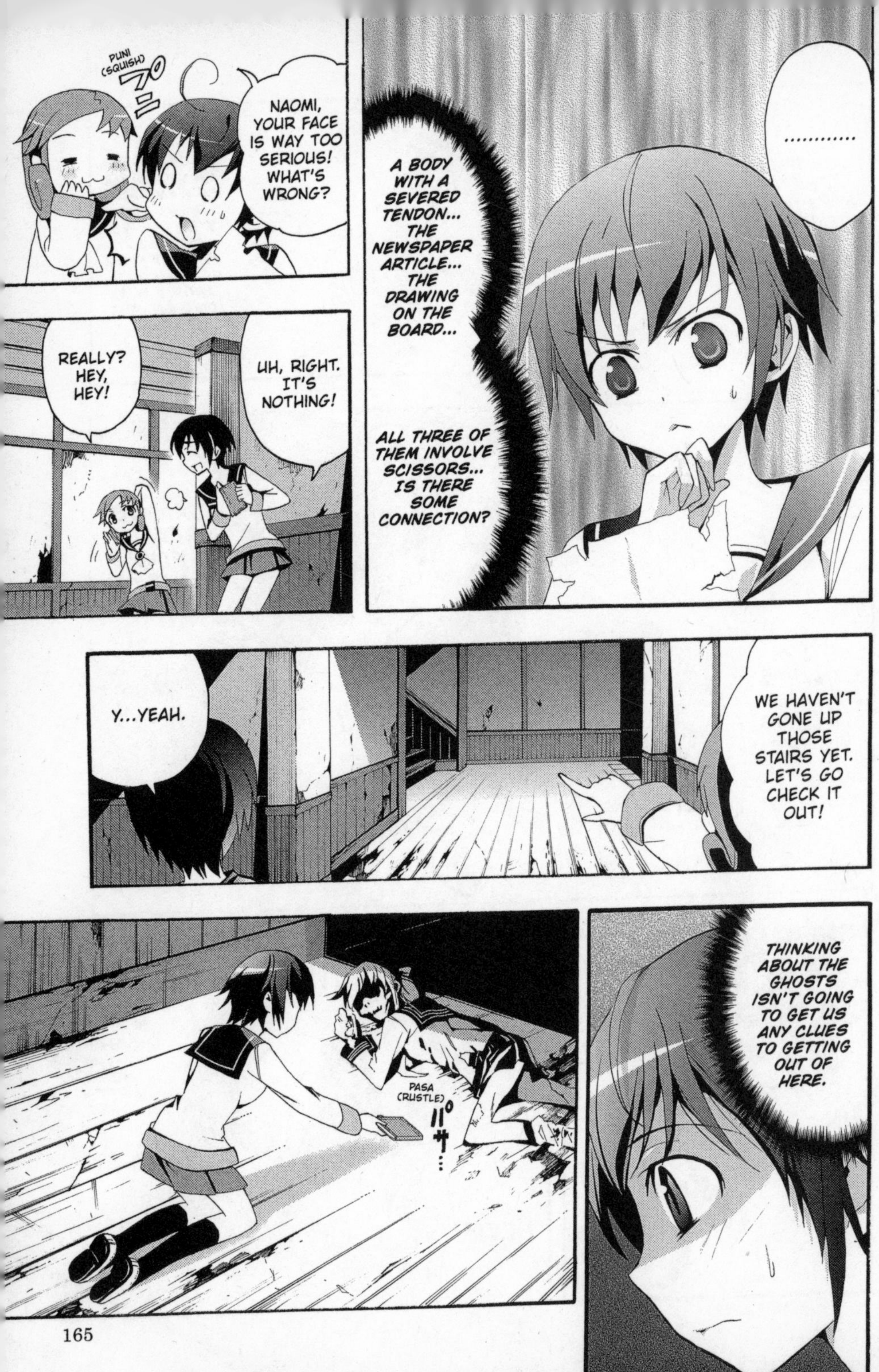
....
A BODY WITH A SEVERED TENDON... THE NEWSPAPER ARTICLE... THE DRAWING ON THE BOARD...
ALL THREE OF THEM INVOLVE SCISSORS... IS THERE SOME CONNECTION?
NAOMI, YOUR FACE IS WAY TOO SERIOUS! WHAT'S WRONG?
PUNI (SQUISH)
UH, RIGHT. IT'S NOTHING!
REALLY? HEY, HEY!
WE HAVEN'T GONE UP THOSE STAIRS YET. LET'S GO CHECK IT OUT!
Y...YEAH.
THINKING ABOUT THE GHOSTS ISN'T GOING TO GET US ANY CLUES TO GETTING OUT OF HERE.
PASA (RUSTLE)

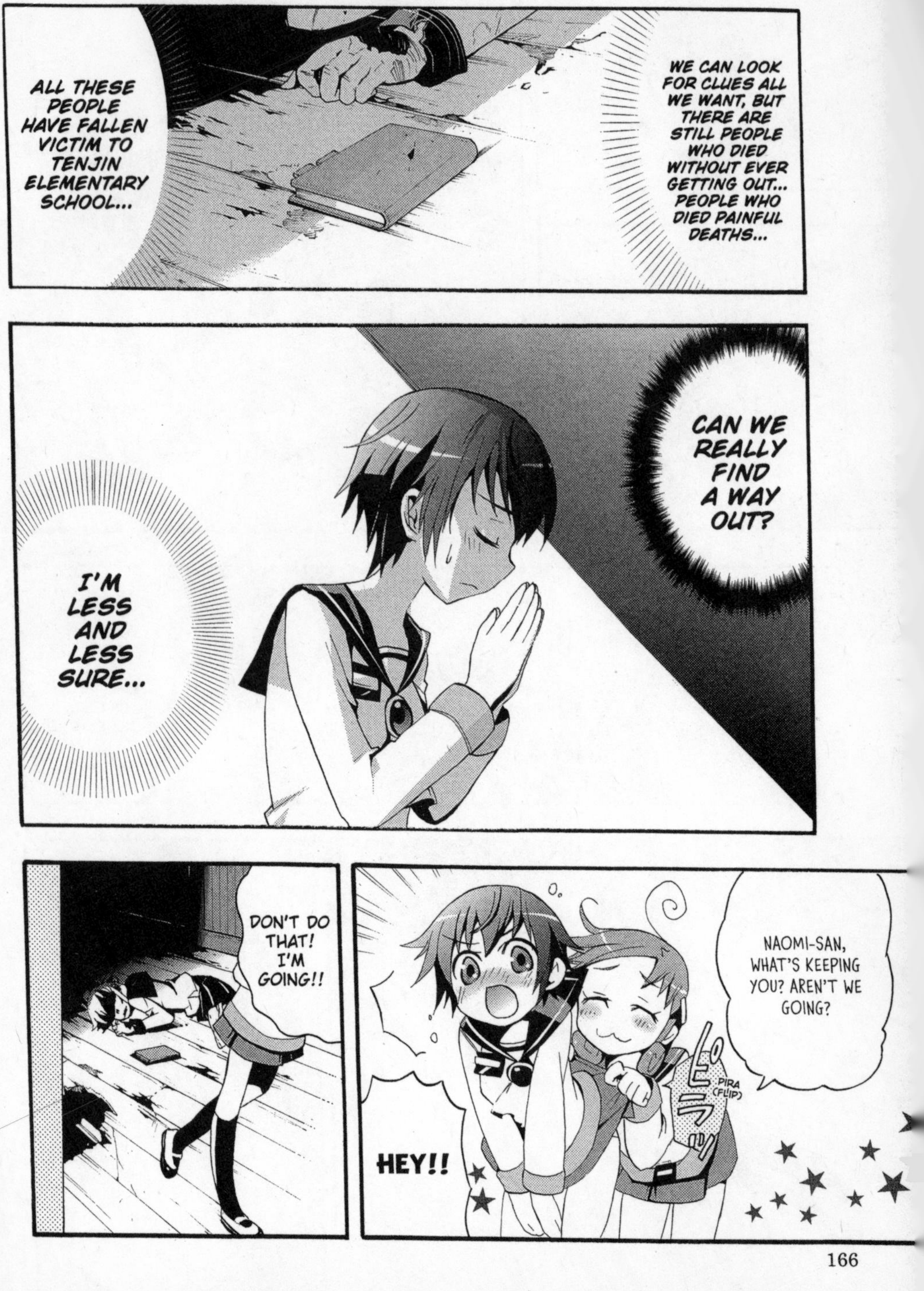
WE CAN LOOK FOR CLUES ALL WE WANT, BUT THERE ARE STILL PEOPLE WHO DIED WITHOUT EVER GETTING OUT... PEOPLE WHO DIED PAINFUL DEATHS...
ALL THESE PEOPLE HAVE FALLEN VICTIM TO TENJIN ELEMENTARY SCHOOL...
CAN WE REALLY FIND A WAY OUT?
I'M LESS AND LESS SURE...
NAOMI-SAN, WHAT'S KEEPING YOU? AREN'T WE GOING?
PIRA (FLIP)
HEY!!
DON'T DO THAT! I'M GOING!!

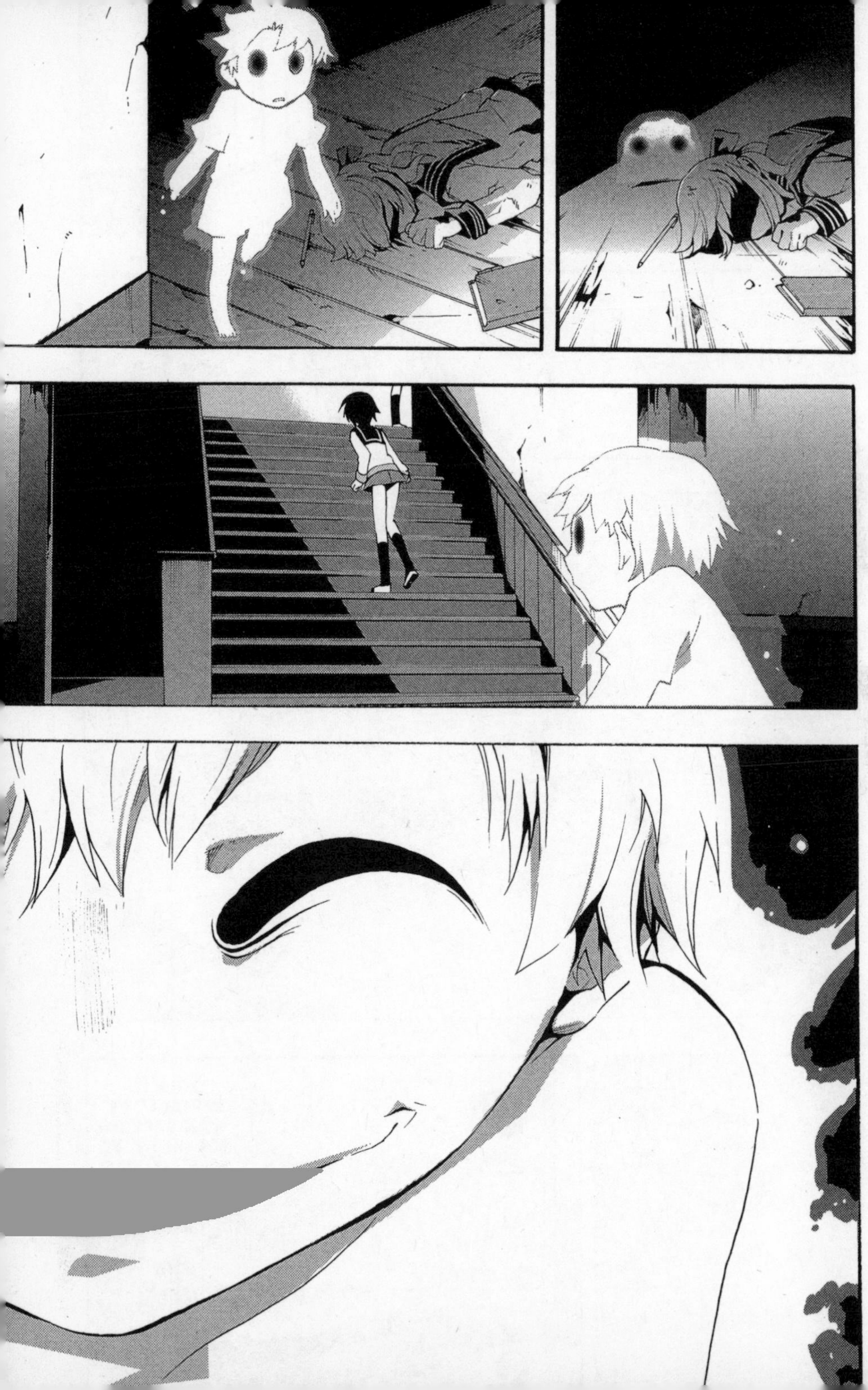

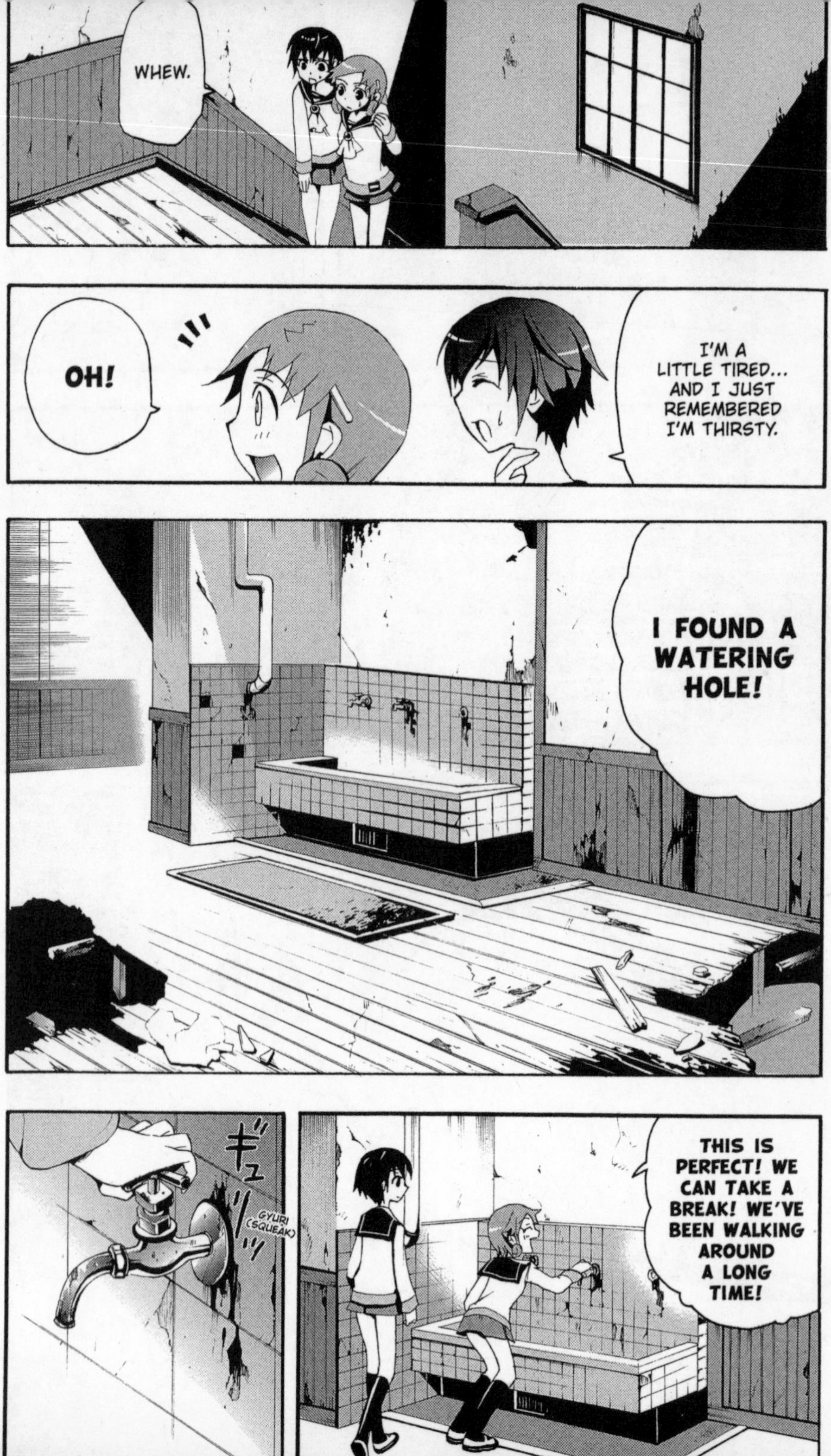
WHEW.
I'M A LITTLE TIRED... AND I JUST REMEMBERED I'M THIRSTY.
OH!
I FOUND A WATERING HOLE!
THIS IS PERFECT! WE CAN TAKE A BREAK! WE'VE BEEN WALKING AROUND A LONG TIME!
ギュリッ
GYURI (SQUEAK)

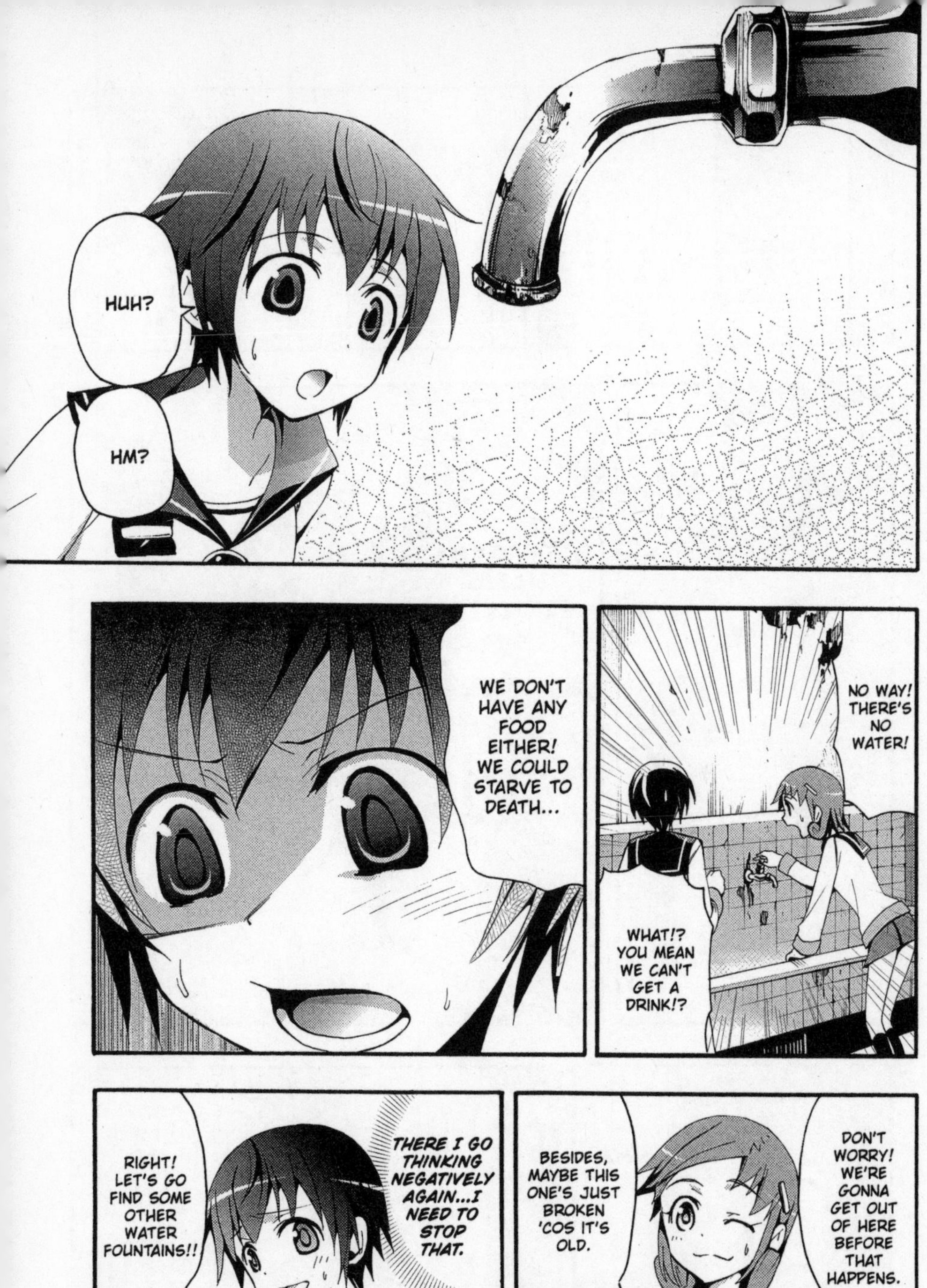
HUH?
HM?
NO WAY! THERE'S NO WATER!
WHAT!? YOU MEAN WE CAN'T GET A DRINK!?
WE DON'T HAVE ANY FOOD EITHER! WE COULD STARVE TO DEATH...
DON'T WORRY! WE'RE GONNA GET OUT OF HERE BEFORE THAT HAPPENS.
BESIDES, MAYBE THIS ONE'S JUST BROKEN 'COS IT'S OLD.
THERE I GO THINKING NEGATIVELY AGAIN...I NEED TO STOP THAT.
RIGHT! LET'S GO FIND SOME OTHER WATER FOUNTAINS!!

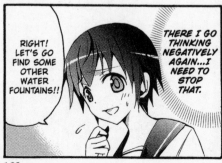

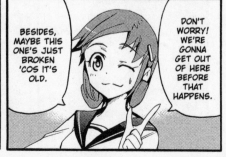

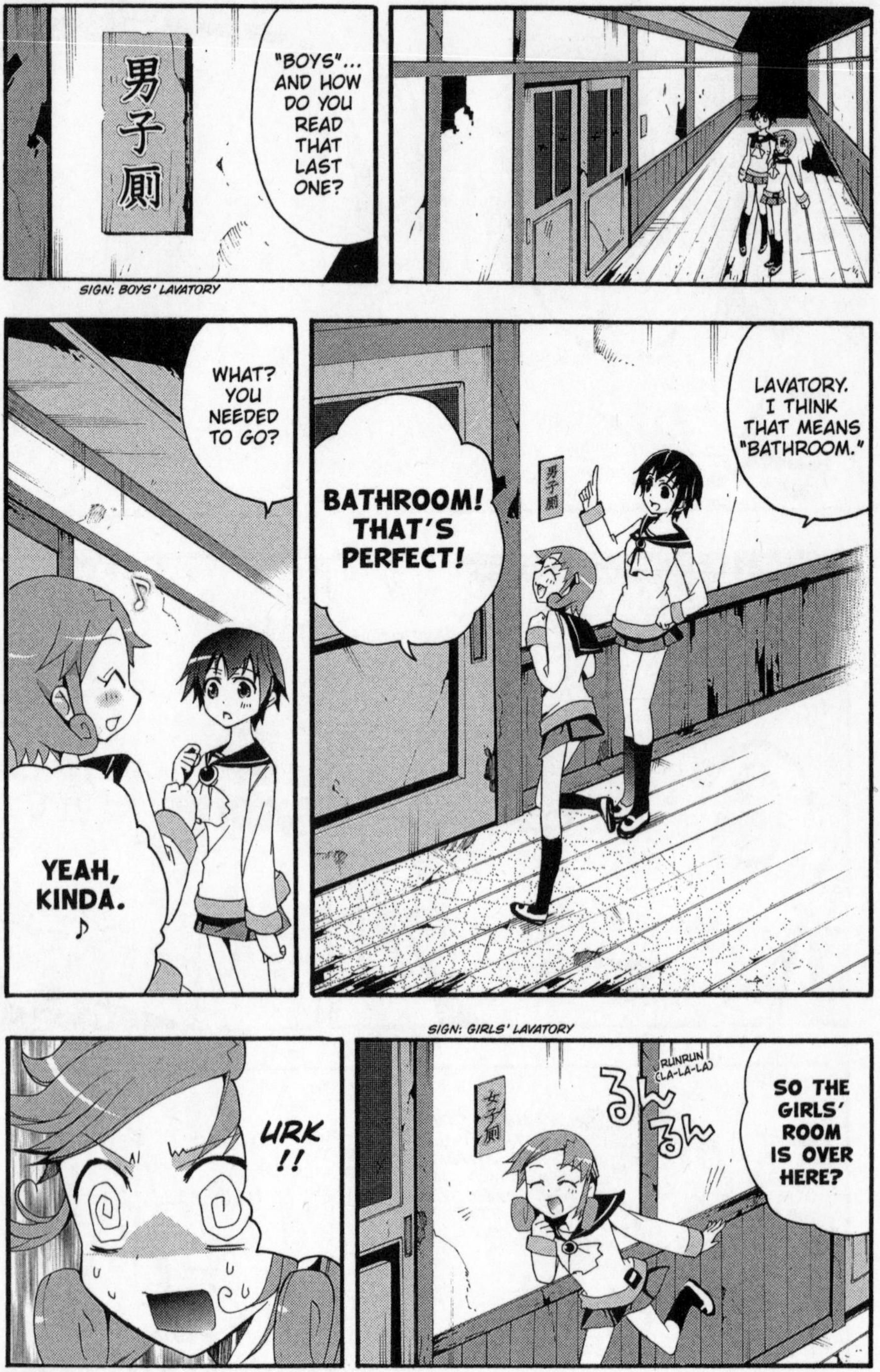
男子厠
"BOYS"... AND HOW DO YOU READ THAT LAST ONE?
SIGN: BOYS' LAVATORY
LAVATORY. I THINK THAT MEANS "BATHROOM."
男子厠
BATHROOM! THAT'S PERFECT!
WHAT? YOU NEEDED TO GO?
YEAH, KINDA. ♪
SIGN: GIRLS' LAVATORY
SO THE GIRLS' ROOM IS OVER HERE?
RUNRUN (LA-LA-LA)
るんるん
女子厠
URK !!

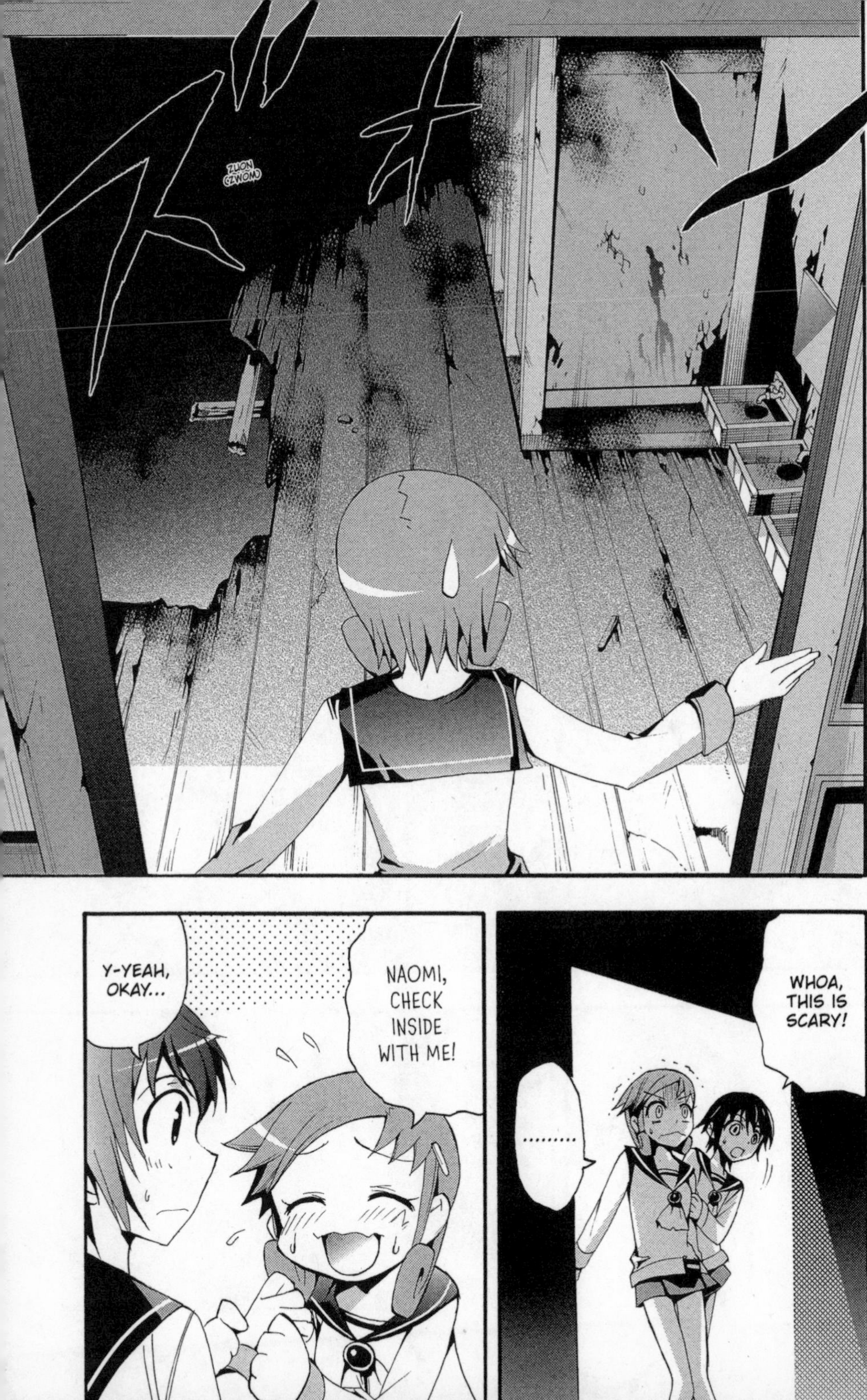
ZUON (ZWOM)
WHOA, THIS IS SCARY!
....
NAOMI, CHECK INSIDE WITH ME!
Y-YEAH, OKAY...

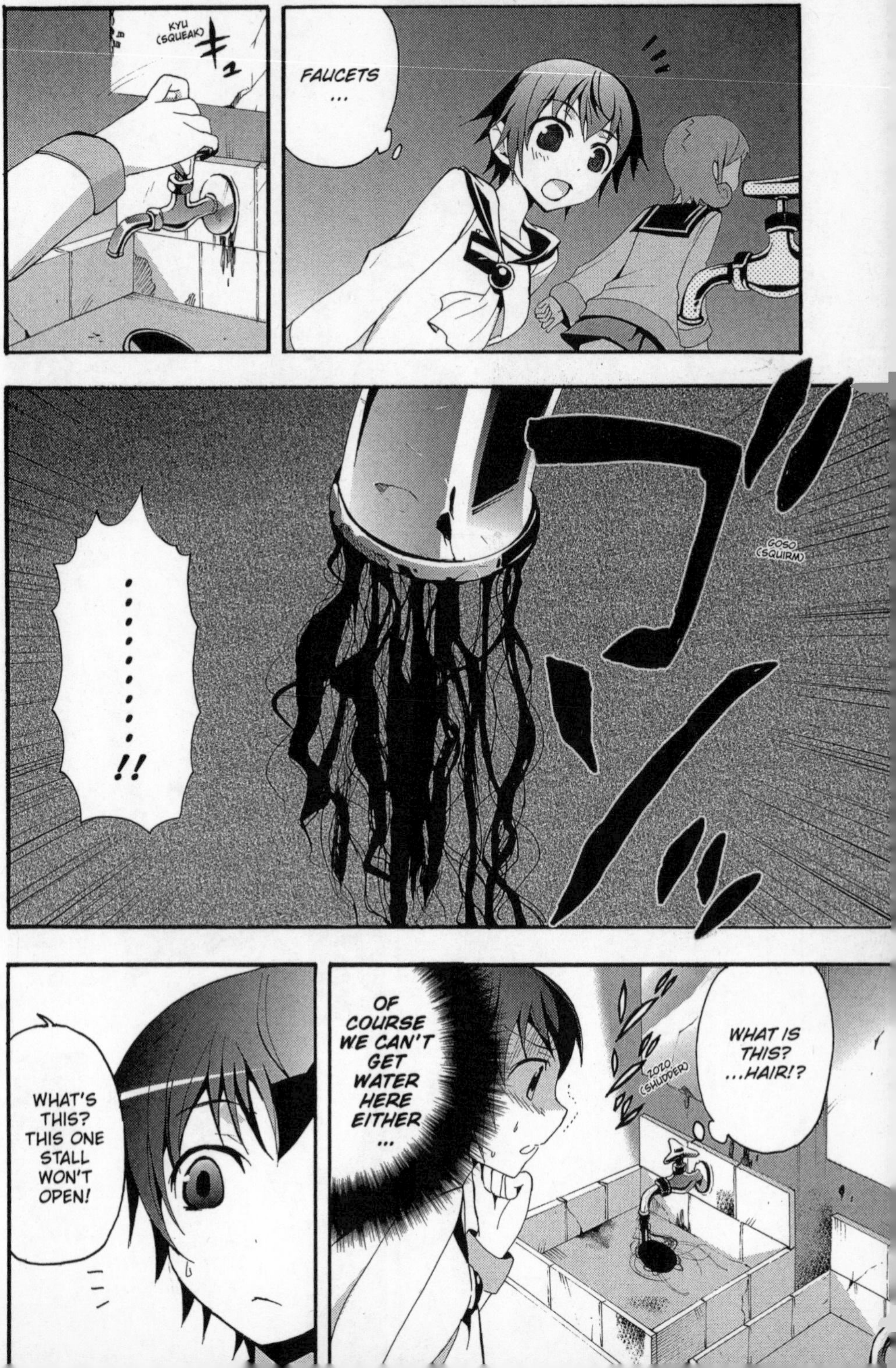
FAUCETS ...
KYU (SQUEAK)
GOSO (SQUIRM)
........!!
WHAT IS THIS? ...HAIR!?
ZOZO (SHUDDER)
OF COURSE WE CAN'T GET WATER HERE EITHER ...
WHAT'S THIS? THIS ONE STALL WON'T OPEN!

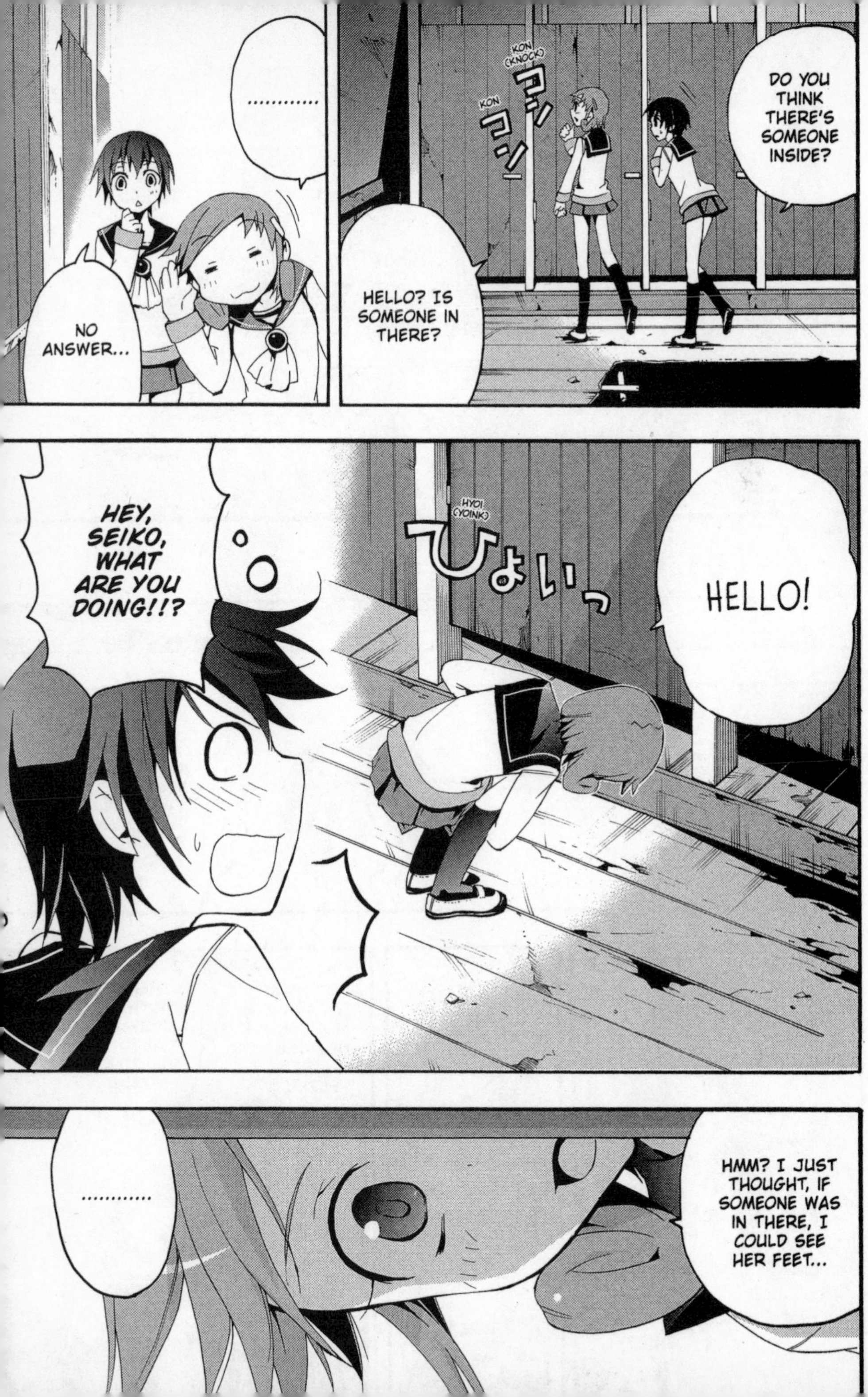
DO YOU THINK THERE'S SOMEONE INSIDE?
KON (KNOCK)
KON
HELLO? IS SOMEONE IN THERE?
....
NO ANSWER...
HELLO!
HYO! (YOINK)
ひょいっ
HEY, SEIKO, WHAT ARE YOU DOING!!?
HMM? I JUST THOUGHT, IF SOMEONE WAS IN THERE, I COULD SEE HER FEET...
....

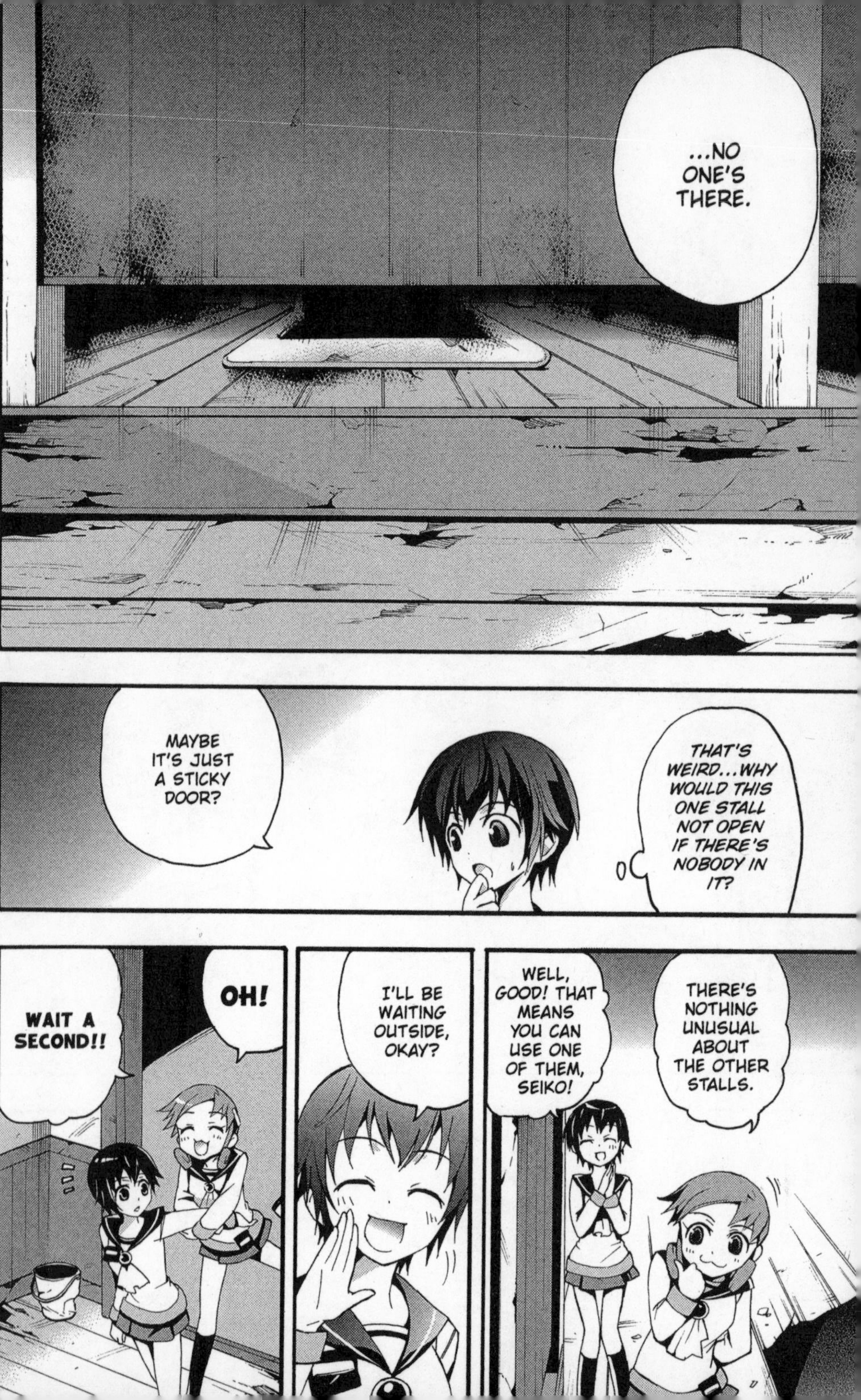
...NO ONE'S THERE.
THAT'S WEIRD...WHY WOULD THIS ONE STALL NOT OPEN IF THERE'S NOBODY IN IT?
MAYBE IT'S JUST A STICKY DOOR?
THERE'S NOTHING UNUSUAL ABOUT THE OTHER STALLS.
WELL, GOOD! THAT MEANS YOU CAN USE ONE OF THEM, SEIKO!
I'LL BE WAITING OUTSIDE, OKAY?
OH!
WAIT A SECOND!!

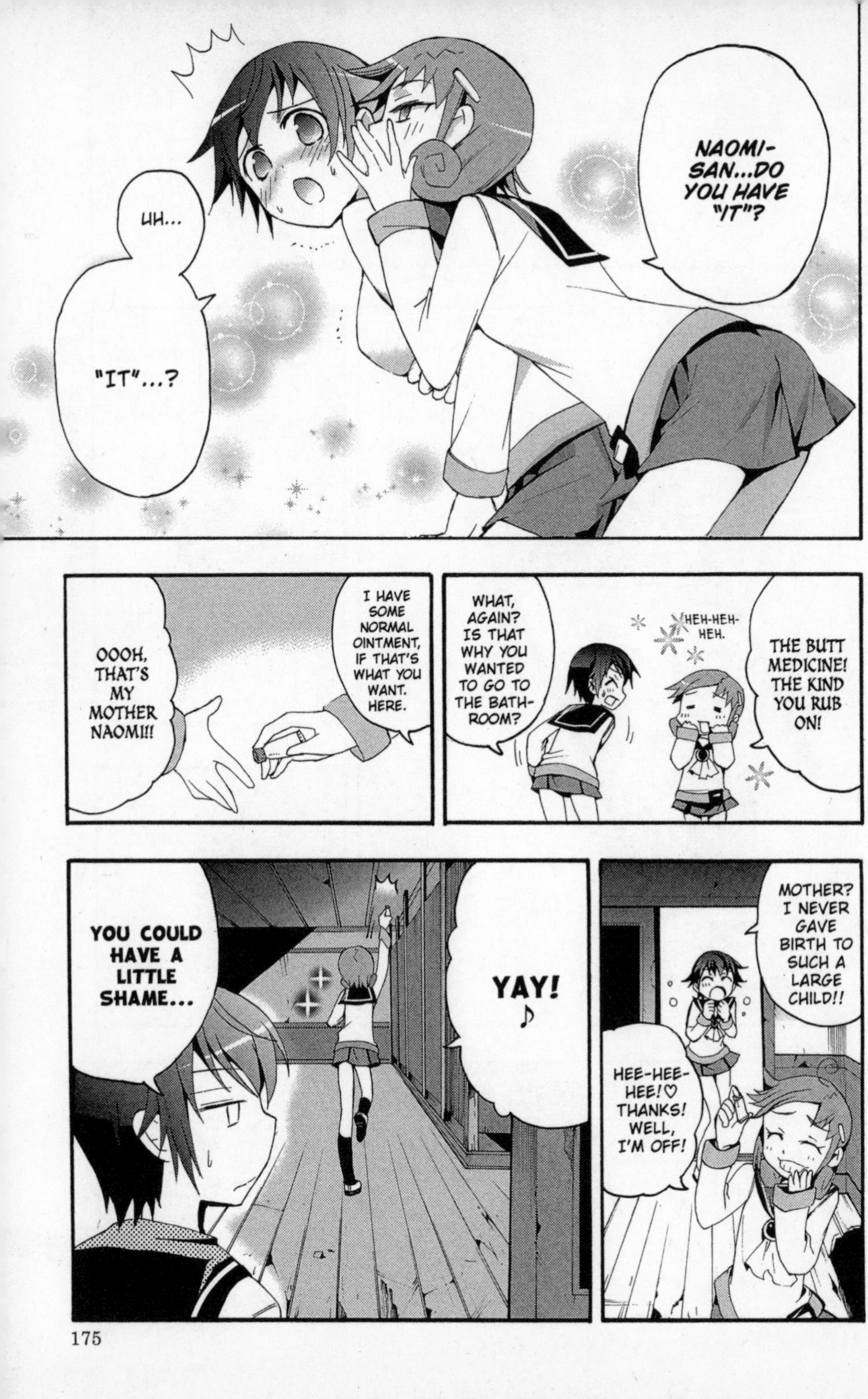
NAOMI-SAN...DO YOU HAVE "IT"?
UH...
"IT"...?
THE BUTT MEDICINE! THE KIND YOU RUB ON!
HEH-HEH-HEH.
WHAT, AGAIN? IS THAT WHY YOU WANTED TO GO TO THE BATHROOM?
I HAVE SOME NORMAL OINTMENT, IF THAT'S WHAT YOU WANT. HERE.
OOOH, THAT'S MY MOTHER NAOMI!!
MOTHER? I NEVER GAVE BIRTH TO SUCH A LARGE CHILD!!
HEE-HEE-HEE!♡ THANKS! WELL, I'M OFF!
YAY! ♪
YOU COULD HAVE A LITTLE SHAME...

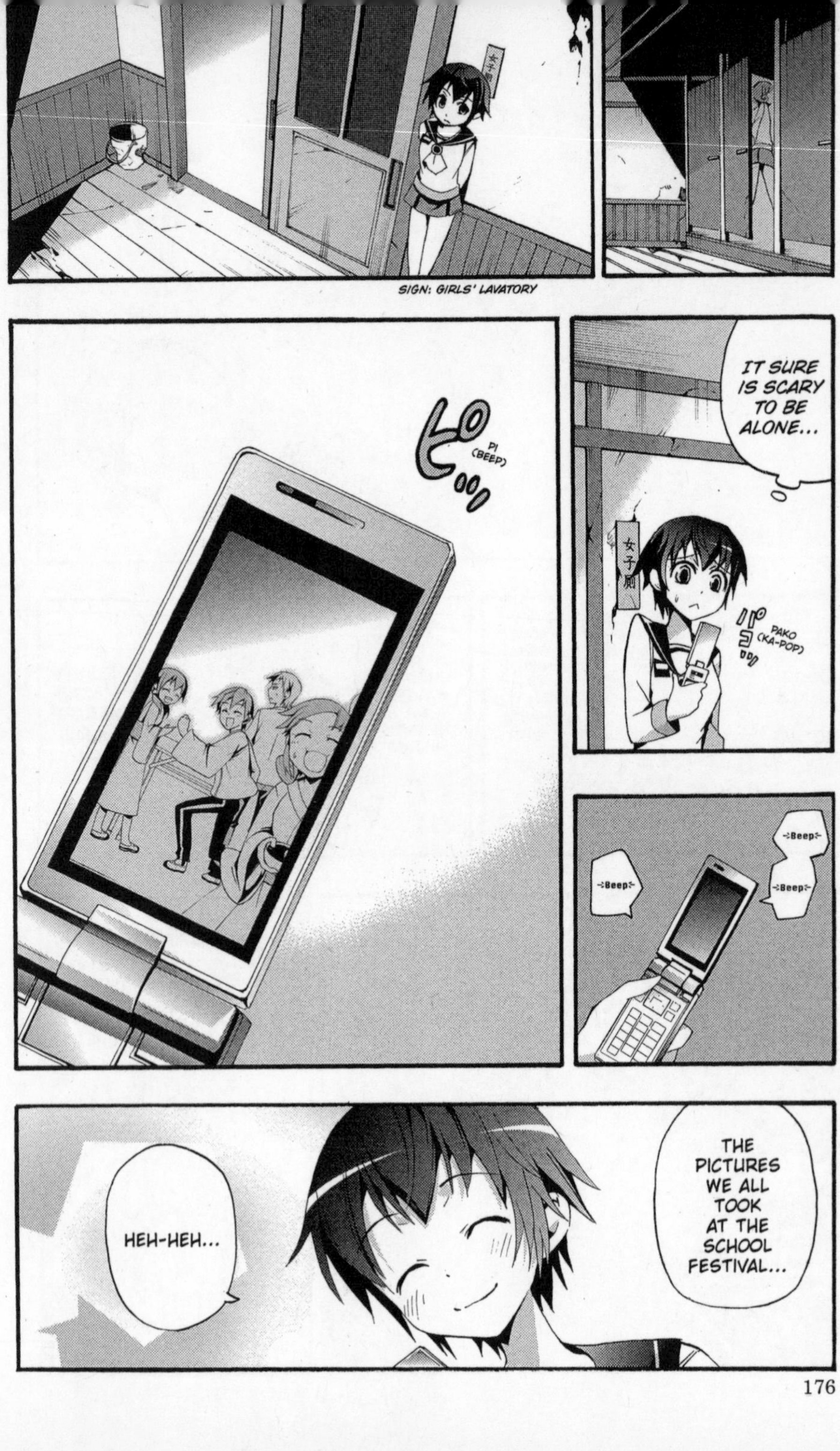
SIGN: GIRLS' LAVATORY
IT SURE IS SCARY TO BE ALONE...
PAKO (KA-POP)
Beep
Beep
Beep
PI (BEEP)
THE PICTURES WE ALL TOOK AT THE SCHOOL FESTIVAL...
HEH-HEH...

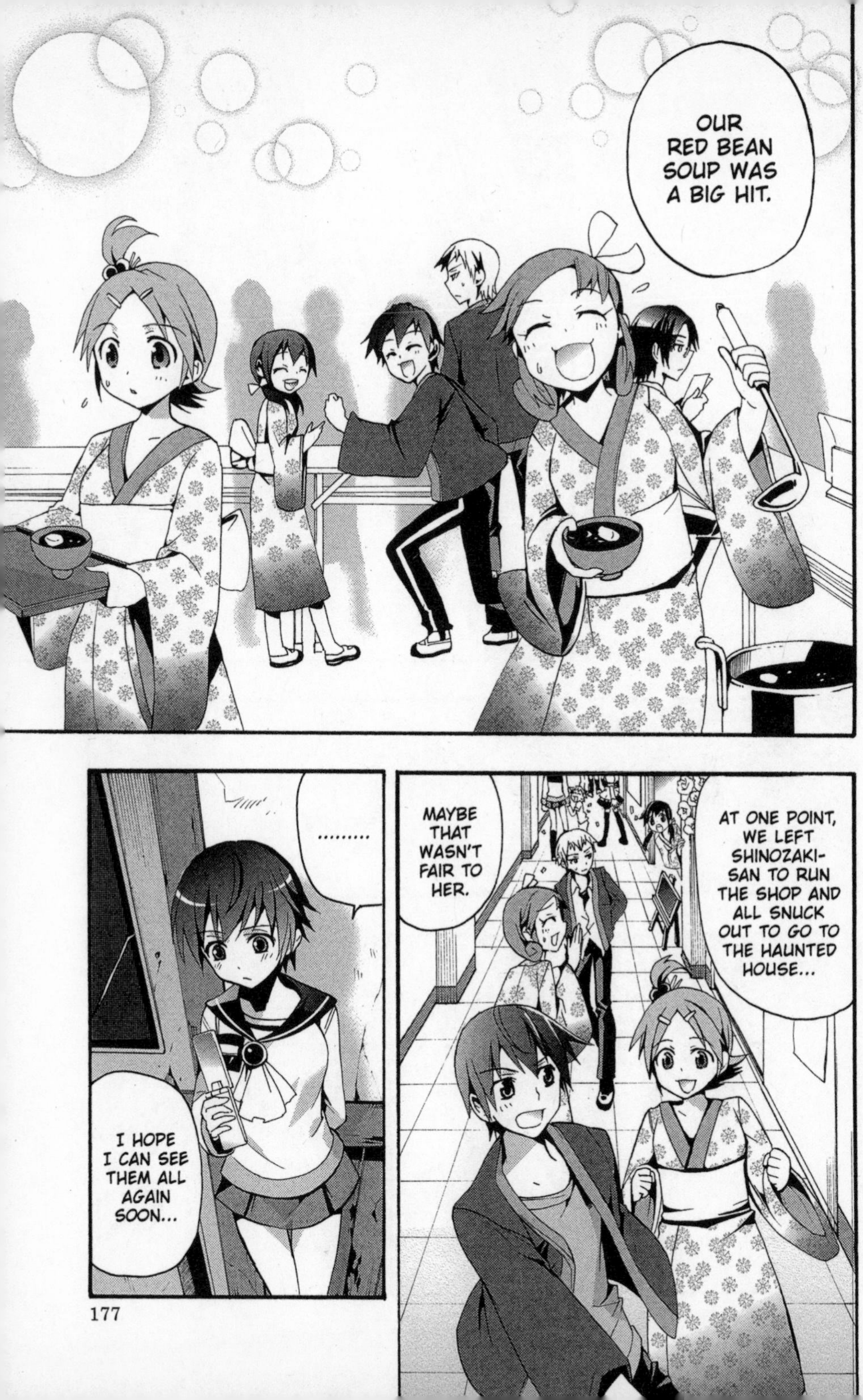
OUR RED BEAN SOUP WAS A BIG HIT.
AT ONE POINT, WE LEFT SHINOZAKI-SAN TO RUN THE SHOP AND ALL SNUCK OUT TO GO TO THE HAUNTED HOUSE...
MAYBE THAT WASN'T FAIR TO HER.
....
I HOPE I CAN SEE THEM ALL AGAIN SOON...

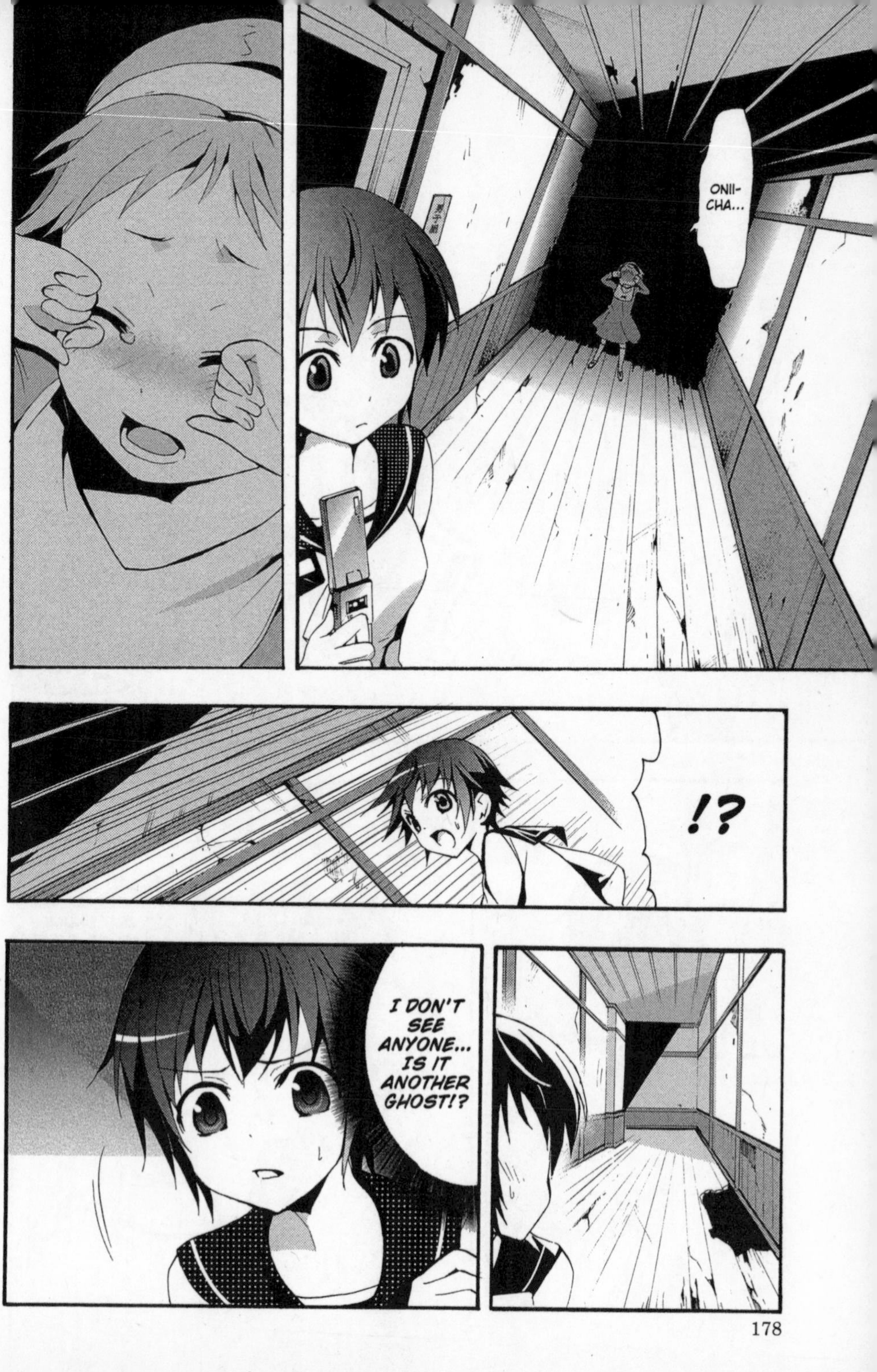
ONII-CHA...
!?
I DON'T SEE ANYONE... IS IT ANOTHER GHOST!?

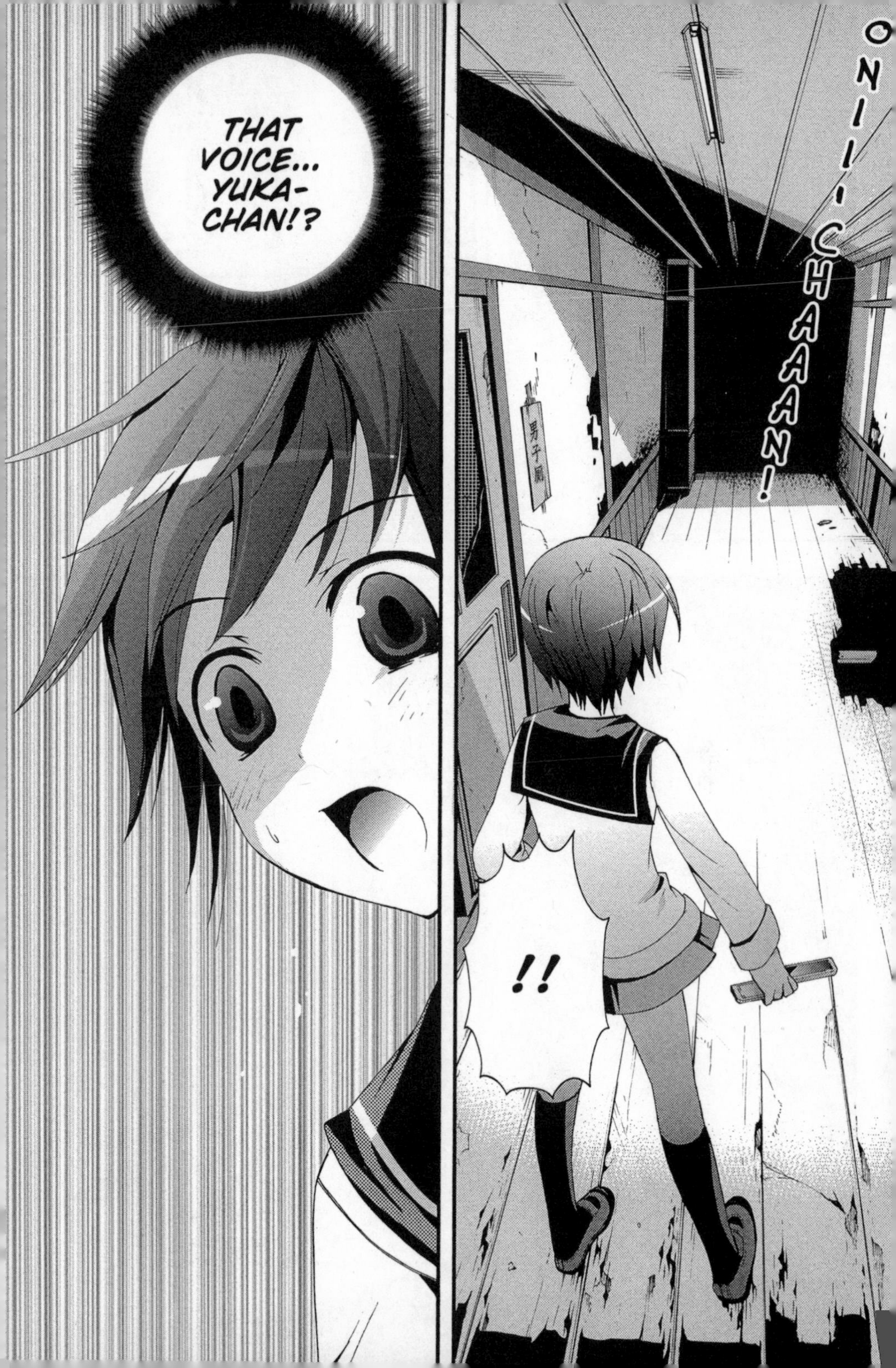
ONII-CHAAAAAN!
男子厠
!!
THAT VOICE... YUKA-CHAN!?

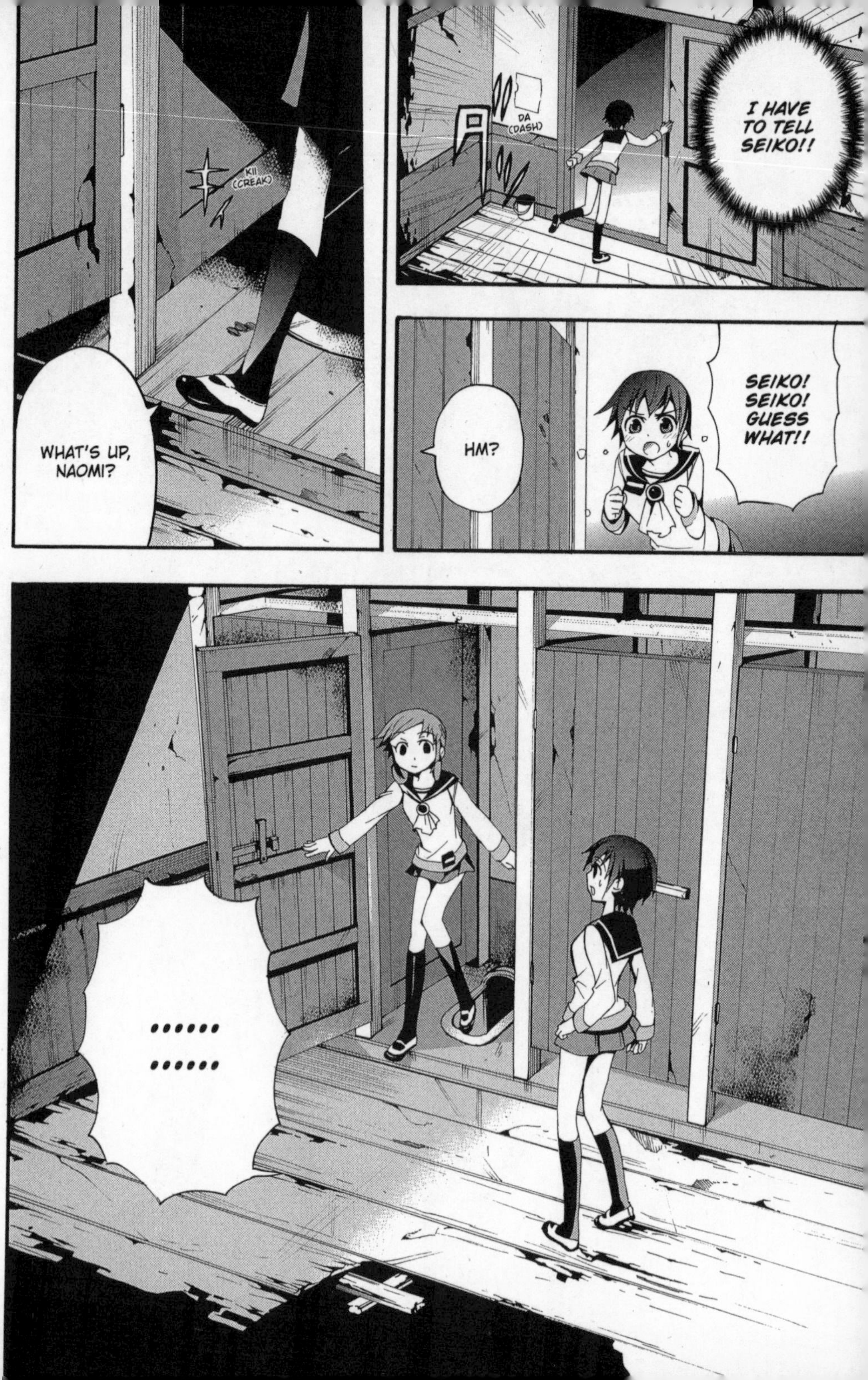
I HAVE TO TELL SEIKO!!
DA (DASH)
SEIKO! SEIKO! GUESS WHAT!!
HM?
KII (CREAK)
WHAT'S UP, NAOMI?
....

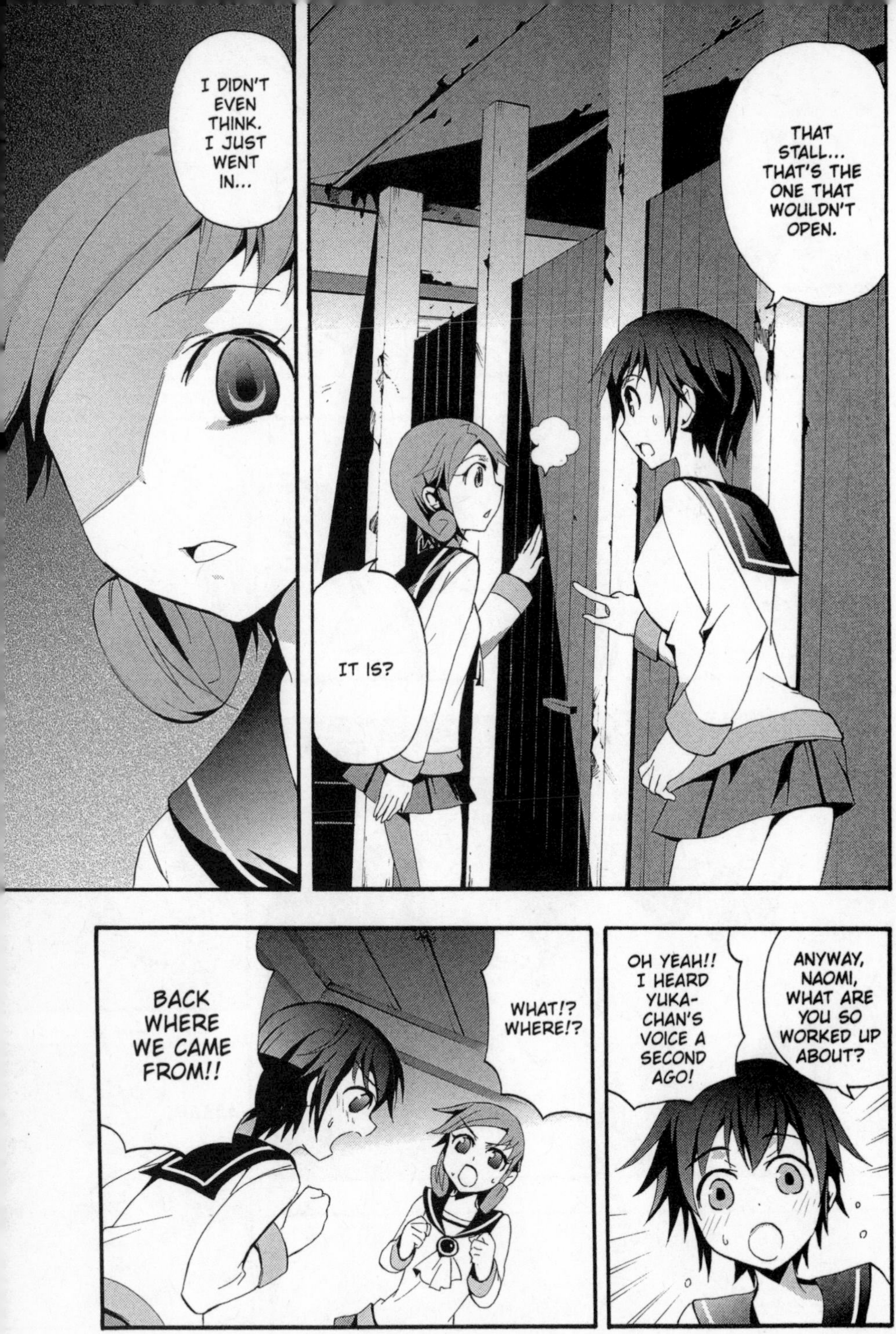
THAT STALL... THAT'S THE ONE THAT WOULDN'T OPEN.
IT IS?
I DIDN'T EVEN THINK. I JUST WENT IN...
ANYWAY, NAOMI, WHAT ARE YOU SO WORKED UP ABOUT?
OH YEAH!! I HEARD YUKA-CHAN'S VOICE A SECOND AGO!
WHAT!? WHERE!?
BACK WHERE WE CAME FROM!!

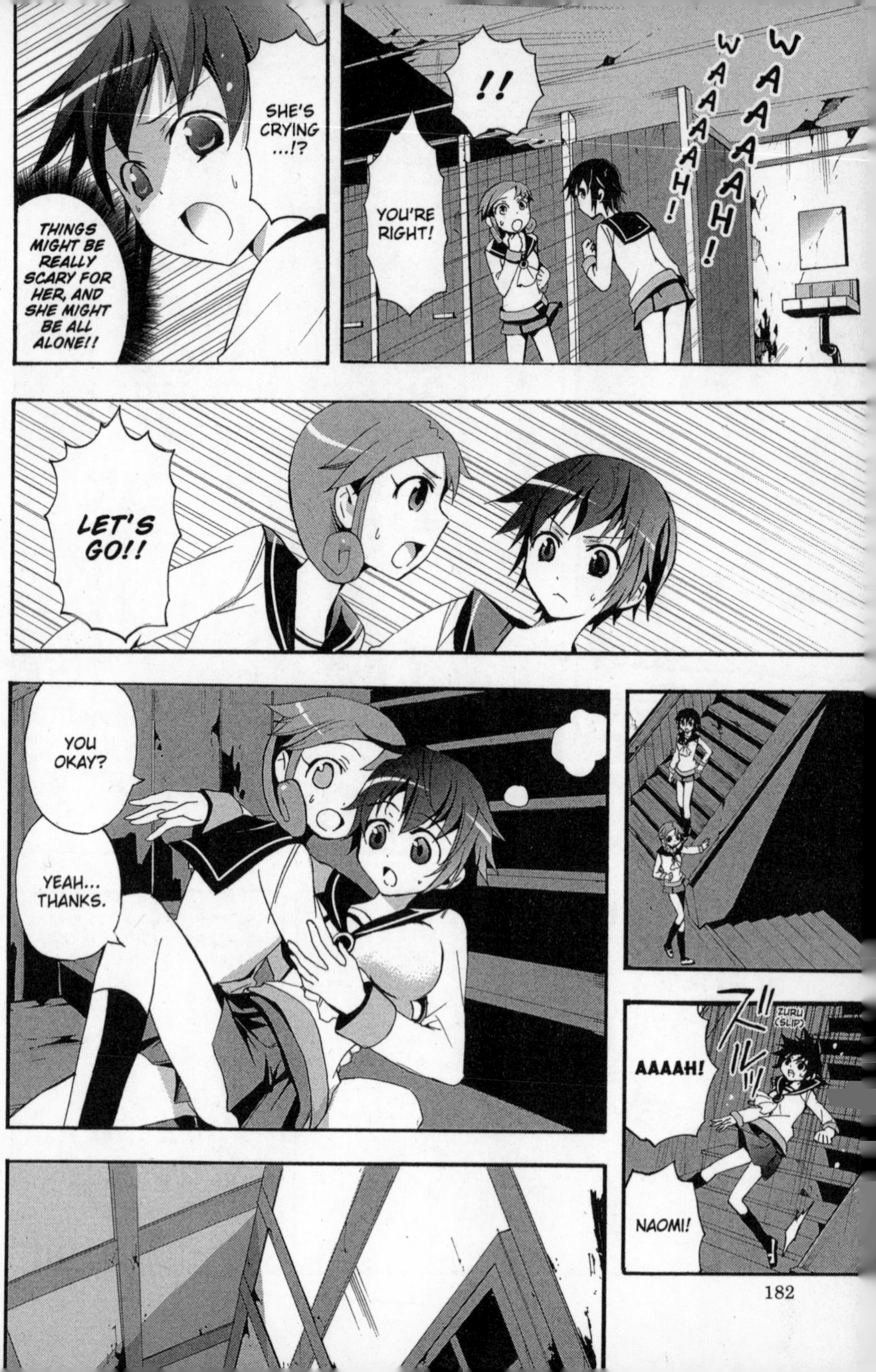
WAAAAAH!
WAAAAAH!
!!
YOU'RE RIGHT!
SHE'S CRYING ...!?
THINGS MIGHT BE REALLY SCARY FOR HER, AND SHE MIGHT BE ALL ALONE!!
LET'S GO!!
ZURU (SLIP)
AAAAH!
NAOMI!
YOU OKAY?
YEAH... THANKS.

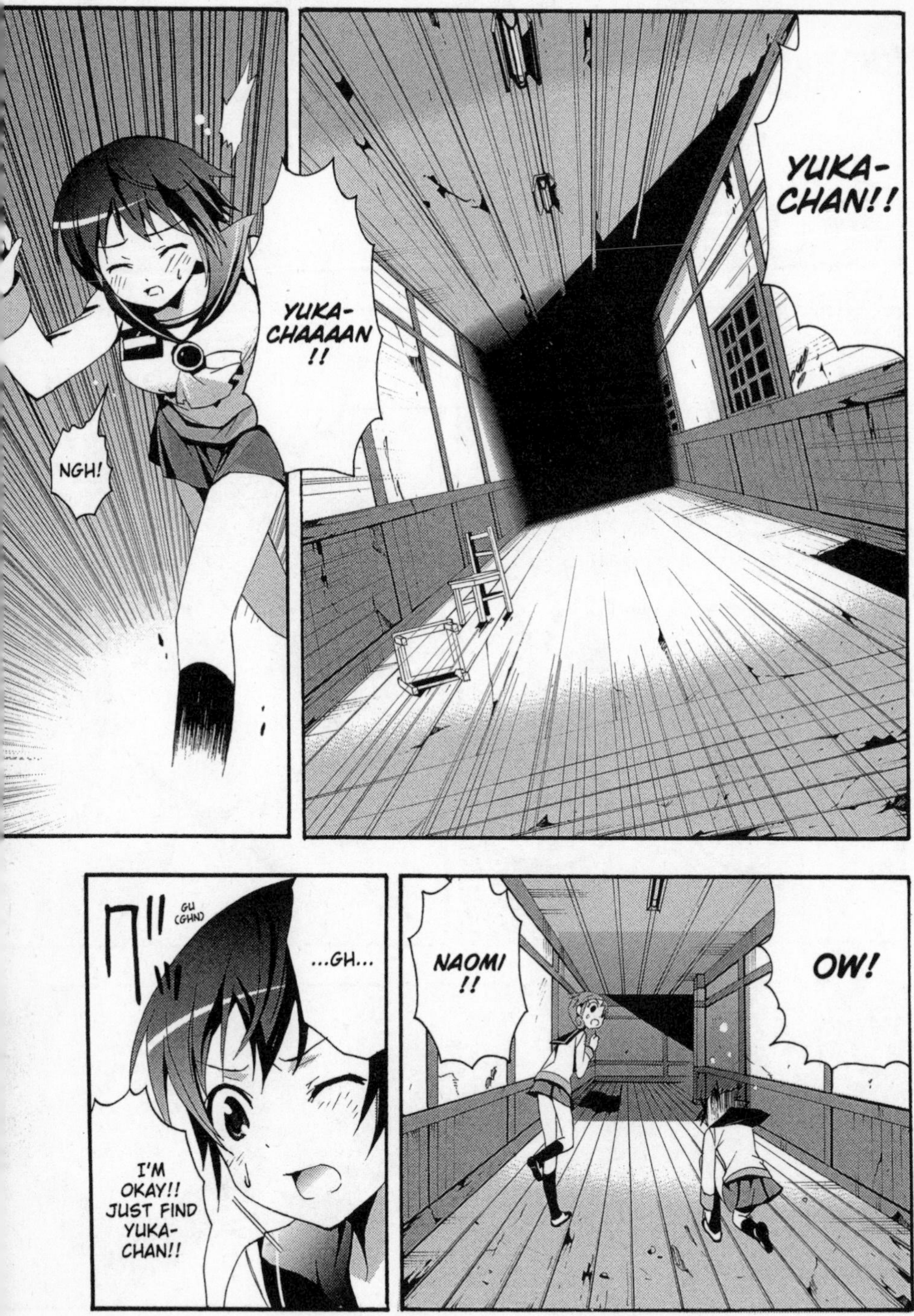
YUKA-CHAN!!
YUKA-CHAAAAN!!
NGH!
OW!
NAOMI!!
GU (GHND)
...GH...
I'M OKAY!! JUST FIND YUKA-CHAN!!

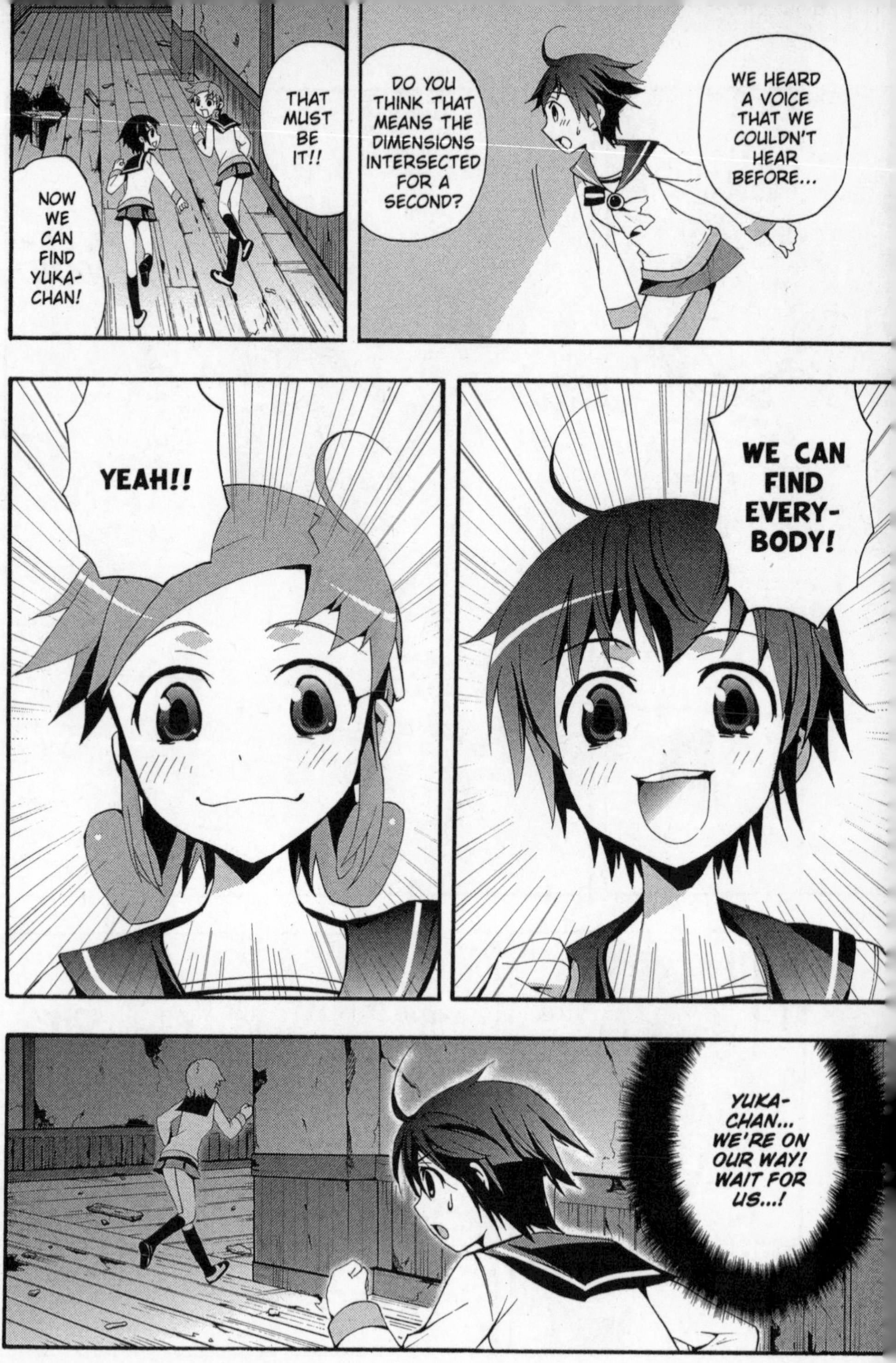
WE HEARD A VOICE THAT WE COULDN'T HEAR BEFORE...
DO YOU THINK THAT MEANS THE DIMENSIONS INTERSECTED FOR A SECOND?
THAT MUST BE IT!!
NOW WE CAN FIND YUKA-CHAN!
WE CAN FIND EVERY-BODY!
YEAH!!
YUKA-CHAN... WE'RE ON OUR WAY! WAIT FOR US...!

GYAAAAAAH!!

プ
チ
ュ
ッ

PUCHU
(SQUISH)

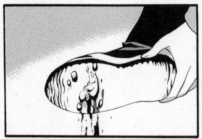

SEIKO!?

I STEPPED ON SOME-THING!!

WHAT... IS THIS?

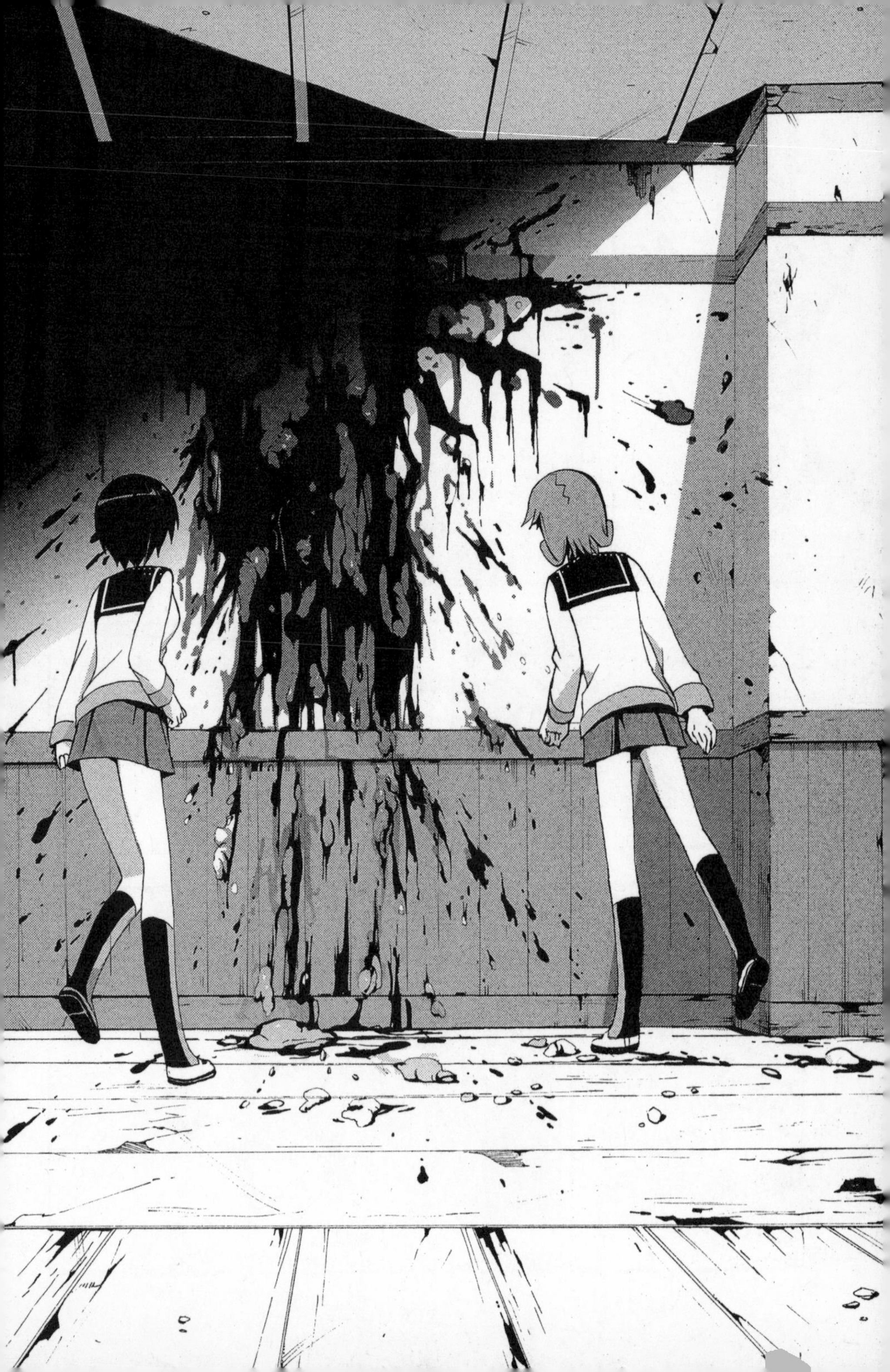

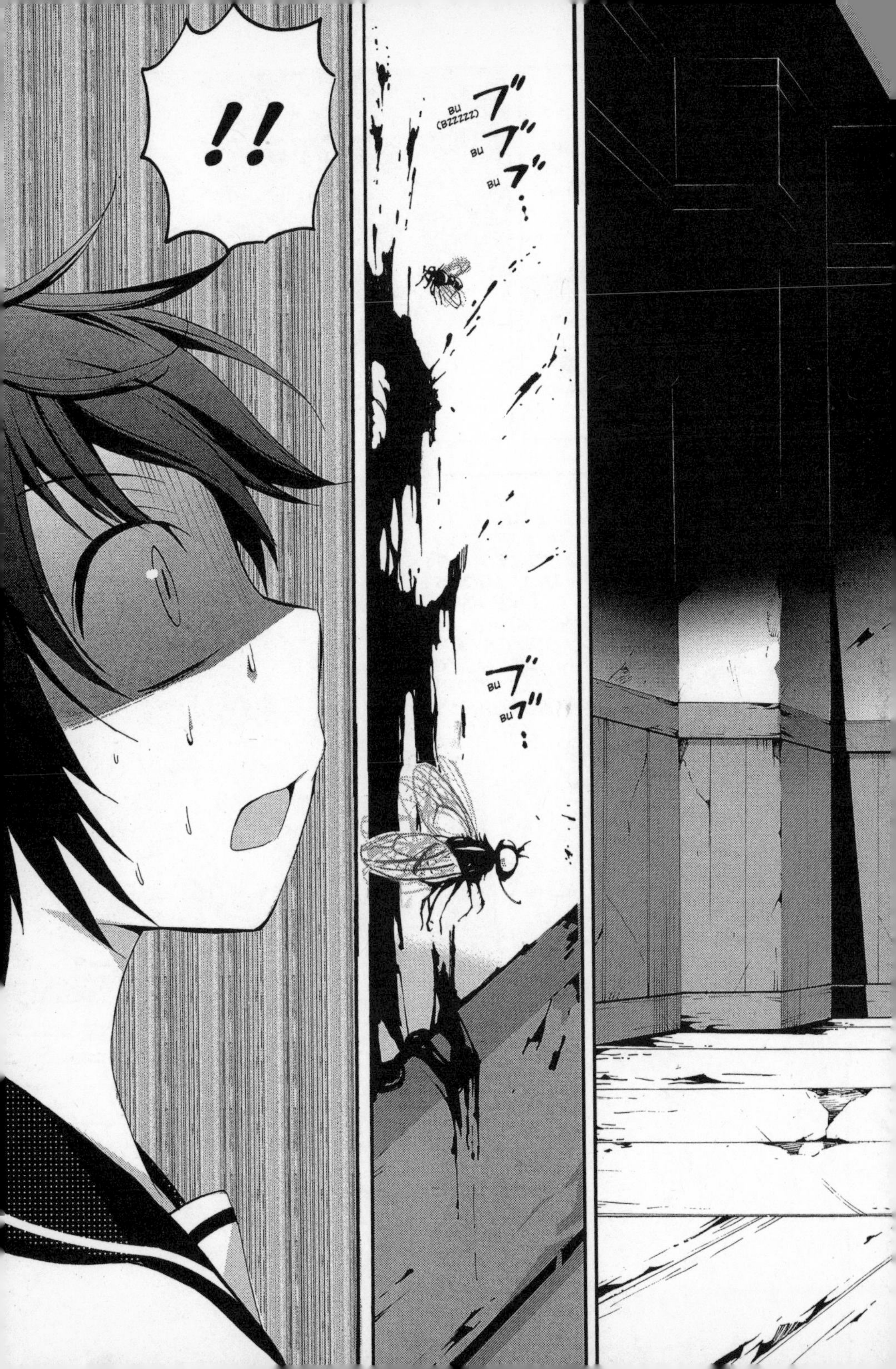
!!
ブブブ…
BU (BZZZZZ)
BU
BU
ブブ…
BU
BU

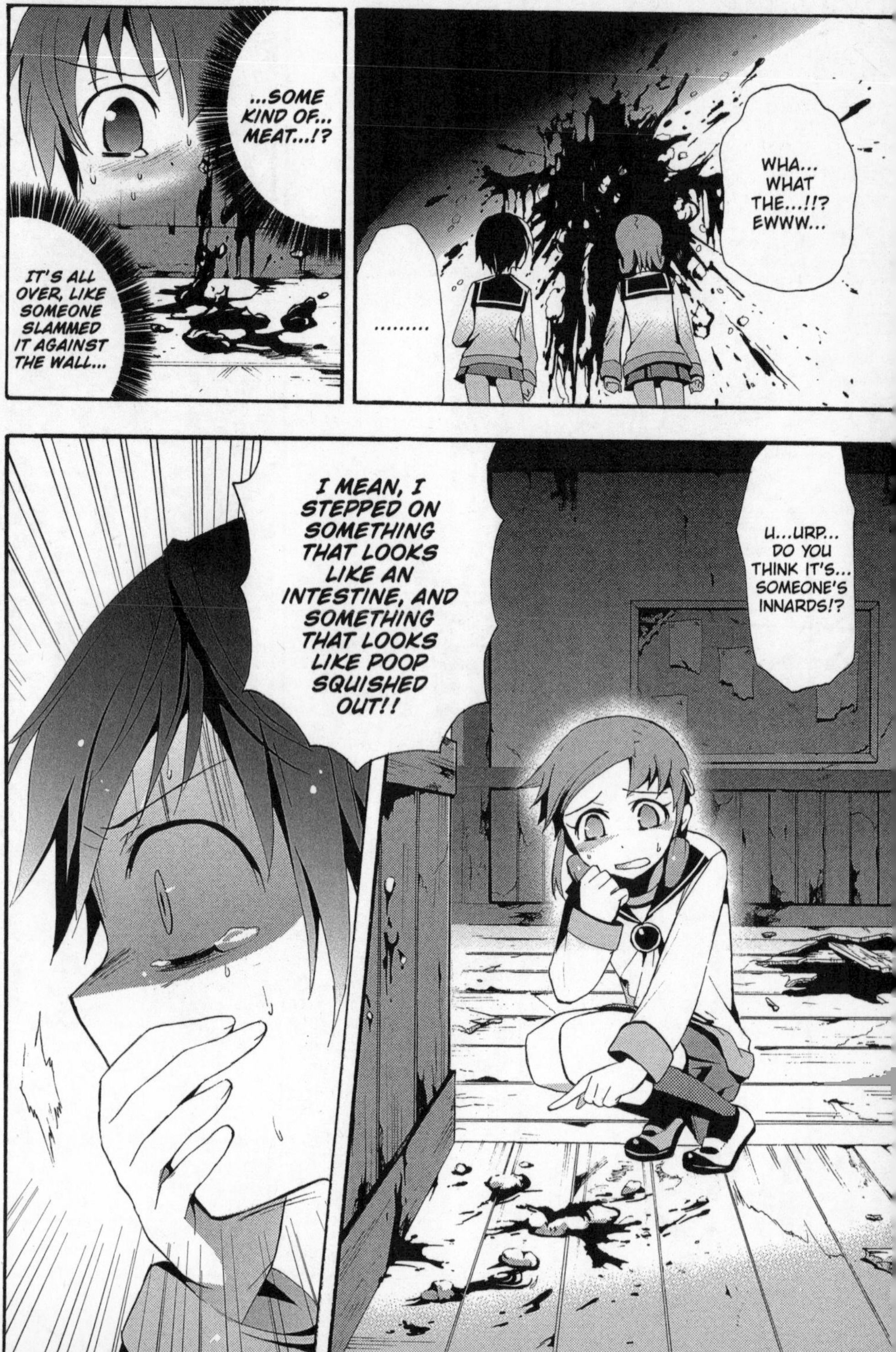
WHA... WHAT THE...!!? EWWW...
....
...SOME KIND OF... MEAT...!?
IT'S ALL OVER, LIKE SOMEONE SLAMMED IT AGAINST THE WALL...
U...URP... DO YOU THINK IT'S... SOMEONE'S INNARDS!?
I MEAN, I STEPPED ON SOMETHING THAT LOOKS LIKE AN INTESTINE, AND SOMETHING THAT LOOKS LIKE POOP SQUISHED OUT!!

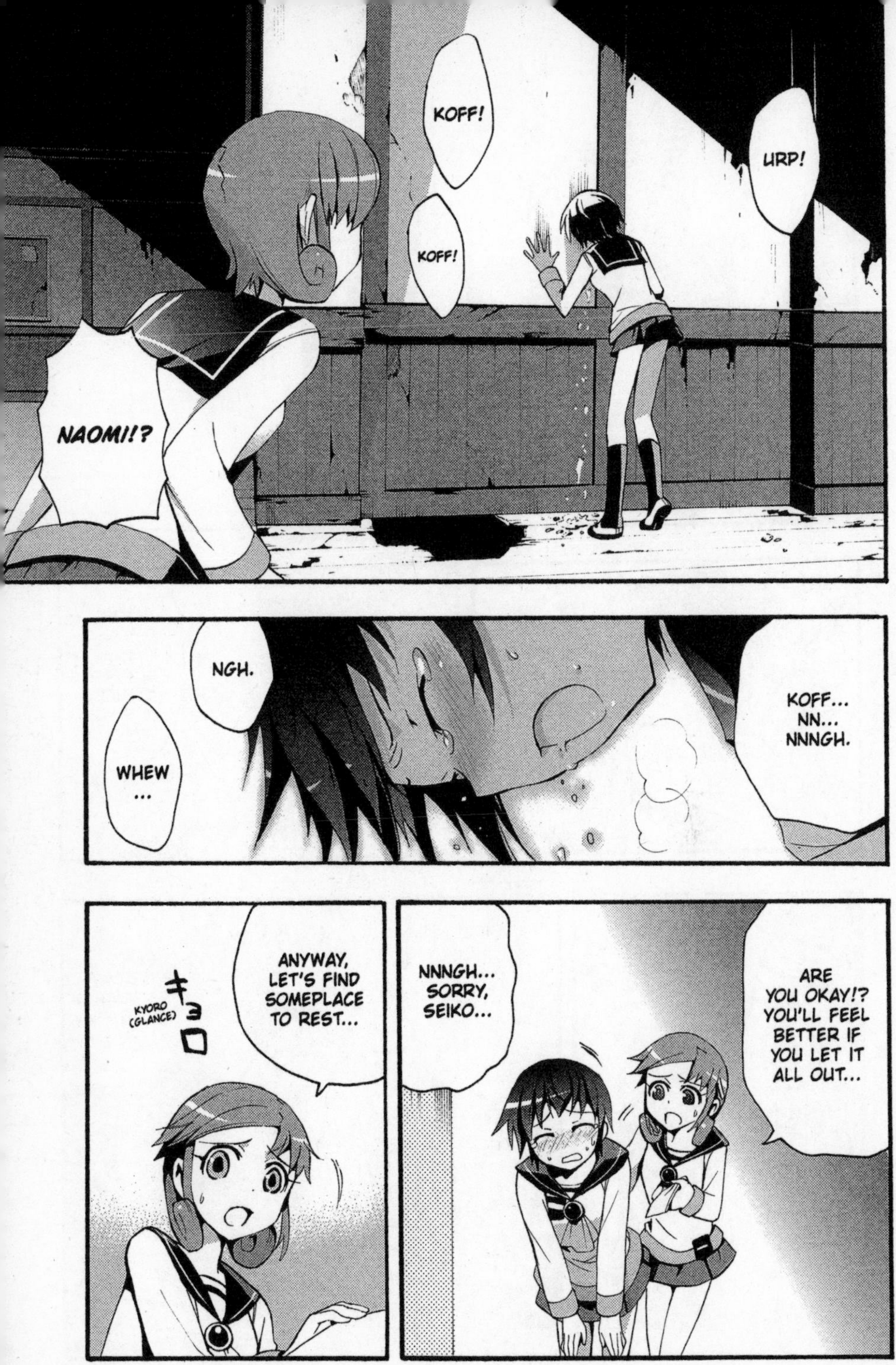
URP!
KOFF!
KOFF!
NAOMI!?
KOFF... NN... NNNGH.
NGH.
WHEW ...
ARE YOU OKAY!? YOU'LL FEEL BETTER IF YOU LET IT ALL OUT...
NNNGH... SORRY, SEIKO...
ANYWAY, LET'S FIND SOMEPLACE TO REST...
キョロ
KYORO (GLANCE)

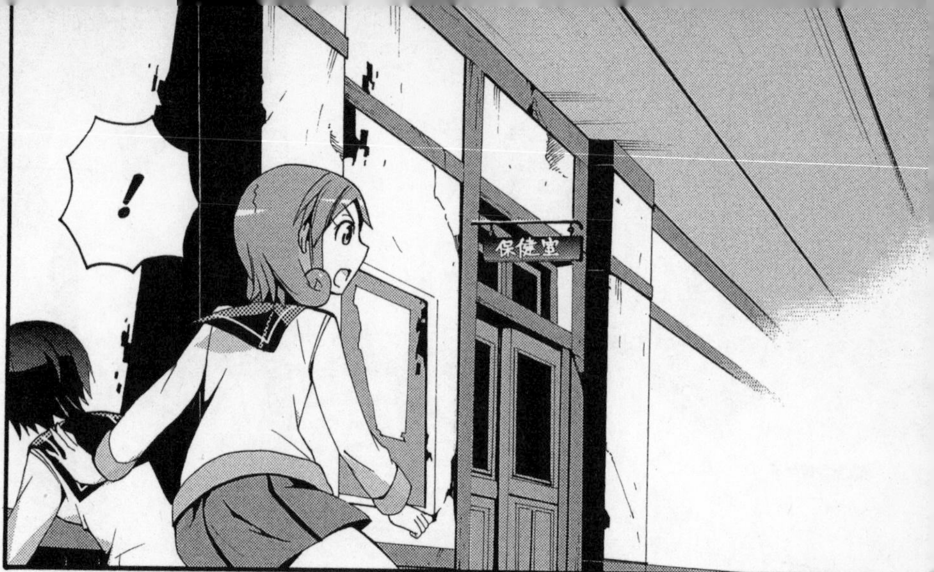
!
保健室

SIGN: NURSE'S OFFICE

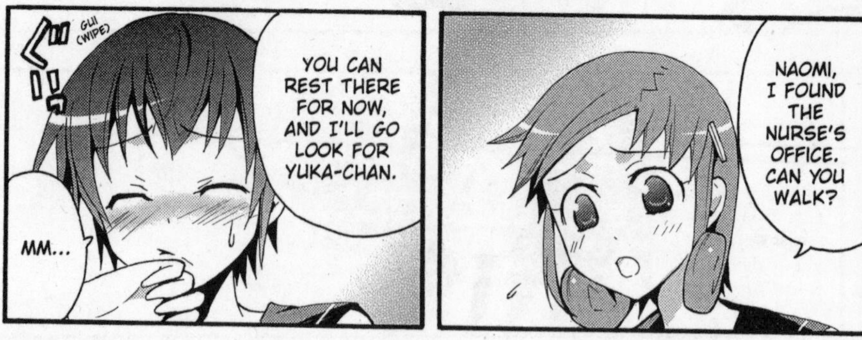
NAOMI, I FOUND THE NURSE'S OFFICE. CAN YOU WALK?
YOU CAN REST THERE FOR NOW, AND I'LL GO LOOK FOR YUKA-CHAN.
GUI (WIPE)
MM...

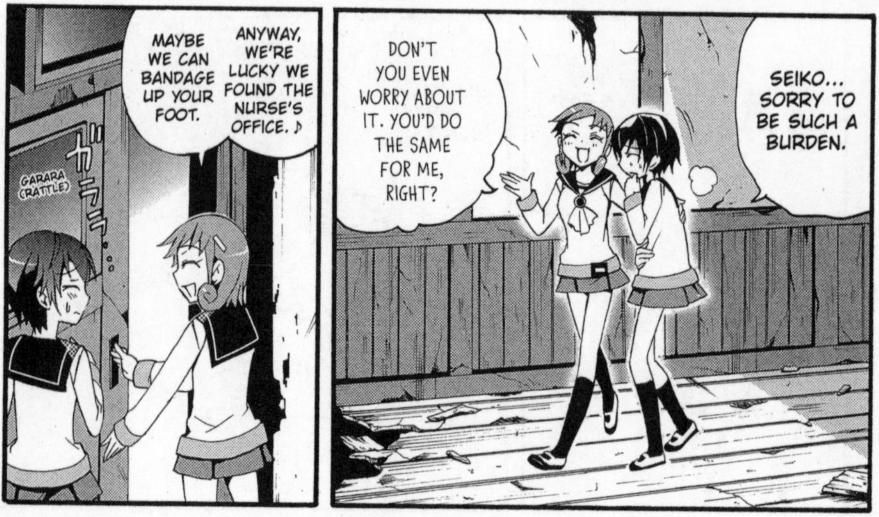
SEIKO... SORRY TO BE SUCH A BURDEN.
DON'T YOU EVEN WORRY ABOUT IT. YOU'D DO THE SAME FOR ME, RIGHT?
ANYWAY, WE'RE LUCKY WE FOUND THE NURSE'S OFFICE. ♪
MAYBE WE CAN BANDAGE UP YOUR FOOT.
GARARA (RATTLE)

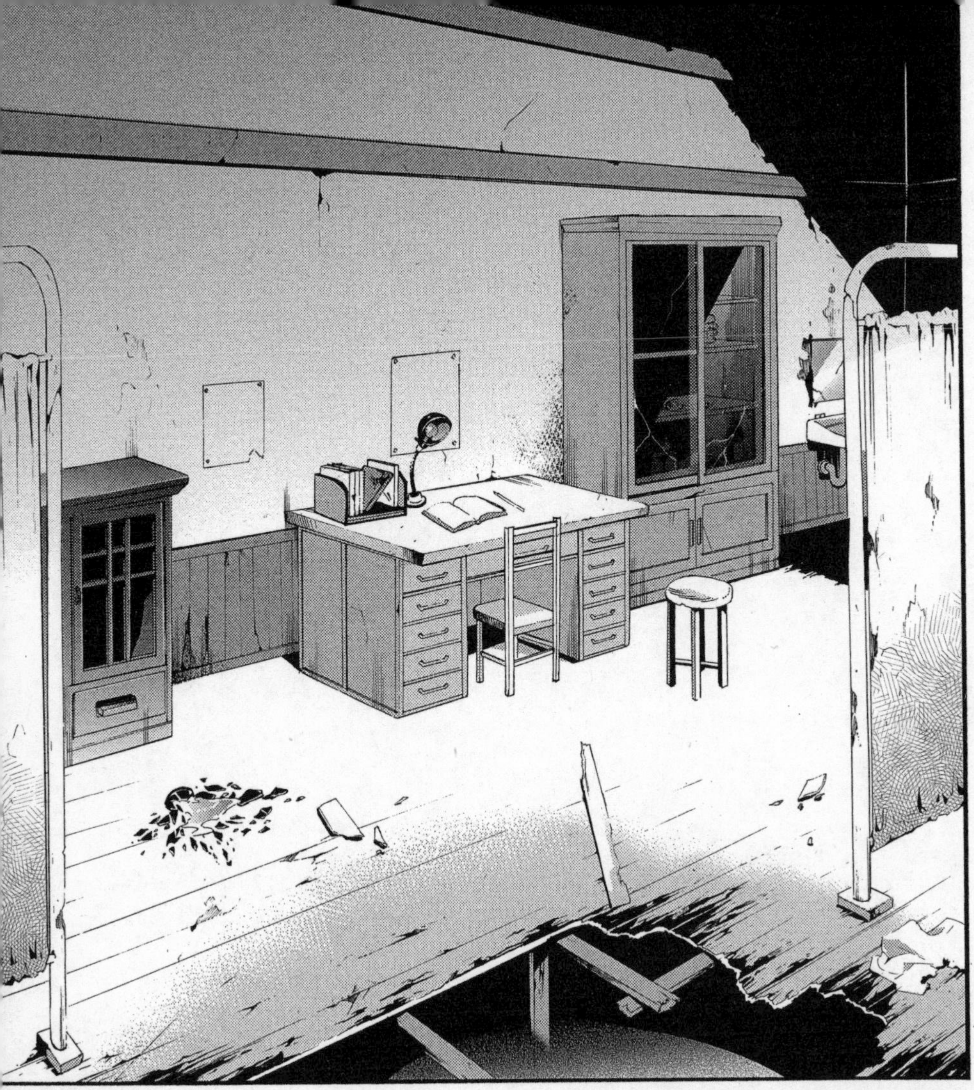

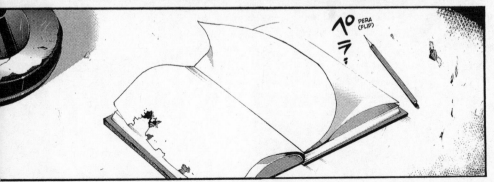

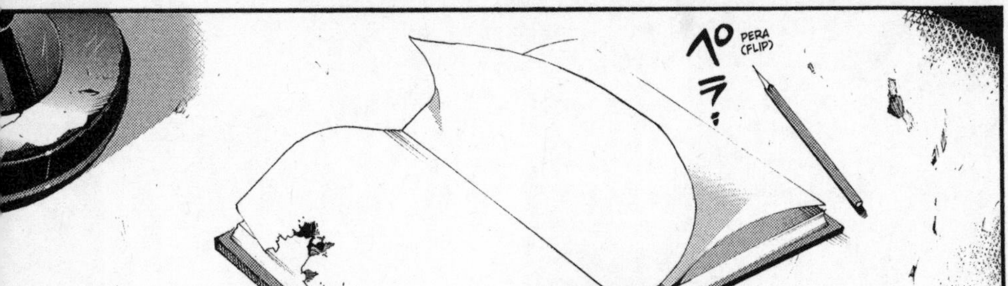
ペラ
PERA (FLIP)

a list of corpses/02

Female student,
Tendo Senior High School, Class II-A

Apparently died from blood loss when
someone used scissors to cut her
Achilles tendon. She was separated
from her elder sister at Tenjin
Elementary School, and she wrote of
her fear of death in her notebook.

← TO THE AFTERWORD...

WHAT SEIKO SAW

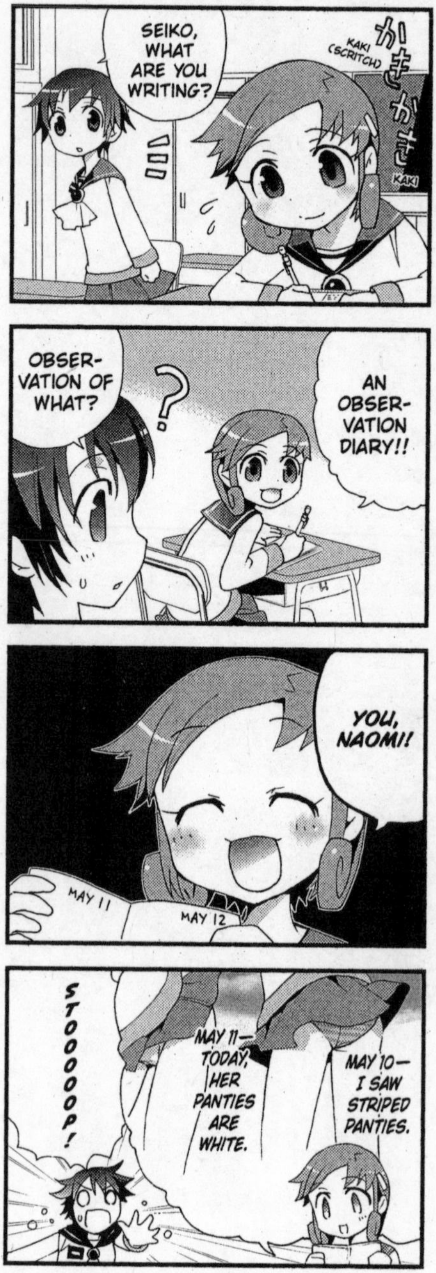
SEIKO, WHAT ARE YOU WRITING?
KAKI (SCRITCH)
KAKI
AN OBSERVATION DIARY!!
OBSERVATION OF WHAT?
YOU, NAOMI!
MAY 12
MAY 11
MAY 10— I SAW STRIPED PANTIES.
MAY 11— TODAY, HER PANTIES ARE WHITE.
STOOOOOOP!

SEIKO ROLLS

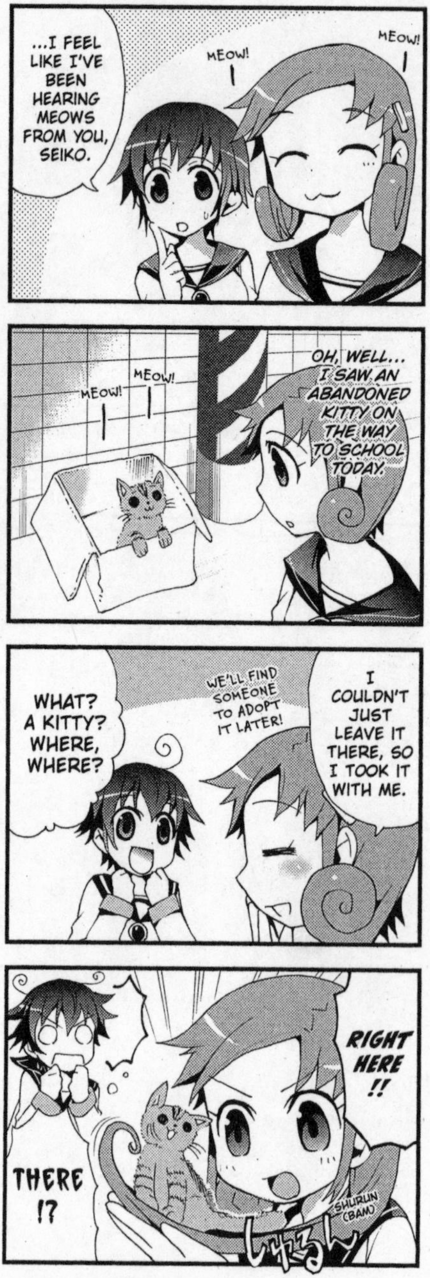
MEOW!
MEOW!
...I FEEL LIKE I'VE BEEN HEARING MEOWS FROM YOU, SEIKO.
OH, WELL... I SAW AN ABANDONED KITTY ON THE WAY TO SCHOOL TODAY.
MEOW!
MEOW!
I COULDN'T JUST LEAVE IT THERE, SO I TOOK IT WITH ME.
WE'LL FIND SOMEONE TO ADOPT IT LATER!
WHAT? A KITTY? WHERE, WHERE?
RIGHT HERE!!
SHURUN (BAM)
THERE!?

Character pickup

Seiko Shinohara

Born December 22, blood type B, 154cm, 44.0kg (5'1", 97.0lbs)

Likes: Hair care, choreography, singing
Dislikes: Alone time
Hobbies: Writing text messages, writing in her Naomi observation diary
Dream Career: Hair and makeup artist

Naomi Nakashima

Born December 14, blood type A, 158cm, 46.4kg (5'2", 102.3lbs)

Likes: Children, her mother, her favorite towel
Dislikes: Crustaceans, ambulance sirens, the smell of disinfectant in the nurse's office
Hobbies: Cooking, playing piano
Dream Career: Preschool teacher

NICE TO MEET YOU AND, HELLO, I'M THE ARTIST, SHINOMIYA. I PRESENT CORPSE PARTY: BLOODCOVERED VOLUME 1. EVERY CHARACTER IN CORPSE IS SO APPEALING, I THINK IT'S FUN TOO. I WANT TO WORK HARD SO AS NOT TO DESTROY THE WONDERFULNESS OF THE ORIGINAL. IF YOU READ THE MANGA AND IT MAKES YOU INTERESTED IN THE GAME, PLEASE GO PLAY IT. I PLAY IT TOO—SHAKING IN THE MIDDLE OF THE NIGHT. I'M SCARED, BUT I HAVE TO KNOW WHAT HAPPENS NEXT!

TOSHIMI SHINOMIYA

SPECIAL THANKS
M KOKKO-SAN, SHIN ARAKAWA-SAN, TAICHI KAWAZOE-SAN, TSUKASA KAGURAI-SAN, TAKATOSHI OGURA-SAN, MASAKI KAWANO-SAN,
AND EVERYONE FROM TEAM GRISGRIS, MAKOTO KEDOUIN-SAN, MY EDITOR, AKIYAMA-SAN, AND KAWANO-SAN,
THANK YOU VERY MUCH!

AFTERWORD

TOSHIMI SHINOMIYA-SENSEI, CONGRATULATIONS ON RELEASING VOLUME 1 OF THIS MANGA. THANK YOU TO EVERYONE WHO PICKED UP THIS BOOK.

THE ORIGINAL IS A HORROR GAME THAT WAS SO TARGETED THAT I GET LETTERS SAYING, "TEN YEARS LATER, IT'S STILL SEXY AND GROTESQUE," SO AT FIRST, WHEN THEY HONORED ME WITH THE OFFER TO MAKE IT INTO A COMIC, I WAS REALLY HAPPY BUT REALLY NERVOUS ABOUT WHETHER OR NOT IT WOULD BE OKAY TO HAVE SUCH CONTENT DEPICTED SO REALISTICALLY.

SHINOMIYA-SENSEI CRUSHED MY GROUNDLESS FEARS WITH A HAMMER AND CAST A LIGHT ON ELEMENTS THAT WERE MISSING IN THE ORIGINAL, WRITING A DETAILED AND POWERFUL NEW *CORPSE* WORLD THAT YOU CAN ONLY FIND HERE! I'M SO IMPRESSED! IF YOU'RE GONNA DO IT LIKE THIS, KEEP GOING ALL THE WAY TO THE END! I LOOK FORWARD TO THE NEXT CHAPTER AS A READER MYSELF.

THE STORY OF THEIR IMPRISONMENT HAS ONLY JUST BEGUN, AND THE CHARMING SMILES OF SEIKO AND NAOMI WILL GRADUALLY FADE AWAY. I HOPE YOU'LL ALL FOLLOW ALONG CLOSELY TO SEE WHAT HAPPENS TO THESE LOVABLE AND PITIABLE CHARACTERS.

MAKOTO KEDOUIN

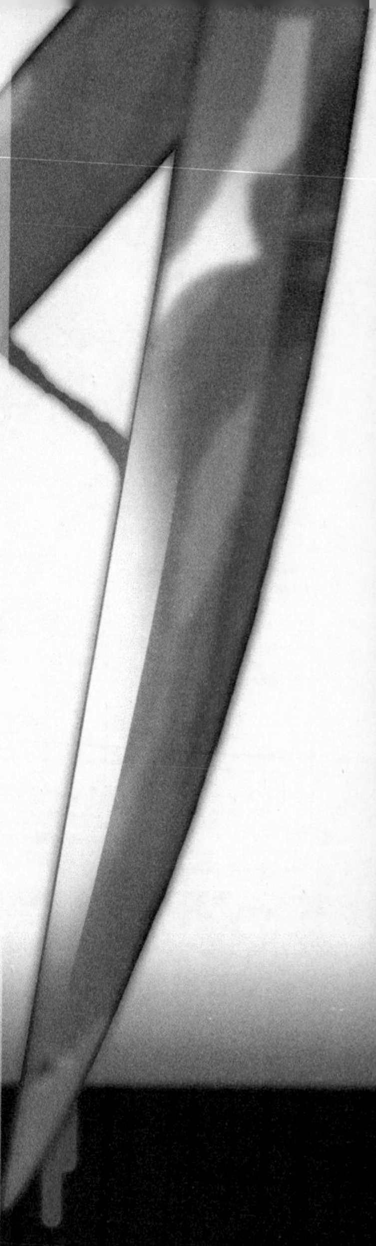

CORPSE PARTY BloodCovered

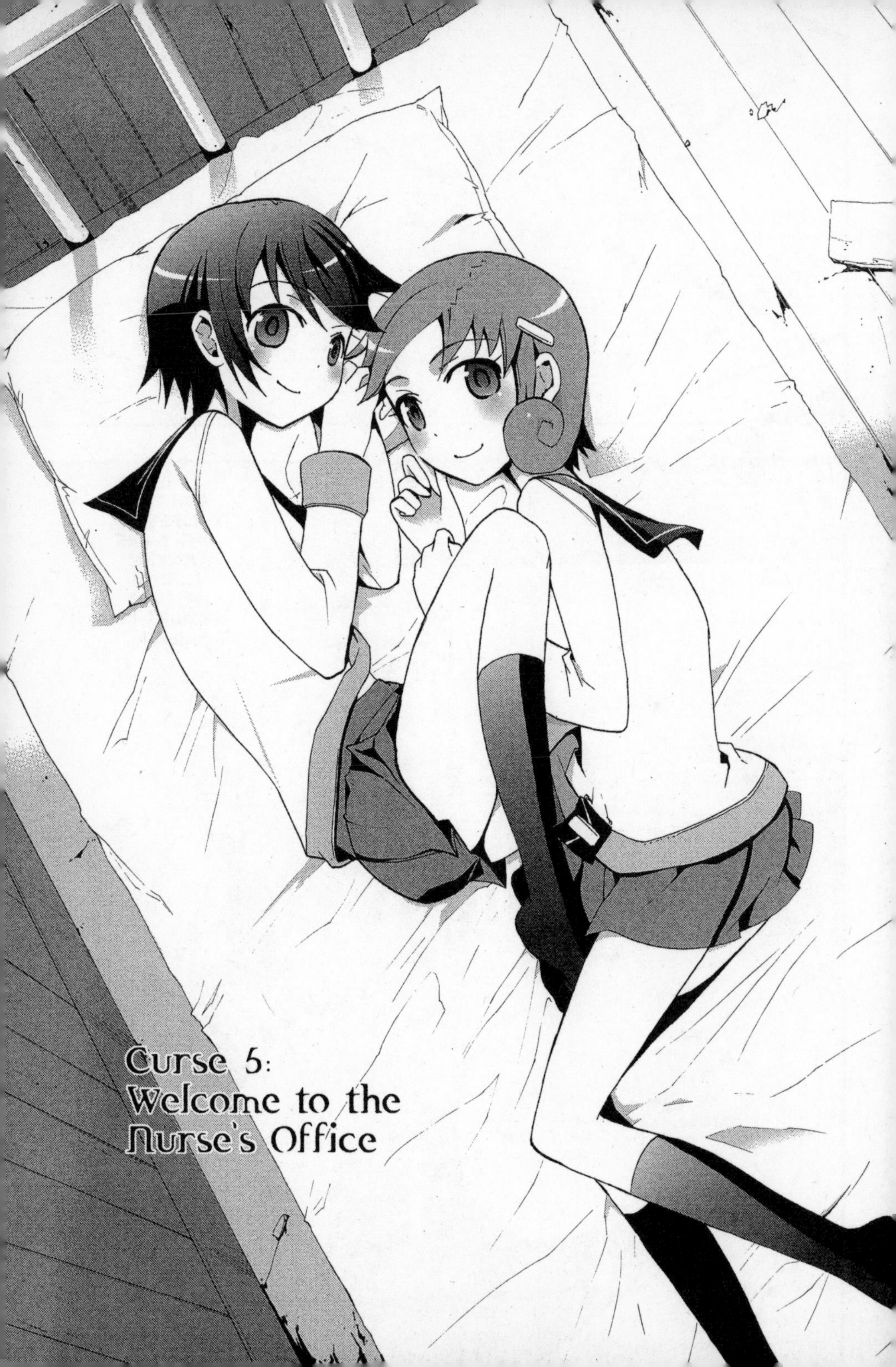
Curse 5:
Welcome to the
Nurse's Office

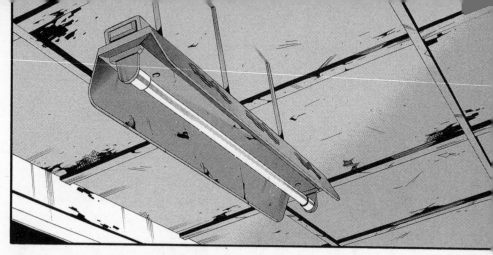

OOH, THE NURSE'S OFFICE HAS WORKING LIGHTS! IT'S SO BRIGHT IN HERE!

AND IT'S CLEANER THAN THE OTHER ROOMS...

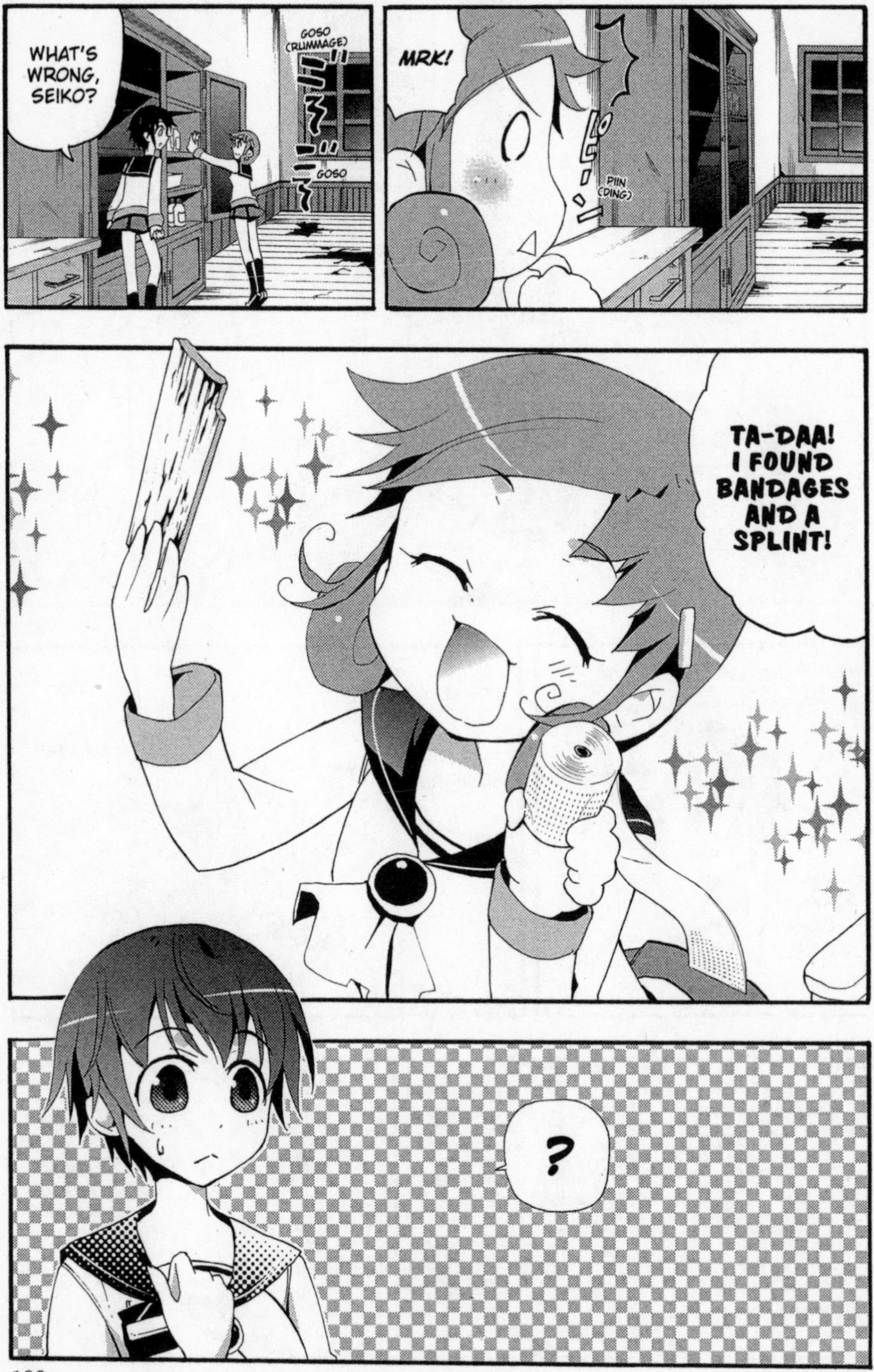
MRK!
PIIN (DING)
WHAT'S WRONG, SEIKO?
GOSO (RUMMAGE)
GOSO
TA-DAA! I FOUND BANDAGES AND A SPLINT!
?

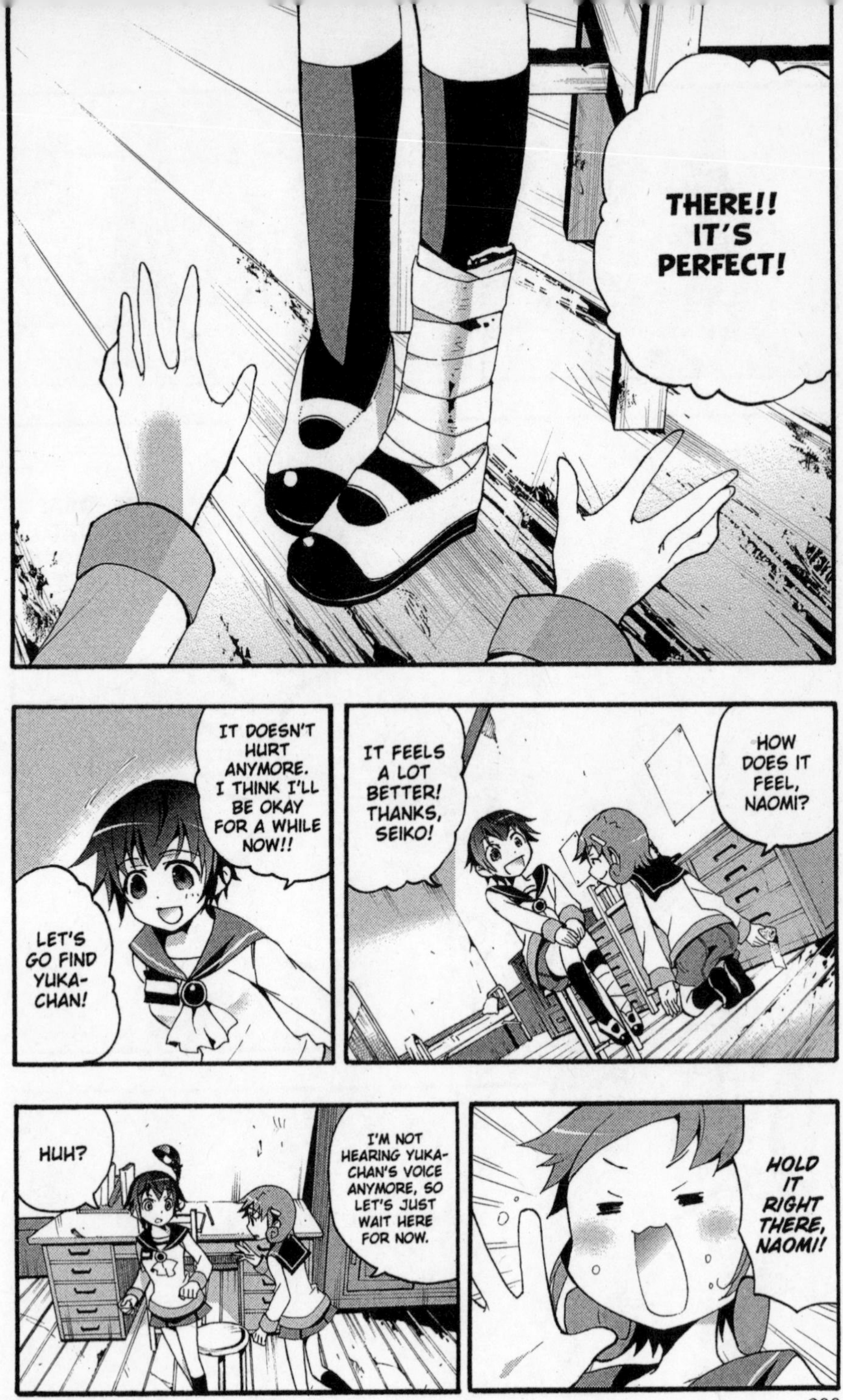
THERE!! IT'S PERFECT!
HOW DOES IT FEEL, NAOMI?
IT FEELS A LOT BETTER! THANKS, SEIKO!
IT DOESN'T HURT ANYMORE. I THINK I'LL BE OKAY FOR A WHILE NOW!!
LET'S GO FIND YUKA-CHAN!
HOLD IT RIGHT THERE, NAOMI!
I'M NOT HEARING YUKA-CHAN'S VOICE ANYMORE, SO LET'S JUST WAIT HERE FOR NOW.
HUH?

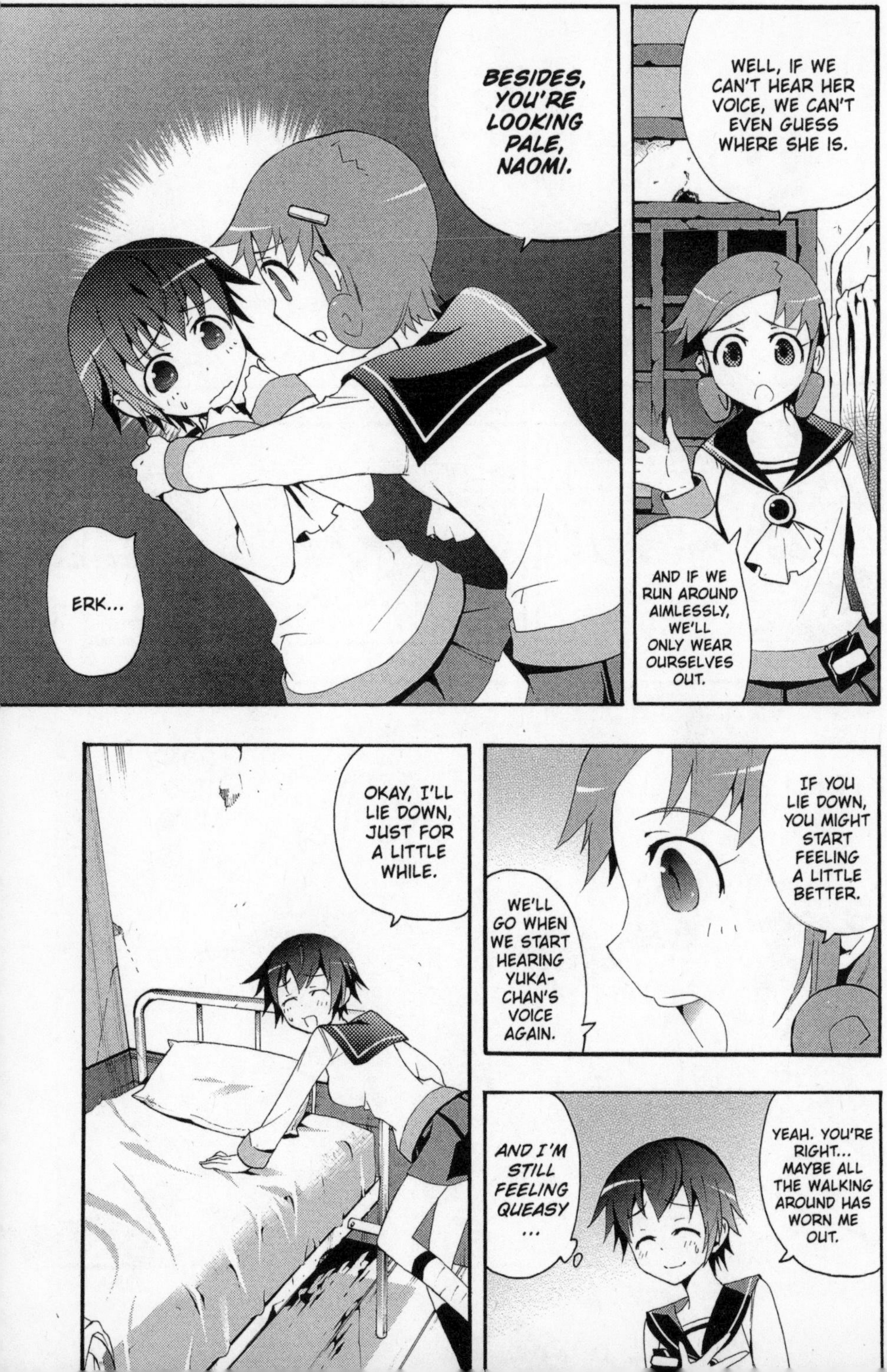
WELL, IF WE CAN'T HEAR HER VOICE, WE CAN'T EVEN GUESS WHERE SHE IS.
AND IF WE RUN AROUND AIMLESSLY, WE'LL ONLY WEAR OURSELVES OUT.
BESIDES, YOU'RE LOOKING PALE, NAOMI.
ERK...
IF YOU LIE DOWN, YOU MIGHT START FEELING A LITTLE BETTER.
WE'LL GO WHEN WE START HEARING YUKA-CHAN'S VOICE AGAIN.
YEAH. YOU'RE RIGHT... MAYBE ALL THE WALKING AROUND HAS WORN ME OUT.
AND I'M STILL FEELING QUEASY...
OKAY, I'LL LIE DOWN, JUST FOR A LITTLE WHILE.

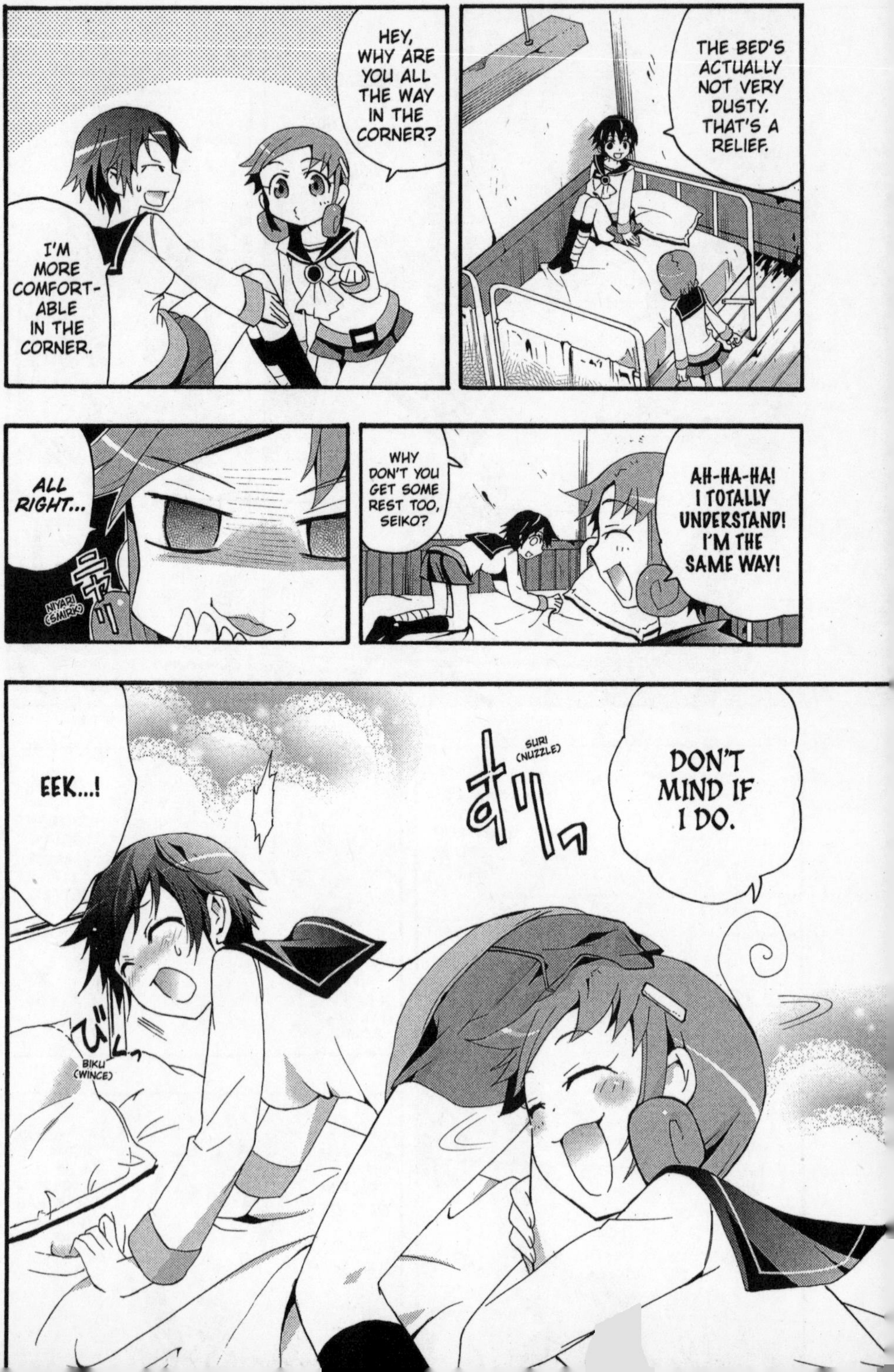
THE BED'S ACTUALLY NOT VERY DUSTY. THAT'S A RELIEF.
HEY, WHY ARE YOU ALL THE WAY IN THE CORNER?
I'M MORE COMFORT-ABLE IN THE CORNER.
AH-HA-HA! I TOTALLY UNDERSTAND! I'M THE SAME WAY!
WHY DON'T YOU GET SOME REST TOO, SEIKO?
ALL RIGHT...
NIYARI (SMIRK)
DON'T MIND IF I DO.
SURI (NUZZLE)
EEK...!
BIKU (WINCE)

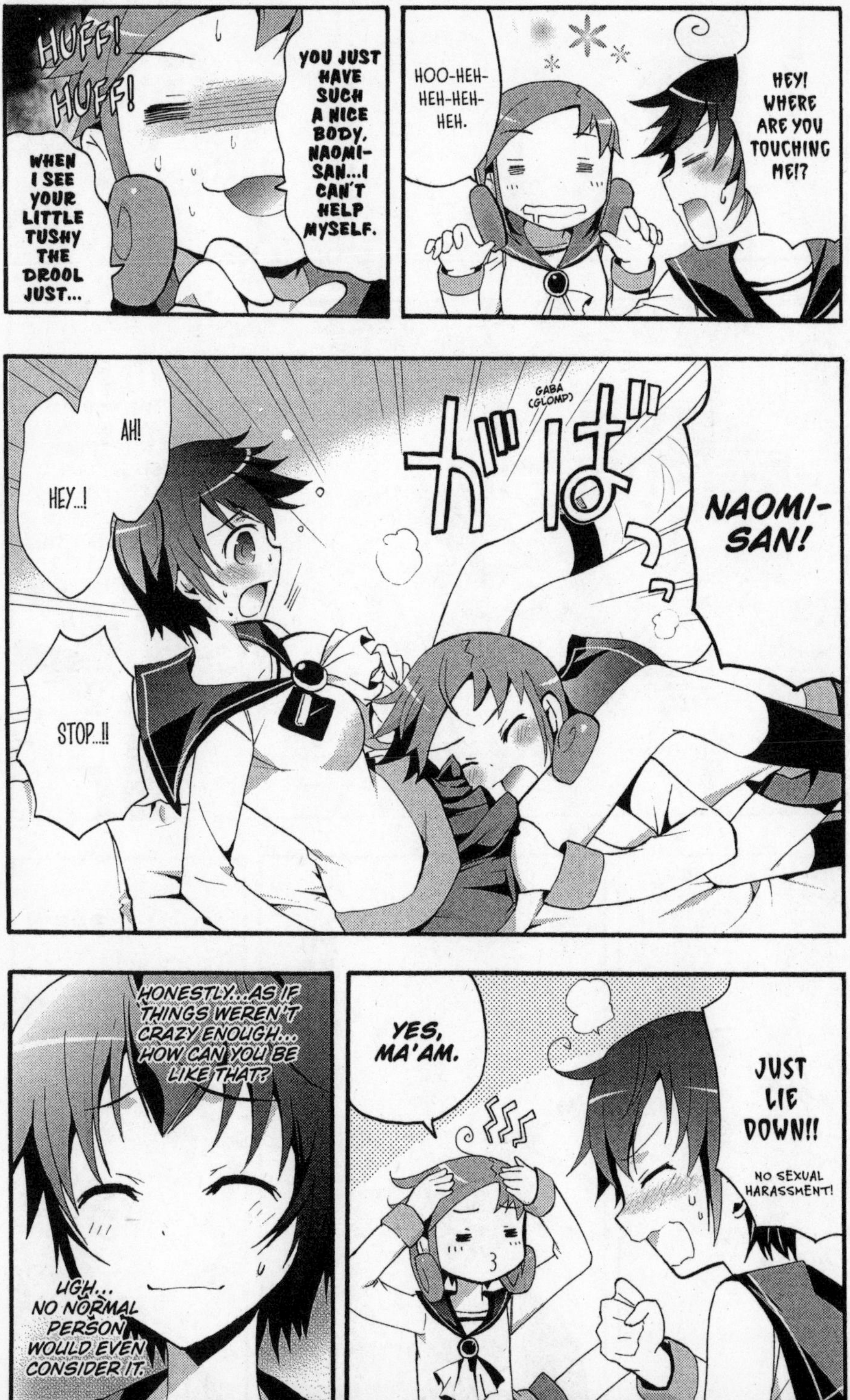
HEY! WHERE ARE YOU TOUCHING ME!?
HOO-HEH-HEH-HEH-HEH.
YOU JUST HAVE SUCH A NICE BODY, NAOMI-SAN...I CAN'T HELP MYSELF.
HUFF! HUFF!
WHEN I SEE YOUR LITTLE TUSHY THE DROOL JUST...
GABA (GLOMP)
がばっ
NAOMI-SAN!
AH!
HEY...!
STOP...!!
JUST LIE DOWN!!
NO SEXUAL HARASSMENT!
YES, MA'AM.
HONESTLY...AS IF THINGS WEREN'T CRAZY ENOUGH... HOW CAN YOU BE LIKE THAT?
UGH... NO NORMAL PERSON WOULD EVEN CONSIDER IT.

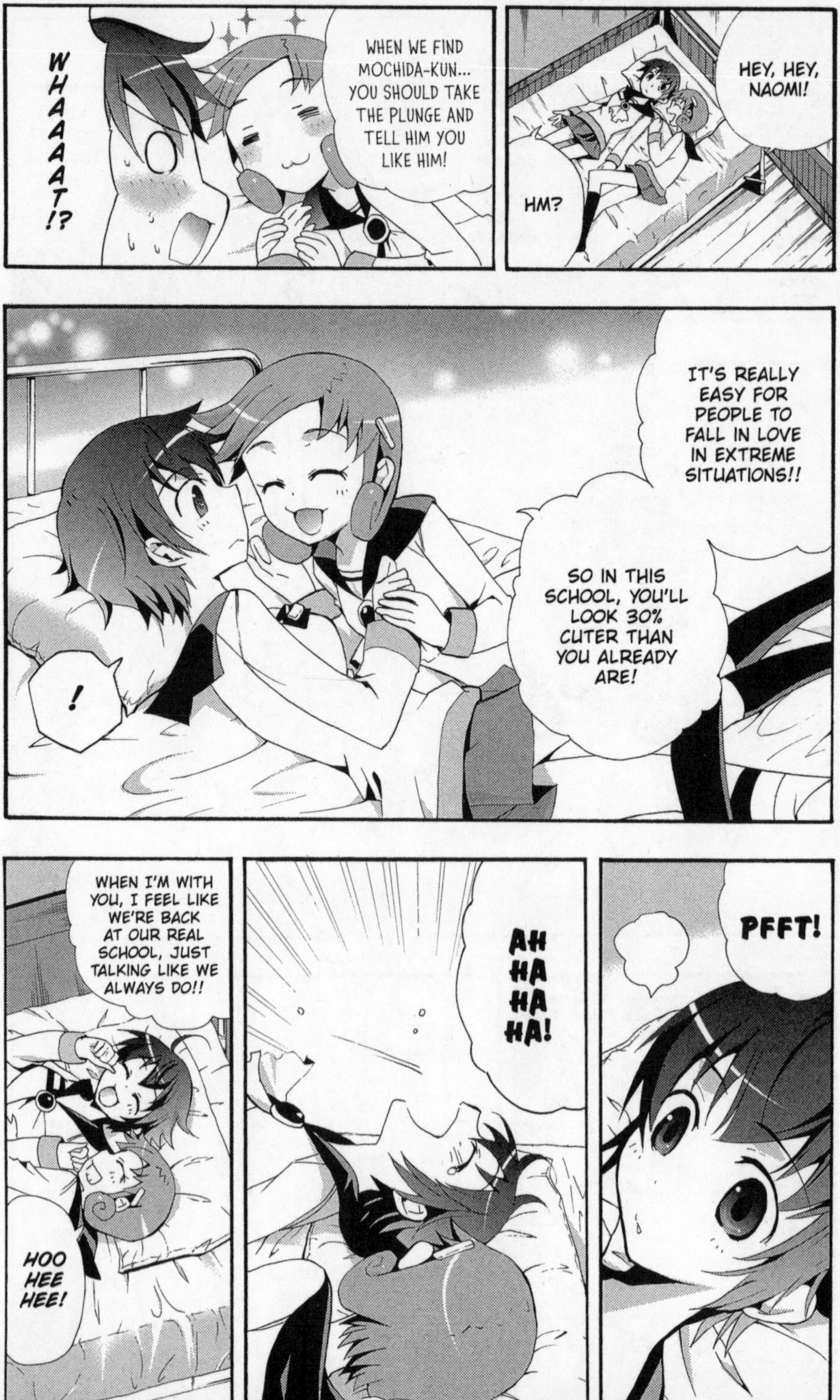
HEY, HEY, NAOMI!
HM?
WHEN WE FIND MOCHIDA-KUN... YOU SHOULD TAKE THE PLUNGE AND TELL HIM YOU LIKE HIM!
WHAAAAAT!?
IT'S REALLY EASY FOR PEOPLE TO FALL IN LOVE IN EXTREME SITUATIONS!!
SO IN THIS SCHOOL, YOU'LL LOOK 30% CUTER THAN YOU ALREADY ARE!
!
PFFT!
AH HA HA HA!
WHEN I'M WITH YOU, I FEEL LIKE WE'RE BACK AT OUR REAL SCHOOL, JUST TALKING LIKE WE ALWAYS DO!!
HOO HEE HEE!

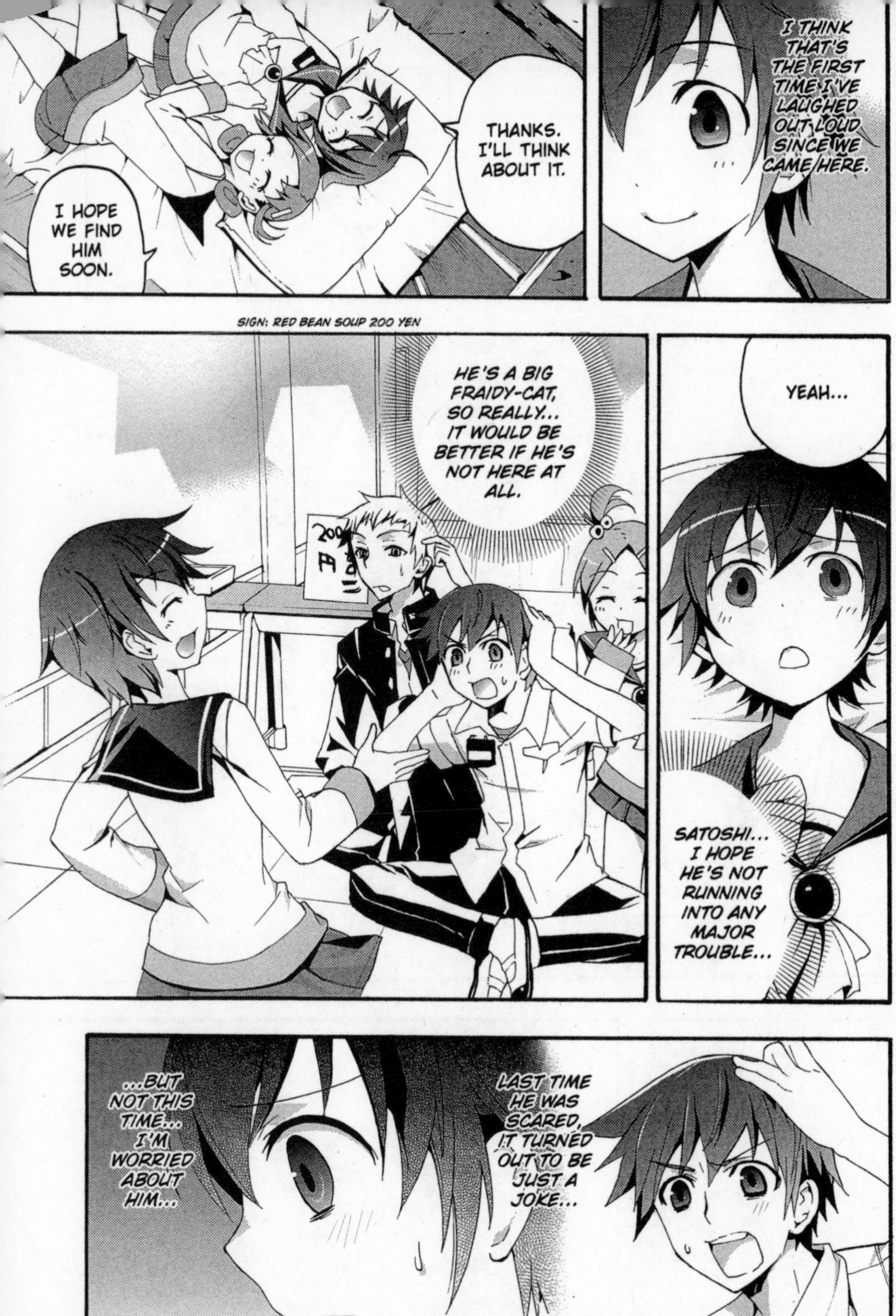
I THINK THAT'S THE FIRST TIME I'VE LAUGHED OUT LOUD SINCE WE CAME HERE.
THANKS. I'LL THINK ABOUT IT.
I HOPE WE FIND HIM SOON.
YEAH...
SATOSHI... I HOPE HE'S NOT RUNNING INTO ANY MAJOR TROUBLE...
HE'S A BIG FRAIDY-CAT, SO REALLY... IT WOULD BE BETTER IF HE'S NOT HERE AT ALL.
SIGN: RED BEAN SOUP 200 YEN
LAST TIME HE WAS SCARED, IT TURNED OUT TO BE JUST A JOKE...
...BUT NOT THIS TIME... I'M WORRIED ABOUT HIM...

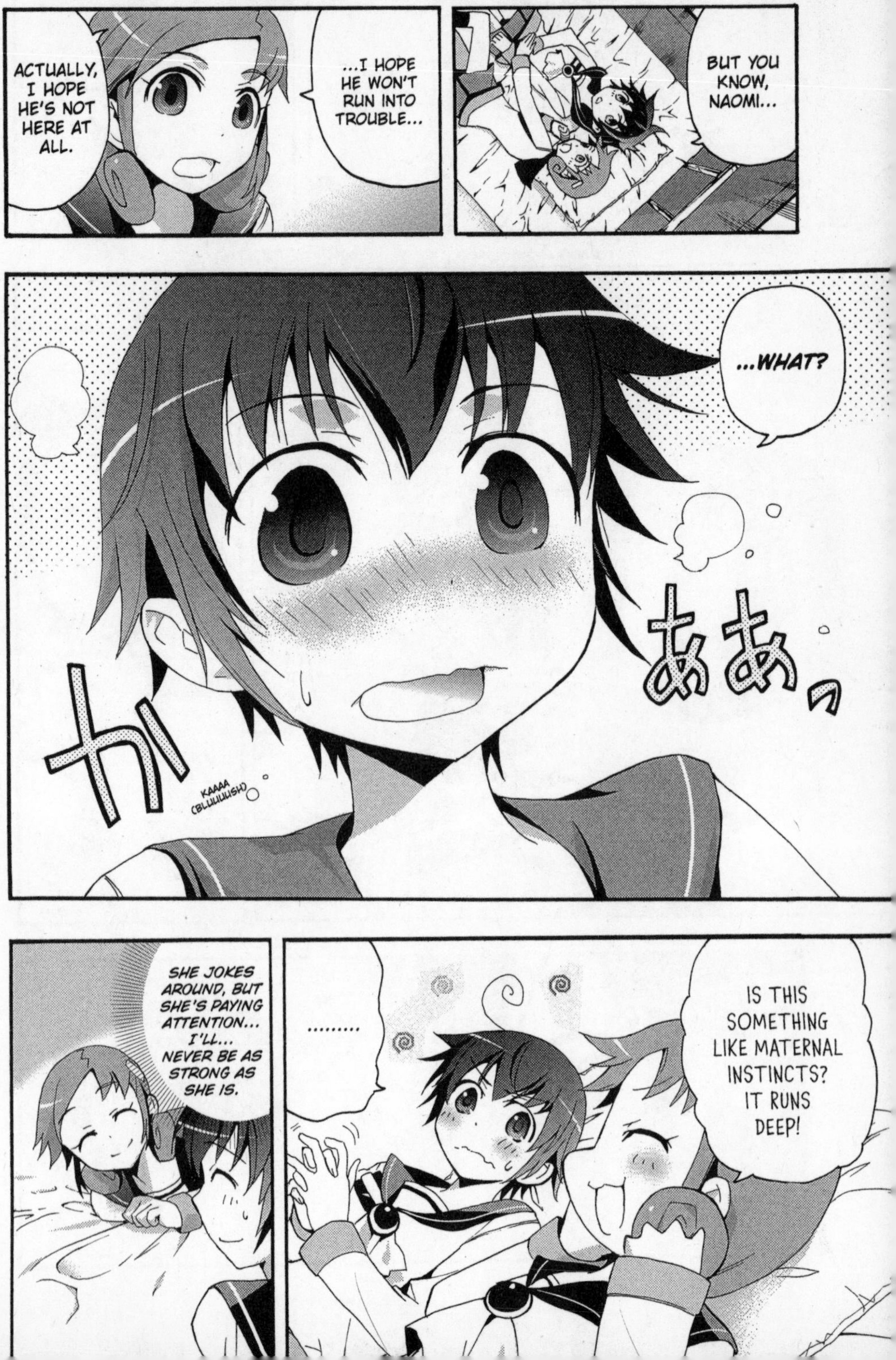
BUT YOU KNOW, NAOMI...
...I HOPE HE WON'T RUN INTO TROUBLE...
ACTUALLY, I HOPE HE'S NOT HERE AT ALL.
...WHAT?
ああっ
か
KAAAA (BLUUUUSH)
IS THIS SOMETHING LIKE MATERNAL INSTINCTS? IT RUNS DEEP!
....
SHE JOKES AROUND, BUT SHE'S PAYING ATTENTION... I'LL... NEVER BE AS STRONG AS SHE IS.

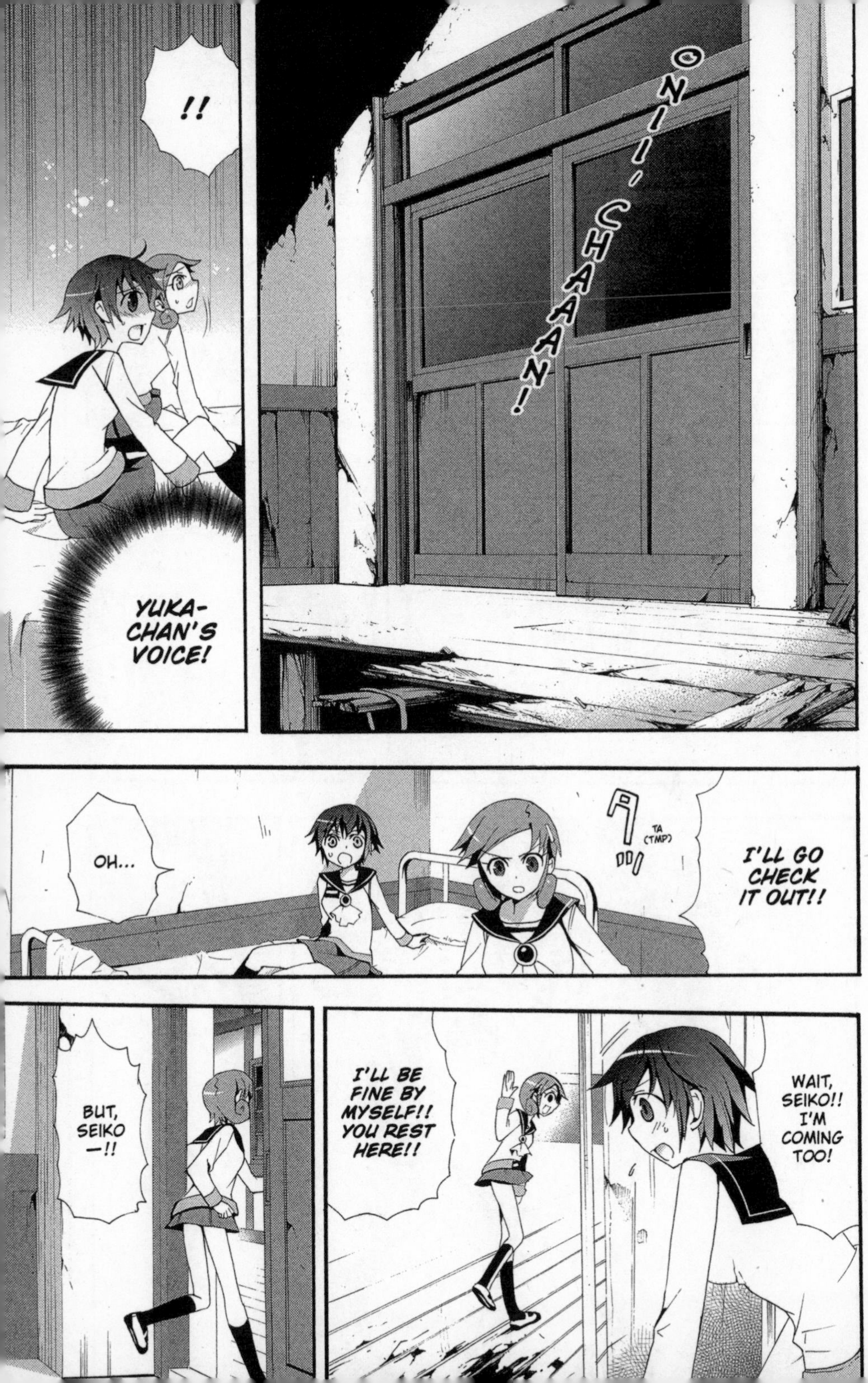
ONII-CHAAAAN!
!!
YUKA-CHAN'S VOICE!
TA (TMP)
I'LL GO CHECK IT OUT!!
OH...
WAIT, SEIKO!! I'M COMING TOO!
I'LL BE FINE BY MYSELF!! YOU REST HERE!!
BUT, SEIKO—!!

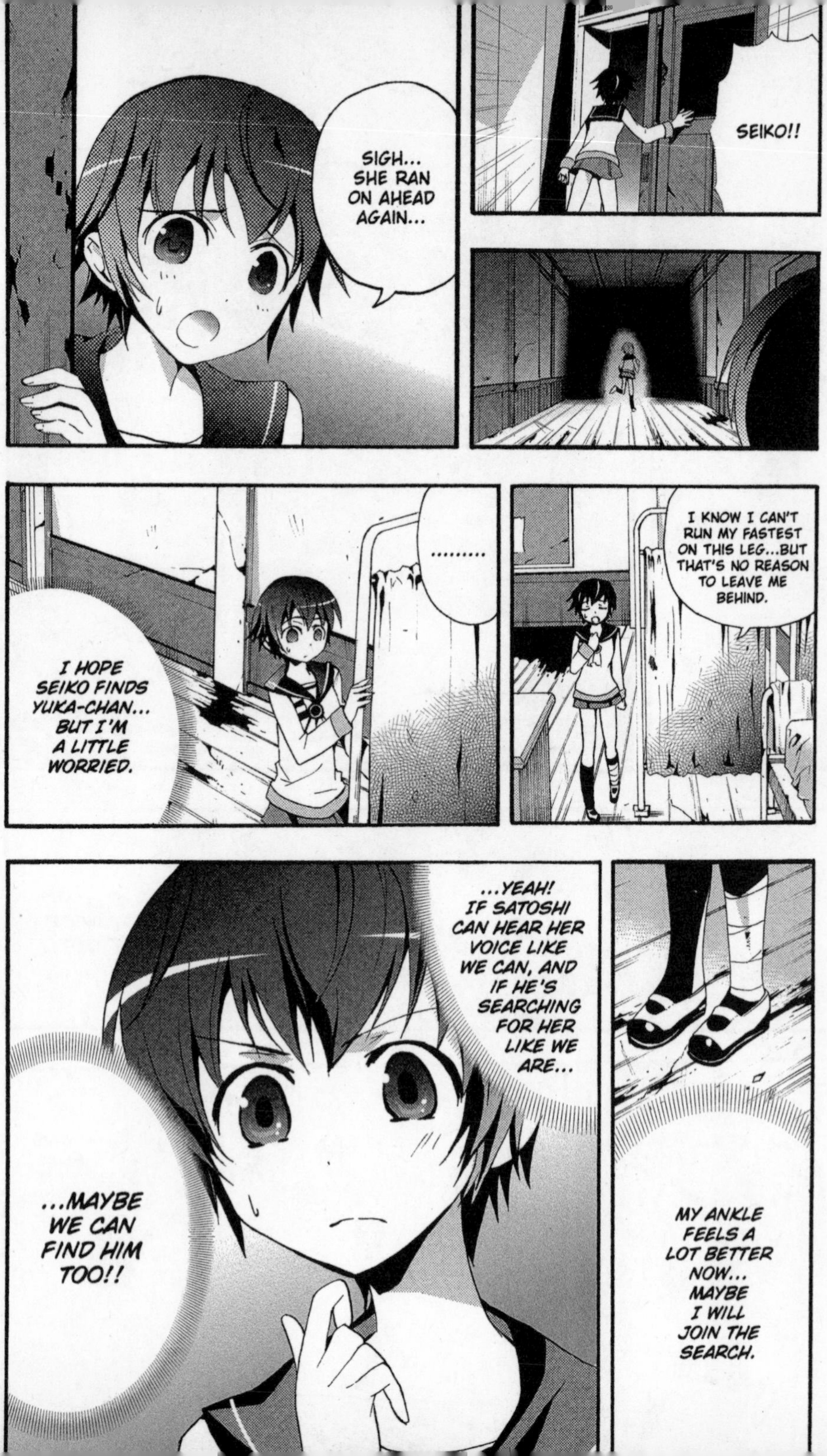
SEIKO!!
SIGH... SHE RAN ON AHEAD AGAIN...
I KNOW I CAN'T RUN MY FASTEST ON THIS LEG...BUT THAT'S NO REASON TO LEAVE ME BEHIND.
....
I HOPE SEIKO FINDS YUKA-CHAN... BUT I'M A LITTLE WORRIED.
MY ANKLE FEELS A LOT BETTER NOW... MAYBE I WILL JOIN THE SEARCH.
...YEAH! IF SATOSHI CAN HEAR HER VOICE LIKE WE CAN, AND IF HE'S SEARCHING FOR HER LIKE WE ARE...
...MAYBE WE CAN FIND HIM TOO!!

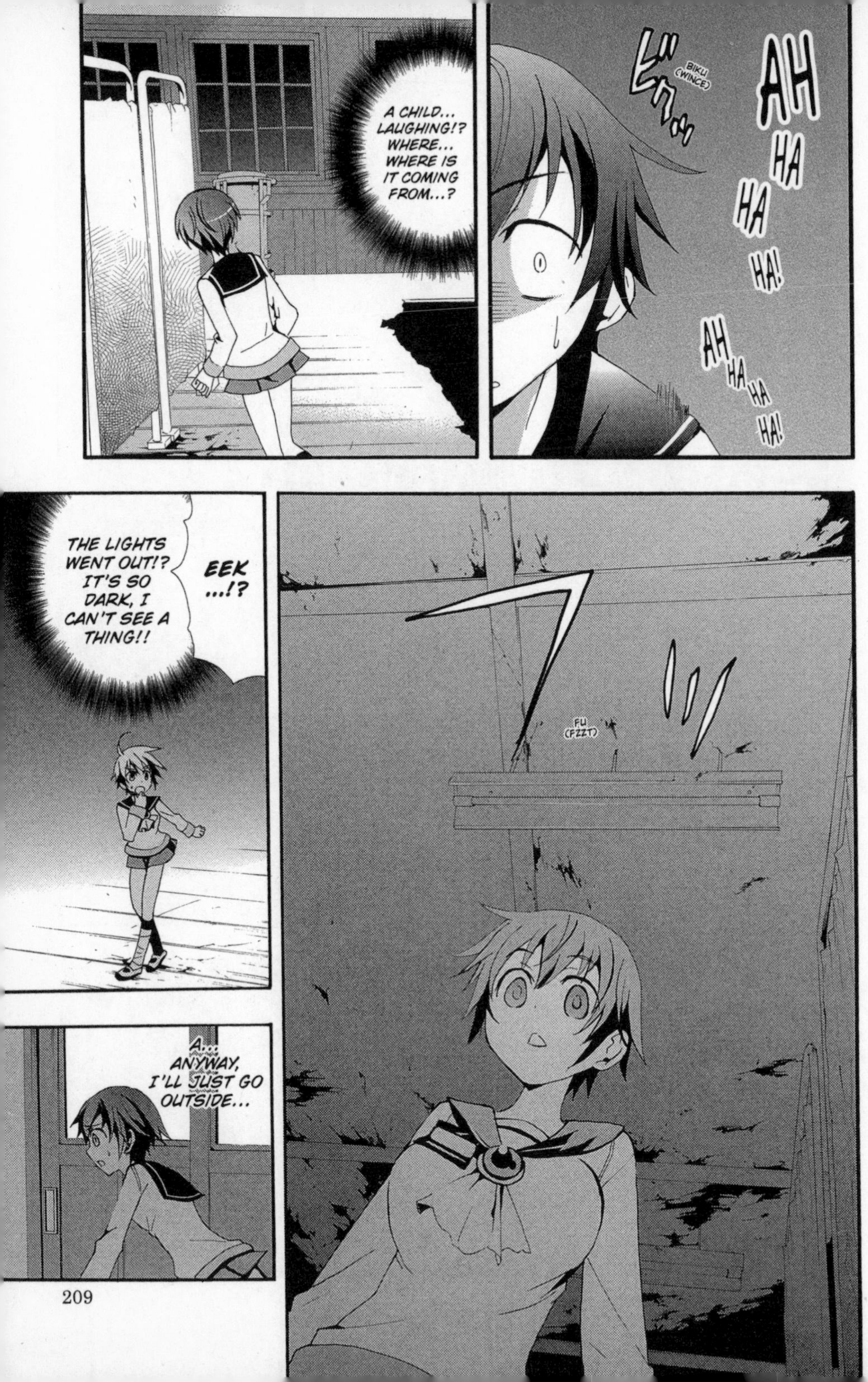
ビクッ
BIKU (WINCE)
AH HA HA HA!
AH HA HA HA HA!
A CHILD... LAUGHING!? WHERE... WHERE IS IT COMING FROM...?
FU (FZZT)
THE LIGHTS WENT OUT!? IT'S SO DARK, I CAN'T SEE A THING!!
EEK ...!?
A... ANYWAY, I'LL JUST GO OUTSIDE...

POSTER: WASH HANDS WITH SOAP.

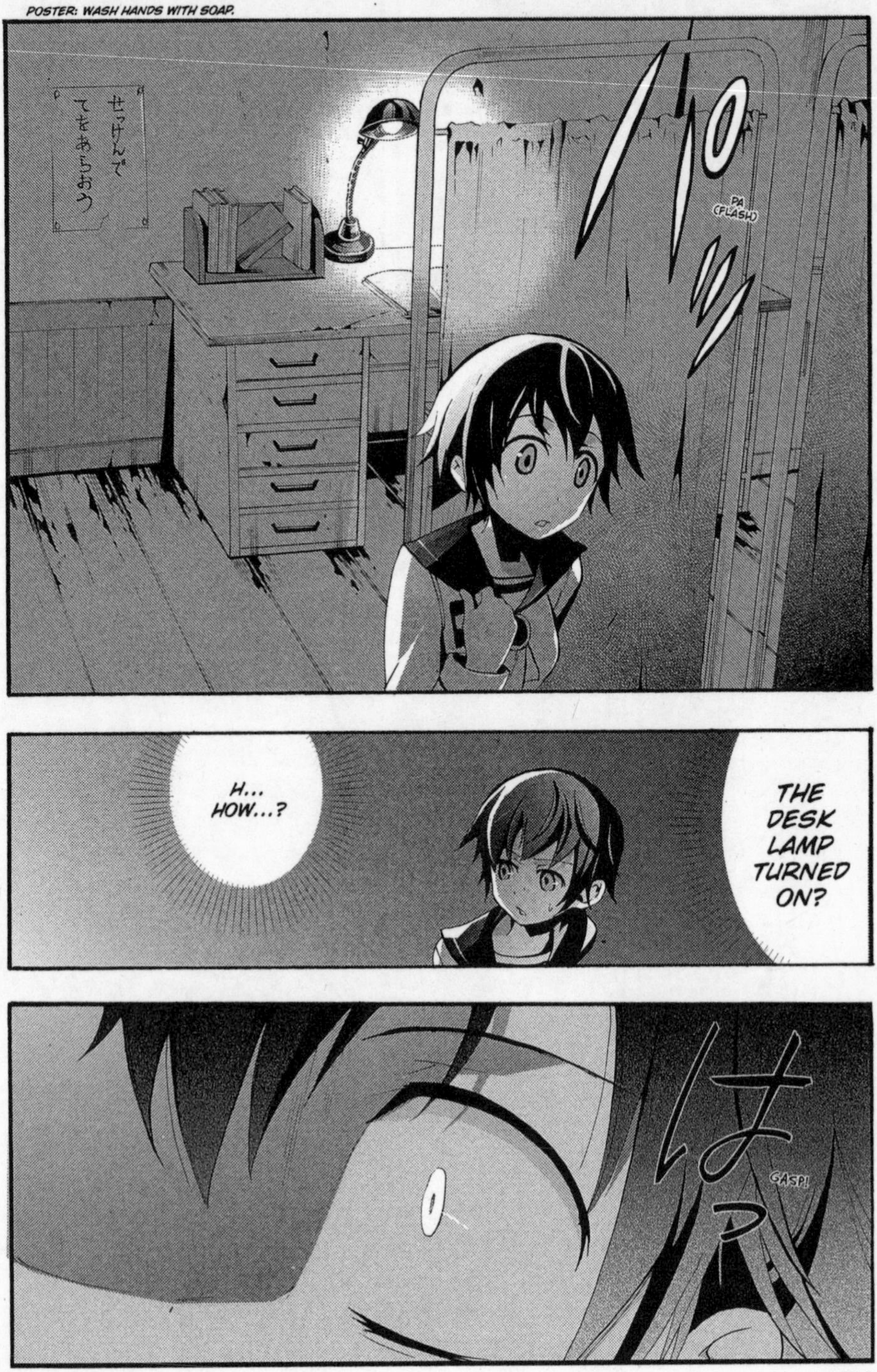
せっけんで
てをあらおう
パッ
PA
(FLASH)
THE DESK LAMP TURNED ON?
H... HOW...?
はっ
GASP!

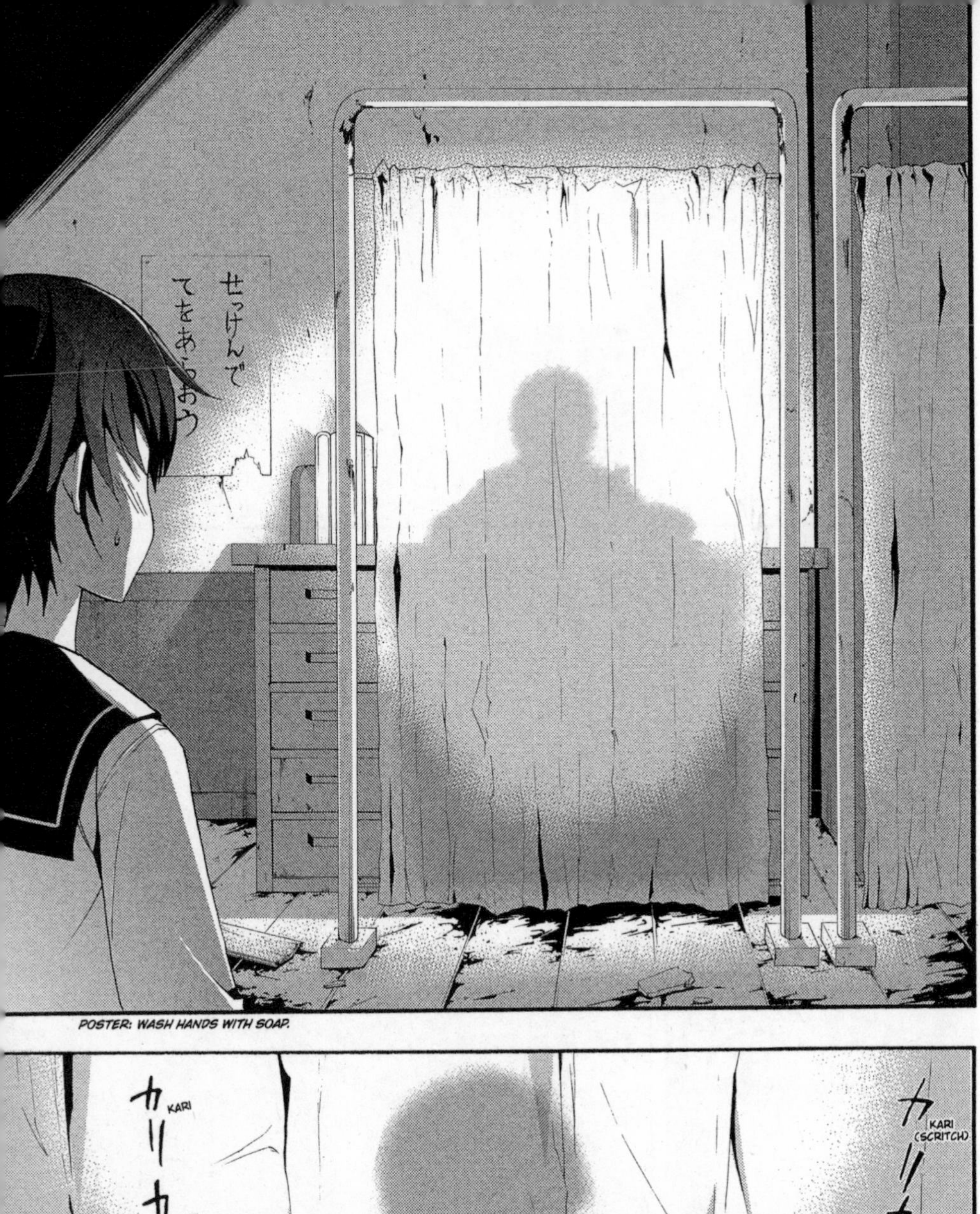
せっけんで
てをあらおう

POSTER: WASH HANDS WITH SOAP.

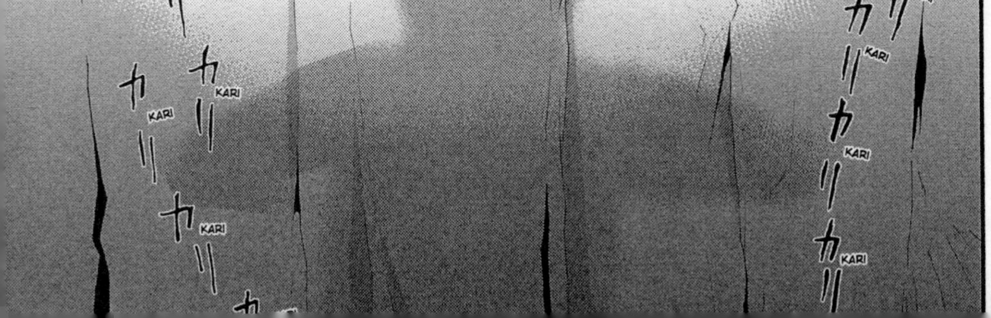
カリ KARI (SCRITCH)
カリ KARI
カリ KARI
カリ KARI
カリ KARI
カリ KARI
カリ KARI
カリ KARI
カリ KARI
カリ KARI

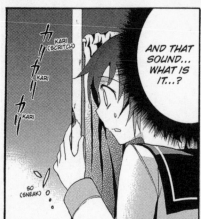

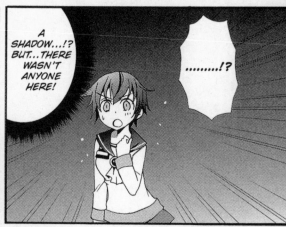

........!?
A SHADOW...!? BUT...THERE WASN'T ANYONE HERE!
AND THAT SOUND... WHAT IS IT...?
KARI (SCRITCH)
KARI
KARI
SO (SNEAK)
WRITING: EVERYONE, LET'S GO ON A PICNIC. HEE-HEE. TEE-HEE-HEE-HEE.
KARI
KARI
KARI
KARI
KARI
KARI
KARI
KARI
KARI
WHAT!? THE PENCIL IS WRITING BY ITSELF...!?

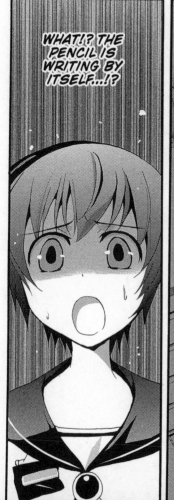

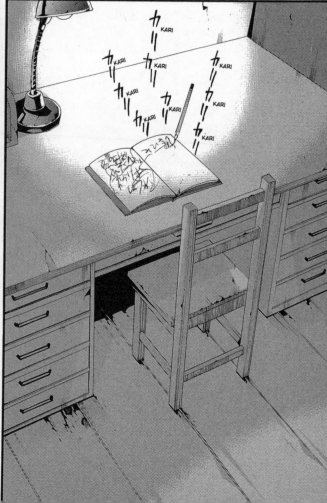

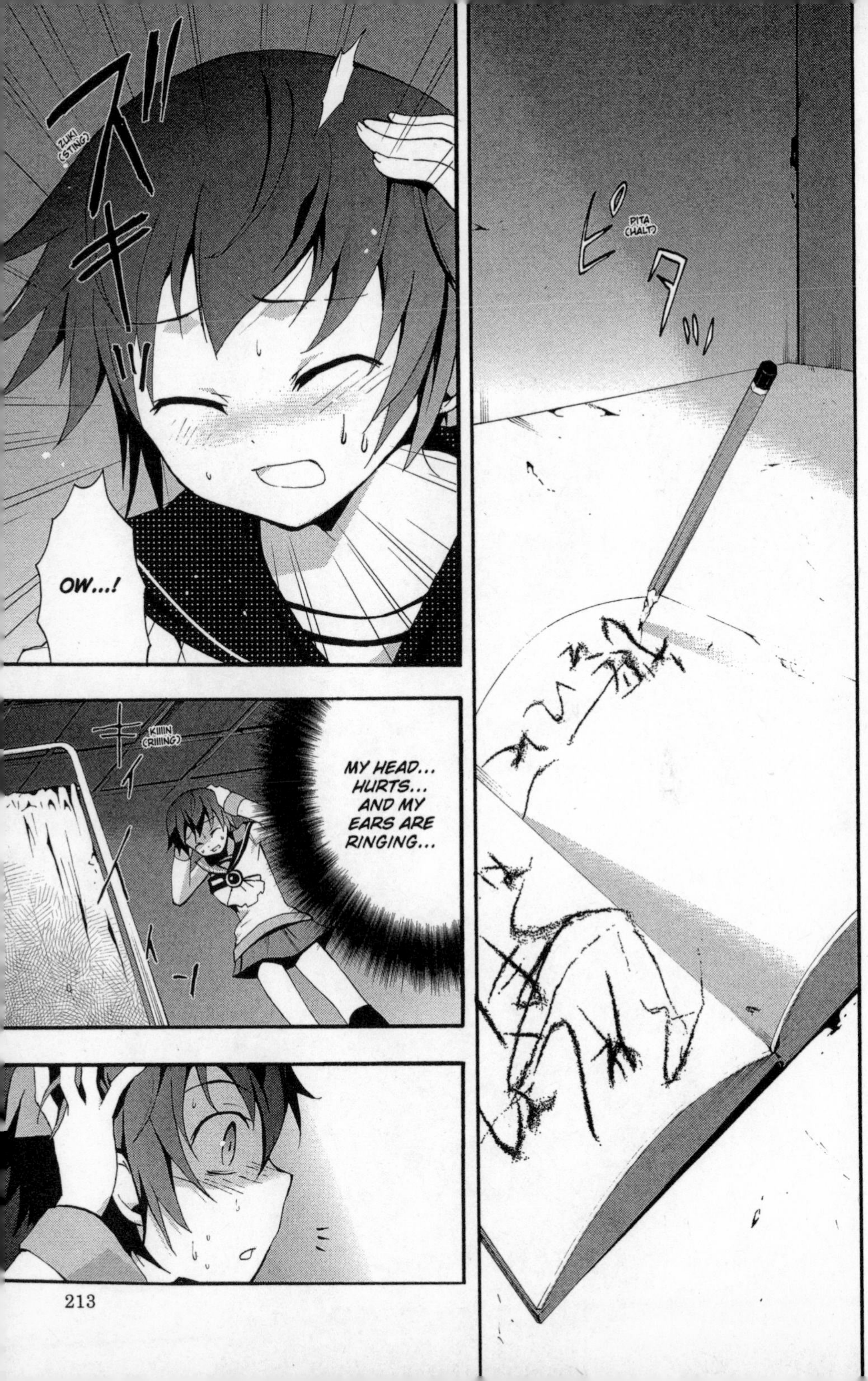
PITA (HALT)
ZUKI (STING)
OW...!
KIIIIN (RIIIIING)
MY HEAD... HURTS... AND MY EARS ARE RINGING...

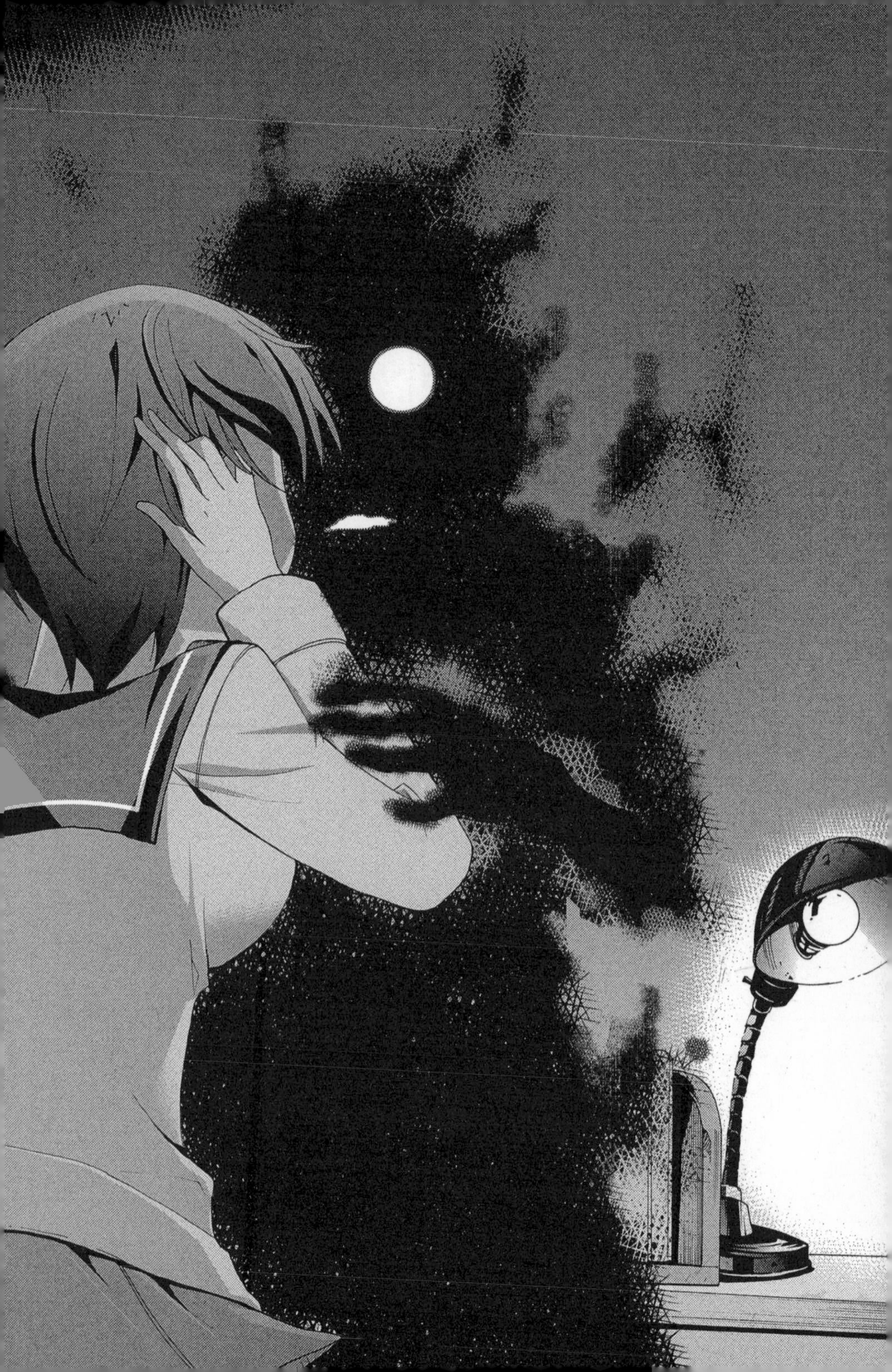

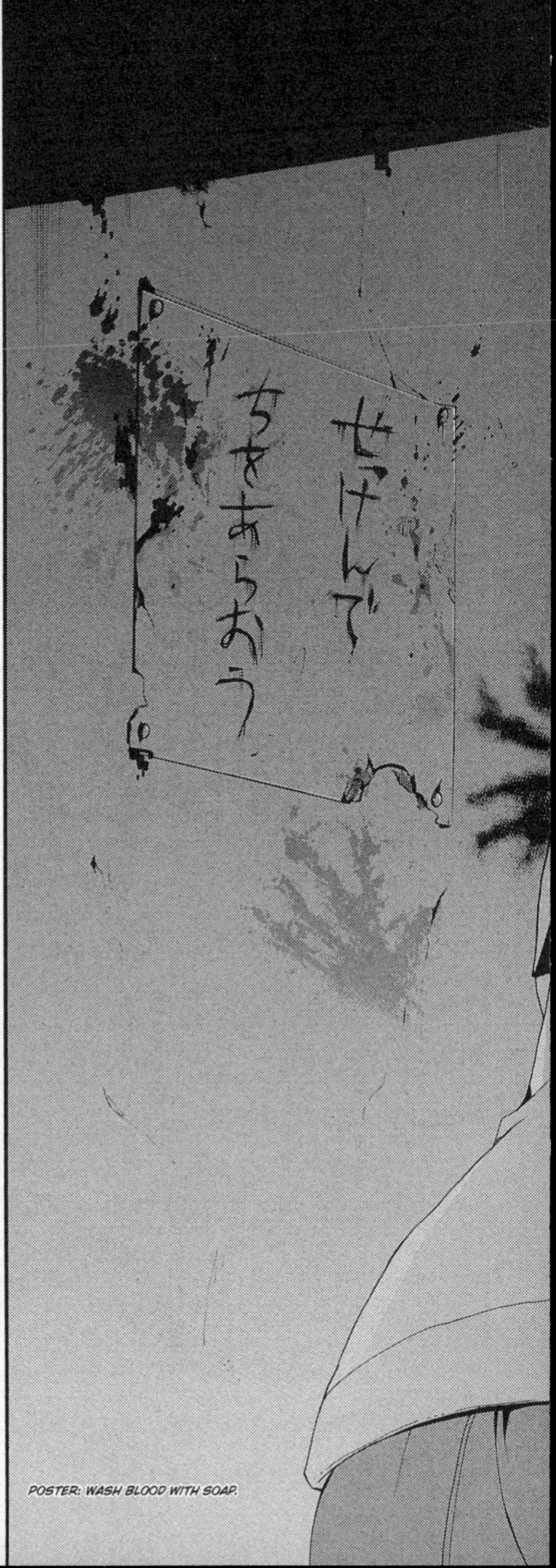
せっけんで ちをあらおう
POSTER: WASH BLOOD WITH SOAP.

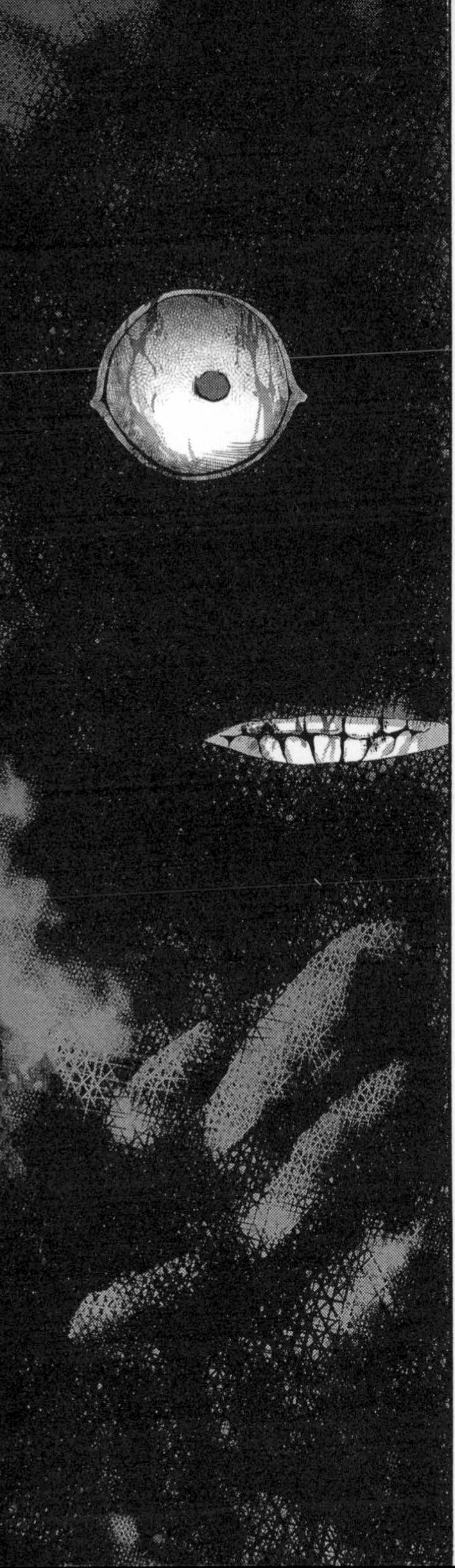

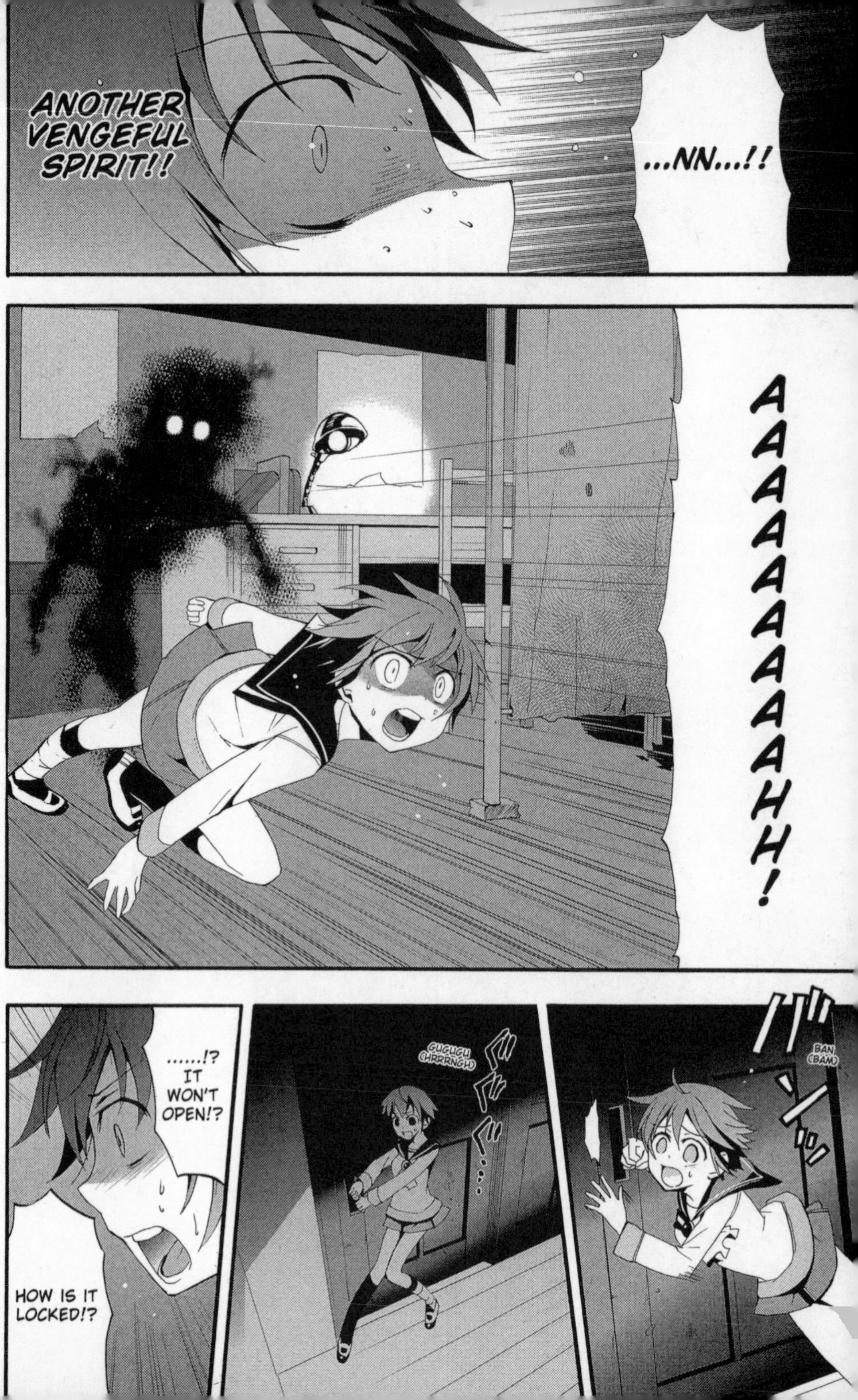
...NN...!!
ANOTHER VENGEFUL SPIRIT!!
AAAAAAAAAHH!
BAN (BAM)
GUGUGU (HRRRNGH)
......!? IT WON'T OPEN!?
HOW IS IT LOCKED!?

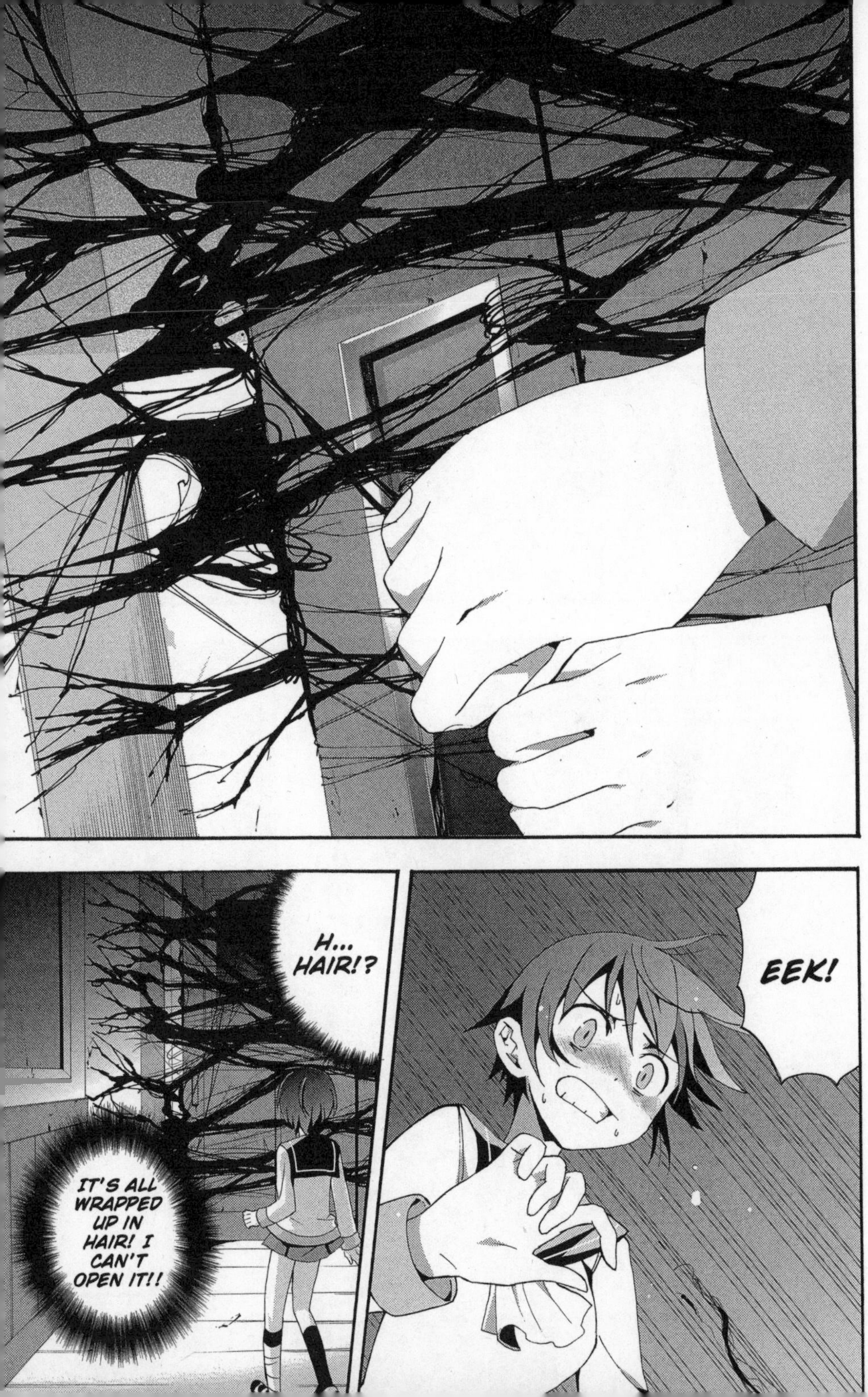
EEK!
H... HAIR!?
IT'S ALL WRAPPED UP IN HAIR! I CAN'T OPEN IT!!

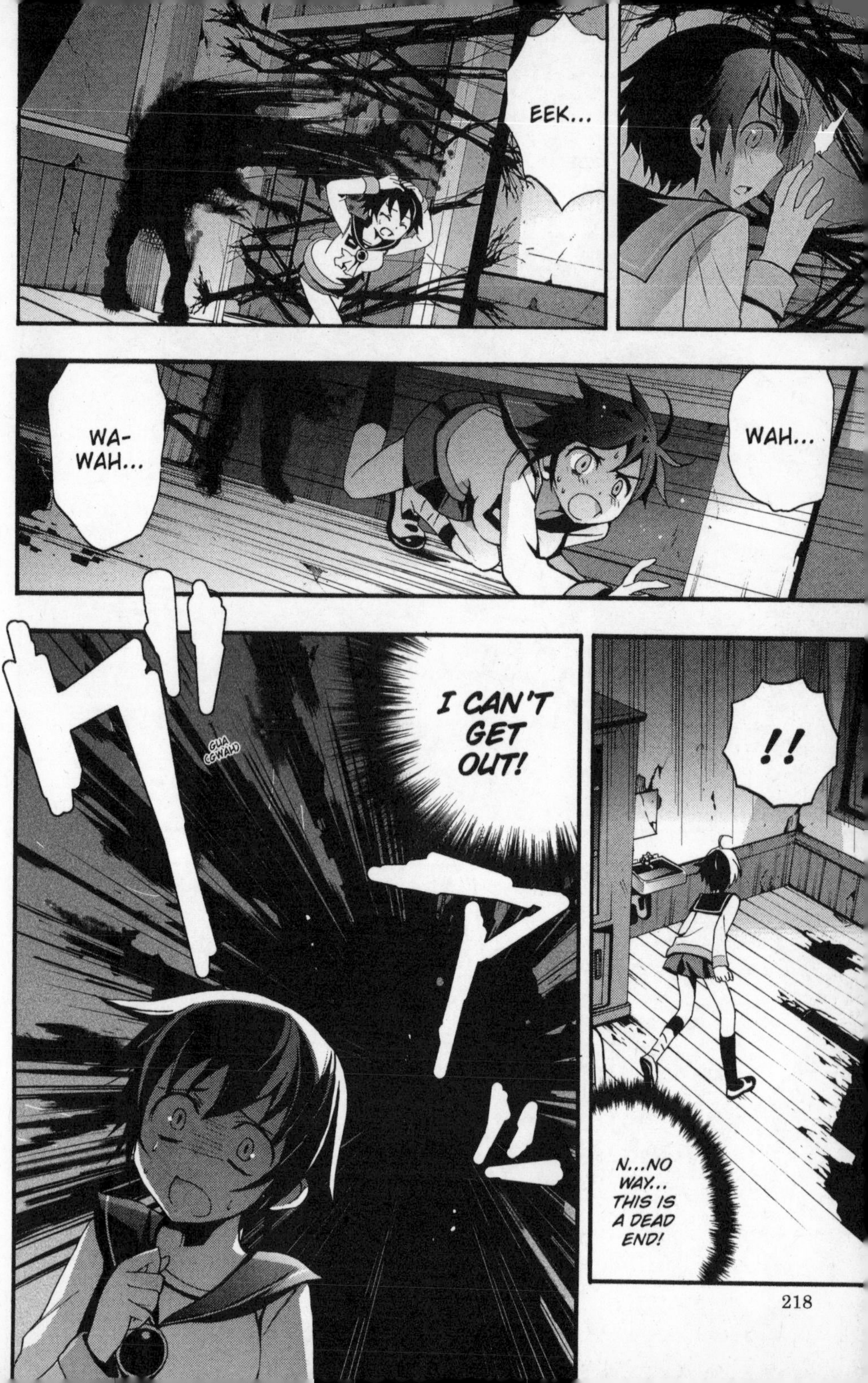
EEK...
WAH...
WA-WAH...
!!
N...NO WAY... THIS IS A DEAD END!
GUA (GWAH)
I CAN'T GET OUT!

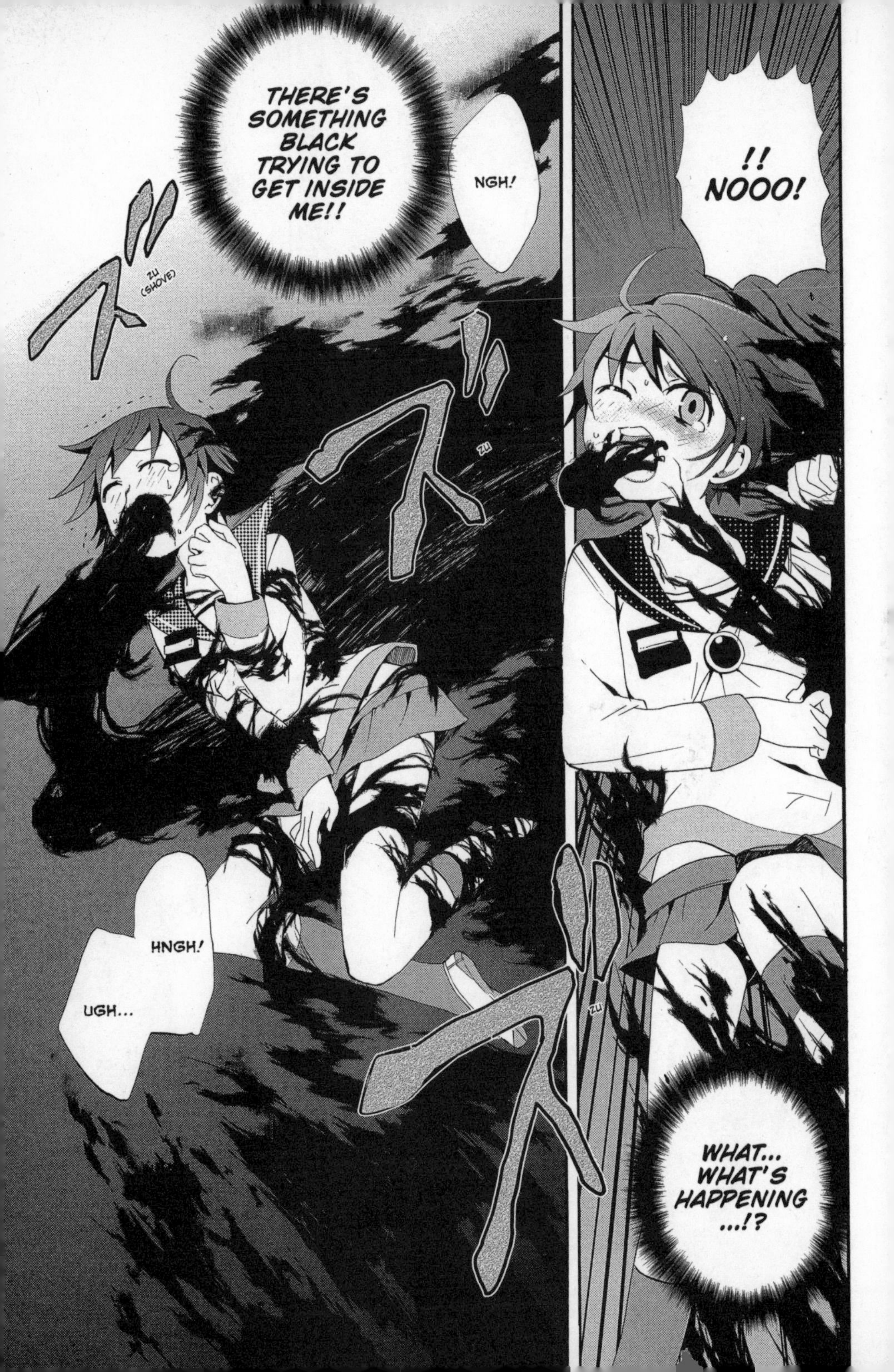
!! NOOO!
WHAT... WHAT'S HAPPENING ...!?
ZU
THERE'S SOMETHING BLACK TRYING TO GET INSIDE ME!!
NGH!
ZU (SHOVE)
ZU
HNGH!
UGH...

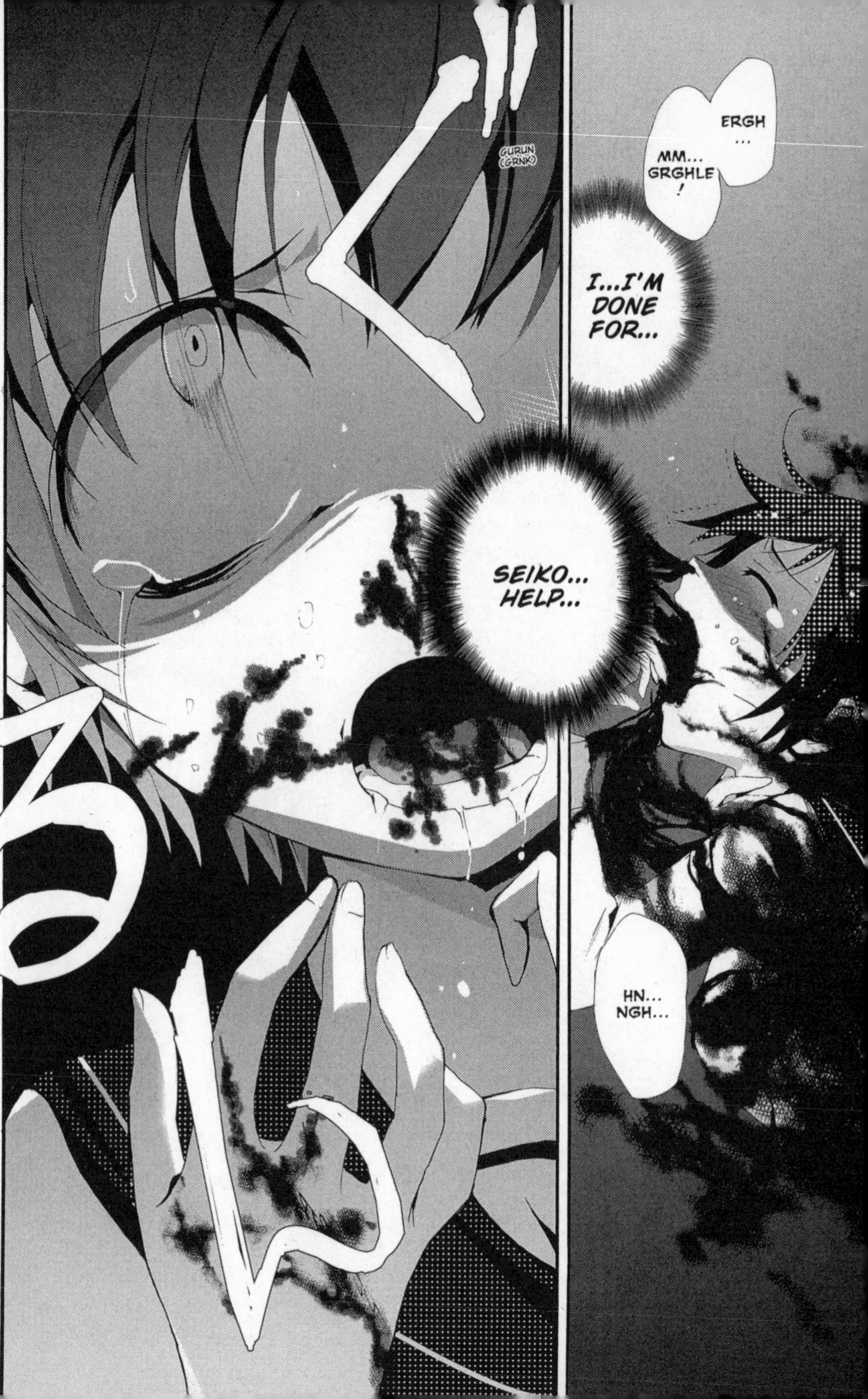
ERGH... MM... GRGHLE!
I...I'M DONE FOR...
SEIKO... HELP...
HN... NGH...
GURUN (GRNK)

...MI!?

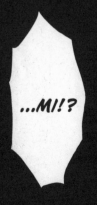

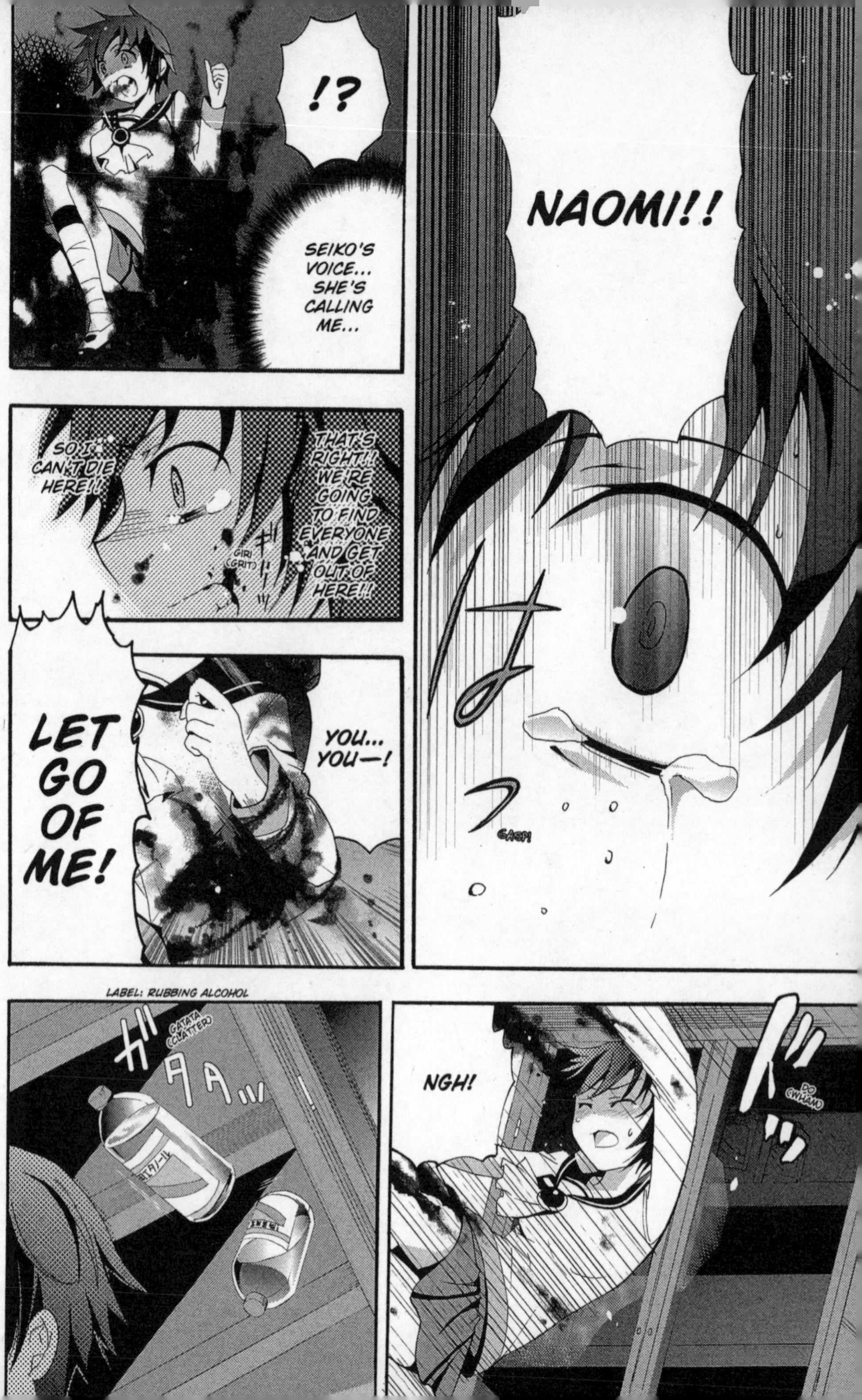
NAOMI!!
GASP!
!?
SEIKO'S VOICE... SHE'S CALLING ME...
THAT'S RIGHT!! WE'RE GOING TO FIND EVERYONE AND GET OUT OF HERE!!
GIRI (GRIT)
SO I CAN'T DIE HERE!!
YOU... YOU—!
LET GO OF ME!
DO (WHAM)
NGH!
LABEL: RUBBING ALCOHOL
GATATA (CLATTER)

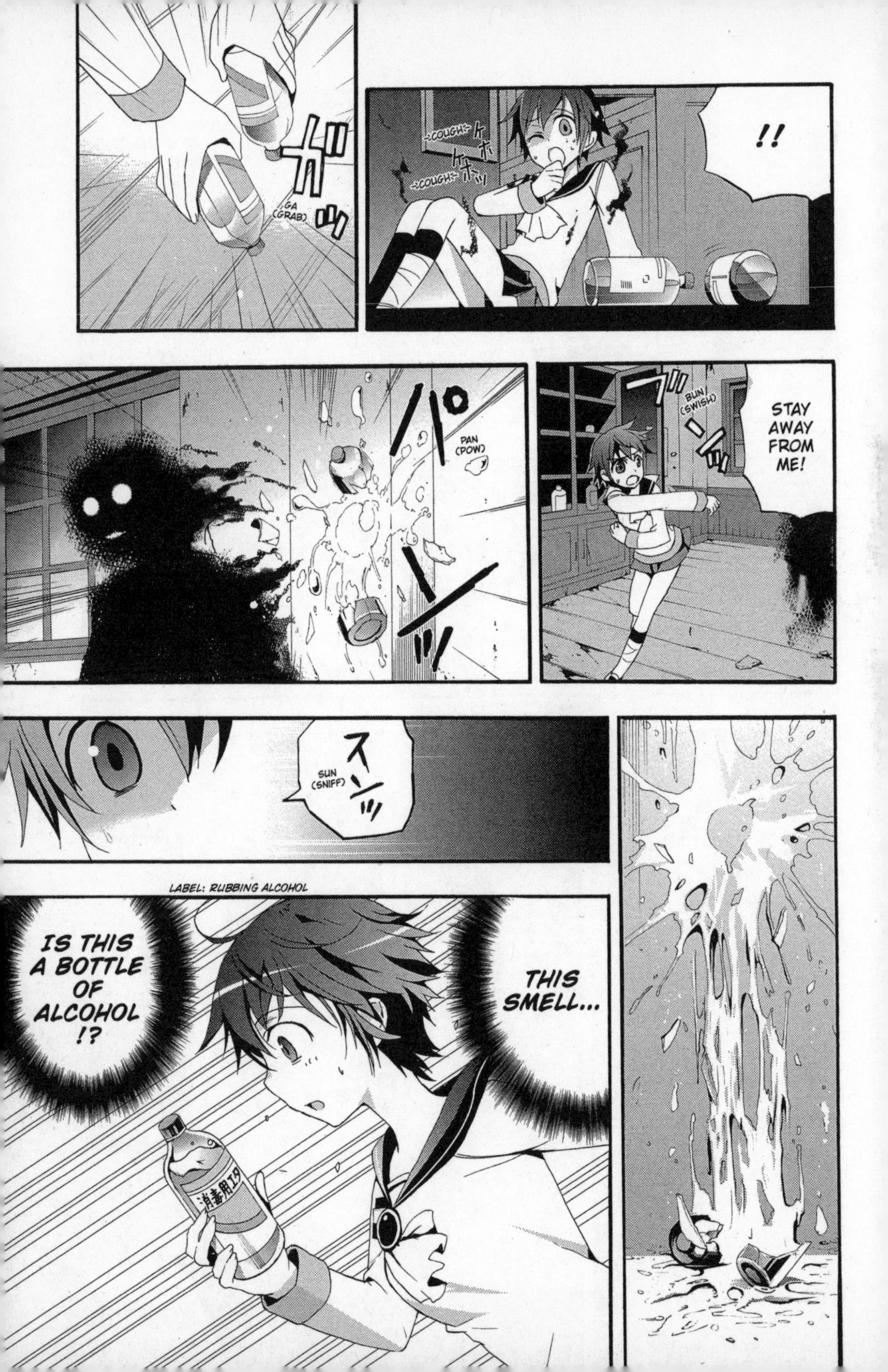
!!
COUGH
COUGH
GA (GRAB)
BUN (SWISH)
STAY AWAY FROM ME!
PAN (POW)
SUN (SNIFF)
LABEL: RUBBING ALCOHOL
THIS SMELL...
IS THIS A BOTTLE OF ALCOHOL!?
消毒用エタ

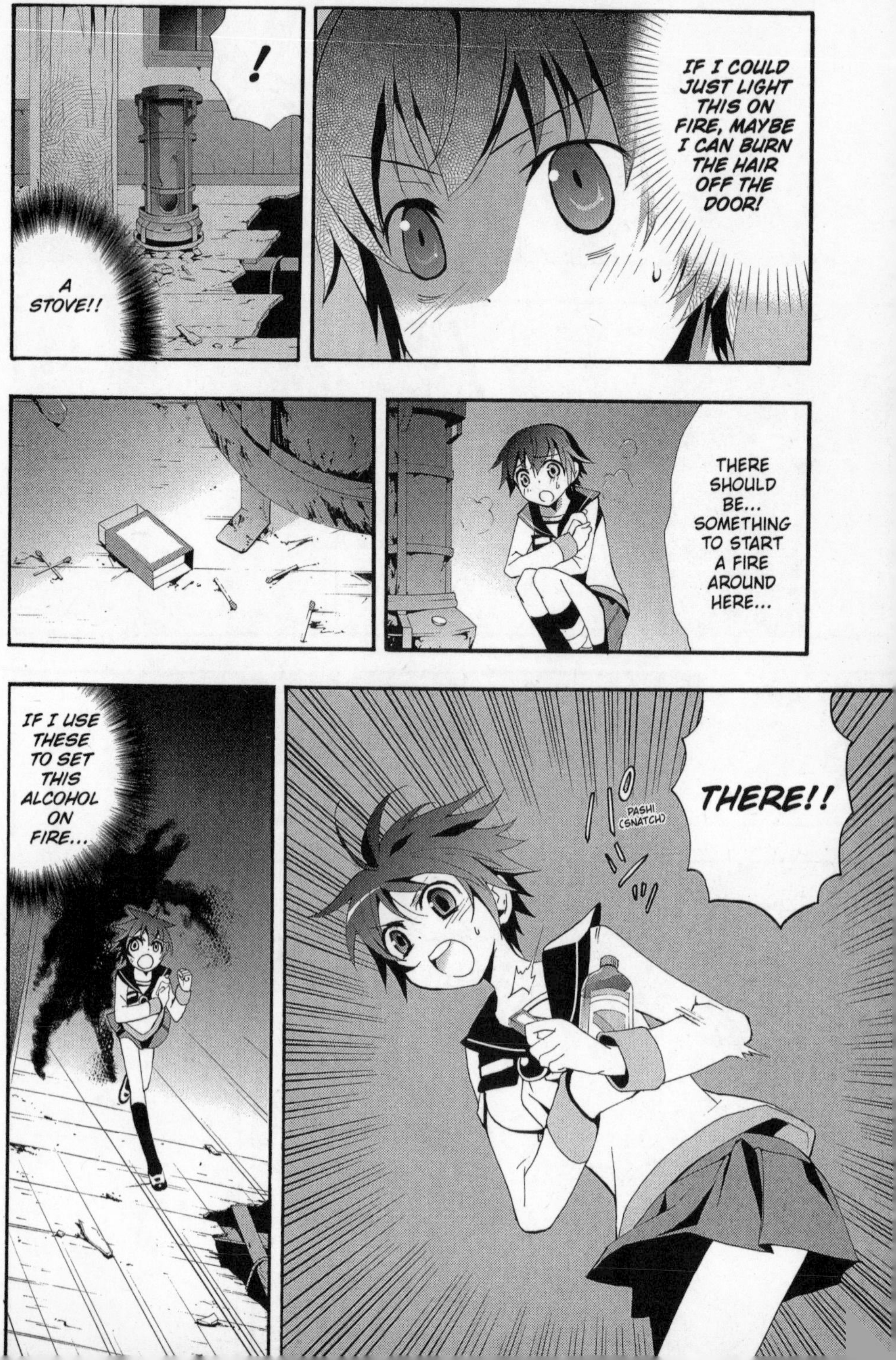
IF I COULD JUST LIGHT THIS ON FIRE, MAYBE I CAN BURN THE HAIR OFF THE DOOR!
!
A STOVE!!
THERE SHOULD BE... SOMETHING TO START A FIRE AROUND HERE...
THERE!!
PASHI (SNATCH)
IF I USE THESE TO SET THIS ALCOHOL ON FIRE...

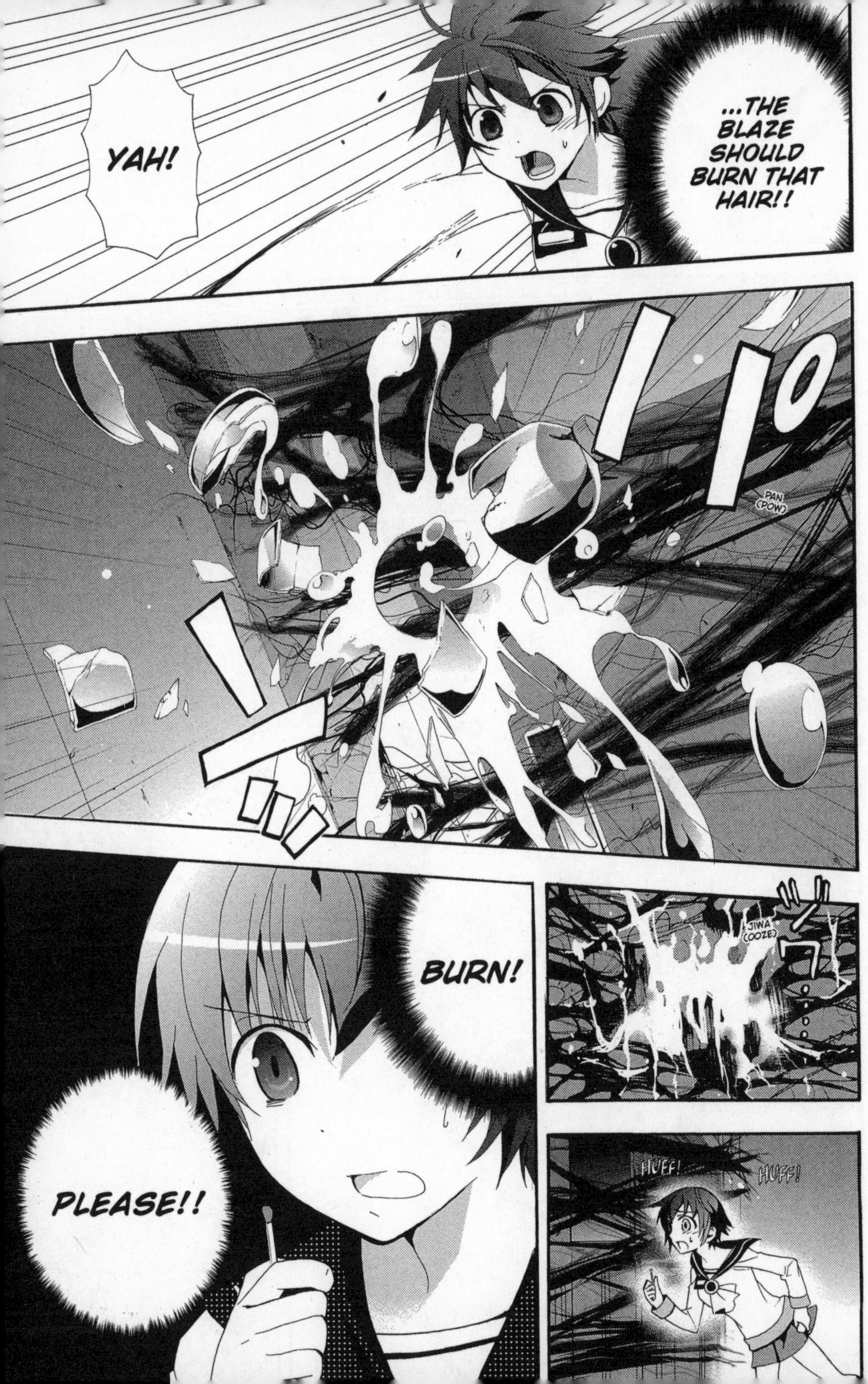
...THE BLAZE SHOULD BURN THAT HAIR!!
YAH!
PAN (POW)
JIWA (OOZE)
HUFF!
HUFF!
BURN!
PLEASE!!

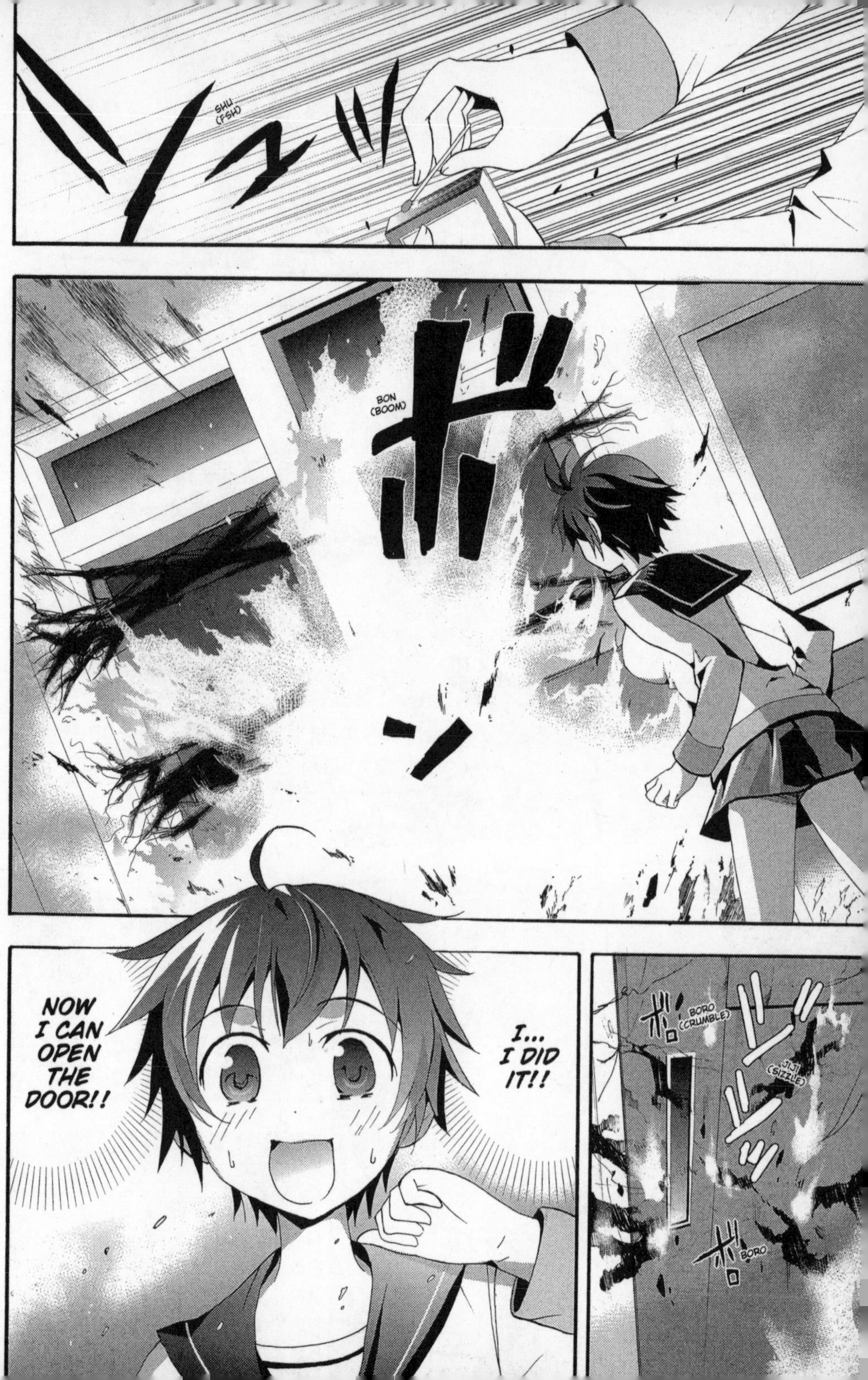
SHU (FSH)
BON (BOOM)
BORO (CRUMBLE)
JIJI (SIZZLE)
BORO
I... I DID IT!!
NOW I CAN OPEN THE DOOR!!

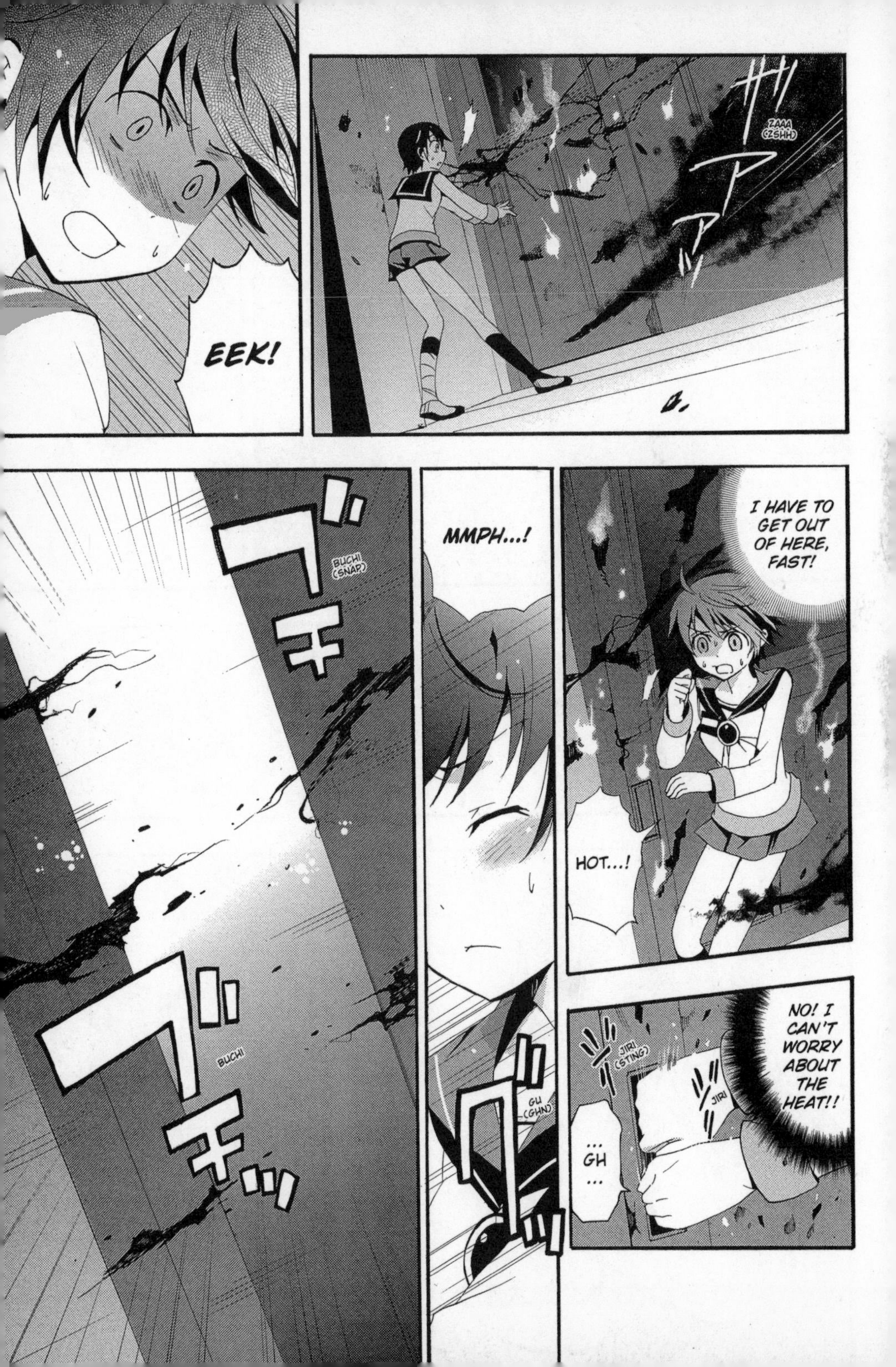
ZAAA (ZSHH)
EEK!
I HAVE TO GET OUT OF HERE, FAST!
HOT...!
NO! I CAN'T WORRY ABOUT THE HEAT!!
JIRI (STING)
JIRI
...GH...
MMPH...!
GU (GHN)
BUCHI (SNAP)
BUCHI

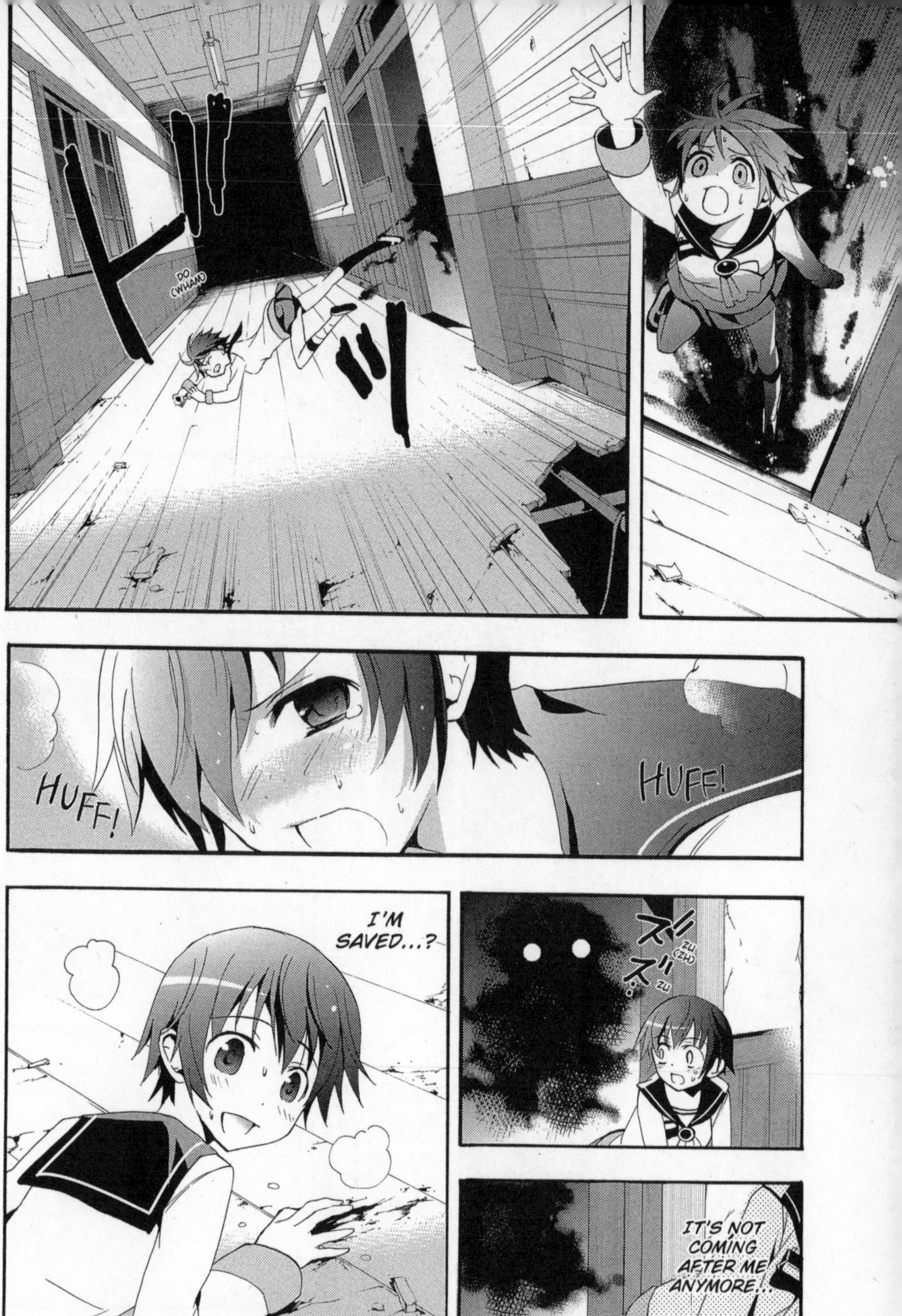
DO
(WHAM)
HUFF!
HUFF!
ズズ
ZU
(ZH)
ZU
IT'S NOT COMING AFTER ME ANYMORE...
I'M SAVED...?

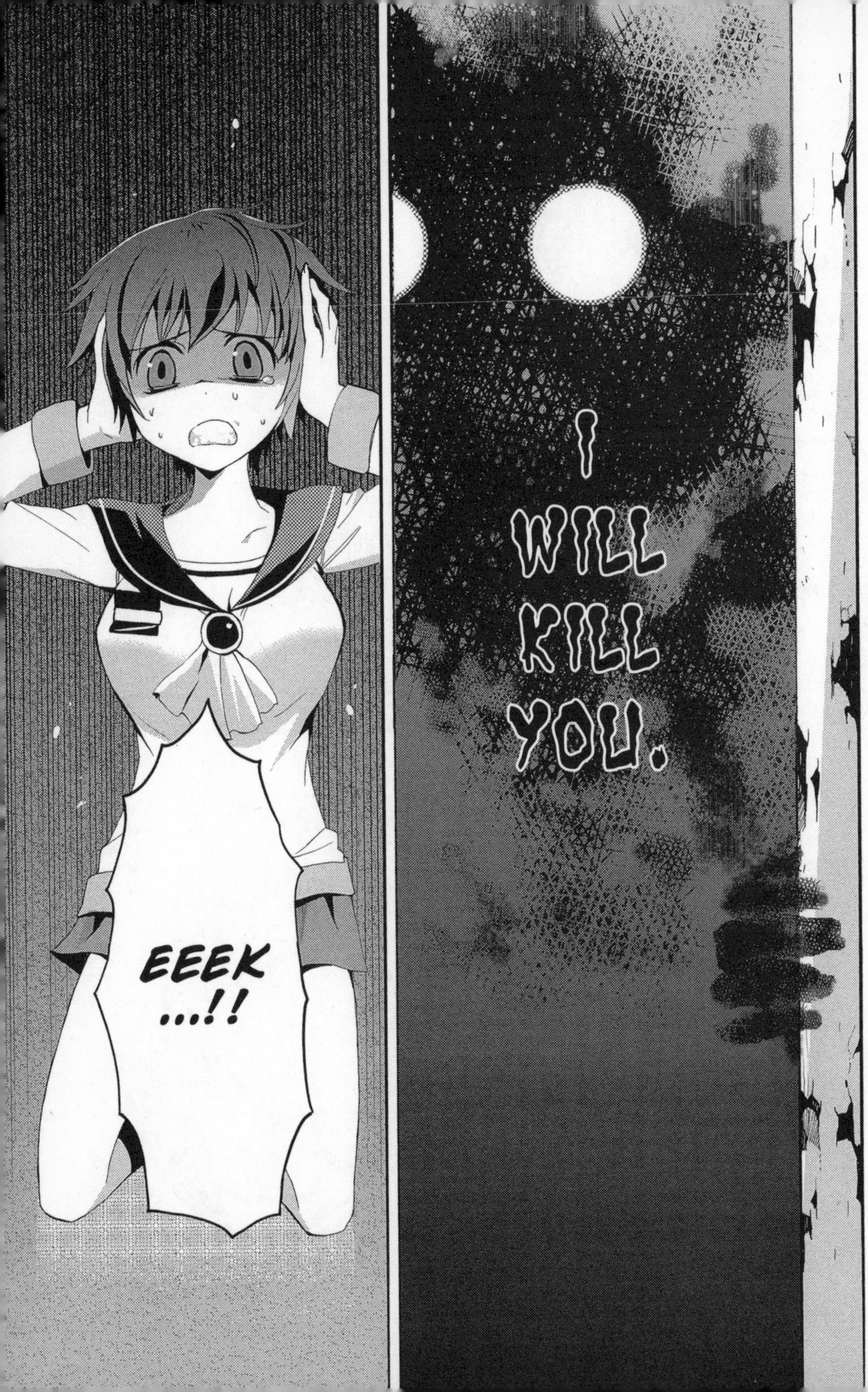
I WILL KILL YOU.
EEEK ...!!

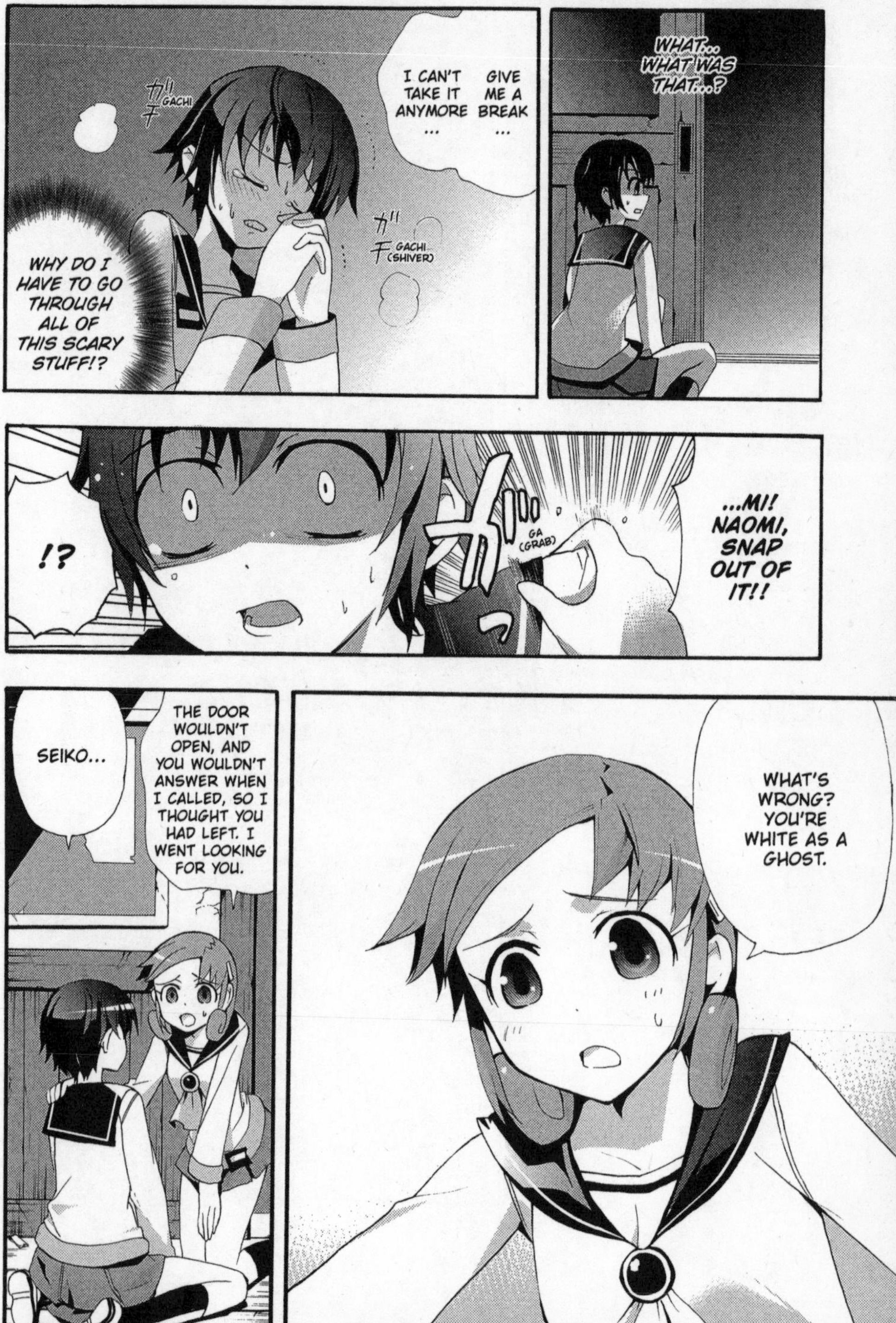
WHAT... WHAT WAS THAT...?
GIVE ME A BREAK ...
I CAN'T TAKE IT ANYMORE ...
GACHI (SHIVER)
GACHI
WHY DO I HAVE TO GO THROUGH ALL OF THIS SCARY STUFF!?
...MI! NAOMI, SNAP OUT OF IT!!
GA (GRAB)
!?
WHAT'S WRONG? YOU'RE WHITE AS A GHOST.
THE DOOR WOULDN'T OPEN, AND YOU WOULDN'T ANSWER WHEN I CALLED, SO I THOUGHT YOU HAD LEFT. I WENT LOOKING FOR YOU.
SEIKO...

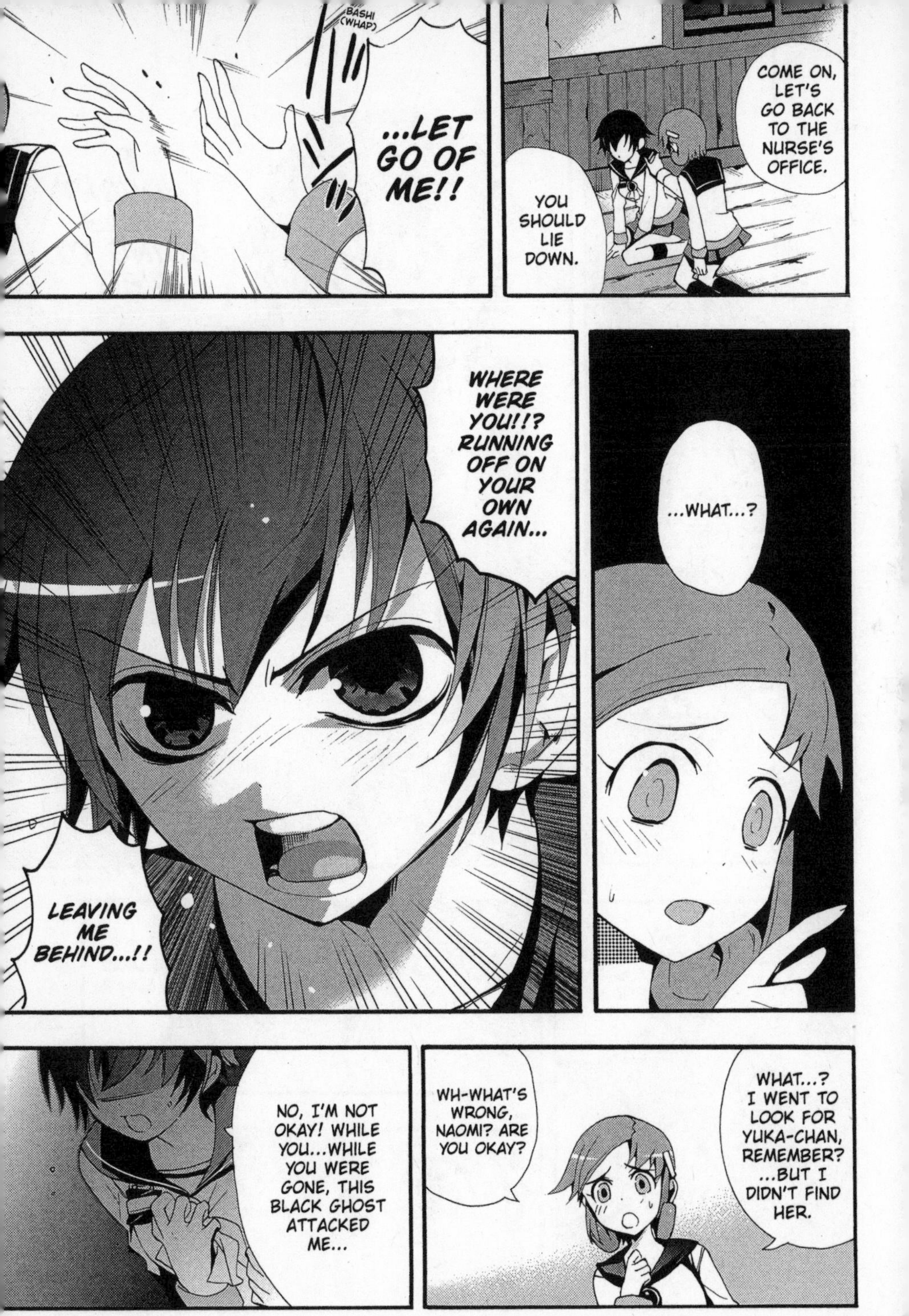
COME ON, LET'S GO BACK TO THE NURSE'S OFFICE.
YOU SHOULD LIE DOWN.
BASHI (WHAP)
...LET GO OF ME!!
...WHAT...?
WHERE WERE YOU!!? RUNNING OFF ON YOUR OWN AGAIN...
LEAVING ME BEHIND...!!
WHAT...? I WENT TO LOOK FOR YUKA-CHAN, REMEMBER? ...BUT I DIDN'T FIND HER.
WH-WHAT'S WRONG, NAOMI? ARE YOU OKAY?
NO, I'M NOT OKAY! WHILE YOU...WHILE YOU WERE GONE, THIS BLACK GHOST ATTACKED ME...

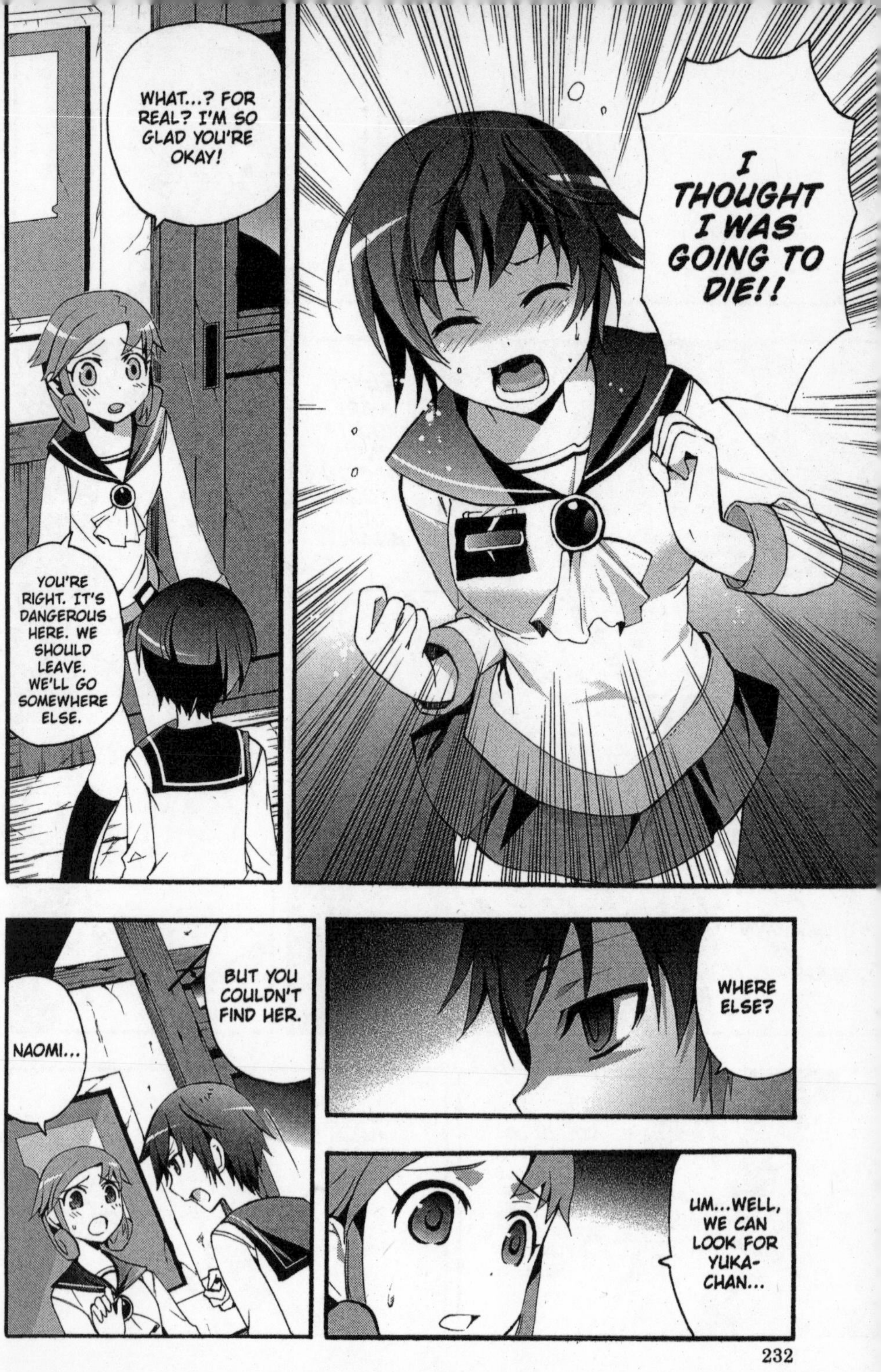
I THOUGHT I WAS GOING TO DIE!!
WHAT...? FOR REAL? I'M SO GLAD YOU'RE OKAY!
YOU'RE RIGHT. IT'S DANGEROUS HERE. WE SHOULD LEAVE. WE'LL GO SOMEWHERE ELSE.
WHERE ELSE?
UM...WELL, WE CAN LOOK FOR YUKA-CHAN...
BUT YOU COULDN'T FIND HER.
NAOMI...

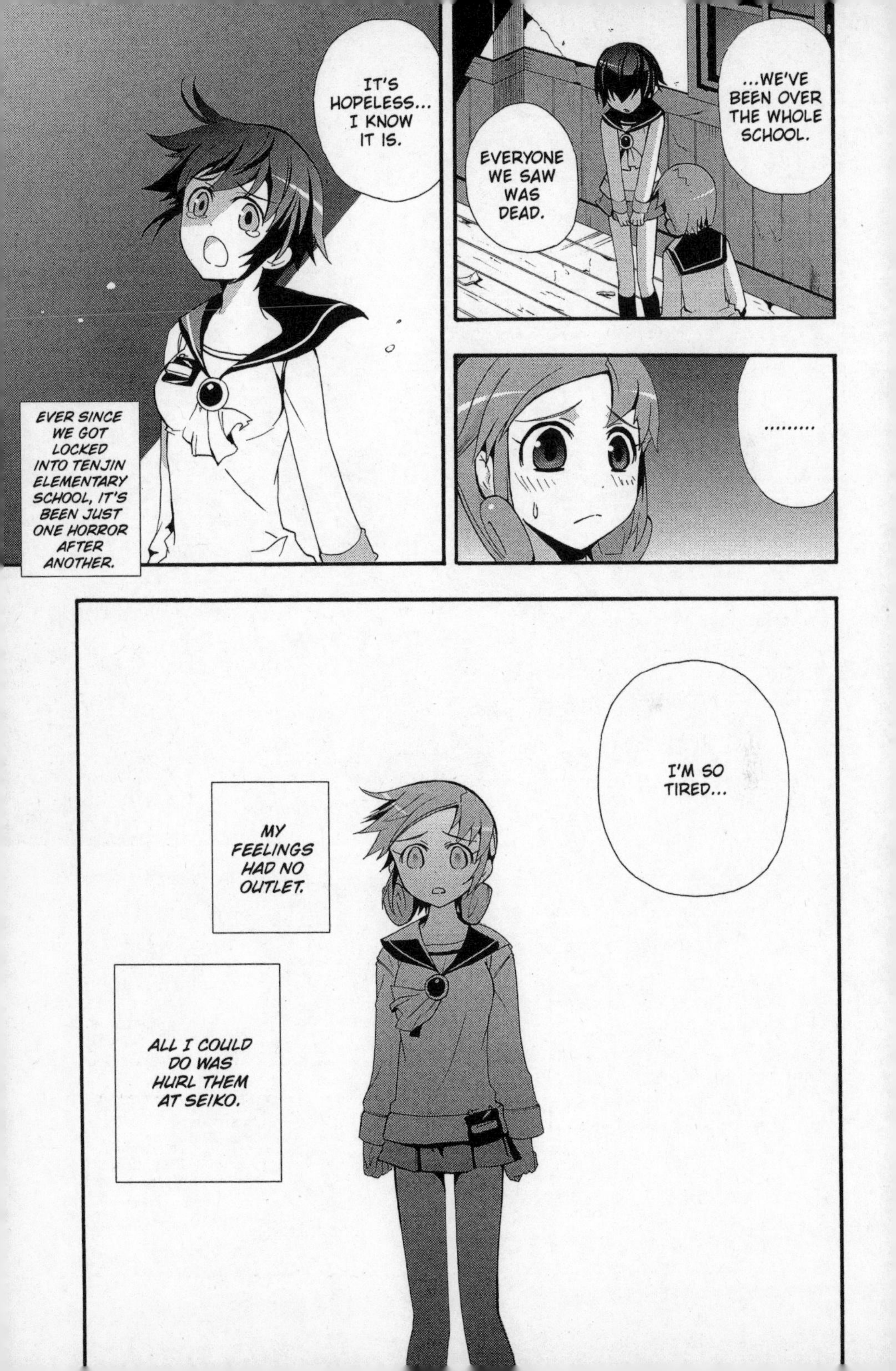
...WE'VE BEEN OVER THE WHOLE SCHOOL.
EVERYONE WE SAW WAS DEAD.
....
IT'S HOPELESS... I KNOW IT IS.
EVER SINCE WE GOT LOCKED INTO TENJIN ELEMENTARY SCHOOL, IT'S BEEN JUST ONE HORROR AFTER ANOTHER.
I'M SO TIRED...
MY FEELINGS HAD NO OUTLET.
ALL I COULD DO WAS HURL THEM AT SEIKO.

The ghost in the nurse's office

A ghost Naomi encountered in the
nurse's office. It was sitting at the
nurse's desk and scribbling something
in a diary. It did not follow her out of
the nurse's office, which could mean it
has some connection to that location.

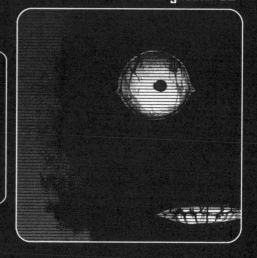

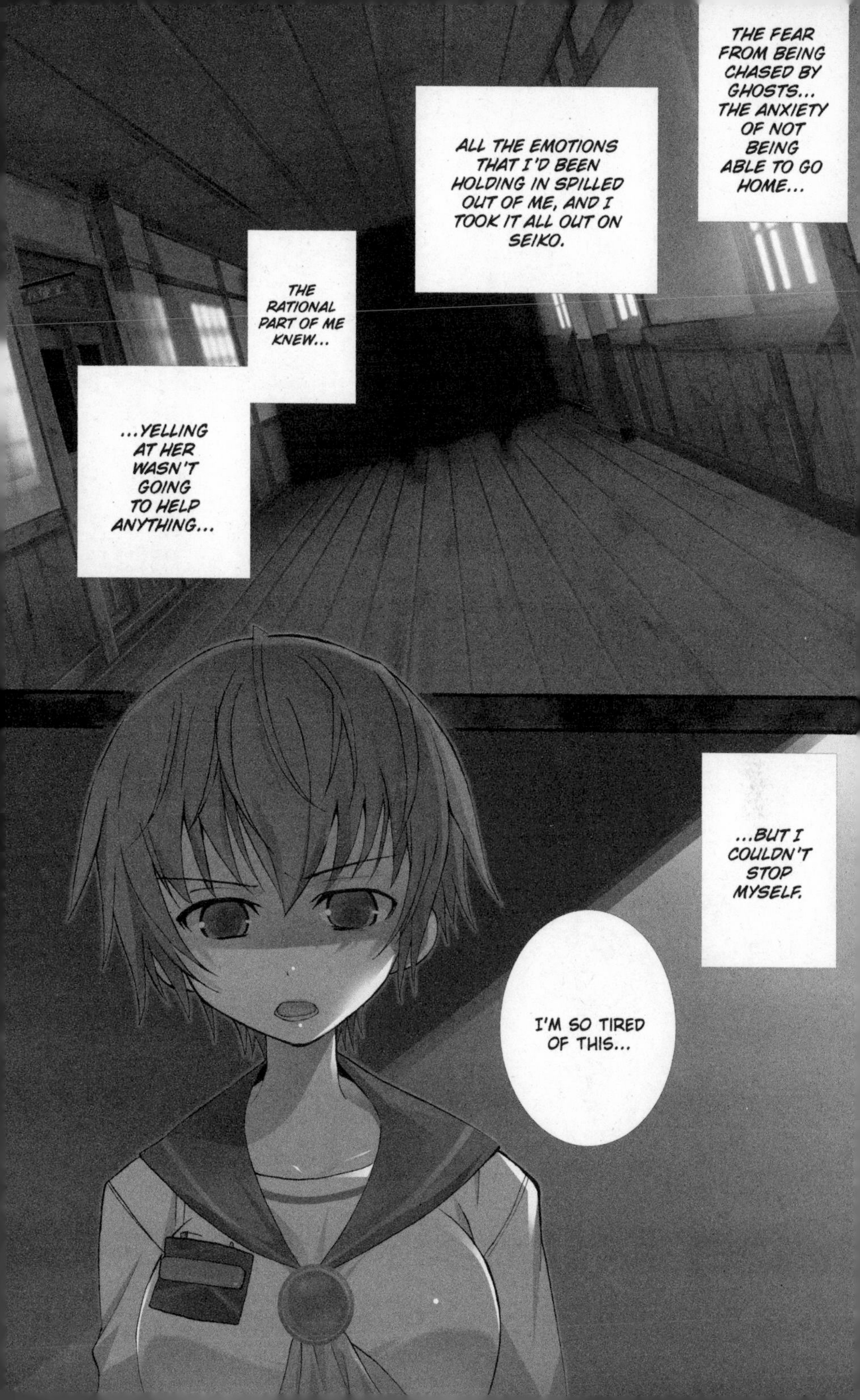
THE FEAR FROM BEING CHASED BY GHOSTS... THE ANXIETY OF NOT BEING ABLE TO GO HOME...
ALL THE EMOTIONS THAT I'D BEEN HOLDING IN SPILLED OUT OF ME, AND I TOOK IT ALL OUT ON SEIKO.
THE RATIONAL PART OF ME KNEW...
...YELLING AT HER WASN'T GOING TO HELP ANYTHING...
...BUT I COULDN'T STOP MYSELF.
I'M SO TIRED OF THIS...

Curse 6: Separation

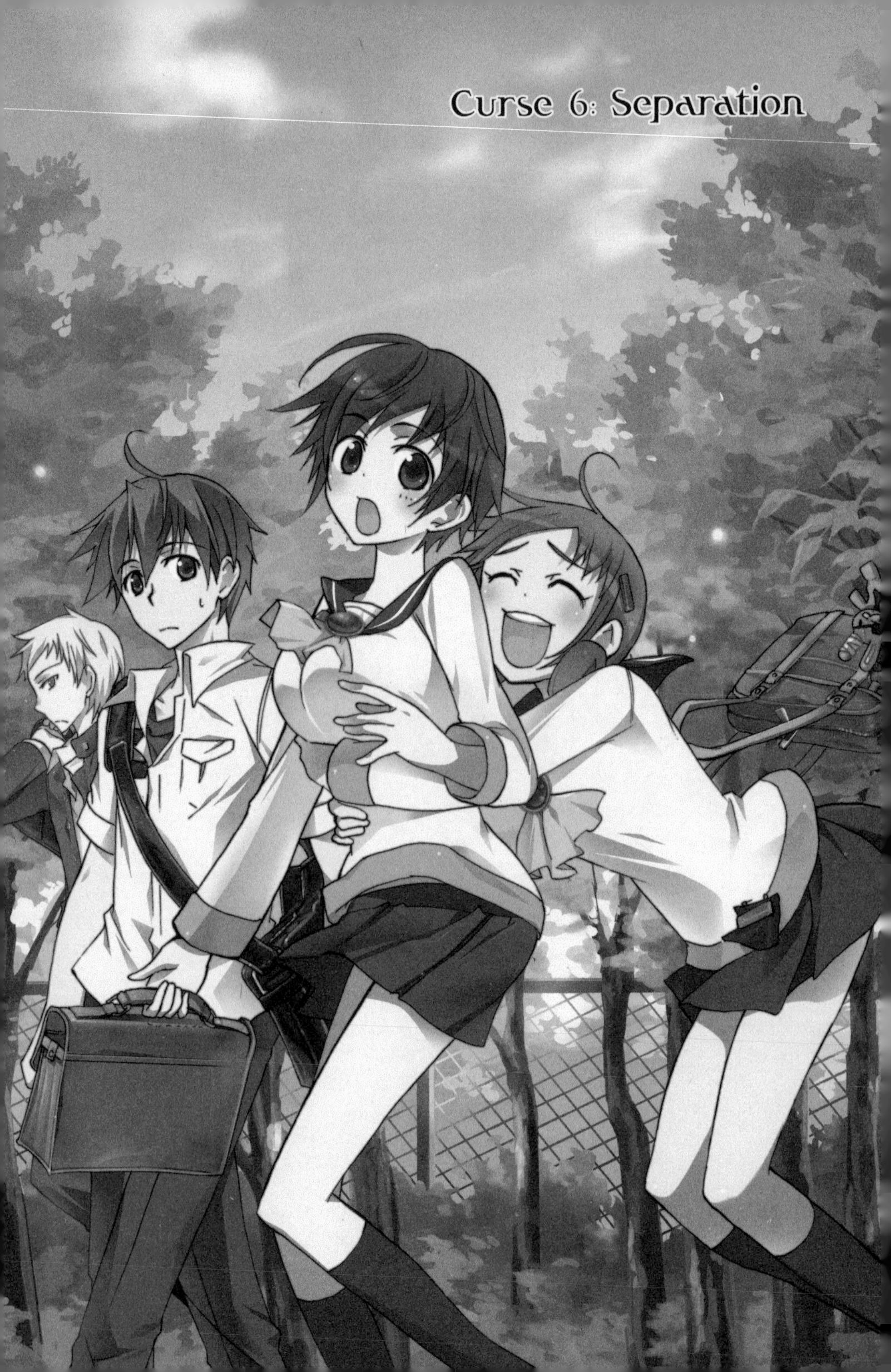

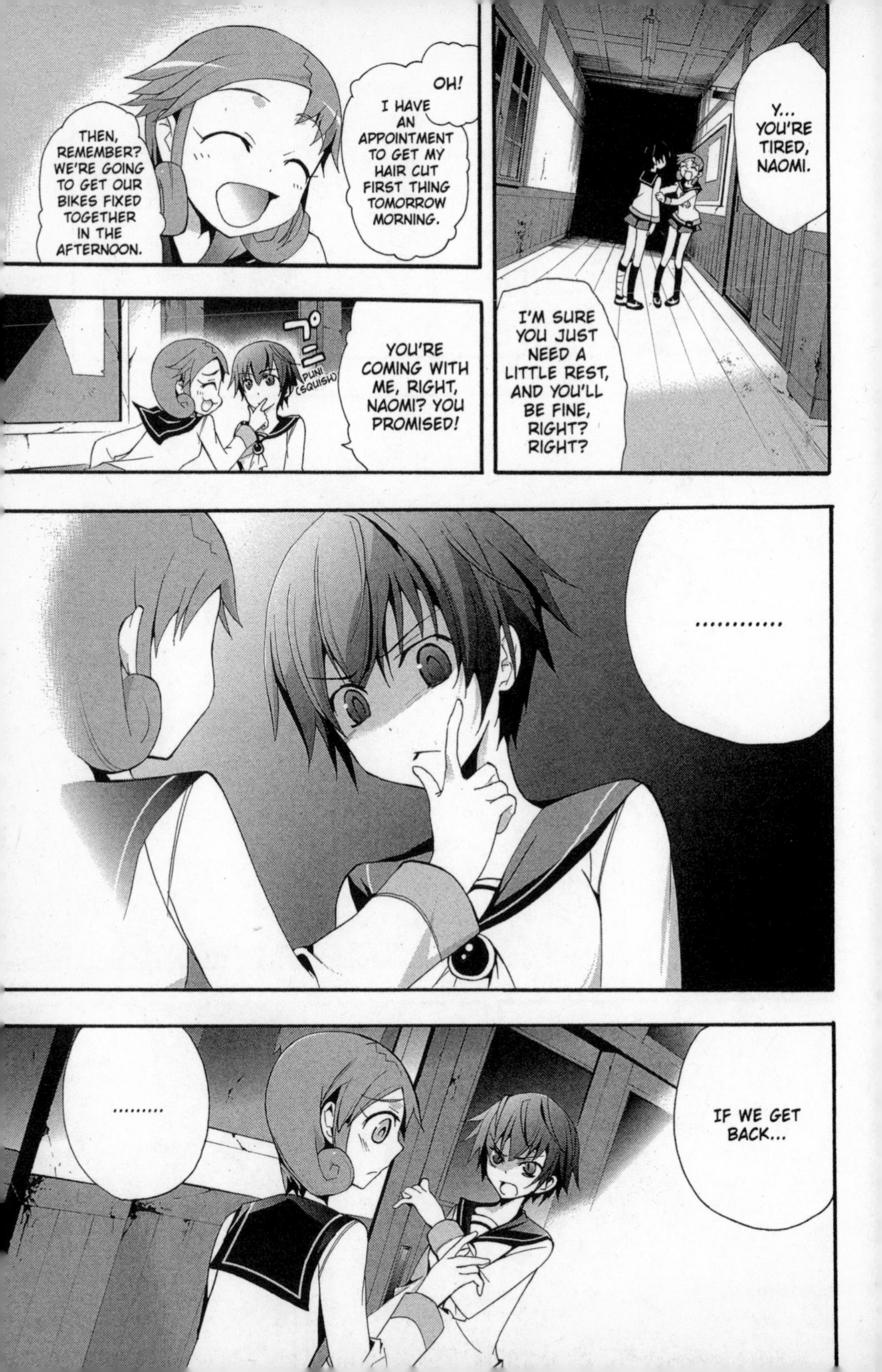

Y... YOU'RE TIRED, NAOMI.
I'M SURE YOU JUST NEED A LITTLE REST, AND YOU'LL BE FINE, RIGHT? RIGHT?
OH!
I HAVE AN APPOINTMENT TO GET MY HAIR CUT FIRST THING TOMORROW MORNING.
THEN, REMEMBER? WE'RE GOING TO GET OUR BIKES FIXED TOGETHER IN THE AFTERNOON.
YOU'RE COMING WITH ME, RIGHT, NAOMI? YOU PROMISED!
プニ
PUNI (SQUISH)
....
IF WE GET BACK...
....

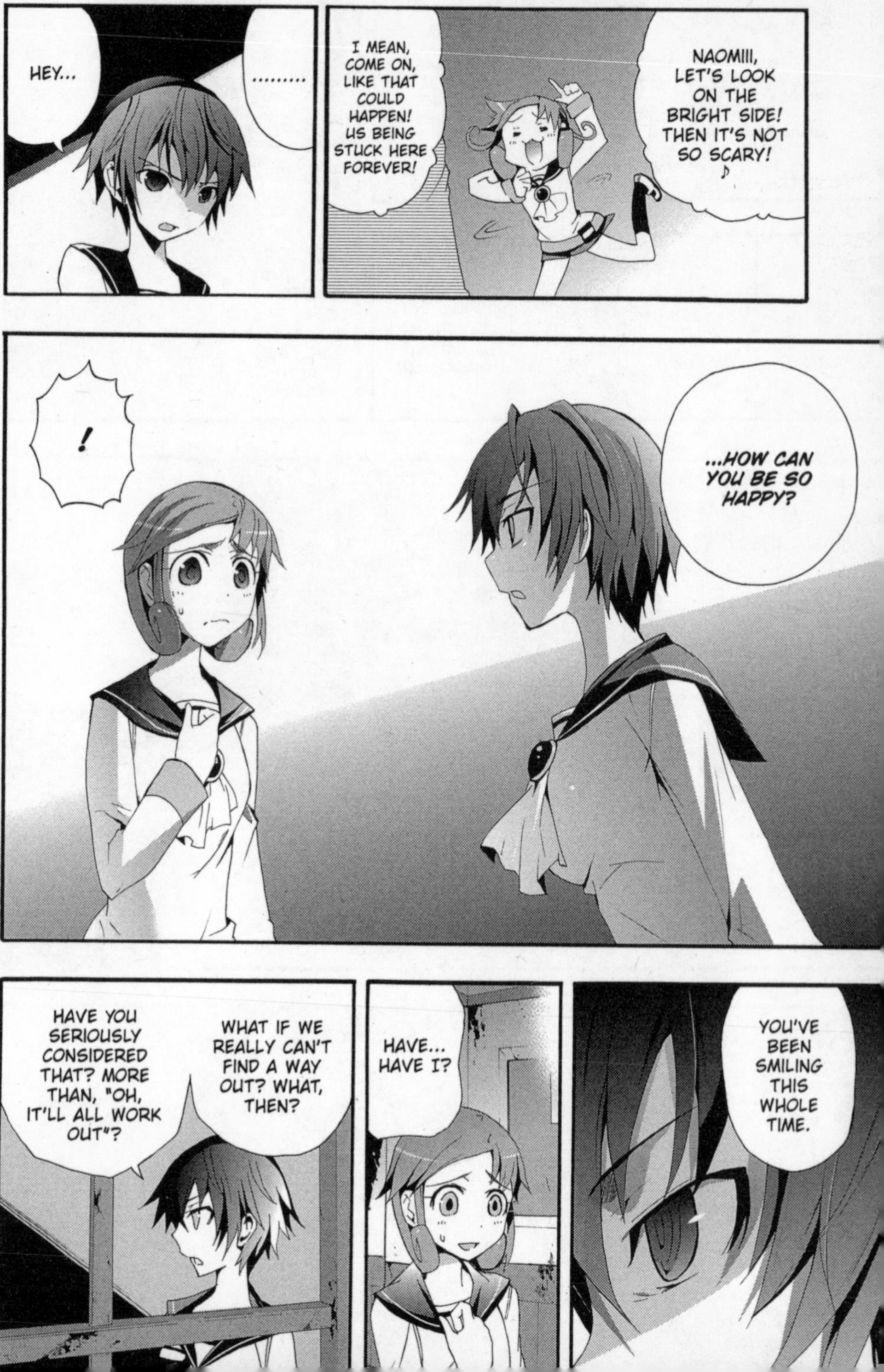
NAOMIII, LET'S LOOK ON THE BRIGHT SIDE! THEN IT'S NOT SO SCARY! ♪
I MEAN, COME ON, LIKE THAT COULD HAPPEN! US BEING STUCK HERE FOREVER!
....
HEY...
...HOW CAN YOU BE SO HAPPY?
!
YOU'VE BEEN SMILING THIS WHOLE TIME.
HAVE... HAVE I?
WHAT IF WE REALLY CAN'T FIND A WAY OUT? WHAT, THEN?
HAVE YOU SERIOUSLY CONSIDERED THAT? MORE THAN, "OH, IT'LL ALL WORK OUT"?

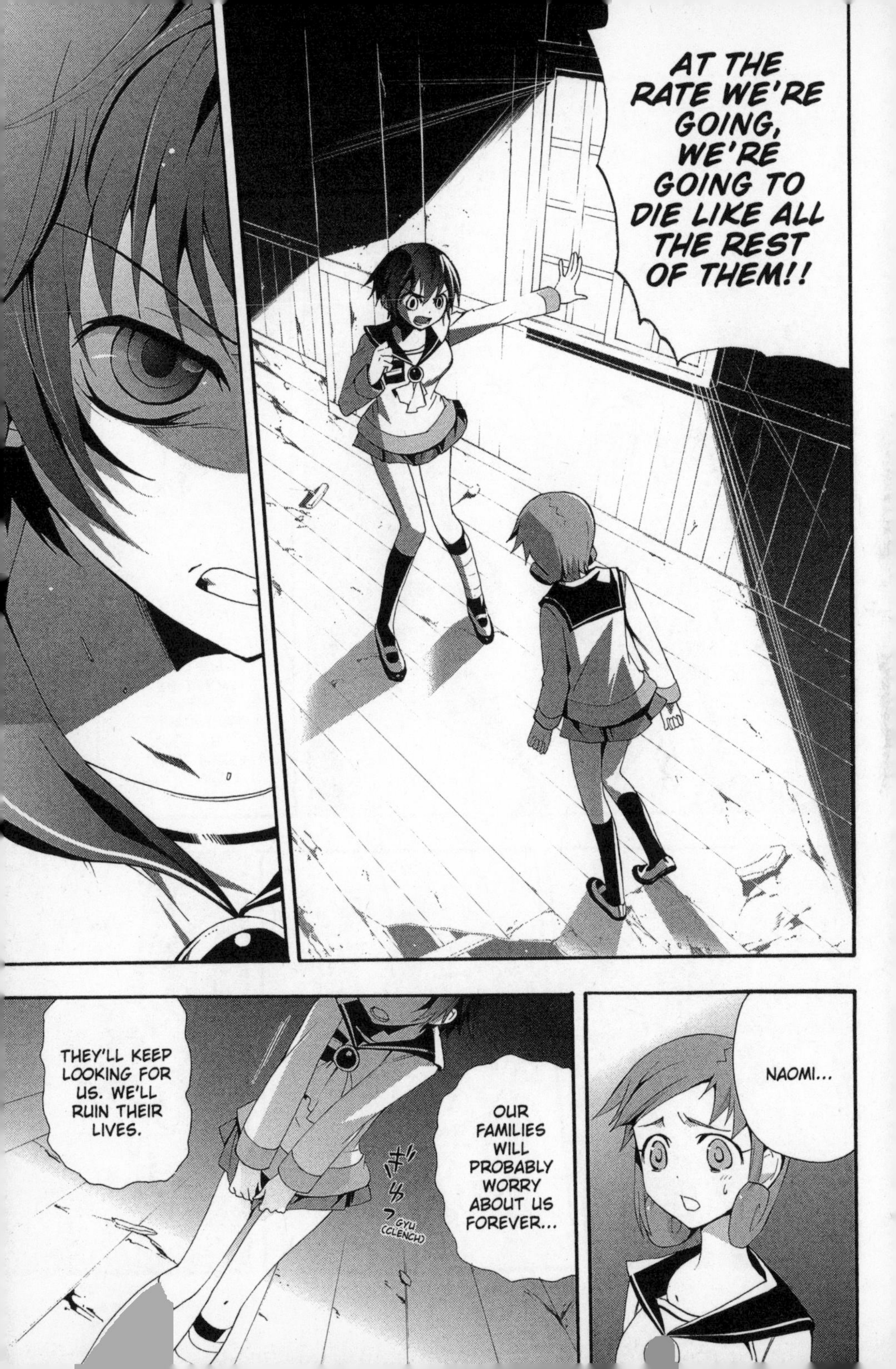
AT THE RATE WE'RE GOING, WE'RE GOING TO DIE LIKE ALL THE REST OF THEM!!
NAOMI...
OUR FAMILIES WILL PROBABLY WORRY ABOUT US FOREVER...
THEY'LL KEEP LOOKING FOR US. WE'LL RUIN THEIR LIVES.
GYU (CLENCH)

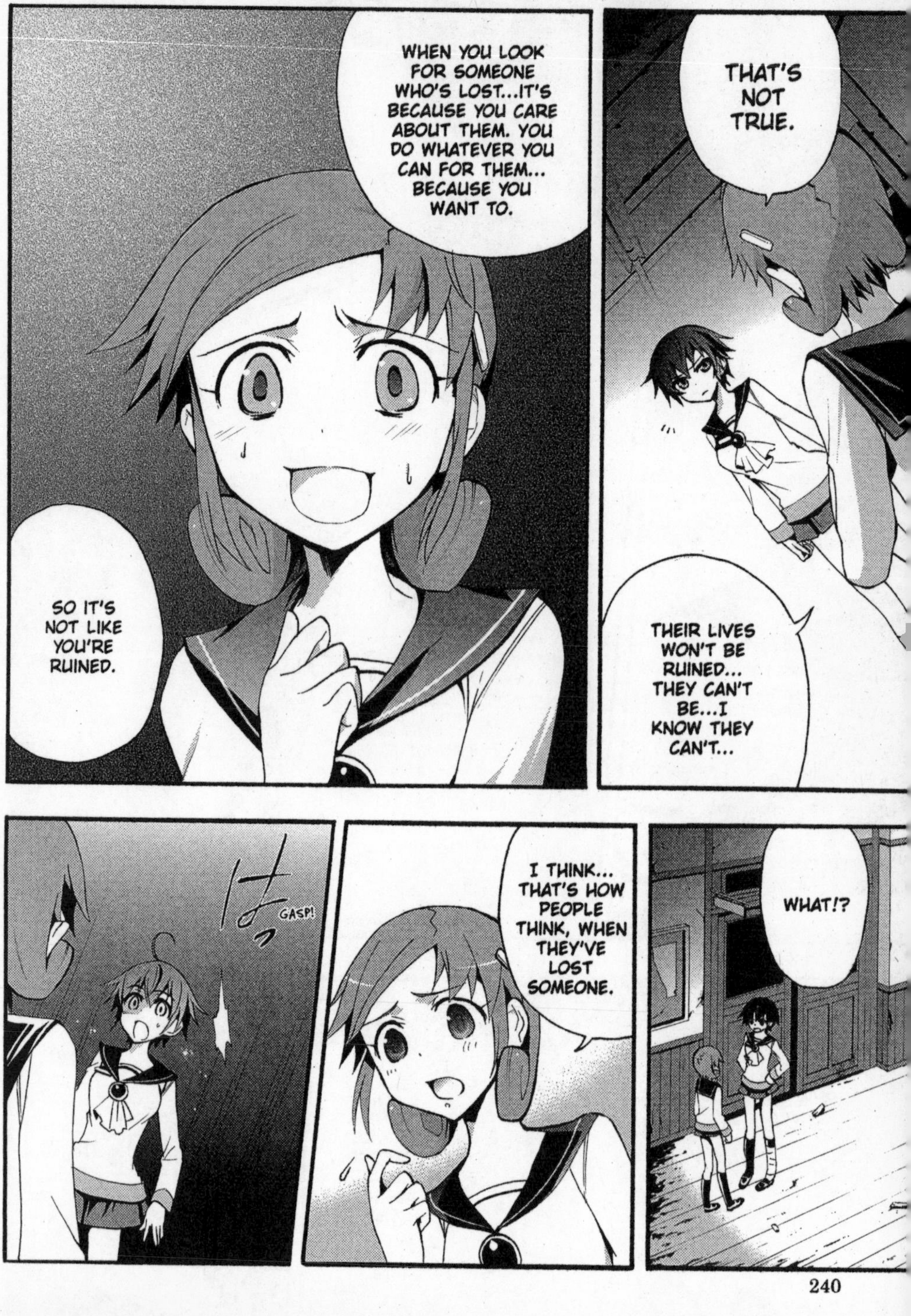
THAT'S NOT TRUE.
THEIR LIVES WON'T BE RUINED... THEY CAN'T BE...I KNOW THEY CAN'T...
WHEN YOU LOOK FOR SOMEONE WHO'S LOST...IT'S BECAUSE YOU CARE ABOUT THEM. YOU DO WHATEVER YOU CAN FOR THEM... BECAUSE YOU WANT TO.
SO IT'S NOT LIKE YOU'RE RUINED.
WHAT!?
I THINK... THAT'S HOW PEOPLE THINK, WHEN THEY'VE LOST SOMEONE.
はっ
GASP!

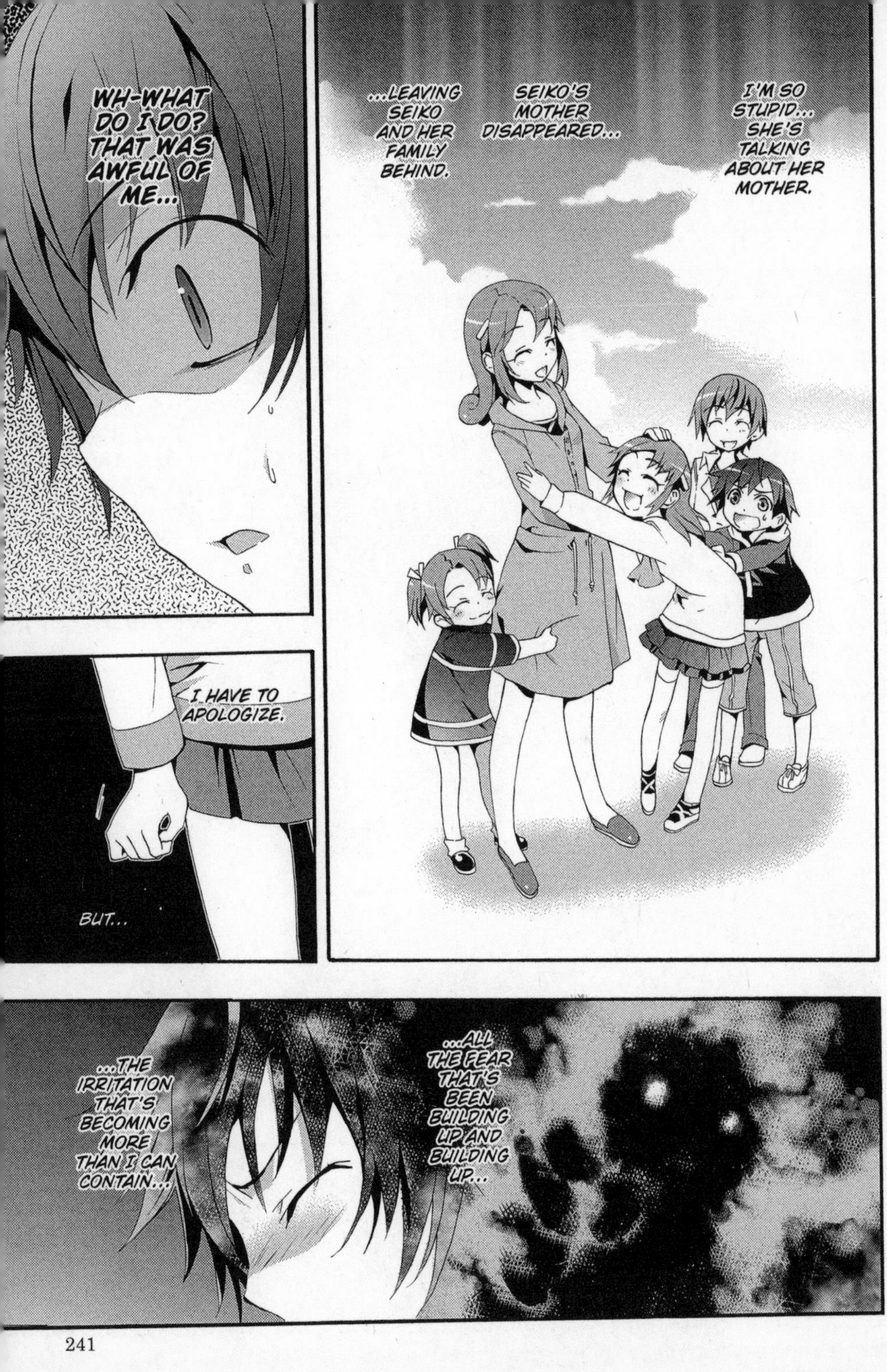
I'M SO STUPID... SHE'S TALKING ABOUT HER MOTHER.
SEIKO'S MOTHER DISAPPEARED...
...LEAVING SEIKO AND HER FAMILY BEHIND.
WH-WHAT DO I DO? THAT WAS AWFUL OF ME...
I HAVE TO APOLOGIZE.
BUT...
...ALL THE FEAR THAT'S BEEN BUILDING UP AND BUILDING UP...
...THE IRRITATION THAT'S BECOMING MORE THAN I CAN CONTAIN...

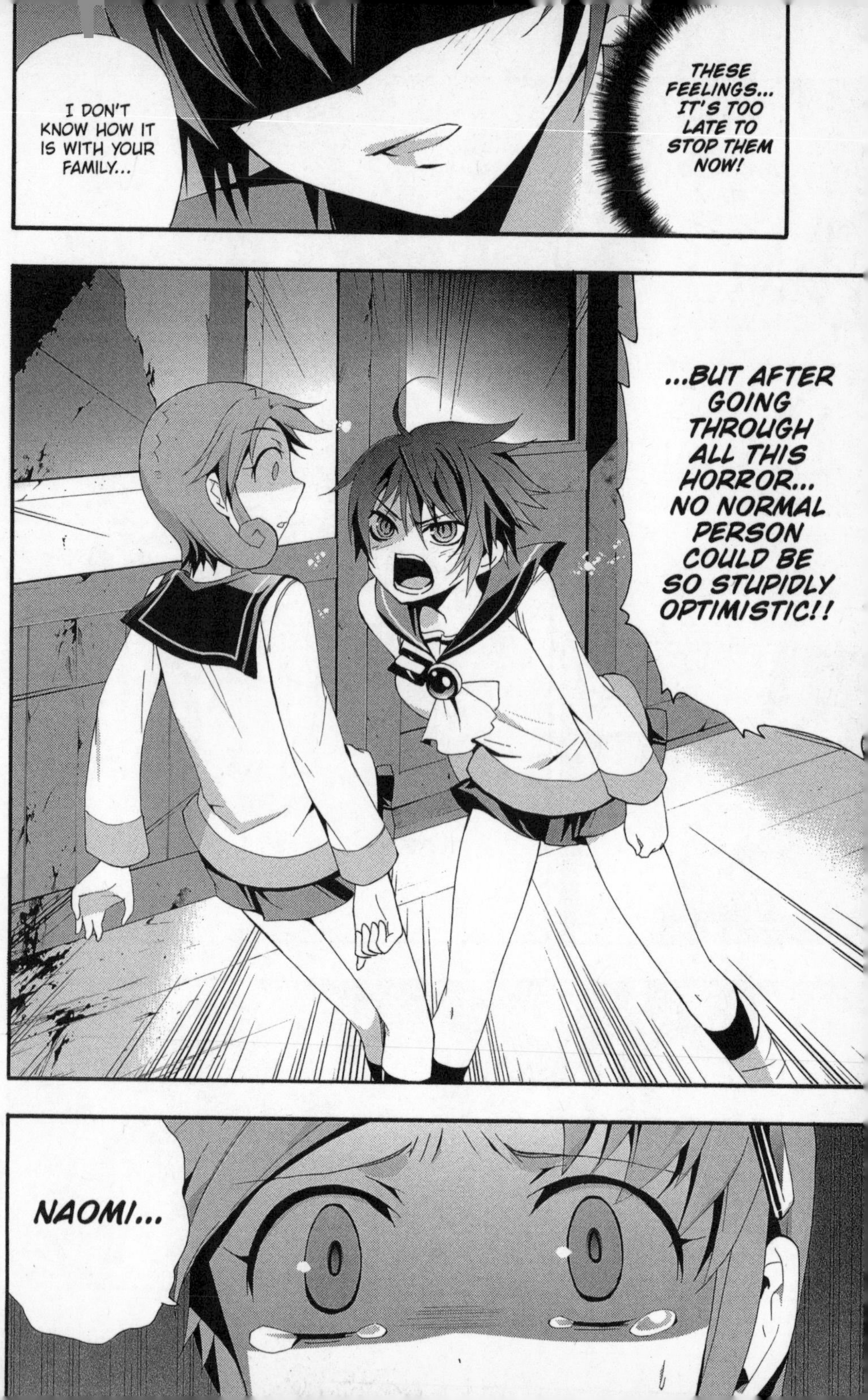
THESE FEELINGS... IT'S TOO LATE TO STOP THEM NOW!
I DON'T KNOW HOW IT IS WITH YOUR FAMILY...
...BUT AFTER GOING THROUGH ALL THIS HORROR... NO NORMAL PERSON COULD BE SO STUPIDLY OPTIMISTIC!!
NAOMI...

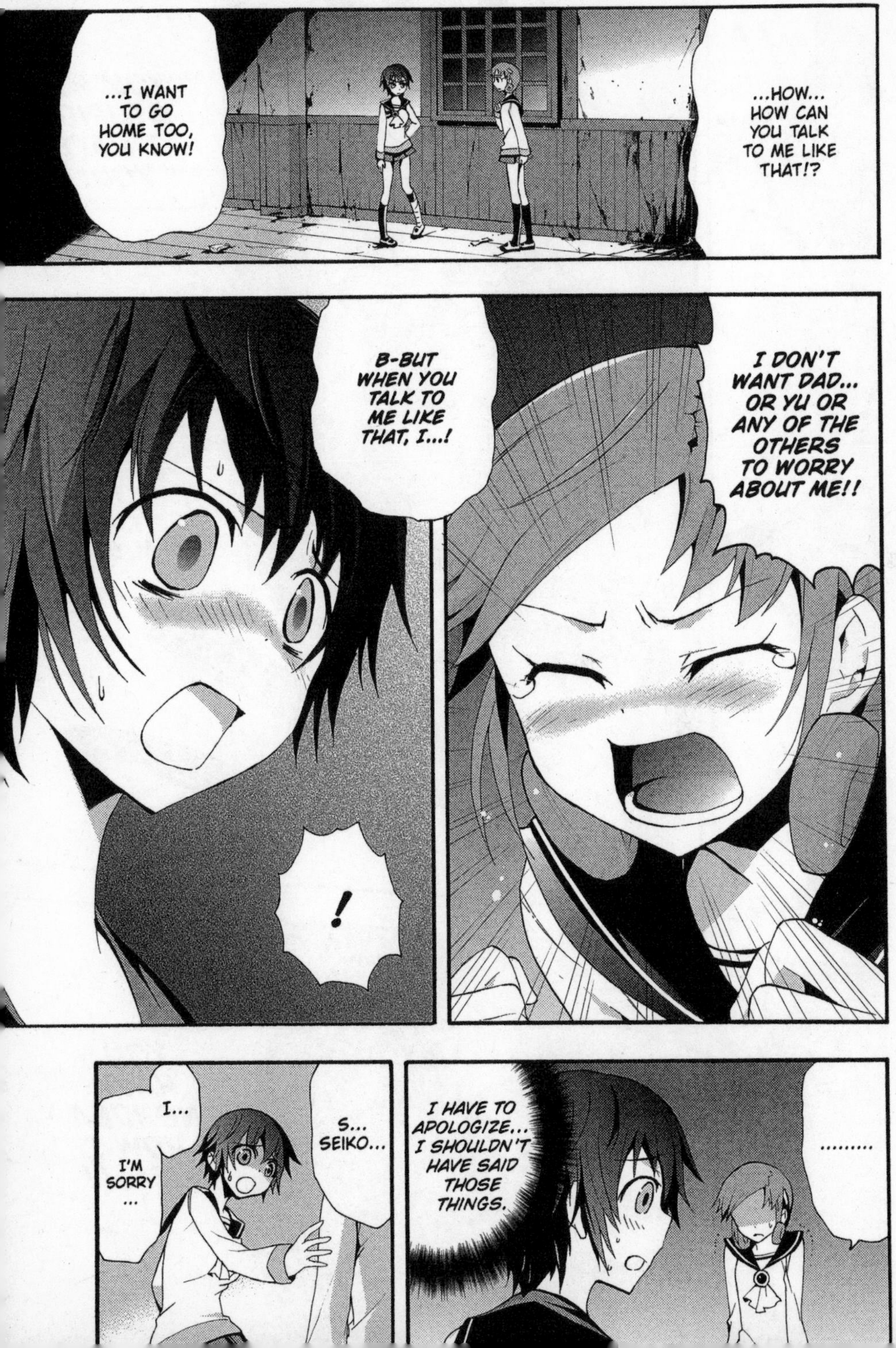
...HOW... HOW CAN YOU TALK TO ME LIKE THAT!?
...I WANT TO GO HOME TOO, YOU KNOW!
I DON'T WANT DAD... OR YU OR ANY OF THE OTHERS TO WORRY ABOUT ME!!
B-BUT WHEN YOU TALK TO ME LIKE THAT, I...!
!
....
I HAVE TO APOLOGIZE... I SHOULDN'T HAVE SAID THOSE THINGS.
S... SEIKO...
I...
I'M SORRY ...

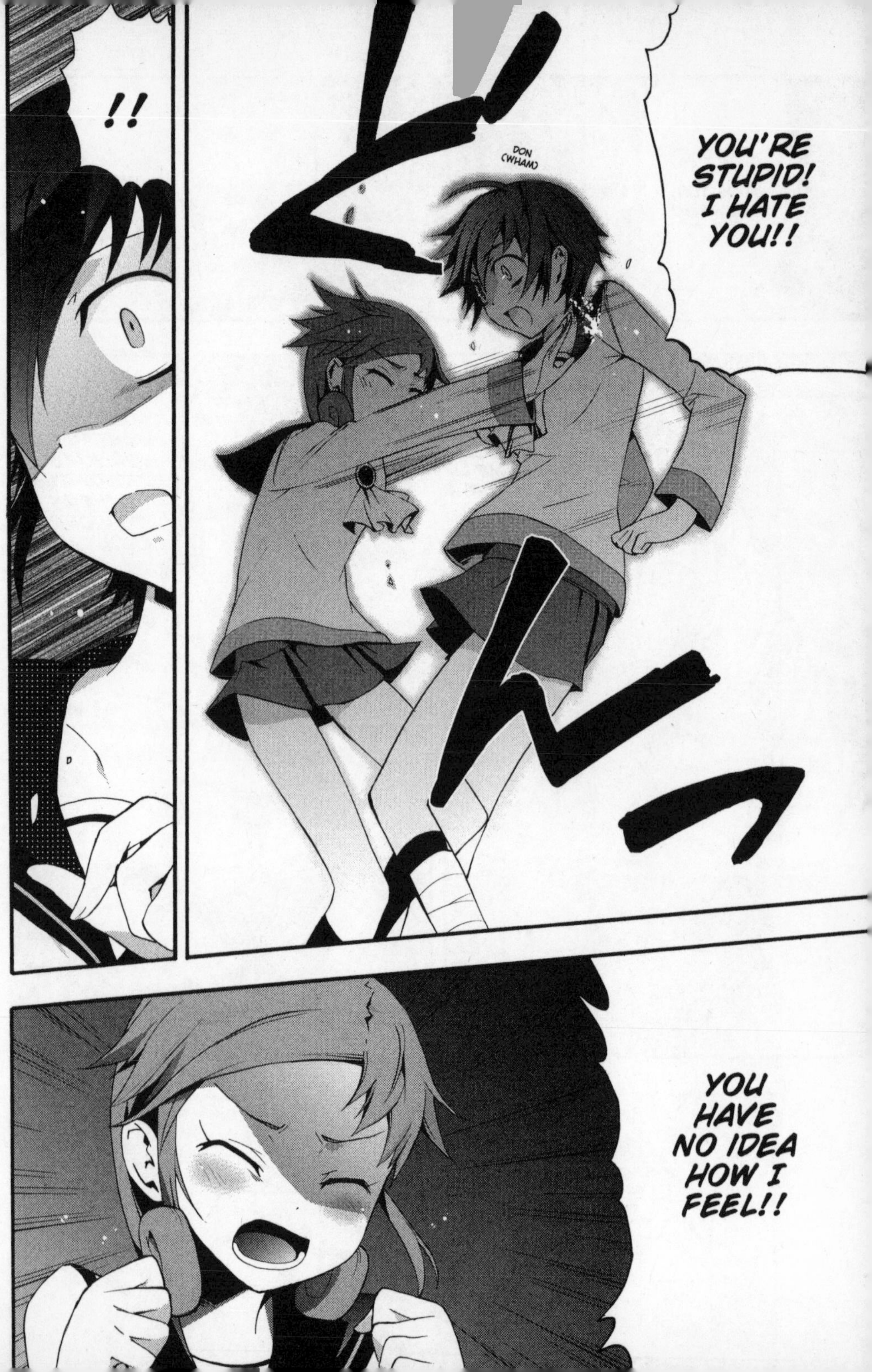
YOU'RE STUPID! I HATE YOU!!
DON (WHAM)
!!
YOU HAVE NO IDEA HOW I FEEL!!

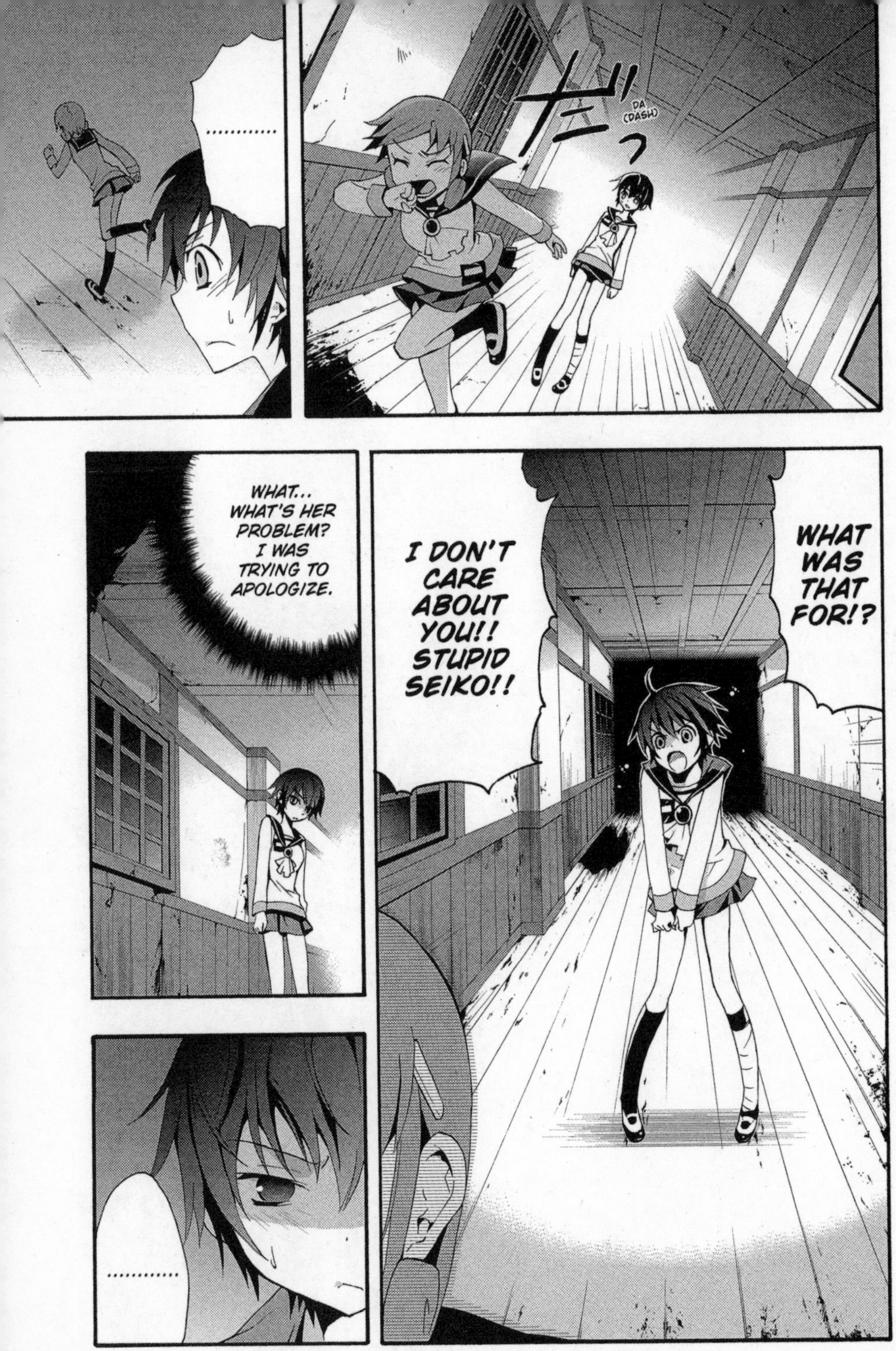
DA (DASH)
....
WHAT WAS THAT FOR!?
I DON'T CARE ABOUT YOU!! STUPID SEIKO!!
WHAT... WHAT'S HER PROBLEM? I WAS TRYING TO APOLOGIZE.
....

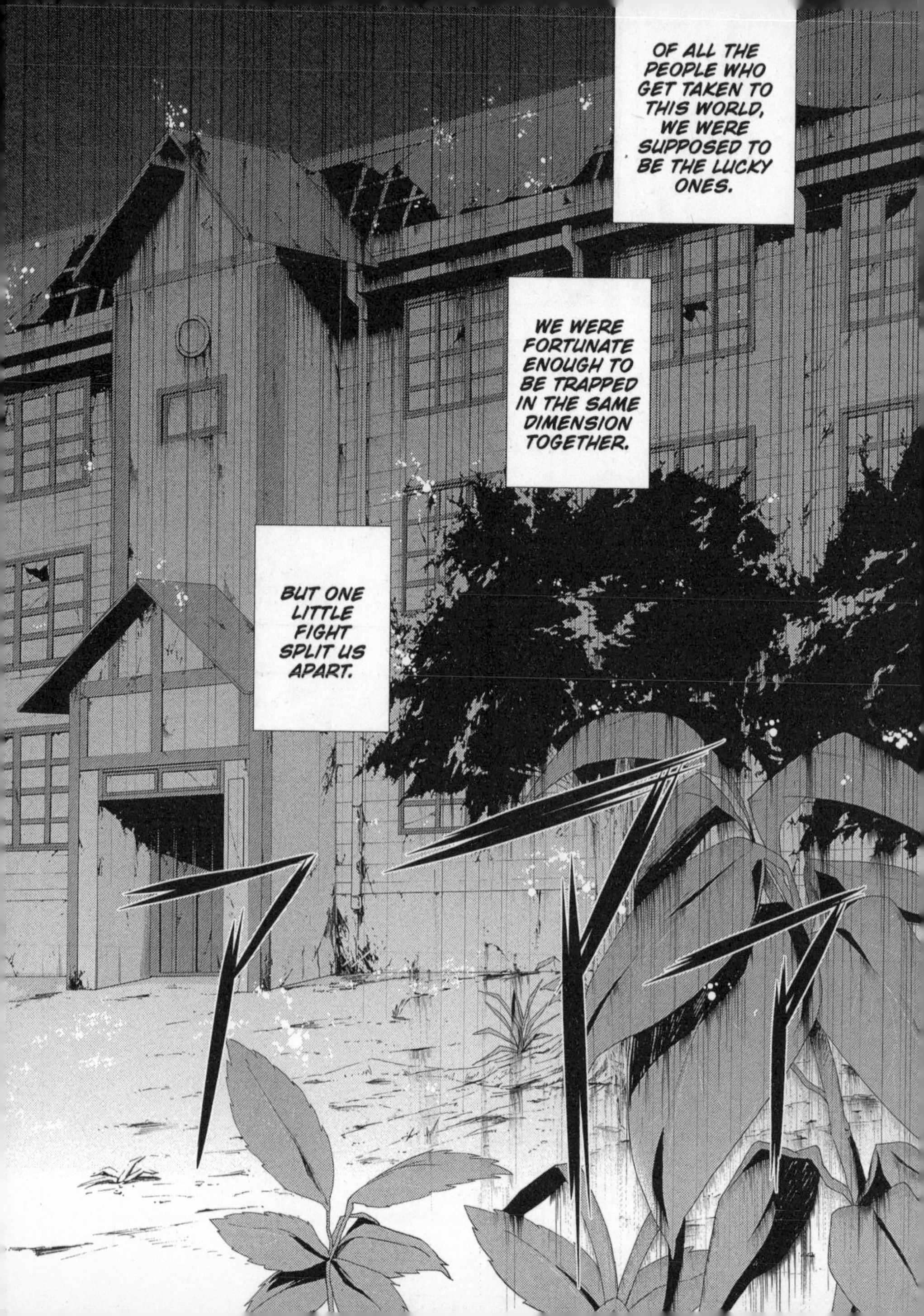
OF ALL THE PEOPLE WHO GET TAKEN TO THIS WORLD, WE WERE SUPPOSED TO BE THE LUCKY ONES.
WE WERE FORTUNATE ENOUGH TO BE TRAPPED IN THE SAME DIMENSION TOGETHER.
BUT ONE LITTLE FIGHT SPLIT US APART.

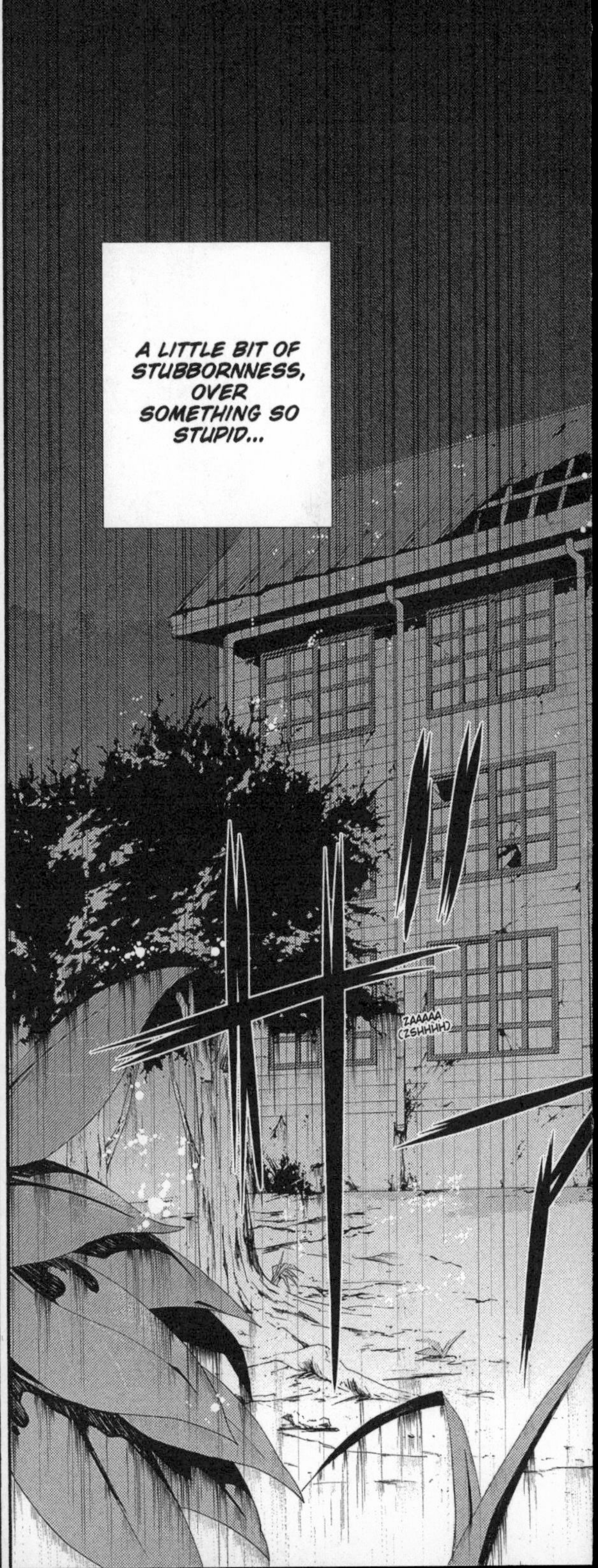
A LITTLE BIT OF STUBBORNNESS, OVER SOMETHING SO STUPID...
ZAAAAA (ZSHHHH)
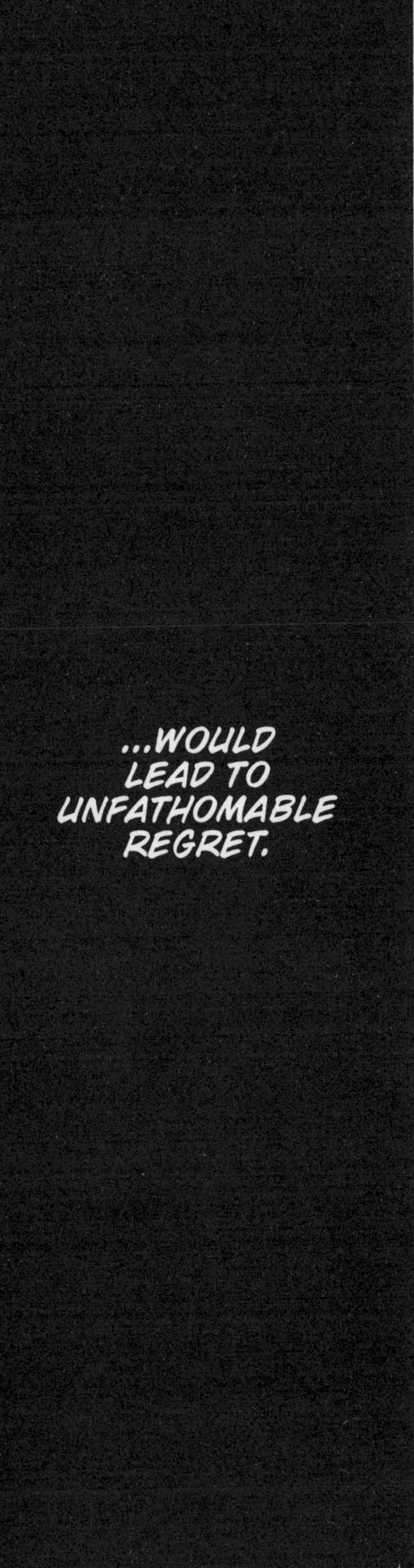
...WOULD LEAD TO UNFATHOMABLE REGRET.

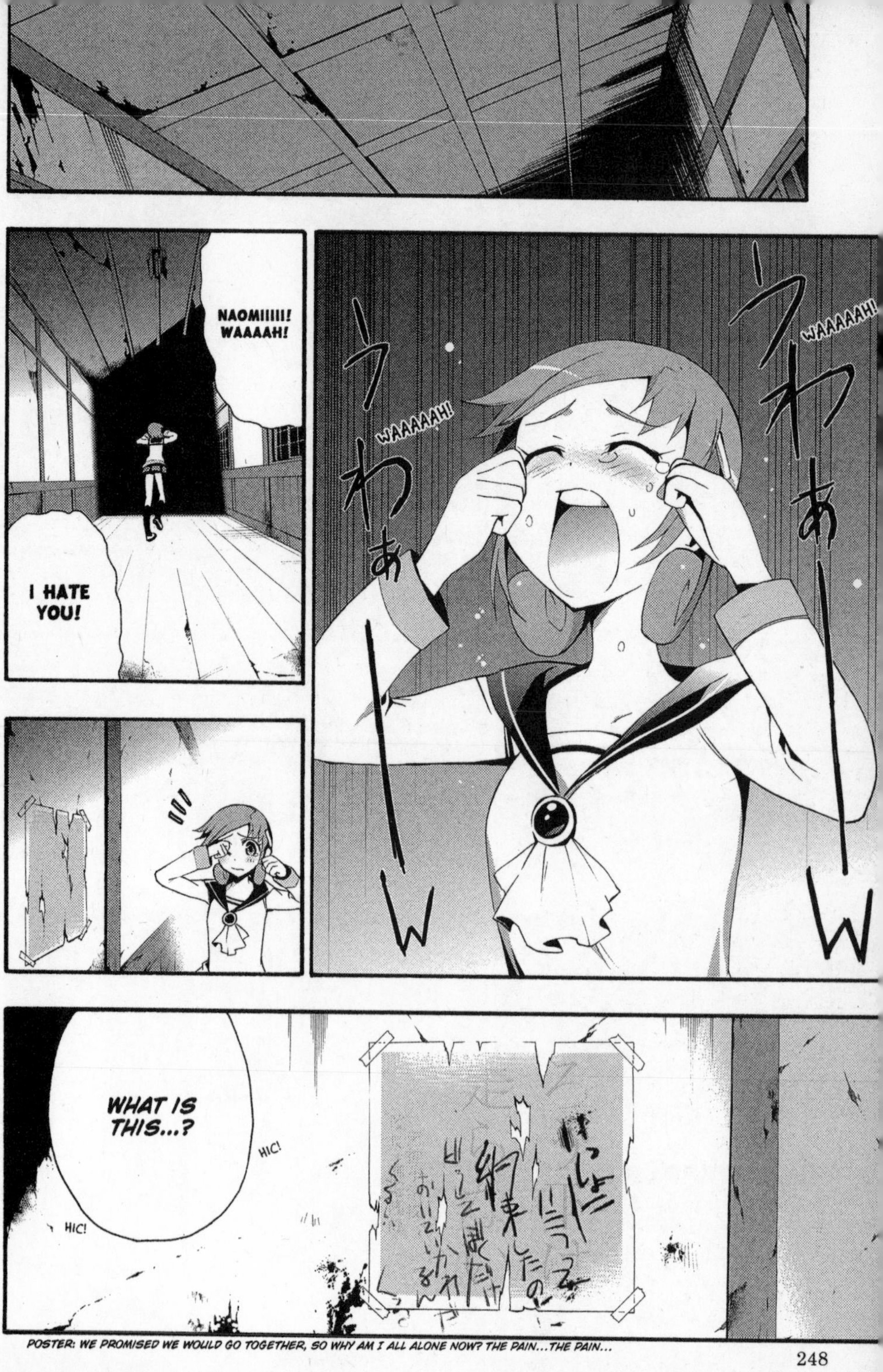
WAAAAAH!
WAAAAAH!
NAOMIIIII! WAAAAH!
I HATE YOU!
WHAT IS THIS...?
HIC!
HIC!

POSTER: WE PROMISED WE WOULD GO TOGETHER, SO WHY AM I ALL ALONE NOW? THE PAIN...THE PAIN...

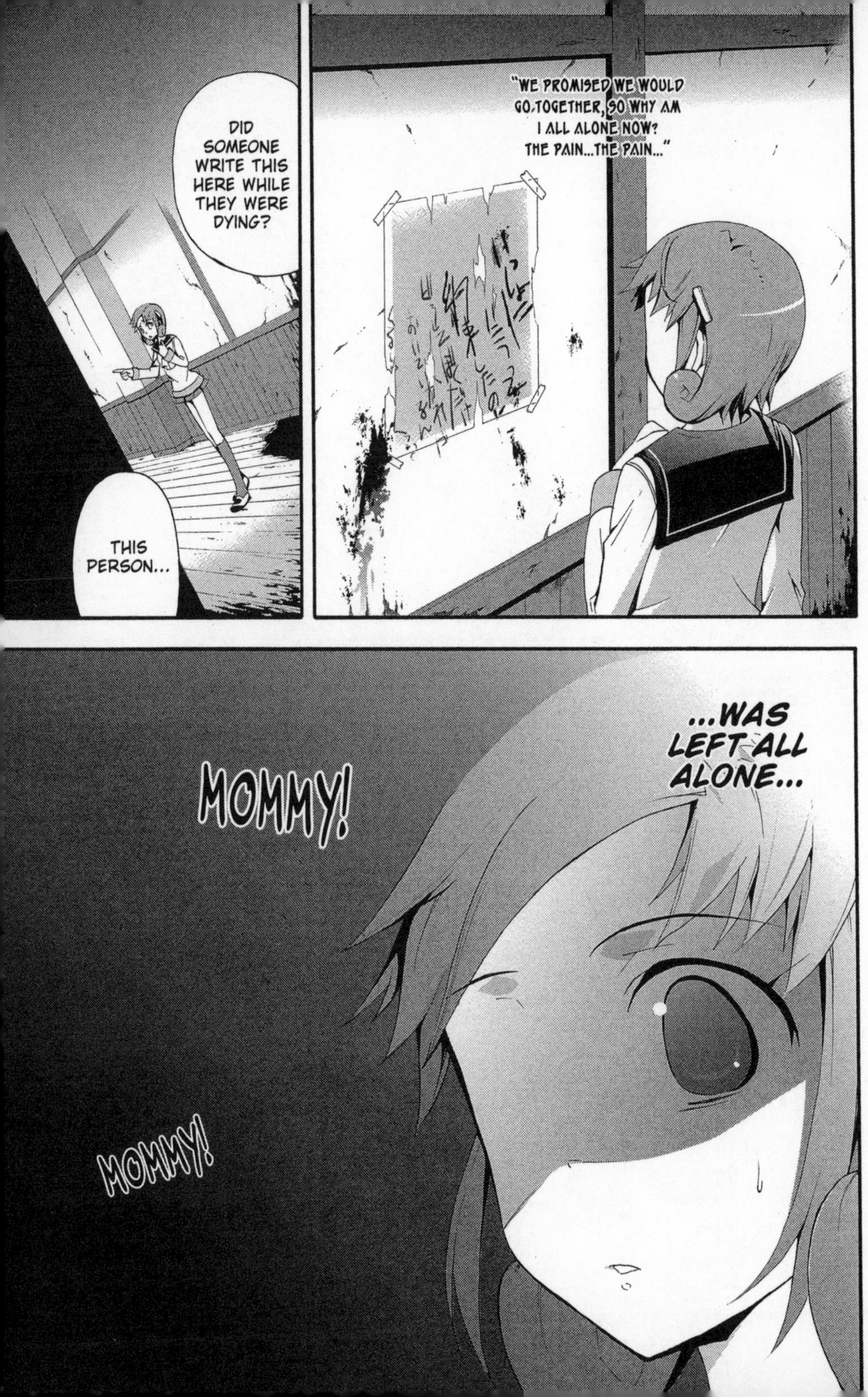
"WE PROMISED WE WOULD GO TOGETHER, SO WHY AM I ALL ALONE NOW? THE PAIN...THE PAIN..."
DID SOMEONE WRITE THIS HERE WHILE THEY WERE DYING?
THIS PERSON...
...WAS LEFT ALL ALONE...
MOMMY!
MOMMY!

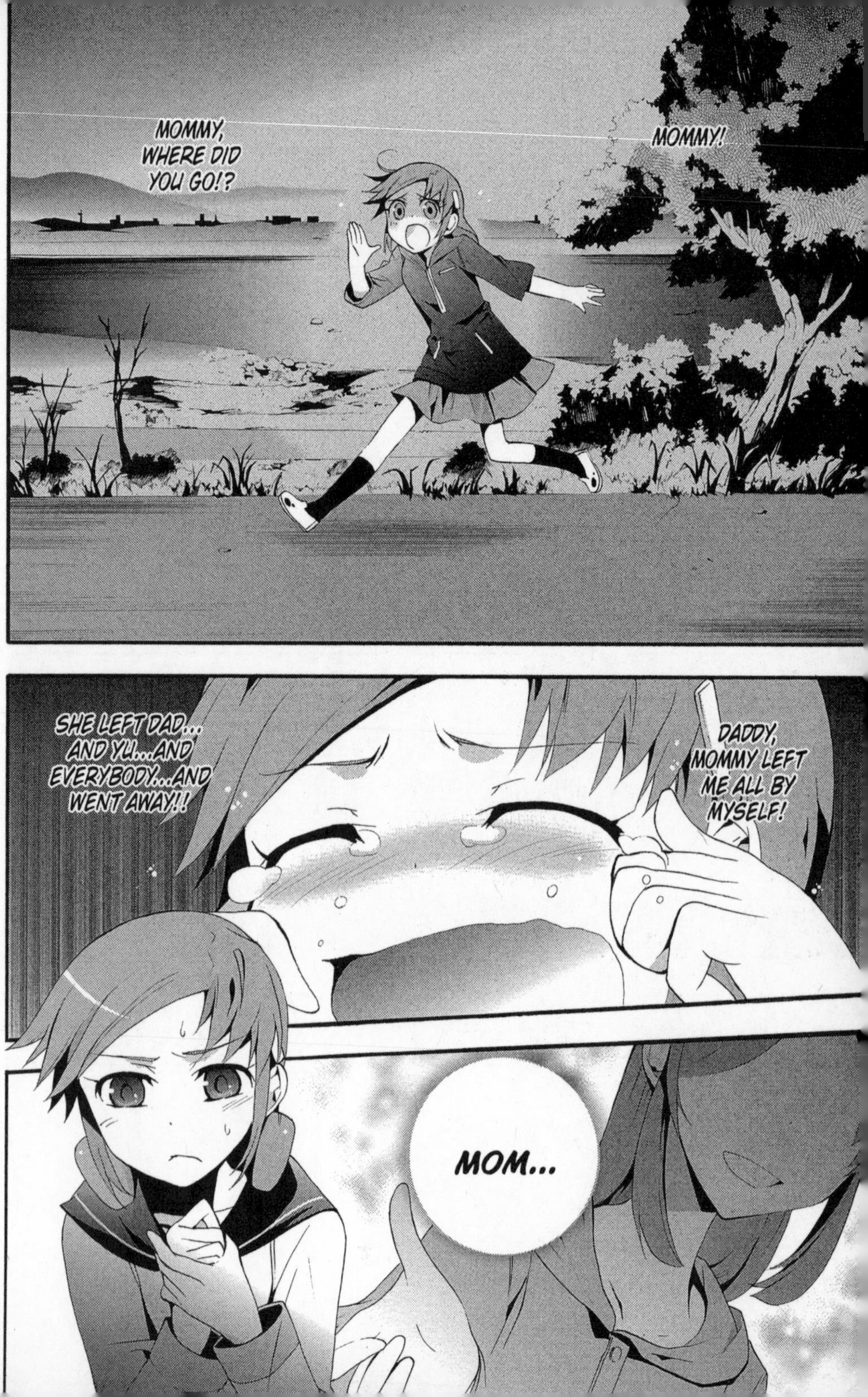
MOMMY!
MOMMY, WHERE DID YOU GO!?
DADDY, MOMMY LEFT ME ALL BY MYSELF!
SHE LEFT DAD... AND YU...AND EVERYBODY...AND WENT AWAY!!
MOM...

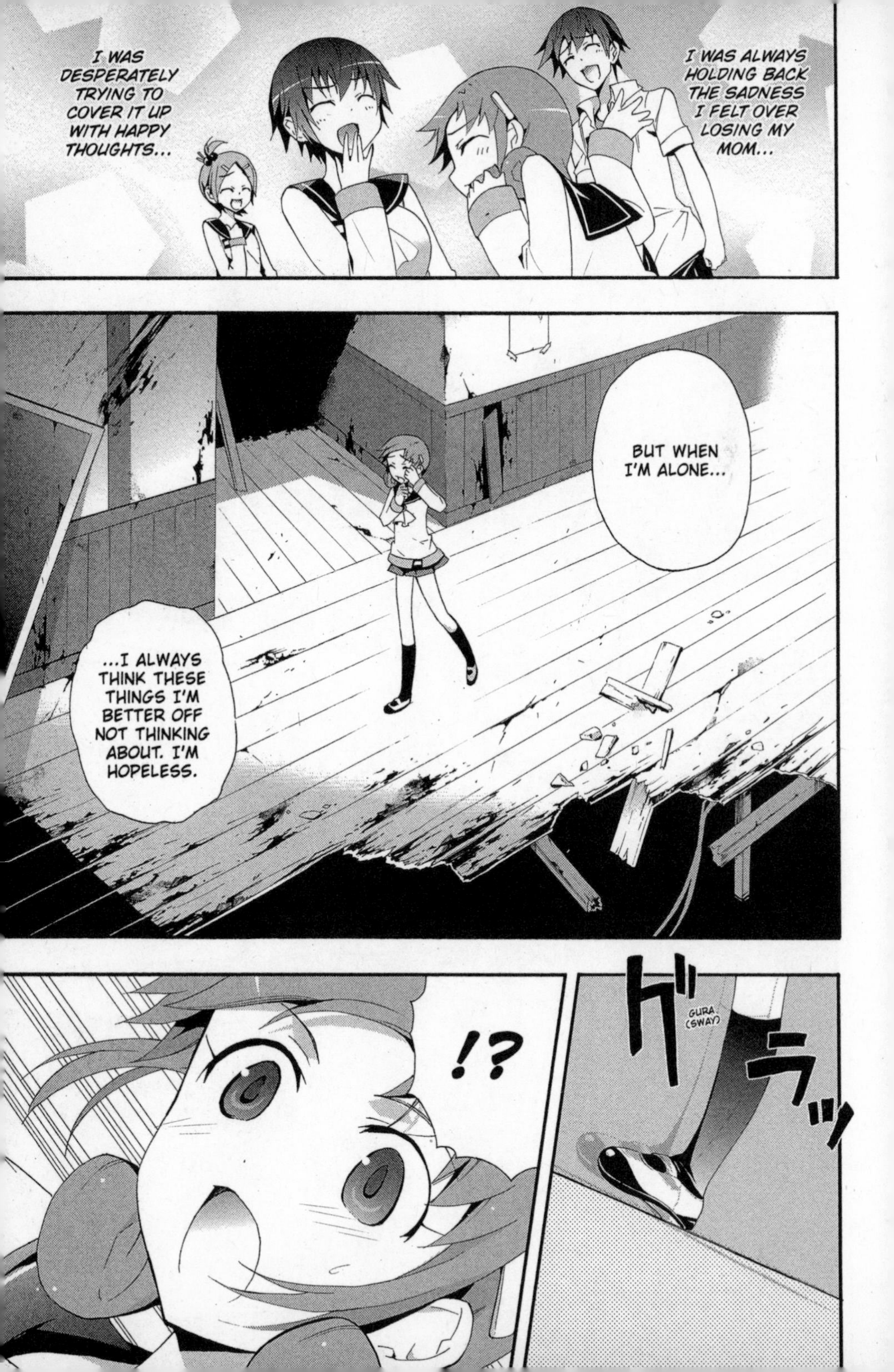
I WAS ALWAYS HOLDING BACK THE SADNESS I FELT OVER LOSING MY MOM...
I WAS DESPERATELY TRYING TO COVER IT UP WITH HAPPY THOUGHTS...
BUT WHEN I'M ALONE...
...I ALWAYS THINK THESE THINGS I'M BETTER OFF NOT THINKING ABOUT. I'M HOPELESS.
GURA (SWAY)
!?

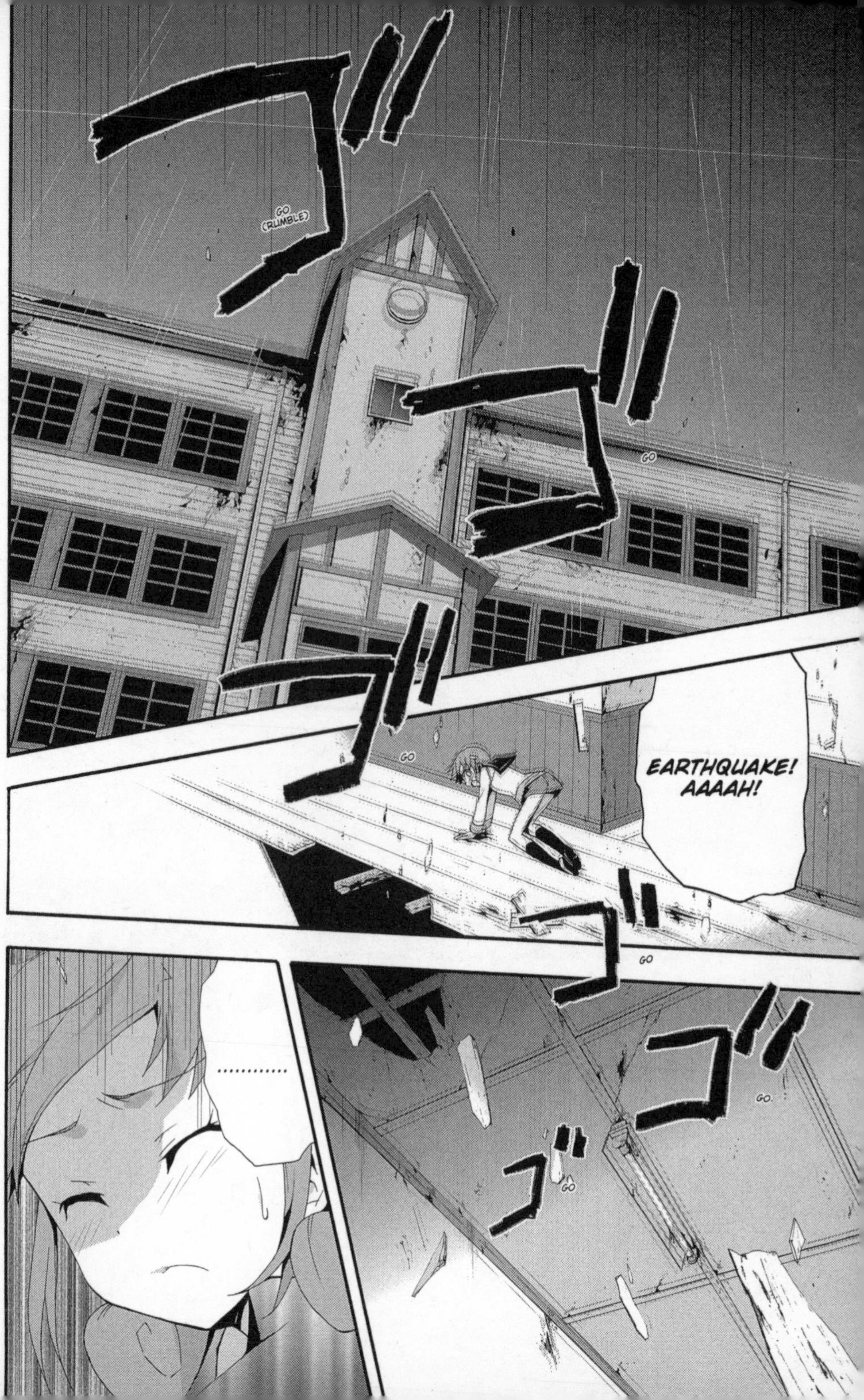
GO
GO (RUMBLE)
EARTHQUAKE! AAAAH!
GO
GO
....
GO.
GO

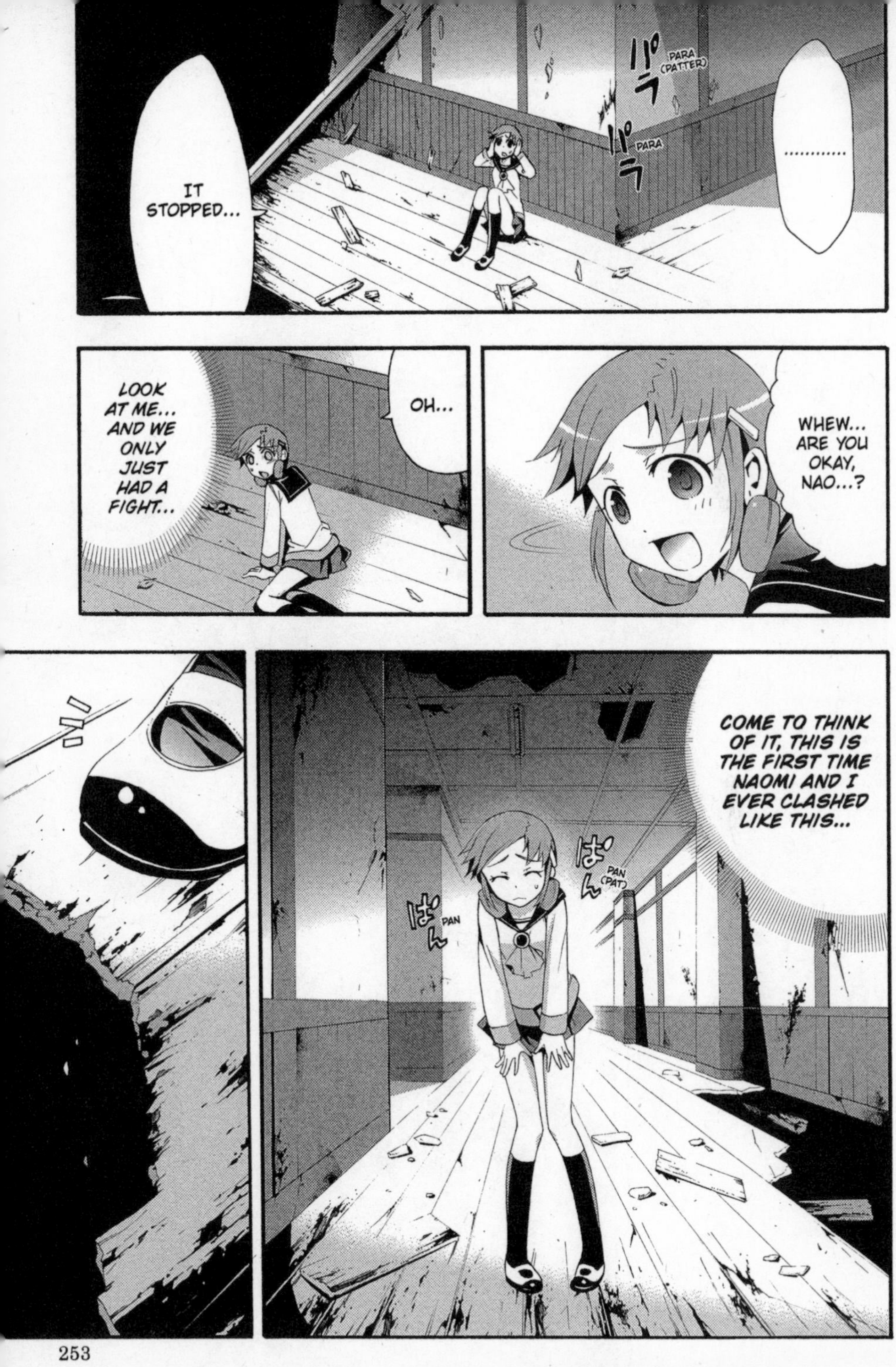

....
パラ PARA (PATTER)
パラ PARA
IT STOPPED...
WHEW... ARE YOU OKAY, NAO...?
OH...
LOOK AT ME... AND WE ONLY JUST HAD A FIGHT...
COME TO THINK OF IT, THIS IS THE FIRST TIME NAOMI AND I EVER CLASHED LIKE THIS...
ぱん PAN (PAT)
ぱん PAN

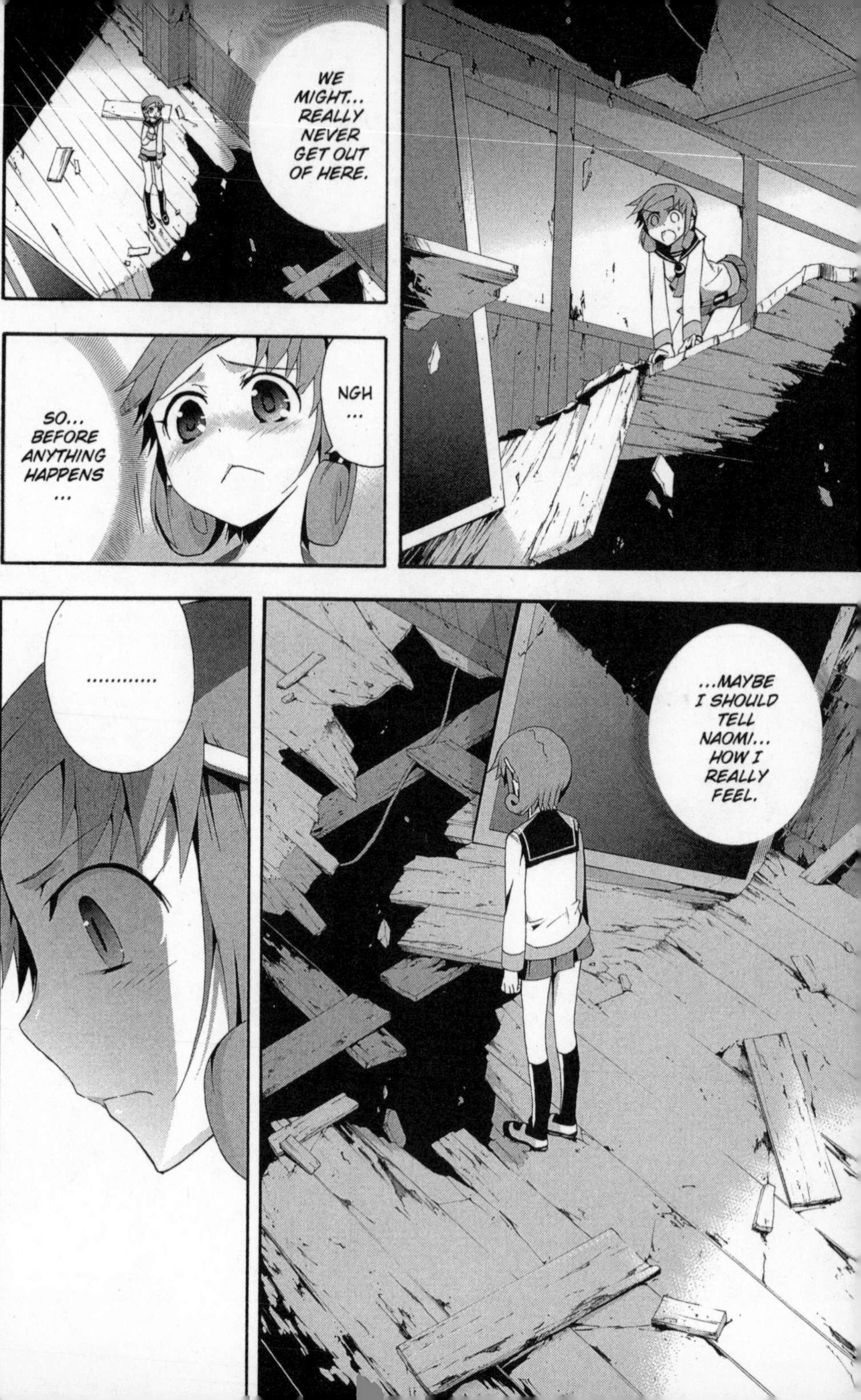
WE MIGHT... REALLY NEVER GET OUT OF HERE.
NGH...
SO... BEFORE ANYTHING HAPPENS...
...MAYBE I SHOULD TELL NAOMI... HOW I REALLY FEEL.
....

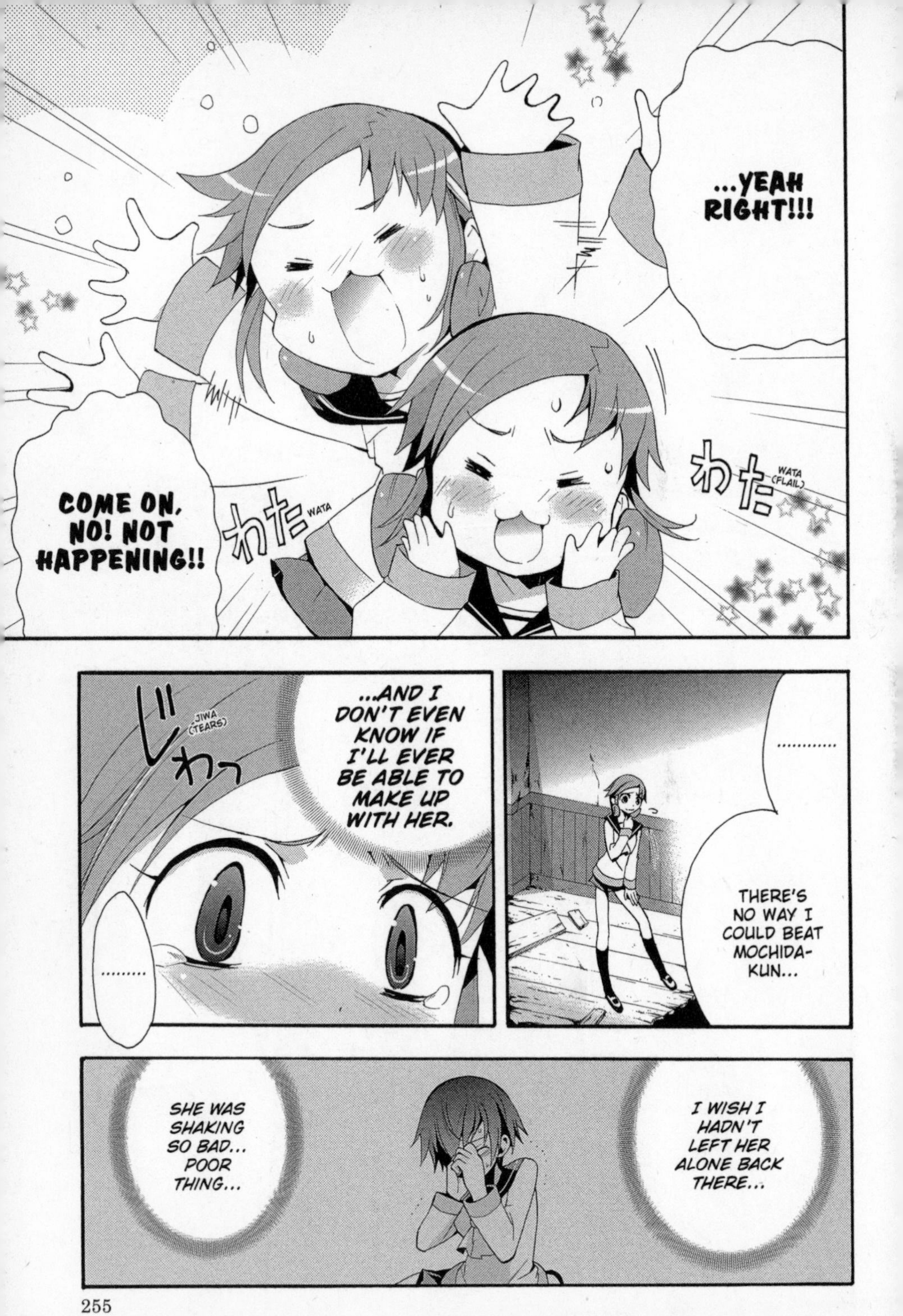
...YEAH RIGHT!!!
わた WATA (FLAIL)
わた WATA
COME ON, NO! NOT HAPPENING!!
....
THERE'S NO WAY I COULD BEAT MOCHIDA-KUN...
じわっ JIWA (TEARS)
...AND I DON'T EVEN KNOW IF I'LL EVER BE ABLE TO MAKE UP WITH HER.
....
I WISH I HADN'T LEFT HER ALONE BACK THERE...
SHE WAS SHAKING SO BAD... POOR THING...

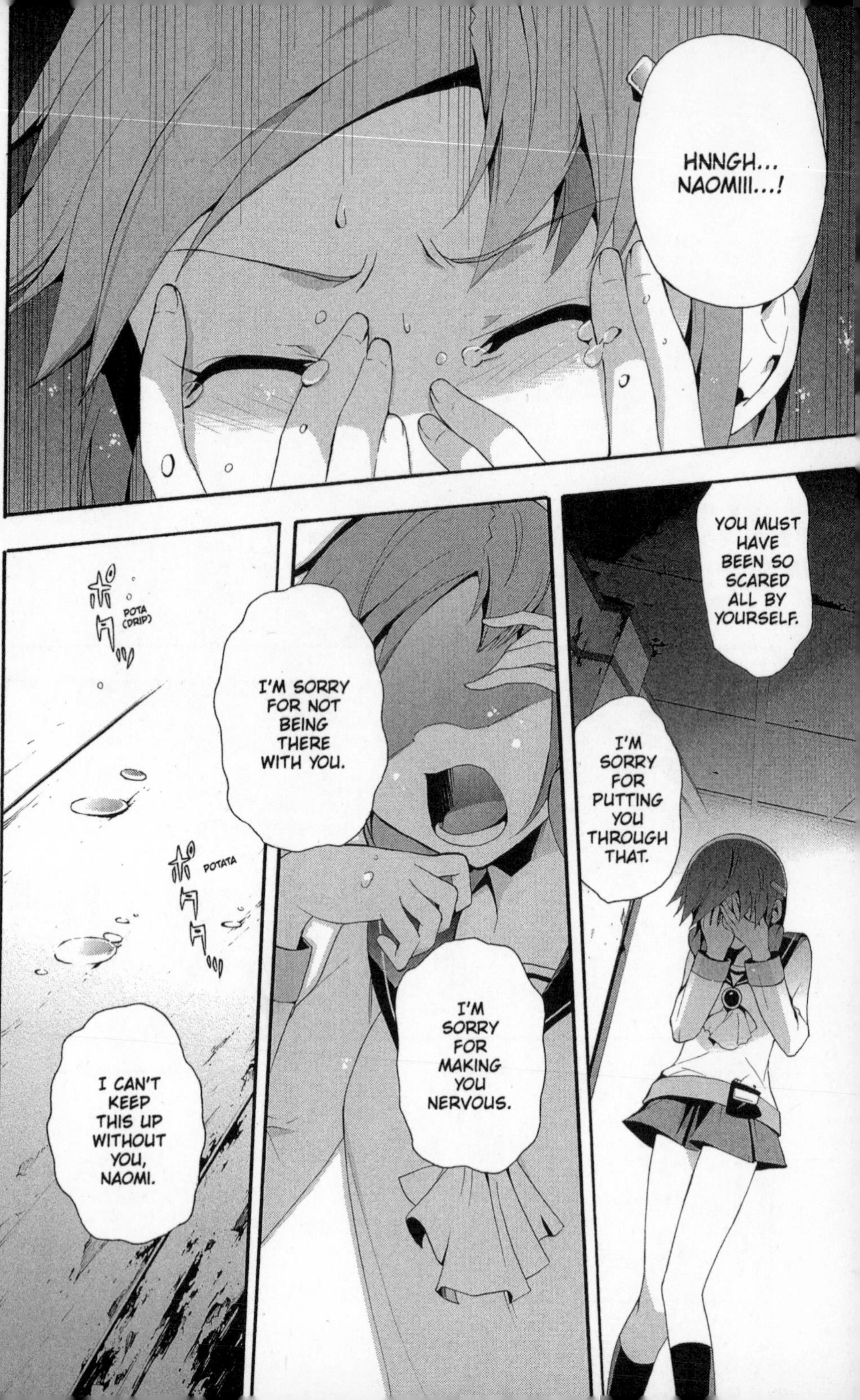
HNNGH... NAOMIII...!
YOU MUST HAVE BEEN SO SCARED ALL BY YOURSELF.
I'M SORRY FOR PUTTING YOU THROUGH THAT.
I'M SORRY FOR NOT BEING THERE WITH YOU.
I'M SORRY FOR MAKING YOU NERVOUS.
POTA (DRIP)
POTATA
I CAN'T KEEP THIS UP WITHOUT YOU, NAOMI.

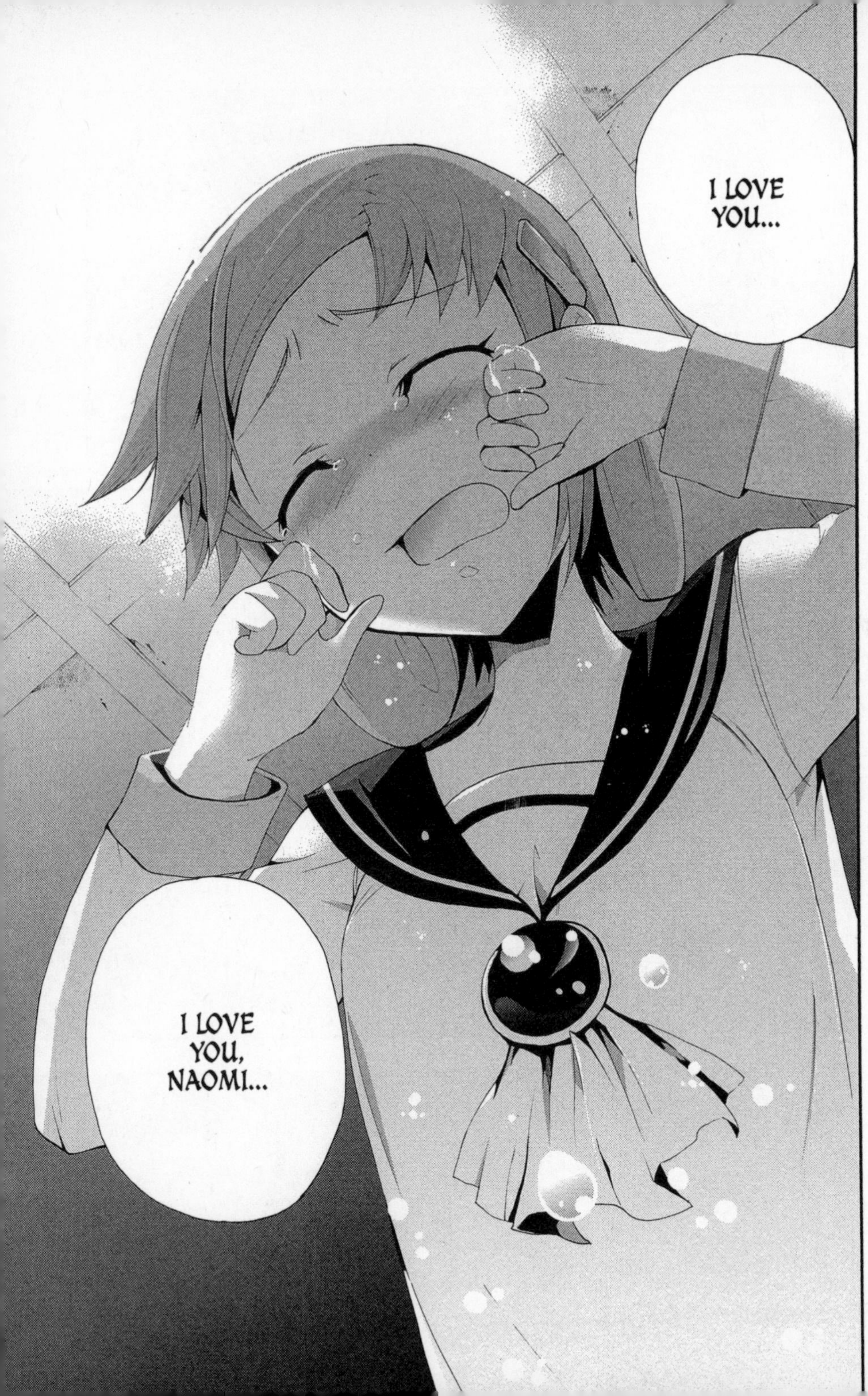
I LOVE YOU...
I LOVE YOU, NAOMI...

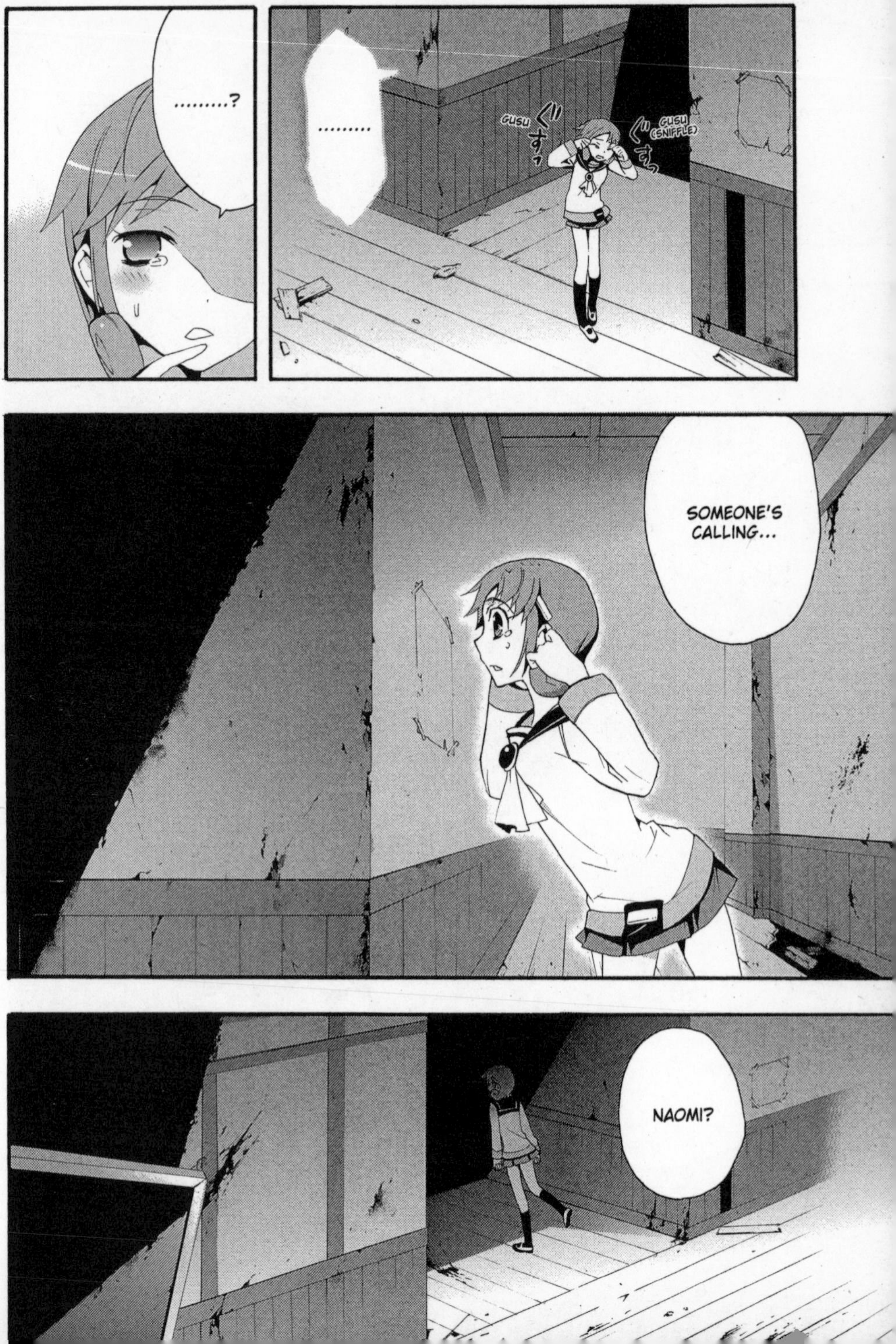
GUSU (SNIFFLE)
GUSU
....
.........?
SOMEONE'S CALLING...
NAOMI?

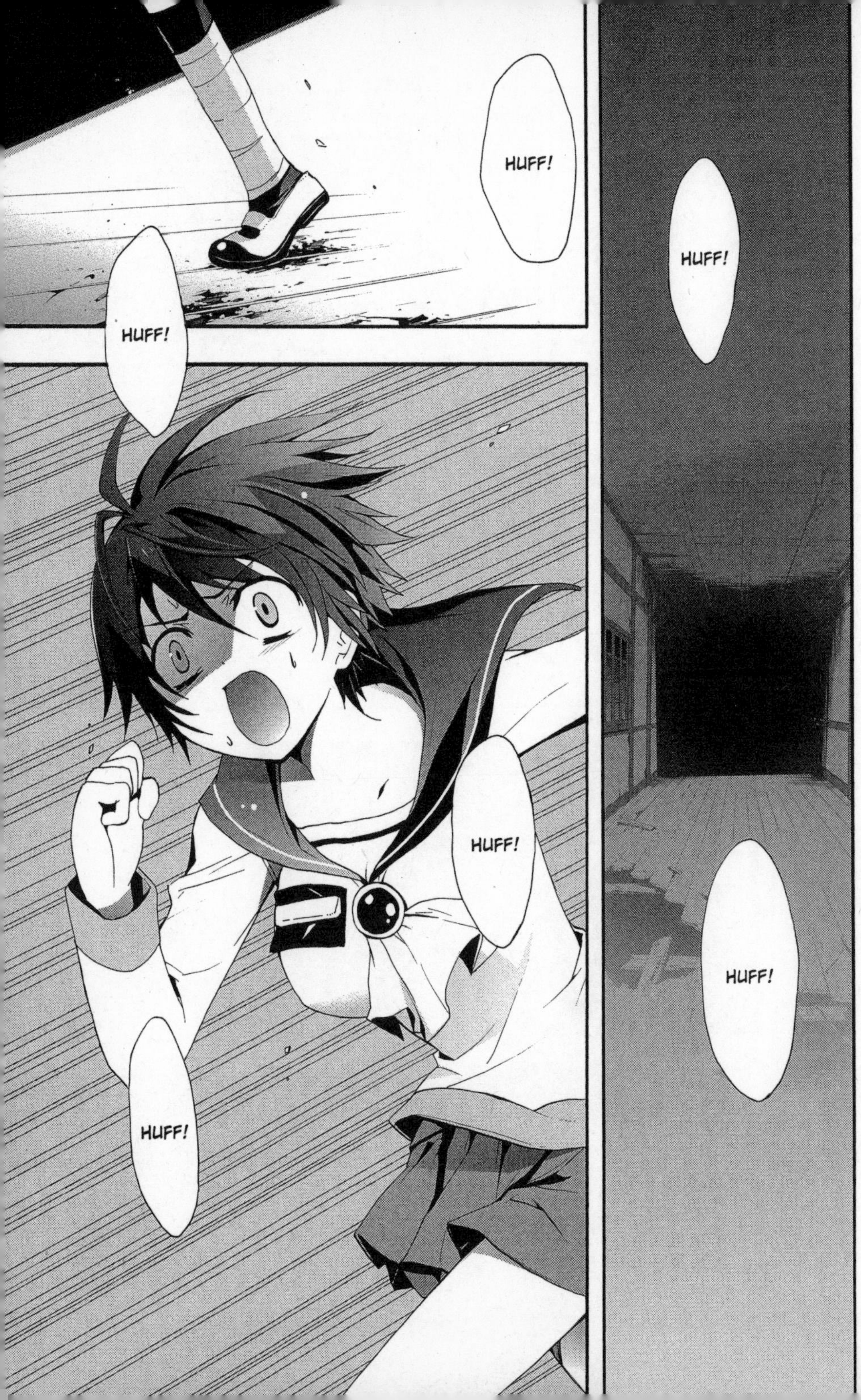
HUFF!
HUFF!
HUFF!
HUFF!
HUFF!
HUFF!

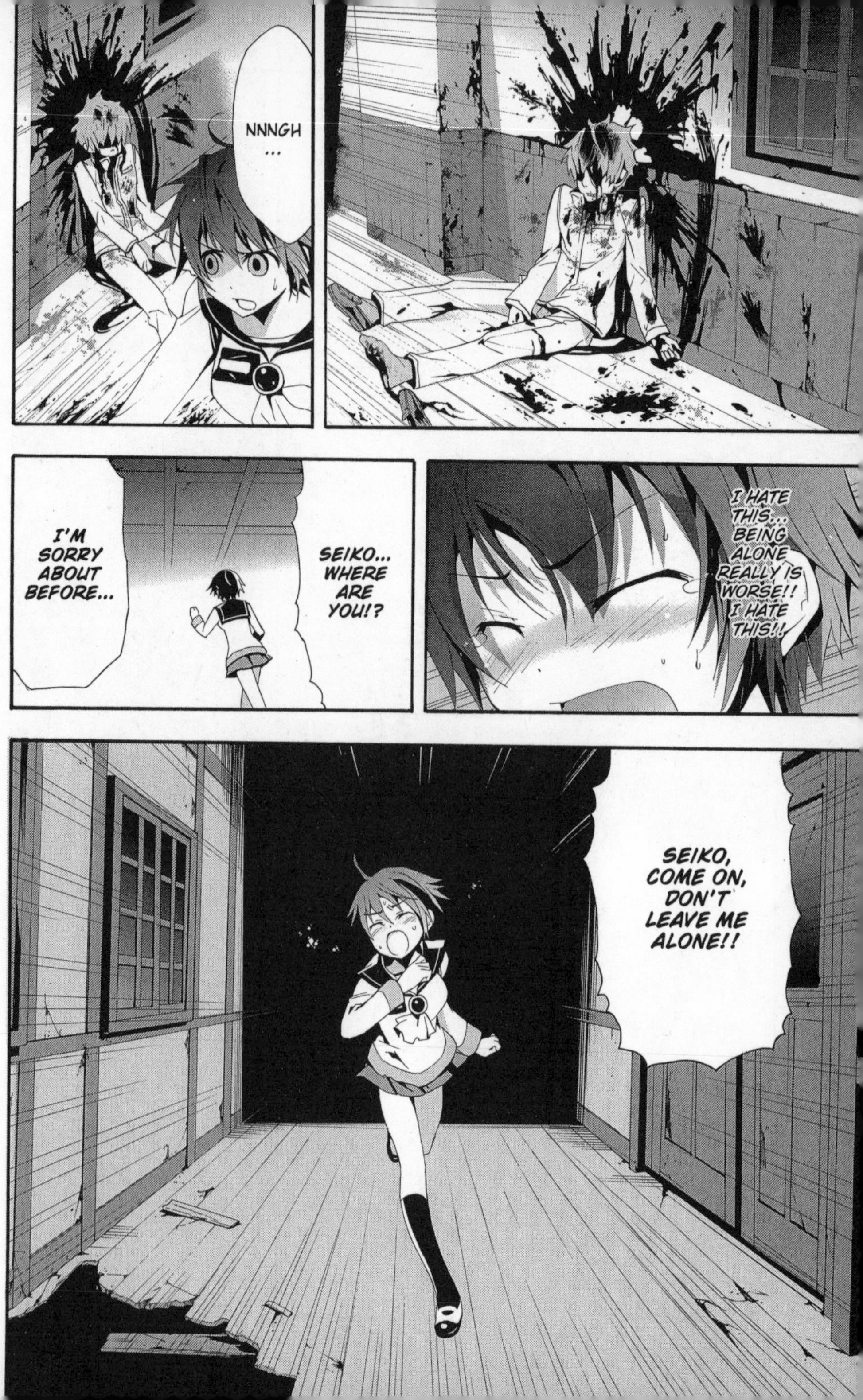
NNNGH ...
I HATE THIS... BEING ALONE REALLY IS WORSE!! I HATE THIS!!
SEIKO... WHERE ARE YOU!?
I'M SORRY ABOUT BEFORE...
SEIKO, COME ON, DON'T LEAVE ME ALONE!!

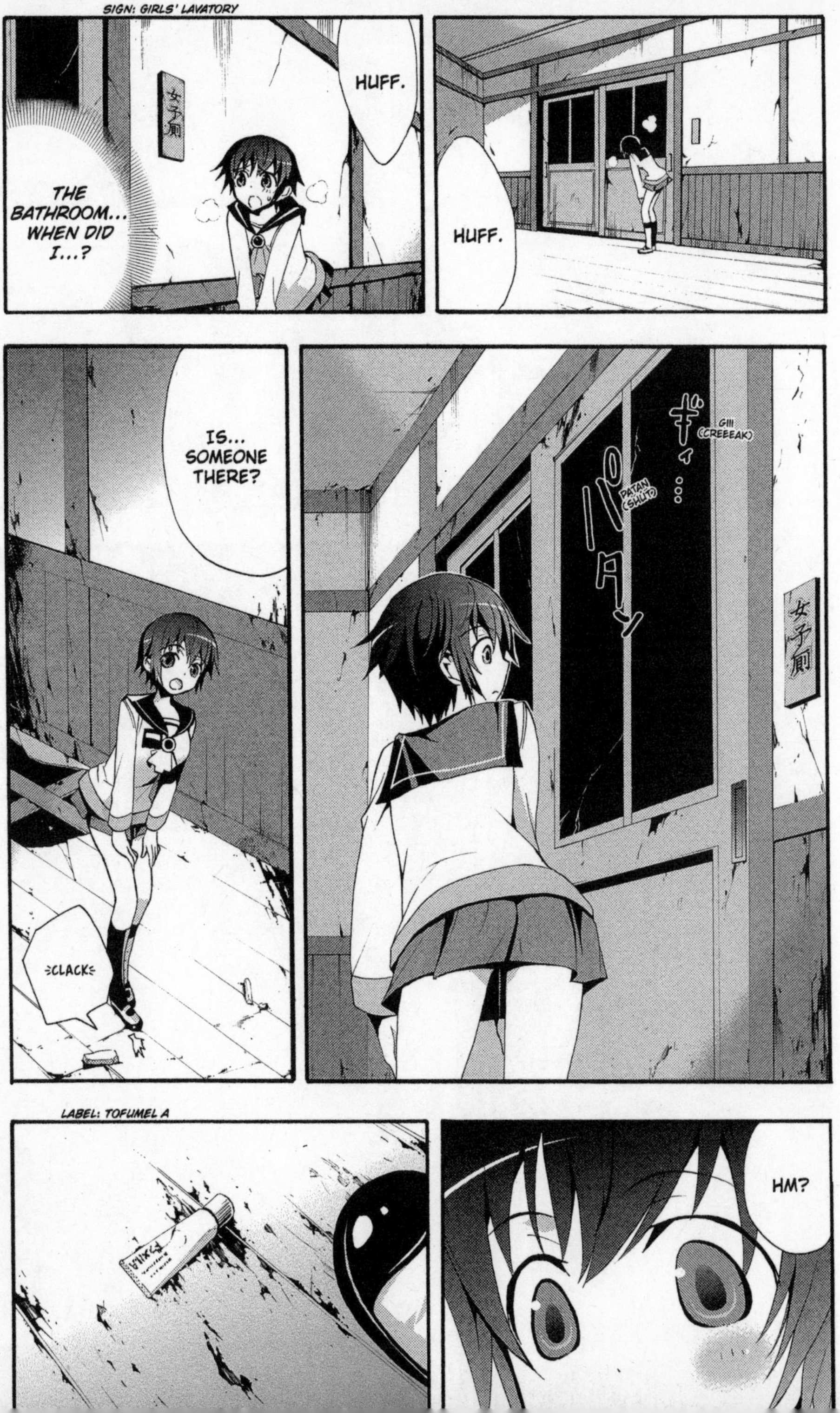
HUFF.
SIGN: GIRLS' LAVATORY
HUFF.
THE BATHROOM... WHEN DID I...?
ギィ…
GIII (CREEEAK)
パタン
PATAN (SHUT)
IS... SOMEONE THERE?
CLACK
HM?
LABEL: TOFUMEL A

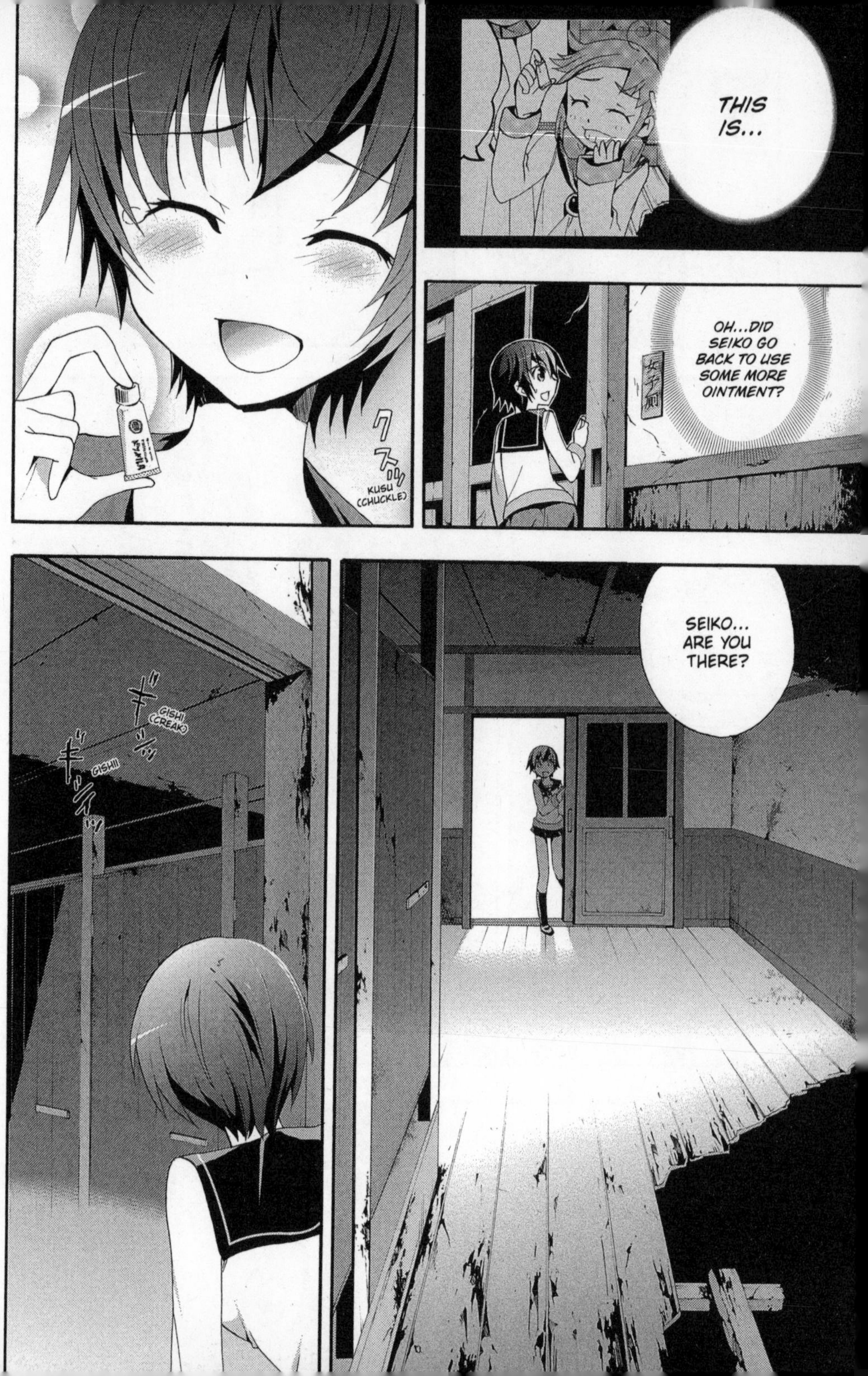
THIS IS...
OH...DID SEIKO GO BACK TO USE SOME MORE OINTMENT?
女子厠
KUSU (CHUCKLE)
SEIKO... ARE YOU THERE?
GISHI (CREAK)
GISHII

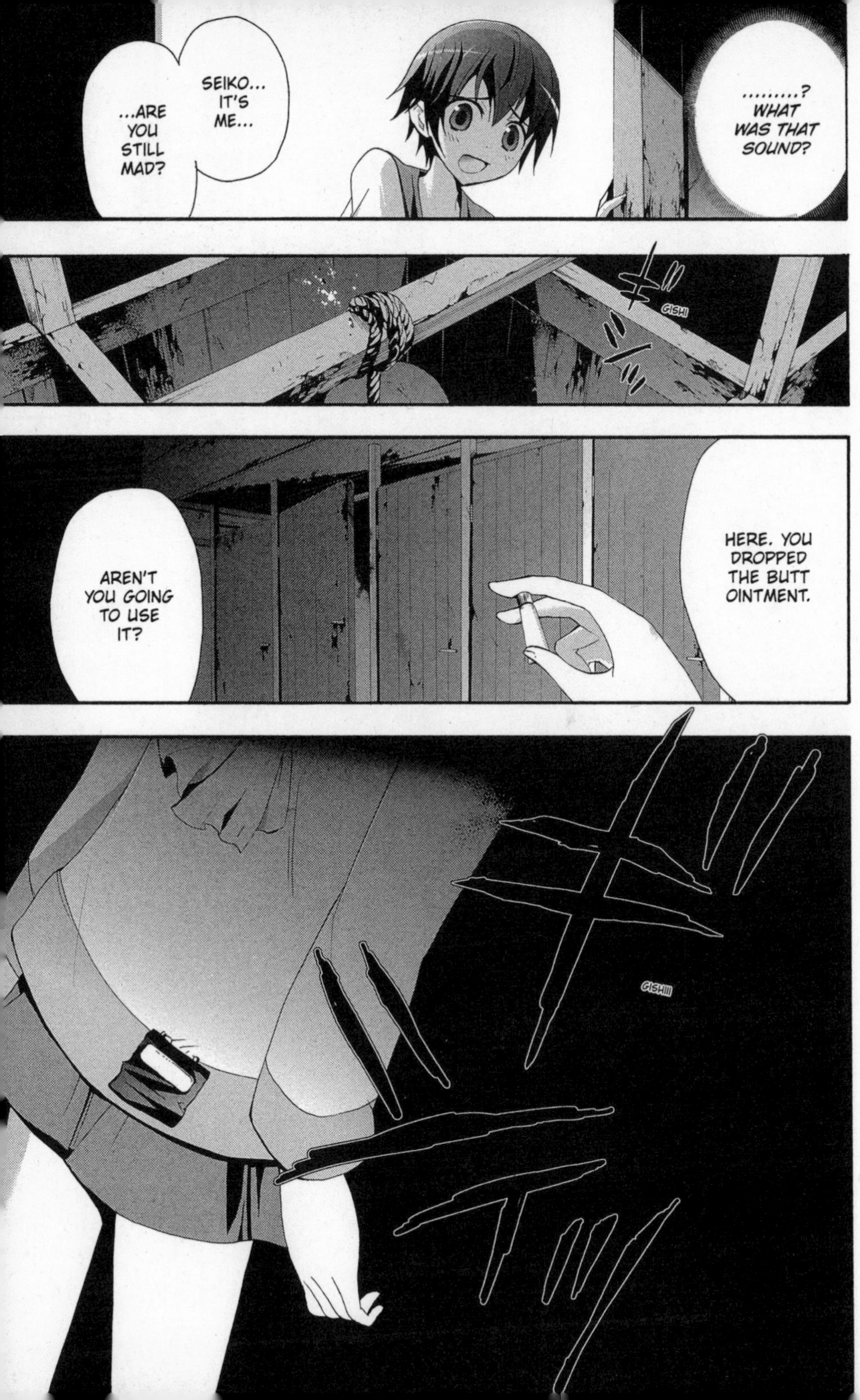
.........? WHAT WAS THAT SOUND?
SEIKO... IT'S ME...
...ARE YOU STILL MAD?
GISHI
HERE. YOU DROPPED THE BUTT OINTMENT.
AREN'T YOU GOING TO USE IT?
GISHIII

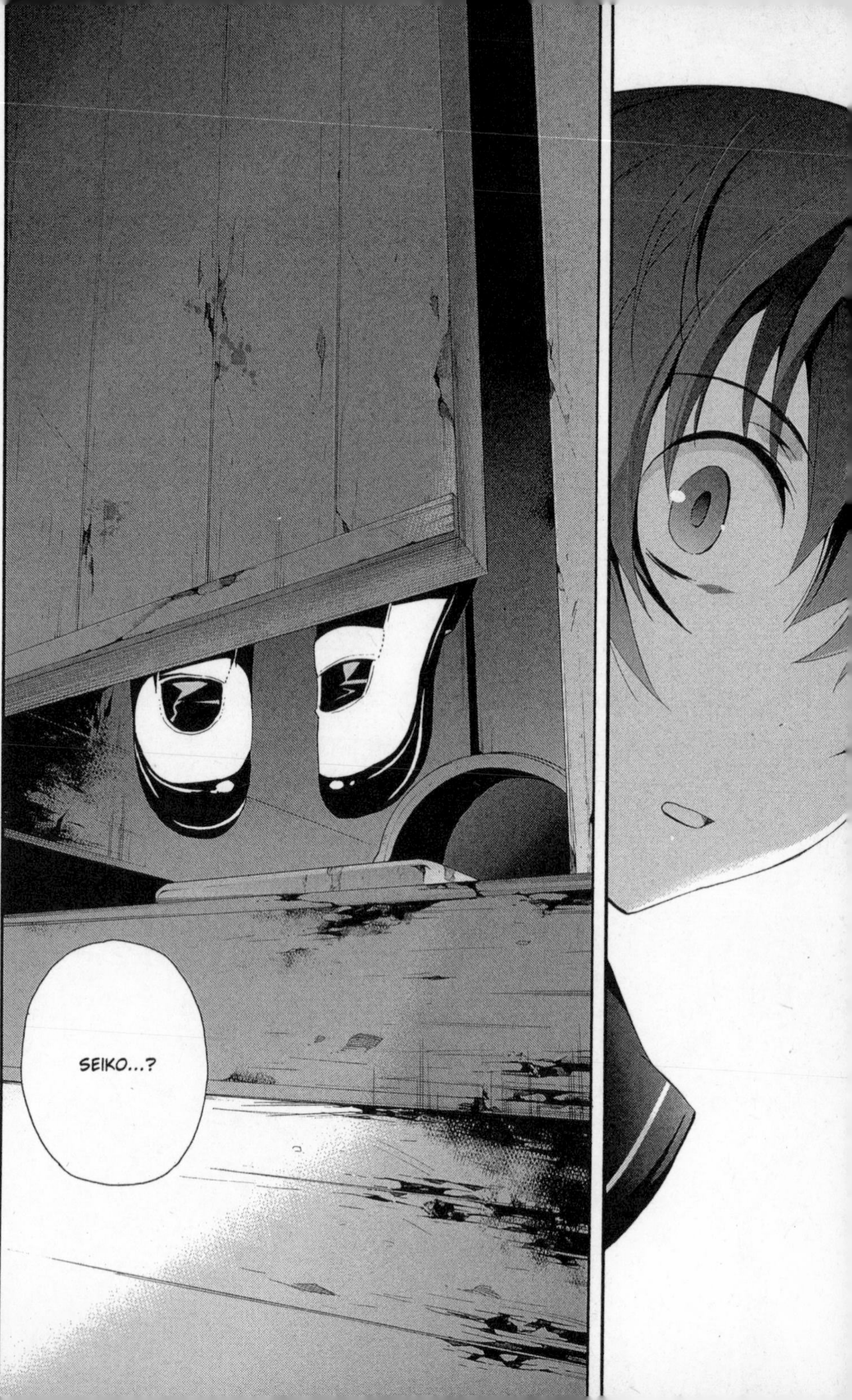
SEIKO...?

a list of corpses/03

Male high school student

From the trail of blood left along the hall floor, it would seem that he got hurt and continued to wander around until he came here, where he took a powerful blow to the head and lost his life. Based on the state of the body, it couldn't have been long since his death.

CORPSE PARTY
BloodCovered

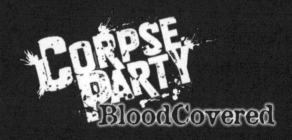

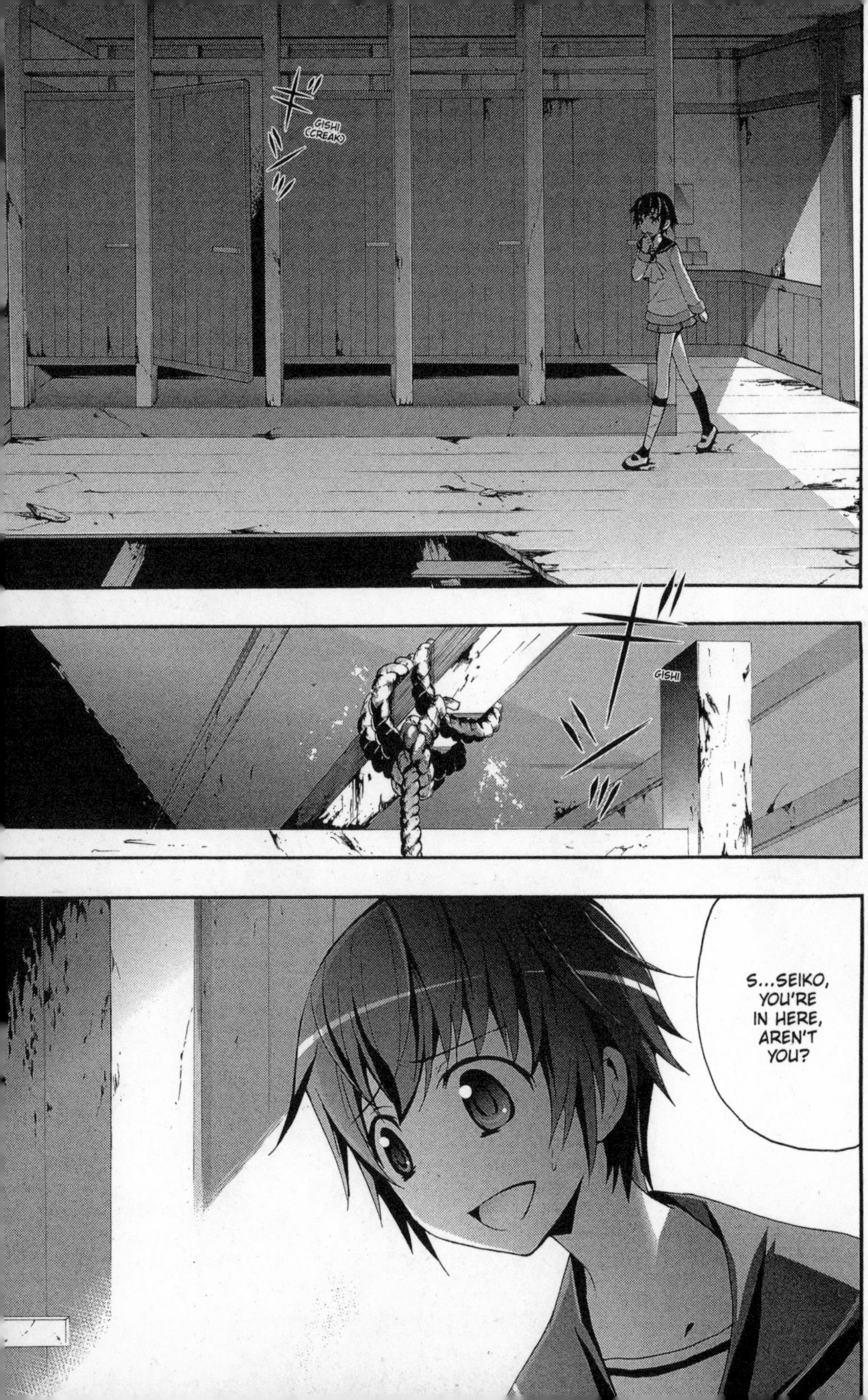
GISHI (CREAK)
GISHI
S...SEIKO, YOU'RE IN HERE, AREN'T YOU?

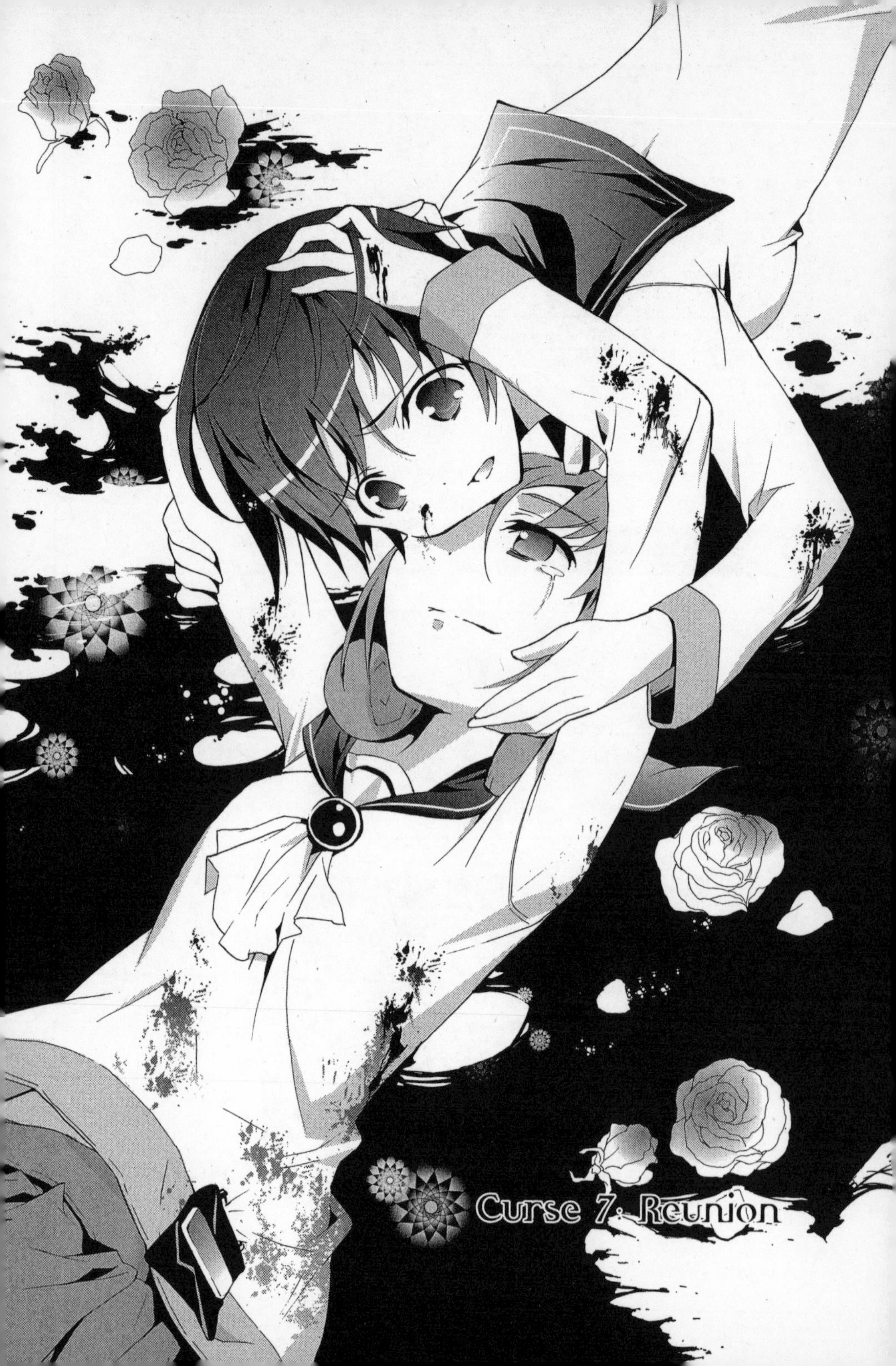
Curse 7: Reunion

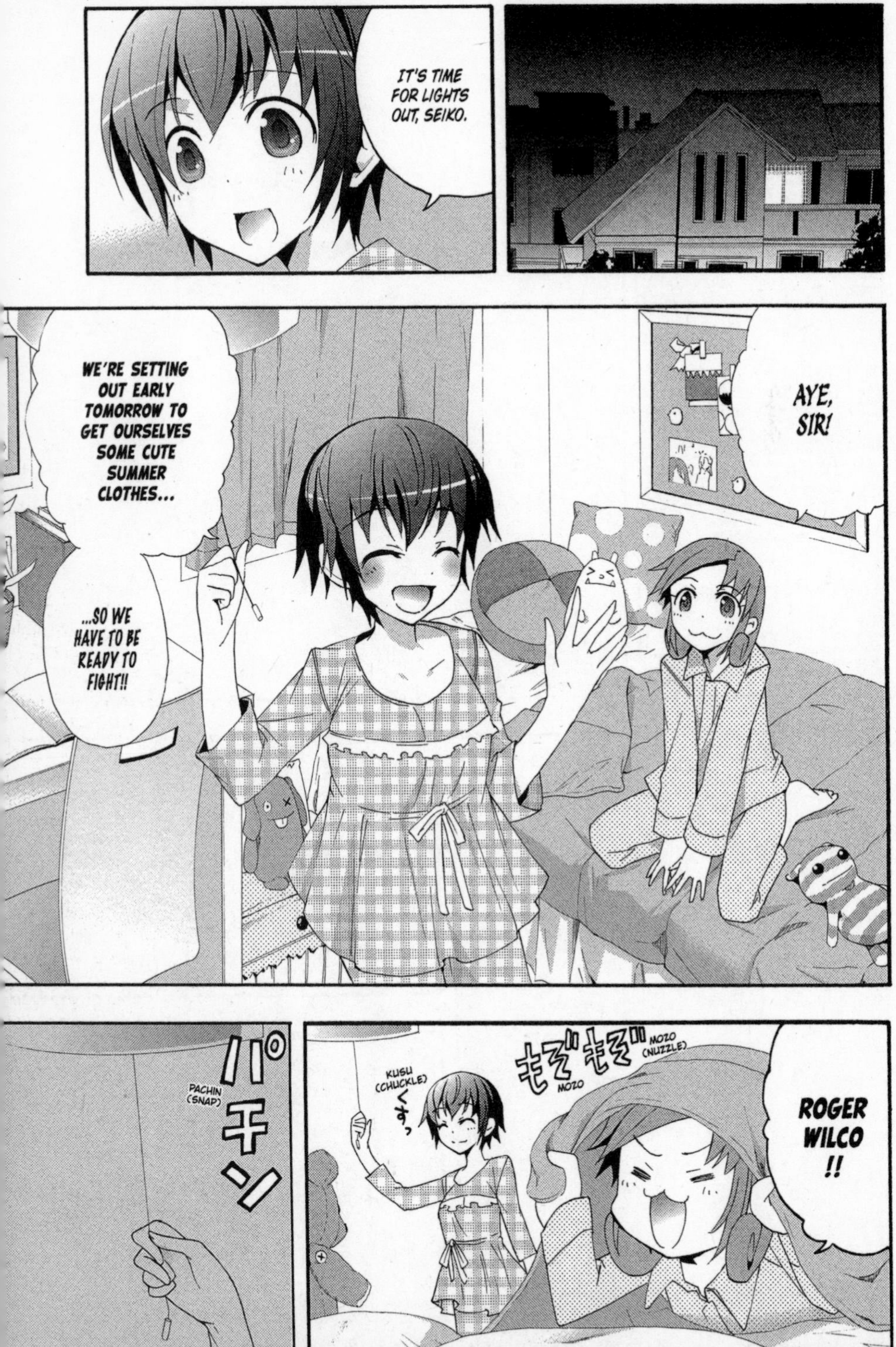
IT'S TIME FOR LIGHTS OUT, SEIKO.
WE'RE SETTING OUT EARLY TOMORROW TO GET OURSELVES SOME CUTE SUMMER CLOTHES...
...SO WE HAVE TO BE READY TO FIGHT!!
AYE, SIR!
ROGER WILCO !!
もぞもぞ
MOZO MOZO (NUZZLE)
くすっ
KUSU (CHUCKLE)
パチン
PACHIN (SNAP)

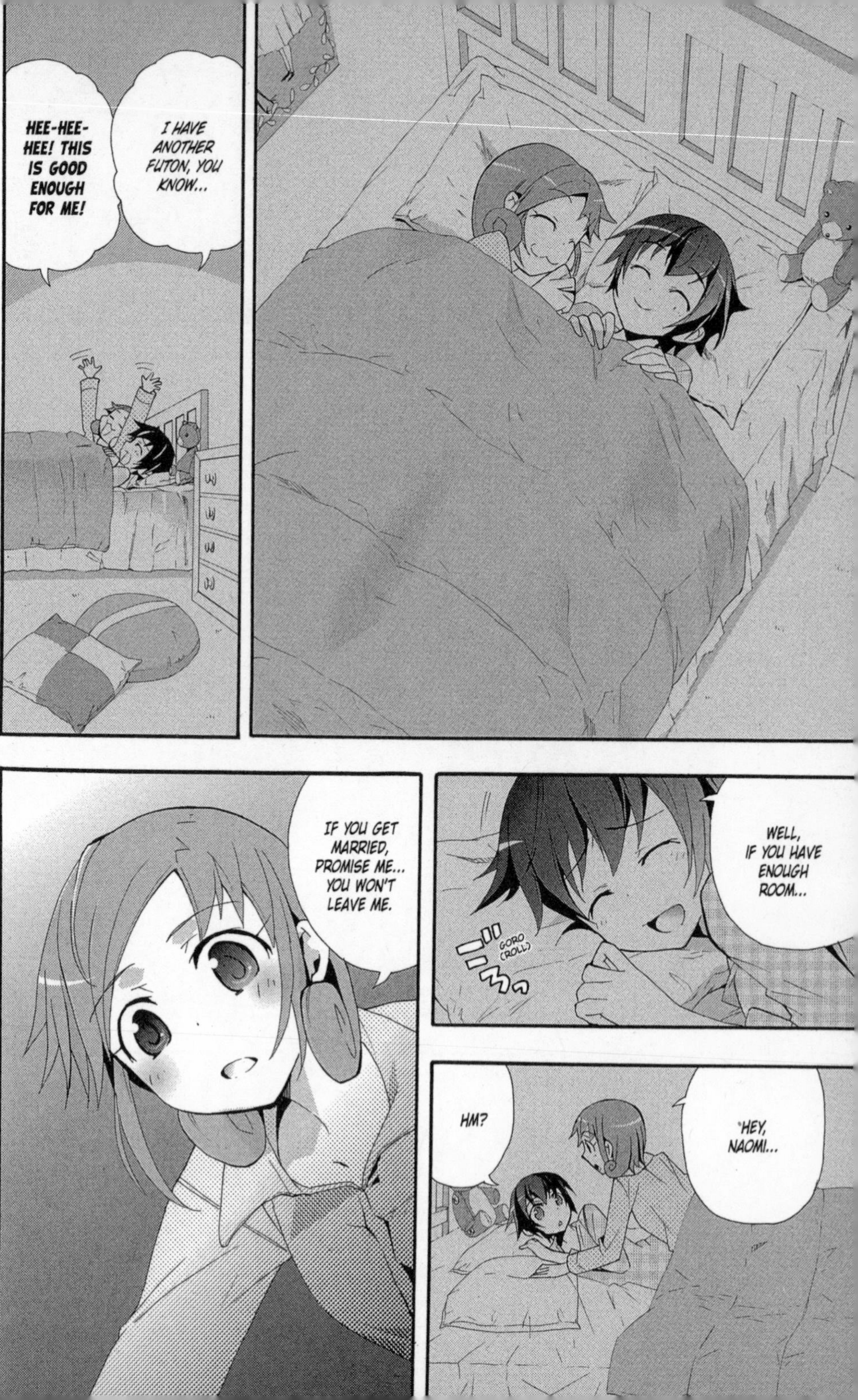
I HAVE ANOTHER FUTON, YOU KNOW...
HEE-HEE-HEE! THIS IS GOOD ENOUGH FOR ME!
WELL, IF YOU HAVE ENOUGH ROOM...
GORO (ROLL)
HEY, NAOMI...
HM?
IF YOU GET MARRIED, PROMISE ME... YOU WON'T LEAVE ME.

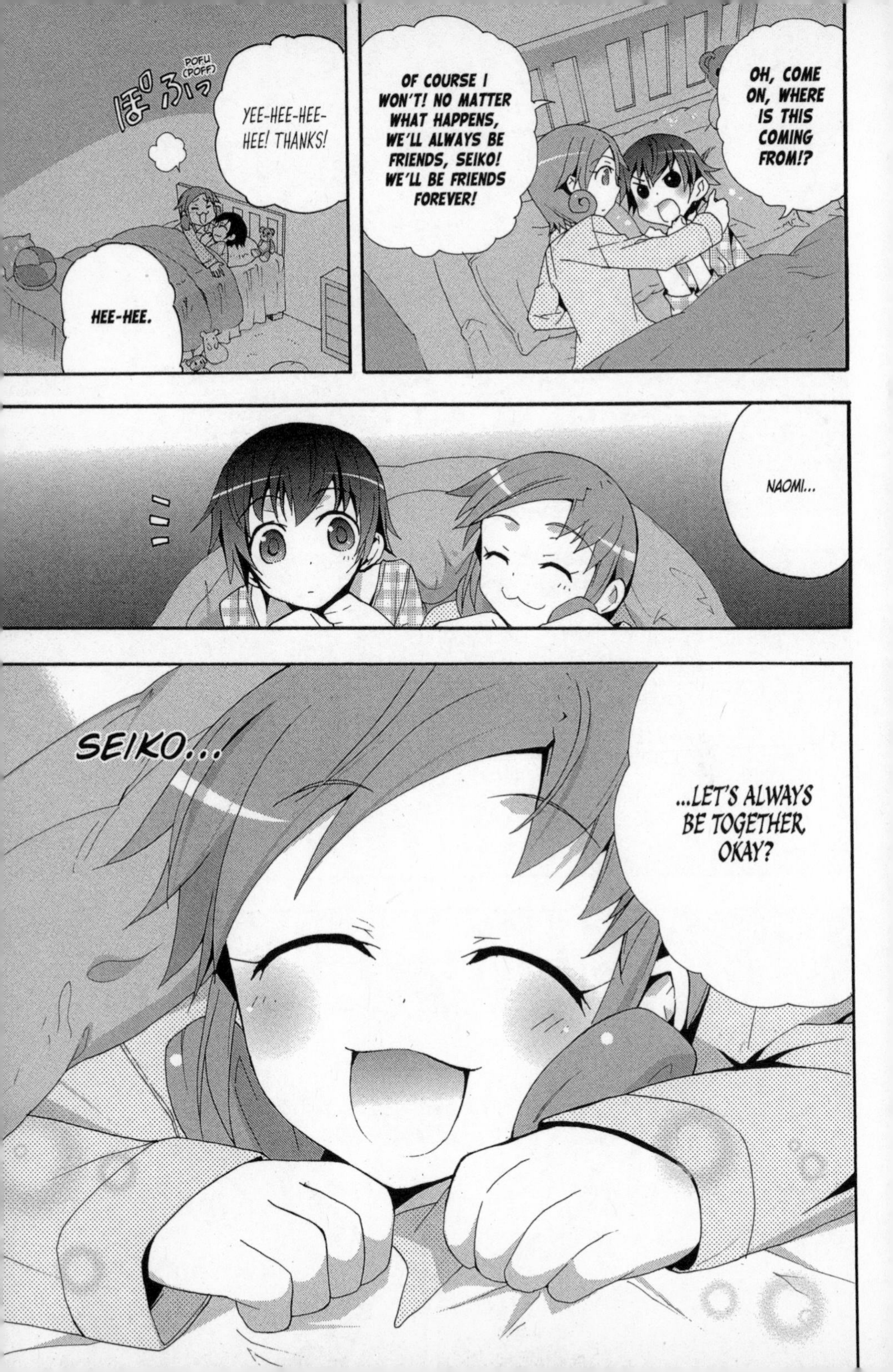
OH, COME ON, WHERE IS THIS COMING FROM!?
OF COURSE I WON'T! NO MATTER WHAT HAPPENS, WE'LL ALWAYS BE FRIENDS, SEIKO! WE'LL BE FRIENDS FOREVER!
YEE-HEE-HEE-HEE! THANKS!
ぽふっ
POFU (POFF)
HEE-HEE.
NAOMI...
...LET'S ALWAYS BE TOGETHER, OKAY?
SEIKO...

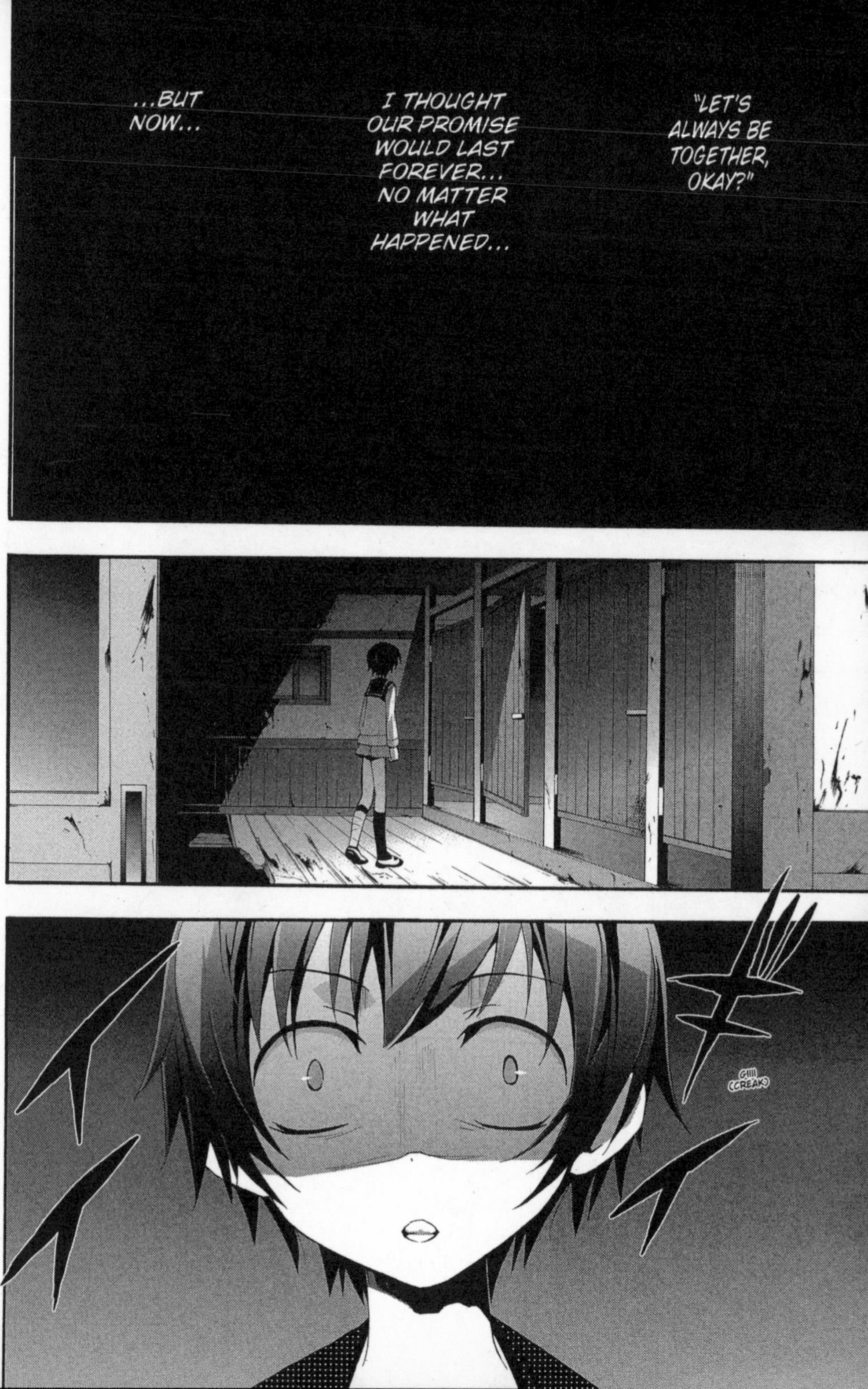
"LET'S ALWAYS BE TOGETHER, OKAY?"
I THOUGHT OUR PROMISE WOULD LAST FOREVER... NO MATTER WHAT HAPPENED...
...BUT NOW...
GIIII (CREAK)

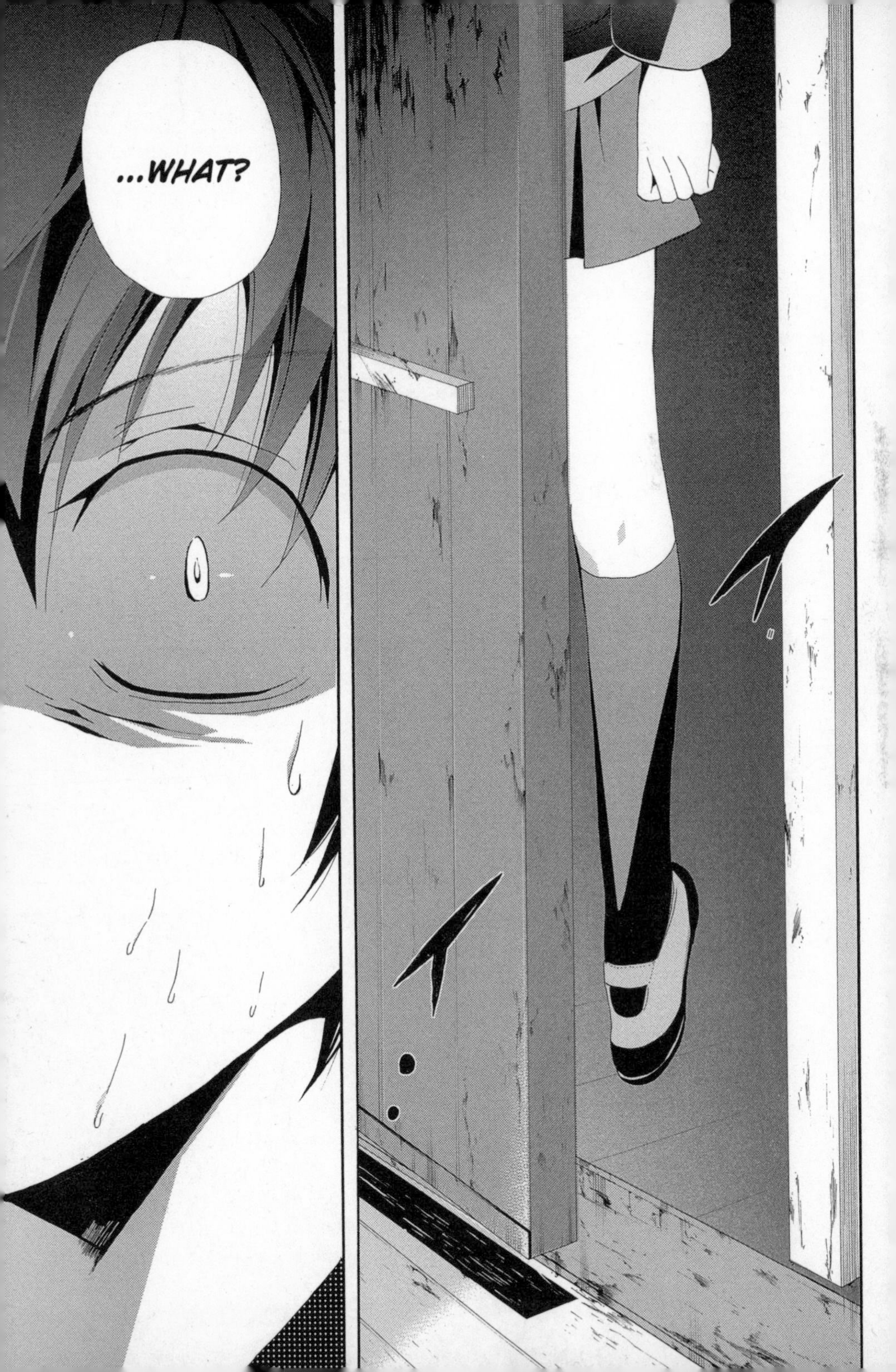
...WHAT?

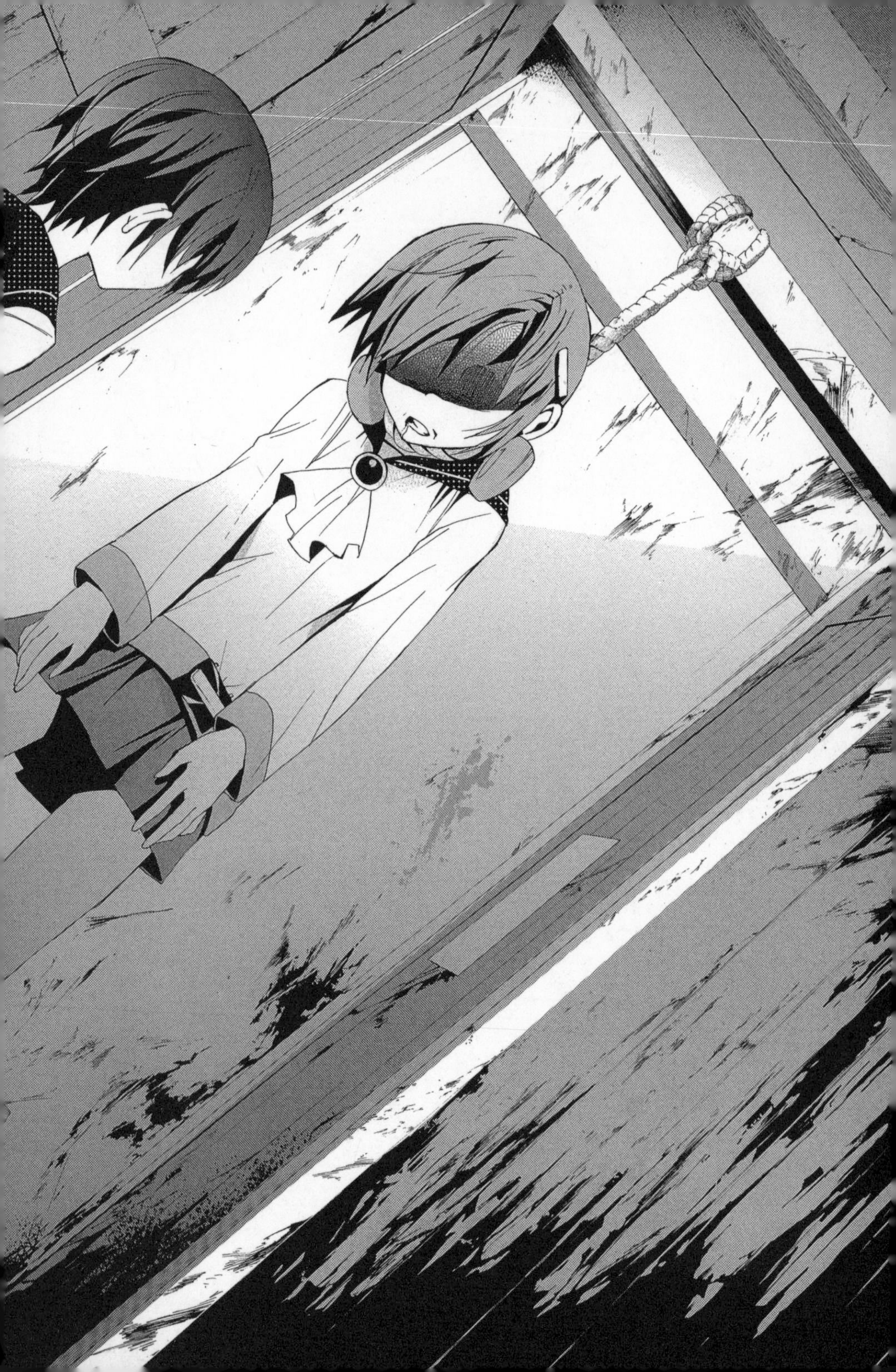

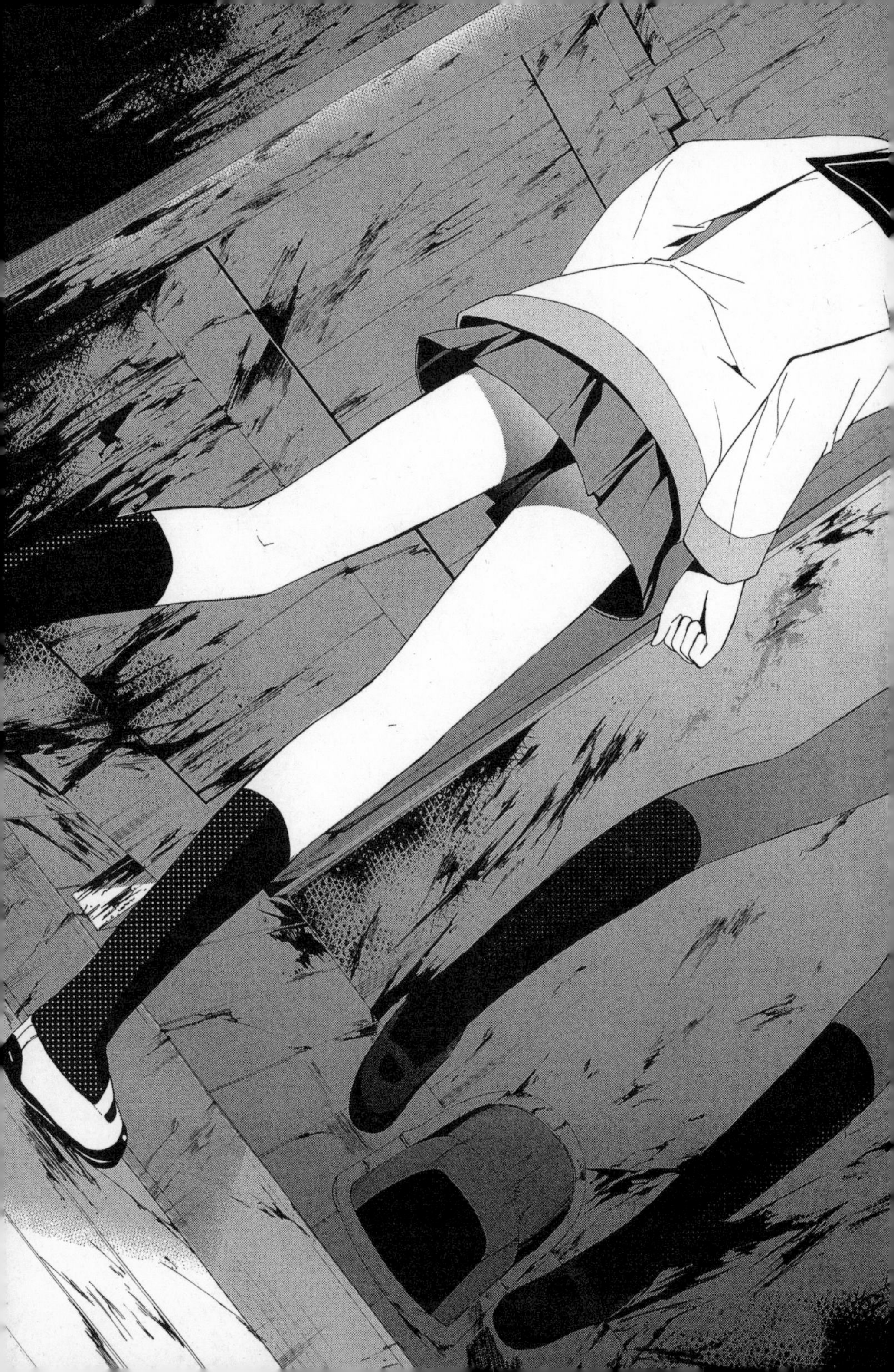

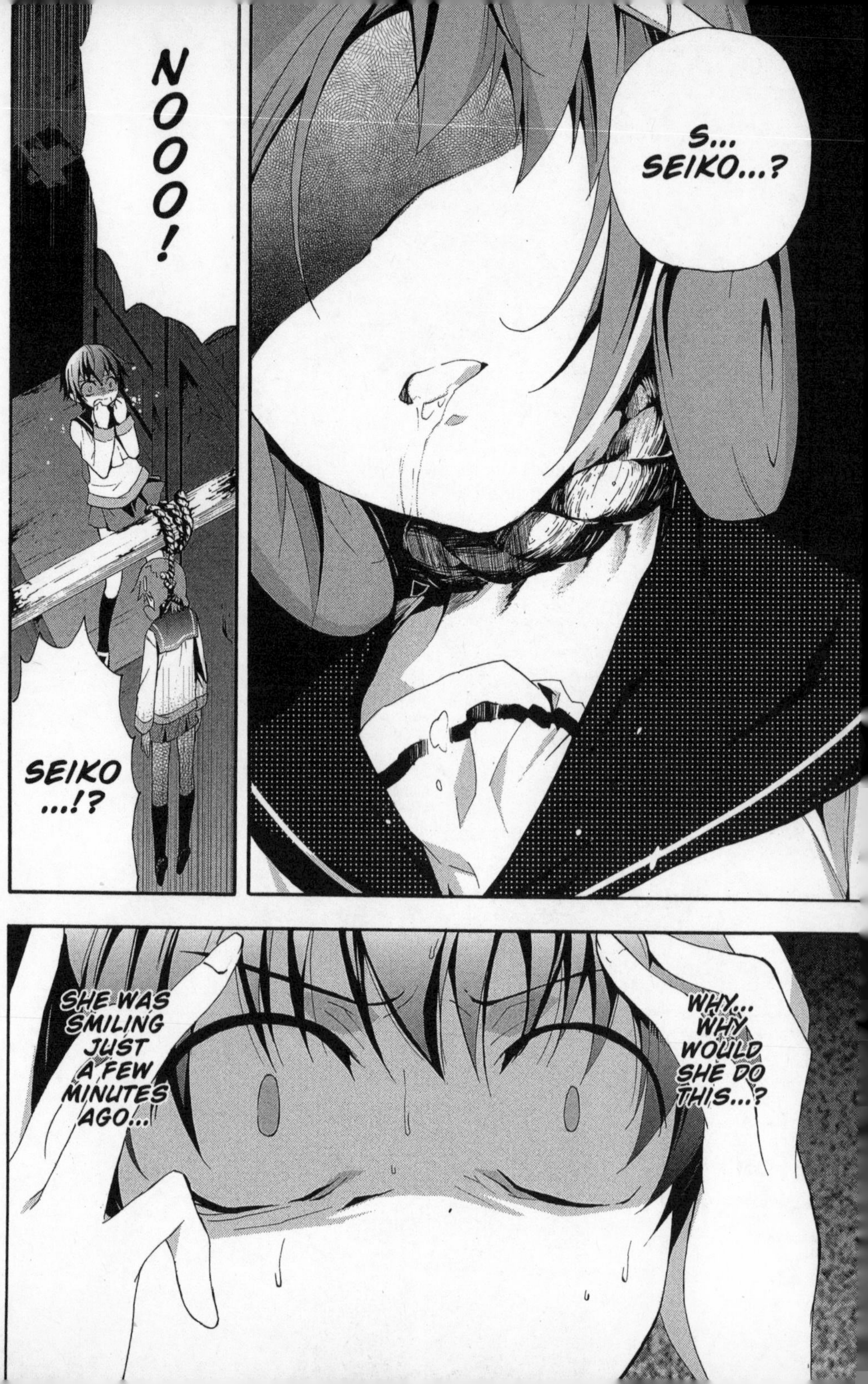
S... SEIKO...?
NOOOO!
SEIKO ...!?
WHY... WHY WOULD SHE DO THIS...?
SHE WAS SMILING JUST A FEW MINUTES AGO...

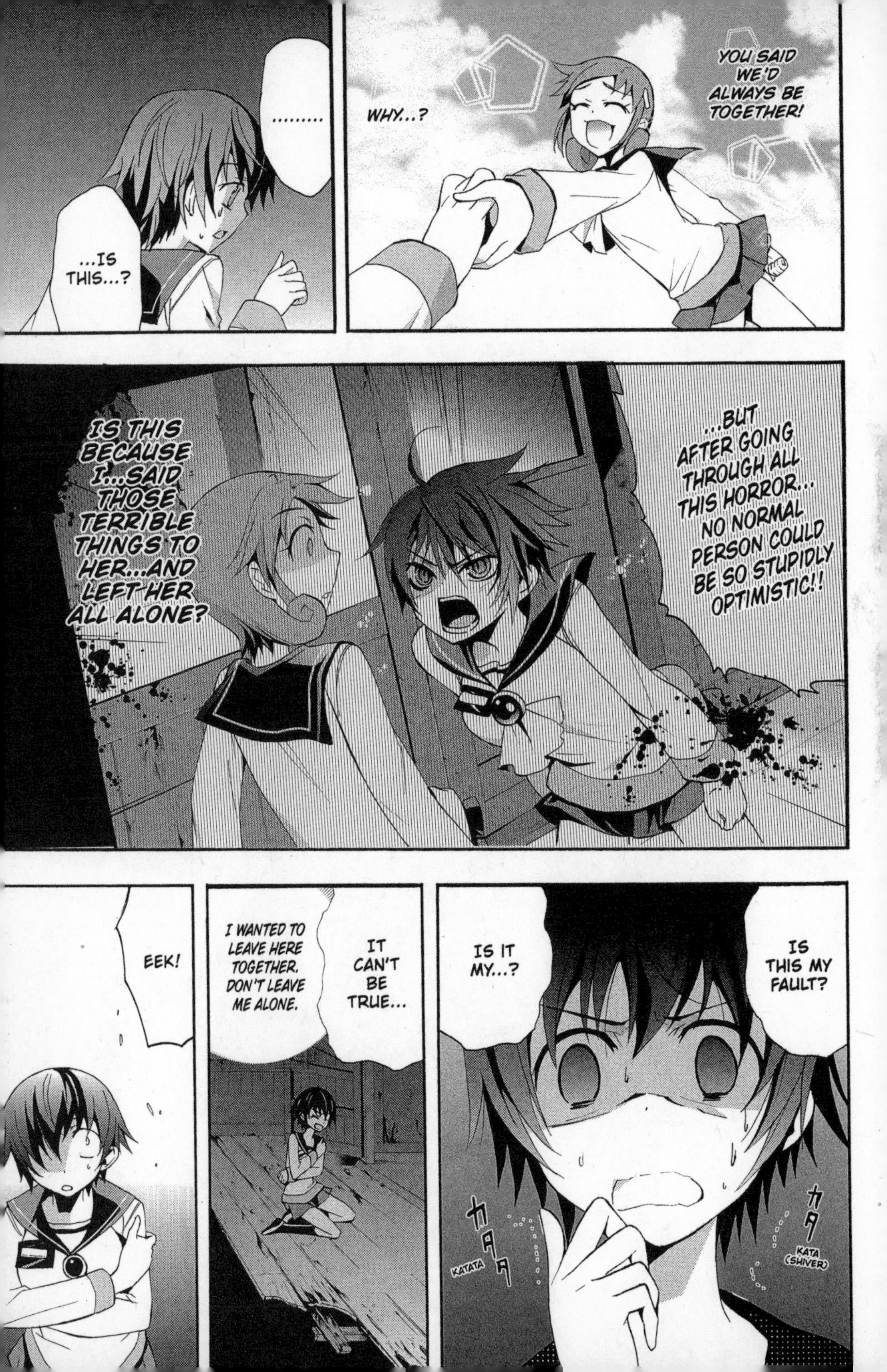
YOU SAID WE'D ALWAYS BE TOGETHER!
WHY...?
....
...IS THIS...?
...BUT AFTER GOING THROUGH ALL THIS HORROR... NO NORMAL PERSON COULD BE SO STUPIDLY OPTIMISTIC!!
IS THIS BECAUSE I...SAID THOSE TERRIBLE THINGS TO HER...AND LEFT HER ALL ALONE?
IS THIS MY FAULT?
IS IT MY...?
カタ
KATA (SHIVER)
カタタ
KATATA
IT CAN'T BE TRUE...
I WANTED TO LEAVE HERE TOGETHER. DON'T LEAVE ME ALONE.
EEK!

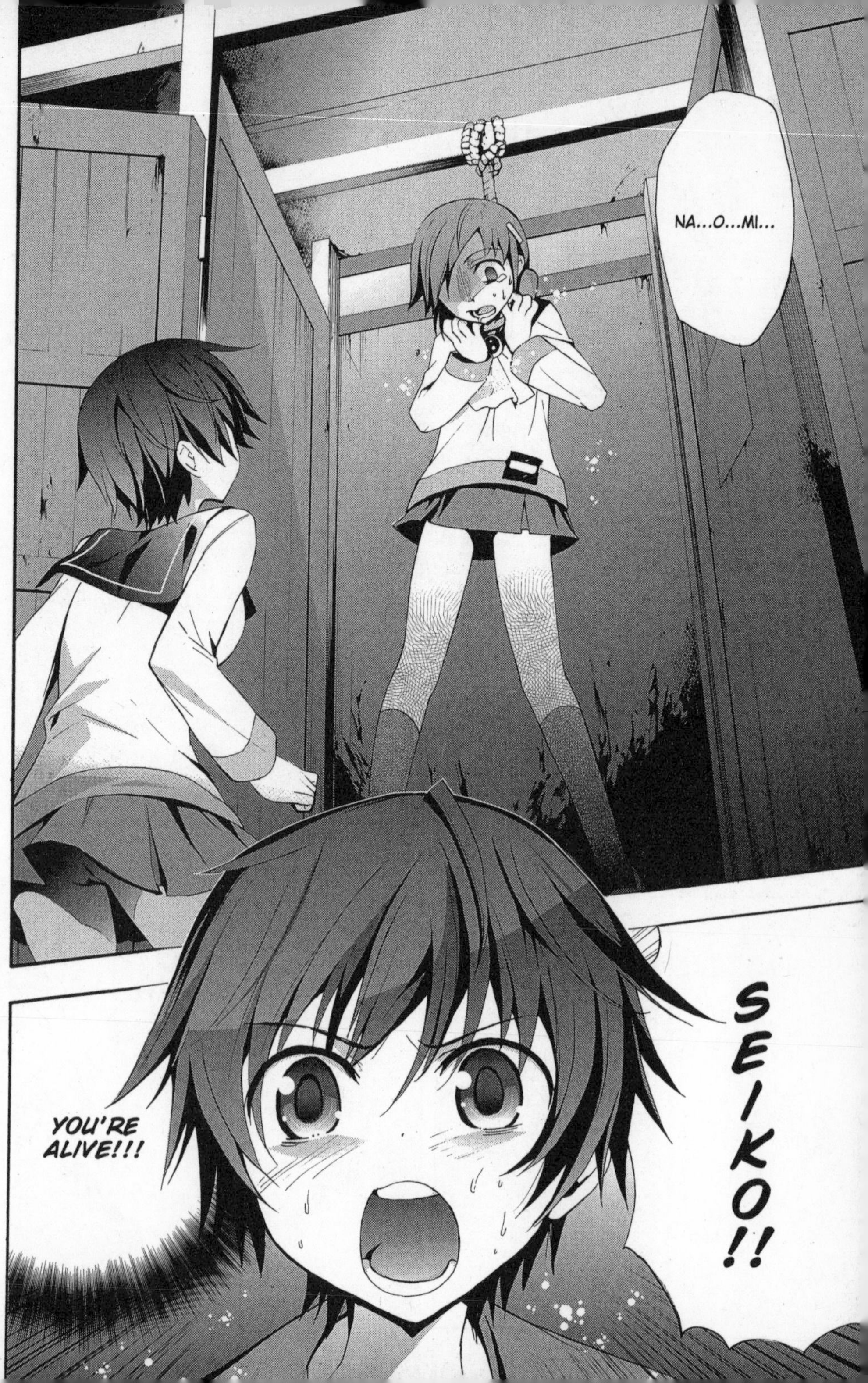
NA...O...MI...
SEIKO!!
YOU'RE ALIVE!!!

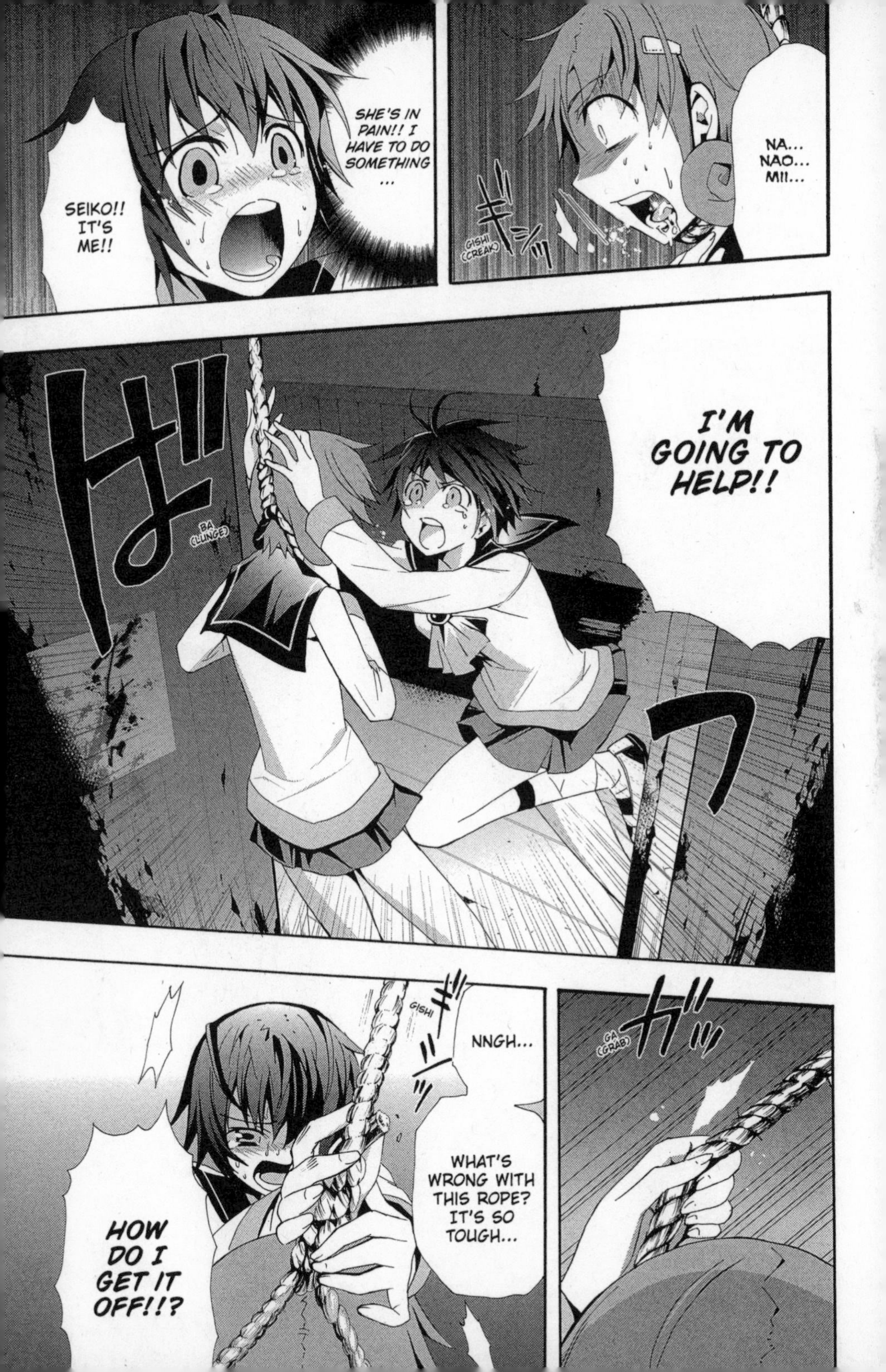
NA... NAO... MII...
GISHI (CREAK)
SHE'S IN PAIN!! I HAVE TO DO SOMETHING ...
SEIKO!! IT'S ME!!
I'M GOING TO HELP!!
BA (LUNGE)
GA (GRAB)
GISHI
NNGH...
WHAT'S WRONG WITH THIS ROPE? IT'S SO TOUGH...
HOW DO I GET IT OFF!!?

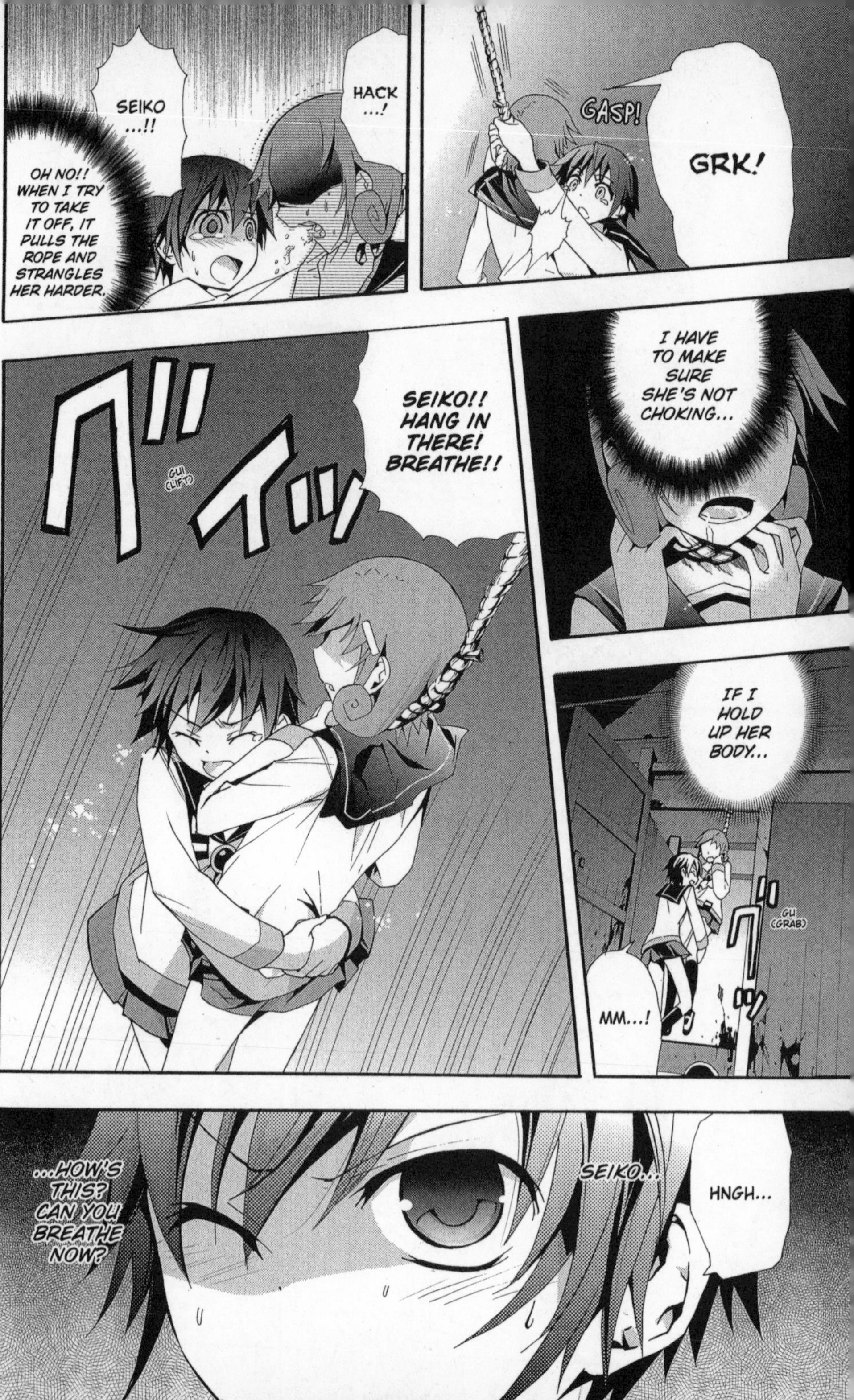
GASP!
GRK!
HACK ...!
SEIKO ...!!
OH NO!! WHEN I TRY TO TAKE IT OFF, IT PULLS THE ROPE AND STRANGLES HER HARDER.
I HAVE TO MAKE SURE SHE'S NOT CHOKING...
IF I HOLD UP HER BODY...
GU (GRAB)
MM...!
SEIKO!! HANG IN THERE! BREATHE!!
GUI (LIFT)
HNGH...
SEIKO...
...HOW'S THIS? CAN YOU BREATHE NOW?

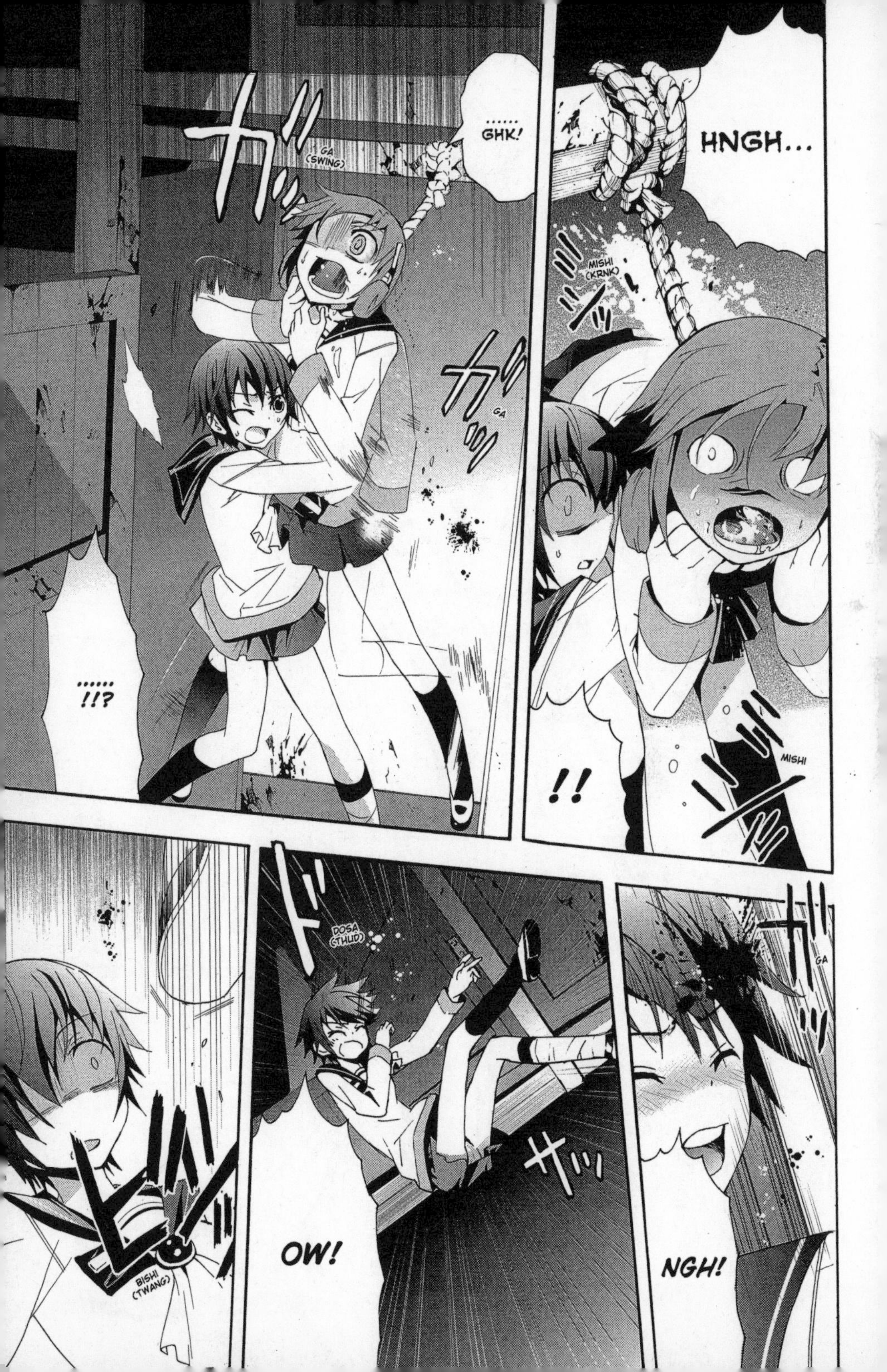
HNGH...
MISHI (KRNK)
MISHI
!!
......GHK!
GA (SWING)
GA
......!!?
GA
NGH!
DOSA (THUD)
OW!
BISHI (TWANG)

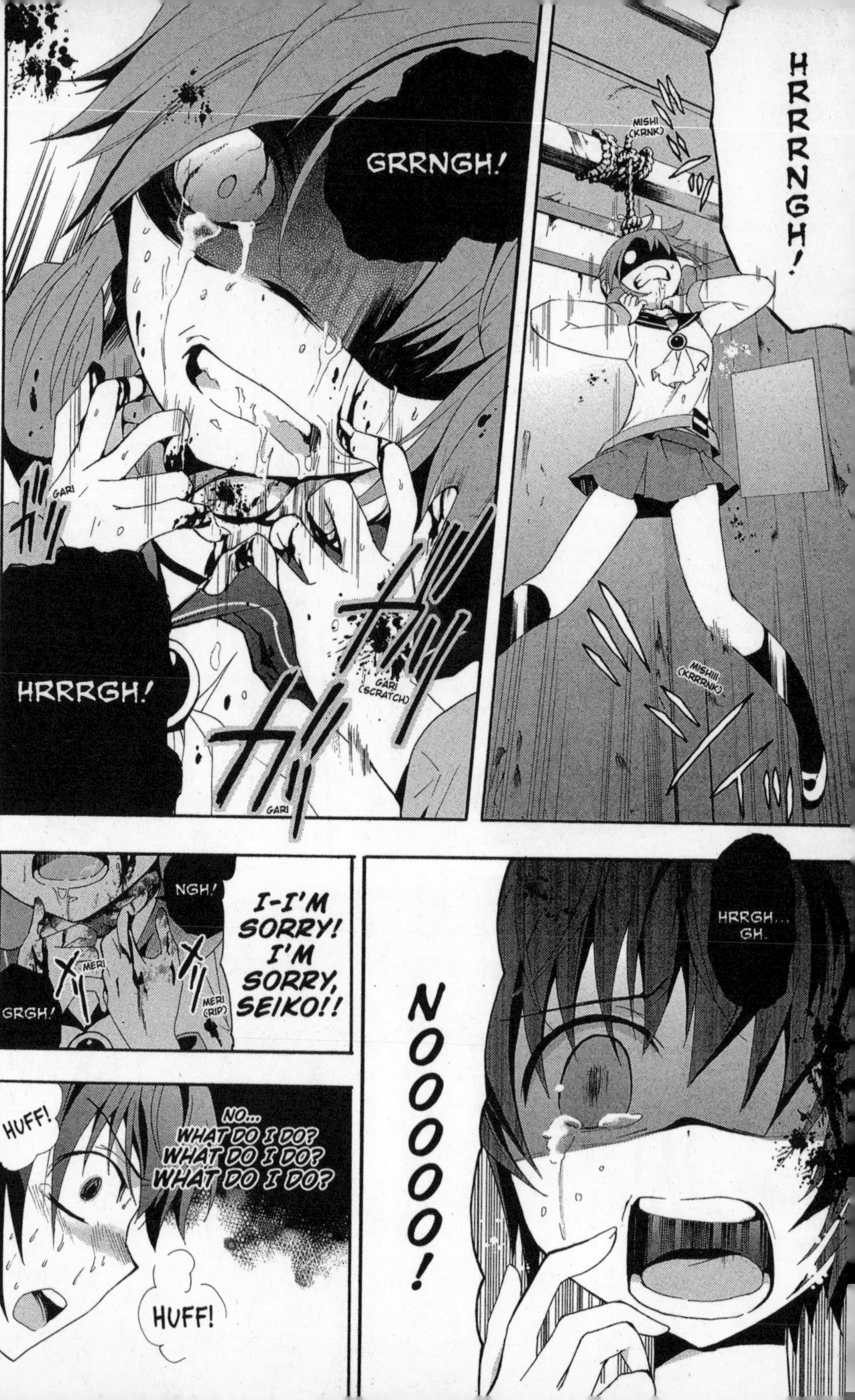
HRRRNGH!
MISHI (KRNK)
MISHIII (KRRRNK)
GRRNGH!
GARI
HRRRGH!
GARI (SCRATCH)
GARI
HRRGH... GH.
NOOOOOO!
NGH!
I-I'M SORRY! I'M SORRY, SEIKO!!
MERI
MERI (RIP)
GRGH!
HUFF!
NO... WHAT DO I DO? WHAT DO I DO? WHAT DO I DO?
HUFF!

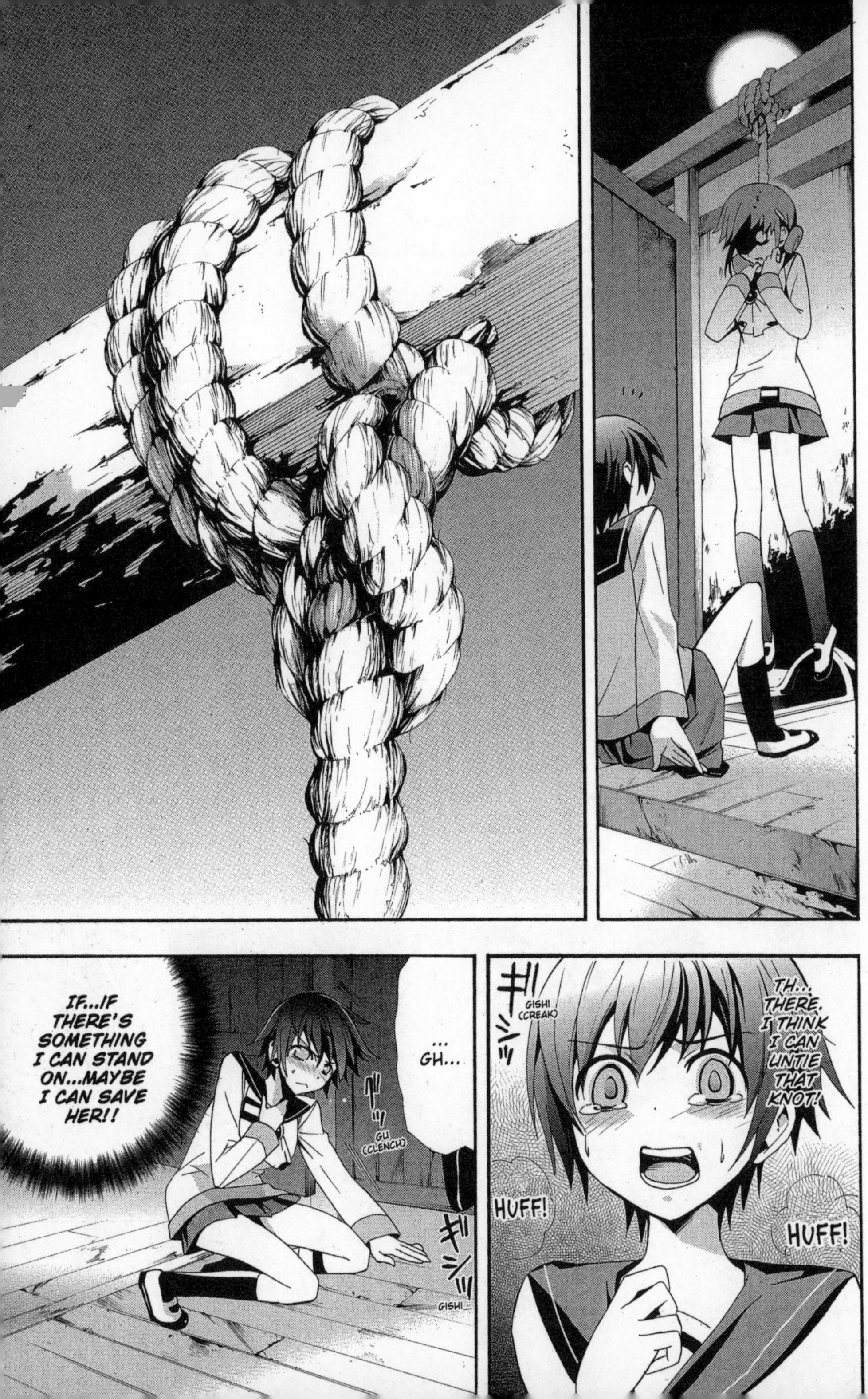
TH... THERE. I THINK I CAN UNTIE THAT KNOT!
GISHI (CREAK)
HUFF!
HUFF!
...GH...
GU (CLENCH)
IF...IF THERE'S SOMETHING I CAN STAND ON...MAYBE I CAN SAVE HER!!
GISHI

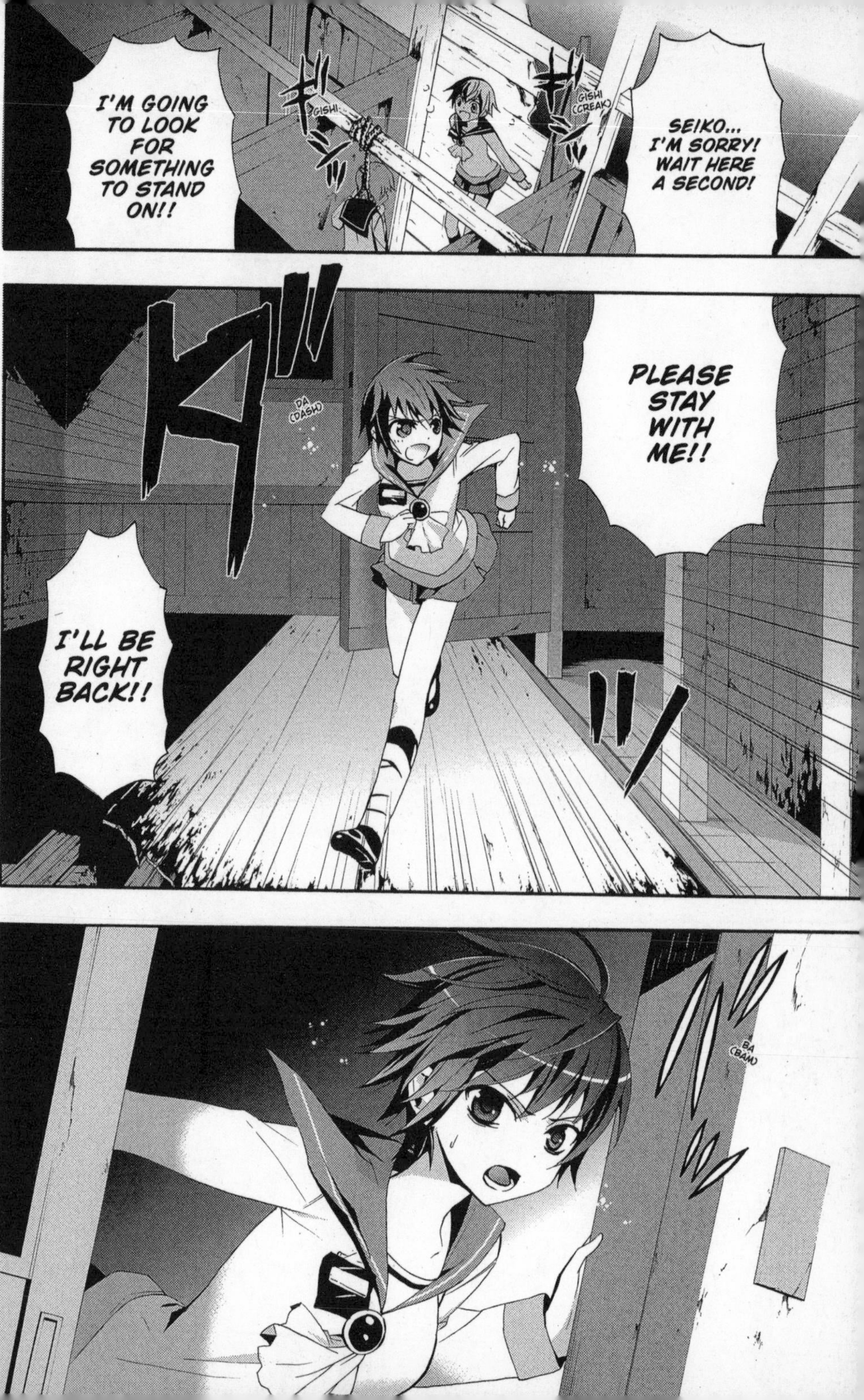
SEIKO... I'M SORRY! WAIT HERE A SECOND!
GISHI (CREAK)
GISHI
I'M GOING TO LOOK FOR SOMETHING TO STAND ON!!
PLEASE STAY WITH ME!!
DA (DASH)
I'LL BE RIGHT BACK!!
BA (BAM)

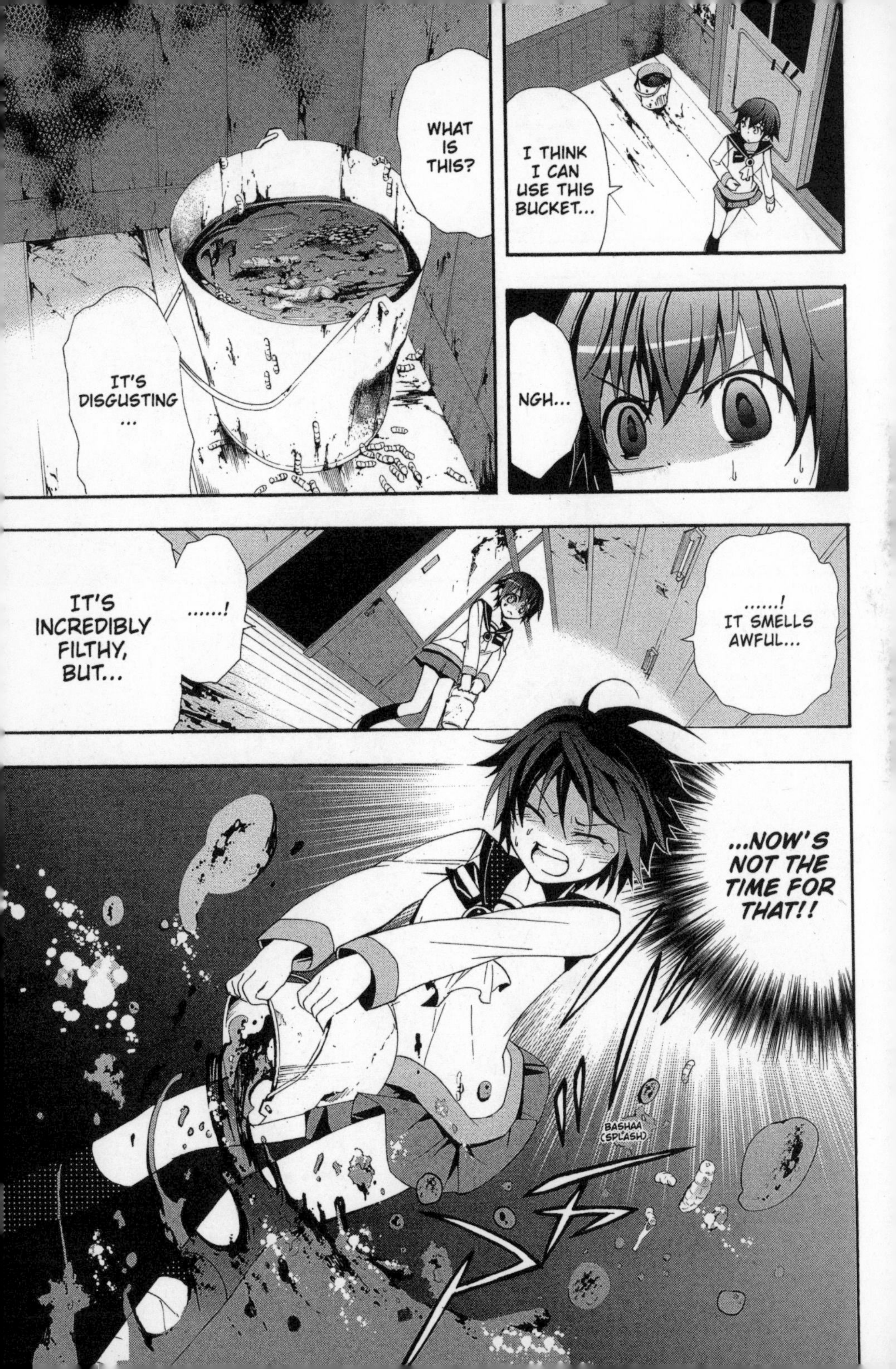
I THINK I CAN USE THIS BUCKET...
NGH...
WHAT IS THIS?
IT'S DISGUSTING ...
......! IT SMELLS AWFUL...
......!
IT'S INCREDIBLY FILTHY, BUT...
...NOW'S NOT THE TIME FOR THAT!!
BASHAA (SPLASH)

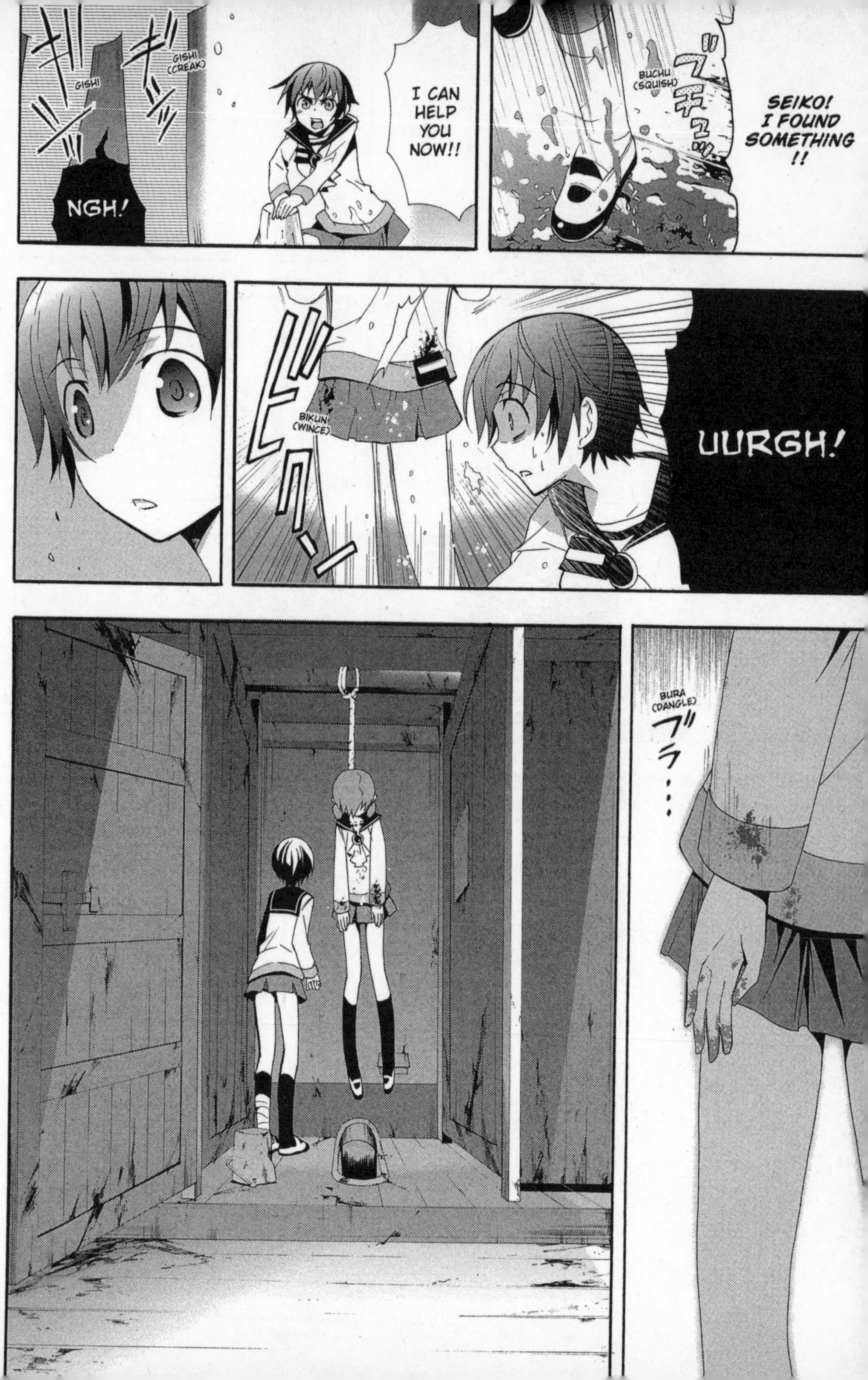
SEIKO! I FOUND SOMETHING !!
BUCHU (SQUISH)
I CAN HELP YOU NOW!!
GISHI (CREAK)
GISHI
NGH!
UURGH!
BIKUN (WINCE)
BURA (DANGLE)
ブラ…

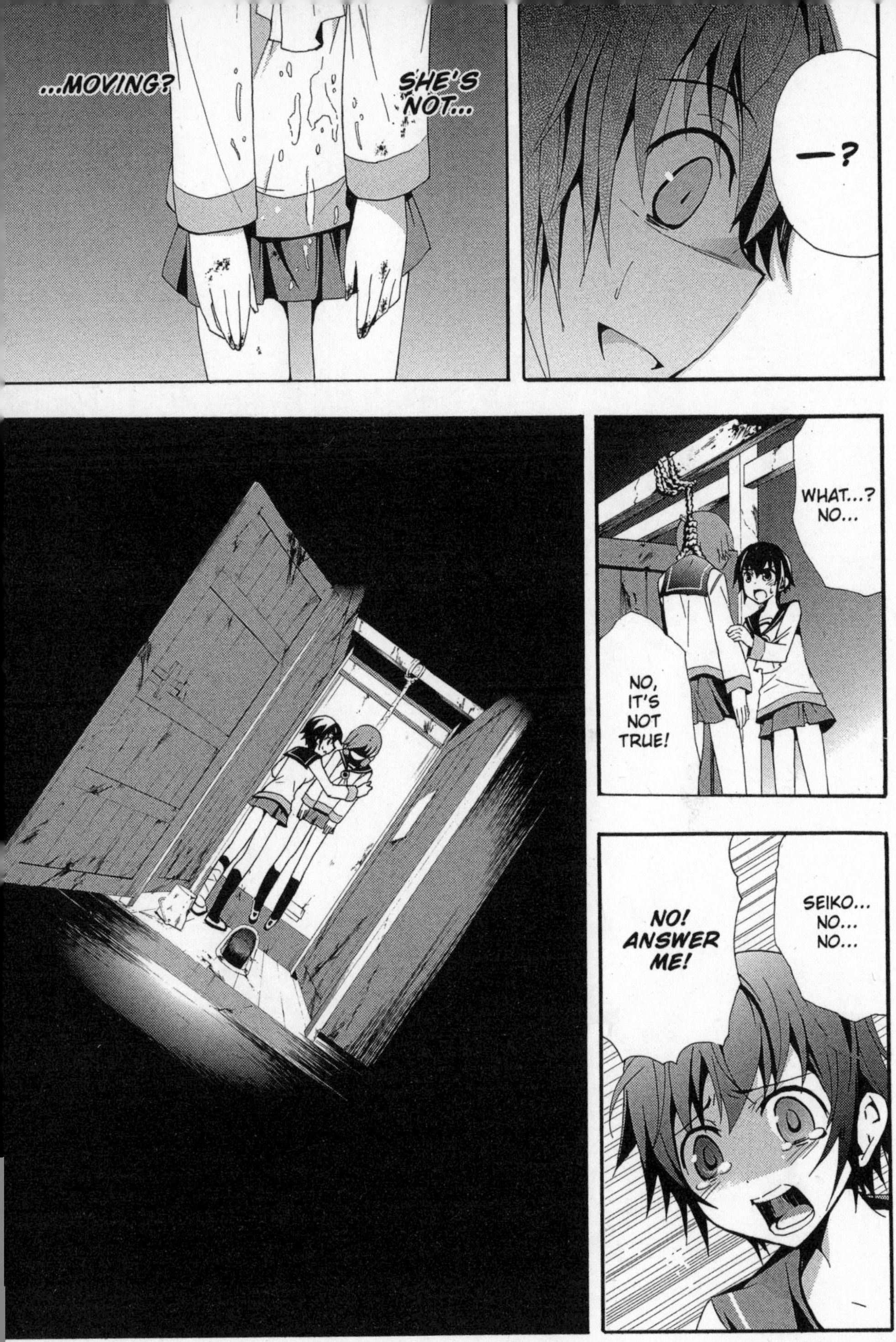
—?
SHE'S NOT...
...MOVING?
WHAT...? NO...
NO, IT'S NOT TRUE!
SEIKO... NO... NO...
NO! ANSWER ME!

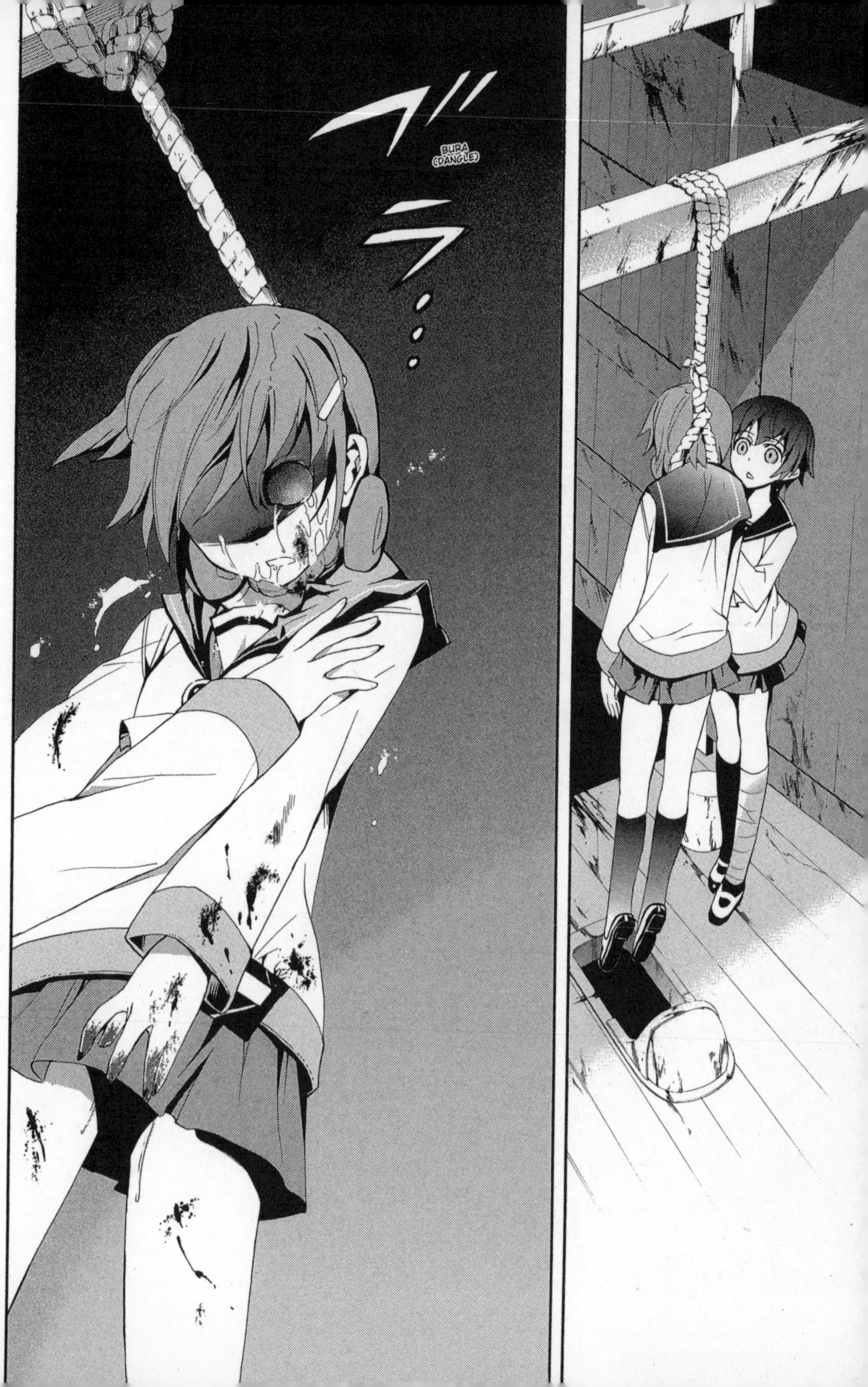
ブラ…
BURA (DANGLE)

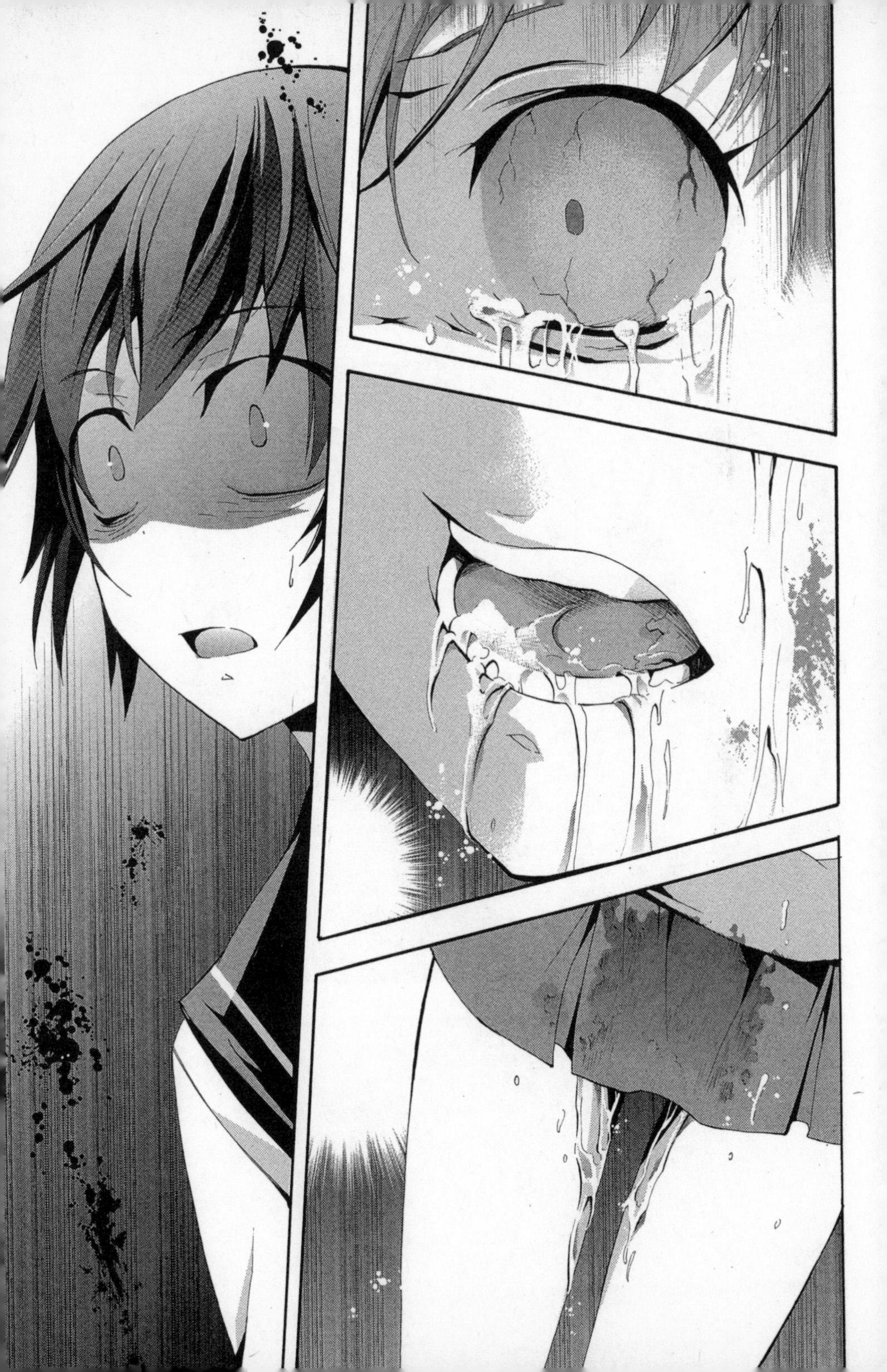

IT-IT CAN'T BE...

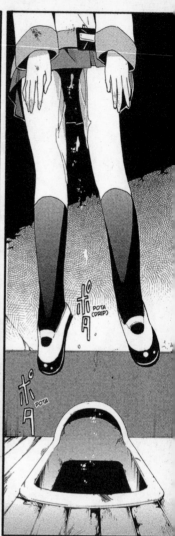

POTA
(DRIP)

POTA

...GH...

SEI...KO...

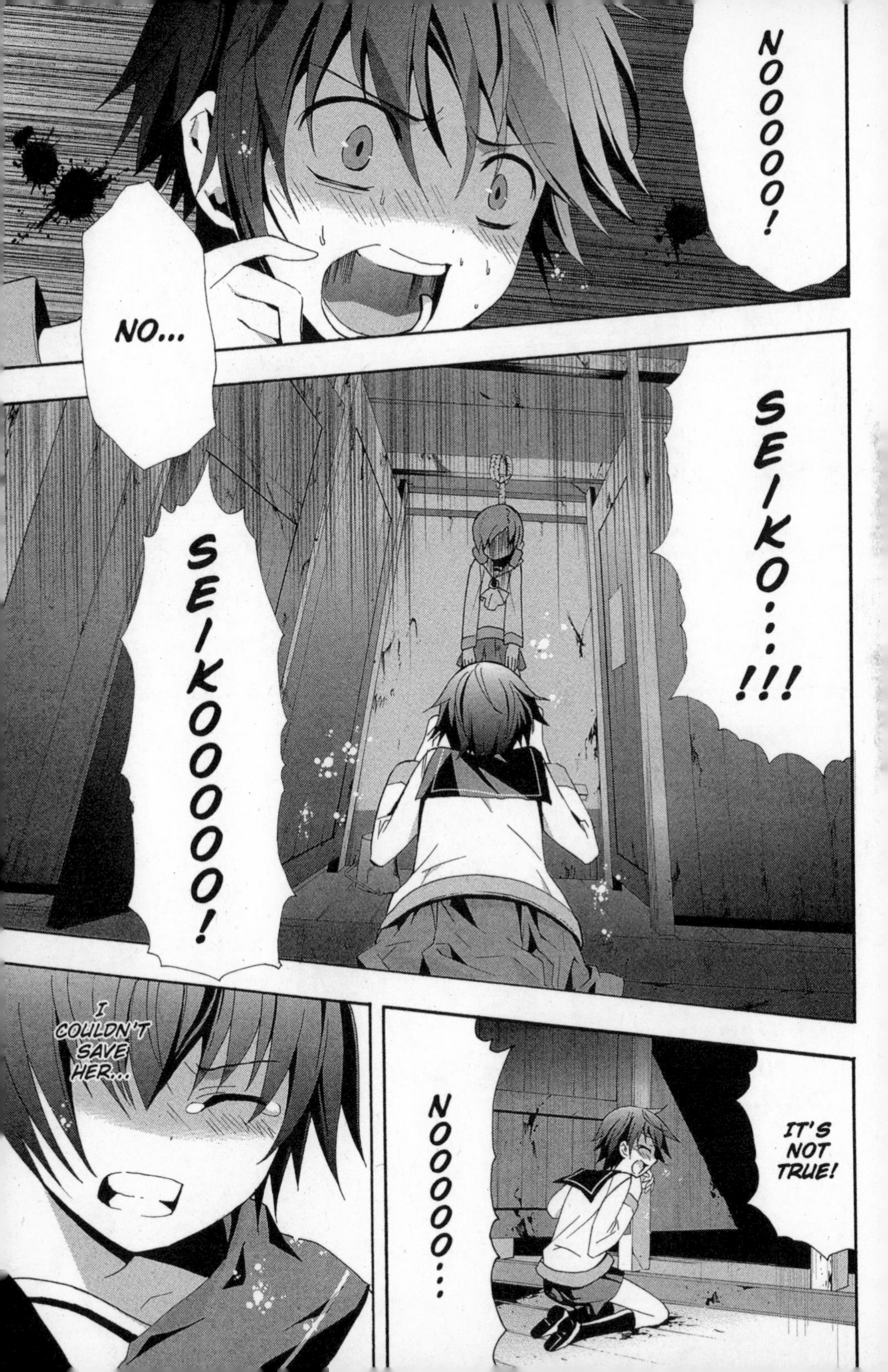
NOOOOOO!
NO...
SEIKO...!!!
SEIKOOOOOOO!
IT'S NOT TRUE!
NOOOOOO...
I COULDN'T SAVE HER...

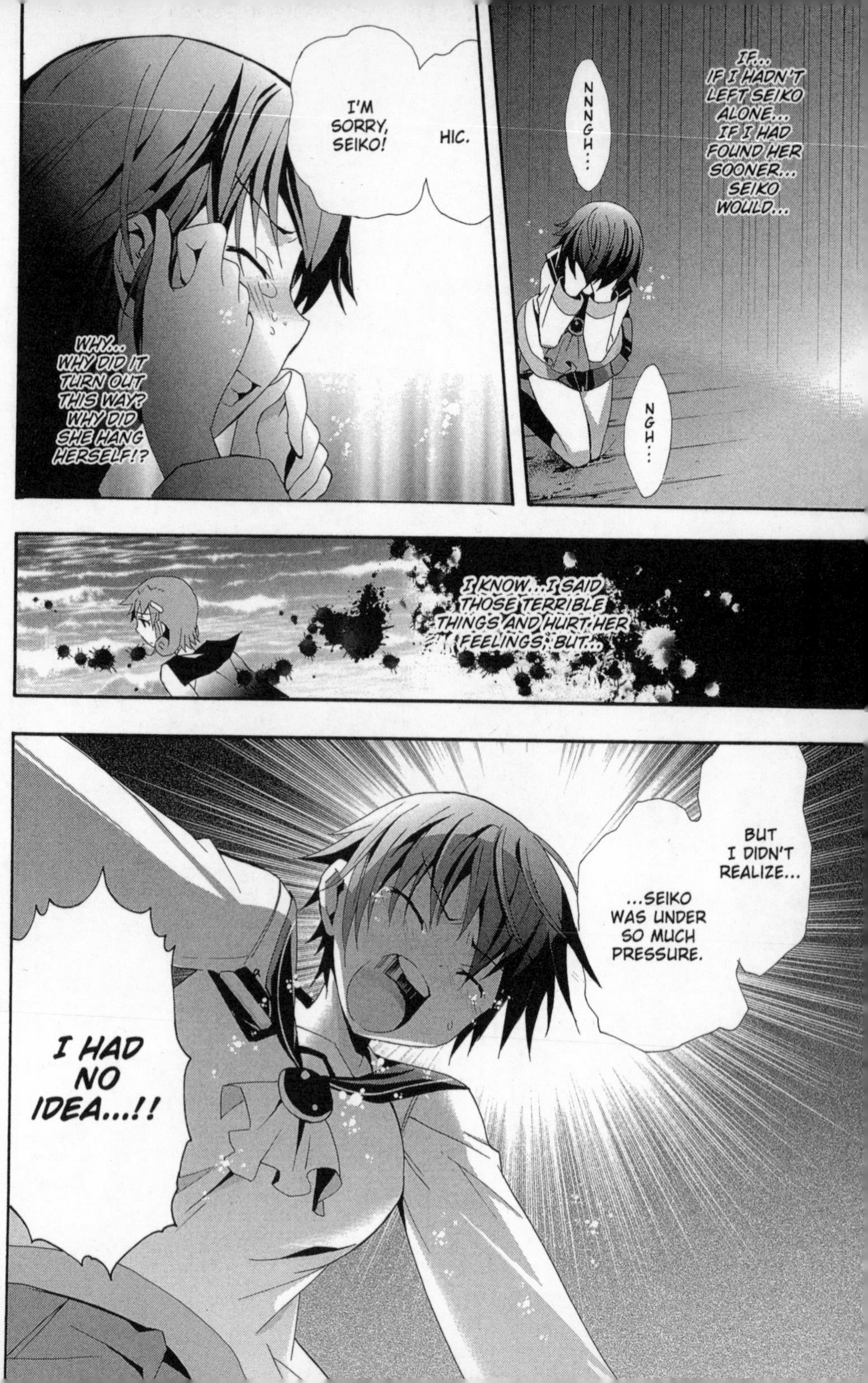

IF... IF I HADN'T LEFT SEIKO ALONE... IF I HAD FOUND HER SOONER... SEIKO WOULD...
NNNGH...
NGH...
I'M SORRY, SEIKO!
HIC.
WHY... WHY DID IT TURN OUT THIS WAY? WHY DID SHE HANG HERSELF!?
I KNOW... I SAID THOSE TERRIBLE THINGS AND HURT HER FEELINGS, BUT...
BUT I DIDN'T REALIZE...
...SEIKO WAS UNDER SO MUCH PRESSURE.
I HAD NO IDEA...!!

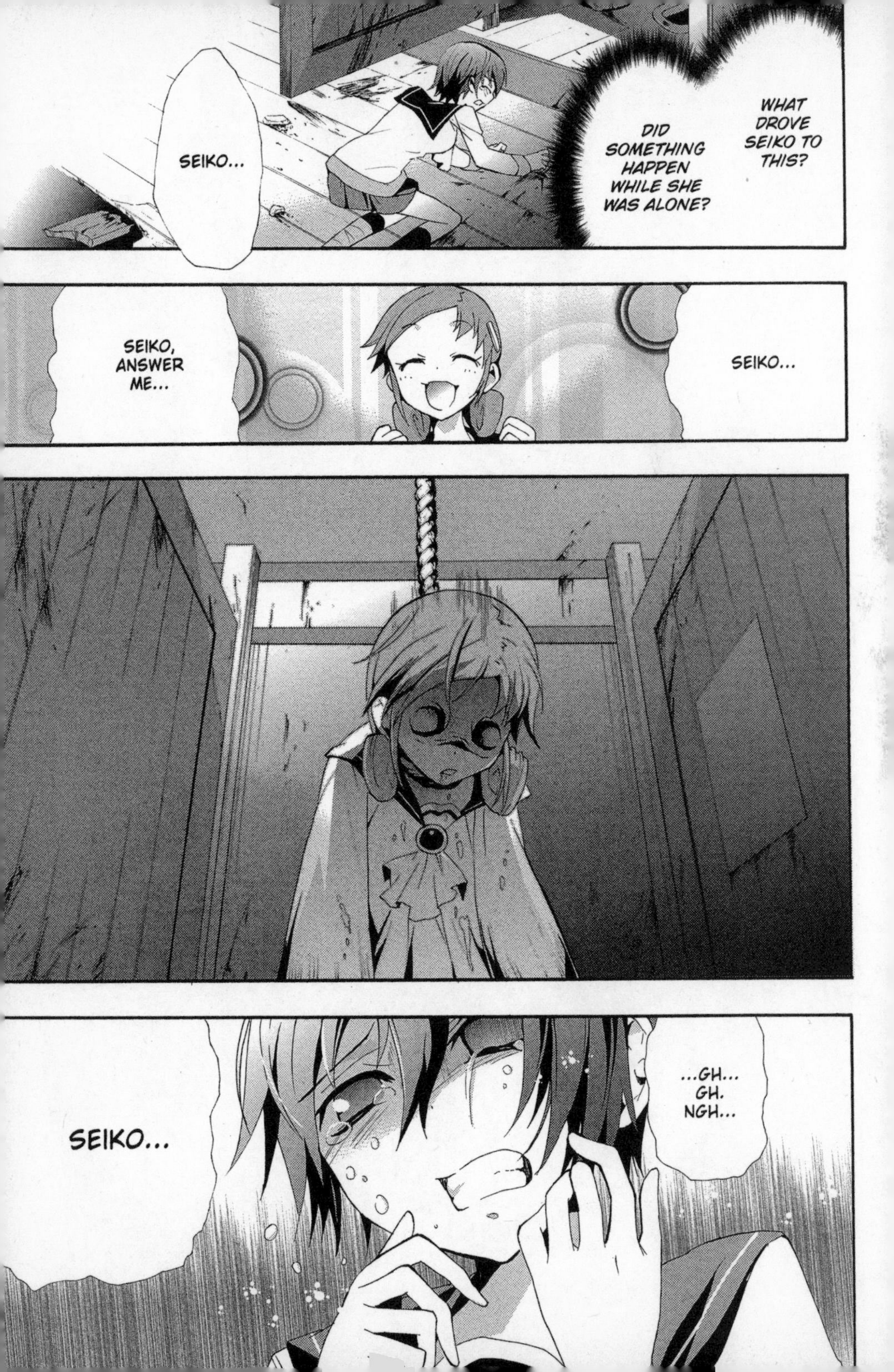
WHAT DROVE SEIKO TO THIS?
DID SOMETHING HAPPEN WHILE SHE WAS ALONE?
SEIKO...
SEIKO...
SEIKO, ANSWER ME...
...GH... GH. NGH...
SEIKO...

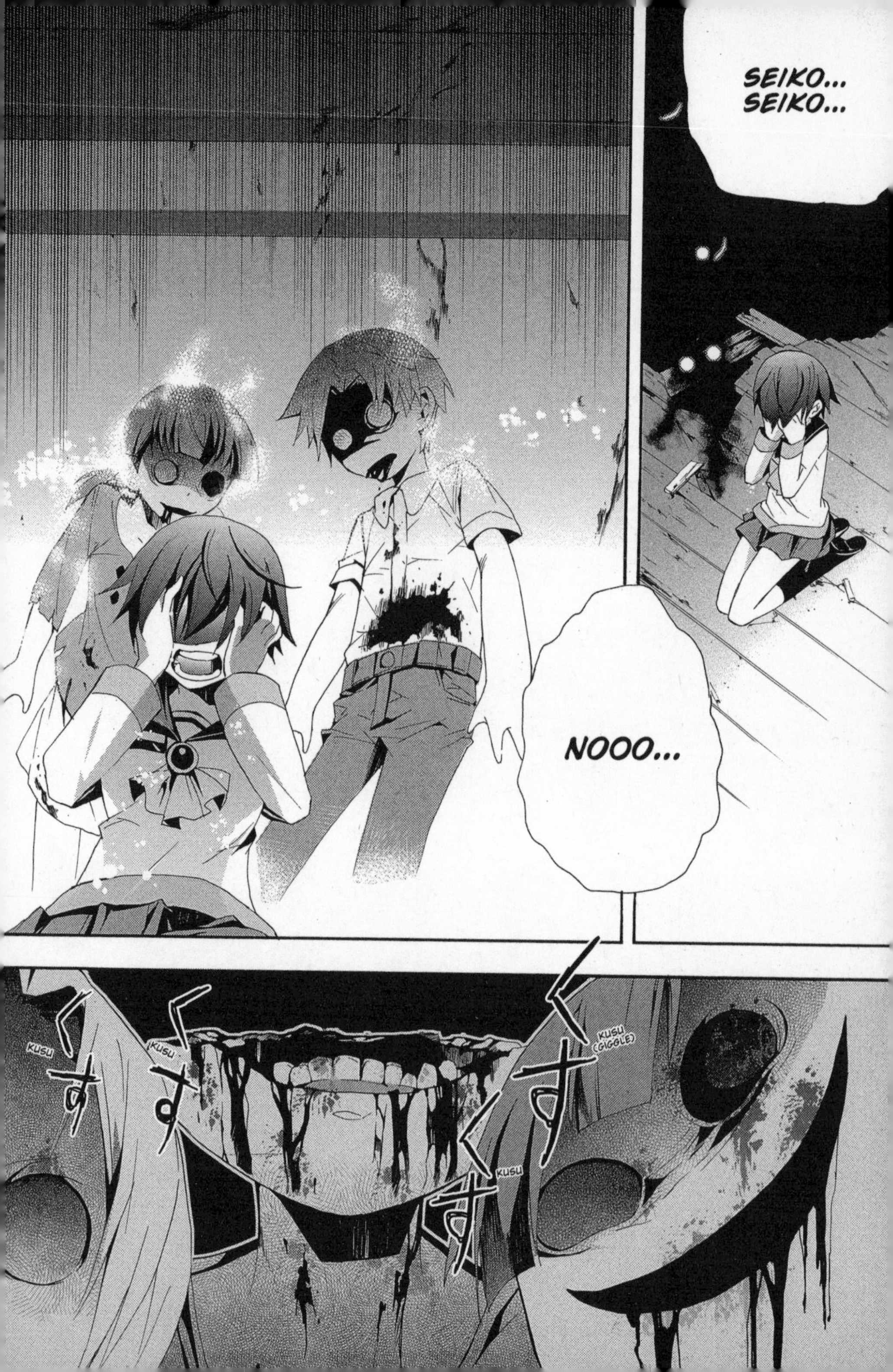
SEIKO...
SEIKO...
NOOO...
くす
KUSU (GIGGLE)
くす
KUSU
くす
KUSU
くす
KUSU

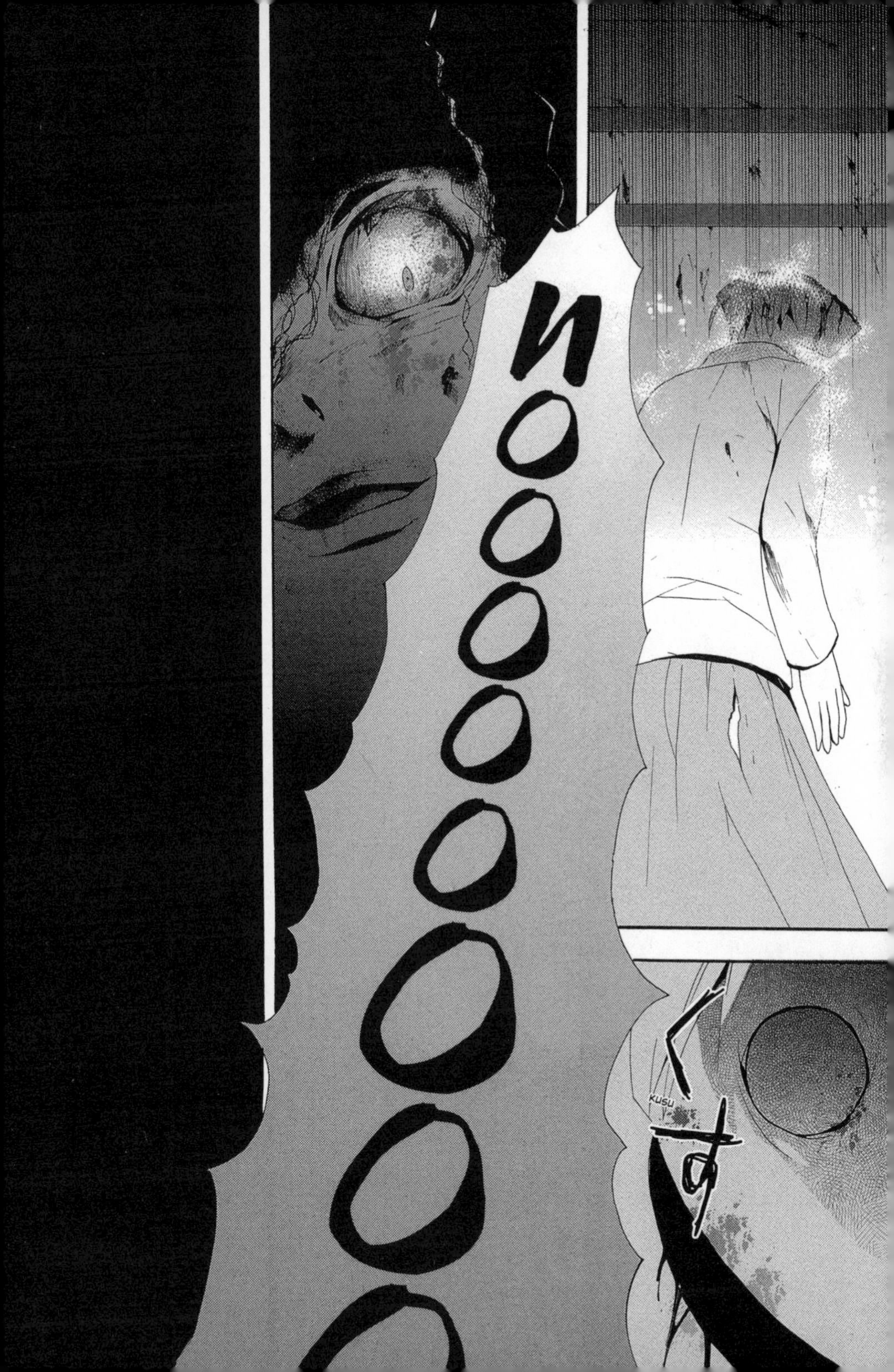
NOOOOOOOOOOO
KUSU

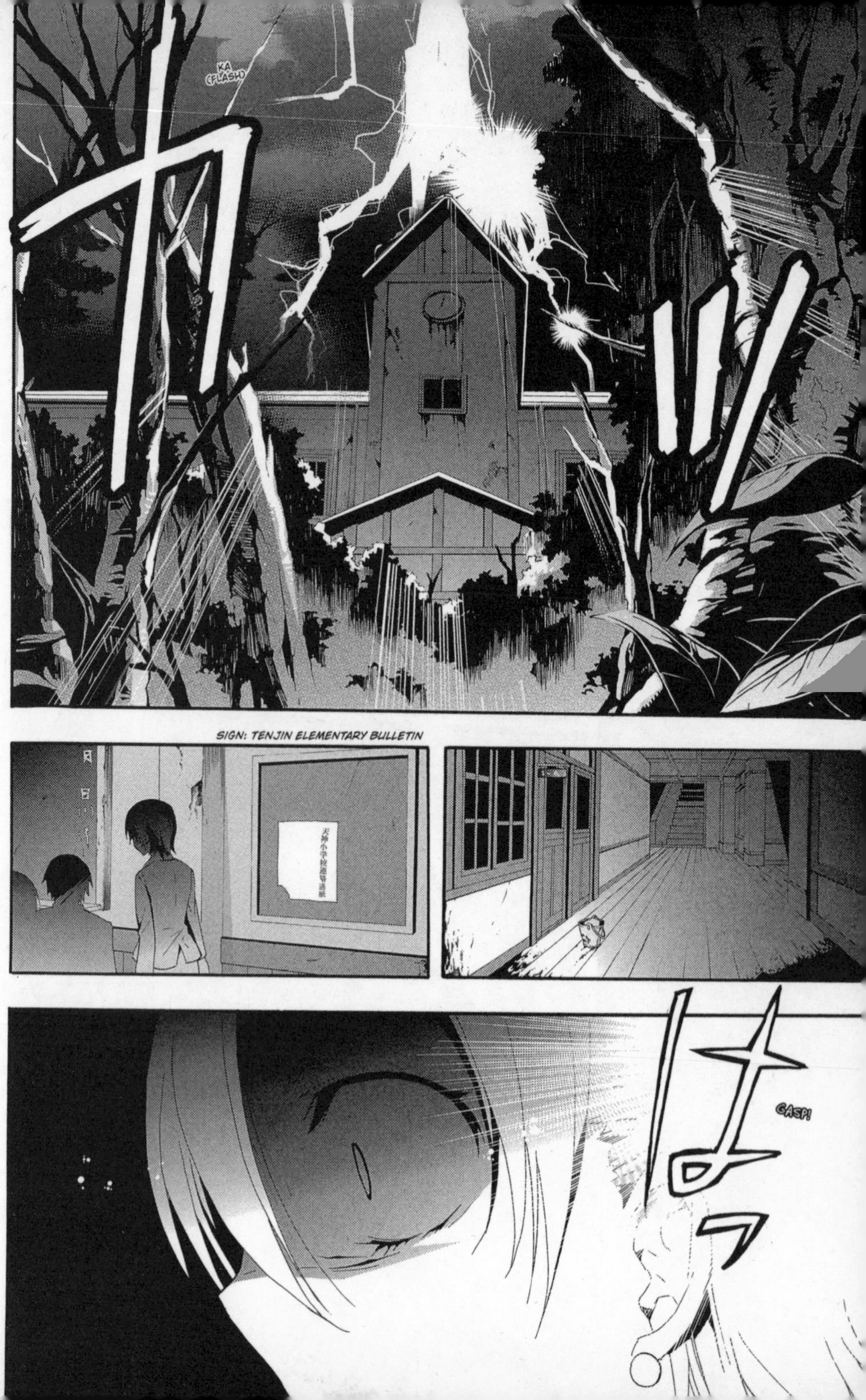
カッ
KA (FLASH)
SIGN: TENJIN ELEMENTARY BULLETIN
はっ
GASP!

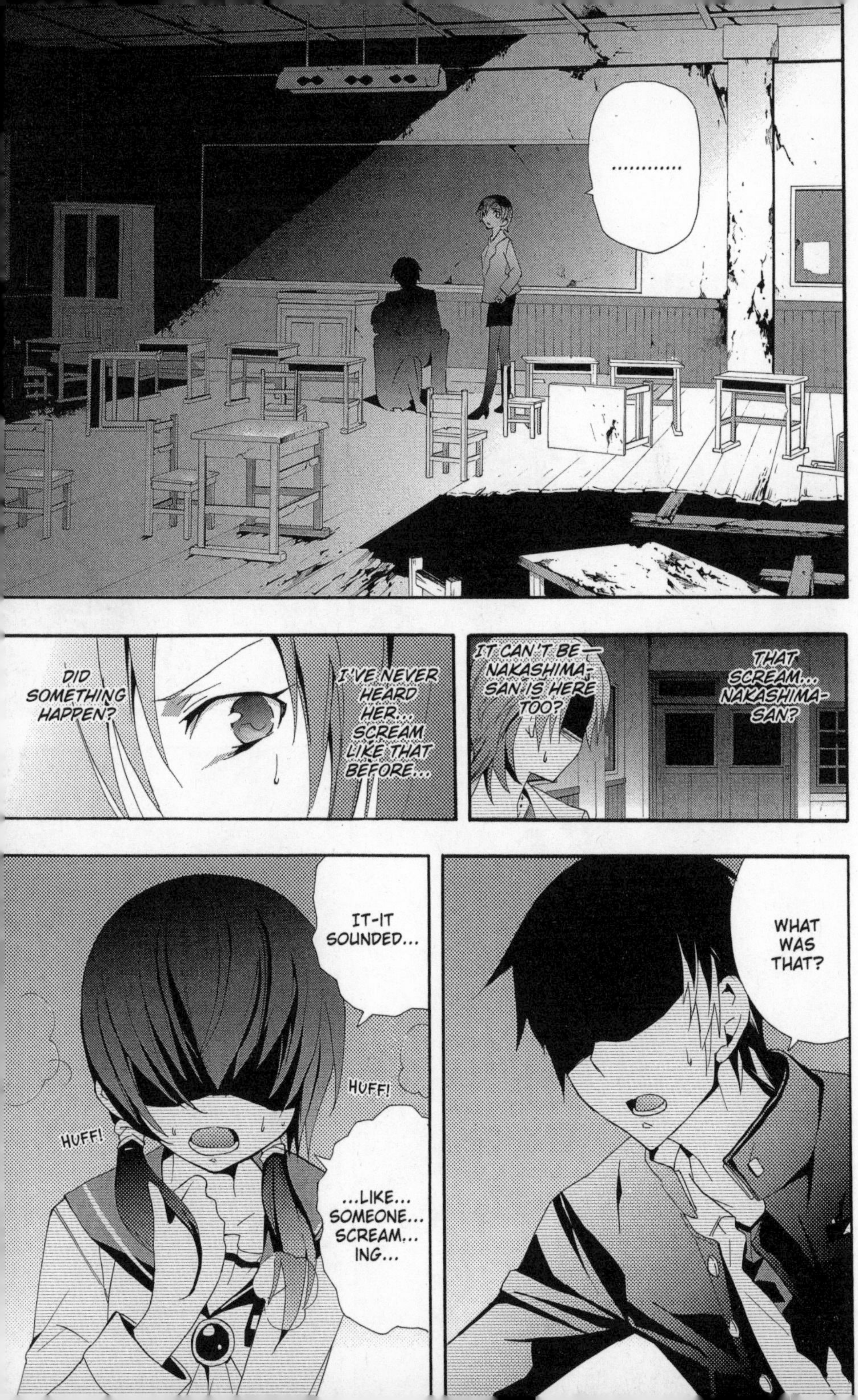
....
THAT SCREAM... NAKASHIMA-SAN?
IT CAN'T BE— NAKASHIMA-SAN IS HERE TOO?
I'VE NEVER HEARD HER... SCREAM LIKE THAT BEFORE...
DID SOMETHING HAPPEN?
WHAT WAS THAT?
IT-IT SOUNDED...
HUFF!
HUFF!
...LIKE... SOMEONE... SCREAM... ING...

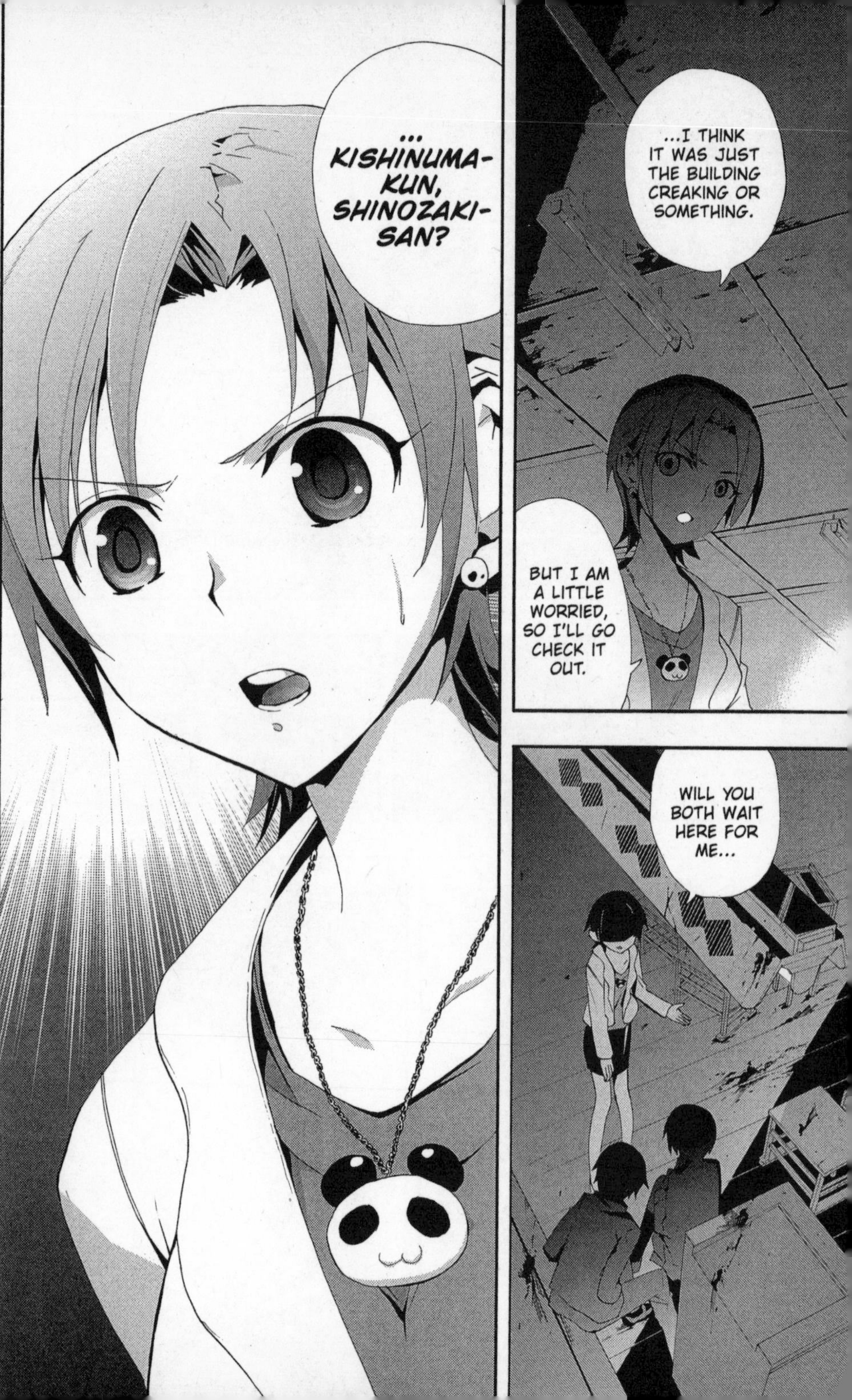
...I THINK IT WAS JUST THE BUILDING CREAKING OR SOMETHING.
BUT I AM A LITTLE WORRIED, SO I'LL GO CHECK IT OUT.
WILL YOU BOTH WAIT HERE FOR ME...
...KISHINUMA-KUN, SHINOZAKI-SAN?

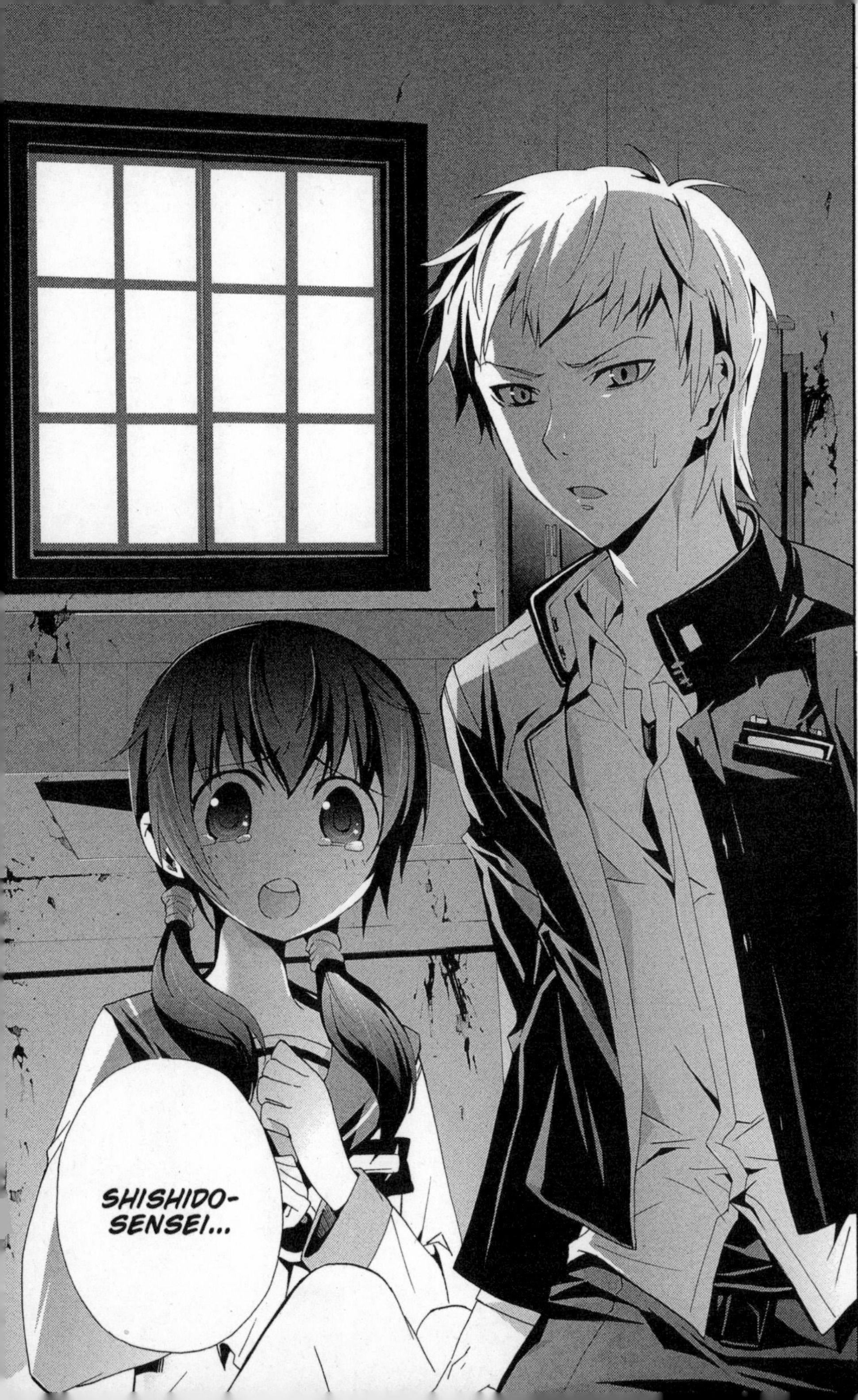
SHISHIDO-SENSEI...

a list of corpses/04

Seiko Shinohara, Class 2-9,
Kisaragi Academy

Died from strangulation after hanging
in the girls' lavatory at Tenjin
Elementary School.

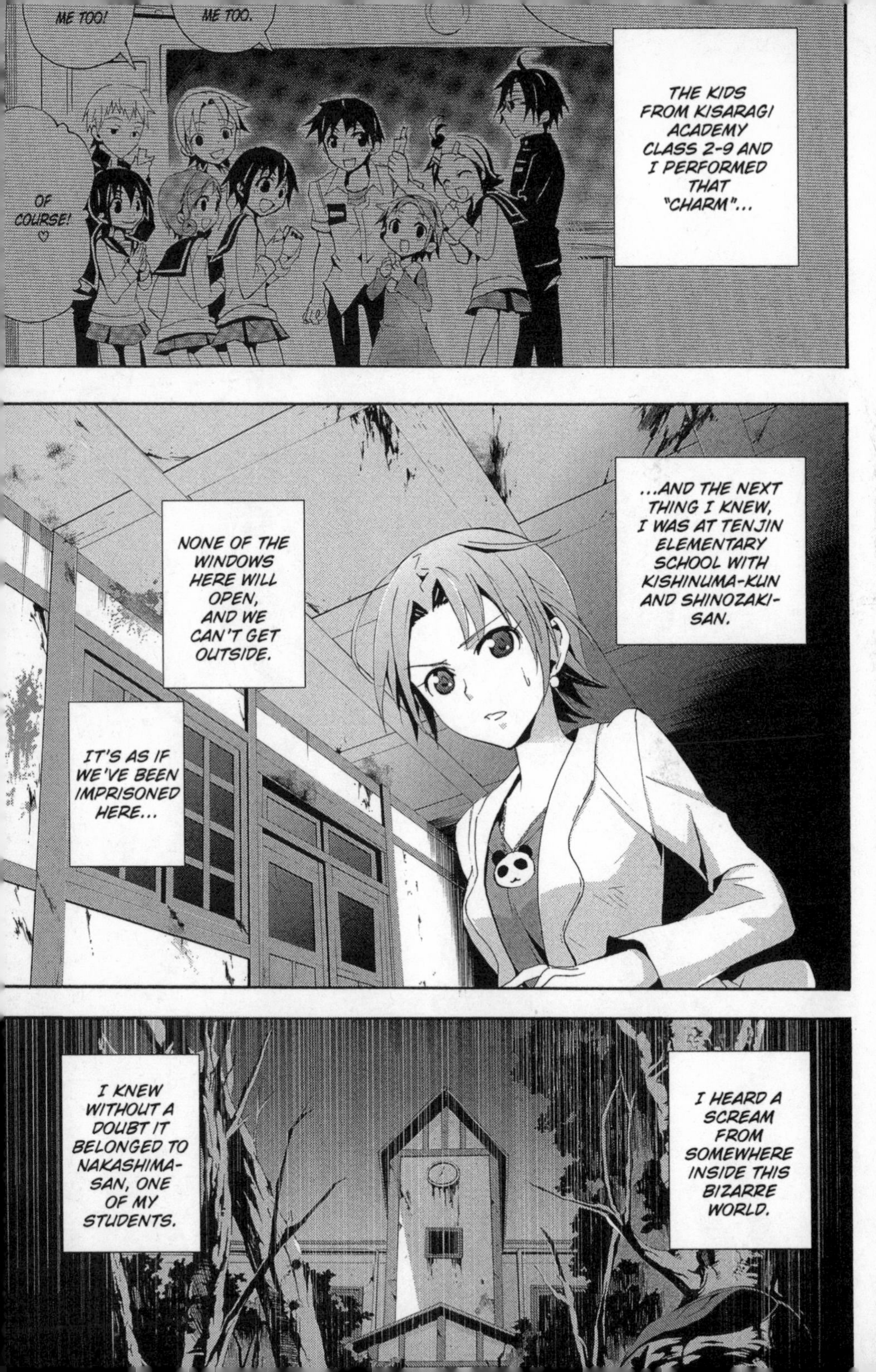
THE KIDS FROM KISARAGI ACADEMY CLASS 2-9 AND I PERFORMED THAT "CHARM"...
ME TOO.
ME TOO!
OF COURSE! ♡
...AND THE NEXT THING I KNEW, I WAS AT TENJIN ELEMENTARY SCHOOL WITH KISHINUMA-KUN AND SHINOZAKI-SAN.
NONE OF THE WINDOWS HERE WILL OPEN, AND WE CAN'T GET OUTSIDE.
IT'S AS IF WE'VE BEEN IMPRISONED HERE...
I HEARD A SCREAM FROM SOMEWHERE INSIDE THIS BIZARRE WORLD.
I KNEW WITHOUT A DOUBT IT BELONGED TO NAKASHIMA-SAN, ONE OF MY STUDENTS.

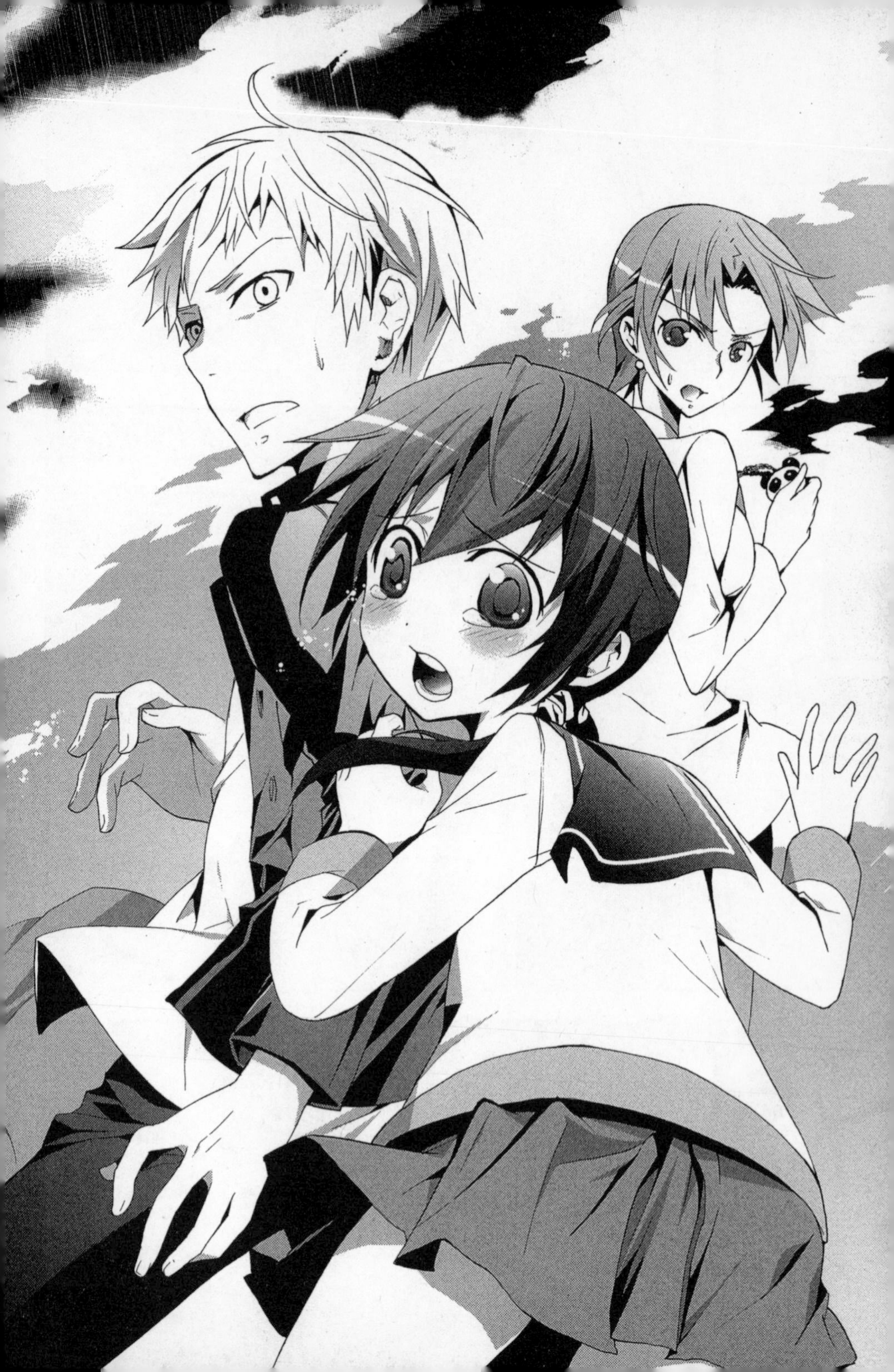

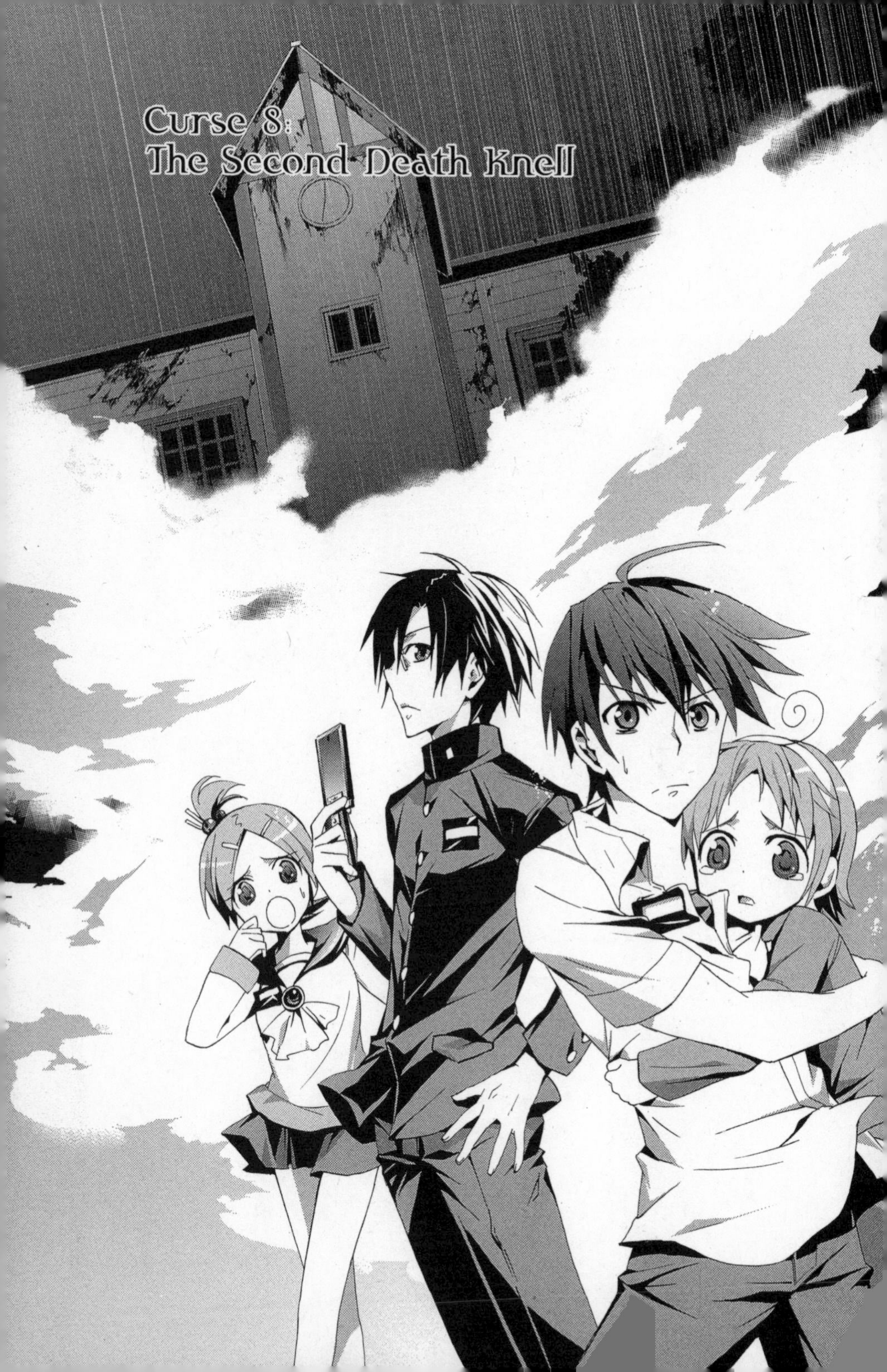
Curse 8:
The Second Death Knell

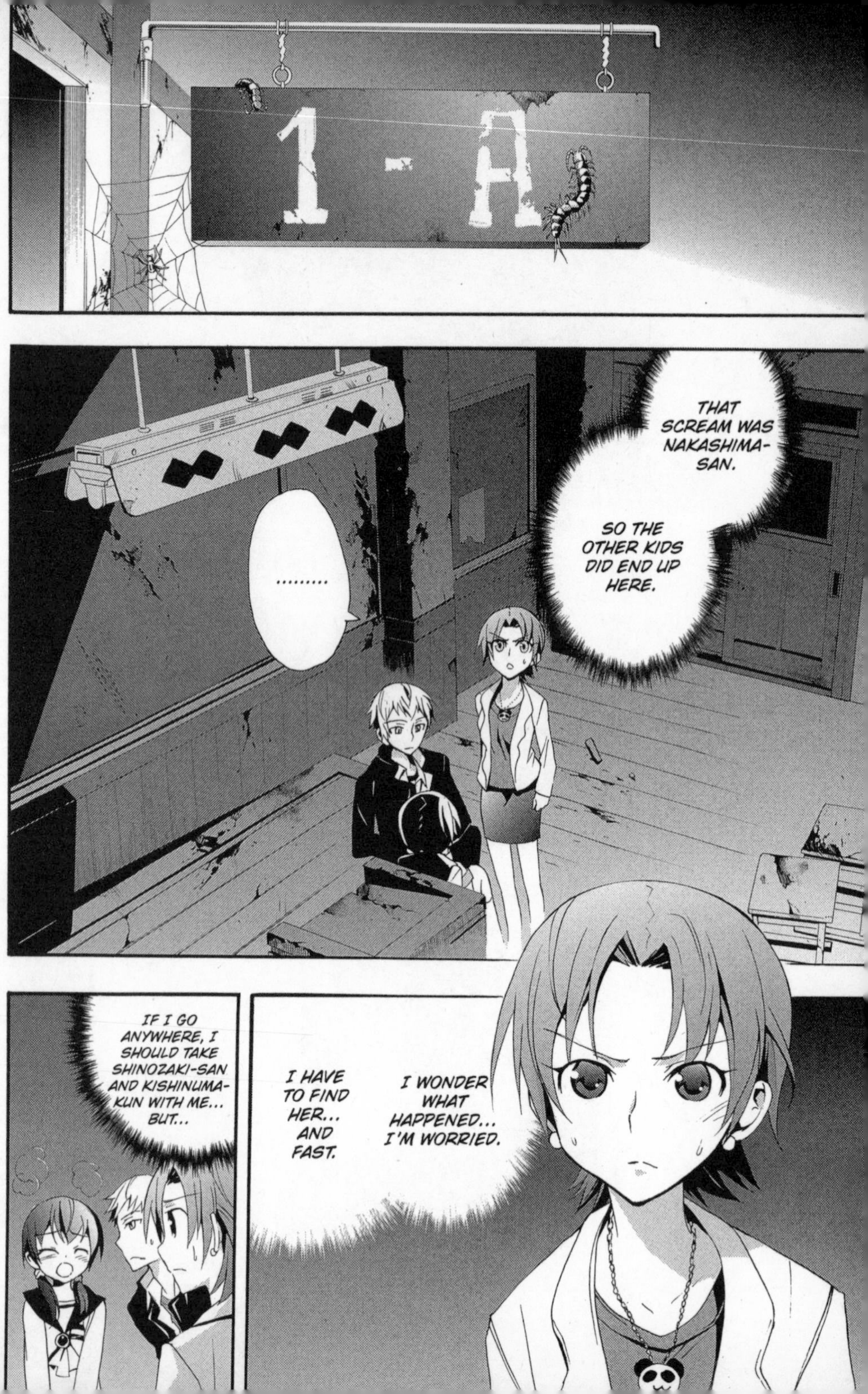
1-A
THAT SCREAM WAS NAKASHIMA-SAN.
SO THE OTHER KIDS DID END UP HERE.
....
I WONDER WHAT HAPPENED... I'M WORRIED.
I HAVE TO FIND HER... AND FAST.
IF I GO ANYWHERE, I SHOULD TAKE SHINOZAKI-SAN AND KISHINUMA-KUN WITH ME... BUT...

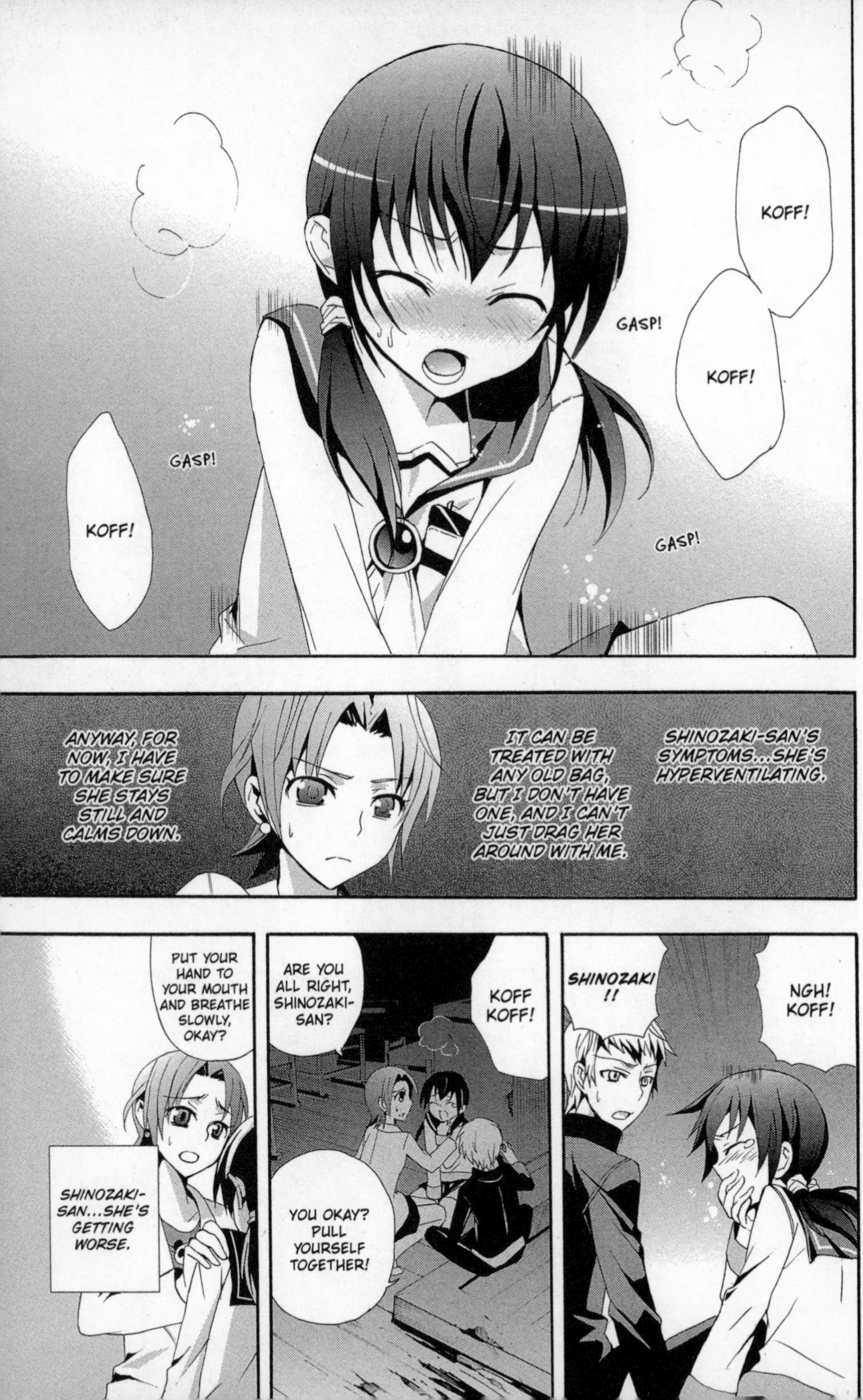
KOFF!
GASP!
KOFF!
GASP!
GASP!
KOFF!
SHINOZAKI-SAN'S SYMPTOMS...SHE'S HYPERVENTILATING.
IT CAN BE TREATED WITH ANY OLD BAG, BUT I DON'T HAVE ONE, AND I CAN'T JUST DRAG HER AROUND WITH ME.
ANYWAY, FOR NOW, I HAVE TO MAKE SURE SHE STAYS STILL AND CALMS DOWN.
NGH! KOFF!
SHINOZAKI !!
KOFF KOFF!
ARE YOU ALL RIGHT, SHINOZAKI-SAN?
YOU OKAY? PULL YOURSELF TOGETHER!
PUT YOUR HAND TO YOUR MOUTH AND BREATHE SLOWLY, OKAY?
SHINOZAKI-SAN...SHE'S GETTING WORSE.

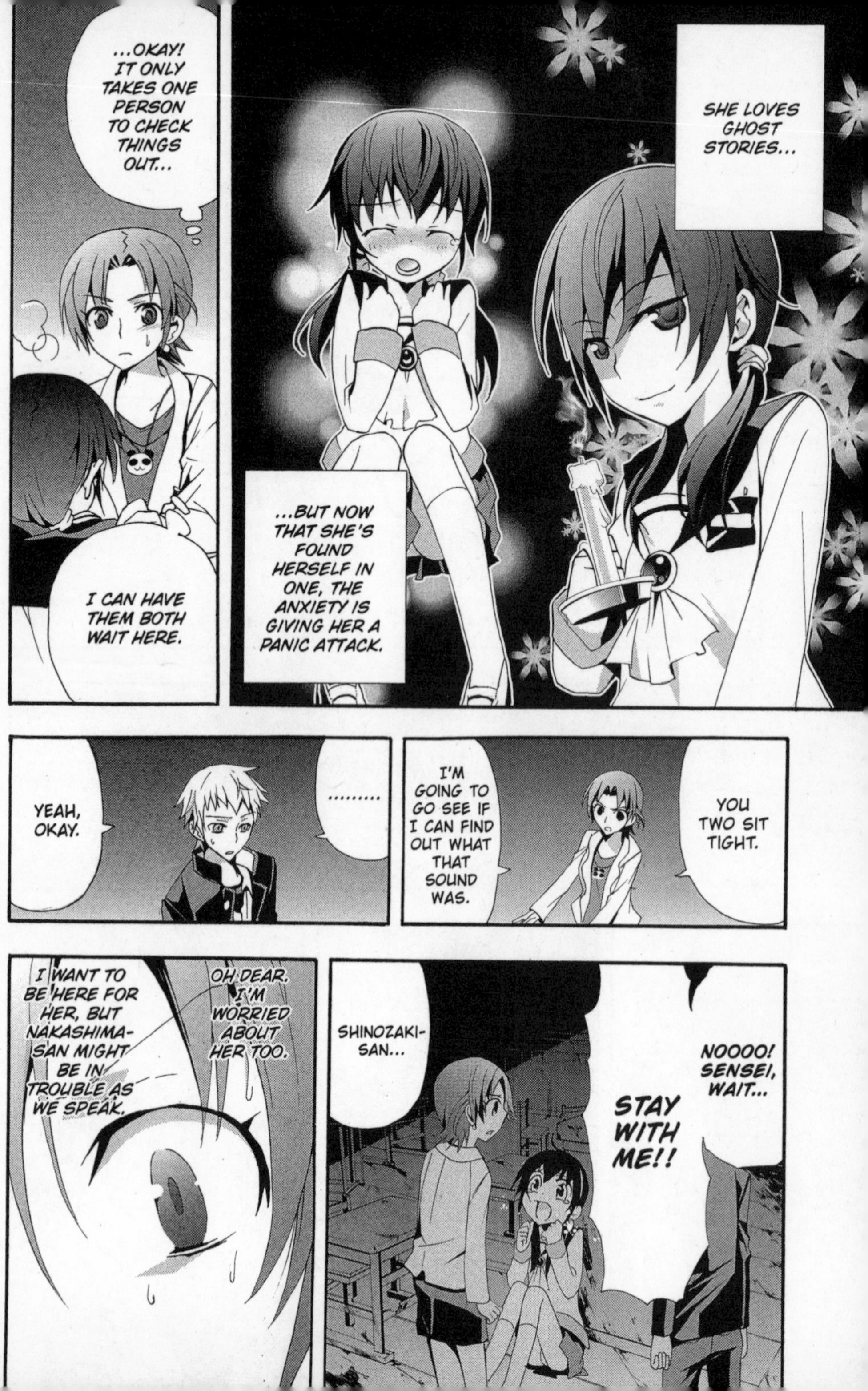
SHE LOVES GHOST STORIES...
...BUT NOW THAT SHE'S FOUND HERSELF IN ONE, THE ANXIETY IS GIVING HER A PANIC ATTACK.
...OKAY! IT ONLY TAKES ONE PERSON TO CHECK THINGS OUT...
I CAN HAVE THEM BOTH WAIT HERE.
YOU TWO SIT TIGHT.
I'M GOING TO GO SEE IF I CAN FIND OUT WHAT THAT SOUND WAS.
....
YEAH, OKAY.
NOOOO! SENSEI, WAIT...
STAY WITH ME!!
SHINOZAKI-SAN...
OH DEAR. I'M WORRIED ABOUT HER TOO.
I WANT TO BE HERE FOR HER, BUT NAKASHIMA-SAN MIGHT BE IN TROUBLE AS WE SPEAK.

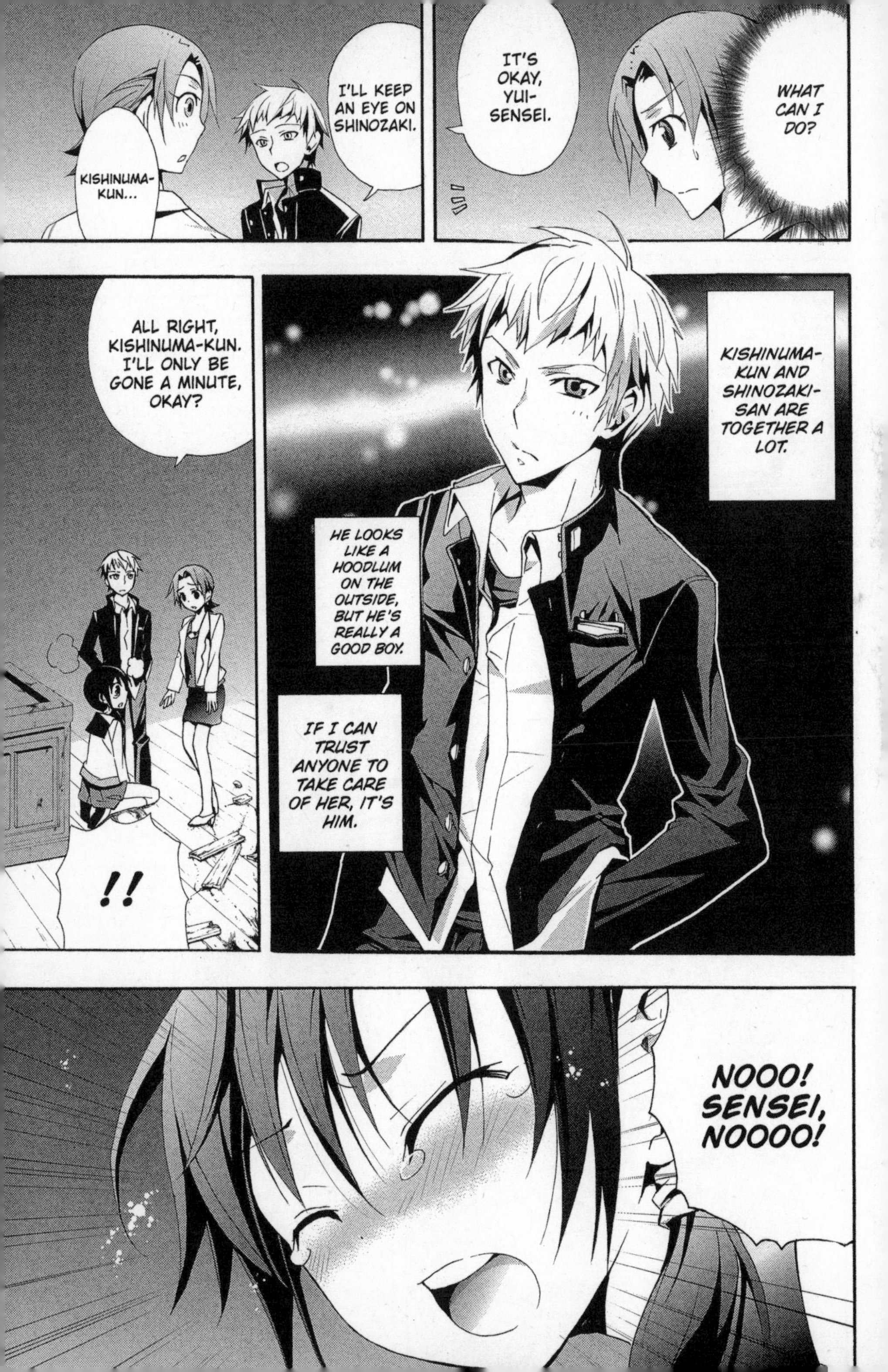
WHAT CAN I DO?
IT'S OKAY, YUI-SENSEI.
I'LL KEEP AN EYE ON SHINOZAKI.
KISHINUMA-KUN...
KISHINUMA-KUN AND SHINOZAKI-SAN ARE TOGETHER A LOT.
HE LOOKS LIKE A HOODLUM ON THE OUTSIDE, BUT HE'S REALLY A GOOD BOY.
IF I CAN TRUST ANYONE TO TAKE CARE OF HER, IT'S HIM.
ALL RIGHT, KISHINUMA-KUN. I'LL ONLY BE GONE A MINUTE, OKAY?
!!
NOOO! SENSEI, NOOOO!

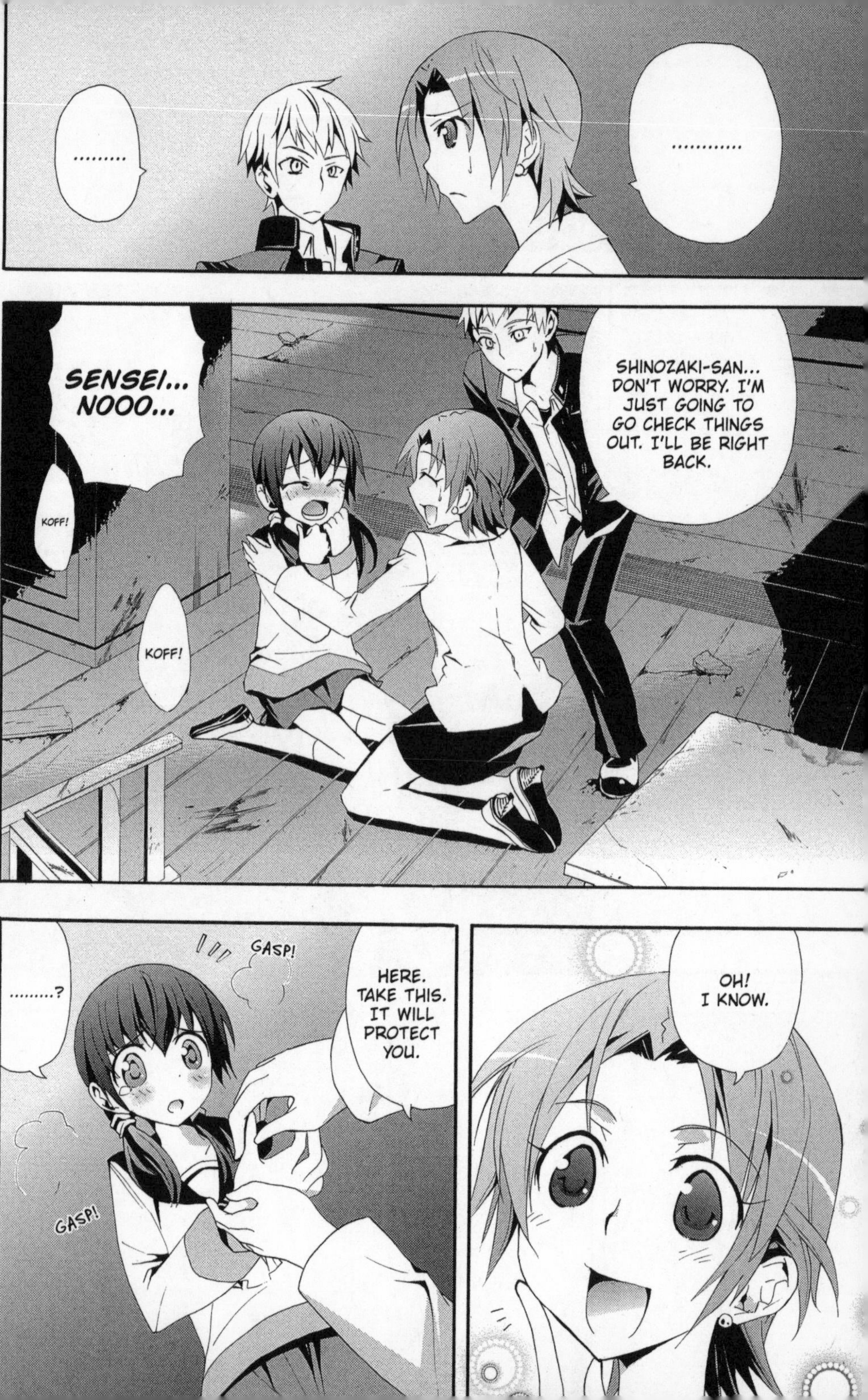
....
....
SHINOZAKI-SAN... DON'T WORRY. I'M JUST GOING TO GO CHECK THINGS OUT. I'LL BE RIGHT BACK.
SENSEI... NOOO...
KOFF!
KOFF!
OH! I KNOW.
HERE. TAKE THIS. IT WILL PROTECT YOU.
GASP!
.........?
GASP!

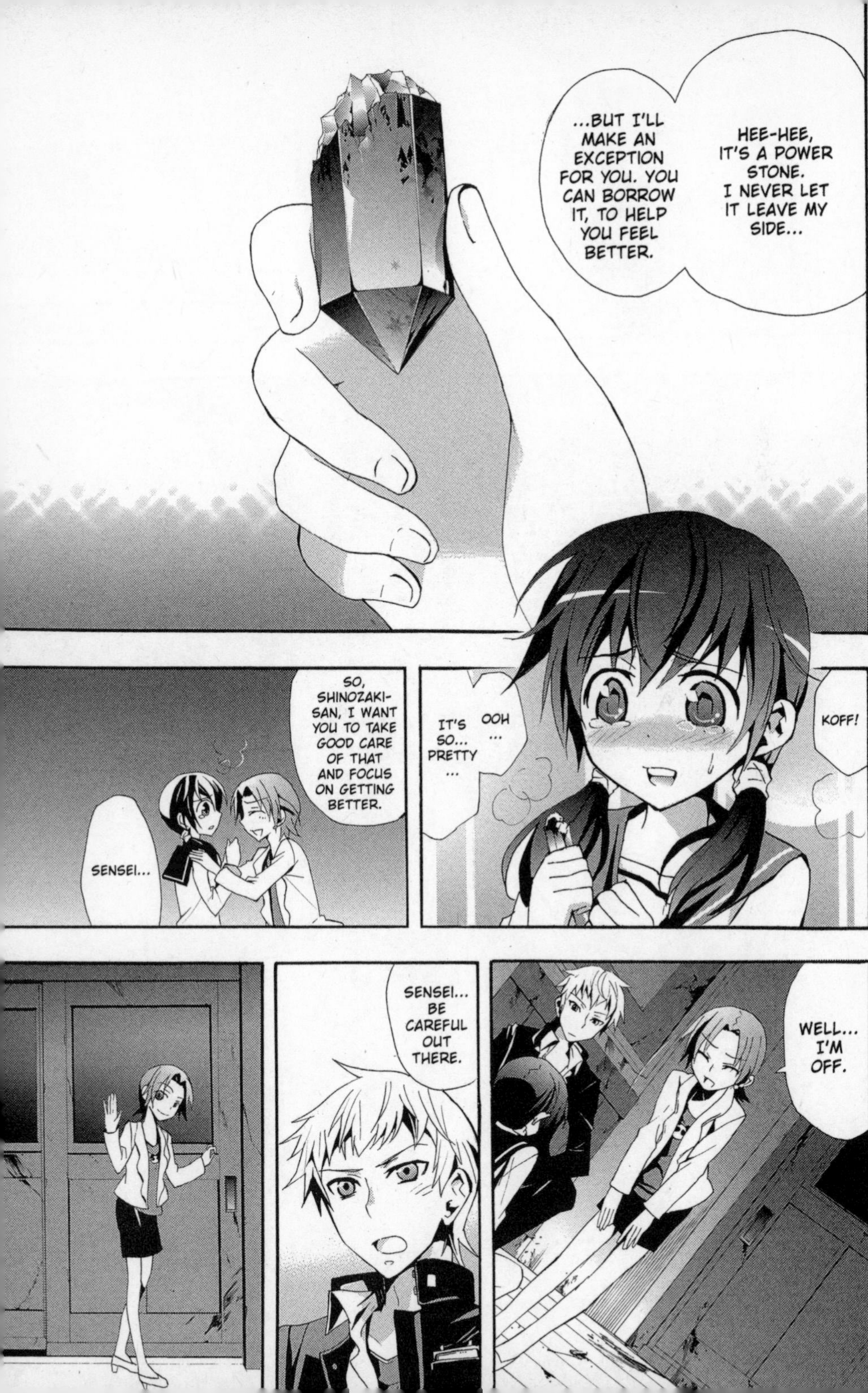
HEE-HEE, IT'S A POWER STONE. I NEVER LET IT LEAVE MY SIDE...
...BUT I'LL MAKE AN EXCEPTION FOR YOU. YOU CAN BORROW IT, TO HELP YOU FEEL BETTER.
KOFF!
OOH ...
IT'S SO... PRETTY ...
SO, SHINOZAKI-SAN, I WANT YOU TO TAKE GOOD CARE OF THAT AND FOCUS ON GETTING BETTER.
SENSEI...
WELL... I'M OFF.
SENSEI... BE CAREFUL OUT THERE.

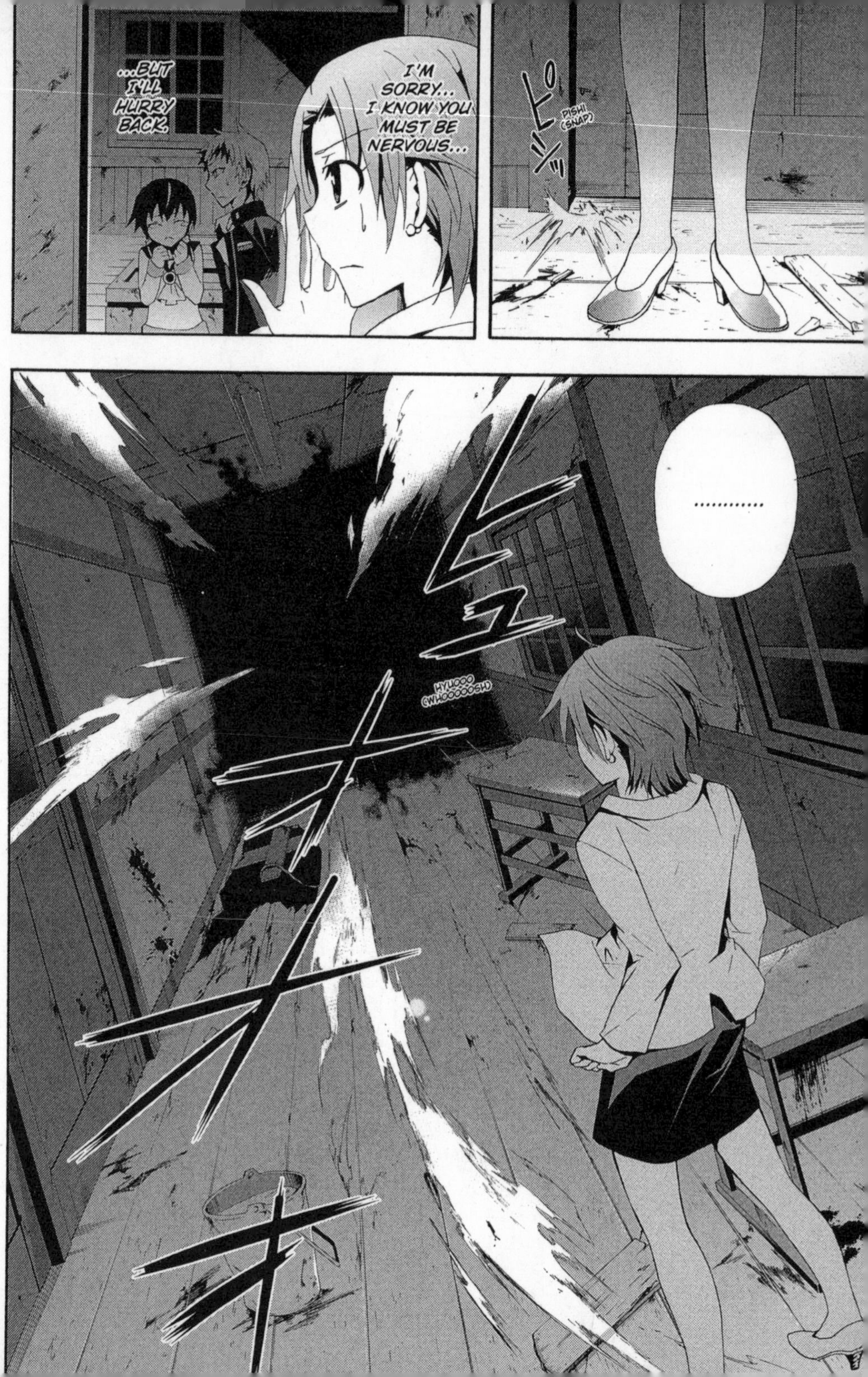
ピシッ
PISHI (SNAP)
I'M SORRY... I KNOW YOU MUST BE NERVOUS...
...BUT I'LL HURRY BACK.
HYUOOO (WHOOOOOSH)
....

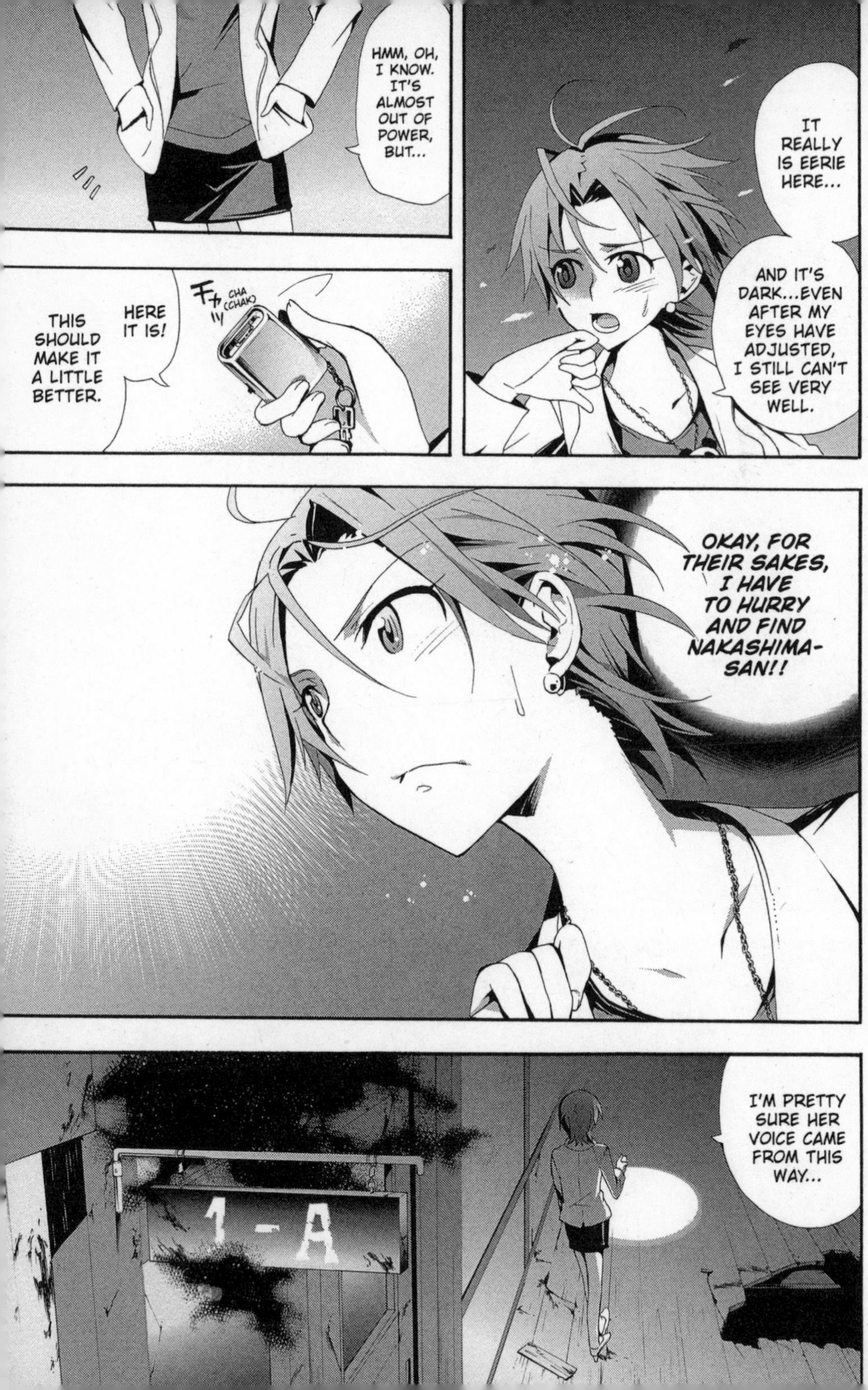

IT REALLY IS EERIE HERE...
AND IT'S DARK...EVEN AFTER MY EYES HAVE ADJUSTED, I STILL CAN'T SEE VERY WELL.
HMM, OH, I KNOW. IT'S ALMOST OUT OF POWER, BUT...
チャッ CHA (CHAK)
HERE IT IS!
THIS SHOULD MAKE IT A LITTLE BETTER.
OKAY, FOR THEIR SAKES, I HAVE TO HURRY AND FIND NAKASHIMA-SAN!!
I'M PRETTY SURE HER VOICE CAME FROM THIS WAY...
1-A

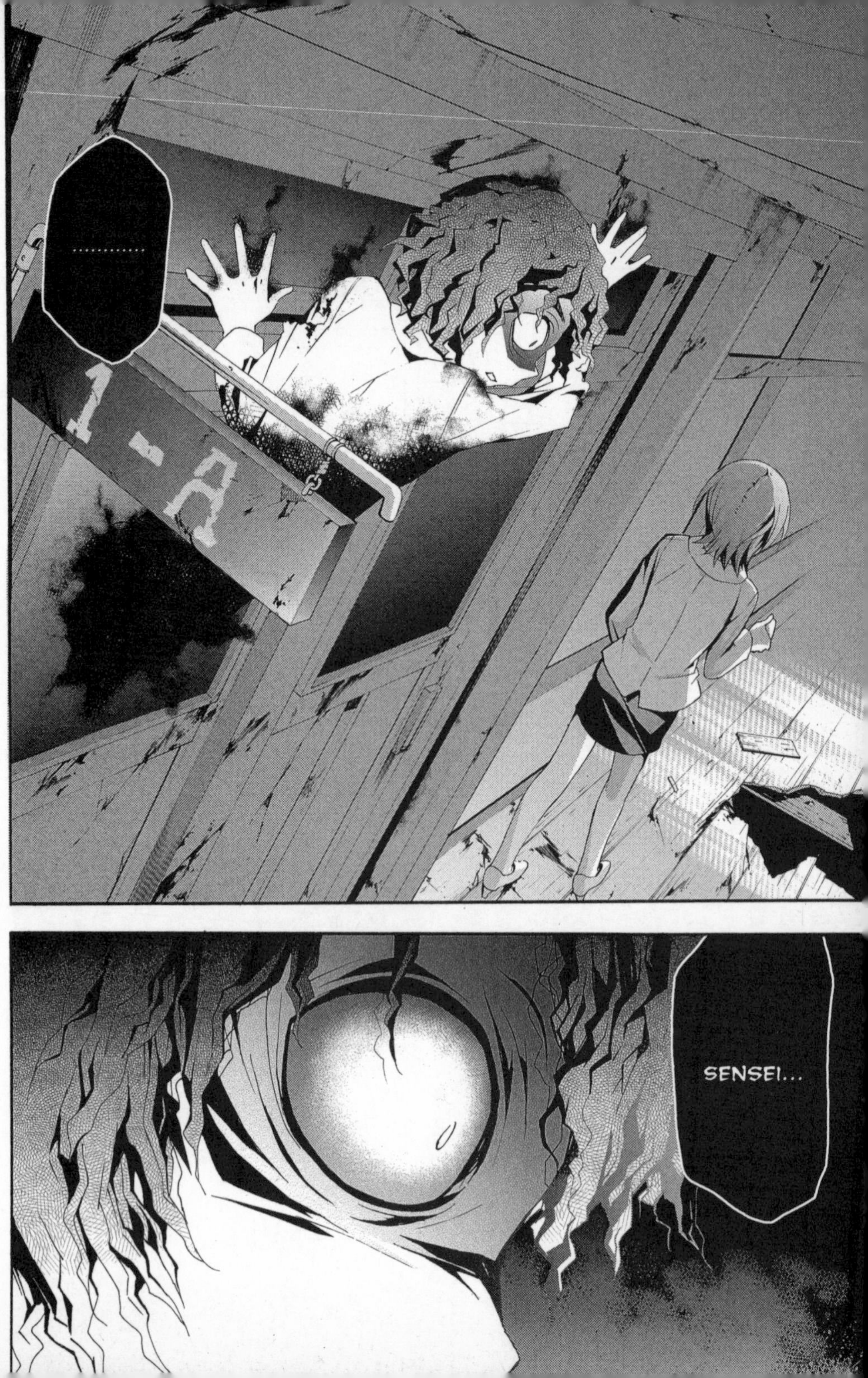
....
SENSEI...

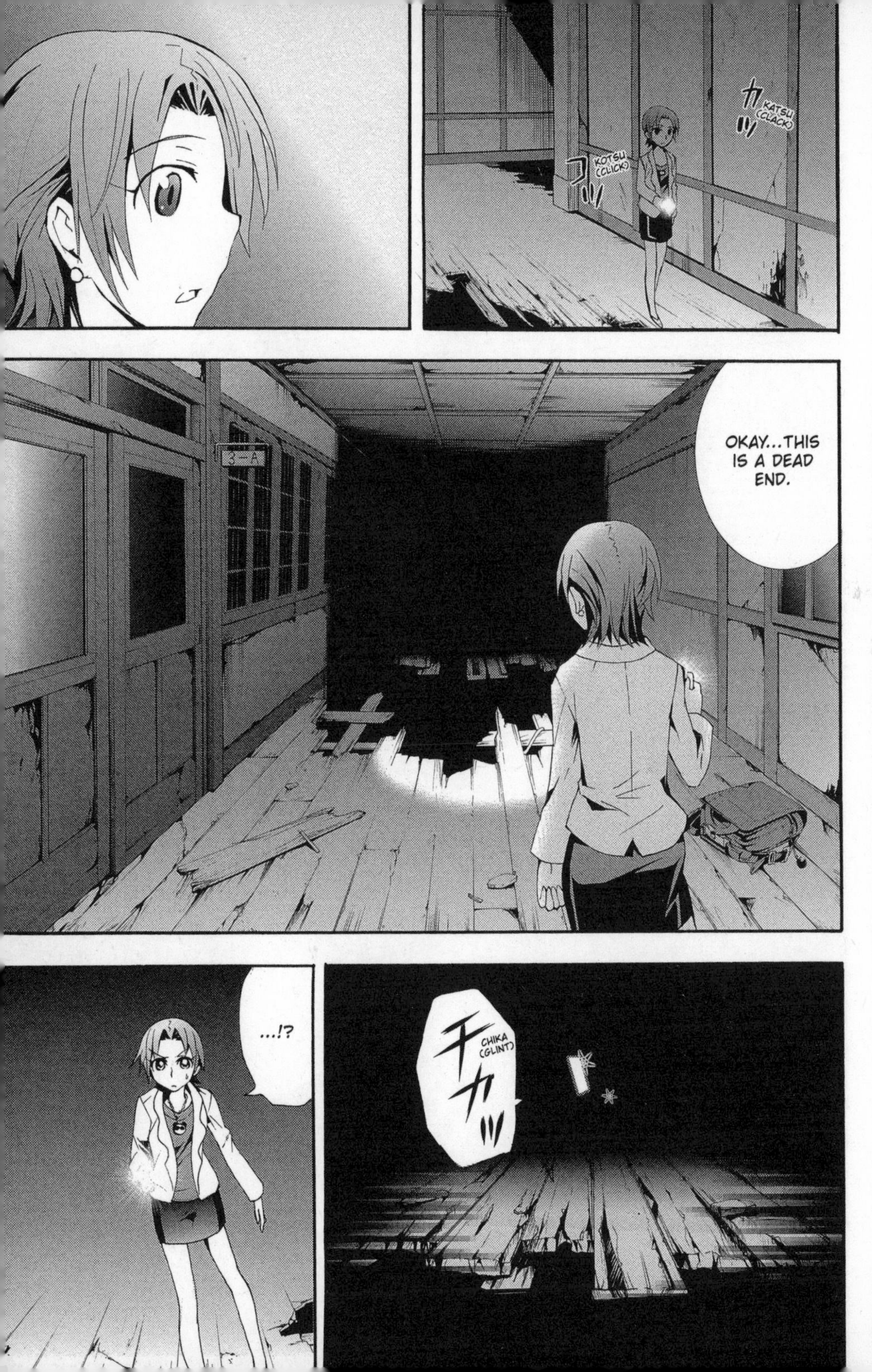
カッ
KATSU (CLACK)
コツ
KOTSU (CLICK)
3-A
OKAY...THIS IS A DEAD END.
チカッ
CHIKA (GLINT)
...!?

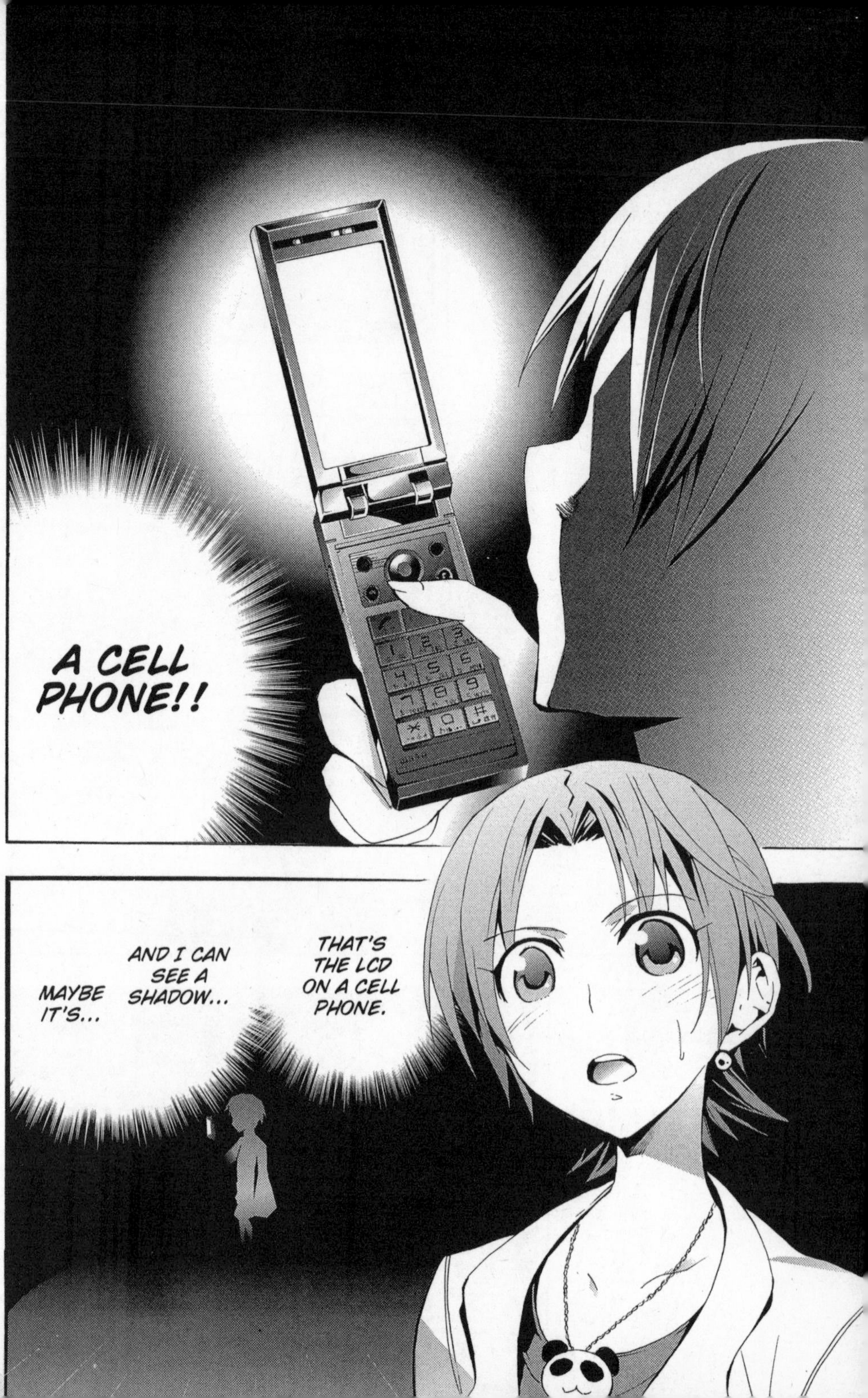
A CELL PHONE!!
THAT'S THE LCD ON A CELL PHONE.
AND I CAN SEE A SHADOW...
MAYBE IT'S...

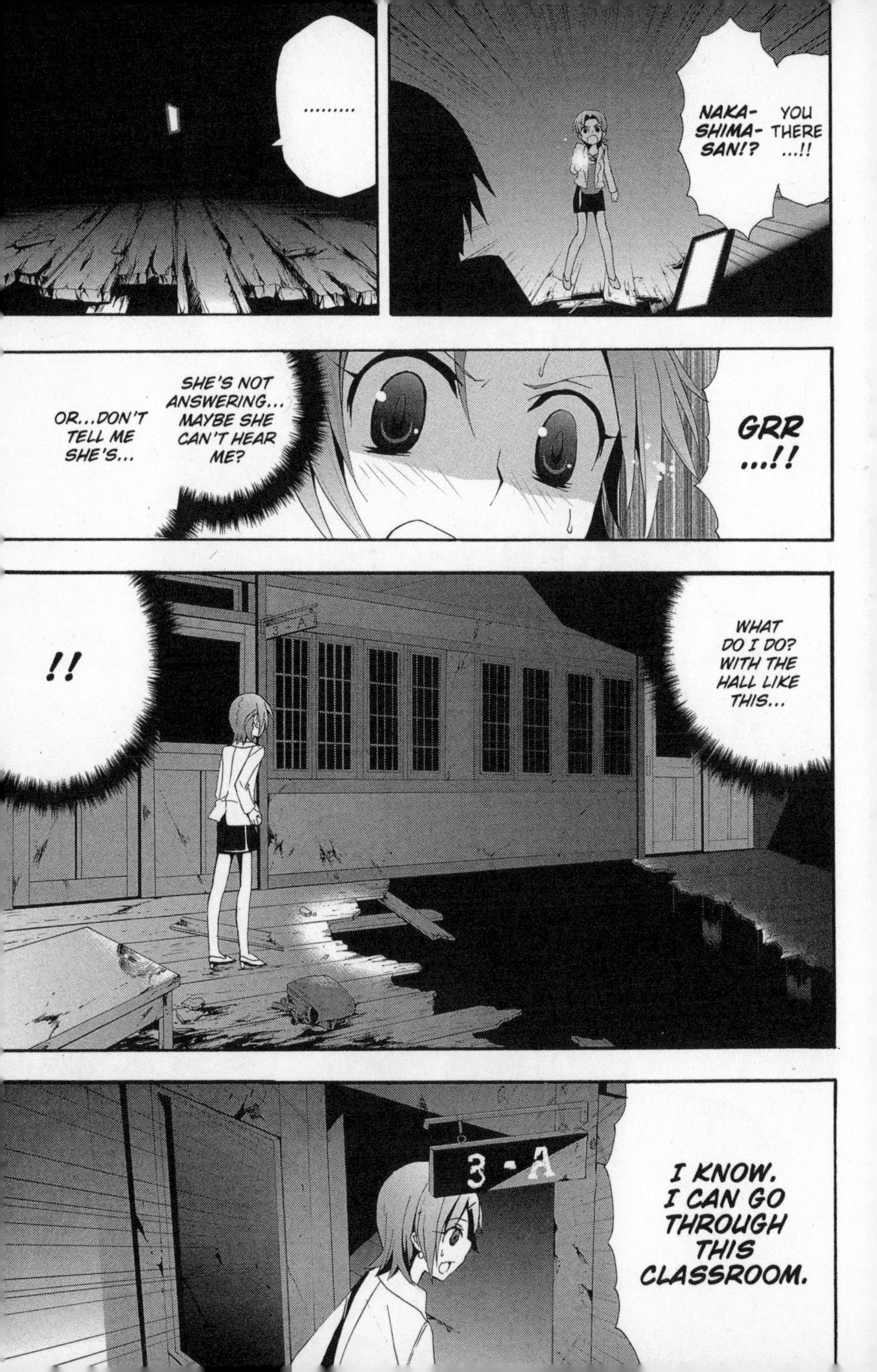
NAKA-SHIMA-SAN!? YOU THERE ...!!
....
GRR ...!!
SHE'S NOT ANSWERING... MAYBE SHE CAN'T HEAR ME?
OR...DON'T TELL ME SHE'S...
WHAT DO I DO? WITH THE HALL LIKE THIS...
!!
3-A
I KNOW. I CAN GO THROUGH THIS CLASSROOM.

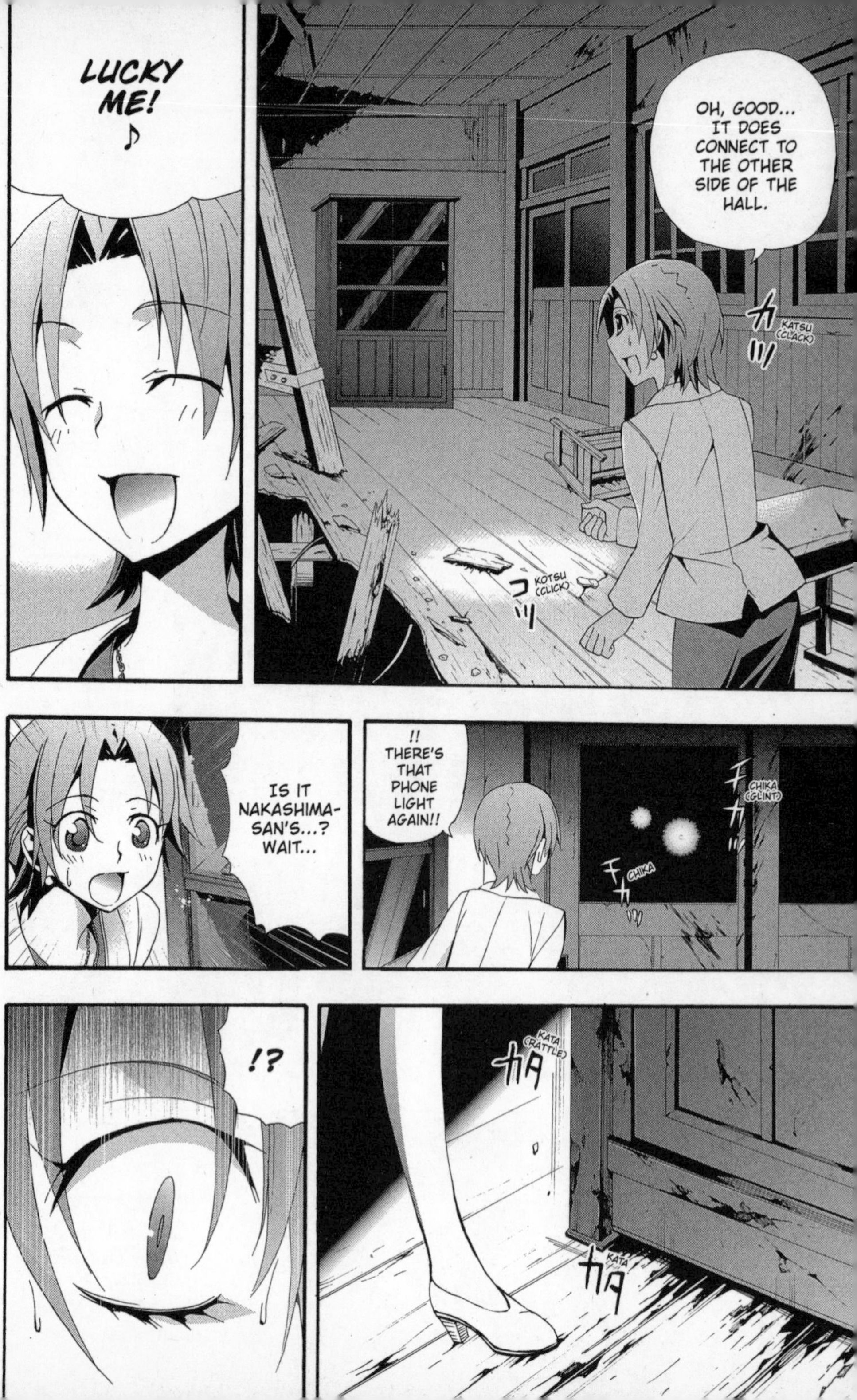
OH, GOOD... IT DOES CONNECT TO THE OTHER SIDE OF THE HALL.
KATSU (CLACK)
KOTSU (CLICK)
LUCKY ME! ♪
!! THERE'S THAT PHONE LIGHT AGAIN!!
CHIKA (GLINT)
CHIKA
IS IT NAKASHIMA-SAN'S...? WAIT...
KATA (RATTLE)
KATA
!?

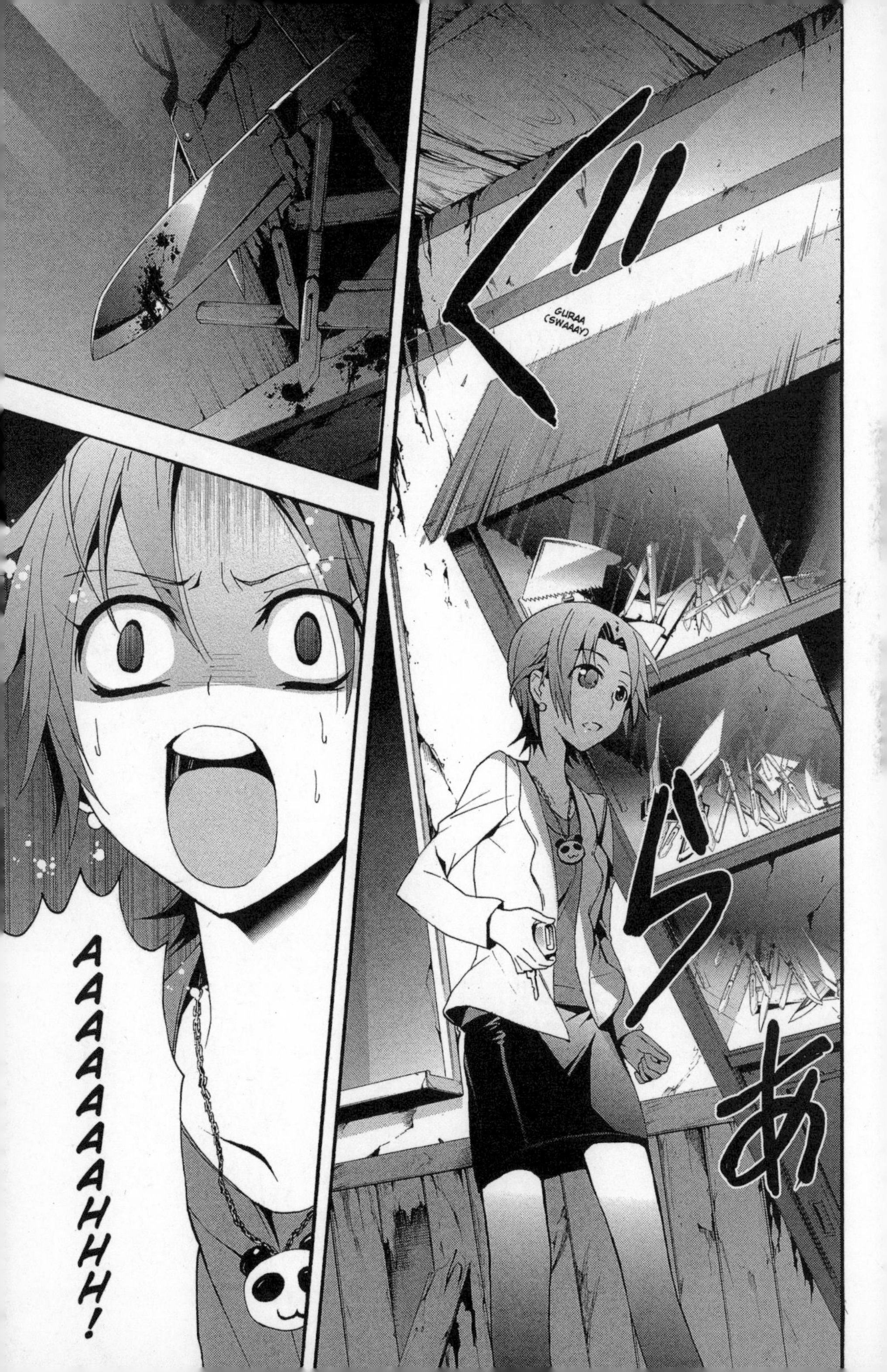
ぐらぁ
GURAA (SWAAAY)
AAAAAAAHHH!

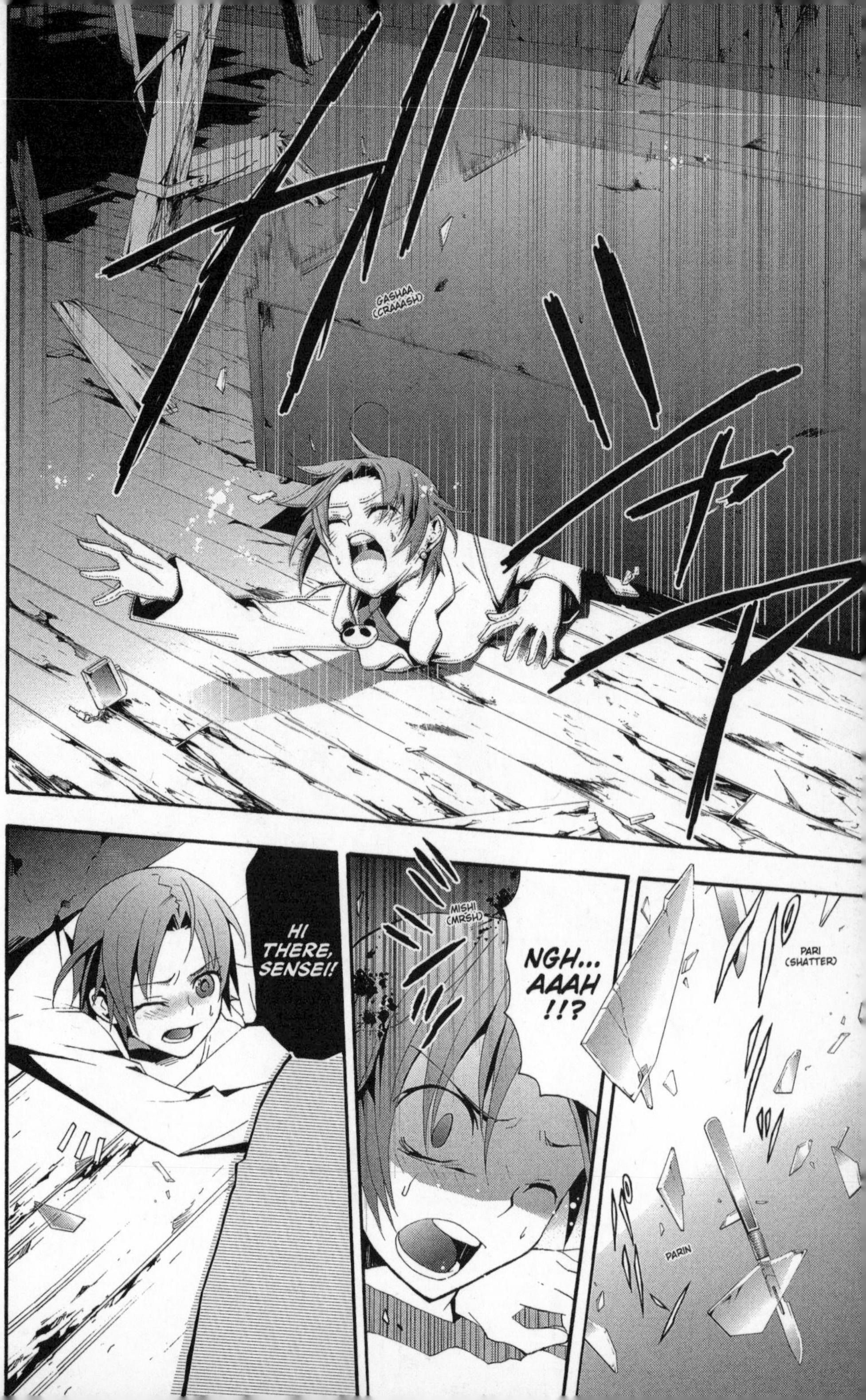
GASHAA (CRAAASH)
PARI (SHATTER)
PARIN
MISHI (MRSH)
NGH... AAAH !!?
HI THERE, SENSEI!!

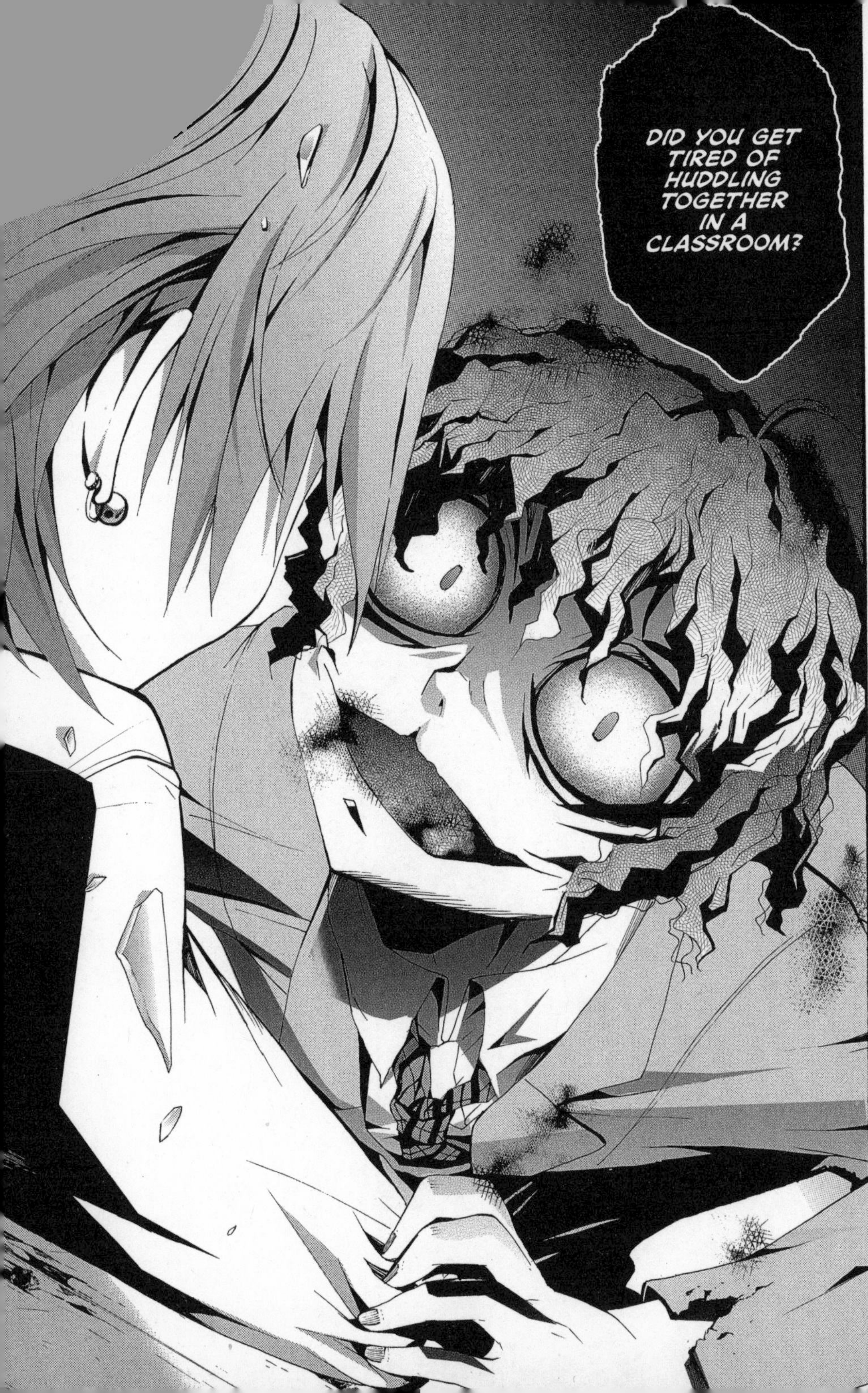
DID YOU GET TIRED OF HUDDLING TOGETHER IN A CLASSROOM?

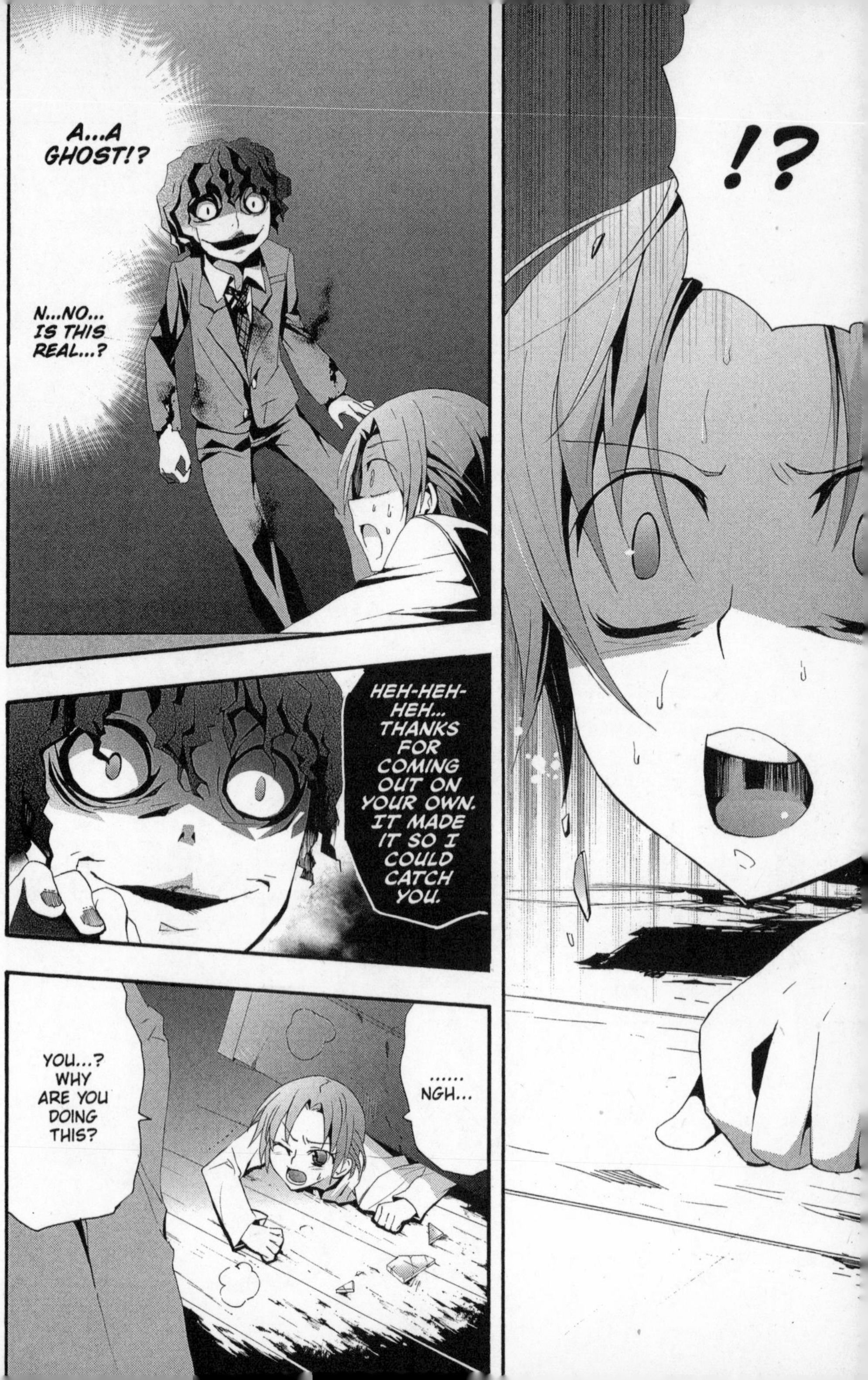
!?
A...A GHOST!?
N...NO... IS THIS REAL...?
HEH-HEH-HEH... THANKS FOR COMING OUT ON YOUR OWN. IT MADE IT SO I COULD CATCH YOU.
...... NGH...
YOU...? WHY ARE YOU DOING THIS?

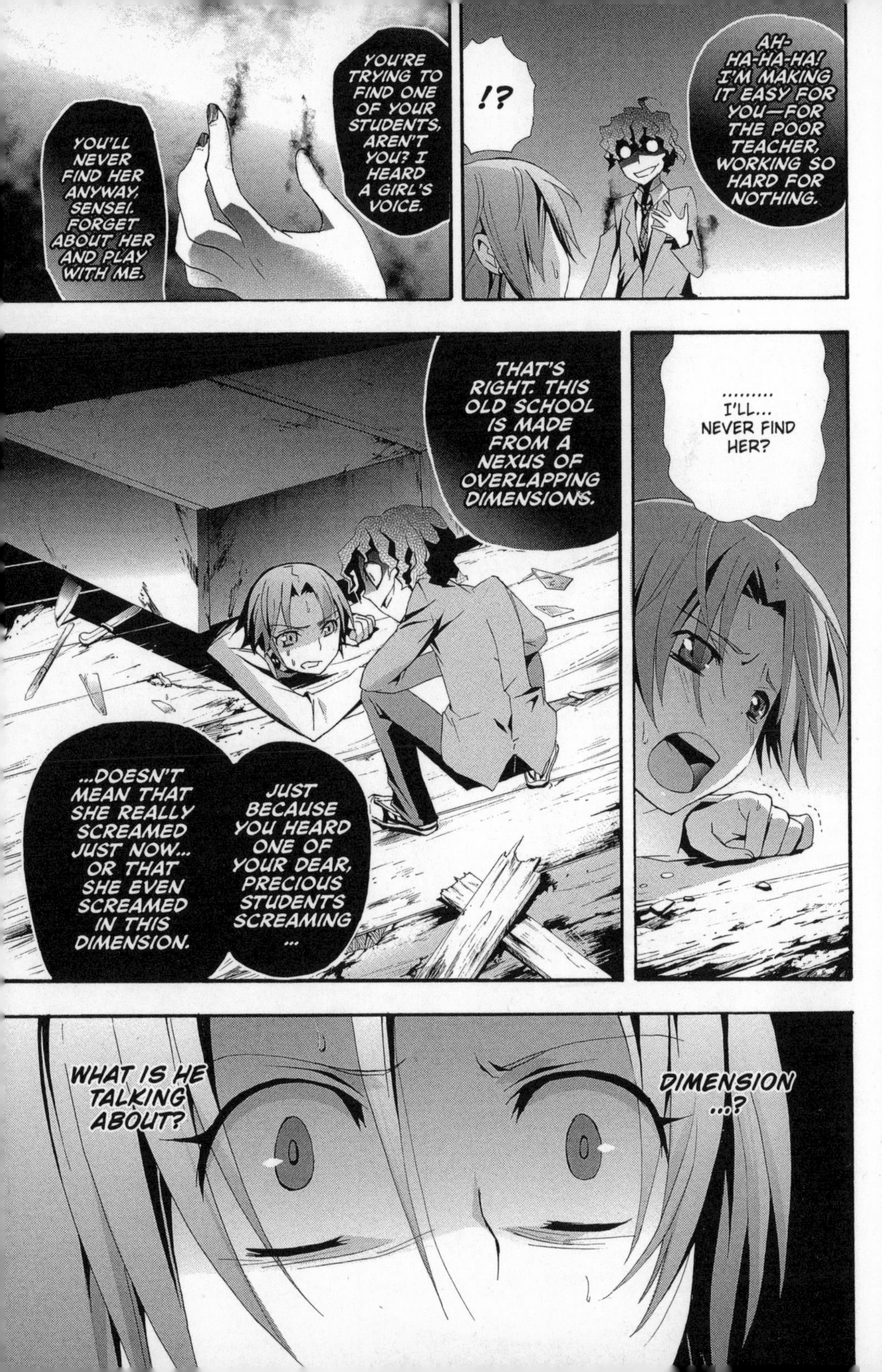
AH-HA-HA-HA! I'M MAKING IT EASY FOR YOU—FOR THE POOR TEACHER, WORKING SO HARD FOR NOTHING.
!?
YOU'RE TRYING TO FIND ONE OF YOUR STUDENTS, AREN'T YOU? I HEARD A GIRL'S VOICE.
YOU'LL NEVER FIND HER ANYWAY, SENSEI. FORGET ABOUT HER AND PLAY WITH ME.
.........I'LL... NEVER FIND HER?
THAT'S RIGHT. THIS OLD SCHOOL IS MADE FROM A NEXUS OF OVERLAPPING DIMENSIONS.
JUST BECAUSE YOU HEARD ONE OF YOUR DEAR, PRECIOUS STUDENTS SCREAMING...
...DOESN'T MEAN THAT SHE REALLY SCREAMED JUST NOW... OR THAT SHE EVEN SCREAMED IN THIS DIMENSION.
DIMENSION...?
WHAT IS HE TALKING ABOUT?

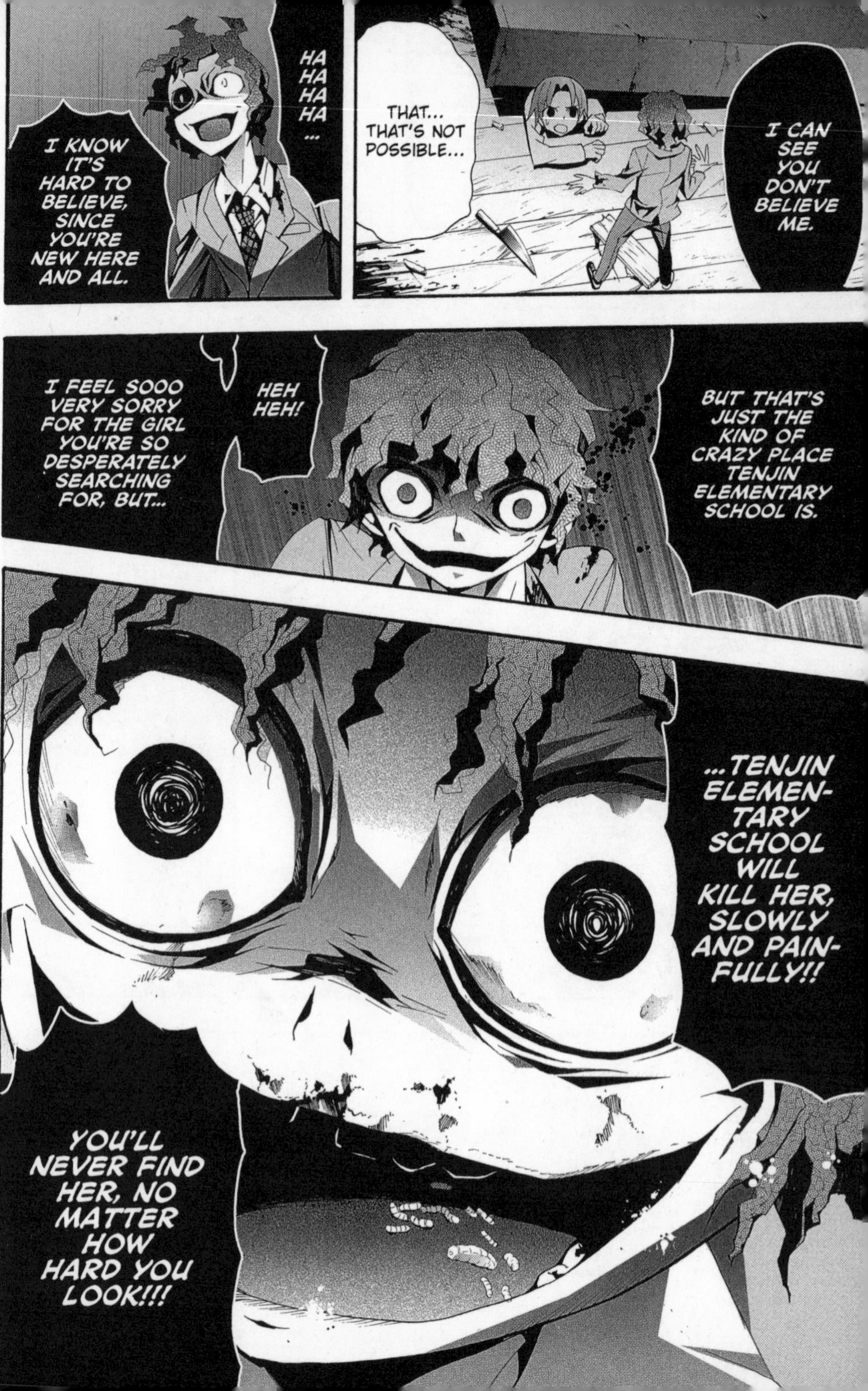
I CAN SEE YOU DON'T BELIEVE ME.
THAT... THAT'S NOT POSSIBLE...
HA HA HA HA ...
I KNOW IT'S HARD TO BELIEVE, SINCE YOU'RE NEW HERE AND ALL.
BUT THAT'S JUST THE KIND OF CRAZY PLACE TENJIN ELEMENTARY SCHOOL IS.
HEH HEH!
I FEEL SOOO VERY SORRY FOR THE GIRL YOU'RE SO DESPERATELY SEARCHING FOR, BUT...
...TENJIN ELEMEN-TARY SCHOOL WILL KILL HER, SLOWLY AND PAIN-FULLY!!
YOU'LL NEVER FIND HER, NO MATTER HOW HARD YOU LOOK!!!

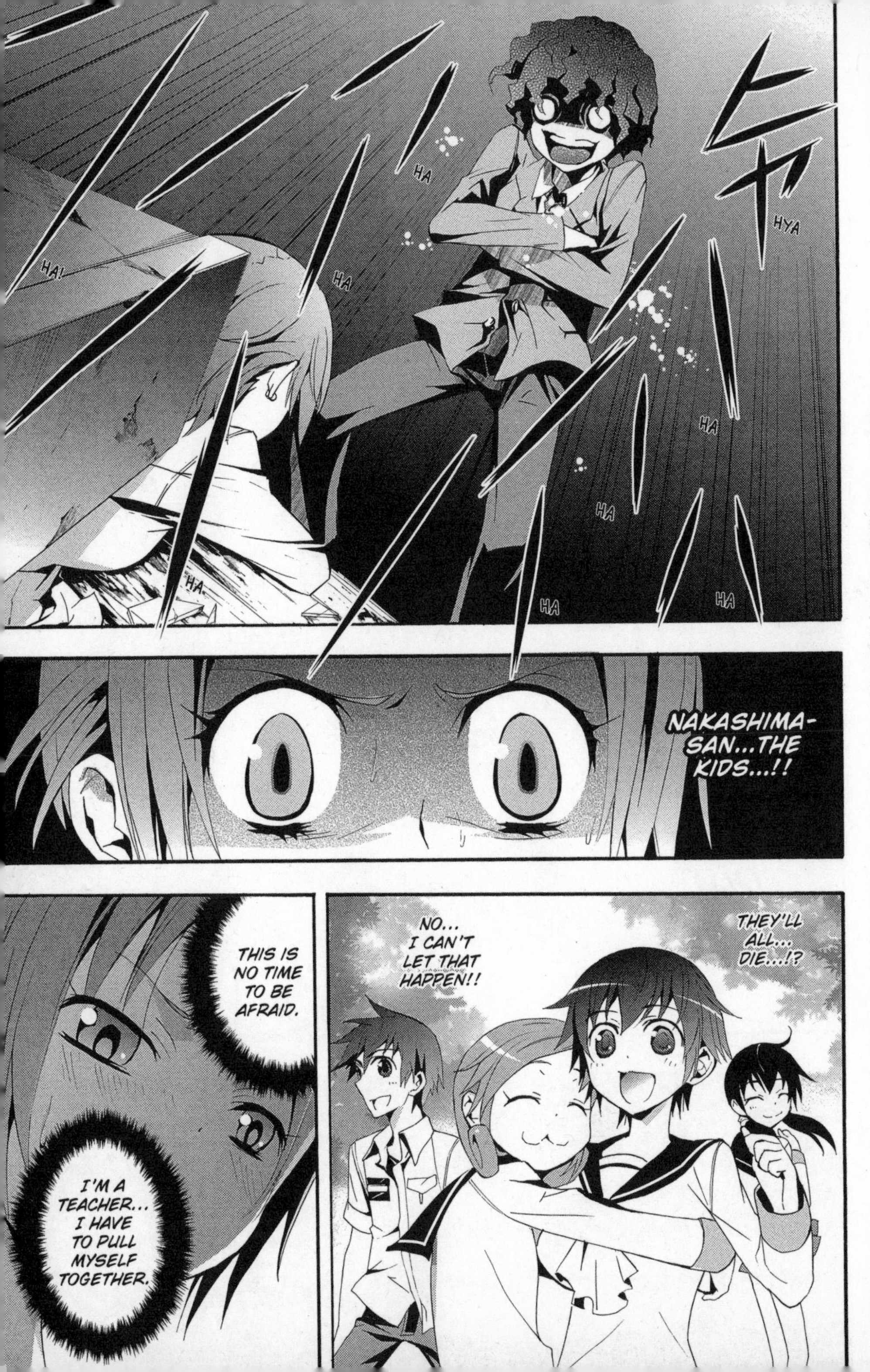
ヒャ
HYA
HA
HA
HA
HA
HA
HA
HA!
HA
NAKASHIMA-SAN...THE KIDS...!!
THEY'LL ALL... DIE...!?
NO... I CAN'T LET THAT HAPPEN!!
THIS IS NO TIME TO BE AFRAID.
I'M A TEACHER... I HAVE TO PULL MYSELF TOGETHER.

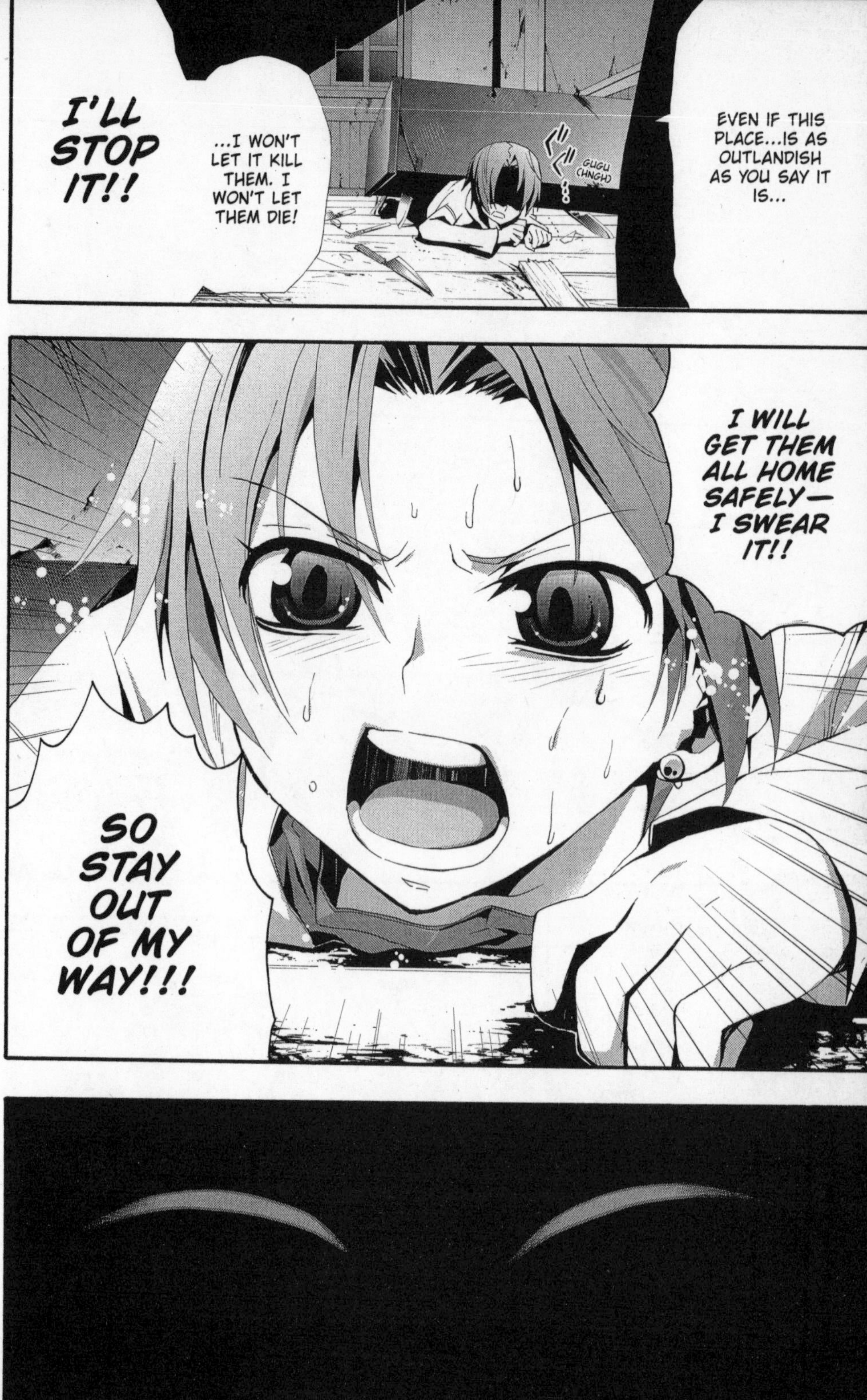
EVEN IF THIS PLACE...IS AS OUTLANDISH AS YOU SAY IT IS...
GUGU (HNGH)
...I WON'T LET IT KILL THEM. I WON'T LET THEM DIE!
I'LL STOP IT!!
I WILL GET THEM ALL HOME SAFELY— I SWEAR IT!!
SO STAY OUT OF MY WAY!!!

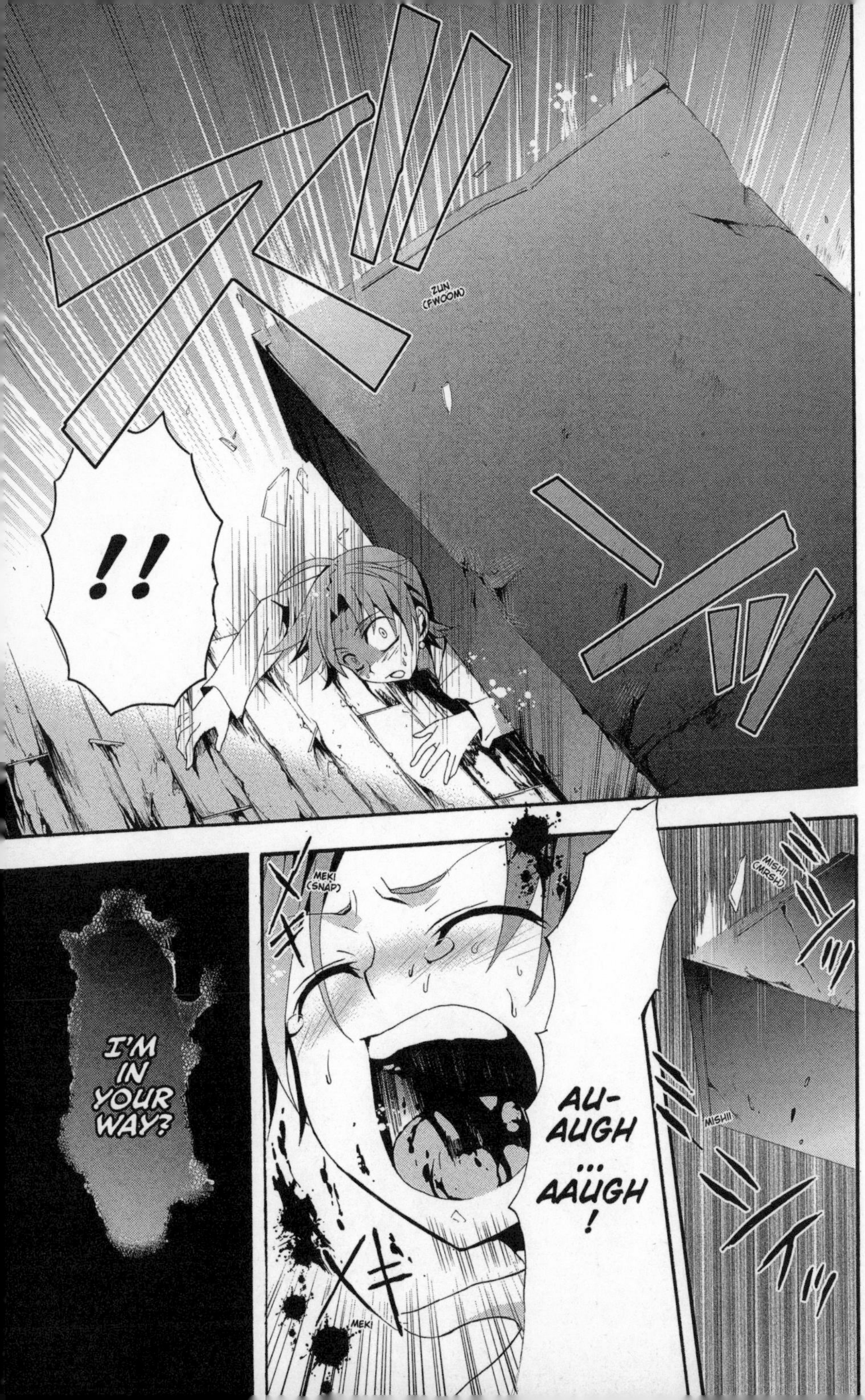
ZUN
(FWOOM)
!!
MISHI
(MRSH)
MEKI
(SNAP)
MISHII
AU-
AUGH
...
AAÜGH
!
MEKI
I'M
IN
YOUR
WAY?

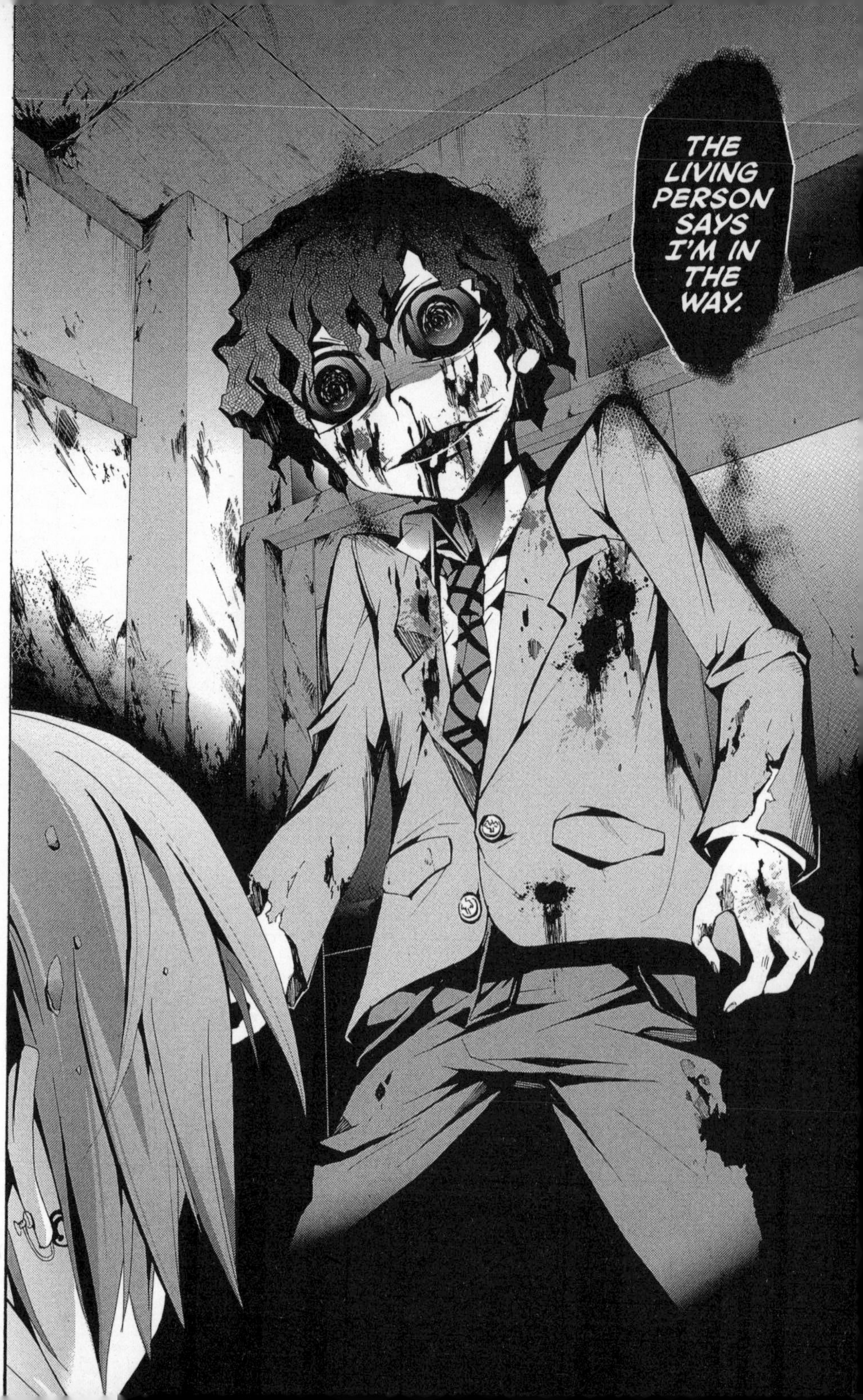
THE LIVING PERSON SAYS I'M IN THE WAY.

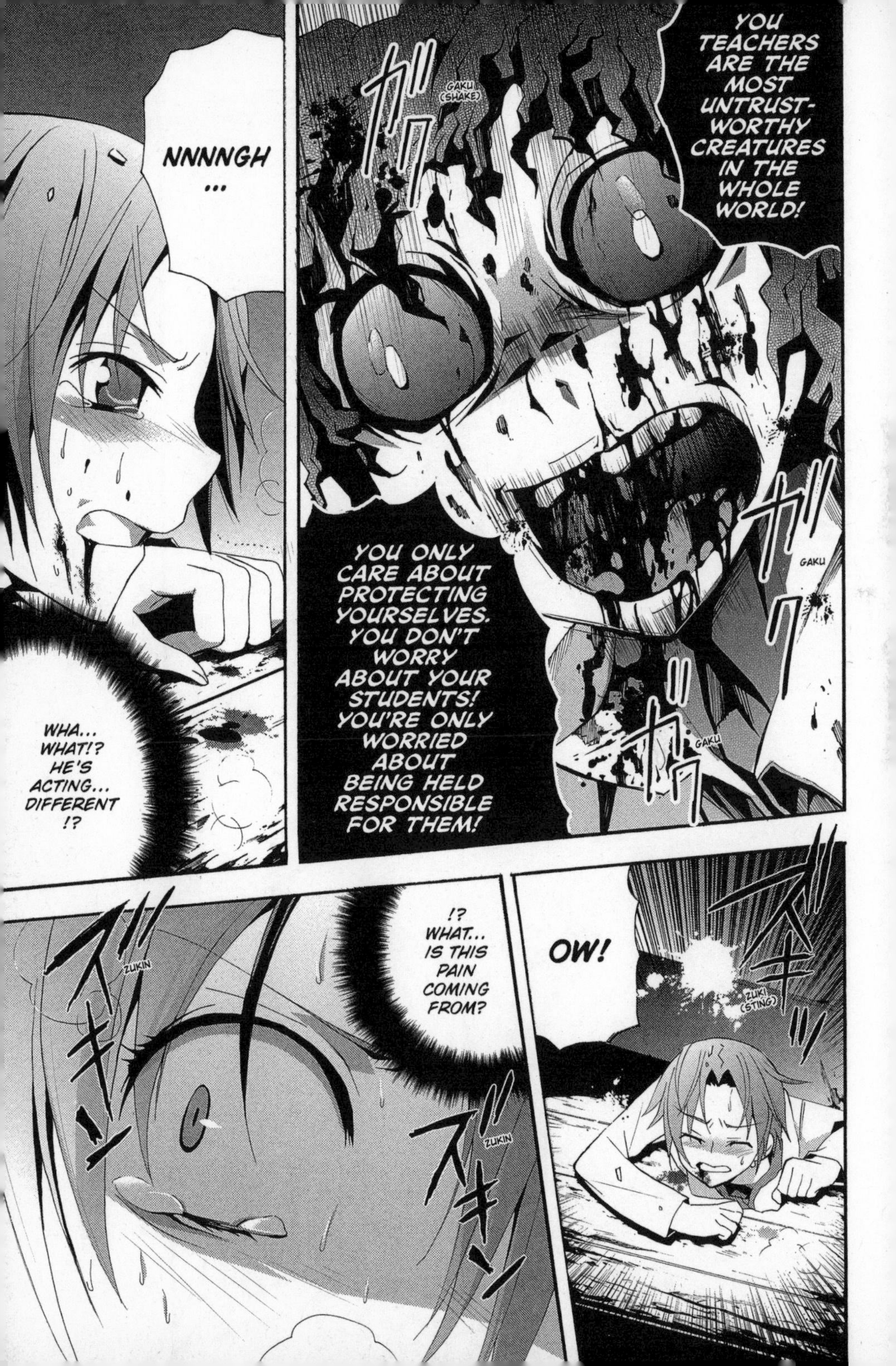
YOU TEACHERS ARE THE MOST UNTRUST-WORTHY CREATURES IN THE WHOLE WORLD!
GAKU (SHAKE)
GAKU
YOU ONLY CARE ABOUT PROTECTING YOURSELVES. YOU DON'T WORRY ABOUT YOUR STUDENTS! YOU'RE ONLY WORRIED ABOUT BEING HELD RESPONSIBLE FOR THEM!
GAKU
NNNNGH ...
WHA... WHAT!? HE'S ACTING... DIFFERENT !?
ZUKI (STING)
OW!
!? WHAT... IS THIS PAIN COMING FROM?
ZUKIN
ZUKIN

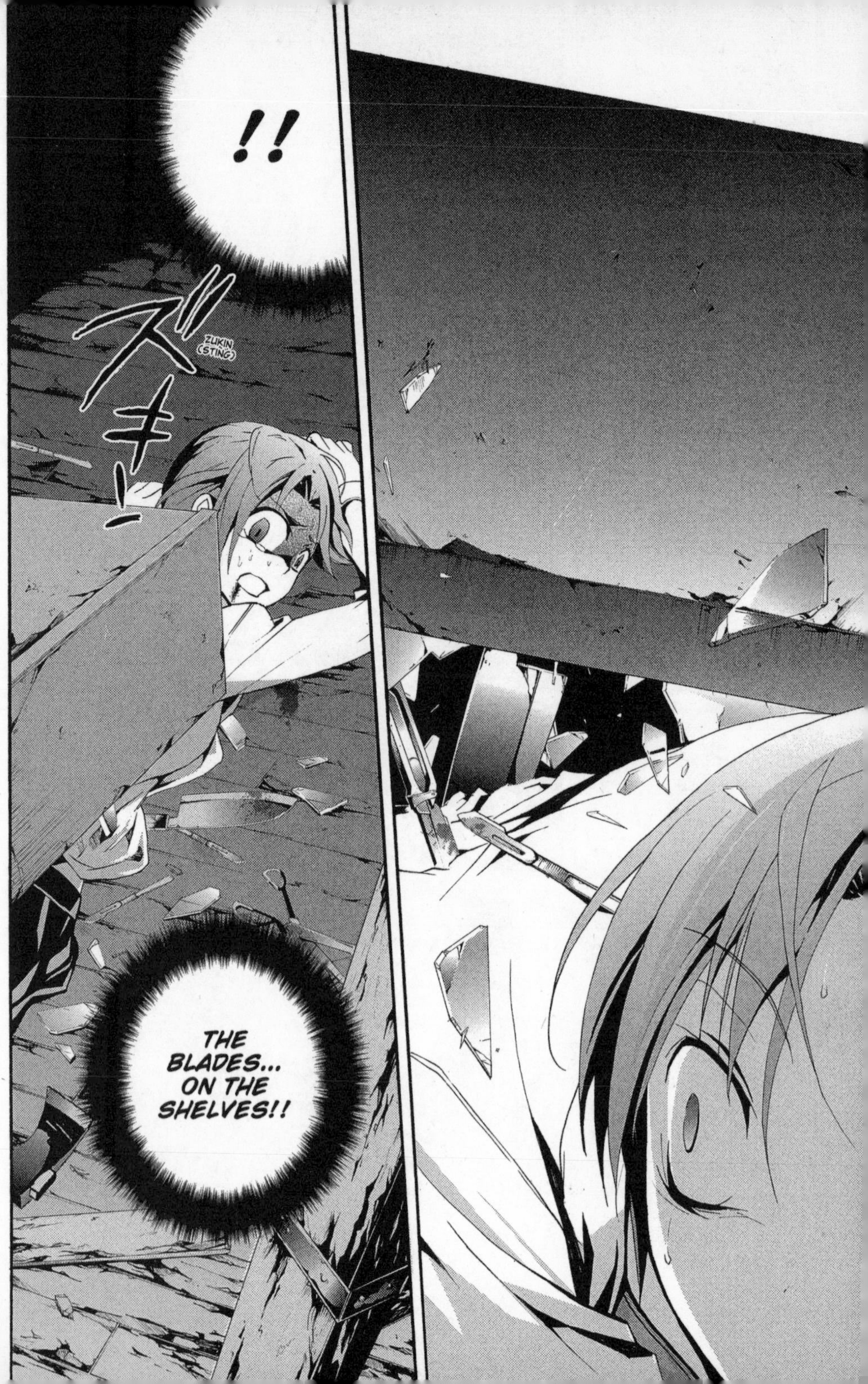
!!
ZUKIN (STING)
THE BLADES... ON THE SHELVES!!

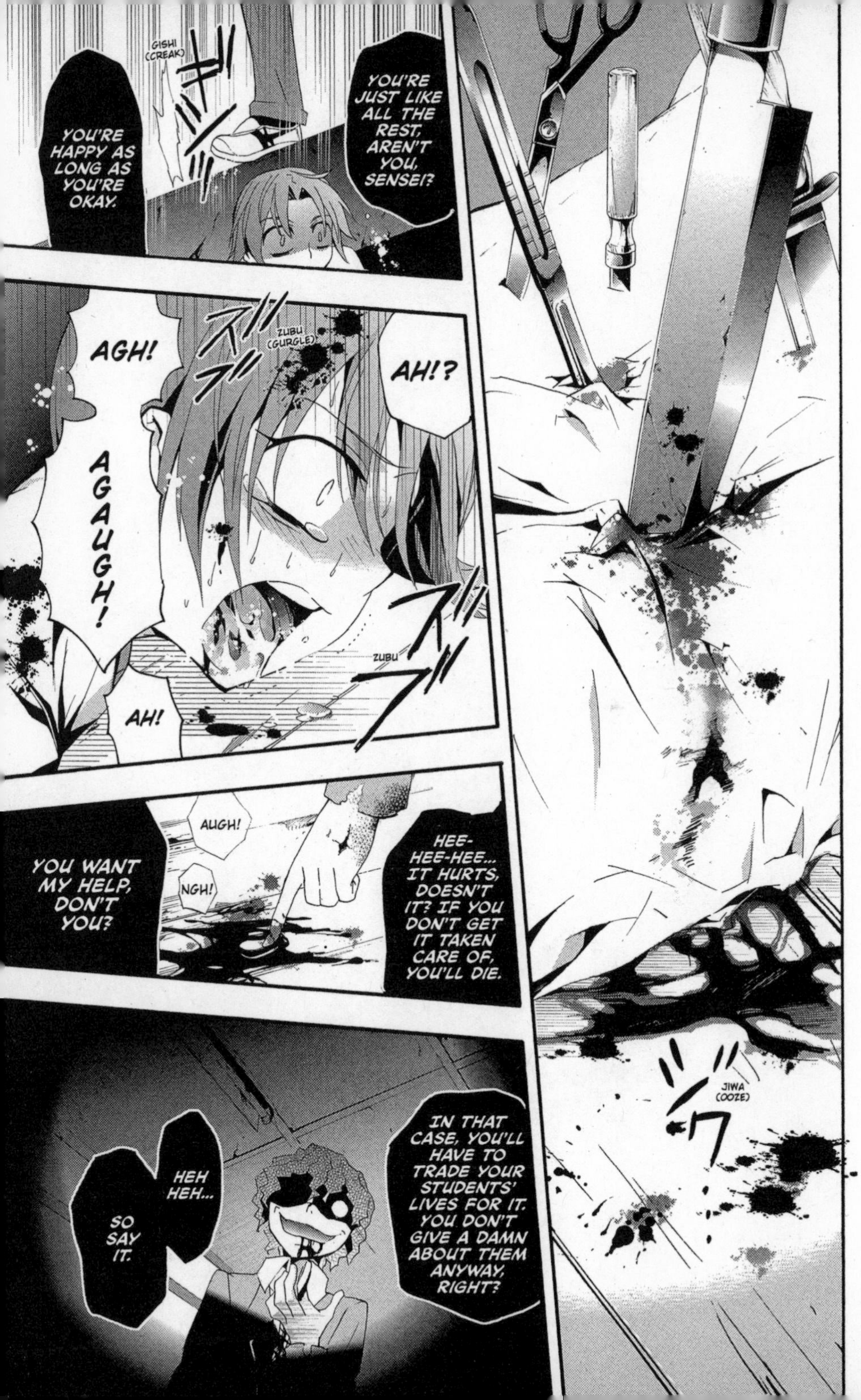
JIWA (OOZE)
YOU'RE JUST LIKE ALL THE REST, AREN'T YOU, SENSEI!?
GISHI (CREAK)
YOU'RE HAPPY AS LONG AS YOU'RE OKAY.
AH!?
ZUBU (GURGLE)
AGH!
AGAUGH!
ZUBU
AH!
HEE-HEE-HEE... IT HURTS, DOESN'T IT? IF YOU DON'T GET IT TAKEN CARE OF, YOU'LL DIE.
AUGH!
NGH!
YOU WANT MY HELP, DON'T YOU?
IN THAT CASE, YOU'LL HAVE TO TRADE YOUR STUDENTS' LIVES FOR IT. YOU DON'T GIVE A DAMN ABOUT THEM ANYWAY, RIGHT?
HEH HEH...
SO SAY IT.

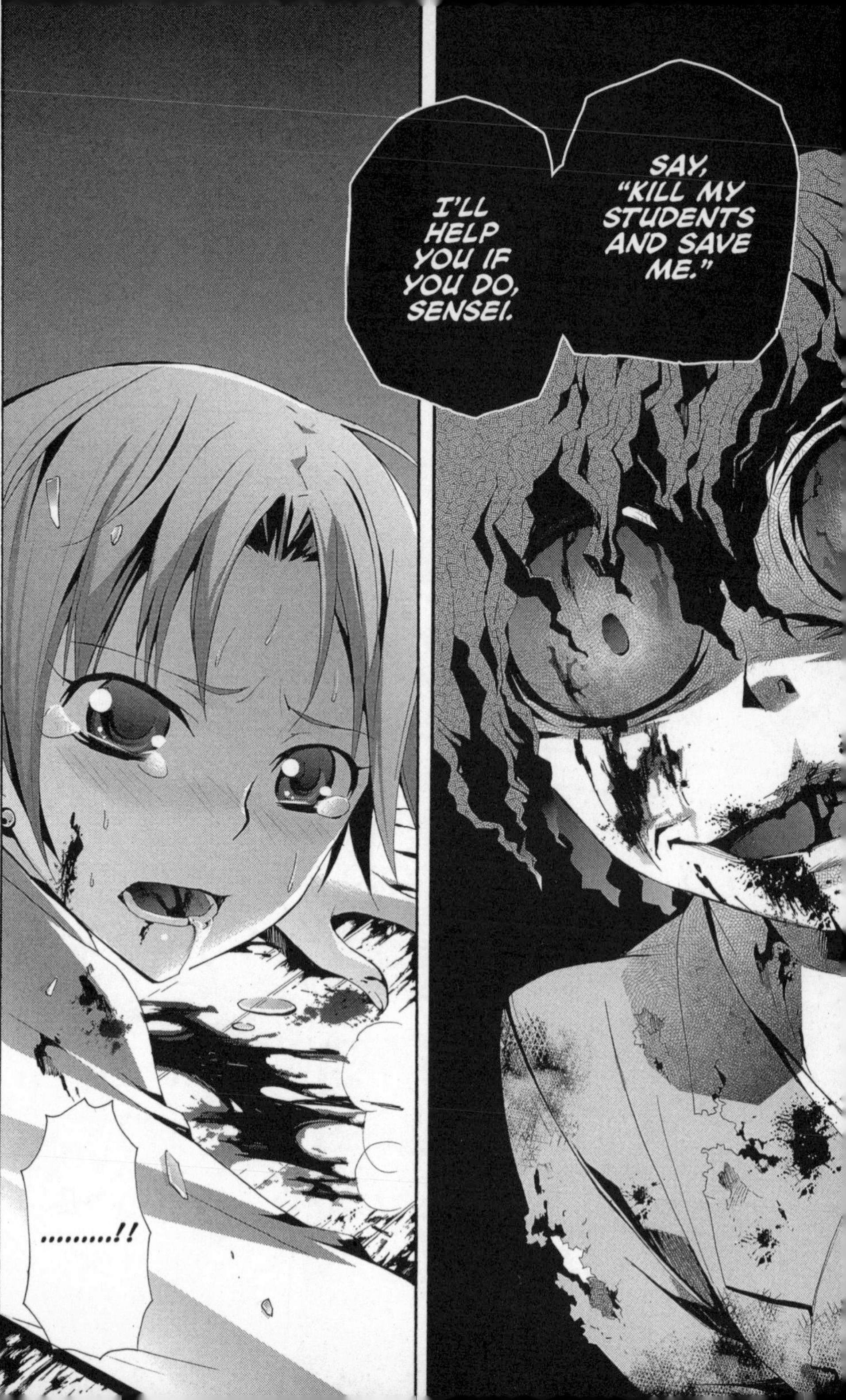
SAY, "KILL MY STUDENTS AND SAVE ME."
I'LL HELP YOU IF YOU DO, SENSEI.
.........!!

a list of ghosts/03

The ghost of a junior high school student

Followed Yui to Class 3-A. Based on
his abnormal obsession with teachers,
it may be that he had some kind of
history with a teacher in life.

CORPSE PARTY
BloodCovered

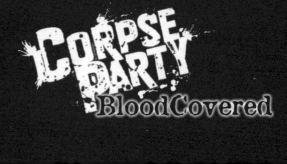

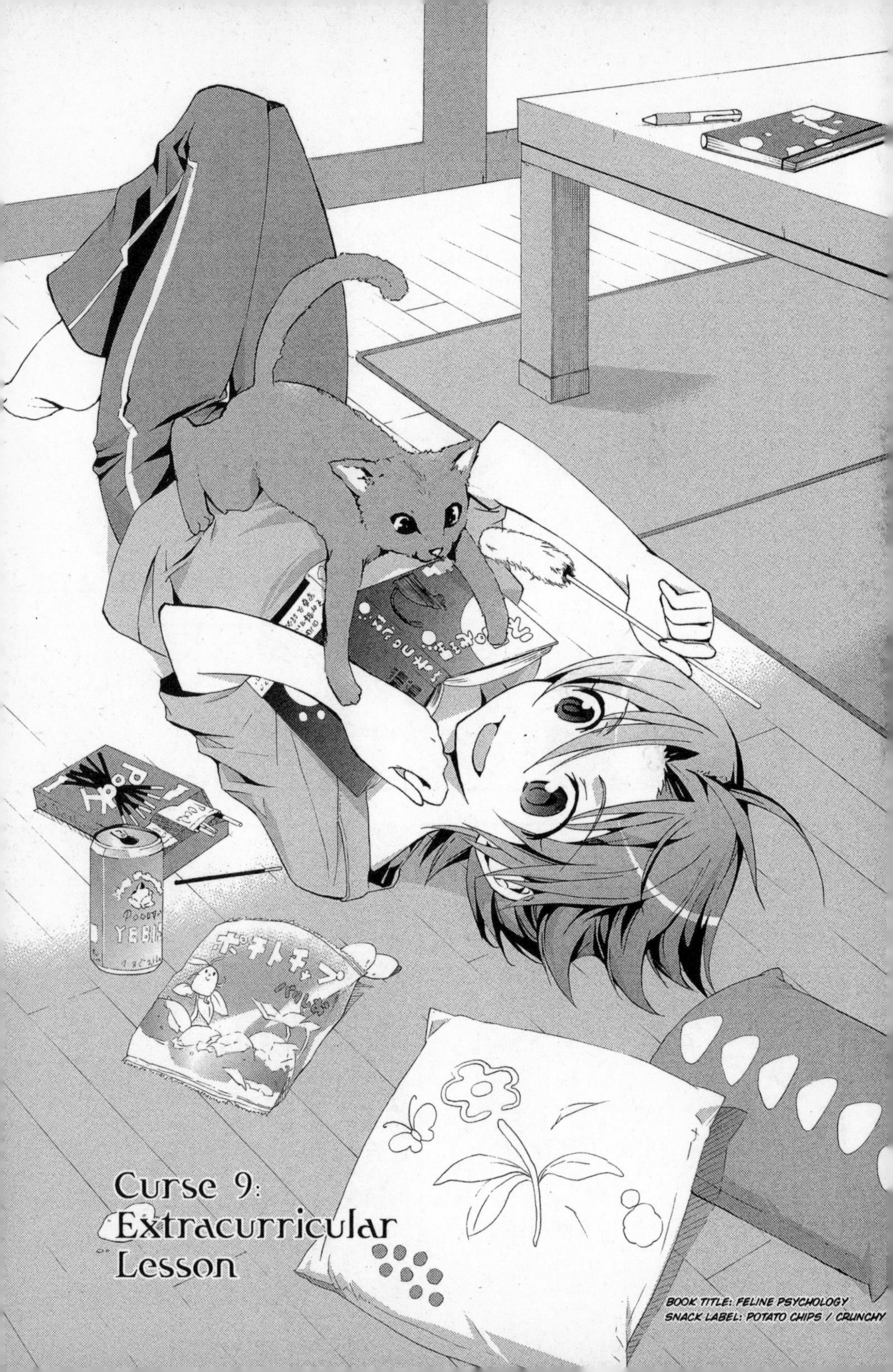
YEBIS
Curse 9:
Extracurricular
Lesson
BOOK TITLE: FELINE PSYCHOLOGY
SNACK LABEL: POTATO CHIPS / CRUNCHY

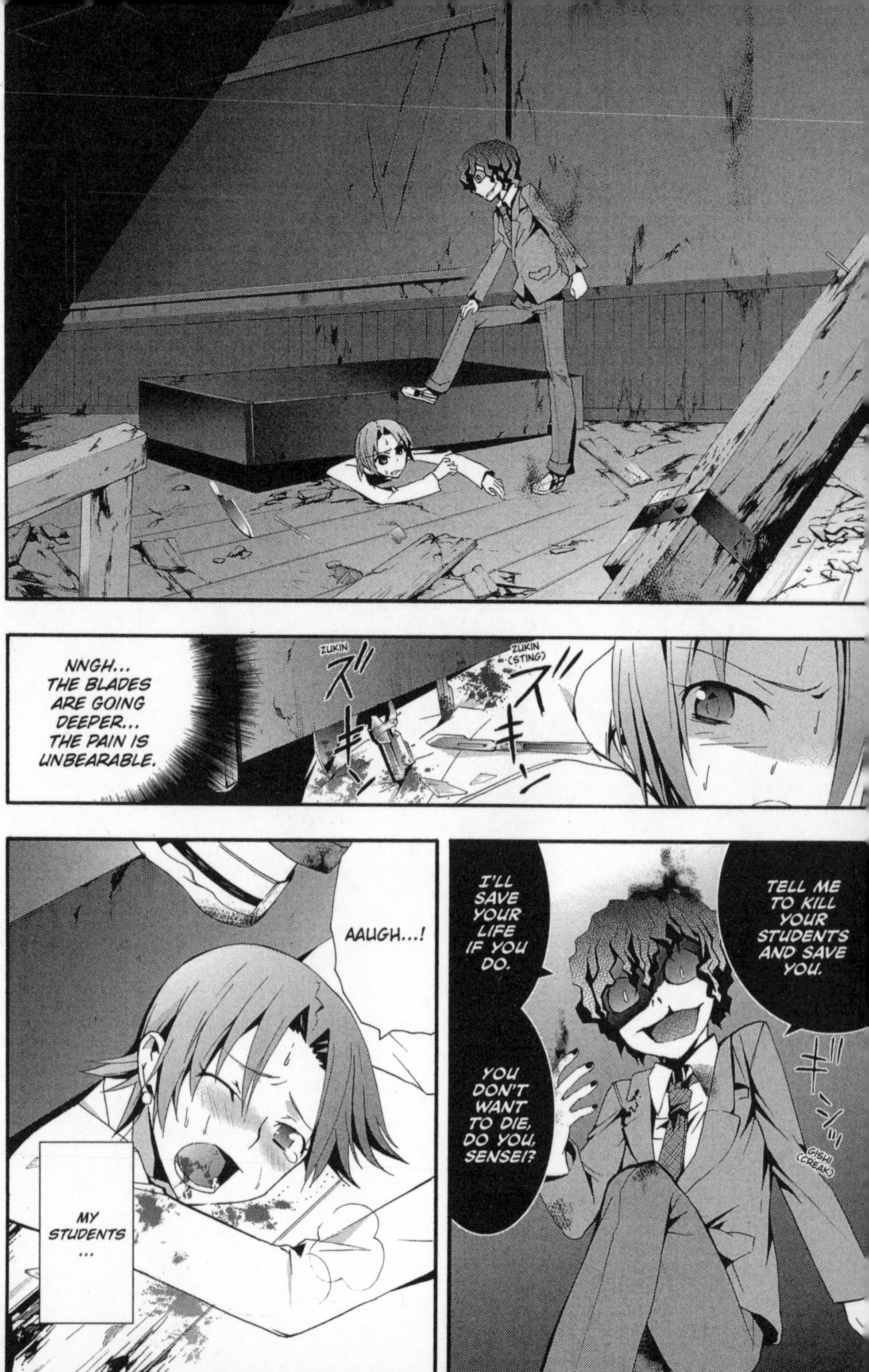
ZUKIN (STING)
ZUKIN
NNGH... THE BLADES ARE GOING DEEPER... THE PAIN IS UNBEARABLE.
TELL ME TO KILL YOUR STUDENTS AND SAVE YOU.
I'LL SAVE YOUR LIFE IF YOU DO.
YOU DON'T WANT TO DIE, DO YOU, SENSEI?
GISHI (CREAK)
AAUGH...!
MY STUDENTS ...

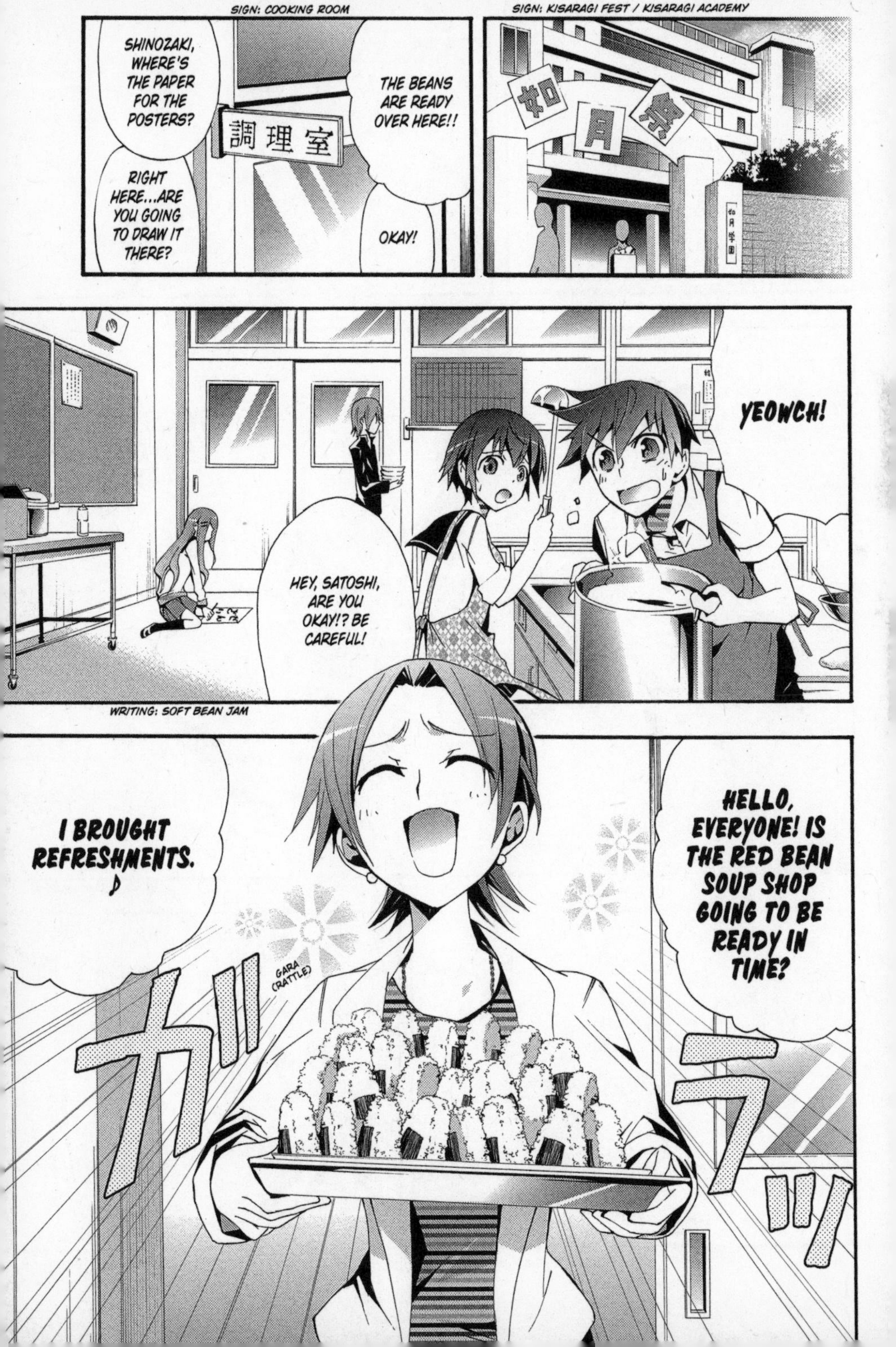
SIGN: KISARAGI FEST / KISARAGI ACADEMY
SIGN: COOKING ROOM
THE BEANS ARE READY OVER HERE!!
SHINOZAKI, WHERE'S THE PAPER FOR THE POSTERS?
RIGHT HERE...ARE YOU GOING TO DRAW IT THERE?
OKAY!
YEOWCH!
HEY, SATOSHI, ARE YOU OKAY!? BE CAREFUL!
WRITING: SOFT BEAN JAM
HELLO, EVERYONE! IS THE RED BEAN SOUP SHOP GOING TO BE READY IN TIME?
ガラッ
GARA (RATTLE)
I BROUGHT REFRESHMENTS. ♪

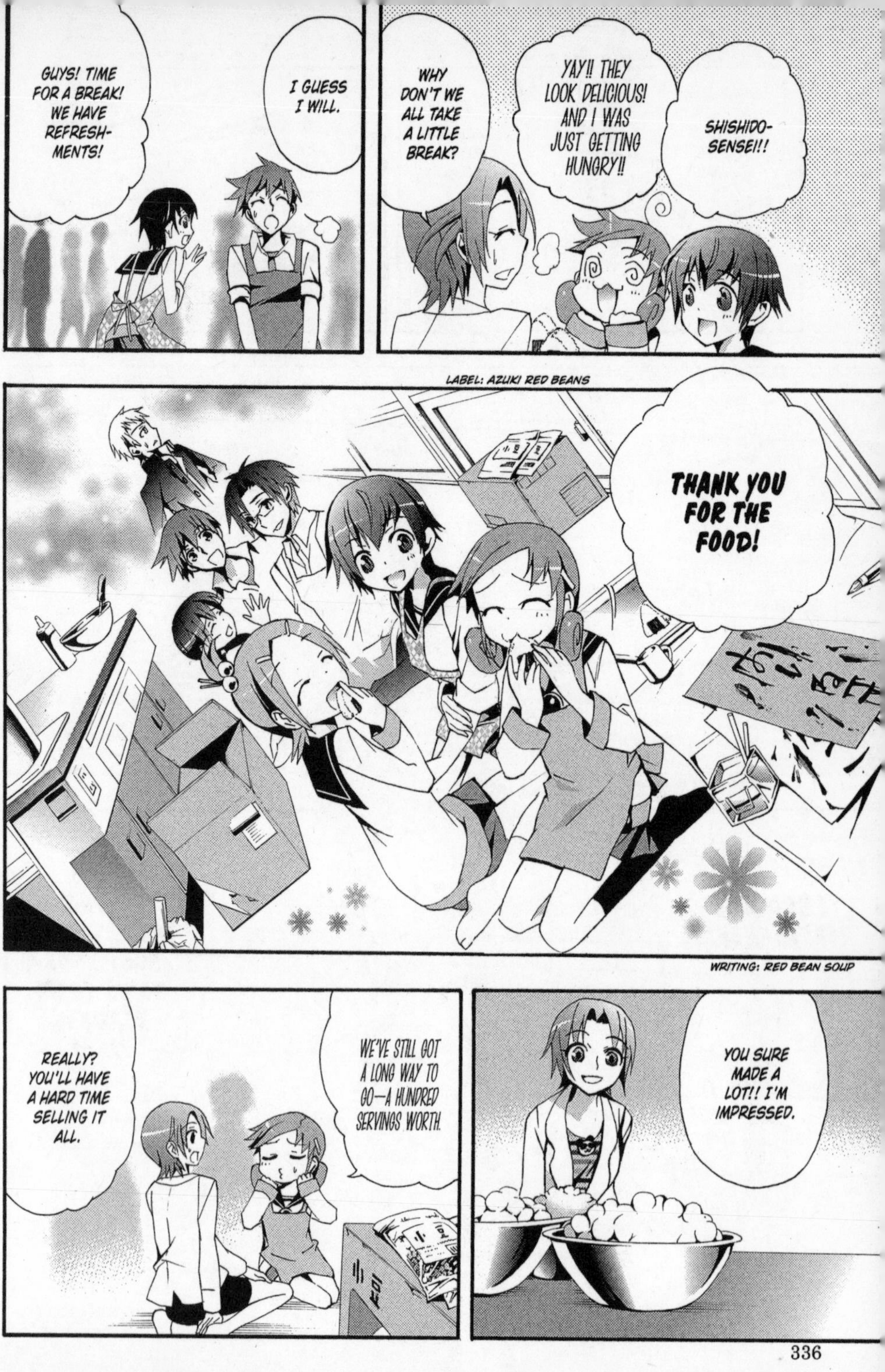
SHISHIDO-SENSEI!!
YAY!! THEY LOOK DELICIOUS! AND I WAS JUST GETTING HUNGRY!!
WHY DON'T WE ALL TAKE A LITTLE BREAK?
I GUESS I WILL.
GUYS! TIME FOR A BREAK! WE HAVE REFRESH-MENTS!
LABEL: AZUKI RED BEANS
THANK YOU FOR THE FOOD!
WRITING: RED BEAN SOUP
YOU SURE MADE A LOT!! I'M IMPRESSED.
WE'VE STILL GOT A LONG WAY TO GO—A HUNDRED SERVINGS WORTH.
REALLY? YOU'LL HAVE A HARD TIME SELLING IT ALL.

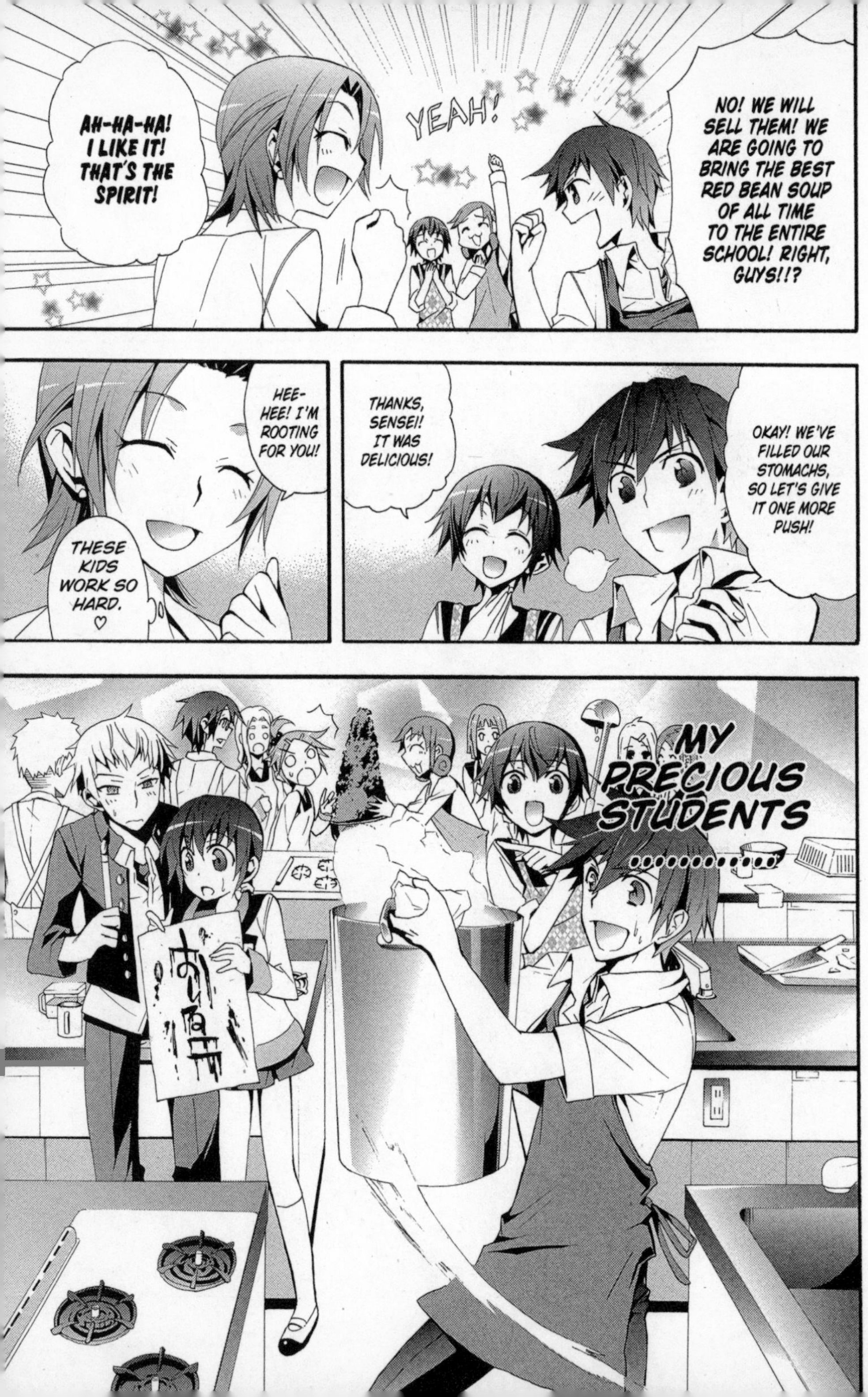
NO! WE WILL SELL THEM! WE ARE GOING TO BRING THE BEST RED BEAN SOUP OF ALL TIME TO THE ENTIRE SCHOOL! RIGHT, GUYS!!?
YEAH!
AH-HA-HA! I LIKE IT! THAT'S THE SPIRIT!
OKAY! WE'VE FILLED OUR STOMACHS, SO LET'S GIVE IT ONE MORE PUSH!
THANKS, SENSEI! IT WAS DELICIOUS!
HEE-HEE! I'M ROOTING FOR YOU!
THESE KIDS WORK SO HARD. ♡
MY PRECIOUS STUDENTS
....

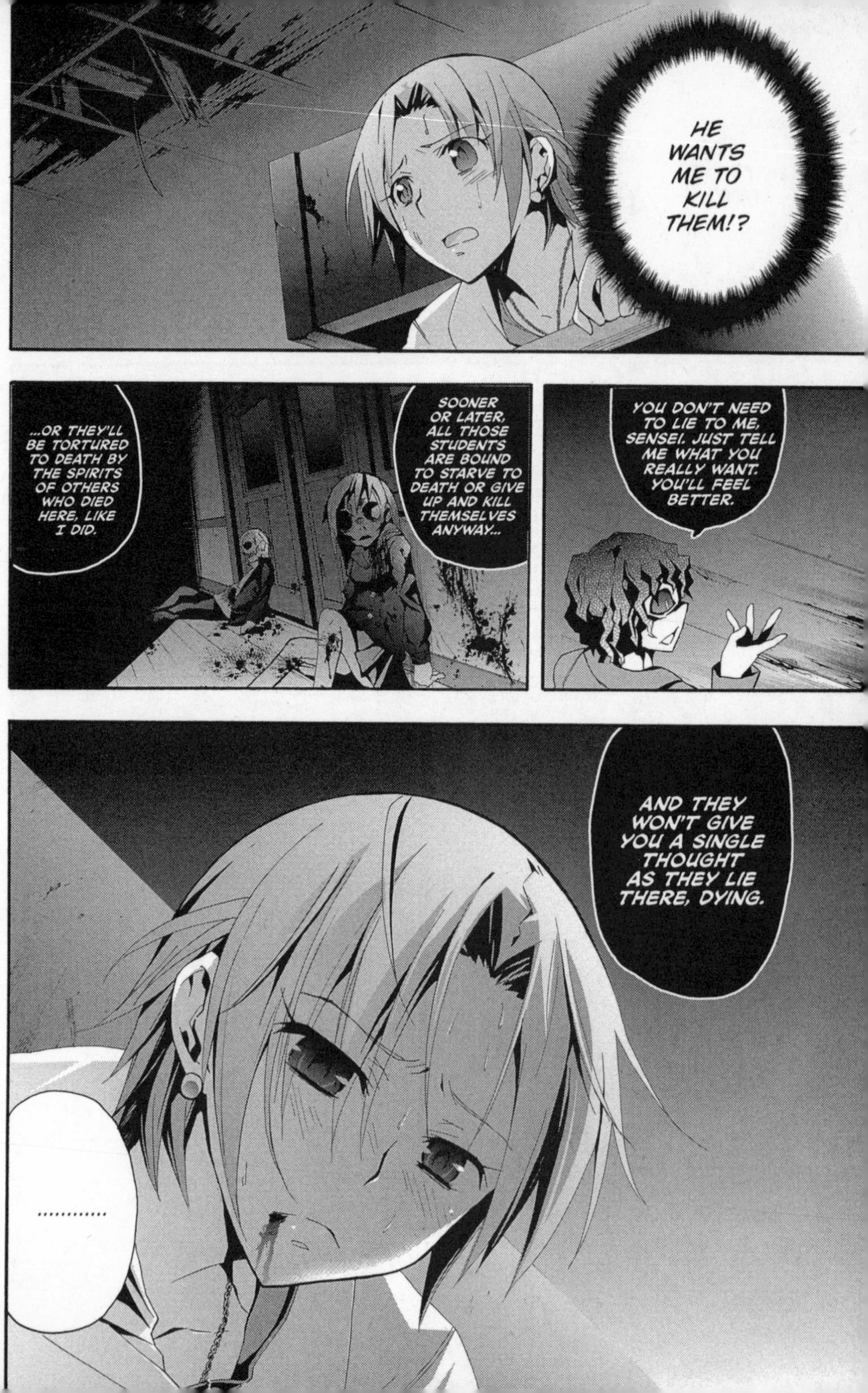
HE WANTS ME TO KILL THEM!?
YOU DON'T NEED TO LIE TO ME, SENSEI. JUST TELL ME WHAT YOU REALLY WANT. YOU'LL FEEL BETTER.
SOONER OR LATER, ALL THOSE STUDENTS ARE BOUND TO STARVE TO DEATH OR GIVE UP AND KILL THEMSELVES ANYWAY...
...OR THEY'LL BE TORTURED TO DEATH BY THE SPIRITS OF OTHERS WHO DIED HERE, LIKE I DID.
AND THEY WON'T GIVE YOU A SINGLE THOUGHT AS THEY LIE THERE, DYING.
....

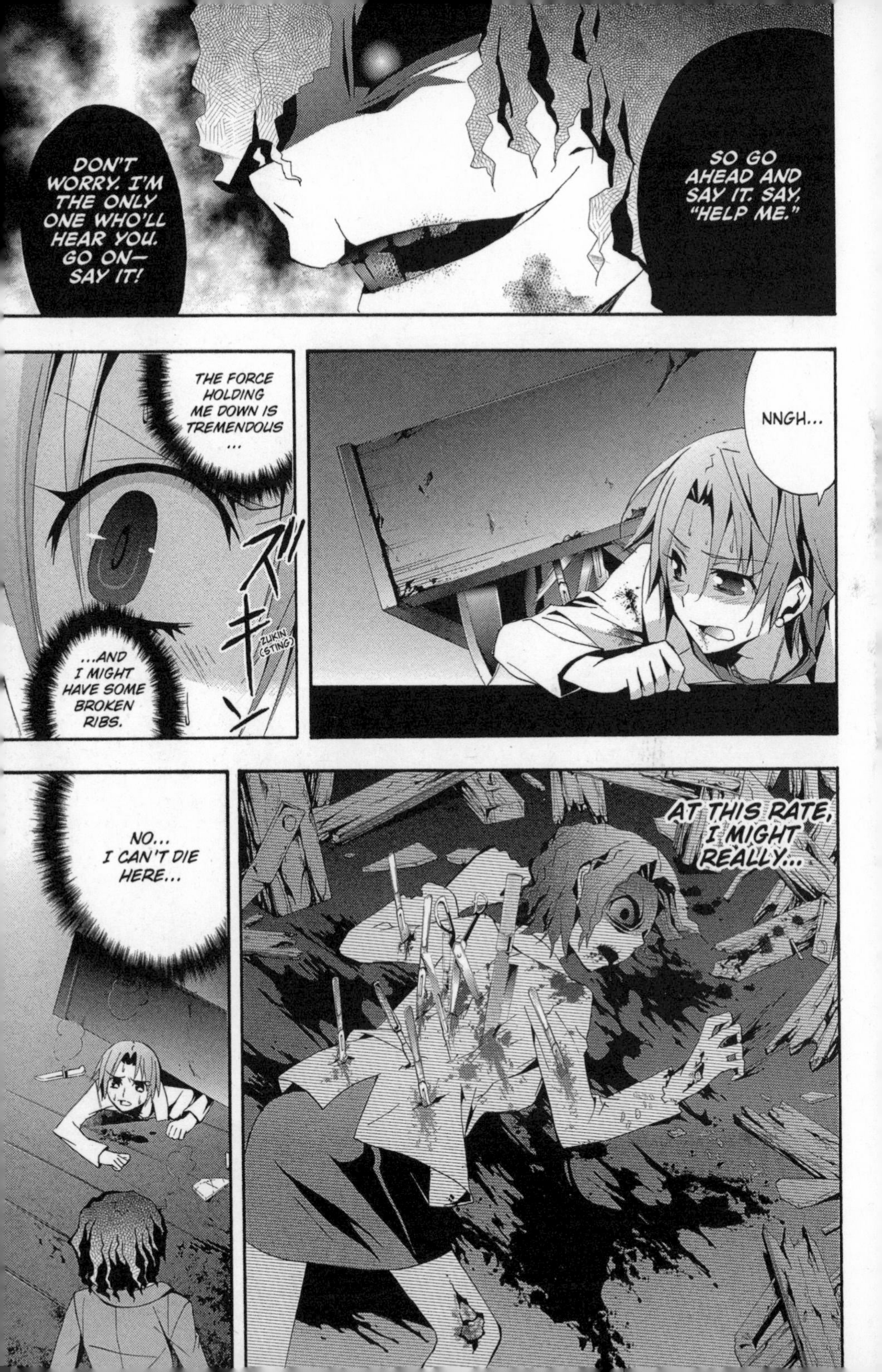
SO GO AHEAD AND SAY IT. SAY, "HELP ME."
DON'T WORRY. I'M THE ONLY ONE WHO'LL HEAR YOU. GO ON— SAY IT!
NNGH...
THE FORCE HOLDING ME DOWN IS TREMENDOUS ...
ZUKIN (STING)
...AND I MIGHT HAVE SOME BROKEN RIBS.
AT THIS RATE, I MIGHT REALLY...
NO... I CAN'T DIE HERE...

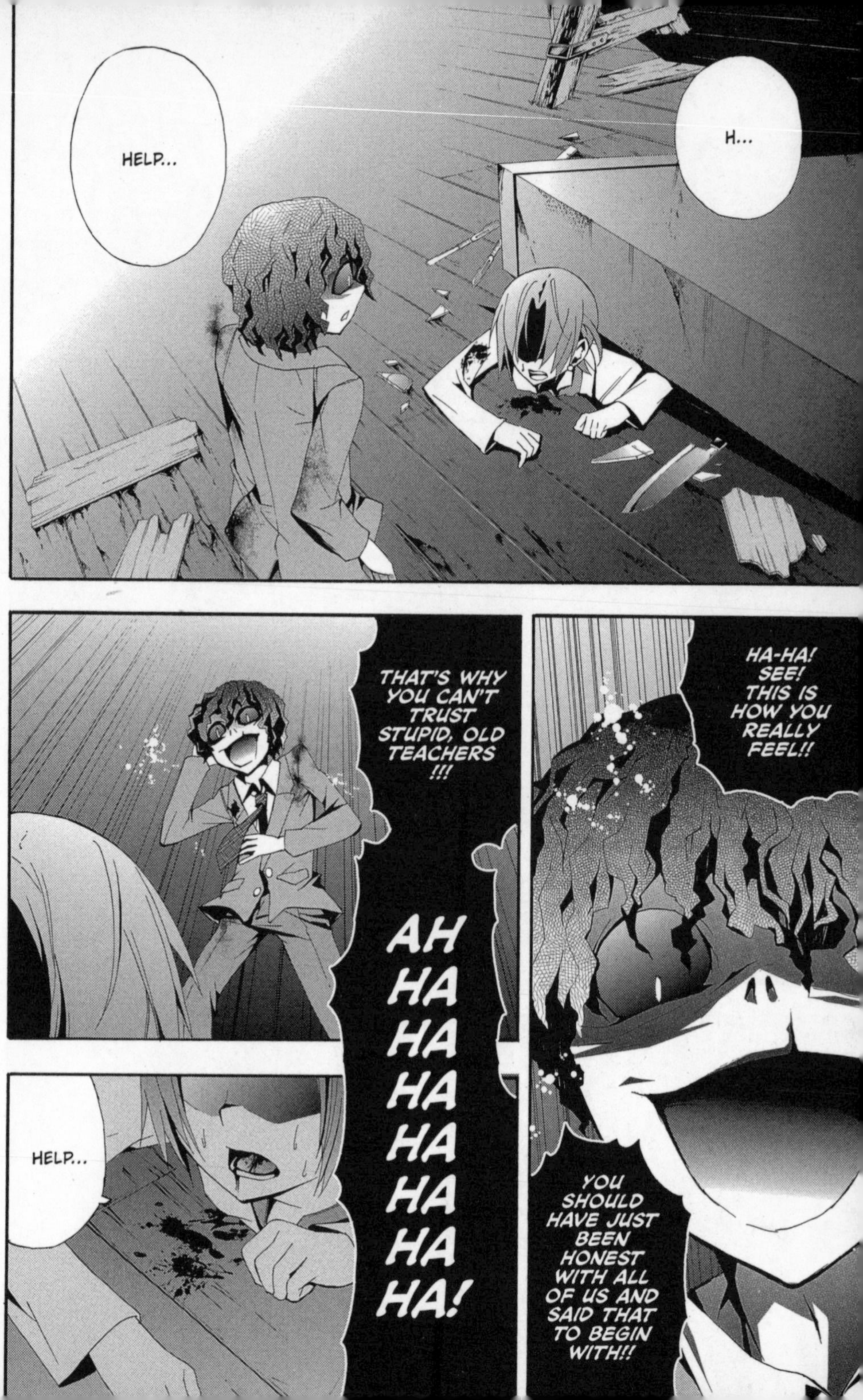
H...
HELP...
HA-HA! SEE! THIS IS HOW YOU REALLY FEEL!!
YOU SHOULD HAVE JUST BEEN HONEST WITH ALL OF US AND SAID THAT TO BEGIN WITH!!
THAT'S WHY YOU CAN'T TRUST STUPID, OLD TEACHERS!!!
AH HA HA HA HA HA HA HA HA HA!
HELP...

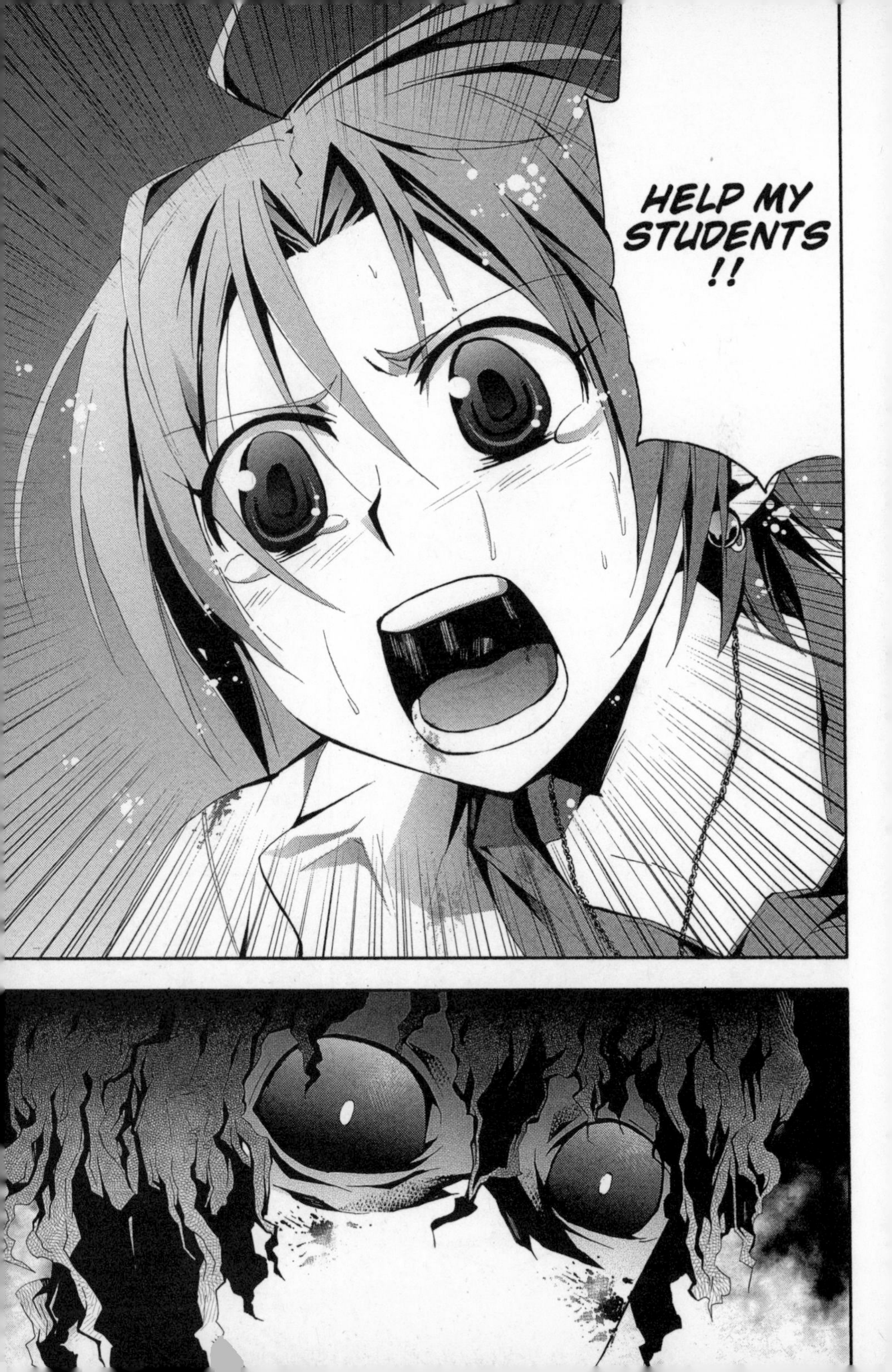
HELP MY STUDENTS !!

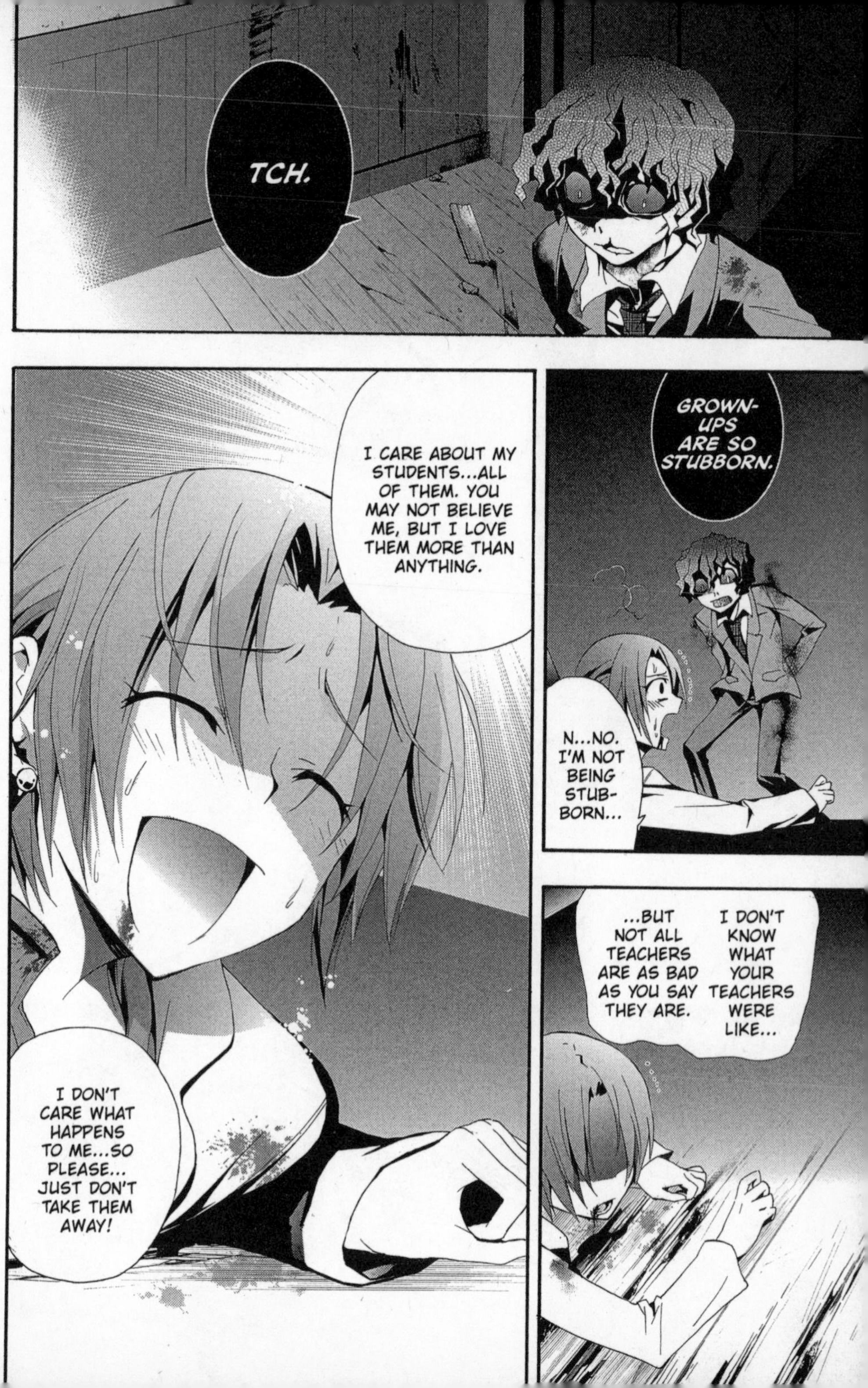
TCH.
GROWN-UPS ARE SO STUBBORN.
N...NO. I'M NOT BEING STUBBORN...
I DON'T KNOW WHAT YOUR TEACHERS WERE LIKE...
...BUT NOT ALL TEACHERS ARE AS BAD AS YOU SAY THEY ARE.
I CARE ABOUT MY STUDENTS...ALL OF THEM. YOU MAY NOT BELIEVE ME, BUT I LOVE THEM MORE THAN ANYTHING.
I DON'T CARE WHAT HAPPENS TO ME...SO PLEASE... JUST DON'T TAKE THEM AWAY!

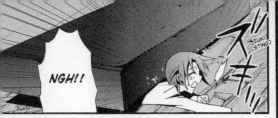

....
NGH!!
ZUKI (STING)
NNN... NGH!
KOFF
KOFF
TSUU (SHHH)
YOU...ACTUALLY CHOSE YOUR STUDENTS AT A TIME LIKE THIS...WHAT A WONDERFUL SENSE OF SELF-SACRIFICE...
YOU'RE THE VERY MODEL OF A GOOD TEACHER.

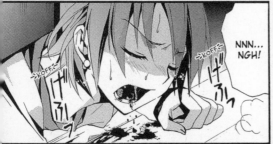

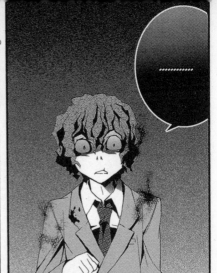

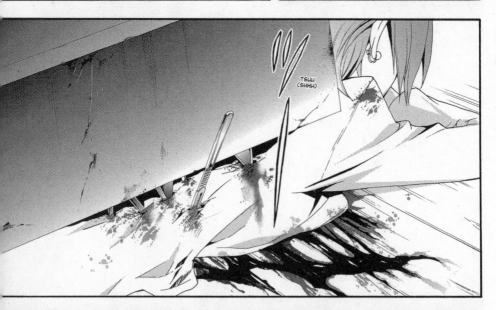

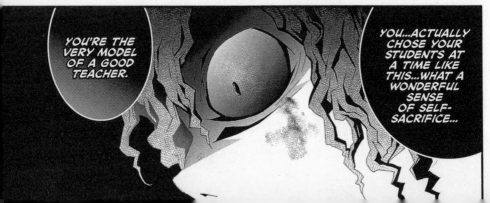

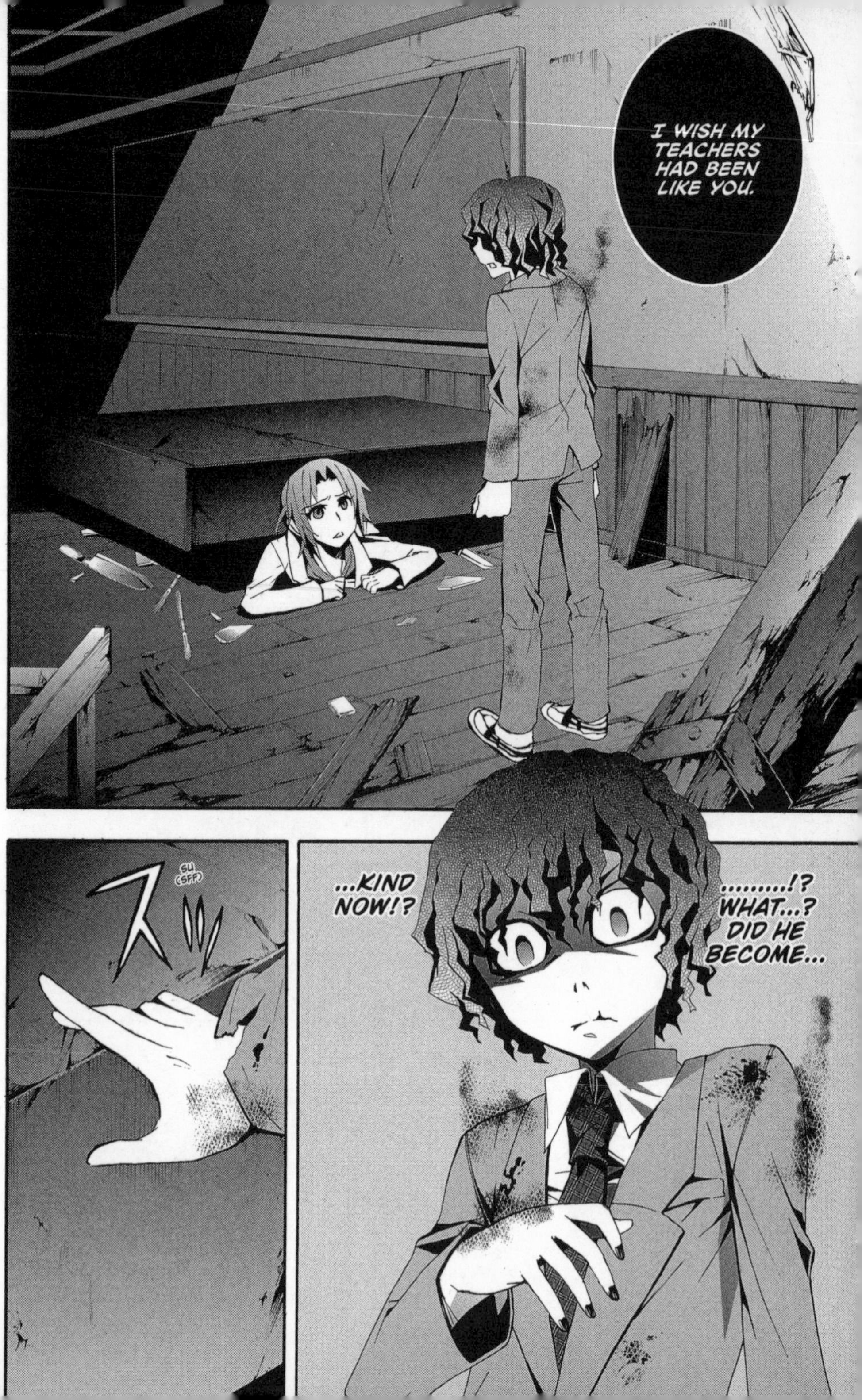
I WISH MY TEACHERS HAD BEEN LIKE YOU.
.........!? WHAT...? DID HE BECOME...
...KIND NOW!?
スッ
SU (SFF)

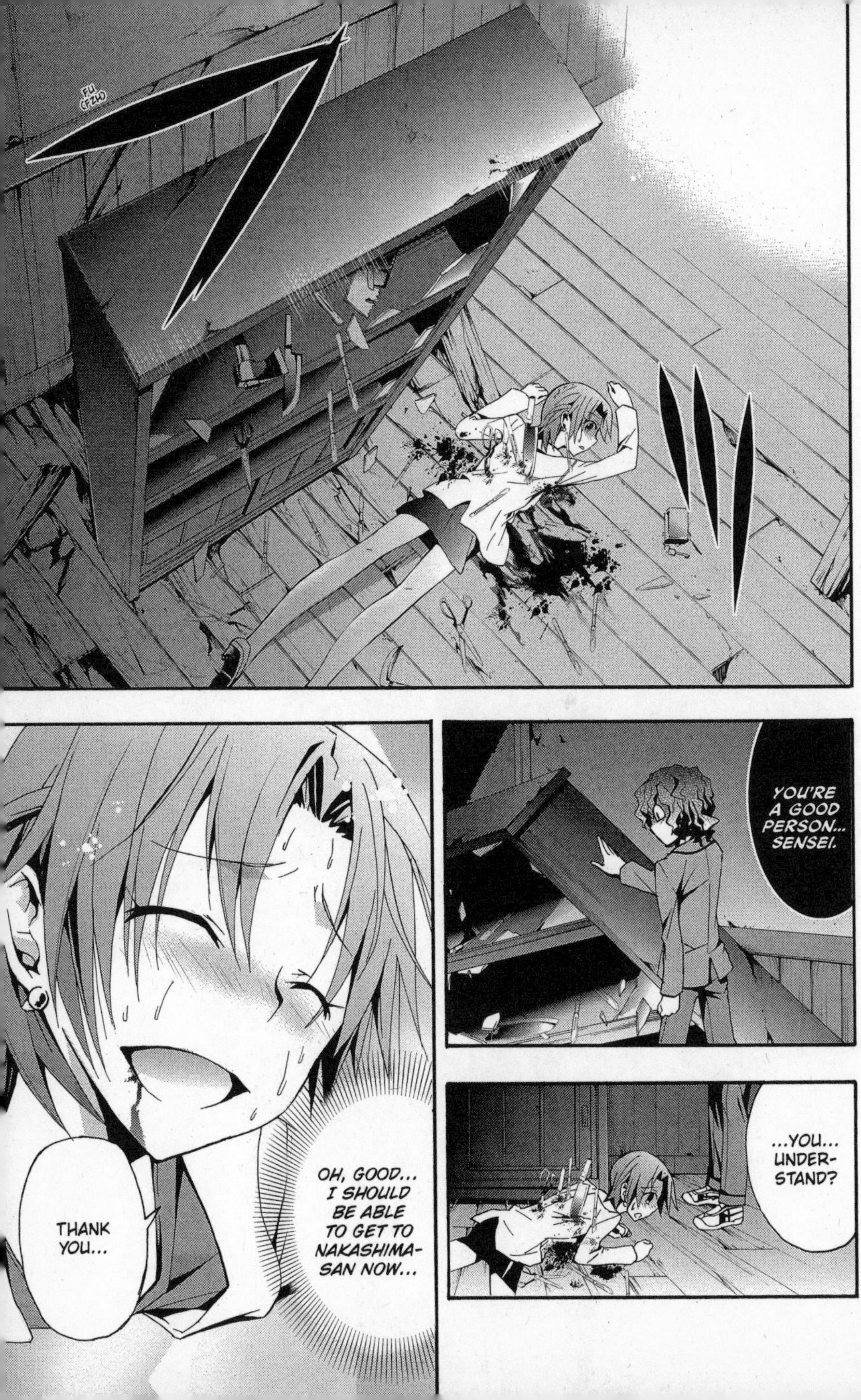
FU (FZH)
YOU'RE A GOOD PERSON... SENSEI.
...YOU... UNDER-STAND?
OH, GOOD... I SHOULD BE ABLE TO GET TO NAKASHIMA-SAN NOW...
THANK YOU...

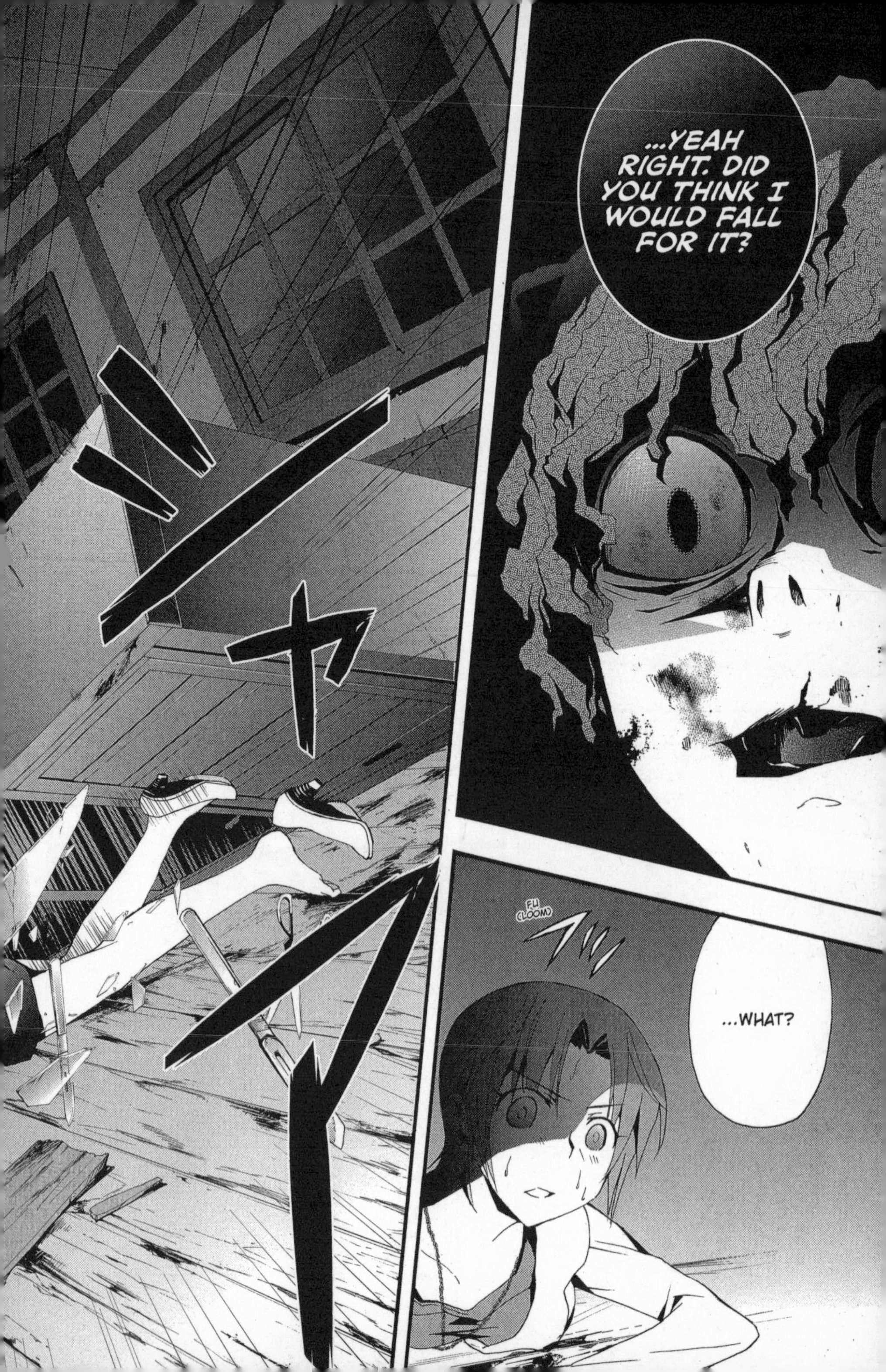
...YEAH RIGHT. DID YOU THINK I WOULD FALL FOR IT?
FU (LOOM)
...WHAT?

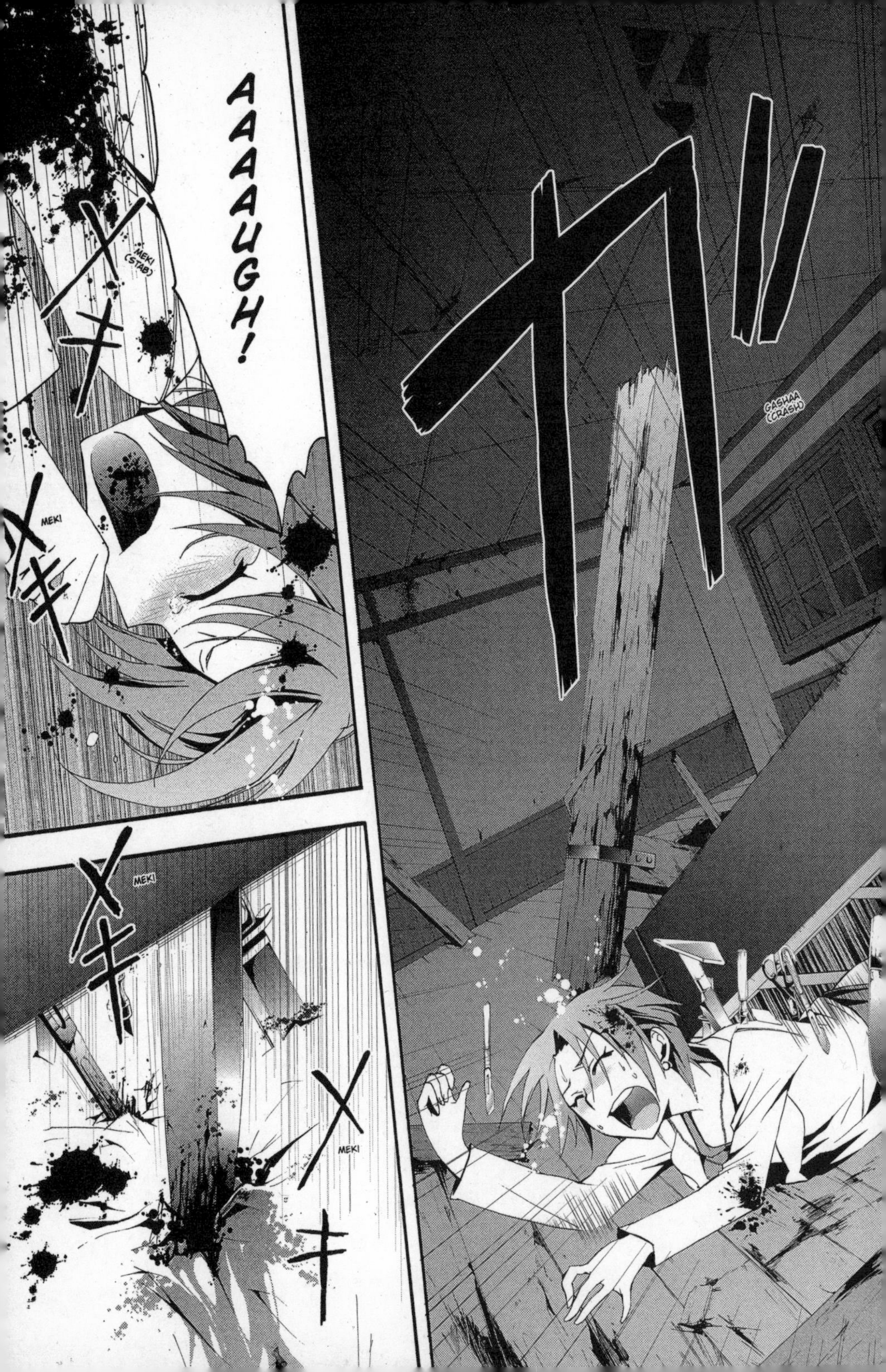
GASHAA (CRASH)
AAAAAUGH!
MEKI (STAB)
MEKI
MEKI
MEKI

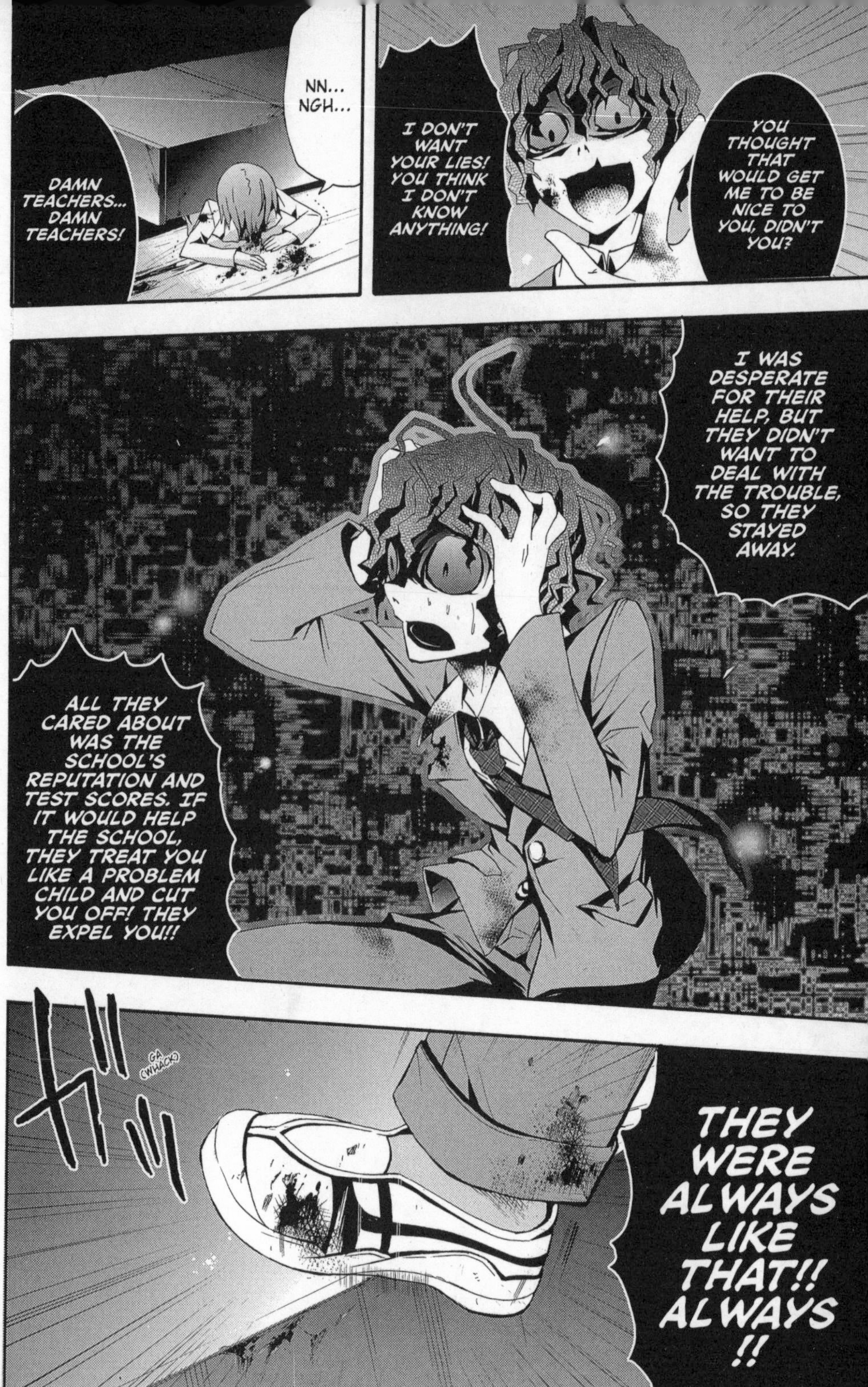
YOU THOUGHT THAT WOULD GET ME TO BE NICE TO YOU, DIDN'T YOU?
I DON'T WANT YOUR LIES! YOU THINK I DON'T KNOW ANYTHING!
NN... NGH...
DAMN TEACHERS... DAMN TEACHERS!
I WAS DESPERATE FOR THEIR HELP, BUT THEY DIDN'T WANT TO DEAL WITH THE TROUBLE, SO THEY STAYED AWAY.
ALL THEY CARED ABOUT WAS THE SCHOOL'S REPUTATION AND TEST SCORES. IF IT WOULD HELP THE SCHOOL, THEY TREAT YOU LIKE A PROBLEM CHILD AND CUT YOU OFF! THEY EXPEL YOU!!
THEY WERE ALWAYS LIKE THAT!! ALWAYS!!
GA (WHACK)

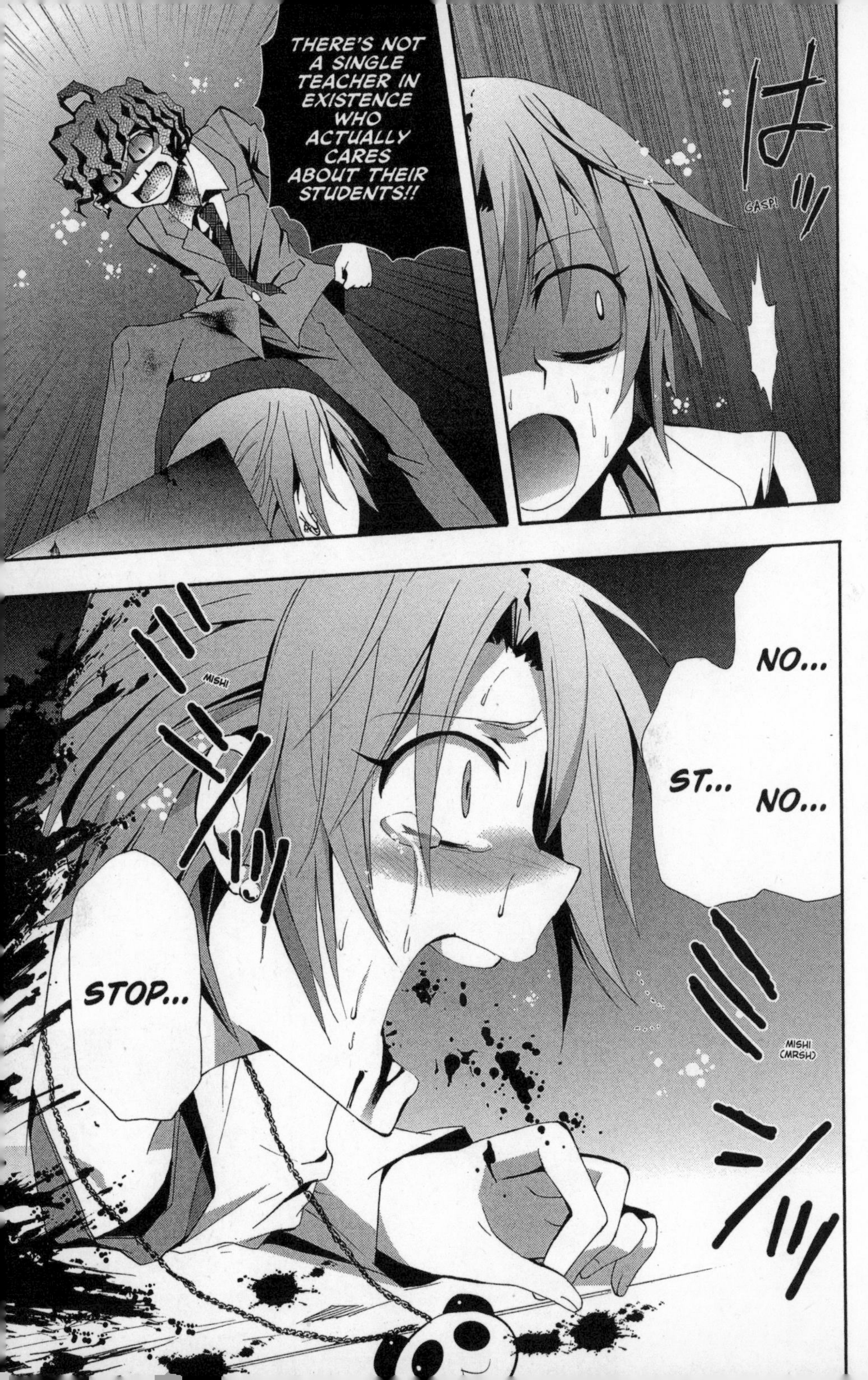
はッ
GASP!
THERE'S NOT A SINGLE TEACHER IN EXISTENCE WHO ACTUALLY CARES ABOUT THEIR STUDENTS!!
NO...
ST... NO...
MISHI (MRSH)
MISHI
STOP...

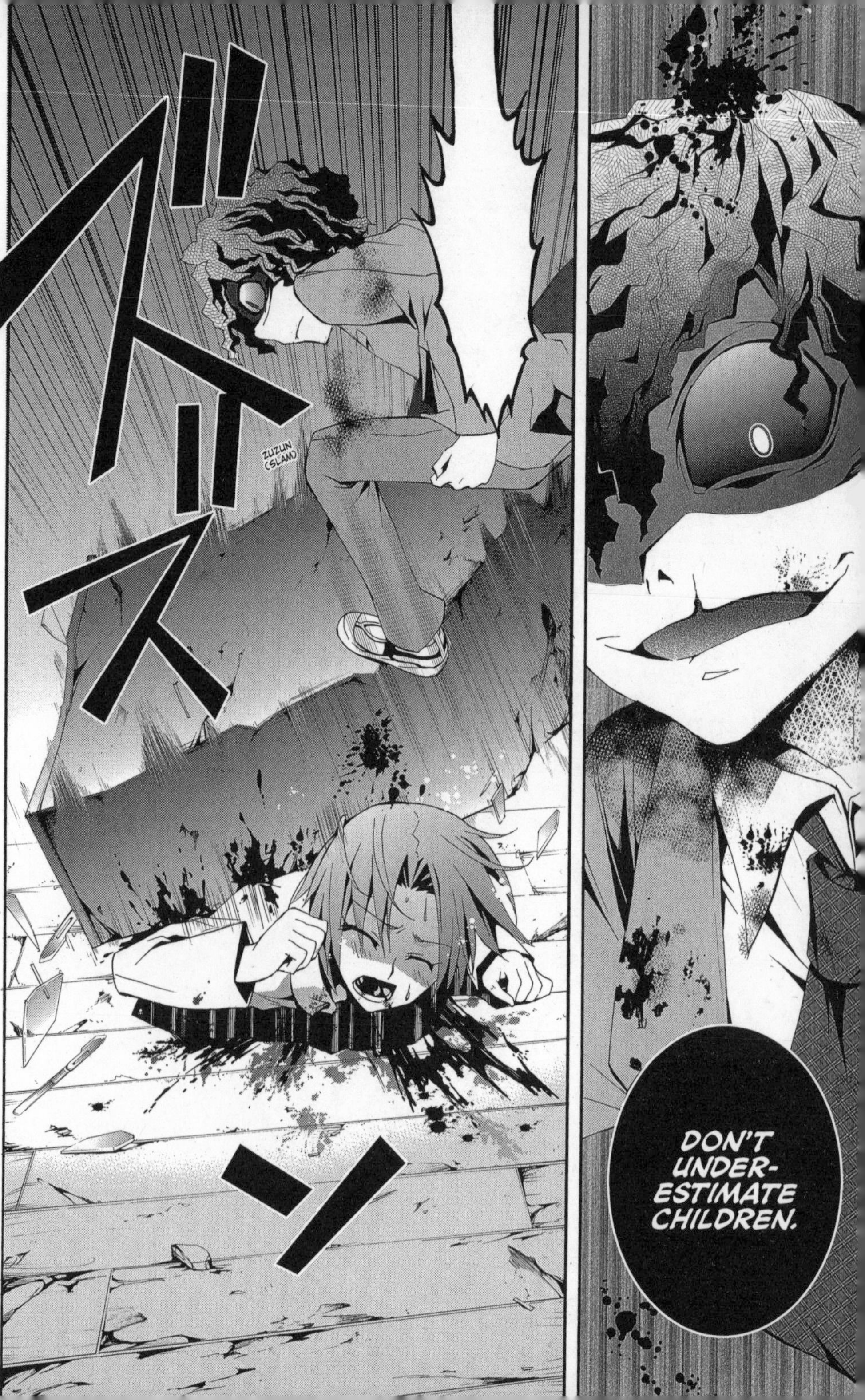
DON'T UNDER-ESTIMATE CHILDREN.
ZUZUN (SLAM)

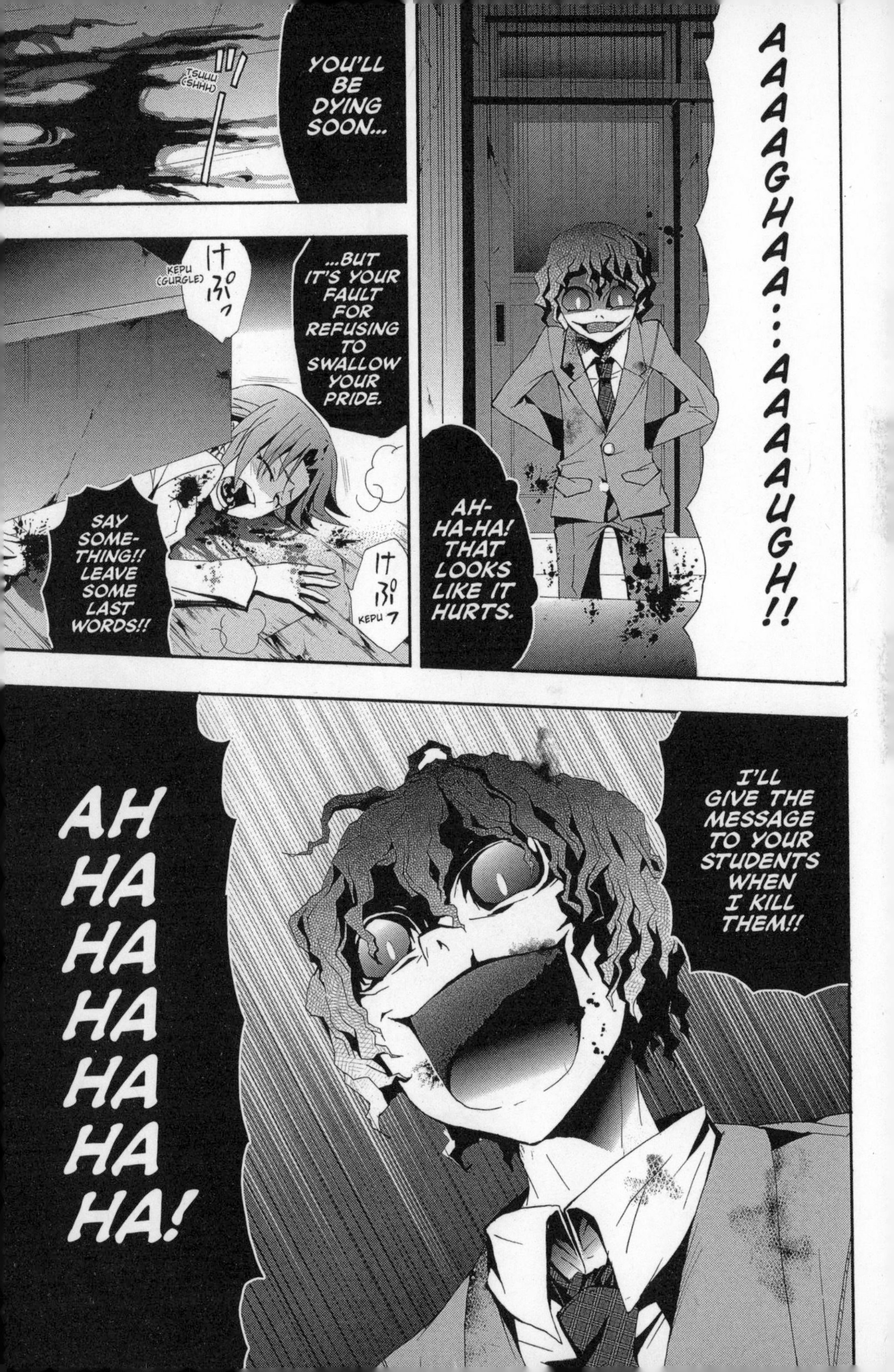
AAAAGHAAA... AAAAAAUGH!!
AH-HA-HA! THAT LOOKS LIKE IT HURTS.
YOU'LL BE DYING SOON...
TSUUU (SHHH)
...BUT IT'S YOUR FAULT FOR REFUSING TO SWALLOW YOUR PRIDE.
けぷっ
KEPU (GURGLE)
けぷっ
KEPU
SAY SOMETHING!! LEAVE SOME LAST WORDS!!
I'LL GIVE THE MESSAGE TO YOUR STUDENTS WHEN I KILL THEM!!
AH HA HA HA HA HA HA HA!

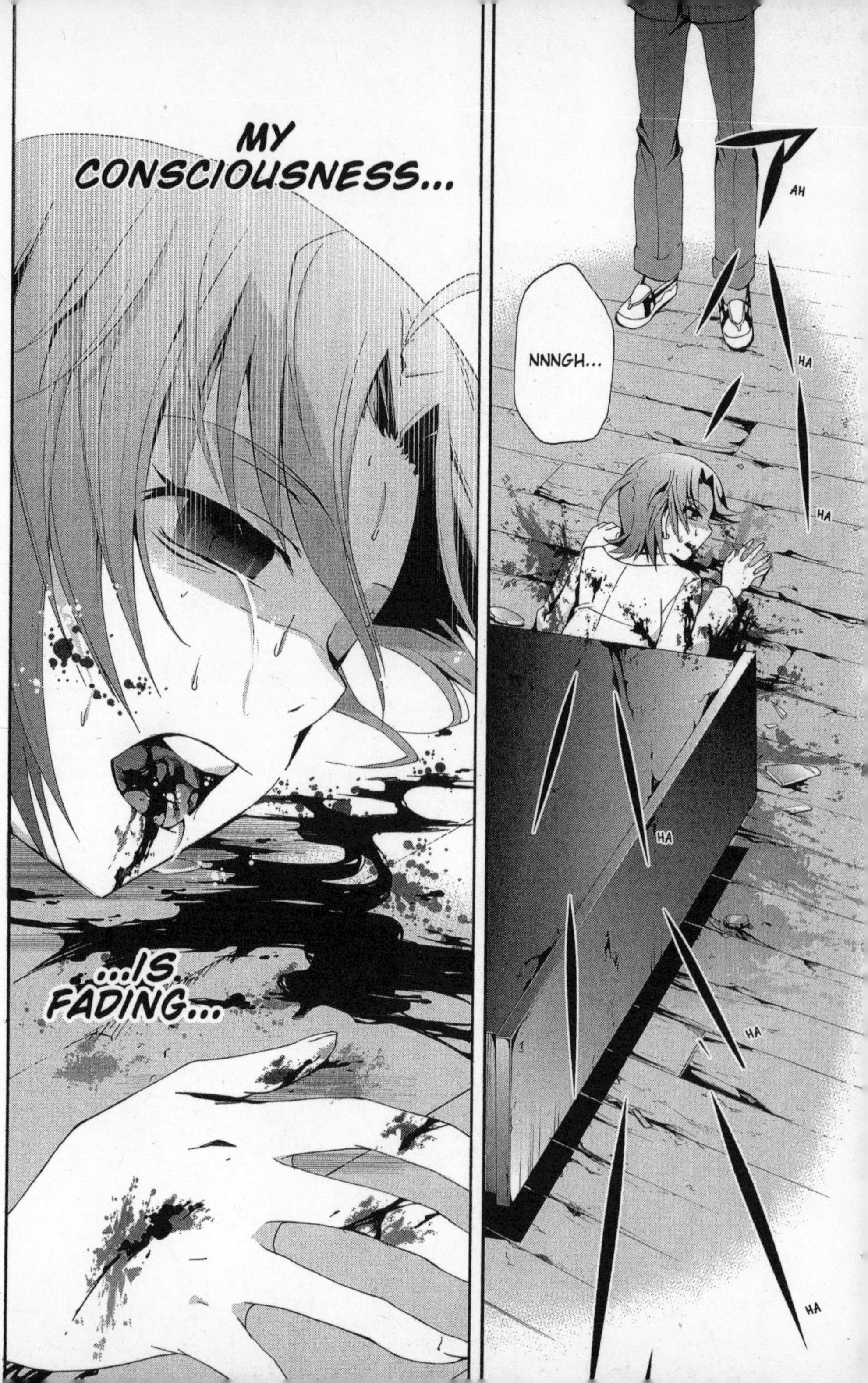
AH
HA
NNNGH...
HA
HA
HA
HA
MY CONSCIOUSNESS...
...IS FADING...

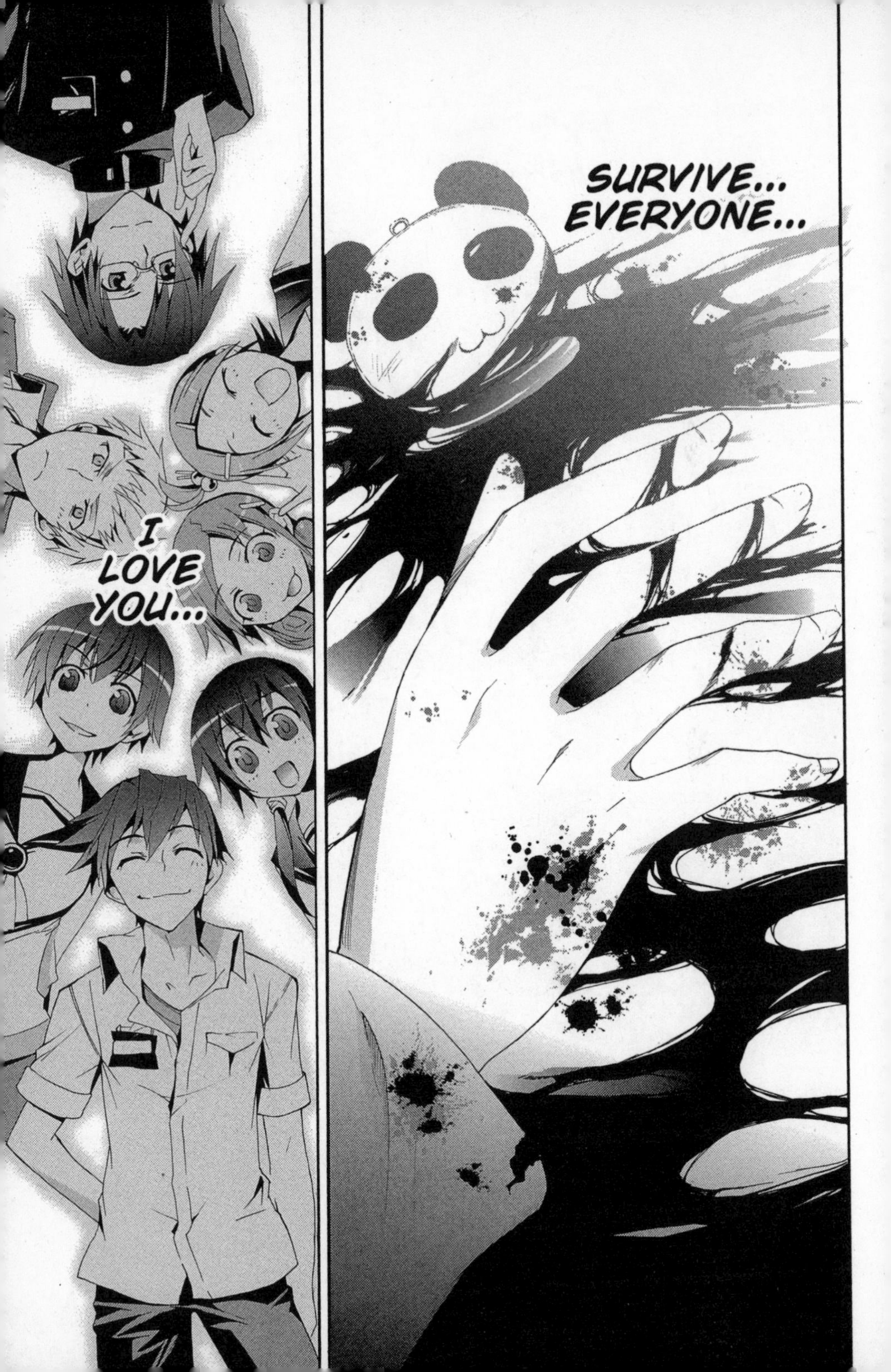
SURVIVE... EVERYONE...
I LOVE YOU...

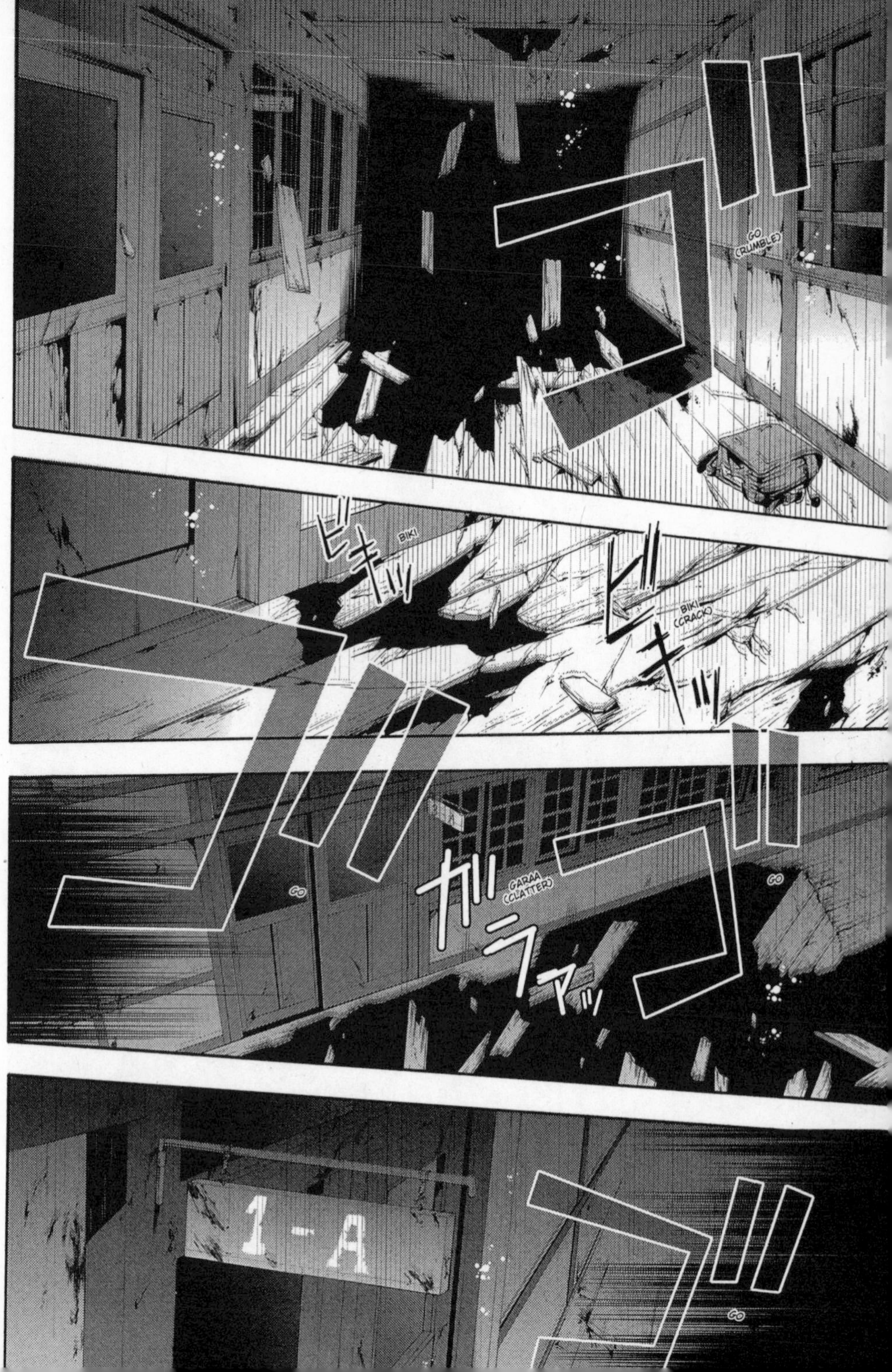
ゴッ
GO (RUMBLE)
ビキッ
BIKI (CRACK)
ビキッ
BIKI
GO
ガラァッ
GARAA (CLATTER)
ゴッ
GO
1-A
ゴッ
GO

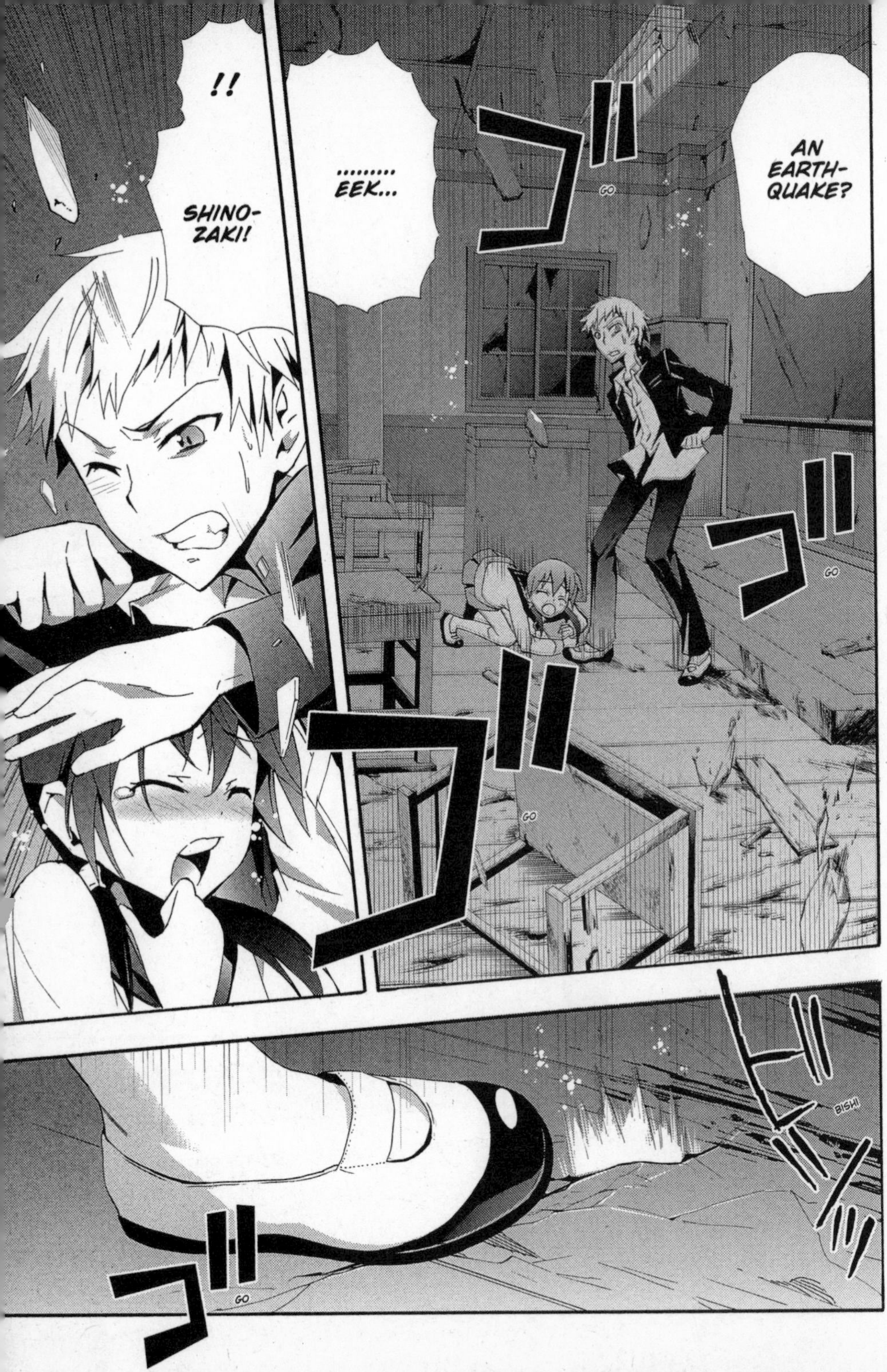
AN EARTH-QUAKE?
GO
.... EEK...
GO
GO
!!
SHINO-ZAKI!
BISHI
GO

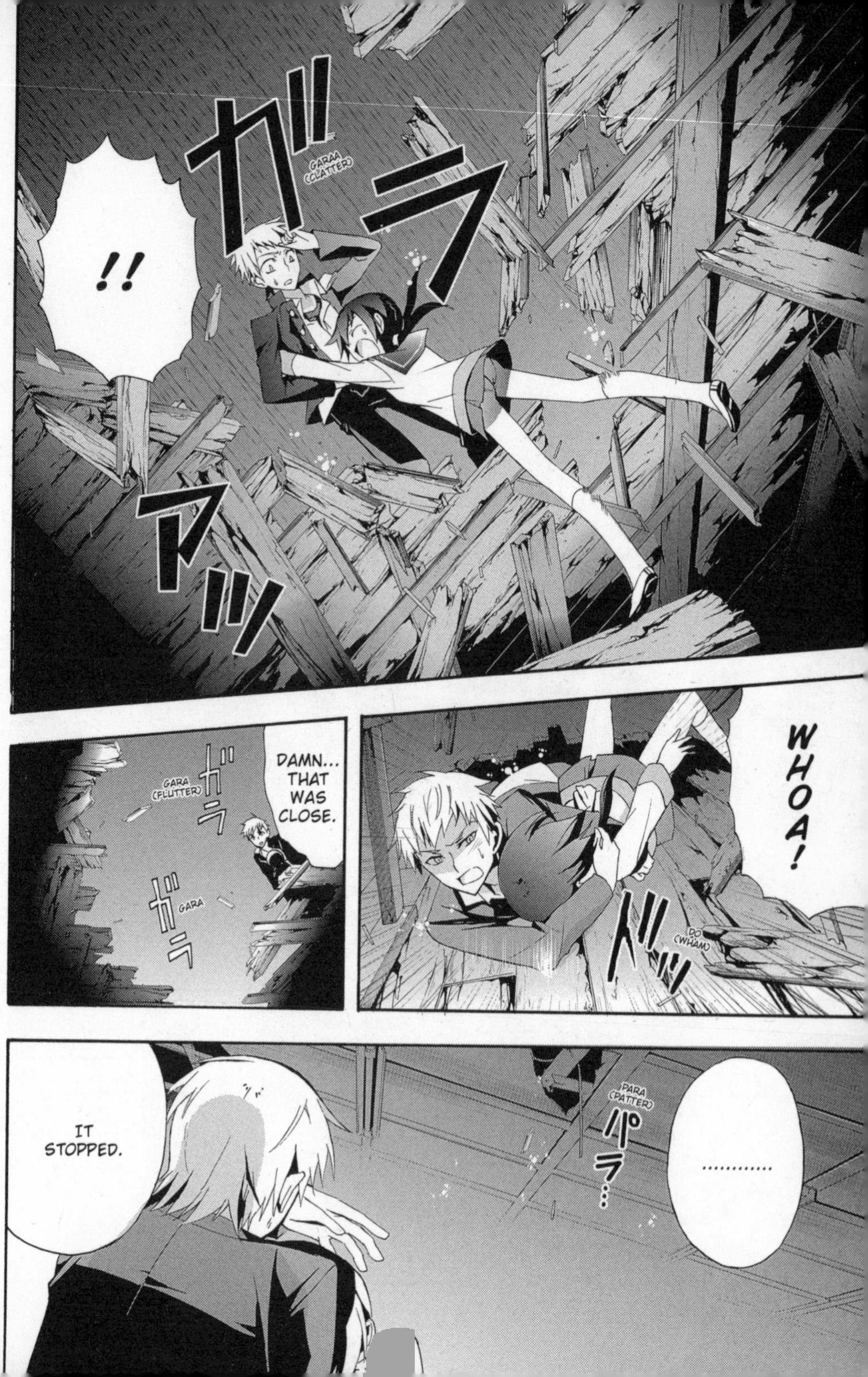
ガラアッ
GARAA (CLATTER)
!!
WHOA!
ドッ
DO (WHAM)
DAMN... THAT WAS CLOSE.
ガラ
GARA (FLUTTER)
ガラ
GARA
....
パラ...
PARA (PATTER)
IT STOPPED.

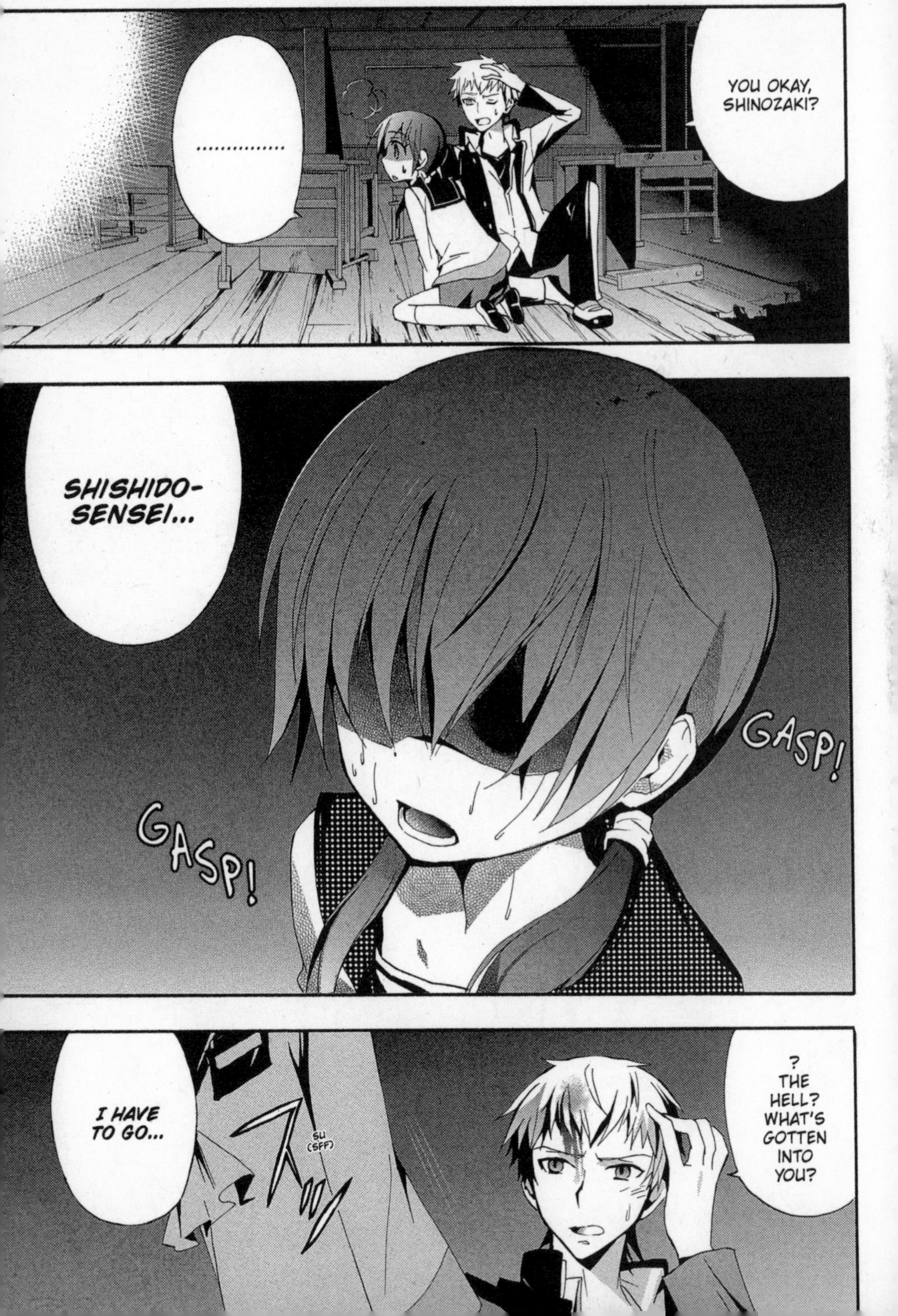
YOU OKAY, SHINOZAKI?
....
SHISHIDO-SENSEI...
GASP!
GASP!
? THE HELL? WHAT'S GOTTEN INTO YOU?
SU (SFF)
I HAVE TO GO...

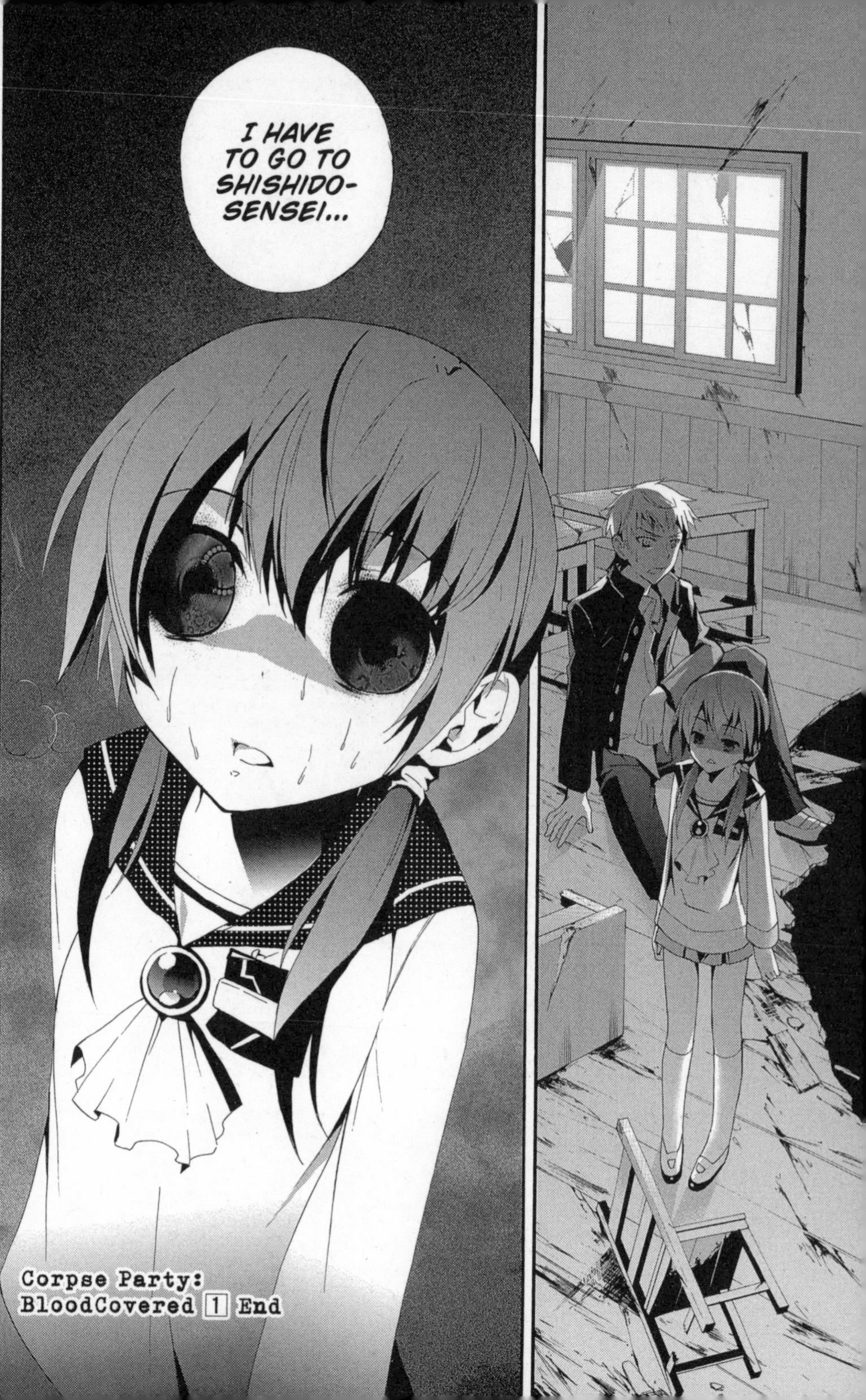
I HAVE TO GO TO SHISHIDO-SENSEI...
Corpse Party: BloodCovered 1 End

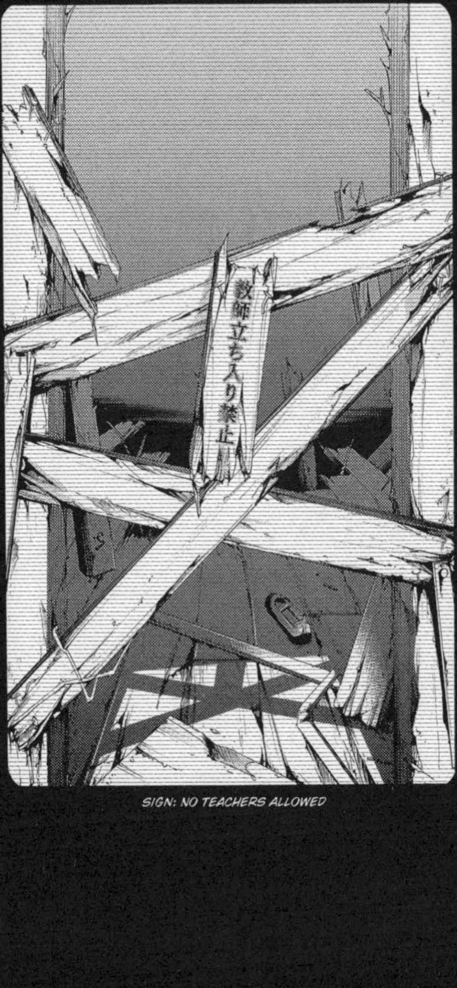
教師立ち入り禁止
SIGN: NO TEACHERS ALLOWED

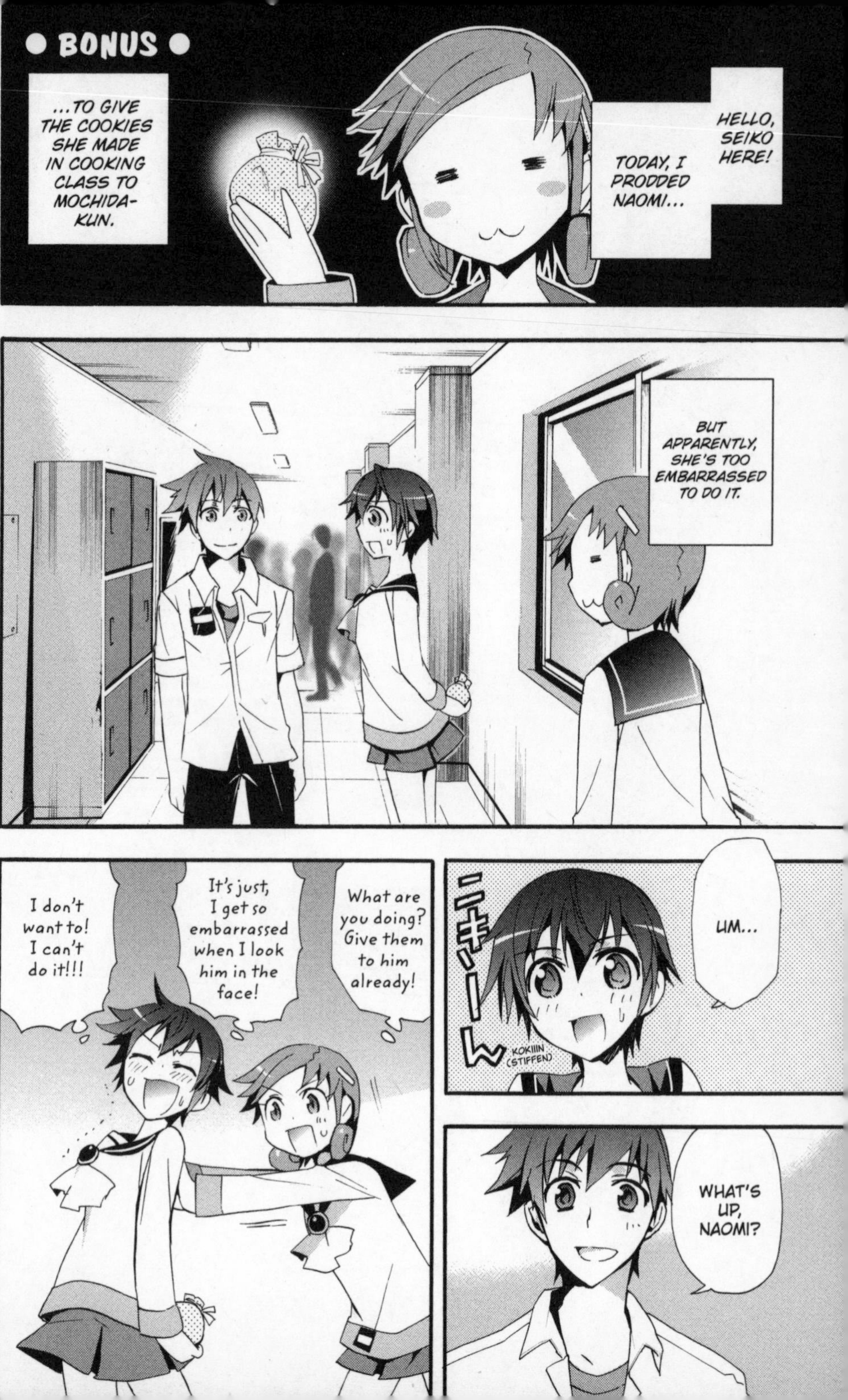
BONUS
HELLO, SEIKO HERE!
TODAY, I PRODDED NAOMI...
...TO GIVE THE COOKIES SHE MADE IN COOKING CLASS TO MOCHIDA-KUN.
BUT APPARENTLY, SHE'S TOO EMBARRASSED TO DO IT.
UM...
KOKIIIN (STIFFEN)
WHAT'S UP, NAOMI?
What are you doing? Give them to him already!
It's just, I get so embarrassed when I look him in the face!
I don't want to! I can't do it!!!

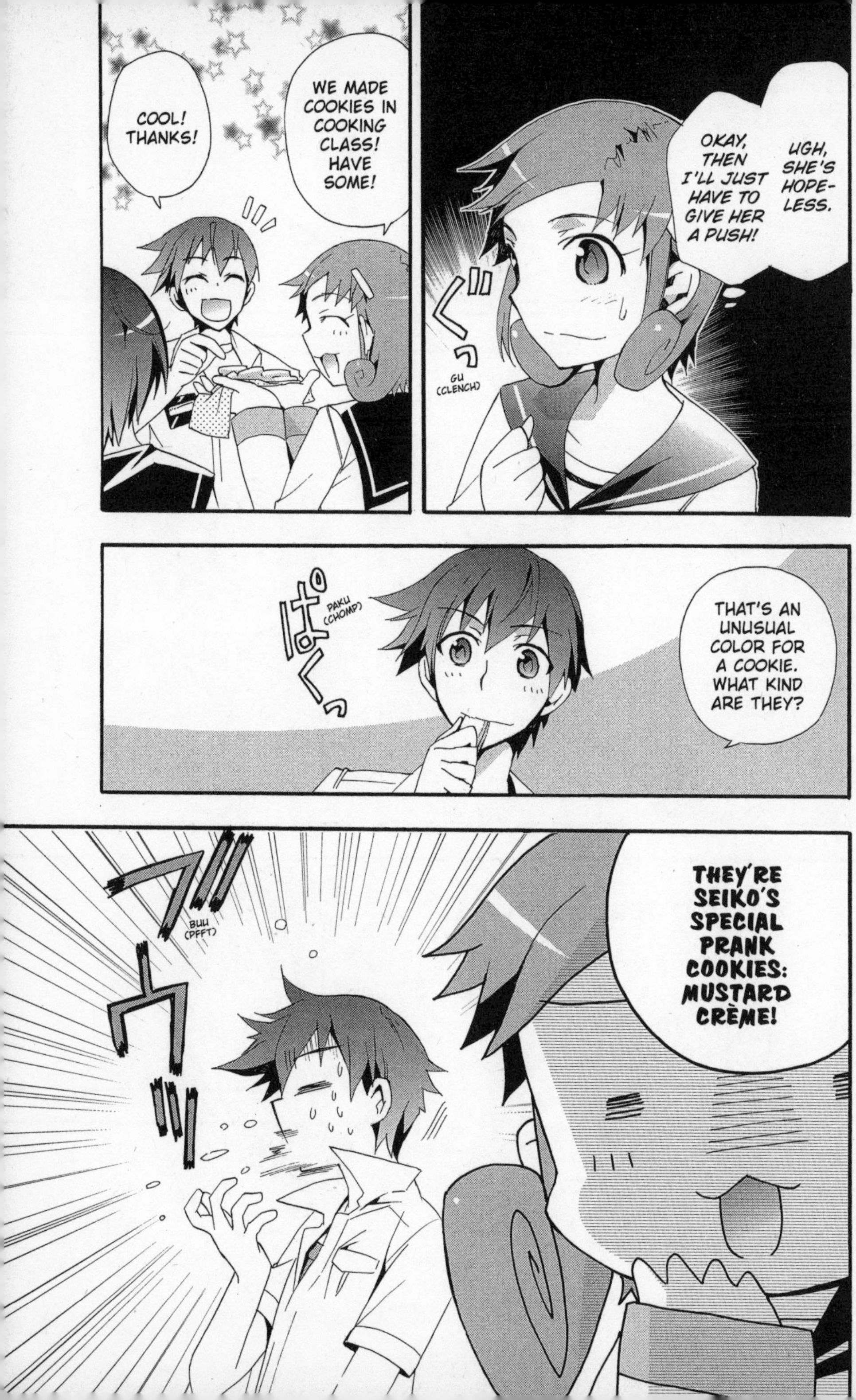
UGH, SHE'S HOPE-LESS.
OKAY, THEN I'LL JUST HAVE TO GIVE HER A PUSH!
GU (CLENCH)
WE MADE COOKIES IN COOKING CLASS! HAVE SOME!
COOL! THANKS!
THAT'S AN UNUSUAL COLOR FOR A COOKIE. WHAT KIND ARE THEY?
PAKU (CHOMP)
THEY'RE SEIKO'S SPECIAL PRANK COOKIES: MUSTARD CRÈME!
BUU (PFFT)

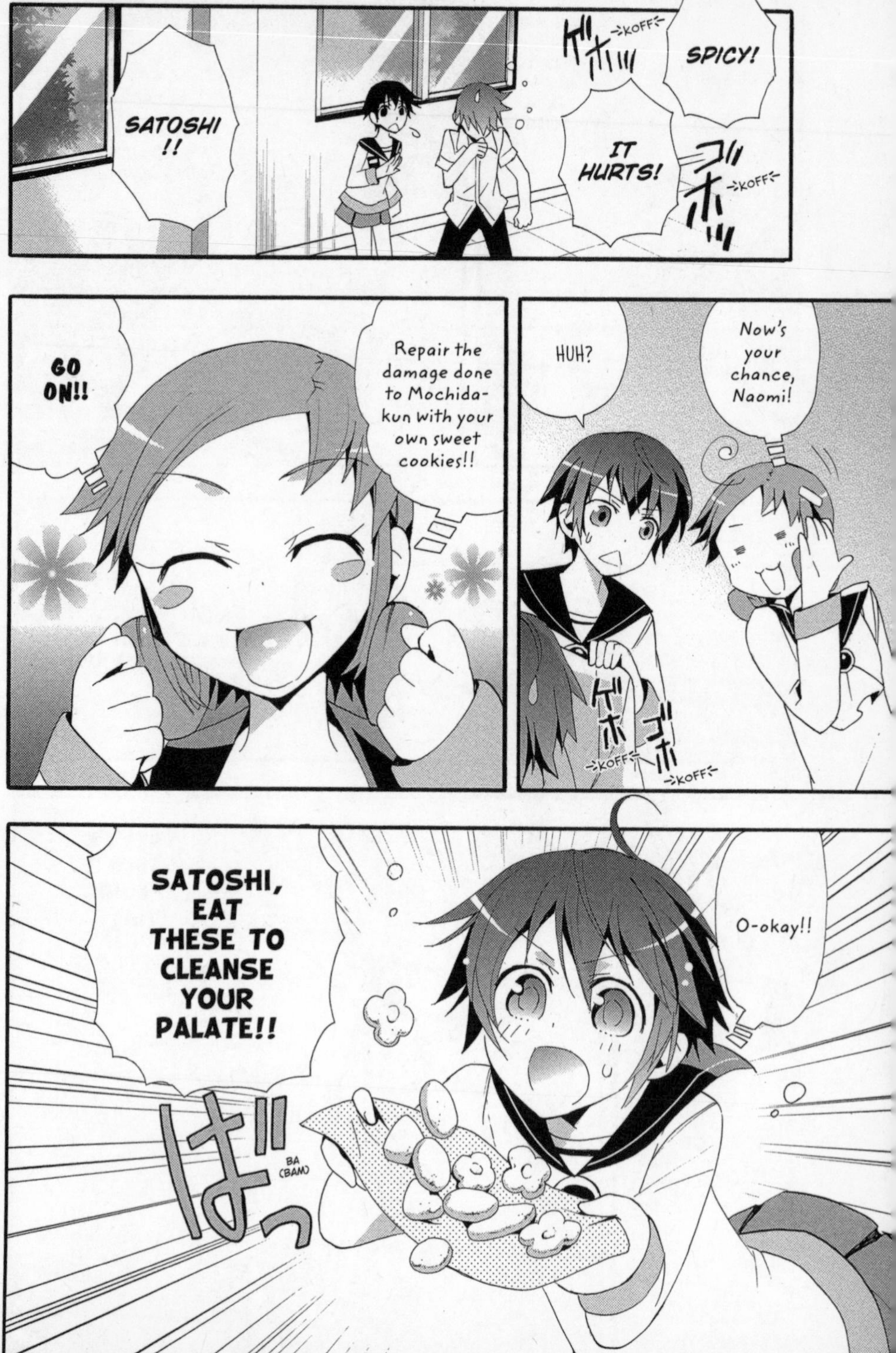
SPICY!
ゲホッ
KOFF
IT HURTS!
ゴホッ
KOFF
SATOSHI!!
Now's your chance, Naomi!
HUH?
ゲホ
KOFF
ゴホ
KOFF
Repair the damage done to Mochida-kun with your own sweet cookies!!
GO ON!!
O-okay!!
SATOSHI, EAT THESE TO CLEANSE YOUR PALATE!!
ばっ
BA (BAM)

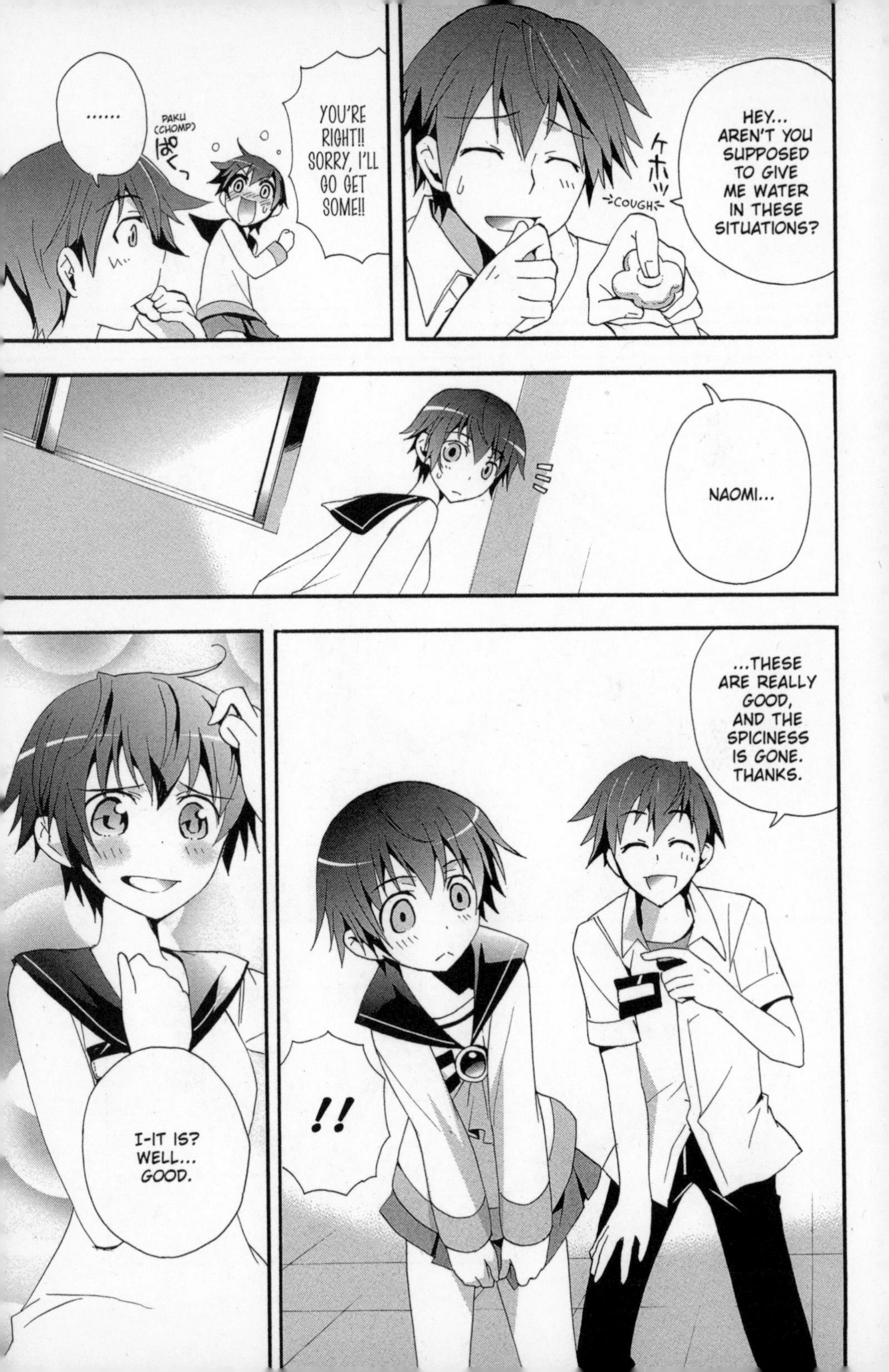
HEY... AREN'T YOU SUPPOSED TO GIVE ME WATER IN THESE SITUATIONS?
ケホッ
-COUGH-
YOU'RE RIGHT!! SORRY, I'LL GO GET SOME!!
PAKU (CHOMP)
ぱくっ
......
NAOMI...
...THESE ARE REALLY GOOD, AND THE SPICINESS IS GONE. THANKS.
!!
I-IT IS? WELL... GOOD.

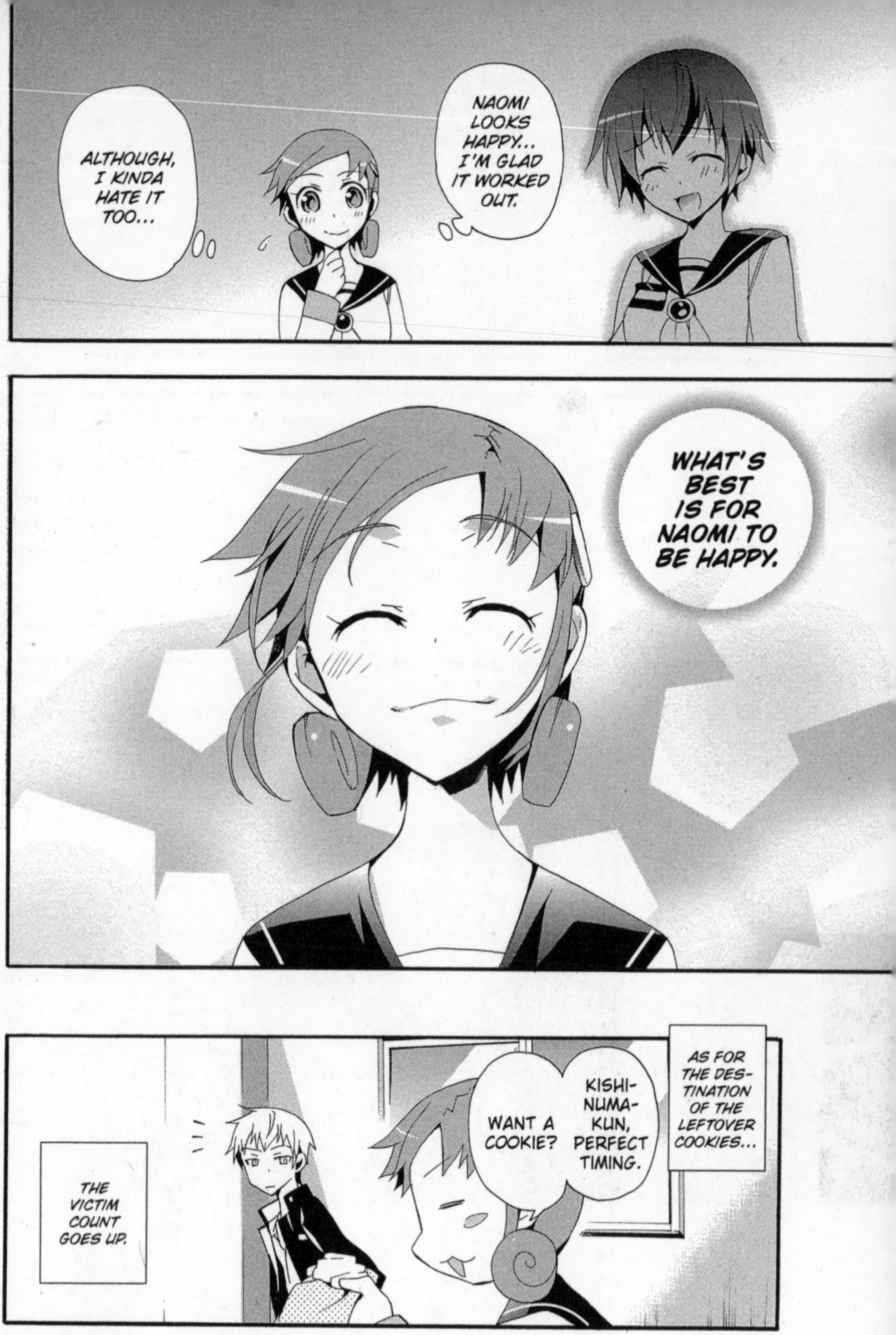
NAOMI LOOKS HAPPY... I'M GLAD IT WORKED OUT.
ALTHOUGH, I KINDA HATE IT TOO...
WHAT'S BEST IS FOR NAOMI TO BE HAPPY.
AS FOR THE DES-TINATION OF THE LEFTOVER COOKIES...
KISHI-NUMA-KUN, PERFECT TIMING.
WANT A COOKIE?
THE VICTIM COUNT GOES UP.

Character pickup

Yui Shishido

Born May 3, blood type O, 164cm, 50.1kg (5'5", 110.5lbs)

Likes: Cats, drinking alcohol, sweets
Dislikes: Unmotivated teachers
Hobbies: Collecting cat toys
Dream Career: To be a teacher until retirement

Yoshiki Kishinuma

Born November 8, blood type A, 172cm, 62.1kg (5'8", 136.9lbs)

Likes: Practicing musical instruments
Dislikes: People with no backbone
Hobbies: Listening to music
Dream Career: Still looking

Ayumi Shinozaki

Born September 12, blood type A, 151cm, 43.2kg (4'11", 95.3lbs)

Likes: Fortune-telling, manga, P*P (hand-held gaming device)
Dislikes: Grown-ups (mostly men)
Hobbies: Ghost stories, collecting horror goods, drawing pictures
Dream Career: Illustrator

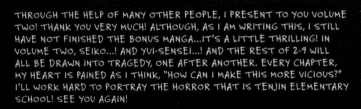

THROUGH THE HELP OF MANY OTHER PEOPLE, I PRESENT TO YOU VOLUME TWO! THANK YOU VERY MUCH! ALTHOUGH, AS I AM WRITING THIS, I STILL HAVE NOT FINISHED THE BONUS MANGA...IT'S A LITTLE THRILLING! IN VOLUME TWO, SEIKO...! AND YUI-SENSEI...! AND THE REST OF 2-9 WILL ALL BE DRAWN INTO TRAGEDY, ONE AFTER ANOTHER. EVERY CHAPTER, MY HEART IS PAINED AS I THINK, "HOW CAN I MAKE THIS MORE VICIOUS?" I'LL WORK HARD TO PORTRAY THE HORROR THAT IS TENJIN ELEMENTARY SCHOOL! SEE YOU AGAIN!

TOSHIMI SHINOMIYA

SPECIAL THANKS
M KOKKO-SAN, SHIN ARAKAWA-SAN, FUMIKO MORIZONO-SAN, TAKATOSHI OGURA-SAN, MASAKI KAWANO-SAN, AND EVERYONE FROM TEAM GRISGRIS, MAKOTO KEDOUIN-SAN, YOSHIKI TONOGAI-SENSEI, MY EDITOR, AKIYAMA-SAN, KAWANO-SAN

AFTERWORD

CONGRATULATIONS ON RELEASING VOLUME 2 OF THE MANGA VERSION! THANK YOU TO EVERYONE WHO PICKED UP VOLUME 1 AND WENT ON TO PICK UP THIS ONE. IT'S GOOD TO SEE YOU AGAIN AFTER SO LONG!

SEIKO-CHAN IS CUTE NO MATTER WHAT THE LOOK ON HER FACE. I SUSPECT THERE AREN'T THAT MANY MANGA THAT CAN SHOW SO MANY DIFFERENT FACES OF ALL OF THEIR CHARACTERS.

I'M CHEERING SHINOMIYA-SENSEI ON AS THE MANGA CONTINUES TO PUSH THE BOUNDARIES OF EXPRESSION, AND I LOOK FORWARD TO SEEING WHAT OUTSTANDING DEPICTIONS ARE IN STORE.

THE SECOND ACT OF THIS IMPRISONMENT TALE, THE INHUMANE BANQUET, AWAITS EVERYONE WITH AN EVEN GREATER UNBALANCE. I HOPE YOU WILL SAVOR THE "BANQUET OF THE DEAD" ALONG WITH THE GIRLS.

MAKOTO KEDOUIN

THE MANY SEVERE EXPRESSIONS...
...A LITTLE LESS SHAME-LESS!
...IN THIS MANGA...
YOU COULD BE...
YAY!!
...COULD BE ATTRIBUTED...
...TO THE MERCILESSNESS OF THE GAME IT'S BASED ON.
BC4
WHAT'S THAT GAME CALLED?
BUT RECENTLY, I GET THE FEELING...
THAT THE SADISM IN THE MANGA SURPASSES THAT OF THE ORIGINAL.
WHAT!? TWICE!?
YOU'RE DROPPING THE SHELF ON HER TWICE!?
I LIKE IT.
I REALLY LIKE IT!
K

CORPSE PARTY
BloodCovered

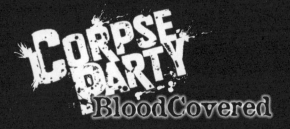

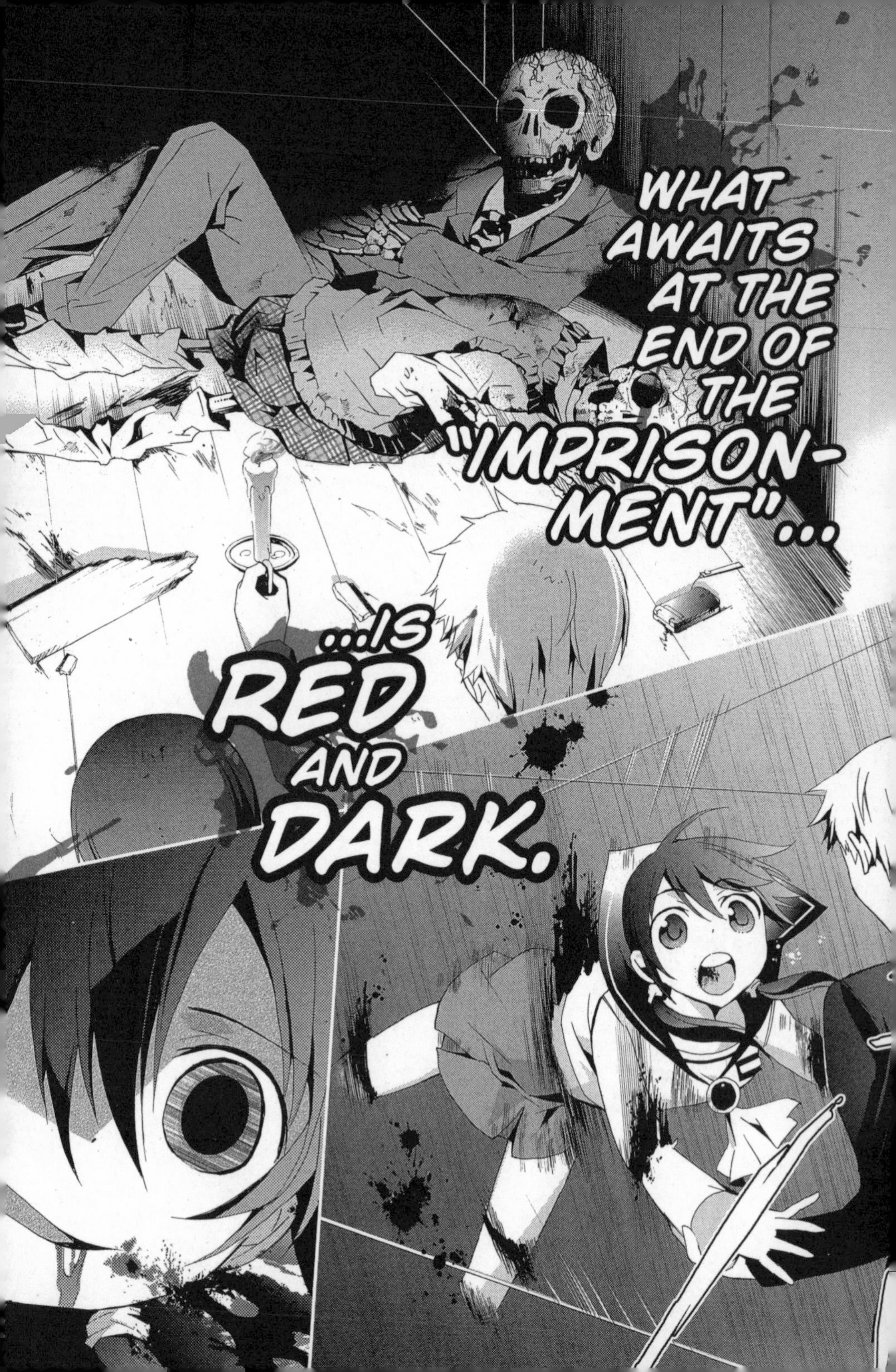
WHAT AWAITS AT THE END OF THE "IMPRISON-MENT"...
...IS RED AND DARK.

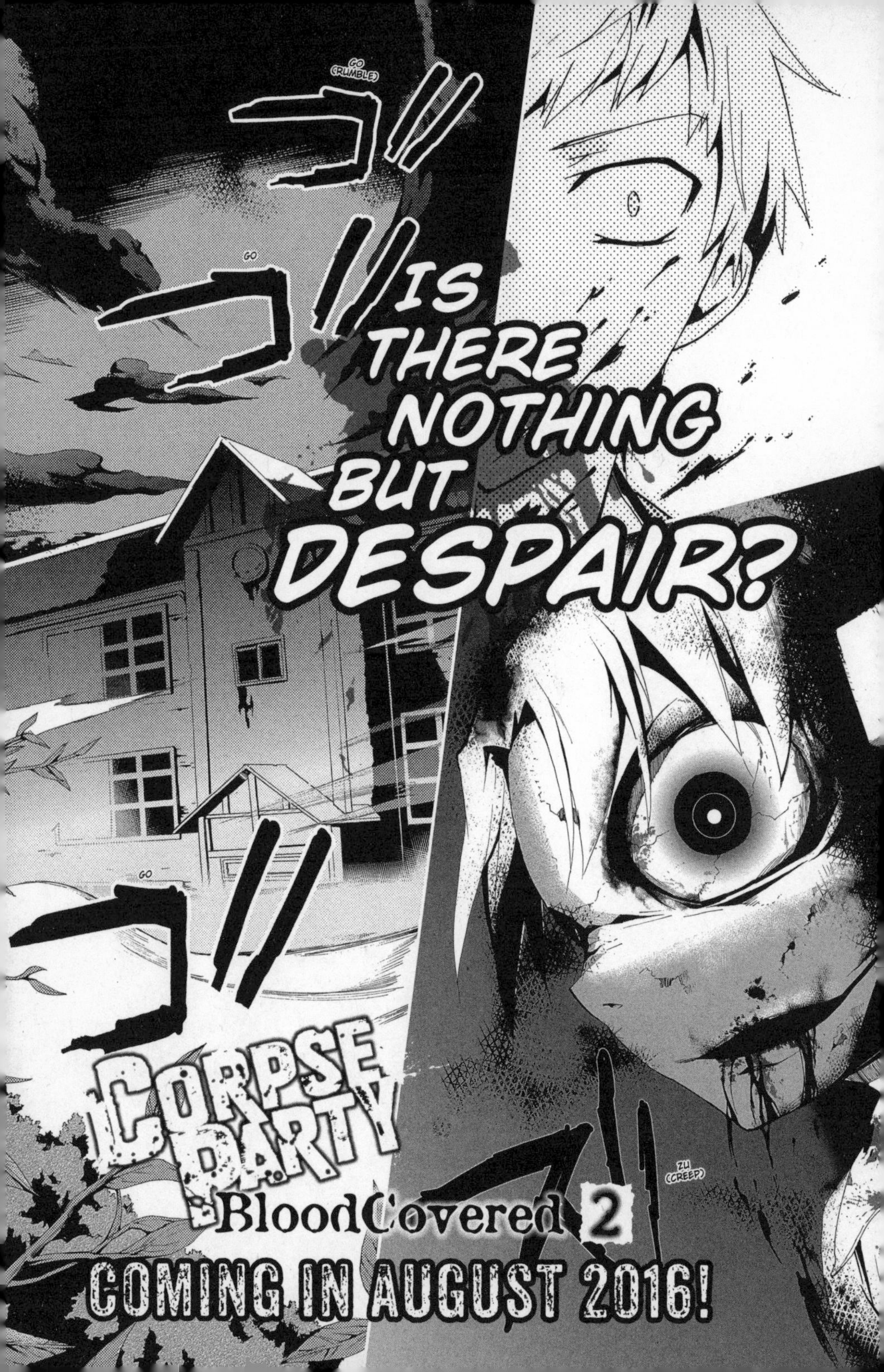
GO (RUMBLE)
GO
IS THERE NOTHING BUT DESPAIR?
GO
ZU (CREEP)
CORPSE PARTY BloodCovered 2
COMING IN AUGUST 2016!

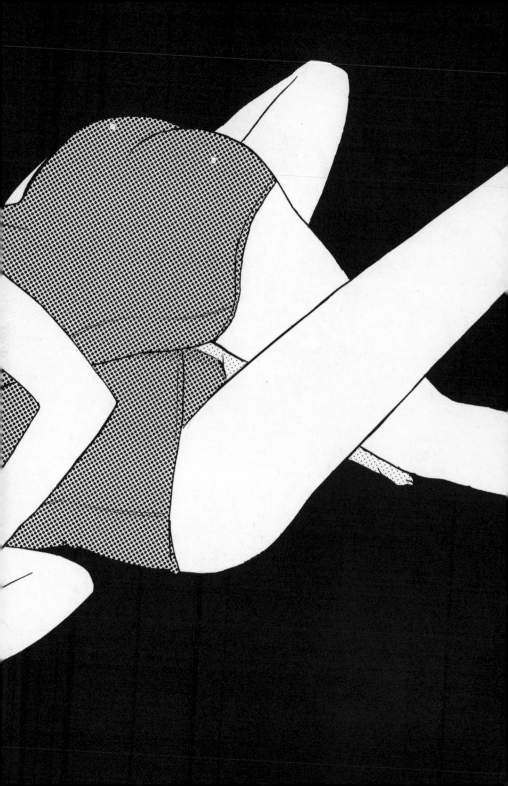

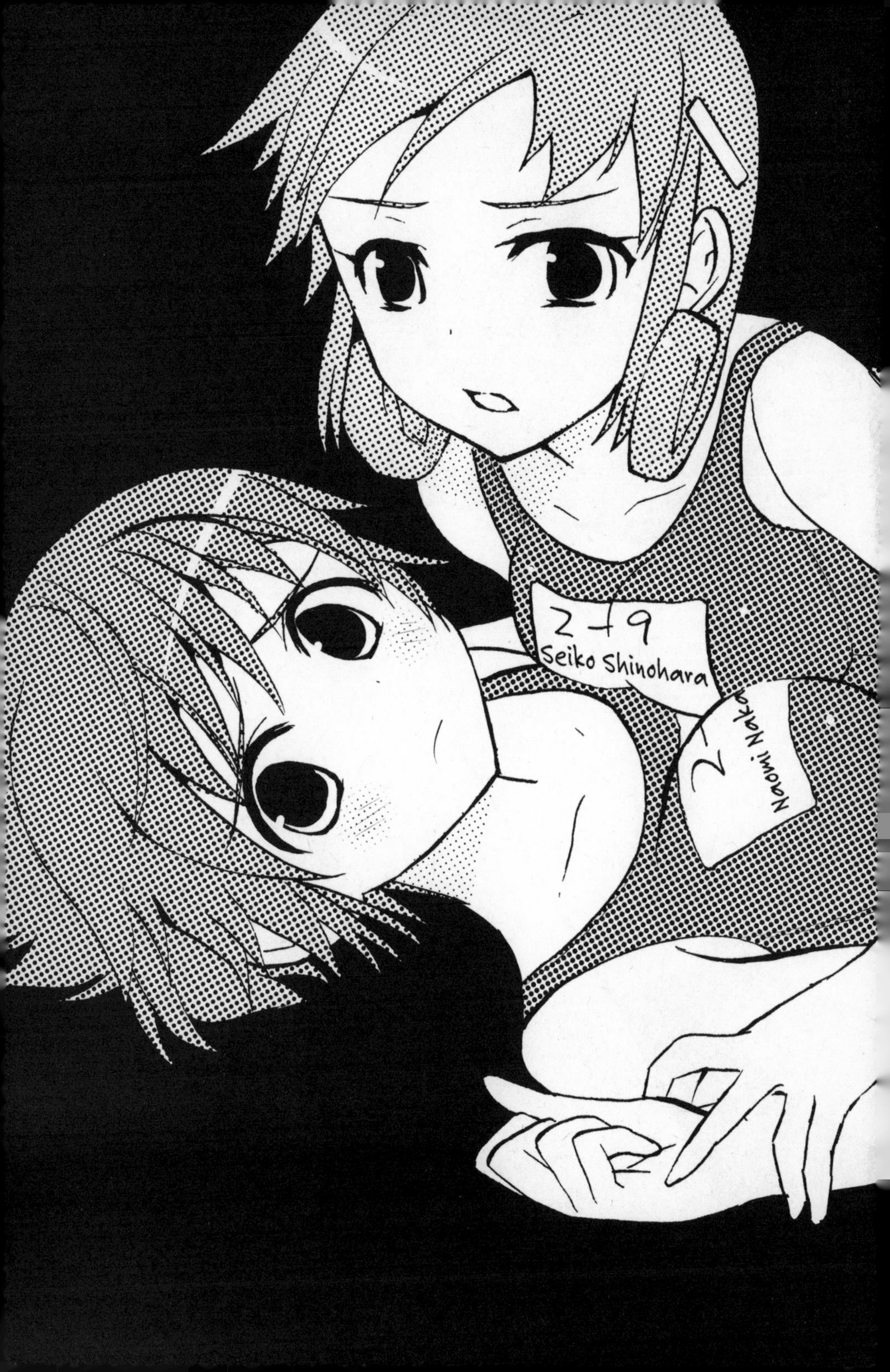
2-9
Seiko Shinohara
2-
Naomi Naka

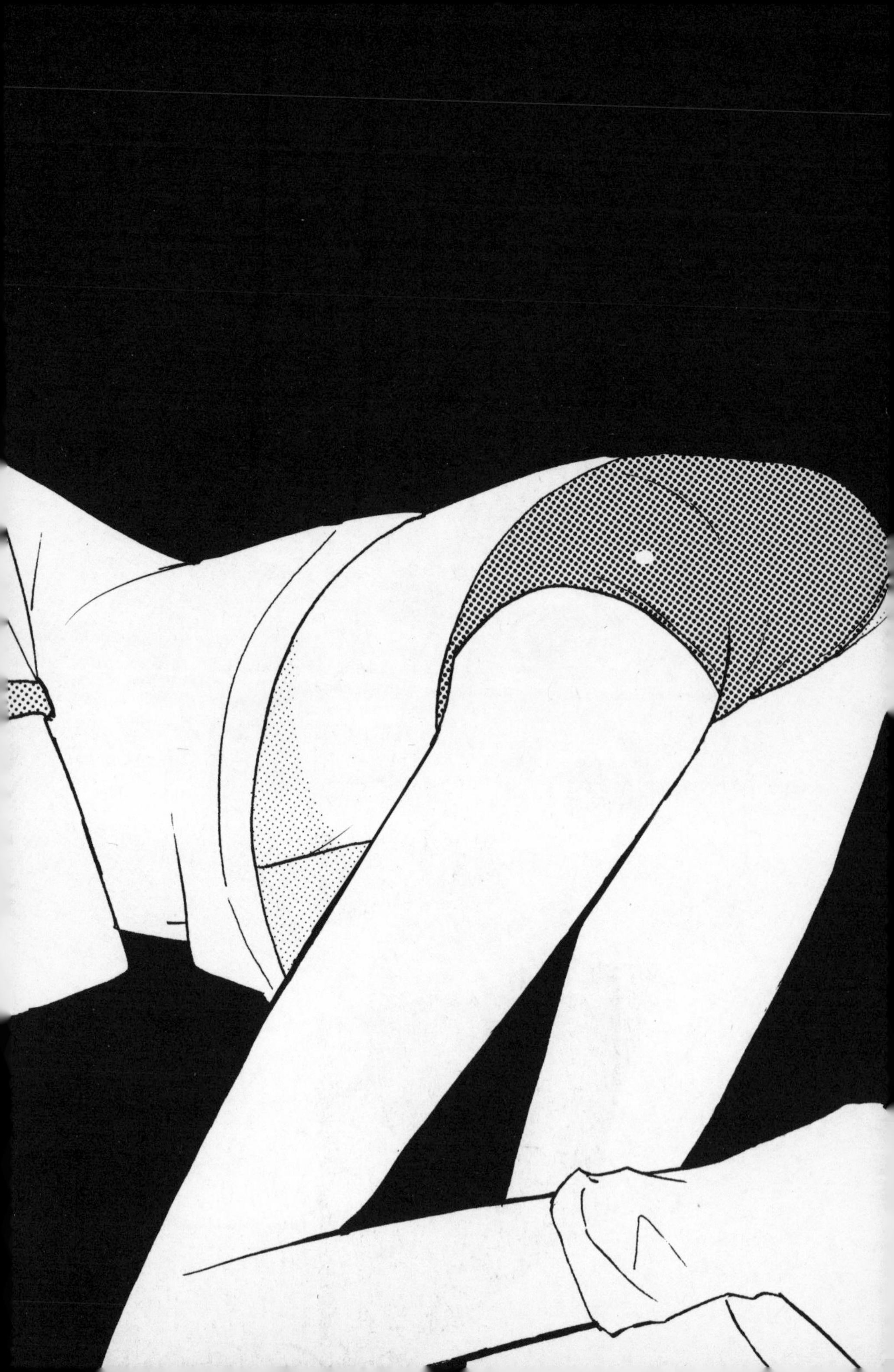

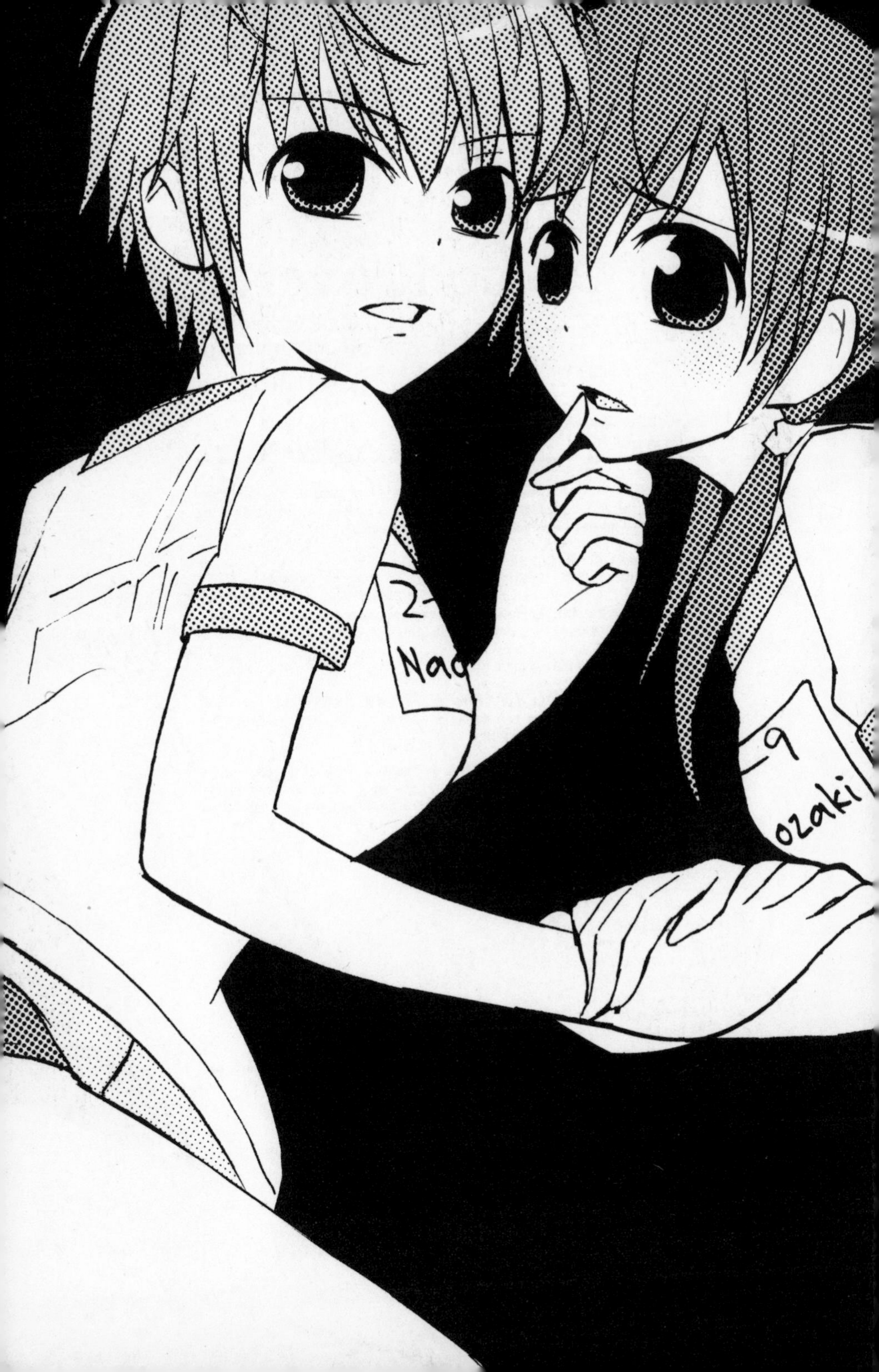
2-
Nao
9
ozaki

BloodCovered

Makoto Kedouin
Toshimi Shinomiya

Translation: Alethea and Athena Nibley
Lettering: D. Kim

CORPSEPARTY BLOODCOVERED Vol. 1
©2008 TeamGrisGris/ALL RIGHTS RESERVED.
©2009 Toshimi Shinomiya/Square Enix Co., LTD. First published in Japan in 2009 by Square Enix Co., Ltd. English translation rights arranged with Square Enix Co., Ltd. and Yen Press LLC through Tuttle-Mori Agency, Inc.

English translation ©2016 Square Enix Co., Ltd.

Yen Press
1290 Avenue of the Americas
New York, NY 10104

Visit us at yenpress.com
facebook.com/yenpress
twitter.com/yenpress
yenpress.tumblr.com

Yen Press is an imprint of Yen Press, LLC.
The Yen Press name and logo are trademarks of Yen Press, LLC.

The publisher is not responsible for websites (or their content) that are not owned by the publisher.

Library of Congress Control Number: 2016930997

First Yen Press Edition: May 2016

ISBN: 978-0-316-27218-6

10 9 8 7 6 5 4 3 2

BVG

Printed in the United States of America